QUEST FOR DISTINCTION

QUEST FOR DISTINCTION

~

Pepperdine University in the 20th Century

W. DAVID BAIRD

Pepperdine University Press

Pepperdine University Press
24255 Pacific Coast Hwy.
Malibu, CA 90263
(310) 506-4125

Ordering Information:
Quantity sales. Special discounts are available on quantity purchases. For details, contact the publisher at the address above.

All photographs are used by permission of Special Collections and University Archives, Pepperdine University.

Project Manager: Markman Editorial Services, www.marlamarkman.com
Editor: Tammy Ditmore, www.editmore.com
Cover Design: Rick Gibson
Interior Design: Marin Bookworks, www.thebookdesigner.com

ISBN: 978-0-9977004-0-4

Printed in the United States of America

Publisher's Cataloging-in-Publication data

Names: Baird, W. David, author.
    Title: Quest for distinction : Pepperdine University in the 20th century / W.
      David Baird.
    Description: Malibu, California : Pepperdine University Press, [2016] |
      Includes bibliographical references.
    Identifiers: LCCN 2016030440 | ISBN 9780997700404 (hardcover)
    Subjects: LCSH: Pepperdine University--History.
    Classification: LCC LD4561.P428 B35 2016 | DDC 378.794/93--dc23
    LC record available at https://lccn.loc.gov/2016030440

First Edition

20 19 18 17 16 / 10 9 8 7 6 5 4 3 2 1

Dedicated to members and former members
of the University Church of Christ
who daily witness Christian community
to Pepperdine students

TABLE OF CONTENTS

FOREWORD

I am honored to write this foreword to *Quest for Distinction: Pepperdine University in the 20th Century* by W. David Baird. It has been my privilege to work closely with David as a colleague during our tenure at Seaver College and Pepperdine University. David and I first began our careers at Pepperdine as faculty colleagues; he came to Pepperdine as holder of the Howard A. White Chair in History, and I came as a professor of religion.

Our paths intersected more frequently when we both served as chairs of our respective divisions. When David became dean of Seaver College, he asked me to serve as his associate dean. When he retired, I succeeded him in the dean's role and advocated with several others that he be drafted to write the official history of Pepperdine University.

The rationale was compelling. A renowned historian, David is best known for his publications relating to Native Americans in the United States. However, for the past several years, he has brought his considerable analytical skills to bear upon the plethora of written documentation relating to the history of Pepperdine while also conducting countless oral interviews of key players involved in that history.

The resulting work is a must-read for anyone who has an interest in the inner workings of a university striving to become a top-tier educational institution known for academic excellence and commitment to Christian mission—or for anyone who is simply looking for a book filled with stories and characters too fascinating to forget. While most institutions have opted for either academic excellence or Christian mission, David ably demonstrates through significant documentation how Pepperdine's leaders steadfastly refused to choose one option to the neglect of the other. He convincingly shows that both laudable goals were in Pepperdine's DNA from the beginning.

In his refusal to focus solely upon the positive moments, David describes clearly the challenging times that threatened the future of the university and provides insight into how decisions were made that impacted the long-term health of the institution. Only a noted historian with a commitment to and love for Pepperdine could accomplish such a needed task—detailing the creation and development of a University committed to an entrepreneurial spirit of innovation and creativity, an institution founded upon fundamental

Christian principles and convictions, and an institution whose ambition for academic excellence has often exceeded the financial resources readily available to achieve its lofty goals.

We all owe David a debt of gratitude for his willingness to tackle this significant scholarly project—and for his courage to narrate a history that describes both the opportunities and challenges faced by flawed humans who were committed to achieving something greater than themselves. The result is the compelling history narrated in *Quest for Distinction: Pepperdine University in the 20th Century.*

Rick R. Marrs
Provost, Pepperdine University

PREFACE

T his is a history of Pepperdine University in the twentieth century. It begins with the story of a Kansas businessman who decided in 1937 to found a small college in south central Los Angeles that he expected would prepare students to serve God and live lives of usefulness. It ends with the onset of the twenty-first century and the inauguration of Andrew K. Benton as the seventh president of the university.

In writing the history of an educational institution, historians can follow many themes. Those might focus on students and alumni, social clubs and sports teams, buildings and donors, and town and gown differences, among others. All of those storylines have a place in the larger narrative of Pepperdine University, but this particular telling focuses on the people who piloted the institution's quest for distinction in academics and in its integration of Christian faith into the learning environment. Telling their stories reveals the tensions that emerged almost from the moment George Pepperdine began dreaming of a college that would be both academically rigorous and connected to Churches of Christ.

This account also seeks to identify the attributes that made Pepperdine a distinctive institution. Among those qualities were its aspiration to be both academically excellent *and* promulgate Christian values, its acceptance of ambiguity in self-definition, its support of traditional American values, its embodiment of an entrepreneurial spirit, its emphasis on international programs, and its Malibu campus setting. The story confirms that this complex of attributes has made Pepperdine University genuinely distinctive as an institution of higher education.

Finally, this narrative tells of an institution's quest for identity. William S. Banowsky, Pepperdine's fourth president, often spoke of the university's "schizophrenia": it has presented itself both as Christian and secular, Church of Christ and nondenominational, liberal arts and professional. It has posited that academic excellence applies to both teaching and research; the school's outreach has been both urban and suburban; it acts as both conservationist and land developer. Pepperdine heartily embraced the Reagan Revolution (free-market economy, a limited central government, and the civil faith of our fathers), but it was also eager to receive government contracts and money.

Schizophrenia of this kind has troubled every presidential administration that has served the university during the course of its history.

This book culminates a seven-year journey that began when current Pepperdine President Andrew K. Benton asked me to write the seventy-fifth anniversary history of Pepperdine University. I accepted the invitation thinking that I could complete the assignment in two years—one to research and one to write. I envisioned the final product as a definitive 400-page monograph that would begin in 1937 and end with 2012.

A funny thing happened on the way to the press. Rather than 400 pages, the first draft ran to 1,400, of which some 15 percent was devoted to footnotes. Rather than two years of research and writing, it stretched into seven plus. And rather than carry the story through seventy-five years, it terminated at 2000. More months of trimming and revising have resulted in this book, *Quest for Distinction: Pepperdine University in the 20th Century.* In completing the manuscript there were many challenges. Foremost was the problem of primary source material. There was a dearth of materials pertaining to the founder, George Pepperdine, as most of his papers were systematically burned by his widow following his death in 1962. The paucity of records was also true of the Batsell Baxter and Hugh M. Tiner presidencies because the official correspondence of the institution seems to have been lost in the move from the Los Angeles campus to Malibu. Fortunately there was a garage full of unprocessed primary materials for M. Norvel Young's tenure as president and chancellor, and a similar amount of processed and unprocessed materials for Banowsky's presidency. A professional historian who understood the importance of documents in reconstructing the past, Howard A. White also left a large collection of primary sources from his years as executive vice president and president.

That was not the case for the David Davenport administration, however, where records of the office of the president were sparse. Much of the communication between President Davenport and his colleagues was by email, the only record of which was a bit of data on a hard drive or in the cloud, a speck that was easily lost and seldom preserved. Consequently, the Pepperdine story conveyed in this book is based upon an abundance of presidential records in its middle chapters but a scarcity of them at its bookend chapters.

This book does not supply the definitive history of Pepperdine University in the twentieth century. These past seven years suggest to me that no such thing is possible. Historians are bound by their sources, which are typically incomplete. The resultant narrative can be, therefore, only partial. The expectation is that future historians will resift the primary resources, study new collections of materials, ask different questions, and write a more complete narrative, or history. Thus, the content of this study is only a first step in a long journey toward discovered truth.

This is not a sun-dial history of Pepperdine University, to use Jerry Rushford's description of his fiftieth anniversary history, that is, one that focuses only on the institution's sunny experiences. This study recounts many cloudy days. Nor does this account attribute a dramatic role for a series of positive developments to the hand of God. As a prayerful Christian and a fifth-generation member of Churches of Christ, I believe firmly that God enters into the affairs of humankind; but as a historian, I am not at liberty to attribute causation to the supernatural. Therefore, I have assiduously avoided drawing conclusions that suggest God has directly favored Pepperdine University, although others have made or could make such a case. Indeed, as a general rule, I try to avoid making independent judgments regarding what is revealed by my sources. My expectation is that readers, given the facts, will make sensible judgments on their own.

Although essentially an administrative history, this is a book that multiple constituencies can enjoy. Faculty and staff serving the university will perhaps benefit most from the study, however. Unconsciously, I have written the book for them. I could have been a better member of the faculty and a better dean of Seaver College had I known then what I know now about the historical roots of Pepperdine University. I think the same thing applies to those who serve the institution today.

This study would not have been possible without the help of numerous colleagues. But special thanks go to Carolyn Hunter, who contributed as a research assistant and editor through the duration of the project; Shirley Roper, who researched the minutes of the Pepperdine University board of regents and preserved important historical documents; Jody Semerau and former Seaver College Dean and now University Provost Rick Marrs, who found budgetary support; Marnie Mitze, who found office space; Melissa Nykanen, Katie Richardson, and Jamie Henricks, who opened the university archives; and Tammy Ditmore, who pored over every line of the text, word by word, and shepherded the manuscript through the printing and production process. Particularly helpful as resource persons were Dean Emeritus James Wilburn, Professor Dan Caldwell, and Professor Emeritus Steven Lemley. And, of course, special thanks go to President Andrew Benton, who first suggested this study, and to my wife, Jane, who gave me the freedom and encouragement to complete it.

W. David Baird

Howard A. White Professor of History Emeritus and Seaver College Dean Emeritus

THE FORMATIVE YEARS
1937–1957

CHAPTER 1

THE FOUNDER

George Pepperdine loved almost everything about Southern California. He reveled in its optimism, utopian ideals, boundless energy, entrepreneurial spirit, Midwestern values, health-restoring climate, and love affair with the automobile. His passion for the region often moved him to poetry: "It's a land of plenty and fortunes bright//It's a land of romance and joyful night//It's a land of hope and heart's delight//California is the land for me," he wrote.[1]

George Pepperdine and his wife, Lena Rose, and daughters Florence and Esther first visited California in 1915. Convinced that the climate would benefit his health and that business opportunities were promising, Pepperdine decided to relocate his auto supply company to Southern California. In January 1916, the family returned to the Golden State, living briefly in San Diego and then moving to Los Angeles. On March 20, 1916, he opened his first Western Auto Supply Agency store at 12th and Main. In the "motorized civilization" that was Los Angeles, the store and its catalog service were immediate successes. By 1939, there were 200 additional stores throughout the West, and George Pepperdine and Lena Rose Pepperdine were major players in the civic life of Los Angeles.[2]

Born on June 20, 1886, George was the second son of John and Mary Lain Pepperdine, Illinois natives who had migrated to Labette County in southeastern Kansas three years earlier and settled on an eighty-acre farm south of Mound Valley. Toward the end of his life, Pepperdine looked back at his Kansas childhood with considerable nostalgia, remembering two transformative influences. The first was the faith of his father, who had been baptized by immersion "into Christ and a newness of life," as he would say, within months of arriving in Kansas. He and his wife were members of a small Church of Christ congregation that met nearby. Living according to New Testament teachings and not "forsaking the assembly of the saints" were fundamental principles in the Pepperdine household, and they remained essential to

George Pepperdine throughout his life, even shaping the character of the college he would found.[3]

The other transformative experience involved trapping rabbits. The Pepperdine farm was inundated with feral rabbits, causing considerable crop loss, so his father suggested that George try trapping them and selling their meat and hide. Rather than limit his enterprise to one trap, George laid out as many as fifty, placing them strategically along a three-mile line. He enjoyed immediate success, earning enough to buy a new saddle. Running the line and processing the catch each morning was hard work, but George learned a principle that would impact his future career: the more units put into production the greater the return.[4]

Concerned about the formal education of his boys, John Pepperdine moved the family to Parsons, Kansas, the principal railroad terminal in the county, in November 1903. George enrolled in Parsons Business College, where he learned shorthand, bookkeeping, and office management skills. He graduated a year later and took a bookkeeper position at a grain elevator in Checotah, Indian Territory, but he became so homesick that he resigned after two months. Another job with a real estate company in Kansas City was also short-lived, and he returned to Parsons, where he stayed for a year raising chickens and trying to impress a young woman named Lena Rose Baker.[5]

Making a Mail-Order Start

Lena Baker, two years younger than George, was the oldest and only daughter of William and Agnes Baker's seven children. Lena grew up on a farm in the same county as George, and her family also was associated with Churches of Christ but in different congregations. George and Lena met at church in Parsons. Lena was keenly intelligent, confident, and outgoing; she was also disciplined and organized. She and George made a handsome couple.[6]

In summer 1907, George returned to Kansas City as bookkeeper for the Southside Garage at a salary of $12 per week. He enjoyed his work, especially watching mechanics repair the cars and craftsmen vulcanize and tread tires. In one of his frequent letters to Lena, he proposed that she come to Kansas City and marry him. She accepted. On October 17, 1907, the two were married in front of a small group made up primarily of church friends. George was twenty-one; Lena was nineteen.[7]

Now a husband and soon a father (Florence was born in 1908), Pepperdine looked for opportunities to supplement his weekly income but found little success for a year and a half. Then, in March 1909, borrowing a concept from Sears, Roebuck & Co., he mailed a circular to 500 automobile owners, offering to provide listed parts and accessories at stipulated cash prices through the U.S. postal service. The response was positive and immediate. George used cash sent by the customer to buy the parts to fill their orders, took the items home where Lena prepared them for shipping, and then mailed the packages to the customers. His only investment in the process was $5 for 500 stamps for the original circular, an investment of about $132 in today's money. By the end of the first month, he and Lena had netted $100; by the end of the year, they had sold $12,000 worth of accessories. A 2016 equivalent would be about $315,000.[8]

Given the success of his enterprise, Pepperdine resigned from the garage and rented a place to process orders and display some merchandise. He began calling his operation the Western Auto Supply Agency. By the end of 1910, he had almost doubled sales of the first year, and within four years, sales totaled $250,000 annually (equivalent to about $6 million today). Pepperdine acquired larger quarters and employed twenty-five workers, three of whom were Lena's brothers; he incorporated his company in Missouri with capital stock of $20,000 (nearly one-half million in today's dollars).[9] His success after 1911 was due largely to his *Ford Owners' Supply Book,* a catalog that offered to replace virtually every part and accessory required to operate a Model T Ford. As the number of Fords on the road grew (15 million were made between 1909 and 1927), so did the Western Auto Supply Agency.[10]

Getting the company up and running was physically taxing for Pepperdine, who developed a tumor on his neck that required surgery in 1910 and 1911. He also contracted a persistent cough, and in June 1914 doctors diagnosed his condition as tuberculosis and recommended Denver as a healthy place to recuperate. Within a week, George, Lena, Florence, and Esther—six and four years old—were on their way to Colorado by car. The change was beneficial, and the family returned to Kansas City after ten weeks. But the humid climate was no place for a tubercular patient, so Pepperdine left Kansas for good, first moving to Colorado, where he started his second store, and then California.[11]

Doing Business in the City of Dreams

Convinced that California offered incredible business opportunities in addition to a more healthful climate, Pepperdine sold 51 percent interest in the Kansas City store to co-worker Don A. Davis for $3,500 and $150 per month for forty-three months: a total of $10,000, or some $250,000 today. He retained ownership of the Denver store and the right to operate Western Auto Stores in the Rocky Mountain and Pacific Coast states.[12]

Before the end of 1916, Pepperdine had established a store in downtown Los Angeles, widely known as the "City of Dreams." By January 1917, the LA store had sold $56,000 worth of goods. The next year that amount increased by 200 percent. By 1919, in an economy stimulated by World War I expenditures,

Pepperdine opened a second store in LA and others in Phoenix, Seattle, San Francisco, Sacramento, Fresno, and Oakland, all with catalog departments. Combined sales in his stores totaled almost $2 million annually.[13]

By incorporating Western Auto Supply Agency in 1920 and recapitalizing three years later, Pepperdine consolidated his eleven stores into one entity and invested in even more stores, opening about twenty-five a year. By 1926, there were 150 stores in the Western Auto chain in Rocky Mountain and Pacific Coast states. Pepperdine also built a headquarters and a model retail store at Grand and 11th streets in Los Angeles in 1923.[14]

The decade of growth following the establishment of the first Western Auto store in Los Angeles was little short of phenomenal. The fifth-largest city in the United States, Los Angeles was the most "automobilized" urban center in the nation. Still, a good portion of the chain's success could also be attributed to the vision and management skills of George and Lena Pepperdine. Foremost of their innovations was the concept of "branch" stores, far-flung stores wholly owned by the parent company and operated by employees of Western Auto.[15]

Equally important was the marriage between Western Auto and Ford automobiles. There was neither a part nor accessory for the ubiquitous Model T that Western Auto did not carry in its catalogue or stock in its Los Angeles store. Its inventory was large enough, chief of sales (and Lena's brother) Hal Baker insisted, to build a Ford right on the floor. To prove the claim, he proceeded to construct one.[16]

Other techniques also contributed to Western Auto's success, including measures taken to recruit and retain talented employees. They also believed strongly in the value of advertising and branding, introducing "Saving Sam," a figure that soon became a company icon. Its big head and little body with one hand extended and the other in his pocket were designed to project serving and saving, while house brands Western Giant and Western Flyer became synonymous with quality tires and bicycles. One of the company's most effective tactics was its "satisfaction-guaranteed policy," an expensive and innovative policy not in wide use by retail companies.[17]

Serving the Community

George Pepperdine and other observers attributed much of the success of Western Auto Supply to Lena.[18] In 1923, just as the new store on South Grand was opening, Pepperdine told a reporter, "Remember, it is Mrs. Pepperdine who is really the Western Auto Supply Company."[19] Lena had joined the company full-time by 1917 and was listed as a director and stockholder when it was incorporated in 1920; she also served as vice president and treasurer with direct responsibility for branch stores in Honolulu. In addition to managing the budget and signing every check that left the Los Angeles office, "L. R.," as she was known to Western Auto employees, hired and directed the activities of more than 100 women, facilitated the work of department managers, and involved herself in the "dealings of human nature," which, she maintained, was where women business executives shone most brightly.[20]

Recognized in the Los Angeles community as one of its most successful and "brainy" businesswomen, Lena Pepperdine was involved with a number of community and charity organizations devoted to a variety of causes, including Prohibition and conservation. Her most notable civic service was as co-chair of the women's division of the Tournament of Roses Association in Pasadena, which earned her a ride in the parade on New Year's Day 1930.[21]

George Pepperdine was no less involved in community affairs, and he was widely recognized as a highly principled, successful businessman, noted

Born in Kansas in 1886, George Pepperdine founded the Western Auto Supply Store in 1909. Because of health issues, he moved with his family to Los Angeles in 1916, where he started another iteration of Western Auto Supply. In 1937, he founded a college named in his honor in south central Los Angeles, dedicating it to "higher learning under the influence of fundamental Christian leadership" and "beautiful Christian living."

for his integrity, modesty, common sense, and fair play whose office was in a "dinky, glassed-in cubbyhole." His friends knew he possessed the sensitivities of a poet, was a bit naïve, generous to a fault, and hopelessly optimistic. He was also recognized as a man with a profound faith in God. Unlike Lena, Pepperdine was ill at ease "in social circles of his own station," that is, among LA's wealthy elite.[22]

Pepperdine championed causes and organizations that harmonized with his strong Christian faith and practical Midwestern values. He was particularly active in the Federated Church Brotherhoods of Southern California—an ecumenical Protestant group organized in 1927 to promote everything from Prohibition to Bible reading and to oppose betting on horse racing and cigarette advertising—and in the Protestant Welfare Association of Los Angeles County, organized in 1923 "to salvage misdirected" boys and girls.[23]

George Pepperdine gave public support to two Los Angeles mayoral candidates, backing former jurist Benjamin Bledsoe, who failed to oust the incumbent in 1925. In 1929, Pepperdine served as finance chairperson of the campaign of John C. Porter, the hand-picked candidate of the Reverend Mr. Bob Shuler, pastor of the huge Trinity Methodist Church in downtown Los Angeles. Shuler recruited Porter because he was from Iowa and a former member of the Ku Klux Klan, an organization that Shuler championed because of its moral agenda. Porter won the election, but Pepperdine later had to defend decisions of the finance committee before a Los Angeles County grand jury. The experience was so unrewarding and Porter's administration so disappointing that Pepperdine never chose to get involved directly in local politics again.[24] He left no record as to his preferences in state or national politics, although it is hard to think of him as supportive of President Franklin Roosevelt.

Their civic involvement did not distract George and Lena Pepperdine from participating fully in their faith community, and they rarely missed a Sunday service. Until 1922, the Pepperdines worshipped primarily with the Church of Christ that met at Ninth and Lime in Long Beach, a very conservative congregation reminiscent of those they had attended in Kansas.[25] That year they became charter members at the Southwest congregation that met at the intersection of SW 64th and Normandie streets in Los Angeles. Pepperdine remained a member of that congregation until his death, serving as an elder after 1938.[26] Records do not indicate that Pepperdine did much actual preaching from the church pulpit, although his thoughts were widely published, most notably in a tract titled *More Than Life*. An estimated 4.5 million copies of that small publication circulated through Churches of Christ around the world.[27]

When he traveled outside of Los Angeles, Pepperdine never failed to find a congregation where he could worship. Consequently, he had considerable knowledge of what was going on and who was who in Churches of Christ throughout the West, especially California. And he was always willing to sustain a preacher, help fund a building, or support a good work like an orphan's home in Ontario.[28] By the mid-1930s, he was helping some fifty congregations in one form or another.[29] He also donated $25,000 to Harding College early in the presidency of George Benson to help the school avoid bankruptcy.[30]

Notwithstanding their admirable generosity and discomfort with the social elite, George and Lena Pepperdine did not eschew the advantages of great wealth. In 1928, Pepperdine purchased as the family home a twenty–year-old mansion of seventeen rooms on two and a half acres at 3320 West Adams, a street of fashion and wealth. Myron Hunt, architect of the Rose Bowl, the Huntington Library, and Occidental College, had designed the house.[31] Florence and Esther were enrolled in elite private schools and came to be considered, at least by the *Los Angeles Times*' society page editor, as sub-debs.[32]

All members of the family traveled worldwide, taking cruises and months-long trips to Hawaii, South America, China, Japan, Europe, and the Holy Lands.[33] In 1928, Pepperdine escorted his mother on a four-month trip around the world, taking several memorable days in Japan to visit Churches of Christ missionaries.[34]

Changes on the Home Front

Significantly, George and Lena traveled separately. For reasons that can only be guessed, the two had grown apart: in late 1927 or early 1928, Lena resigned her executive position at Western Auto Supply Agency and left the family home.[35] In January 1929, George sued Lena for divorce on the grounds of abandonment. Neither Lena nor her attorney appeared to contest the action, so the Superior Court judge granted a bill of divorce to George Pepperdine to be final after a year and subject to an amicable property settlement. George and Lena had been married twenty-one years.[36]

In the wake of the divorce, Lena planned a lengthy cruise of South America with daughter Esther. Before she left, however, she prepared a will naming her ex-spouse as executor of her estate. At Buenos Aires, one of many ports-of-call on the cruise, she bought a pair of colorful parrots, commonly known as love birds. Before the ship returned to Los Angeles in mid-December, one of the parrots sickened and died. Despite a bit of fever, Lena was unconcerned about her own health when she returned to Los Angeles. She met her social obligations in the city, which included riding in the Rose Bowl parade on January 1, 1930. Immediately after, Lena and Esther embarked on *The City of Los Angeles* for Hawaii to visit Florence and her husband, Randolph Crossley, who were living in Honolulu. By the time she reached the islands, Lena was quite ill; on

January 18, 1930, she died of psittacosis, or parrot fever. Her body was returned to Los Angeles and buried in Forest Lawn Cemetery.[37]

At Lena's death, the Western Auto Supply company controlled by George Pepperdine consisted of 170 stores with annual sales totaling $14 million.

Pepperdine left little to indicate his feelings in the wake of his divorce and Lena's subsequent death, not even permitting mention of it in his authorized biography. His mother lived with him in the Adams Street mansion until her death in 1932. Shortly after her death, Pepperdine met his future wife, Helen Louise Davis, at a social affair organized by the Protestant Welfare Association. Sixteen years younger than George, Helen was Indiana-born, the daughter of a dentist, and—according to Pepperdine—the most beautiful woman in the world.

He was pleased with her passion for social work and even more impressed with her faith in God and her willingness to work and worship in Churches of Christ although she had grown up in the Christian Church. After a two-year courtship, George and Helen married on June 17, 1934. W. C. Pearce, a distinguished leader of the interdenominational Sunday school movement and Pepperdine's personal friend, administered the vows.[38]

George considered Helen a "blessing, a joy, and a dynamo of helpful energy" and made a habit of sending her affectionate notes and cards, such as at Christmas 1956 when he wrote, "Of all sweet words, I must confess, The sweetest were yours when you said 'yes.'"[39] The couple's relationship was one of mutual respect and devotion, and it lasted for twenty-eight years.

Together they had three children: Marilyn (1935), George II (1936), and Wendell (1941). They were loving and supportive parents but pretty inflexible when it came to patterns of behavior, best described as a list of *don'ts*. All three children attended George Pepperdine College, pursued postgraduate studies, and had successful careers. Not all, however, imitated the religious faith of their parents. Marilyn once confessed to "skeptic notions" and to being embarrassed by half-intelligent articles published in religious periodicals, which left her so ashamed she did not want to be "associated in anyway with the . . . so-called 'flock'."[40]

Keeping through Sharing

Throughout the Great Depression and establishing a new marriage and family, Pepperdine retained his philanthropic interests. Indeed, he had come to accept as a principle of his Christian faith that anyone who acquired a large amount of money had a positive duty to society and to God to see that the money was used to benefit mankind rather than passed on to heirs. He was convinced that wealthy men really kept only what they gave away.[41]

In 1931, therefore, he established the George Pepperdine Foundation to channel his gifts to religious, charitable, and educational organizations, funding it with gifts of dividend-paying Western Auto Supply Agency stock.[42] There were tax advantages to the foundation too: first, any income (dividends) from his gifts was tax-free, and, second, it was a way to transfer his wealth to the support of preferred philanthropies without the impediment of inheritance taxes. The board of trustees for the foundation were George Pepperdine, his mother, and R. C. Cooper, an elder of the Southwest Church of Christ.[43]

For the first two years, the foundation had virtually no money to distribute, but by the end of 1939, the foundation had a net worth of $5.2 million, or some $89 million in today's currency.[44] It had also added a staff person, A. J. Dumm an elder of the 12th and Hudson Church of Christ in Los Angeles and former vice president of the local branch of the Federal Reserve Bank. Beneficiaries of the George Pepperdine Foundation included the Helen Louise Girls Home, the Casa Colina Convalescent Home for Crippled Children, the Pacific Lodge, the Boy Scouts, the YMCA, forty or more Churches of Christ, and an unknown number of ministers. After 1937, its foremost beneficiary would be George Pepperdine College.

To bolster the assets of the foundation, Pepperdine sold his controlling interest in Western Auto Supply Agency in July 1939 after receiving a "fair" proposal from Gamble-Skogmo Company of Minneapolis. It was a sale he had contemplated for several years, especially as he got deeper into charitable, religious, and educational activities. He was wholly convinced "that his life should not be given to the making of money, but that a large part of his efforts and time should be devoted to the best possible use of the money already earned . . . for the benefit of humanity."[45]

How much George Pepperdine netted from the sale of Western Auto was never published, although there was a lot of speculation that set Pepperdine's fortune at the $10 million level ($166 million in today's currency).[46] Helen Pepperdine would later say that George's estate was half what some people thought and that he gave away twice as much as most people believed.[47] Whatever the size of his fortune, Pepperdine set about putting it to good use.

First, however, he took care of the future needs of his family, establishing trust funds for his children. He also made a substantial gift of stock and property to Helen, never dreaming that the income from the gift would have to sustain the two of them completely just twelve years later.

The Foundation Dries Up

George Pepperdine himself made the decisions as to how best to reinvest the foundation's assets. Up to that point, those decisions had been tempered by the experience and wisdom of A. J. Dumm, but he had died in 1939. Men who did not necessarily have the best interests of the foundation in mind now advised Pepperdine. They encouraged him to move the assets into various kinds of businesses, ranging from aircraft equipment, chemical producers, and tool and tire makers to dry ice plants, lumber mills, and companies mining for gold, petroleum, gypsum, fluorspar, and sodium sulphate.

Most of these investments, it turned out, required far more working capital than contemplated to generate a significant return. Eager to arrange for a big payday so that the work of the foundation would continue, Pepperdine endorsed a strategy of borrowing money to meet the need for additional capital. Indeed, an ethic of borrowing pervaded the foundation, and in some cases Pepperdine pledged his personal assets as collateral for loans.

The majority of the foundation's ventures, even with additional capital, never turned the corner that Pepperdine anticipated. By December 1950, he and the foundation found themselves unable to pay all the notes given for the

A native of Indiana, Helen Louise Davis was the beloved second wife of George Pepperdine, who helped him establish the college named in his honor. Helen Pepperdine was a member of the governing boards of the university until her death at the age of 87 in 1990.

money borrowed. Pepperdine appeared before Los Angeles County Superior Court and petitioned that the foundation be dissolved, "its purposes having been accomplished," and a referee appointed to liquidate its assets and pay 104 individuals and companies who were creditors of the organization.[48] The petition was granted the following January, and court-supervised liquidation began almost immediately.

It was a painful process for all parties concerned. There simply were not enough assets, gathered through something like a fire sale, to meet the foundation's liabilities.[49] And Pepperdine's personal assets, the loss of which left him penniless, were inadequate to cover the difference. It deeply troubled him that he not only owed people money he could not pay, but also that the foundation assets intended to build a large endowment for his college had been swept away.[50]

In addition to indignities and insults, a dizzying array of lawsuits followed. In one famous case, five creditors of the foundation sued Pepperdine and other former directors for gross negligence in managing the affairs of the organization, having wasted a $3 million endowment and incurring $551,300 in debts. In the Superior Court as well as the District Court of Appeal, judges ruled against the plaintiffs, with the appellant judge writing a blistering decision that became a judicial landmark. There was in the pleadings, said the judge, "not a chirp . . . that intimates at a corrupt motive that marred the character or inspired the acts" of Pepperdine or the directors. Instead, the losses of the foundation were "the product of impoverished thought or inaccurate calculation and [was] on a parity with [its] improvident, ill-conceived investments."[51]

In 1953, twenty-six creditors of the foundation sued George Pepperdine College, charging that it had been the recipient of properties from the foundation that should have been used to satisfy their claims and asking for a judgment of $260,000.[52] The case created considerable consternation on the campus of the college, but the suit was settled out of court for $22,000 four years later.[53]

The collapse of his foundation and the loss of his fortune reduced George Pepperdine to circumstances that he had not known since he was a boy in Kansas. He and Helen were forced to sell the mansion on West Adams Street for $75,000 and to make a down payment on a much smaller house at 1614 Wellington Street. For living expenses, they had to rely on a modest income of less than $9,000 per year from assets belonging to Helen. Those were so limited, however, that Pepperdine could not even pay debts he owed his brothers, much to the consternation of his sisters-in-law.[54]

Remarkably, the Pepperdines never declared bankruptcy nor repudiated a debt, convinced that was something that Christians did not do. Nor did they blame others for their circumstances. Pepperdine came to understand that many of his investments were "foolish." "I have plenty of time now to regret those things," he wrote to his sister-in-law, "but that does not bring back the money. I am praying much these days that the Lord will forgive my errors, which were many and bad, although made with good intentions and hopes of gain."[55]

Telling His Story

George Pepperdine hoped to regain some of his stature by publishing a biography, and he approached Richard L. Clark, then a professor at George Pepperdine College, about writing the book. Clark started with the early chapters, using notes prepared by Pepperdine, but for some unknown reason withdrew from the project before it was completed. Pepperdine then persuaded Jack W. Bates, formerly a faculty member at the college but then dean at Lubbock Christian College in Texas, to take up the challenge.

Bates spent part of 1957 and much of 1958 completing his part of the manuscript, but it was a continuing challenge because Pepperdine was never certain about what he wanted to include. He wanted the simple stories of his childhood to be told because those carried a moral message of faith, family, and hard work. But he was not sure that accounts of his business failures should be spread across the pages of his biography. Ultimately, he agreed to include part of that story, but he permitted no word regarding his failed marriage to Lena.[56]

To reveal his religious beliefs, Pepperdine merely included the tract he co-wrote some years earlier with Hugh Tiner, "More than Life." To document his commitment to private property, the free-market economy, and the American Way, he inserted "The Miracle of the American Way of Life," an essay inspired and largely written by George Benson, president of Harding College in Searcy, Arkansas. Also appended were personal letters written during his world tour in 1927–1928 and some farewell thoughts on what he was thinking at the sunset of his life. Published in 1959, the book revealed a man endowed with the spirit of humility, love, and service; however, as a biography or autobiography, it did not do the man or its readers justice.[57]

As the 1950s progressed, Pepperdine regained his reputation as a notable civic leader. California Governor Goodwin Knight declared June 20, 1956—Pepperdine's seventieth birthday—as George Pepperdine Day, and the Los Angeles County Board of Supervisors honored him with a resolution of appreciation. In March 1960, the Freedom's Foundation of Valley Forge, Pennsylvania, granted Pepperdine its George Washington Medal for his essay, "The Miracle of the American Way of Life." In May 1961, the Los Angeles County Board of Supervisors gave Pepperdine its first Distinguished Service Medal for outstanding and extraordinary public service.[58]

Within his church community, George Pepperdine lost little standing because of his financial troubles. Indeed, how he handled those woes actually elevated his standing. When Pepperdine had nothing left, Don Miller recalled, "he was still the same trusting, Christian gentleman" as when he had money. He knew how to deal with adversity. Such losses, historian Bill Youngs wrote, "did not ruin his serene and trustful spirit, dull his enjoyment of the good work being continued, nor rob him of his optimism and happiness or his faith in God and men."[59]

That godly attitude endeared Pepperdine to his brothers and sisters among Churches of Christ, and that respect was best demonstrated when George Pepperdine College hosted Bible lectures that attracted Churches of Christ faithful from across the nation. Attendees greeted Pepperdine as if he were a famous movie star. This outpouring of respect and affection was never more apparent than in March 1962 when the 12,000 people attending the lectureship at the Los Angeles Sports Arena teared up when George Pepperdine rose from his gurney and spoke of his joy at being there among his brethren, "perhaps for the last time."[60] Kenny Hahn, a former student at the college, best expressed how they felt: "He was a humble man, who made a fortune and gave it away for the benefit of others before he died."[61] A few months, later, on July 31, 1962, George Pepperdine died from an aneurysm of the aorta.

Like that of most, Pepperdine's legacy was mixed. He succeeded in business, engaged in notable philanthropies, dedicated himself to his church, loved his family, and practiced Christian values. Despite the best of intentions, however, his record as a foundation manager and even as a husband and father was less enviable. But his mark was lasting, nevertheless, thanks to his founding of a college dedicated to rooting young men and women in Christian character and faith and preparing them to live lives of usefulness in a competitive world.

CHAPTER 2

THE MIRACLE ON VERMONT AVENUE

A strand of anxiety ran through the United States in 1937. President Franklin Roosevelt's New Deal programs had provided some relief from the heavy hand of the national depression, but efforts for serious social and economic reform had yielded little more than rancorous criticism. In Europe, Adolf Hitler was building the greatest war machine in history and had tested its capacity by bombing Guernica, a peaceful Basque village in northern Spain, killing or wounding 1,600 innocents. The nervous tension was not lessened by the disappearance of Amelia Earhart in the vastness of the Pacific Ocean.

But notable accomplishments mitigated some of that anxiety. The Golden Gate Bridge opened for traffic; Dale Carnegie published *How to Win Friends and Influence People*; Hormel Company launched Spam; Margaret Mitchell published *Gone with the Wind*; Fred Astaire sang "They Can't Take That Away from Me"; and Joe DiMaggio hit forty-six home runs.[1] No doubt George Pepperdine took note of these and other events, but any anxiety was overshadowed by optimism. For him, 1937 would be a year of joy, hope, abundant blessings, and virtual miracles that culminated in September with the opening of George Pepperdine College.

Birth of an Idea

Every Sunday morning, Hugh Tiner hosted *Take Time to Be Holy* on radio station KFVD in Los Angeles. Sponsored by Churches of Christ within Southern California, the program gave Tiner an occasion to deliver a biblical-based message and promote the work of sponsoring congregations. One of the supervisors in the county educational system, Tiner also preached regularly for the Sichel Street Church of Christ, the oldest congregation in Los Angeles. George Pepperdine was a faithful listener, and sometime in mid-1936 invited Tiner to his office at the Western Auto Supply headquarters in Los Angeles.[2]

A native of La Vernia, Texas, and a graduate of Abilene Christian College, Tiner had come west to secure a master's degree at Stanford and then found employment as a teacher and administrator in the Los Angeles County public schools. Only twenty-eight, Tiner was a tall, handsome man with considerable presence in both private and public settings. He and Pepperdine related on several levels, and Pepperdine liked him immediately. Both were immigrants to California, both had parents of modest means, both had been baptized as teenagers, and neither was afraid of hard work. Tiner, for example, had paid for his college education by working as a pressman in dry cleaning shops. Above all, the two related because of their common commitment to Churches of Christ.[3]

Pepperdine asked Tiner how he had retained his Christian faith and practices and his allegiance to Churches of Christ. The young educator instantly attributed it all to attending a Christian college. That was not the answer Pepperdine expected. His religious mentors had taught him that churches could not support colleges because the practice was not mentioned in scripture. Moreover, Christian colleges brought dangers from worldliness, flawed teaching, softness in doctrine, and domination of individual congregations.[4] Tiner's active faith and church record, however, contradicted that teaching.

Tiner was not the first person to suggest to Pepperdine that Christian colleges could have benefits. George Benson, an old missionary friend he had visited in Japan was the new president of Harding College, and he had convinced Pepperdine, through his foundation, to donate $25,000 to the Arkansas school in 1936.[5] A. M. Burton, a Nashville, Tennessee, life insurance underwriter millionaire, spoke just as effectively regarding David Lipscomb College, which he supported heavily.[6] Clinton Davidson, a New Jersey advisor of Benson and another wealthy insurance broker, had spoken of the value of Christian education as well.[7] Even Pepperdine's minister at the Southwest Church of Christ, T. W. Phillips II, had said good things about Christian education—so long as it was considered adjunct to the home rather than the church.[8]

Although willing to concede that Christian higher education merited the support of individual Christians, George Pepperdine was not sure it was the right investment for him. Individually and through his foundation, he had long supported Church of Christ ministers, evangelists, missionaries, and church building programs. But that support was limited and noncontroversial. However, given the financial resources at hand and his conviction that one should not use a great fortune selfishly, he wanted to do something of more lasting benefit to humanity. The more he talked to Tiner, who became like a son to him, the more Pepperdine thought that lasting legacy could come from ensuring young people had a chance for a collegiate education in a Christian environment with believing professors and a "sound" curriculum.[9]

A Decision Built on Faith

By Christmas 1936, George Pepperdine had pretty much decided to make Christian education his philanthropic priority.[10] Whatever reservations he might have had were resolved after Hugh Tiner arranged a personal conversation with Batsell Baxter, the former president of both Abilene Christian College and David Lipscomb College, in February 1937. Tiner had lived in the Baxter home when he was a student at ACC and knew the venerable churchman and educator well. Baxter listened intently to Pepperdine's dream of a four-year liberal arts college on the West Coast that would be academically sound and based on Christian faith, but not dependent upon the churches for support. He then asked only two questions: how will you finance the institution and when do you expect to begin?[11]

Pepperdine's answers were as clear as they were bold. His foundation would supply funds to cover the initial costs and a good part, if not all, of the annual budget. And he thought September, eight months thereafter, was feasible. Clearly, there was no time to lose.[12]

Even so, the issue was not yet settled, at least in Pepperdine's mind. He wrote to Hugh Tiner early in March that he was willing to "help" finance a college but only if:

- The project was recognized from the beginning as a private institution, not connected with the church in any manner.
- The church under no circumstances would ever be asked for contributions to the college.
- The perpetuation of the work was assured by an adequate endowment.
- The institution from its very beginning would be able to qualify as a standard-grade, four-year college.
- The board of trustees and faculty would be composed of devout "Christians," meaning members of the Church of Christ, thereby safeguarding and deepening the faith of the students.

He raised these contingencies, he said, because he wanted "to avoid the possibility of any scriptural question ever arising over the establishment of such an institution" and because he had no interest in supporting an educational program that was not rooted in a "safe Christian environment." Moreover, he did not want to finance something that Christian parents in Southern California did not "unanimously" support. Pepperdine asked Tiner to determine whether that support existed.[13]

On March 15, Tiner sent a letter to as many "Christian Parents and Friends" in California for whom he could find addresses. Would they, he asked, "like to see a college started in Southern California similar to Harding or David

Lipscomb or Abilene Christian?" The response to his inquiry is unknown, but it was clearly positive enough to affirm Pepperdine's intention to open a new four-year college six months later.[14] At the March meeting of the Los Angeles Chamber of Commerce, Pepperdine announced to the community at large his plans to build a college, and Tiner distributed a mimeographed press release describing those plans.[15] The story was picked up quickly by the Los Angeles press and national periodicals, including *Time Magazine*.[16] Now there could be no turning back.

Doubtless, members of the Chamber of Commerce and prospective patrons wanted to know the name of the new college. George responded to such inquiries with a measure of honest embarrassment, for the school was to be named "George Pepperdine College." Presumably he had agreed to that name reluctantly, and only after friends insisted.[17] Since Pepperdine was a man of genuine humility, it is hard to discount this traditional story. Perhaps he did not protest too much, however. After all, he did also name the foundation after himself; a new home for girls after his wife, Helen Louise; and the women's residence hall at the college after his daughter, Marilyn.

Constructing a Dream

By May 1937, the new college not only had a name but also a location, architectural plans, a construction contractor, a board of trustees, administrative officers, and a faculty. After considering several options, George Pepperdine and his wife, Helen, purchased for $150,000 thirty-four acres of land in south central Los Angeles on 79th Street between Vermont and Normandie Avenues. Known as the Connelly estate, the property was the remnant of an old Spanish land grant and featured an elegant, twenty-five-year-old mansion known for its wood paneling and beautiful cabinetwork. The Pepperdines envisioned the mansion as the home of the college president and as a site of special events for students. Most important, the property was directly accessible via street cars to central Los Angeles and part-time jobs.[18]

Pepperdine chose as the architect and builder of the campus John M. Cooper, well-known in Los Angeles for his art deco structures, including Western Auto Supply headquarters. Cooper began work on the four initial buildings—the administration building, the dining hall, and men's and women's residence halls—in early June, anticipating completion on September 20, the date of the college's expected opening.[19]

Pepperdine also established a governing structure for the new college. With the help of attorney Eli Bush, he wrote articles of incorporation for George Pepperdine College that—curiously—never once referred to it as a Christian college. It did provide that a board of trustees would be composed of from five to thirty men or women who were members in good standing of Churches of Christ. It would be the trustees' responsibility to see that the college fulfilled its Christian mission, having the authority to select a president, fix salaries, and prescribe courses of study, among other things.[20] Five organizing trustees were named: George Pepperdine; Clarence Shattuck, a vice president of National Cash Register and subsequently business manager of the George Pepperdine Foundation; A. J. Dumm, a vice president of the Federal Reserve Bank of Los Angeles; Donald V. Miller, a vice president of the Security National Bank of Pasadena; and Hugh M. Tiner. The board had its first meeting on July 7, 1937, when it ratified the articles of incorporation and adopted bylaws.[21]

Batsell Baxter led the opening prayer of the initial meeting of the trustees. Pepperdine had offered him the presidency of his new college with an annual salary of $3,600. Despite ill health, Baxter found it impossible to decline what he considered to be a virtual "Macedonian call." To be the founding president of a well-funded college offering a standard four-year curriculum in a Christian environment was the opportunity of a lifetime, and more importantly, a chance to expand the kingdom of God. By April 22, he had moved his family to Los Angeles and begun to recruit a faculty, organize a curriculum, and recruit a student body—all tasks that needed to be complete within five months. Fortunately, he was soon joined by Hugh Tiner, who had agreed to serve as the first dean of George Pepperdine College, also at a salary of $3,600.[22]

Since Pepperdine expected that the faculty would be members of the Churches of Christ in good standing, Baxter had to be selective in recruiting. First, he looked for prospects on faculties of other Church of Christ colleges, telling them about Pepperdine's vision for Christian higher education and of his generosity in underwriting the cost of that vision. He appealed to their pioneering spirit and Church of Christ loyalties. For example, to E. V. Pullias he wrote:

> Churches of Christ [in California] are small in number, but strong in faith . . . [and they] are looking to George Pepperdine College as the greatest power and influence for good that has ever come to this section. . . . In making the college possible, [George Pepperdine] has opened to [Churches of Christ] a field that challenges the best and finest there is in us. He plans to make this college the major work of his life. It can become the major project of our lives . . . [and] there is no human mind capable of measuring the good that, by the help of God, we can accomplish.[23]

With such a message, President Baxter was an effective recruiter.[24] By September 15, he had gathered a faculty of twenty-one men and women. Among these were Callie Mae and R. R. Coons, J. Herman Campbell, Hubert Derrick, Francis Hinds Easley, Dederich Navall, E. V. Pullias, Wade Ruby,

Russel N. Squire, J. Eddie Weems (dean of men), and Martha Middlebrooks (dean of women).

Four members of the first faculty had doctorates, eleven had master's, and six had bachelor's degrees. If they were full-time, a faculty person was typically paid $250 per month, a salary that varied only a little over the next decade.[25] As Pepperdine had directed, all were members of Churches of Christ with the exception of Navall, who was a Mennonite. All presumably confessed their belief in the virgin birth, deity and miracles of Christ, "the Biblical account of creation," and the inspiration of the Bible.[26] They would also have embraced what Pepperdine called the doctrine of "the Church and conversion of sinners," which to the founder meant accepting scriptures that taught belief, confession, repentance, and baptism into "Christ's body, the Church." Members of the Churches of Christ would have celebrated the Lord's Supper weekly and worshipped without the aid of instrumental music.[27]

To prepare a four-year curriculum for George Pepperdine College (GPC) in a matter of months required pragmatic creativity. Baxter took the most recent annual catalogs of Occidental College, UCLA, and the University of Southern California (USC), tore out the degree requirements and course listings for particular majors and asked the appropriate Pepperdine faculty person to blend the three programs into one suitable for GPC and for publication in the college's first catalog.[28] It was taken for granted that GPC would base its curriculum on the quarter system since most regional schools already utilized that structure.

Baxter also used suggestions from the new faculty to help build the library collection. The accrediting agency recommended that start-up colleges have a library with a minimum of 10,000 volumes. E. V. Pullias supplied a list of 1,000 titles needed to support the psychology and education majors; other faculty members presumably provided similar suggestions.[29]

All of this, of course, required an enormous amount of money. Pepperdine had the necessary assets, but most were tied up in Western Auto. His foundation also had obligations to additional philanthropies, including a new one, the Helen Louise Home for Girls on Westmoreland Street in Los Angeles, that he and Helen launched simultaneously with GPC. To handle the finance and investment issues of the foundation, Pepperdine recruited trustee A. J. Dumm, one of the elders of the Central Church of Christ at 12th and Hoover in Los Angeles. He so capably managed the assets of the foundation that the cash necessary to fund the construction of the campus and recruitment of the faculty was at hand. He would spend some $600,000 on the property and physical facilities of the campus and gather another $1 million into an endowment for the college.[30]

Gathering a Student Body

With the campus, faculty, and curriculum under construction, Baxter, Tiner, and Pepperdine turned their attention to recruiting a student body, targeting Church of Christ students who were either expecting to attend or had attended colleges related to Churches of Christ. They inserted large ads in church publications, visited the campuses of "sister" schools, and circulated widely the first bulletin for GPC, which promised the college would offer a well-rounded education to prepare students "for a life of usefulness in a competitive world" while providing "a foundation of Christian character and faith which [would] survive the storms of life."

The bulletin also assured prospective students that the environment on the campus was designed so that "Christian character, loyalty to Jesus, and faith in God [would] increase." Yet Pepperdine also declared that the new college would "not be connected with any church" or "solicit contributions from the churches."[31]

Exceptional for Church of Christ colleges, all others of which were situated in the U.S. South, GPC announced that it would welcome qualified students of color, although they could not live on campus until the college built a dormitory for international students. Put differently, black students could attend classes with white students but not live with them in the same residence hall.

The residential restriction aligned with the views of most Churches of Christ members in the 1930s—the majority of whom lived in the South—but the open admission policy certainly did not. That remarkable exception to policies of other colleges associated with the Churches of Christ speaks highly of the Christian spirit of George Pepperdine, President Baxter, and Dean Tiner. Even the separate living restrictions did not survive long, disappearing from the catalog in 1944.[32]

Emphasizing a "Useful" Education

The recruiting bulletin demonstrated that Baxter and Tiner had taken seriously Pepperdine's wish that the college's curriculum should prepare students for *useful* lives in a competitive world. There was no reference at all to liberal or general education. Instead, students were assured that the college would prepare them for careers in business administration, law, medicine, engineering, teaching, ministry, and home economics.

The administrators may have emphasized "practical arts" because they expected the majority of their first class would be transfers from two-year institutions who would have completed general education requirements and be ready for advanced training in major fields. Then, again, it may have been the genesis of a conviction that undergraduate education at GPC, and its successor, Seaver College, would be essentially pre-professional, and that by design of the founder.

George Pepperdine College was marketed as "an economical school." For nine months, tuition and fees were $140; board and room were $270, and the college promised to help students find part-time work if they needed it. Costs were higher than for some schools, but prospective students, the bulletin commented, should consider the strength of the faculty, the advantages of location, the environment, the modern dormitories, and "the prestige and educational standing of the school." Moreover, it was "sound policy to charge a reasonable tuition, as no one should expect 'something for nothing.'"[33]

In addition to personal appeals, print ads, and the college bulletin, President Baxter also utilized radio ads to market the new college, no doubt influenced by the successful Western Auto Supply and George Pepperdine Foundation advertising campaigns. The college was promoted on the *Take Time to Be Holy* radio show and subsequently featured weekly on a KFWB show devoted solely to the college.[34] Indeed, the young college was featured so frequently on California's airways that Baxter feared negative repercussions from schools like UCLA and USC.[35]

Dedicating a Dream

George Pepperdine College opened its doors for the first time in mid-September 1937 with 162 students. None of them were persons of color, although during the second year at least one was, freshman Ed Anderson. Eighty-two students lived in residence halls; seventy-six were day students. Forty-nine were from states outside California; a majority were members of Churches of Christ.

Barbara Vance from Hollywood, California, was the first student to register. Seaborn Kennamer of Montgomery, Alabama, was the first student to reserve a room in the men's dormitory, and Sue McMahan of Springfield, Tennessee, was the first to reserve a room in the women's dormitory. Ninety-two were classified as freshmen; twenty-six were sophomores; thirty-two were juniors; and five were seniors. Thirty-four of the students were transfers, with nineteen coming from David Lipscomb, nine from Abilene Christian, and six from Harding.[36]

Classes began Monday, September 27, in the mostly completed administration building. It was another three weeks, however, before both women and men occupied residence halls—Marilyn for the women and Baxter for the men—or had use of the dining hall.[37]

President Baxter presided over an impressive dedication ceremony on the afternoon of September 21, 1937. Some 2,000 persons, among them the most influential politicians, businessmen, and religious leaders in the city and state, assembled with faculty and students at the center of the campus under a bright sun. On a specially-built platform were Baxter, who served as master of ceremonies; G. C. Brewer, minister of the Central Church of Christ in Los Angeles, who led the invocation; Frank Shaw, mayor of the city of Los Angeles, who delivered a welcome to all guests; Hugh Tiner, who reflected on the events that led to the founding of the college; Frank Merriam, California governor, who delivered the principal dedicatory address; and T. W. Phillips II, minister of the Southwest Church of Christ, who offered the benediction.[38]

On the platform, too, was George Pepperdine. It was a glorious moment for him. The dream of a lifetime was unfolding before his fifty-one-year-old eyes. His fortune was seeding a harvest that he believed would bless his church, his family, his community, his nation, and his world in this and future generations. When it was his turn, he spoke briefly, simply, and profoundly. An educated person without Christianity, he said, was like a car without a

Batsell Baxter was the founding president of George Pepperdine College, serving from 1937 to 1939. Baxter, who had previously served as president of Abilene Christian and David Lipscomb, played a large role in transforming a dream into a reality: an accredited liberal arts college in a little more than two years.

steering gear. He was endowing the college, therefore, so that young men and women could prepare for lives of usefulness as they also built foundations of Christian character and faith. All instruction, he assured his hearers, would "be under conservative, fundamental Christian supervision" by faculty whose lives would be "noble examples of Christian living."

Finally, he dedicated the college to the twin causes of "higher learning under the influence of fundamental Christian leadership" and "beautiful Christian living." In so doing, he believed he was doing his "small bit to glorify the name of God in the earth and extend his Kingdom among the children of men."[39]

Pepperdine Pioneers

With the dedication of the campus accomplished, administration, faculty, and students went about the work of turning the buildings and grounds into a college. Students launched into academic programs structured around general education (GE) courses during the first two years and major courses during the last two years. For GE credit, they had to take courses in English, religion, science, social science, and a foreign language. One half of their academic work was devoted to a major and a minor field. Students graduated with 192 quarter hours. Those requirements changed little over the next decade.[40]

Faculty typically taught sixteen units, or three courses, each quarter. Over a nine-month period, therefore, a single faculty member would teach nine courses, although not always nine different classes. Whatever the mix of classes, nine courses an academic year represented a substantial teaching responsibility, especially when compared to teaching loads of five to six courses a year in the early 2000s.[41] Typically, classes were small, although the GE courses could be bigger. J. Eddie Weems, an instructor in English and the GPC track coach, taught the largest classes in the early years; even so, he probably had fewer than seventy-six students per term.

Fifty percent of the first class of students worked at on-campus jobs for part of their school expenses. Twenty-seven percent worked off campus.[42] The work-study activity of the students warmed Pepperdine's heart. He saw it as an expression of personal dedication on the part of students, as evidence of the college's commitment to making an education possible to anyone willing to work, and a demonstration of the social conscience of the free-market system.

Dean Tiner took responsibility for organizing or establishing most of those trappings that turned buildings and space into a college. Under his leadership, a student newspaper, the *GraPhiC*, published its first issue on October 20, 1937. The name cleverly imbedded the initials of the college, GPC.[43] The next month, at Tiner's suggestion, students designated the athletic teams, initially basketball, as the "Waves."[44] He also orchestrated a referendum of the student body that established blue, the color of the Pacific Ocean, and orange, the color of the fruit that ripened in the groves of Southern California, as the school's colors.[45] The college yearbook, *The Promenade*, was launched a year later.[46]

Under the watchful eye of deans Weems and Middlebrooks, students organized themselves into social clubs, service clubs, and groups with interest in particular academic or vocational fields. The All-Student Association represented the student body as a whole; its nine members included a student-elected president, representatives from each of the classes, and the editors of the *Graphic* and *Promenade*. Its purpose was to act as a medium between faculty and students, promote cooperation among campus organizations, encourage a closer association between day and boarding students, and maintain a deep and enthusiastic school spirit. Those duties would increase over time, as would the prestige of the student body president. College administrators came to rely upon that officer to such an extent that they felt justified in giving him or her a partial scholarship.[47]

Aware that "real" colleges had sports teams, President Baxter and Dean Tiner were eager to create some at GPC. Putting together a sports program in a matter of months, especially when the campus lacked a gymnasium, was a logistical challenge, but they were able to organize both a track team and a basketball team, which practiced on church playgrounds and played games at the Manchester Playground.[48] The basketball program took a quantum leap forward with the construction of a new gymnasium in the summer of 1938. The first baseball and tennis teams were fielded in the second year, 1938–1939; neither club had much success.[49]

Four students qualified for a degree at the first commencement of the infant college on June 11, 1938. These included Carmen Landrum, a business administration major; Paul Tucker, an English major who intended to preach; Malcom Hinkley, a history major; and Richard Gibson, a language major. They received their diplomas on the front lawn of the president's home following a commencement address by E. H. Ijams, president of David Lipscomb College. All four were enthusiastic about their experiences at GPC. Said Gibson: it "is everything that I expected to find in a Christian school and a Christian environment."[50]

Ensuring a Christian Environment

George Pepperdine and President Baxter expected all elements of college life, whether curricular or extra-curricular, to strengthen the Christian character and faith of the students. That outcome, as Pepperdine articulated in his founding address, would be supported by faculty members who lived and practiced their faith before their students on a daily basis. It would also be enhanced by requiring all students to take four to six Bible courses before graduation.[51]

Finally, the faith and character of students would be enhanced by participating in a campus lifestyle organized according to Christian principles.

Supporting the Christian ethos of the campus were rules and regulations that students might have found in their homes. Initially, church attendance of boarding students was required, a rule "unenforced" because students went to church on their own volition. Rowdy behavior and hazing were not permitted, nor was dancing. Alcoholic drinks, cards, and dice games were forbidden. Smoking was not allowed on campus except in the dormitory rooms of boarding men who were addicted to tobacco. "Smoking [was] not tolerated among women," addicted or not.

Curiously, the early GPC bulletins make no mention of chapel requirements, although chapel services were a fundamental part of the Christian ethos of the campus. Every morning at 10 a.m. the campus stopped its "secular" activities for about thirty minutes and gathered for chapel. Services included hymns, scripture readings, prayers and inspirational messages, but they also included campus announcements and sometimes a presentation by a notable public figure, often secured by Pepperdine. According to the *Graphic,* chapel was the outstanding feature of college life that inspired and unified students and faculty. It gave the college its "real character."[52]

As important as daily chapel was to the founder and the administration, attendance does not seem to have been mandatory. Until the auditorium was constructed in 1940, there was no room large enough to hold everyone. Even at that, chapel attendance disappointed Baxter. He understood why students with jobs, who lived off campus, or were Catholic did not attend, but he could not understand why boarding students had such poor records of attendance. Chapel attendance became a major issue on campus once the auditorium was completed.

The nearby presence of a Church of Christ congregation helped sustain the Christian ethos on campus. Initially, GPC students who were Church of Christ members attended services of the Southwest congregation. In 1938, Tiner, Pullias, Jimmy Lovell, Russel Squire, and other faculty members organized a congregation adjacent to the campus on Vermont Avenue, purchasing a surplus Catholic church building and moving it in halves to the property. Tiner was the congregation's first minister, followed in 1939 by J. P. Sanders, who also headed the religion department on campus. Most boarding students who were members of the Churches of Christ attended it.[53]

The Vermont Avenue congregation was more than just an ancillary enterprise for George Pepperdine College. It played an important role in the college's complicated relationship with Churches of Christ. Pepperdine utilized its services to print and circulate some four million copies of his tract, "More than Life."[54] But he did not want the college to be accused of meddling in the affairs of independent congregations. For that reason, he asked the leadership of the congregation rather than the faculty of the college to mentor and help find speaking appointments for young men interested in ministry.[55]

For similar reasons, college administrators limited faculty participation in the *Take Time to be Holy* radio show.[56] The board of trustees even declined to participate in a campaign to advertise Christian education with Abilene Christian, David Lipscomb, Harding, and Freed-Hardeman colleges, all sister institutions who looked to Churches of Christ to support them financially.[57] But attempts to separate church from college were not always successful at the Vermont Avenue church, where faculty provided leadership and students filled the pew. Indeed, church-related periodicals came to insist that the college dominated the congregation, to the extent that it chose elders scripturally unqualified for the office.

Cultivating Recognition and a Reputation

George Pepperdine had said from the beginning that he wanted the college fully recognized by the proper accrediting agency, meaning the Northwest Association of Secondary and Higher Schools (NASHS) in Spokane, Washington. Accreditation was important in that it assured students that their classwork would be accepted by other institutions. Baxter contacted NASHS soon after he arrived in Los Angeles, informing them of the birth of the college and its desire to meet the standards of the association.

NASHS representatives visited Los Angeles in March 1938 to evaluate the campus and its programs. On April 5, the association informed Baxter that it would recognize George Pepperdine College provisionally, with a final review scheduled for the next year. Even provisional recognition was unusual for a school that had not yet completed its first year, a testimony to the founder, Baxter, and the faculty.[58]

To achieve full standing in NASHS, the association wanted GPC to meet certain requirements. Before the close of the 1938–39 academic year, the college was to complete the construction of the gymnasium and library. Moreover, it was to transfer control of the endowment fund, presumably $1 million, from the George Pepperdine Foundation to the direct control of the college. And it was to guarantee that the foundation would provide $25,000 annually for operating expenses, to increase to $50,000 when enrollment reached 500.[59]

All steps were accomplished—and more. The $40,000 gymnasium opened in November 1938.[60] The following month, the college broke ground for the new $48,000 library, which was also designed with art deco features by H. I. Gogerty.[61] It was completed early in 1939, with its 10,000-plus books ready for use by the spring term.[62] For good measure, wings were added to the men's and women's residence halls, doubling on-campus housing capacity.[63] To provide the $25,000/$50,000 cash subsidy required by the accreditors, the George Pepperdine Foundation formally contracted to deliver the stipulated amount to the college annually. The promise of those developments satisfied NASHS. On April 5, 1939, with Baxter present at the meeting in Spokane, the association granted unqualified membership.

Baxter's Surprise

Pepperdine and his fellow trustees were impressed. They re-elected Baxter as president and told him that "so far as they could see now," he would be at the college as long as he wanted. Baxter responded that the "set up" at the school was most satisfying. It was the first time in his career as a college president, he wrote to a friend, that he had not had to worry about finances, for the "heavy endowment" took "care of everything in a financial way."[64]

But the pressure of starting a college from scratch and operating it so that it could be fully accredited within two years was incredibly stressful, even for a fifty-three-year-old man. In addition to his administrative feats, Baxter had made himself accessible to students and faculty at the college, opening up the president's mansion to receptions, dinners, weddings, classes, and young married couples in need of housing.[65] He also preached each Sunday at the Central Church of Christ in Los Angeles, where he served as an elder. He took joy from the fact that his son served on the GPC faculty with him, but his wife's chronic illness was a constant sorrow. In March 1939, Baxter asked for a year's leave of absence beginning in June so that he could calm his nerves and help his wife regain her health.

He expected to return to the faculty at the end of the year as head of the religion department rather than as president of the college. The board of trustees readily agreed to the request, committed to pay Baxter a professor's salary during the absence, and promised to let him know early in 1940 about returning to the faculty.[66] But by late December 1939, the board had decided that there would be no place on the faculty for the former president. George Pepperdine, as chairman of the board, conveyed that information to Baxter on January 8, 1940.[67] His letter was very formal: because the religion department was fully staffed and Baxter's health was problematic, "it would not be best for [him] to return next September."

Baxter's response later that month was equally formal: your letter "closes the matter of my return. . . . My best wishes shall ever be with the effort there. . . ."[68] Given Baxter's services to the college and his credentials as a Christian educator, the correspondence, not to mention the turn of events, was surprising. In addition, the board's action opened it to severe criticism from powerful members of the Churches of Christ establishment.[69]

So why the unexpected decision? Apparently, President Baxter enjoyed hugging the young women who surrounded him as staff and students, some of whom he hugged too long. When the board learned of his penchant, it withdrew its invitation for Baxter to return to the campus.[70]

Nevertheless, Baxter served George Pepperdine College admirably. Bringing it from a mere idea to an academically accredited liberal arts college in two years was no mean accomplishment, even with the help of a large staff and robust budget. It was a testimony to vision, experience, hard work, and leadership.

Baxter attributed the success he experienced to God's grace. Some of his peers, however, saw it as something more: a virtual miracle, the "miracle on Vermont Avenue."

CHAPTER 3

WAR ABROAD—AND BATTLES AT HOME

S
ervices at the Vermont Avenue Church of Christ were especially somber on the evening of December 7, 1941. Worshippers had learned earlier in the afternoon that Japanese planes had bombed Pearl Harbor. Some of the young men in the audience, including Los Angeles County supervisor-to-be Kenneth Hahn, were deeply troubled; they wanted to defend their country, yet as Christians they were opposed to war.

After services, they walked to the nearby home of Dean E. V. Pullias and began a discussion that extended long into the night. Their conversation helped them clarify their options about whether to serve and how to justify that service, and all were calmed by the opportunity to talk the problem through with a mentor like Dean Pullias.[1]

George Pepperdine College was influenced by World War II but not defined by it. It was able to retain its uniqueness in large part because of the good leadership of its president and dean. Hugh Tiner succeeded Batsell Baxter as president of GPC on August 1, 1939. Only thirty-one, he was one of the youngest—if not *the* youngest—college president in the United States at the time. But he was not inexperienced. Tiner had been a member of the college's first board of trustees, part of the team that had built the college *ex-nihilo*, and had served as dean during the college's first two years. He was also well connected in the Los Angeles educational community and in Southern California Churches of Christ. Moreover, he had the personal confidence of George Pepperdine.[2]

Tiner was also active in local civic clubs, serving on the boards of directors of the YMCA, the Southside Chamber of Commerce, and the Ontario Orphan's Home. He served as president of the Southwest Rotary Club in Los Angeles and later (1946–1947) as governor of District 107, a prestigious position in the Rotary organization. His service in Rotary probably brought more publicity to GPC than any other single development in its first decade.

Tiner also had a long-lasting interest in international relations. In due time, he would hold positions of leadership with the American Council of the Institute of Pacific Relations, the United Nation's Committee of Southern California, and the Southern California Council on UNESCO. He spoke widely on such topics as "Alternatives to World War III" and "Challenge of Leadership in Today's World." Newsman Chet Huntley interviewed Tiner on Middle Eastern issues following his trip to Egypt in 1952. In that same year, he took a courageous stand against loyalty oaths being demanded of textbook writers by the supporters of Joseph McCarthy. In 1960, after he left Pepperdine, Tiner would run unsuccessfully for the California state assembly as a Democrat in a San Diego district.[3]

Tiner was so deeply involved in civic affairs that he drew criticism from some prominent churchmen. Foy E. Wallace Jr., a Church of Christ evangelist and editor of the influential *Bible Banner*, thought such heavy involvement distracted Tiner from his presidential duties, reflected a serious preoccupation with self, and demonstrated an obsession with worldliness. All of this suggested to Wallace that Tiner was too "green" to be president and that the college's board of trustees had made a serious mistake in letting Batsell Baxter leave.[4] But the board, especially George Pepperdine, did not agree with Wallace, siding instead with Jimmy Lovell who said Tiner was "the most known, respected and sought after gospel preacher in California. . . . If there [was] a young man in America in the church or out of it who ha[d] accomplished more in fewer years than this Tiner fellow," he would like to know where he lived.[5]

A New Dean

A year after taking the presidency, Tiner chose E. V. Pullias as the academic dean of the college. A native of Tennessee with deep roots in Churches of Christ, Pullias had attended David Lipscomb College before taking a BA degree from Cumberland College in 1928. He earned an MA at the University of Chicago two years later, after which he entered Duke University to pursue a PhD in psychology. He completed the doctorate in 1936 and he took a staff position in the psychiatric clinic of the Duke University hospital. He accepted a position on GPC's initial faculty as a professor of psychology, with the proviso that he could take the first year, 1937–1938, with full pay to pursue postdoctoral study at the University of London and Oxford University. Pullias arrived at GPC in August 1938 as one of four PhDs on the faculty, and he assumed the dean's position a year later.[6]

Personality-wise, Pullias and Tiner were cut from different cloth. Tiner was comfortable in a crowd; Pullias was not. Tiner most often acted from instinct; Pullias acted deliberately after reflection. Tiner was pragmatic; Pullias was philosophical. Tiner was lighthearted and informal; Pullias was sober and formal. Tiner was athletic; Pullias was scholarly. But there were also some notable similarities between the two. Both were young and green when it came to running a college. Both valued their Church of Christ heritage and were active churchmen, Tiner as a preacher and Pullias as an elder. Both were committed to building a first-rate liberal arts college in a Christian—as opposed to denominational—environment. Apparently their commonalities outweighed their differences, because Pullias later said that he and Tiner never had a misunderstanding in the seventeen years they worked together.[7]

Building a Respected Academic Institution

Pullias and Tiner wanted to build an institution that would be highly respected in Southern California's educational community. The dean considered himself charged to develop GPC academically. Almost everything that happened on campus fell under his purview, but he directed his attention toward activities associated with mission, faculty, curriculum, co-curriculum (including intellectual enrichment and athletics), and student quality. Tiner focused on representing the college to its external constituencies, raising the profile of the college in the community, working with Pepperdine and the board of trustees, supervising the build-out of the campus, and soliciting additional funding.

Tiner and Pullias were surprisingly effective in achieving the recognition they coveted for GPC. The college was admitted to full membership to the American Association of Colleges in 1941.[8] The same year it was accepted as a member of the Western College Association (WCA), an organization primarily of California schools that would become GPC's preeminent accreditor. Tiner was elected to its executive board.[9] Subsequently, Pullias served on a WCA team that accredited the University of Southern California.[10]

Fairly quickly, Tiner and Pullias subtly broadened Pepperdine's vision for the college. Rather than focusing merely on vocational goals and a Christian foundation, they spoke of stimulating students "to the highest level of intellectual achievement," of fostering "Christian character and ideals," and of learning and living "the great principles of democracy."[11] Beginning with 1944–1945, the *George Pepperdine College Bulletin* embellished these institutional goals, identifying as important the development of a Christian personality, of civic intelligence and competence, of opportunities for democratic living, of the value of lifelong learning, and of the sanctity of the Christian home.[12] Subsequently, there were paragraphs about sportsmanship.[13]

Under the leadership of Pullias, the number of faculty increased from thirty-three to fifty between 1940 and 1945.[14] Faculty credentials improved too. The number of PhDs serving on the faculty increased from four to thirteen, including three part-time instructors, by the end of World War II. All but three department heads held a doctorate.[15] Given a sixteen-unit teaching load, only a few members of the faculty did any scholarship, most notably Pullias in educational psychology, Callie Mae Coons in home economics, and Dederich Navall in German Mennonite studies.[16]

Through the course of World War II, the total faculty compensation package improved. Salaries remained steady at $3,000, but the teaching schedule covered by that amount was reduced from twelve to nine months.[17] The college added health insurance for all employees in fall 1944.[18] It added a retirement program with TIAA as of September 1, 1946, contributing 5 percent of the employee's salary if the employee contributed 5 percent.[19] The relationship with TIAA lasted for sixty-two years.

According to Pullias, faculty morale improved during the war years due to an attractive teaching environment, competitive salaries, a new benefits package, and—beginning in the academic year of 1940–1941—a committee structure that permitted faculty involvement in the decision-making of the college. Some nineteen faculty committees operated during the 1940s, with the professional problems committee being arguably the most important. It had recommended the health insurance and retirement programs, and it also was responsible for adjudicating salary disputes. Other important committees included ones on curriculum, chapel, scholarship, and student publications.[20]

The faculty grew in direct proportion to the increase of the student body. GPC had enrolled 192 students during its first year; by 1940, its fourth year, that number had more than doubled to 407. During World War II, enrollments remained around 400, with females making up 62 percent of the student body. In 1944–1945, enrollment jumped to 592, with returning veterans accounting for the dramatic increase.[21]

As enrollments grew, Pullias made every effort to improve the academic ability of the student body. His most effective tool was the strategic use of scholarships. Working through the faculty scholarship committee, the college offered nineteen full-tuition and thirty-four half-tuition scholarships beginning in 1940. Sixty percent of those were given on the basis of academic ability; 40 percent on character. Four years later, the college handed out fifty full and partial scholarships, although the total amount of money involved was not much different. Grants were also made for "special achievements," given to students with highly regarded talents in drama, music, and journalism, among others.[22] The scholarship committee also awarded a limited number of named scholarships funded by Harry K. Nowlin and Mr. and Mrs. John Marble.[23]

But there were always more needy students than the college had resources to help, which was why President Tiner was so pleased to meet prospective student Olaf Tegner in fall 1939. The son of Swedish parents who were faithful members of the Salvation Army, Tegner lived five blocks from GPC and had worked on one of the crews constructing some of the campus buildings. He determined to attend the college, but his application was received coolly because he lacked some prerequisites. Tegner walked dejectedly from the registrar's office to encounter President Tiner, who asked if he could be of service. Tegner explained his predicament, whereupon the president asked, "How are you planning to pay your own tuition?" When the prospective student said "in cash," Tiner reputedly said, "Welcome to Pepperdine!"[24]

Broadening Opportunities for Students

The basic outline of degree requirements offered GPC students did not change dramatically between 1940 and 1945. The 192 quarter units required for graduation remained the same; degrees still came out of twelve academic departments. What did change was that degree programs were enriched with new courses and opportunities. The home economics department, for example,

Hugh M. Tiner was George Pepperdine College's founding dean (1937–1939) and second president, serving in that role from 1939 to 1957. A native of Texas who also had an abiding interest in international relations, Tiner quickly and effectively led the infant school to a place of recognition and respect in higher education.

added a practice house where six girls for six weeks enjoyed a practicum in home management.

The completion of the auditorium in fall 1940 enabled the speech and dramatic arts department to offer sophisticated theater productions, musical events, operas, and opera workshops. Because of additional faculty and courses in the psychology and education department, the California State Department of Education certified GPC's teacher education training program in fall 1943, meaning that students no longer had to arrange practice teaching through UCLA.[25]

GPC took special pride in its debate program. Batsell Barrett Baxter, the son of the college's first president, joined the faculty as an instructor in speech and coach of the debate team during the academic year 1938–1939. He organized his students into a formidable squad over the years, garnering hundreds of awards in national competitions in everything from debate to extemporaneous speaking.[26] Successor coaches, Albert Lovelady among them, continued the tradition through World War II. The Founder's Day oratorical contest, established in June 1938, drew hundreds of contestants from major colleges across the American West for several years.[27] Pi Kappa Delta, the national honorary society in speech communication, recognized the quality of GPC's program by granting it a chapter in 1942, the first national honorary organization on the campus.[28]

Other evidence of curricular maturation was the emergence of a special events series that complemented the academic program, especially in the fine arts. Sponsored by Associated Students and inaugurated in 1944, the series presented artists of national and international reputation at no cost to students. The Community Town Hall met monthly, featuring international speakers and musical acts of distinction. In addition to these headline attractions, various academic departments presented a rich offering of lectures, plays, art exhibits, and concerts.[29]

The addition of a graduate program in religion also suggested that the college was moving rapidly toward academic credibility. In December 1943, W. B. West Jr., head of the department of religion, suggested to the board of trustees that the school offer a master of arts degree in religion. Such a program, he argued, would better train young men for ministry and qualify them to pursue advanced degrees elsewhere. It would also attract additional students from Churches of Christ for no sister college offered a graduate degree of any kind. The resources to implement the program, he reported, were minimal. The University of Chicago School of Religion and the Pacific School of Religion had agreed to recognize the MA degree if the religion program at GPC had four full-time teachers, three of whom with a PhD, and if the library would add 3,000 religious volumes over three years and spend $750 annually on books thereafter. Despite the uncertainties during a time of world war, the trustees boldly endorsed West's proposal.

The college admitted its first graduate class in fall 1944, pursuing a curriculum distributed over biblical, doctrinal, historical and practical fields. In addition to West, the full-time faculty included Ralph Wilburn and Woodrow Wasson, both graduates of Chicago, as well as C. H. Roberson, then on the faculty at Abilene Christian. William Green, on the faculty at University of California, Berkeley, taught part-time. With the exception of Roberson, all had or would soon have their doctorates.[30] With such a faculty, it was no surprise that the undergraduate program with the largest number of seniors was religion, at least in 1944.[31]

George Pepperdine College offered its first summer school session in 1942. The addition was designed to help students with their academic progress, and also to give members of the faculty a way to increase their incomes. With fewer than 100 students the first two summers, the term cost the college money. By the summer of 1944, however, enrollments increased 20 percent and budget expectations were met, which in summers to follow happened more often than not.[32]

When students reflected upon academic developments at GPC, they usually gave the school fairly high marks. Average class size seldom exceeded 16. Not only had the school been accredited, but programs in religion, education, and speech had received recognition within their individual disciplines. And students were being recognized too. Beginning in fall 1941, *Who's Who in Colleges and Universities* included George Pepperdine College students.[33] Numbers in the senior class increased from nineteen in 1937 to sixty-one in 1949, with averages of forty-six graduates per commencement in the last three years of World War II.[34]

Building School Spirit

Like the curriculum, the co-curriculum also matured. According to the 144-page 1945–1946 *Student Handbook,* certain traditions and ideals had presumably emerged to anchor the co-curriculum in the previous seven years. Among those were a spirit of reverence and devotion, an appreciation of the beauty of the campus, a sense of courtesy based on respect, a commitment to democracy and cooperation, an ability to balance freedom and self-control, a desire to exhibit friendliness, a wholehearted commitment to the task at hand, the rendering of genuine service, an infectious sense of humor, and promotion of sportsmanship based upon the Golden Rule. These traditions, the handbook stated, made the Pepperdine community "a place where it [was] a joy to work, to worship, to play, and to grow."[35]

Much of the work of student body organizations was designed to strengthen school spirit, an energy that presumably would bring students to GPC, keep them enrolled there, and keep alumni attached. President Tiner and Dean Pullias encouraged students and faculty in spirit-building activities. In 1941–1942, GPC welcomed to campus Dolores, a small statue of a demure young girl who came to represent the innocent potential of the college. She was placed on a pedestal in a newly constructed fountain central to the campus quadrangle.[36] That same year, students opened the "Oasis," a nonprofit student union supervised by the student board and the dean of men, which quickly became a major hangout for GPC students.[37]

Recognizing that school spirit both promoted and benefitted from a successful athletic program, President Tiner encouraged formation of a pep band and a pep squad and promoted athletic teams and programs.[38]

A. E. Duer, a Kansas native, came to coach in 1939. Duer was not recruited as a coach; he was hired as an assistant professor of physical education, who would also coach, serve as dean of men, and subsequently as director of athletics. Duer's job description demonstrates that the basketball program, like all sports programs, was part of the academic division of physical education with definite educational objectives. Among these, of course, was building school spirit, but it was also expected to give training in sportsmanship to both participants and spectators while placing the college before the public eye and giving first-rate competition to the highly skilled athletes.[39]

With those objectives in mind, Duer would transform the Pepperdine basketball program into one of the premier programs on the West Coast. Under his leadership, GPC became a member of the Southern California Basketball League, which included UCLA, Caltech, and Occidental, by 1942.[40] In 1942 and 1943, Duer's "Wavemen" received invitations to compete in the National Association of Intercollegiate Basketball (NAIB) national tournament in Kansas City. As champions of the Southern California Basketball League in 1944, the Pepperdine team was invited to represent the West Coast in the NCAA regional playoff. Undoubtedly the "biggest thing to happen" to the "little school on Vermont Avenue," Duer's team unfortunately lost in the first round to Iowa State.[41]

Although baseball and tennis teams were first fielded in the academic year of 1938–1939, neither thrived until after the war, although the tennis program enjoyed exhibition matches on campus by the reigning Wimbledon and U.S. champion, Bobby Riggs. Riggs' father was a pioneering Church of Christ preacher in Los Angeles, and his brother was an instructor at the college.[42]

A Living Workshop in Christian Living

George Pepperdine, President Tiner, and Dean Pullias all spoke and wrote about the college being a workshop in "Christian living," and none had any intention of altering the Christian ethos President Baxter had inaugurated on campus. Tiner and Pullias took pride in forbidding cursing and drinking, even if that inconvenienced some students or discouraged prospective students.[43] But establishing rules of forbidden behavior was not the heart of the matter for the leadership; the college's goal was the development and guidance of the Christian personality "through provisions of Christian environment, courses of instruction, and religious experiences on the campus."[44]

Given this objective, daily chapel services on campus were important, and an average of 68 percent of all students attended.[45] However, Tiner, Pullias and others were disappointed that not all students appreciated "this central aspect of our college life." In a letter to all students, the president and dean noted that those who did not participate in chapel were part of the college and would eventually be graduated as finished products of the college's educational program. Yet, sadly, they would not have received the benefit of the very experience that was "most typical" of Pepperdine. The administration did not want to force any student to participate, but they asked how the college could accept responsibility for the development of a student who consistently failed to participate in what the administration and faculty considered most significant in a student's development?

Hoping to persuade students to attend, Tiner and Pullias encouraged the *Graphic* to run stories on how meaningful chapel had been to graduating seniors and to Pepperdine college alumni serving in World War II.[46] The 1942–1943 *Promenade* created a moving segment on the value of chapel services, and the 1943–1944 college catalog carried a description of the purpose and practice of chapel.[47] Either Tiner or Pullias lectured every new student on the importance of attending chapel. Despite their best efforts, chapel attendance remained far below the 100 percent desired by the administration.

Some students saw a direct relationship between chapel attendance and an unnecessarily restrictive social environment. To them, chapel, dress codes, prohibition against dancing and card playing, and restricted visiting hours in the women's residence halls all seemed to flow from an undemocratic, "holier than thou" attitude manifested by administrators and "preacher boys."[48] From that perspective, it was not much of a stretch to blame all unappreciated rules on the faith and practices of Churches of Christ, to which most administrators, faculty, and 49 percent of students belonged in 1941.[49]

Churches of Christ Identity Crises

The tendency to divide the college into two different camps troubled President Tiner greatly. He tried to address the matter at multiple levels. By fall 1940, he had eliminated the rule that boarding students "must" attend church. Instead students were merely "urged" to attend worship services on Sunday.[50] He also launched a campaign to admit even more members of Churches of Christ, whose numbers had decreased after the first year.[51]

At the same time, Tiner and Pullias emphasized the fact that GPC was not organically connected with any church, that it was Christian but not denominational.[52] As interpreted and implemented on campus, that emphasis mitigated some of the latent criticism, but it opened up a new source of censure off campus, specifically from some Churches of Christ leaders.

The most vocal critic was Foy Wallace. The editor of the *Bible Banner* held a revival for the Central Church of Christ in Los Angeles in 1940. During that and other revivals in Southern California, he formed some definite opinions about GPC and its leadership. As already mentioned, he was absolutely certain that President Tiner was too young and inexperienced for his job. He was astounded that Tiner, Pepperdine, and other dignitaries associated with the college supported the nondenominational Federated Church Brotherhood of Southern California instead of advancing the cause of the true Church of Christ.

Moreover, Wallace was pretty certain that the college, specifically some of its professors, was not sound doctrinally. He suspected Wade Ruby, professor of English and baseball coach, held views of premillennialism, the belief that Jesus Christ would literally and physically return to the earth and take the righteous back to heaven with him. In Church of Christ circles in 1940, being called a premillennialist held similar connotations as being called a communist a decade later.

Over the next several years, Wallace intensified and expanded his criticisms. He considered Dean Pullias a "modern" who did not believe in social discipline and who was "not grounded in the truth." Moreover, Wallace charged Pullias with having been disloyal to Churches of Christ during his doctoral studies at Duke University by attending a Christian Church during that period. President Tiner, Wallace further complained, had permitted more non-Church of Christ than Church of Christ preachers to speak in GPC chapel, one of whom he had introduced as "Reverend."

According to Wallace, Tiner had even permitted a Presbyterian minister to teach Calvinism without comment but then had rebuked a faculty person who had read and commented on a text regarding baptism. And the peace of the Vermont Avenue Church of Christ had been troubled by men wanting to bring the congregation under the domination of the college. According to

Wallace, this low standard of conduct and lack of spirituality had "distressed" both students and faculty.[53]

Wallace never aimed his criticism at George Pepperdine, who had been personally generous to him, but he considered the George Pepperdine Foundation fair game. The foundation, he said, directed Pepperdine's philanthropies away from the "cause of Christ," meaning the Churches of Christ. And he was disturbed by how the foundation supported thirty or so preachers or congregations of Churches of Christ, comparing it to a one-man missionary society that circumvented supervision by a local congregation.[54]

Publicly, the GPC leadership mostly dismissed Wallace's charges as the fuming of a man with little influence in California. Privately, however, they moved quickly to counter his charges and to demonstrate that GPC valued a relationship with Churches of Christ. Pepperdine wrote directly to Wallace trying to ameliorate his concern regarding the foundation. Indeed, he even mandated that the foundation's support of preachers and congregations be funneled through the elders of the Southwest Church of Christ in Los Angeles, Pepperdine's home congregation.

The college also launched an initiative to demonstrate that cordial ties with Churches of Christ were desired, even necessary. The college catalog for 1940–1941 noted that Pepperdine had founded GPC to prepare leaders for the church, and that he and the board of trustees were members of the "church of Christ." Moreover, "It [was] the policy of the College to select the faculty from the members of this institution," the catalog proclaimed. Similar assurances remained in the college catalog until 1951–1952.[55]

In addition, in April 1942 the board of trustees authorized creation of an advisory board of up to twenty-five members to advise the college on matters of concern to the church. They selected John Allen Hudson, who also served on the board of the foundation, as chairperson.[56] With the input of this board, the college organized its first forum and lectureship for members of Churches of Christ in January 1943. C. R. Nichol, a well-known evangelist and author and soon to be minister of the Vermont Avenue church, presented the plenary address.[57] This gathering of the Church of Christ faithful on the college campus became an annual event, the Bible Lectures, that has continued into the twenty-first century. The trustees also added the MA degree in religion designed specifically to prepare ministers for Churches of Christ pulpits.

A Foundational Relationship

The board's most notable response to Wallace was the contract it negotiated with Pepperdine's foundation. In 1939 when the Northwest Association of Secondary and Higher Schools (NASHS) granted GPC full accreditation, it did so on the assurance that the foundation would support the college with an annual cash subsidy of $25,000, an amount that would increase to $50,000 when the student body reached 500. The foundation paid the stipulated subsidy by virtue of a gentleman's agreement until April 1943. At that time, Pepperdine and the college trustees insisted that the transaction be formalized into a contract whereby the foundation committed to an annual payment of at least $50,000, or 75 percent of the foundation's yearly net income, whichever was larger.

As quid pro quo for this guarantee, the trustees would agree that its membership, its chief officers (the president and dean), and a strong majority of faculty and instructional staff would be members of the Church of Christ "so long as the college exists."[58] Presumably, the existence of a contract calling for a critical mass of church members at the school would quiet critics like Wallace who questioned whether George Pepperdine College was really connected to Churches of Christ.

President Tiner and Dean Pullias were in harmony with the intent of the contract. In the 1942–1943 academic year, for example, just 64 percent of the GPC faculty were members of Churches of Christ. The next year, however, the school's leadership increased the number to 78 percent.[59] For churchmen like Jimmy Lovell, that development was worthy of praise and illustrated the administration's continuing efforts to build a faculty committed to transforming "hopeless young men and women into leaders, not only leaders in material things but leaders for Christ."[60]

The remarkable response of the college to the censure of Wallace and others did not quiet the critics, however. Early in 1945, L. O. Forsythe circulated a four-page newspaper-like broadside containing stinging criticisms of GPC, claiming it did not exercise strict discipline and allowed immoral conduct unbecoming of a Christian college campus.[61]

For its part, the board was quite confident that the administration and the college disciplinary committee had matters well in hand. It did not, therefore, need to respond to Forsythe's charges publicly or even to take them up with the faculty.[62] This apparently disturbed a few of the faculty. Young Batsell Barrett Baxter, for example, agreed with Forsythe that discipline on campus was lax and wondered why Pepperdine remained supportive of Tiner and Pullias. History professor M. Norvel Young held similar views, as did faculty couple Callie Mae and R. R. Coons, who resigned their positions at GPC and accepted appointments at Harding College.[63]

The esteemed C. R. Nichol also departed. Nichol was part of the religion faculty who also preached weekly at the Vermont Avenue Church of Christ. In 1945 that congregation appointed men as elders (E. V. Pullias, A. O. Duer, and Russel Squire) and deacons (Hugh Tiner) whom he did not consider scripturally qualified, specifically that they were not the fathers of believing children.[64] They were selected as elders of the church, Nichol believed, because of their standing at the college, a clear indication that fears of men like Wallace—that colleges would dominate the local church—had materialized.

Nichol even queried Pepperdine in a letter about his views on the qualifications of elders, specifically whether they had to be parents of believing children. In a gentle but ironic letter that quoted Nichol's own book, *Sound Doctrine*, Pepperdine said no, on the principle that you do not have to be 100 percent blameless to serve. He then asked Nichol to support the college even though there were disagreements between him and the administration regarding discipline methods and enforcement.[65] Nichol could not be pacified, however. He resigned from the college and the Vermont Avenue church, even refusing to complete the academic term. He returned to Texas where he took up full-time evangelistic work.[66]

Endowed with Blessings, Burdens

For President Tiner, the college's finances were a constant challenge. When he took charge in 1939, the value of the school was calculated as $2,027,218, which included $1,237,115 in investments (managed by the George Pepperdine Foundation as an endowment account) and $673,479 for campus land and buildings.[67] The total figure did not change substantially through World War II, although components varied from year to year.

Operating budgets increased steadily. In 1939–1940, revenue from all sources totaled $212,625. This included $47,182 from tuition and fees, $56,210 from auxiliary enterprises, $72,114 from endowment earnings, and $35,379 from gifts. In 1941–1942, the operating budget totaled $265,862; in 1945–1946, it reached a historic high of $412,253.[68]

Student tuition and fees covered only one-half of the operating expenses in any one year. The expenses not covered by tuition Pepperdine paid either by personal gifts or through the endowment he had established. His gifts always covered the budget deficits that occurred virtually every year: $82,641 in 1939, $53,379 in 1940, $50,000 in 1941, $40,000 in 1942, and $29,307 in 1944.[69]

Of course, the fiscal integrity of the college depended upon annual payouts from the college's endowment. Calculated as totaling $1.2 million through 1940, it had decreased in value to $1 million by 1942. In the year 1941–1942, income realized from the endowment totaled $56,628, which was nearly $14,000 less than anticipated.[70] Two years later, it generated $53,674, about a 5 percent payout.[71]

Although President Tiner and the board of trustees often spoke of the college's "endowment," it does not seem to have existed as an entity in and of itself. Instead, the endowment was just a folio of assets—apartment buildings and stock certificates—held and managed by the George Pepperdine Foundation. Of course, this arrangement had troubled the accrediting team in 1938, and it continued to trouble President Tiner through the first decade of his administration. By 1943, the board of trustees of the college could identify a list of "College Investments" and did deliberate on how best to enhance them. But those investments remained under the general management of the George Pepperdine Foundation and were included in published statements of the foundation's net worth.[72]

Judging from board meeting minutes, the trustees were well aware of the college's investment portfolio. And it is clear they wanted to be good stewards of those assets. Some of their decisions, however, were questionable. One example involved the Pacific Tire and Rubber Company, in which GPC held considerable stock. The company's principal plant had been closed by a strike in mid-1941, and was in danger of collapsing, despite good contracts with the federal government. George Pepperdine, who knew the owners of Pacific Tire and Rubber well, proposed that the college loan the company $50,000. The board voted unanimously to borrow the money from the Union Bank of California, which it promptly did. In this case, the company eventually repaid the loan, but the transaction raised questions about how the college endowment was managed.[73]

The symbiotic relationship between Pepperdine's college and Pepperdine's foundation had advantages and disadvantages. Early on, of course, the foundation provided as much as 25 percent of the college's annual budget. After 1943, as already mentioned, Pepperdine obligated the foundation to annually pay the college at least $50,000 or 75 percent of all income it generated from assets not assigned to the college. By such an arrangement, he hoped to provide another 25 percent of the annual revenue needed by the college to meet expenses, an amount that he had heretofore given from personal funds. Put differently, Pepperdine wanted the foundation to generate enough revenue from the college endowment and other foundation assets to cover one-half of the operational costs of the college, or at least $100,000 per year. Clearly, the George Pepperdine Foundation was an advantage to the college.

But it was also a disadvantage. The foundation was widely known in Southern California for its support of institutions designed to improve the status of young men and women. It was also known as an organization willing to invest in business opportunities that would yield higher than usual returns. Indeed, it was willing to liquidate apartment house properties, where return on investments were depressed because of rent controls, and invest in high-yield opportunities that many in the business community considered risky. Rumor had it that the new investments were not working out and therefore that the financial status of George Pepperdine College was problematic. The board of trustees worked hard to establish the fact that the foundation and the college were two different legal entities, but it was a difficult sale.[74]

Shaken by War

Whether it be curriculum, co-curriculum, church relationship or college finances, World War II touched almost everything on the campus of George Pepperdine College. Within Churches of Christ ran a deep river of pacifism that assumed Christians were not citizens of any worldly state but of the kingdom of God. They would pay taxes, of course, but they found no reason to vote, participate in government programs, or fly a national flag within their assemblies. Above all, they would not participate in any war that would jeopardize the life of human beings.

Dean Pullias embodied some of the traditional reservations about Christians participating in warfare and even favored an amendment to the U.S. Constitution that would require a majority vote of the people to approve U.S. participation in any foreign war. In his view, there had never been a "war sufficiently justified to secure the support of the majority of a reasonably common sense nation."[75]

The question of whether or not to serve in the military ceased to be an academic one with the bombing of Pearl Harbor on December 7, 1941. Apparently, most of the George Pepperdine College men who gathered in Dean Pullias's home that fateful night leaned toward registering for military service but in noncombatant roles. Other students or alumni registered as conscientious objectors but also claimed a ministerial exemption from the draft. More than likely, some students refused to register for the draft. But the majority registered or enlisted in one of the military services, and some 300 GPC students ultimately served in the United States armed forces during the war; at least six never made it home.[76]

President Tiner kept in touch with the GPC students on active duty around the world. He put together a newsletter titled "On the Beam," published it periodically, and sent it to homesick servicemen and women. To many of these newsletters, he attached personal notes. Coach Duer was just as active in staying in touch, sending out "uncountable [numbers of] personal letters of news and encouragement." Servicemen and women responded to these communications with letters of their own, some of which found their way into the columns of the *Graphic.* All remembered their experiences at the college as among the best in their life, and many particularly cherished the memory of daily chapel, to the extent that some at chapel time actually stopped whatever they were doing around the world and had their own devotion.[77]

Surprisingly, the number of GPC students remained fairly steady during the war years at just above 400. The gender ratio, however, did change; after the spring of 1943, there were two females for every male.[78]

War preparedness activities became a part of campus life, and in 1942, the faculty added to the curriculum a course in basic engineering, which was part of the Engineer, Science, and Management War Training program. Fifty-five students enrolled in the initial offering, probably including students in the Army Enlisted Reserve Corps and V-1 programs.[79]

The pages of the *Graphic* did not make much of V-Europe day on May 8, 1945, and V-Japan day on August 15, 1945. More exciting was the promise of a much larger student body. The academic year beginning fall 1945 would include twice as many students as had enrolled the previous year. That enrollment, fueled by returning veterans, not all of whom were former GPC students, would fill the sleepy little school on Vermont Avenue with unusual measures of confidence and pride.

CHAPTER 4

Standing on the Summit

In 1945 at the close of World War II, British Prime Minister Winston Churchill observed that "America at this moment stands at the summit of the world." What Churchill said about the United States could have also been applied to George Pepperdine College.

Thanks to the GI bill, total enrollments had more than doubled, reaching 1,839 in 1948–1949. Forty-five percent of the students that year were veterans; two-thirds were men, and 38 percent were freshmen.[1] Within two years, enrollments tapered off to 1,285, subsequently dropped to 850, and later stabilized at 1,050. The decline was somewhat associated with a negative accrediting review, but also with the Korean War, economic inflation, competition from public colleges, crowded campus conditions, and tension created by the college's Christian mission.[2]

The enrollment bubble generated by World War II veterans literally changed the complexion of the student body. By 1956, 10 percent of the 1,100 students at GPC were African American. Twenty-two of the black students lived in Baxter Hall, and several were members of social clubs. Eight percent of the student body were Asian; 2 percent were Hispanic; and 5 percent were not U.S. residents.[3] And there was an emerging racial sensitivity on campus as well. When one skit in the 1957 Spring Sing portrayed Africans in a negative stereotype, criticism from the student body caused the organizers of the skit to apologize.[4]

Although the board of trustees preferred a college with a limited, relatively small student body that embraced the Christian mission, President Tiner and Dean Pullias clearly saw value in enrolling as many students as possible.[5] In fall 1953, GPC received 400 applications for admission and admitted all but 35.[6] Of the 365 accepted, 267 enrolled, a remarkable yield rate of 73 percent. Four years later, 205 seniors graduated, a rate of nearly 80 percent, which was a much higher retention and graduation rate than had been seen at the height of veteran enrollment.[7]

Larger enrollments brought a larger faculty. Although measures used to identify "faculty" were fluid, the fifty members who had taught a student body of 529 at the end of World War II increased to 125 at the height of enrollment in 1948 and decreased to fifty-seven full-time faculty for an enrollment of 1,097 in 1957.

Significantly, the credentials of the faculty improved as more were hired. After World War II, 22 percent of the faculty possessed a PhD or equivalent, and 36 percent had MA degrees.[8] By 1957, the number of doctorates had increased to 42 percent, while those with an MA degree constituted 40 percent of the faculty.[9] In addition, some faculty members engaged in substantive research and scholarly publications. In 1952, for example, chemist George Campbell received funding to do research for the U.S. Army, the first government grant in the college's history.[10] These measures support Dean Pullias's contention that the GPC faculty compared favorably with the faculty of other small colleges in California.[11]

Lagging Faculty Pay

Although faculty numbers and credentials were increasing, their basic pay was not much higher than it had been a decade earlier. In 1948–1949 professors teaching sixteen units per term earned $3,000 to $3,800 for nine months; associate professors received $2,700 to $3,600; assistant professors from $2,400 to $3,000, and instructors from $2,000 to $2,700. The salary of department heads, whose contract was for twelve months, ranged from $3,400 to $5,000.[12] Given the large enrollments and additional tuition revenue, the board of trustees showed its appreciation in 1947 and again in 1948 by voting a 10 percent cost-of-living bonus to each faculty and staff member. It was able to do so because the college ended those fiscal years with a budgetary surplus. After 1950, the school would not even balance its budget for almost a decade.[13]

When the George Pepperdine Foundation crumpled in late 1950 and George Pepperdine was reduced to destitution, the faculty and staff at his namesake college were widely recognized as among the poorest paid at comparable schools in Southern California. This troubled President Tiner and the board of trustees, but declining enrollment after 1950–1951 made it difficult to make dramatic adjustments. Following a study by the faculty's professional problems committee in 1952, however, the board did approve a salary scale that capped department heads at $5,600, professors at $5,200, associates at $4,400, assistants at $3,800, and instructors at $3,400. Four years later the caps were increased further: to $6,000 for professors, $5,500 for associates, $4,500 for assistants, and $4,000 for instructors. Overall, salaries increased 40 percent or more, surpassing the rate of inflation, but at the cost of substantial annual deficits for the institution.[14] A 1956 Ford Foundation grant of $142,900, specifically to endow salaries for ten years, decreased the deficits only marginally.[15]

Why did the faculty remain at their posts given the minimal level of compensation? Dean Pullias attributed it to the faculty's sacrificial spirit and commitment to the college's Christian mission.[16] Members of the staff truly saw themselves as ministers, and Pullias embodied that role himself. Paid only a few hundred dollars more than department heads, he, his wife, and two sons led the disciplined, reflective, and frugal life of a Christian ascetic. Pullias had misgivings about his world view, but in his pride, he confessed to his journal, he persevered.[17]

Athletics as Education

The postwar athletics teams produced mixed results, with large numbers of veterans changing the focus and success of the programs. A football team established after World War II enjoyed significant success from 1946 through 1948, but faltered after Warren Gaer left the coaching position. The baseball squad experienced its first winning season in the history of the college in 1946–1947, when veterans largely filled the roster, and made it to post-season play a few times in the 1950s. Although it was less visible on campus, the tennis program was far stronger following the war than it had been earlier.

The basketball and track programs enjoyed the most success in this era. Wave basketball teams seldom turned in anything but a winning season under Robert L. "Duck" Dowell, who assumed the coaching responsibilities in 1948, and the track team under J. Eddie Weems also enjoyed considerable success. The basketball and track programs competed in regional and national events, bringing much favorable attention to the small college in south Los Angeles.

In the new demands and expectations of the postwar world, GPC upgraded its athletic conference, first in basketball and then in other sports. Seeking a league that offered a Division I level of competition but did not demand participation in football, the college joined the California Basketball Association conference in 1955. A year later, the CBA changed its name to the West Coast Athletic Conference; in 1989, the word "athletic" was dropped from the conference name. Today the WCC sponsors intercollegiate competition for all sports teams at Pepperdine except men's volleyball and water polo and women's swimming and diving.[18]

Unlike those at other institutions, especially big-time sports institutions, Pepperdine athletics were envisioned as essential parts of the academic and spiritual mission of the college. Dean Pullias deemed sports programs to be part of the physical education department's curriculum. The director of athletics was also the chairperson of the PE department, and what student athletes did on the court or the field was considered part of their academic training. GPC administrators vigorously objected when a 1951 accrediting team member classified the Pepperdine athletic program as an instrument of institutional publicity, instead of defining athletic competition as an educational internship that prepared graduates for lives of usefulness.[19]

Athletics were not only integrated into the academic curriculum, they were also structured to further its Christian mission. Athletic Director Al Duer, especially, emphasized the importance of sportsmanship for both athletes and fans, claiming it was "but another manifestation of Christianity on our campus."[20] However valuable the GPC athletic program was to the academic and spiritual mission of the college, it had detractors among students and faculty, with most critics complaining about its costs. The athletic budget in 1949–1950 was $90,000, or about 10 percent of the total college budget, to be offset by no more than $40,000 in revenue.

The deficit of $50,000 was roughly the amount of the annual deficit of the college.[21] Duer recommended significant cutbacks in the budget and special efforts to increase revenue and even took himself off the budget by accepting the position of executive secretary of the National Association of Intercollegiate Basketball (NAIB) in 1949.[22] The athletic budget deficit remained, however.

Veterans in the Classroom

As in the athletic program, the enrollment of a large number of veterans had a significant impact upon GPC's academic curriculum. Returning veterans embraced the school's disposition toward pre-professional education, the curricula that prepared students to live "lives of usefulness," to use George Pepperdine's phrase. Consequently, the preponderance of GIs majored in business administration, education, or physical education. Very few went into the liberal arts, especially religion. Of the 300 graduates in 1949, for example, 59 percent were business administration, education, or physical education majors, while just 3 percent were religion majors. The same percentages held for 1950.[23] Clearly, the veterans reinforced a vocational orientation in undergraduate education that remained strong through the remainder of the century.

To facilitate the educational process for the GIs and other students, GPC made some substantive institutional changes, including establishing the Office of Student Personnel, an idea that Hugh Tiner had advanced in his doctoral dissertation. The student personnel office directed all student affairs, including social issues, housing matters, and other areas of campus life that required personal counseling. The office also coordinated various campus services such as admissions (through the registrar's office) and financial aid (from the business office). The Office of Student Personnel functioned very much like a hybrid version of what would be later called the Office of Student Affairs and One Stop.[24]

At the urging of registrar Russell A. Lewis, the college changed from a quarter system to a semester system.[25] It began to schedule night classes primarily for nonresidential and working students in 1949, and in addition to a full complement of summer classes, it also offered off-campus summer sessions at Camp Tanda. Located at Big Bear Lake and organized by Church of Christ men and women as a summer camp, Camp Tanda was a perfect location for environmentally based courses like biology but also for classes in art, physical education, and reading and discussion in the social sciences. Professor of history and chair of social sciences Woodrow Whitten coordinated the Camp Tanda program initially, even organizing on-campus fund-raisers to help sustain the camp.[26]

Encouraging Intellectual Participation

Other programs were initiated to encourage greater student involvement in the intellectual life of the community. Most important was the Campus-Community Forum, which promoted discussion on world affairs, initially for just enrichment, but subsequently for credit. Organized by Professor Whitten, the forum was open to the community for a fee, met each Wednesday evening, and attracted an array of distinguished scholars and public figures to campus. The series opened in September 1947 with Professor Alonzo Baker of USC speaking to an audience of 600 on the subject, "The UN, a Rip-Snorting Success."[27] Over the academic year, attendance averaged 250–300 per session.

Congressman James Roosevelt, the eldest son of President Franklin Roosevelt, and actress Myrna Loy also spoke on campus that year but at different venues.[28] Well-known philosopher Will Durant spoke at the forum in February 1949.[29] In the forum's third year, presentations ranged from the beauty of Kashmir to the dangers of international communism.[30]

Interest in the Campus-Community Forum remained high until late in the 1950s, although actual attendance was a bit anemic after its inaugural year. To rekindle attendance, Dean Pullias and Professor Whitten in 1950 offered the program for one unit of academic credit and changed its focus from world affairs only to the arts in general.[31] Some of the series' better years followed, and participants included artist Norman Rockwell, actor Charles Laughton, sociologist Margaret Meade, U.S. Senator Estes Kefauver, Lord Arthur Balfour,

U.S. Secretary of Agriculture Charles Brannan, U. S. Senator Paul Douglas, and newscaster Chet Huntley—just to name a few.[32]

GPC also continued to offer a notable concert series, more for enrichment than credit. Among others appearing in the postwar period were the Los Angeles Philharmonic, Boy's Town Choir, and U.S. Naval Band.[33] The fine arts department also used this series to showcase the college's community orchestra, various ensembles, the choirs, and student solo instrumental or vocal performances.

Although Dean Pullias and Professor Whitten had broadened the focus of the Campus-Community Forum series beyond foreign affairs, matters involving global issues remained of intense interest on the GPC campus. President Tiner, of course, was well-known in UNESCO and was in demand as a dinner speaker on the prospects of world peace.[34]

Tiner's enthusiasm for global issues was widely shared on the GPC campus. In 1948, for example, following a chapel presentation on the United Nations as the alternative to world chaos, the student body unanimously voted to call upon the United States government to take the lead in getting the United Nations to organize a world conference on peace.[35] Demonstrating this enthusiastic interest, along with frequent letters and reports in the *Graphic*, were three student-faculty groups: the international relations club, the collegiate council for the United Nations, and the council on atomic implications.[36] In October 1949 and subsequent years, those groups celebrated a United Nation's Week, and the college hosted an international relations conference attended by 300 students from 30 colleges in 1950, boosting President Tiner's contention that GPC was "the 'most internationally minded' school for its size anywhere in the United States."[37]

This interest in international relations would translate into the genesis of international studies program that became the envy of almost every institution in the United States before the turn of the century. In summer 1953, Professor Whitten took fifty-three students on a tour of Europe, preceded by an eight-session institute that would provide students with a historical context for what they were about to see. He was accompanied on the tour by Professors Russel Squire of Pepperdine and Adolph Purvey of USC.[38] The tour was so gratifying to both students and faculty that they replicated it in successive summers. Within two years, GPC had organized the Institute of Travel Education and offered academic credit for courses taught in conjunction with the University of Lausanne and later the University of Geneva.[39] In the 1960s, the travel programs Whitten inaugurated would grow into residential programs centered in European cities.

Clearly, both the United States and GPC stood on a summit in the aftermath of World War II, and changes that occurred in its wake ensured that the college—like the country—would never be the same. Returning veterans spurred changes in the curriculum, co-curriculum, student life regulations, ethnic relations, Christian disciplines, the athletic program, physical plant, and global worldview. The GIs even transformed the faculty, accounting for an increase in numbers, better pay, greater benefits, and professionalization. For GPC, the view from the summit seemed encouraging, but it was also deceiving.

CHAPTER 5

PEERING OVER
THE PRECIPICE

The U.S. summit Winston Churchill described in 1945 was not always high enough to raise the country above the muck and mire of daily living. The emerging civil rights campaign and the crusade against international communism, among other things, exposed deep divisions in American society. George Pepperdine College also stood on a summit. But it proved to be more of a precipice than a mountain top. After a period of greater enrollments and steady institutional advances, the bottom dropped out, resulting in a financial quagmire and loss of academic accreditation.

The *Los Angeles Times* revealed the reality on Thursday, February 15, 1951, with front-page headlines that screamed "Pepperdine Says He's Penniless Now." The story related the disturbing news that George Pepperdine, a "one-time multimillionaire," was unable to pay a court-ordered judgment of $10,000. His once ample assets, he had revealed in court, had been pledged as collateral for investments of the George Pepperdine Foundation. Those investments had soured, and his personal fortune had disappeared. He was forced to live on an allowance extended to him by his wife.[1]

The *Times* article also noted that the Superior Court had recently dissolved the George Pepperdine Foundation and appointed trustees to carry out closure to satisfy the creditors. Assets not owed creditors were to be transferred to George Pepperdine College, which had received $2.5 million from the foundation between 1937 and 1940 and other significant gifts in the ensuing years. The assets of the foundation presumably totaled more than $1 million, but most of those were paper assets that had no actual value, much like George Pepperdine's personal balance sheet. Not part of the foundation's assets, although established by it, was the million-dollar endowment of George Pepperdine College. Presumably it was beyond the reach of any of the foundation's or Pepperdine's personal creditors.[2]

President Tiner was not so sure he could trust the assurances from legal counsel that the college would not be affected. In the public mind, the relationship between George Pepperdine Foundation and George Pepperdine College was indistinguishable. Financial instability in one meant financial instability in the other, and he believed the college's creditability was in jeopardy. Tiner had reason to be concerned. The college was hosting a visit by an accrediting team from the Western Association of Colleges as the news broke.

GPC had expanded its academic programs in the postwar world. These were designed less to accommodate veterans than to attract new students who would replace graduating veterans. Dean Pullias and his colleagues, for example, offered chemistry as a stand-alone degree in 1950 and added master's degrees in psychology, American history, and speech in 1951–1952.

Accreditation Problems

But appealing to a new generation of students proved difficult. The second-largest major at GPC was education. It was popular primarily because it qualified graduates for jobs in elementary or secondary schools as teachers of business education, art, physical education, or homemaking.[3] To make the program even more attractive, Dean Pullias wanted to offer a general secondary credential and asked the California department of education to certify it in 1949.

To his surprise, the state agency refused, citing the inadequacy of the library, the lack of a graduate program in education, and the questionable financial status of the college. It even questioned the validity of the existing credential programs.[4] A year later, the state department did reaffirm approval of the elementary and special secondary certification programs, but it rejected GPC's petition to offer a general secondary credential and expressed concern again over the financial condition of the college.[5]

The decision of the state board of education was trivial when compared to the setback perpetrated by the Western College Association (WCA) in 1951. Twenty-seven years earlier, the WCA had organized as a professional organization in support of higher education, especially the liberal arts. Its charter members were UCLA, Occidental, Cal Poly, Pomona, Redlands, and Whittier. In January 1941, Pepperdine had been admitted to membership following an on-campus visit by a team headed by Gordon Watkins, dean of arts and sciences at UCLA. According to Watkins, the financial resources and educational program of the school qualified it for membership, and he believed membership "would have a very beneficial effect upon the college itself," providing it with "guidance and assistance" that only more mature institutions could provide.[6]

President Tiner and Dean Pullias attended the annual meetings of the association. In October 1948, they readily agreed with the majority of members when the WCA assumed the responsibility of accrediting institutions of higher education as one of the regional agencies recognized by the U.S. Department of Education. The association began its first accrediting visits in June 1949, combining its visit with the California State Department of Education to evaluate teacher education programs. WCA scheduled just such a visit with GPC on March 5 and 6, 1951. Although GPC had been accredited by the Northwest Association of Secondary and Higher Schools since 1938, the administration welcomed the WCA visit because it would be far more convenient to be accredited by an association that focused on California.[7]

But the date of the visit could not have been worse. For weeks, newspapers had been running stories about the dissolution of the George Pepperdine Foundation and George Pepperdine's financial ruin. Rumors circulated widely suggesting that the college would soon declare insolvency too. Rather than preparing to host an accrediting team, President Tiner and Dean Pullias were busy with damage control, encouraging the trustees to present a united front, to protect the good name and reputation of George Pepperdine, and to rededicate themselves to the purposes and ideals of Christian education.[8] There is no record that the distracted Tiner and Pullias ever informed the trustees about the WCA visit, and no reports about the visit made it into the *Graphic*.

Since the WCA visit occurred simultaneously with the state education department visit, the college submitted the same 90-page self-study to both teams. In the document, the college administration envisioned several new buildings, a larger endowment, and a student body of 1,000 to 1,200. With GPC committed to providing "high quality . . . instruction in a wholesome Christian environment," the report described the general education program; the qualities sought in selecting faculty; and how faculty members promoted the objectives of the school, taught sixteen units, and accepted an ad hoc tenure policy. The document also spoke to the quality of students attracted by the college, the high GPAs they earned, and the postgraduate programs they matriculated. In general, the report implied, the college stood on the summit of academic respectability.[9]

Serious Reservations in Thirteen Pages

Assuming that a single report would satisfy the requirements of both visiting teams, however, was a mistake. One team was looking at teacher preparation issues, while the other was surveying the quality of the liberal arts program.[10] The WCA team, chaired by UCLA dean of letters and sciences Paul Dodd, had serious reservations about GPC. In a thirteen-page report, the visitors praised the strong Christian atmosphere, the enthusiasm and loyalty of faculty and students, the quality of facilities, and the beauty of the campus grounds.

The team, however, devoted most of its report to criticism. Salaries were far too low, negatively impacting faculty morale and performance in the classroom. It was little wonder there was no American Association of University Professors (AAUP) chapter on campus! It charged that the college spent too much on things other than education, such as "publicity"—which included athletics—and facility maintenance. Moreover, the general education requirements were not basic enough, lacking a mandatory laboratory class and a required social science and literature class. The report was also critical of the limited number of PhDs on staff, especially in business administration, and the minimum level of research activity within the entire faculty.[11]

The visitors had other concerns as well. They believed that there was an imbalance between pre-professional programs (business administration, physical education, and art and music) and liberal arts programs (philosophy, English literature, history, biology, chemistry, and physics) that had to be corrected "if the College [was] to offer a genuine liberal arts program." Their report criticized the disparity between the number of courses offered in the catalog and the number actually taught. Finally, the committee concluded that academic expectations of students were not high enough, either as applicants for admission to the college or as graduates of it. GPC did not stand at the summit but on a precipice. The WCA visiting team unanimously recommended that GPC's request for accreditation be denied.[12] The executive committee of the association accepted the recommendation on April 6, 1951.[13]

Battling the WCA Report

President Tiner and Dean Pullias were "greatly disappointed and somewhat perturbed over the report." "To refuse accreditation to an institution when there [were] no minimum standards employed in the evaluation program [was], to say the least, dangerous," Tiner wrote to Lawrence Nelson, the chair of the association's committee on membership and standards. "Passing judgment on the basis of generalizations or cursory visits to classes [was] a practice which could prove disastrous to our Association."[14]

After a personal meeting with Nelson in August, Tiner and Dean Pullias prepared a lengthy response, dated September 1, 1951, to the findings of the visitation committee.[15] They wanted to persuade the WCA to work with GPC in developing new evaluation procedures and to have the previous report tabled and judgment suspended on the Pepperdine case until new procedures were developed.[16]

In careful detail, Tiner and Pullias defended the work and record of the college. They identified some of its achievements, including GPC graduates who had done well in graduate and professional schools. Equally notable were the positive accreditation reviews by the Northwest Association and the American Medical Association for twelve years and the California Department of Education for ten years. Tiner and Pullias also noted that Pepperdine students regularly won coveted journalism competitions and were nationally recognized for their debate talents and that the academic qualifications of the faculty had improved steadily, now equaling those at any similar college. In light of these accomplishments, especially over such a short time, they wrote, the "unqualified rejection" of the college "without warning [and] without consultation . . . was altogether unexpected."[17]

Having enumerated the positives, the president and dean then turned to the misunderstandings and errors they found in the committee's report. Those ranged from complaints regarding how much money the college invested in "promotion and public relations," to the presumption that the faculty was "poorly-trained, incompetent, and professionally inactive," to the assumption that GPC was primarily a vocational school. Tiner and Pullias argued that the committee had erroneously classified the athletic program and the annual catalog as public relations, that it erroneously assumed the faculty was unprofessional because it was poorly paid, and that it had failed to understand the importance of general education in the GPC curriculum.[18]

The discrepancies in the report were blamed on several factors. Among these were WCA's lack of minimum standards to be applied impartially to all institutions, the small size of the team that visited GPC, the brevity of its visit, and its unfamiliarity with factual material. Unfortunately, the team "consciously or unconsciously undertook to settle *ex cathedra* numerous controversial issues in education"; it failed to check its facts with the college to guarantee accuracy; and members tended to compare Pepperdine College with their own institutions or an imagined ideal. Finally, GPC had received inadequate provision for self-evaluation.

These circumstances, Tiner and Pullias argued, were not trivial and had resulted in "a serious, far-reaching injustice." Leaked news of the report had been used to damage the reputation and good name of GPC. Faculty and alumni had been chided; prospective students had been urged not to attend because the college "had been kicked out of the Western College Association and would probably have to close"; and donors had been urged to reconsider bequests to the college. In all, Tiner and Pullias believed that the report would cost the college fifty to 100 students in fall 1951.[19]

In concluding their response, the president and dean listed a series of "normal developments" taking place on the Pepperdine campus, including efforts to improve the school's fiscal status and trim athletic expenditures, the sacrificial service of the faculty, advances in faculty governance (including organization of an AAUP chapter) and faculty scholarship, the reduction of the faculty's teaching load, a stronger general education curriculum, and declining interest in pre-professional degrees. All these developments illustrated that the president and his faculty colleagues possessed the "fixed ambition to build an excellent small college in basic harmony with the noble tradition of the American church-related college." Moreover, they believed it was in the best interest of WCA "to allow a reasonable amount of freedom and self-determination on the part of institutions in developing and evaluating their programs when they [were] directed by men and women of acceptable training and reasonable integrity."[20]

Getting a Second Chance

The WCA committee met in San Francisco to consider Tiner's and Pullias's response on Nov. 2, 1951. It was received coolly. The committee rejected the implication that the visitors were prejudiced, noting that they had rendered a unanimous decision and that their report was "in essence, fair." It also expressed doubt that new procedures of self-evaluation would be beneficial, but it agreed to a resurvey of the college.

The membership committee voted not to reverse its denial of accreditation to GPC but also voted that the committee chosen to resurvey the college be recruited chiefly from Northern California.[21] The WCA executive committee accepted the report, agreeing to stand by its previous vote of non-accreditation but also to authorize a new visit of the college within a year.[22]

Throughout the lengthy interaction with the accrediting agency, neither Tiner nor Pullias let the faculty or the board of trustees know about the negative report or their response. In Pullias's view, the report would remain "incomplete" until a new committee made a second visit sometime during the spring. He was willing to discuss some of the WCA recommended improvements with the faculty but unwilling to share the unpurged report until after the visit. Then, he said, the committee's report could be studied by department heads, and "perhaps by the faculty as a whole." But the dean believed a faculty member could best contribute "by operating in the area of his [sic] competency" rather than by dabbling in administrative matters. And he felt the same way about the board of trustees.[23]

The resurvey occurred exactly one year after the initial WCA visit, March 5 and 6, 1952. This team was composed of four members, two from Northern California and two from Southern California, with J. Paul Leonard, the president of San Francisco State College, serving as chair. Rather than review every element of the college, the committee focused only on matters found problematic the previous year. It found that:

- the catalog was being revised to reflect the true instructional program of the college;
- an improved system of accounting had been put in place;
- the amount spent on athletics had been reduced;
- the general education program had been improved and a lab science was now required;
- major departments had reviewed and improved their offerings (religion, for example, had dropped thirty different courses from its catalog);
- it was appropriate for GPC to offer pre-professional or vocational programs; and
- the admissions program, which seemed to have no clear-cut standards, was comparable to other accredited programs in California.[24]

But the review team also said further improvements were warranted:

- the general education program needed further strengthening;
- the course sequence in all fields needed continued study;
- faculty salaries needed serious increases, and
- additional facilities were needed for science instruction.

Nevertheless, the committee recommended full accreditation for Pepperdine College "in view of the gains made at the college the past year and the present status" of comparable programs of "other accredited colleges in the state."[25]

At their Phoenix meeting on April 4, 1952, both the committee on membership and standards and the executive committee accepted the visiting team's report, voting to extend GPC full accreditation "for a period the termination of which shall coincide with the next state review of the institution for the elementary credential."[26] Eleven days later, and surely with a measure of relief, President Tiner was able to tell the board of trustees that the institution was fully accredited by the WCA. He said nothing about the fight that had preceded the approval.[27]

In effect, the WCA approval was good only for about eighteen months as the next state department of education accreditation was scheduled for late 1953. President Tiner and his colleagues spent much of 1953 preparing a 326-page self-study. The document demonstrated considerable institutional maturity and evidence that previous criticism had been taken seriously.

On January 28, 1954, the WCA's committee on membership and standards recommended that GPC be granted full accreditation for five years. But the decision was not without reservation. Some committee members thought Pepperdine's accreditation was being granted "on the basis of good intentions" rather than "actual achievement." However, the executive committee affirmed WCA accreditation for the college until 1958.[28]

Affirmation also came from the state department of education, with that visiting team recommending reaccreditation of the general elementary credential and the special secondary credentials in art, business education, homemaking, music, and physical education. It also approved an additional special secondary credential in speech, but did not award the general secondary credential. That would have to wait for another two years, by which time GPC had also added an MA degree in education.[29]

Financial Problems

The concerns of the WCA and the state department of education about the college's financial standing were legitimate. Despite—or perhaps because of— the additional enrollment generated in the postwar era, the college operated with an annual deficit through 1958, except for three years in the late 1940s. The minutes of the board of trustees reveal that the financial survival of the college was often month to month, if not week to week. College officials carried short and long-term bank loans just to meet daily expenses.[30] Toward the end of the period, those bank loans totaled as much as $175,000, or almost 20 percent of the annual operating budget.[31]

The financial constraints were surprising for an institution that had an endowment of at least $1.1 million in 1946. George Pepperdine had begun to set aside investments just for the benefit of the college as early as 1937, and these were enhanced to the $1 million level after he sold his interest in Western Auto Supply two years later. The college's investments were separated from the George Pepperdine Foundation in 1949, but the relationship remained confused because the senior foundation not only harbored the assets of the junior but borrowed money from it.[32]

That close relationship proved unwise when the George Pepperdine Foundation dissolved and Pepperdine found himself penniless in 1951. Some of the creditors of both the foundation and Pepperdine sued the college for $260,000, assuming the college had benefitted from the largess of both. The suit was settled out of court for $22,000 in 1956, but the negative publicity associated with the case and with Pepperdine's personal financial losses tarnished the general reputation of the college. This crisis can explain why enrollments declined 30 percent after fall 1952 and why accrediting teams thereafter were so skeptical about the college's future.[33]

The collapse of the George Pepperdine Foundation and the dramatic decline in enrollment also accounted for the college's difficulty in borrowing capital in the 1950s. On one occasion in early 1952, the college treasurer was lectured by a local banker on fiscal responsibility when he sought to extend for six months the due date of a $5,000 note.[34] Moreover, the college could find no lenders in its search to borrow $200,000 on a long-term basis to consolidate a number of short-term notes.[35]

Spurned by commercial banks, GPC's only available source of cash was the school's endowment, from which it borrowed regularly, with the endowment selling equities to generate necessary cash.[36] These transactions showed initially on the college's financial records as interfund liabilities, but they were always written off eventually.[37] The practice reduced the total value of the endowment, which by 1957 was some 50 percent less than it had been twelve years earlier. The annual payout continued at about 5 percent, but the amount in 1957 was less than half of the payout at the beginning of the decade.

The endowment was just one of the revenue streams available to the college. The college derived the bulk of its annual income, or 47 percent, from student tuition and fees, which had risen substantially after World War II, from $350 to $550 per academic year. Board and room, along with other auxiliary enterprises, supplied another 30 percent of the college's annual revenue. But altogether those sources fell short by about 12 percent of providing the revenue necessary to balance the budget.[38]

Looking for Big Donors

Unless expenditures were cut, a balanced budget required annual gifts totaling $100,000 or more. Through the 1940s, George Pepperdine had covered much of the annual deficits through personal contributions booked at $50,000 per year, most coming as gifts of commercial real estate or natural resource property that produced little or no income. Most notable was a gift of six natural gas wells, booked with a value of $200,000, but paying no royalties at all, making it a gift that looked good but did not help the bottom line. After 1951, Pepperdine could not even offer those kinds of gifts. Lacking income from other sources, George Pepperdine College operated with annual deficits, eroding the value of its endowment to cover the costs.[39]

Everyone involved with the college, including the board of trustees, President Tiner, and members of the faculty, agreed that the financial health of GPC required support from major external donors. The school was just months old when the George Pepperdine Foundation launched a campaign to encourage donors to help support the college, and similar efforts were undertaken through World War II. The efforts, however, had little impact other than to provide scholarship aid for a limited number of years. Alumni director Oly Tegner organized a "Friends of Pepperdine College" campaign in spring 1948 to raise $250,000 for construction of a campus student union, but it fell far short of its goal.[40] As an explanation for this lack of success, college friends often reasoned that the school would not be able to raise external money so long as George Pepperdine, presumably a man of wealth, was alive.[41]

The need to generate gifts became more urgent as the college deficits grew after the foundation failed and Pepperdine found himself without financial resources. With the approval of the board, President Tiner enlisted the help of two professional fund-raisers, John H. LeGrand and Hal Thomas. For a percentage of what they raised, they were to solicit $1,000 gifts from friends of board members, community-minded philanthropists, alumni, and others.[42] Tiner and board member Jimmy Lovell volunteered to identify and solicit donors in Texas, especially among Church of Christ members.[43]

Apparently, this initiative yielded a disappointing harvest, as operating deficits continued at the college, and some academic departments were reduced to selling Christmas cards, hawking discount passes, and begging for 25-cent donations to carry on the work of the college.[44] Similar results came from the $2.4 million endowment campaign proposed in 1951 by Hal Thomas, who grounded the effort in the college's strong support of Americanism, commitment to freedom, and advocacy of a market economy.[45]

Jimmy Lovell: Marksman, Salesman, Churchman

Of all those directly associated with the college, none was more helpful in the postwar era than Jimmy Lovell. A Tennessee native and World War I veteran, Lovell was a marksman with few peers. His skill earned him a position with the DuPont Company, traveling throughout the American West demonstrating DuPont gunpowder and shells in shooting exhibitions. He eventually joined the sales staff, traveling the world selling explosives to miners, builders, and oilmen, crossing one ocean or another twenty-one different times and living in Salt Lake City, Denver, and finally Los Angeles.[46]

Lovell was a crack shot and a super salesman, but above all else he was a churchman. He never missed an assembly of the church if he could help it, despite his travel. At one time, Lovell estimated—probably correctly—that he had attended the services of more Churches of Christ than any other person in the world. He solidified his connections by publishing the *Colorado Christian*, the *West Coast Christian*, and *Action*. The latter journal was aptly named as Jimmy Lovell was a man of action.[47]

He joined the George Pepperdine College board of trustees in 1950 with at least three objectives: (1) to honor George Pepperdine, with whom he had a long-lasting working relationship; (2) to ensure that GPC retained its Christian mission and its relationship with Churches of Christ; and (3) to use his extensive business connections to bring major donors to the college. The board felt Lovell's presence almost immediately.

Lovell turned his attention first to the matter of fund-raising. With the full knowledge of the board, he contacted Clinton Davidson, a very successful New Jersey insurance broker and churchman, who had helped George Benson and Harding College build a substantial endowment. Choreographed by Davidson, Benson had committed Harding to anticommunism and the free-market economy, promoting and defending those positions in a weekly column that appeared in hundreds of small-town newspapers across the United States. On record as a defender of Americanism and free enterprise, Benson then called upon leading industrialists along the East Coast seeking support for his crusade and his college. The strategy worked wonderfully, and Jimmy Lovell wanted GPC to replicate it.[48]

Building a Builder's Recognition Program

While developing that approach, Lovell also acted to organize the American builders' recognition program, something he had envisioned as early as 1948. The initial idea was for GPC to publish a book featuring stories of the U.S. heavy construction industry, highlighting companies that had built major projects such as the Hoover Dam and the Metropolitan Aqueduct. Such recognition, he believed, would attract the builders' attention and might persuade them to support George Pepperdine College. As Lovell joined the board of trustees, his idea morphed into a yearly publication and an annual recognition night where a notable builder would be honored at a formal banquet and granted an honorary doctor of law degree from George Pepperdine College.[49]

With the support of three prominent corporations, Pepperdine College published the first edition of *America's Builders* magazine in September 1950.[50] The first recognition banquet occurred the evening of May 8, 1953, on the Vermont Avenue campus. Honored that night was the Six Companies, Inc., that had constructed Hoover Dam; attendees included families from major construction companies, such as W. A. Bechtel, Henry J. Kaiser, MacDonald & Kahn, Pacific Bridge, and J. F. Shea. Edgar F. Kaiser delivered the principal address, and President Tiner awarded the honorary doctorate to Ann Morrison, the "first lady of construction."[51] Interest in the event grew, and some 800 individuals came to campus in 1956 for the fourth annual recognition night, requiring that a tent be set up to accommodate them. Attendance remained robust, although never quite so strong.[52]

Under the umbrella of the America's Builders Recognition Night, Pepperdine College would honor and extend doctorates to Thomas J. Walsh, builder of the Grand Coulee dam; William P. Johnson, CEO of American Pipe and Construction Company; Lucian Earl Dixon, builder of the Los Angeles Memorial Coliseum and Shrine Auditorium; Edgar F. Kaiser, industrialist extraordinaire; and Edward T. Foley, a retired Santa Barbara builder and benefactor of Loyola University.[53]

Although the sums were not great, the builder's program did result in some "real" money, perhaps as much as $100,000, not an inconsequential amount, but not as much as Lovell and the board had hoped.[54]

The "American Way" of College Financing

Lovell and Tiner hoped the approach recommended by Clinton Davidson would be more productive.[55] Because Davidson preached that prospective donors would only be interested in an educational institution that supported their personal and corporate agendas, GPC strove to position itself as a champion of the "American Way" and worthy of the favor of the corporate establishment. In April 1954, for example, the board of trustees went on record reaffirming its faith in the free-market economy:

> In keeping with the traditional purposes of the Founder of Pepperdine College to provide "adequate preparation for a life of usefulness in a competitive world," the Board of Trustees unanimously reaffirms its faith in this great objective and in the free enterprise system which has made the College possible.[56]

The trustees also authorized establishment of a board of leading industrialists who would provide support and advice to the college.[57] On February 2, 1955, at the California Club in downtown Los Angeles, fifteen men met to form the President's Council of George Pepperdine College. According to President Tiner, it was the most significant step in the development of the college since its founding eighteen years earlier.

Hosted at the club by Bryant Essick, whose company built heavy construction equipment, the group included such notables as Lee Atwood, president of North American Aviation Company; Donald Douglas, Jr., vice president of Douglas Aircraft Company; Charles R. Fleishman, president of A. J. Bayer Company; Edgar Kaiser, president of Kaiser Motor Company; Charles Luckman, partner in a renowned architectural firm; and R. E. Smith, oil producer from Houston. Within ten months, the council had forty members.[58]

Paul G. Hoffman, the current board chair of the Studebaker-Packard Corporation, previous administrator of the Marshal Plan in Europe, and subsequent chair of the Ford Foundation, addressed the group. His message was clear: independent, private colleges were the primary bulwarks of the freedoms—the market economy and the Bill of Rights—that made America great and unique. Interestingly, neither Hoffman nor Tiner appear to have referenced the significance of the college's Christian mission in their remarks.[59]

Tiner was constantly challenged to decide how to utilize the council. He had promised members that he would not ask them for money but instead would seek their advice on policy and strategy and identifying prospects who might partner with Pepperdine College in perpetuating political and economic freedom. Tiner kept his promise easily, for he despised having to ask anybody for money.[60] Consequently, despite the wealth represented on the council, the number of major gifts to the college did not increase. Edwin W. Pauley, a member of the University of California board of regents and a benefactor of UCLA, was an exception. After being elected to the council and receiving Pepperdine's honorary doctorate, he pledged a gift for scholarships of $30,000 over six years. Leonard Firestone was another exception, although his major gift lay several years in the future.[61]

Also a member of the President's Council, Clinton Davidson was convinced that George Pepperdine College's message to the council was uncertain

A native of Tennessee, Jimmy Lovell joined the George Pepperdine College board of trustees in 1950 and had an immediate impact on the school's fund-raising efforts. A prominent Church of Christ layman and publisher who was well-known for his skills as a marksman, Lovell served as a part of Pepperdine's governing board into the 1980s.

if not unsound and believed there should be greater clarity on how the college could help members. He volunteered to come across the country and address the council. "I think that I can show the majority of them how Pepperdine College can be of great help to them and I am certain that each one who is helped will immediately want to provide substantial financial help for the college.[62] The college trustees were a bit uneasy about the offer, however, fearful that Davidson wanted the college to become a "propaganda agency for business" rather than merely a servant "of business, labor, government [and] . . . the church."[63]

Davidson was a bit put off by the hesitancy of the trustees. He reminded Jimmy Lovell of something he had told George Pepperdine in 1938 and Hugh Tiner many times since: "If the college wants these businessmen to contribute financially in a big way, it [must] . . . first . . . do something that these men would like to have done." George Benson and Harding College had followed this principle, resulting in $250,000 of annual income and several millions for buildings. There might be a better way, Davidson wrote, but he was quite certain that the fund-raising efforts at George Pepperdine College yielded less than at any college controlled by Churches of Christ.[64]

Davidson was probably correct, but President Tiner and the trustees were not quite ready to convert GPC into the kind of bastion of anticommunism and right-wing politics as Harding College had become. The reason is unclear. Perhaps they saw George Pepperdine College itself as less doctrinaire and more tolerant and urbane. Perhaps they feared that the work of the college, which heretofore had been free from external interference, even from its own trustees, would be compromised. Perhaps they saw members of the president's council as less narrow than those who supported Harding as many of them headed companies that depended upon government contracts for their profit margins. Or, perhaps President Tiner, strongly committed to world peace through international cooperation, objected to a fund-raising posture that divided the world into two camps—communist and noncommunist, east and west, red and blue, good and evil.

For whatever reason, Tiner and the board declined Davidson's invitation to mimic Harding's admittedly successful fund-raising scheme. GPC would learn from the Harding experience, back down from the financial precipice, and follow its own path to financial sufficiency.

So George Pepperdine College's post-World War II summit of hope proved to be little more than a precipice that descended to academic censure and financial insolvency. And there was more: some leaders of Churches of Christ questioned the school's commitment to traditional Christian values.

CHAPTER 6

THE CHURCH CHALLENGES

Significant financial challenges and major accreditation issues caused George Pepperdine College considerable grief and anxiety in the postwar era. But even more disturbing were questions as to how it manifested its Christian mission and nurtured its relationship to Churches of Christ.

Descriptions of the Christian mission of the college did not change significantly in the school's bulletins between 1945 and 1957. However, Christian mission was identified as one of several purposes of the college, rather than its *raison d'être* as articulated in its founder's statement. In 1949, for example, a public relations bulletin stated that "George Pepperdine College is wholly dedicated to the ideals and practices of democracy and Christianity." The declaration was followed by a ringing defense of political freedom, equal opportunity, and the "age old virtues" of hard work, honesty, fair play, tolerance, faith, and selfless service, or the so-called "American Way."[1]

Three years later, the catalog spoke of "education with a purpose," defined as "the development of a wise, rich character for full, abundant living; of vocational skills that would enable one to make an honest, adequate living; and of attitudes and proficiencies supporting effective citizenship in a democracy." To this mix, George Pepperdine College added a Christian environment, which brought a wholeness or completeness to the educational process.[2]

How the Christian mission manifested itself on campus also changed, although most of the behavioral rules were still in place. But by the 1950s, college administrators no longer held students accountable to a particular dress code. The centrality of chapel changed, too.

Probably nothing about George Pepperdine College was more difficult to explain to the influx of veterans than daily chapel. Veterans had no problems with the college having a Christian mission, or having to take required Bible courses, or even *having* chapel services every day. But to expect them to attend every day, even on a voluntary basis, was deemed unrealistic, and it offended their ideas of freedom.[3]

To increase attendance, Tiner and Pullias tried several approaches, including changing the name, format, and objective of chapel. The newly christened "Chapel Assembly," began with a fifteen-minute devotional followed by outstanding speakers and artists, some of whom were students.[4] This reconstitution of chapel did not improve attendance, however, and Tiner and Pullias finally acted to make chapel mandatory.

Beginning fall 1950, all students had to attend at least one chapel assembly each week. On other days, attendance was voluntary. Although attendance improved, there was a lot of student pushback to any form of mandatory chapel, with complaints that sectarian expectations of Churches of Christ had influenced administrators. Partly because of this hostility, Tiner and Pullias replaced required chapel for everyone with mandatory daily chapel for each student enrolled in the first required Bible course. Other students could attend as they wanted.[5]

Critics Find Cause for Alarm

For leaders of Churches of Christ, the decreased chapel attendance requirements at George Pepperdine College led to more basic questions: Was the college losing its Christian focus? Was it in the process of severing ties with Churches of Christ? Leaders like Foy E. Wallace Jr., James Bales, S. H. Hall, Reuel Lemmons, and Walter Adams feared that it was.

Church critics argued that the environment at GPC was not Christian. Local minister L. O. Forsythe was convinced there was little Christian deportment on campus and absolutely no Christian discipline. An Idaho woman was outraged that the college was sponsoring "dancing classes" (actually summer cheerleading camps).[6] Others had serious questions about classes instructing future teachers in "folk dances." Jimmy Lovell could not understand why only women were forbidden to smoke.[7] The absence of a dress code prohibiting women from wearing short pants on campus disturbed Walter Adams, dean at Abilene Christian College.[8] It was probably a good thing that he did not know that the Kappas, a women's service sorority, had actually modeled bathing suits in President Tiner's on-campus home![9]

Critics also pointed to the declining number of Church of Christ members within the student body and faculty. In fall 1946, 302 of 1,109 students identified themselves as members of Churches of Christ. A decade later, only 160 of 1,097 students were associated with Churches of Christ.[10]

The percentage of full-time faculty who were members of Churches of Christ had increased from 59 percent in fall 1949 to 71 percent in fall 1956, but the critics believed that all full-time faculty should be members of the founder's church.[11] Moreover, all references to Churches of Christ had been deleted in the 1951–1952 bulletin.[12] Assurances in the fall 1956 bulletin that GPC was "operated by members of the Church of Christ although not organically connected with or subject to any church" did not quiet the critics.[13]

Modernism in Religion Department?

Of particular concern to the church critics, however, was what they thought was going on in the religion department. There had been encouraging developments during World War II when the college added an MA degree in religion, the first graduate program of its kind in Churches of Christ. Its religion faculty, anchored by W. B. West Jr. and Ralph Wilburn, was highly trained and well respected as the postwar era began. Both were published scholars, excellent teachers, and respected mentors. Under their direction, the Timothy Club—made up of men and women preparing for ministry—and Monday night religious forums prospered. However, the editors of *The Bible Banner,* first Wallace and then Roy E. Cogdill, thought the good reputation of the Pepperdine faculty was undeserved as they found it rife with theological modernism.

In May 1947, former GPC student John F. Wolfe wrote an article for the *Banner* titled "What I Found at George Pepperdine." A 1926 graduate of Abilene Christian College and a forty-three-year-old preacher in the Los Angeles area, Wolfe was a graduate student who took five religion courses at GPC between 1944 and 1946. In those classes, he wrote, modernism as a way of understanding the Bible prevailed. He claimed that religion faculty attributed most miracles to natural causes and taught that God's revelation of himself was shaped by time and space rather than divine plan, that Isaiah 53 was not a prophecy about Christ, and that the Church of Christ was just another denomination.[14]

President Tiner replied almost immediately to Wolfe's accusatory article although Wallace chose not to publish that response until February 1948. Tiner expressed sorrow that Wolfe had clearly misunderstood the purpose and nature of some things taught in one or two graduate classes and that his article would confuse people who did not have first-hand knowledge of the Pepperdine religion department. Tiner listed what the religion faculty taught and believed: the Bible was inspired; miracles occurred; God revealed himself over time, ending with Jesus Christ; Christ died for our sins; belief in the resurrection was the cornerstone of our faith; there was one hope, one faith, and one baptism; education benefited preachers; and Christian teachers must be informed.[15]

Tiner's rejoinder had no impact upon Wolfe, however. Clearly, Wolfe said, "the spirit of compromise [was] abroad in the school." He rejected Tiner's invitation to meet with him and members of the religion faculty, believing the issue would not be settled in private conversations, but by "the enlightened opinion of the church at large."[16]

"Scandalized" by Faculty Views

In the midst of the Wolfe controversy, at least eighteen ministers of Los Angeles-area Churches of Christ met at the YMCA building in Long Beach on December 2, 1947. Among them were four GPC faculty members who were also part-time preachers: Wilburn of the religion department, Wade Ruby of the English department, Hubert Derrick of the language faculty, and Woodrow Whitten of the social sciences department.

Cogdill, publisher of *The Bible Banner*, addressed the group on "What Should We Preach," emphasizing that there was only one faith, which had been delivered once for all. The discussion that followed confirmed to Cogdill that Wolfe was right: modernism reigned at Pepperdine College. Ruby had said man could learn of God through means other than divine revelation or Scripture. Whitten observed that Jesus gathered some of his teachings like the Golden Rule from human philosophers who had lived before him. Ruby, Whitten, and Derrick all argued that there were children of God, people who have obeyed the gospel, in human denominations. All three agreed, Cogdill reported, "that we cannot positively know the truth" in matters of faith and practice.

Cogdill was scandalized by what he heard. "Brethren," he wrote to the church at large, "it is apparent to me that instead of just one modernist on the faculty of Pepperdine College, they have a whole nest full of infidelity up there." He printed a written summary of the meeting and had eleven of his colleagues witness by signature the accuracy of his account. The document was then forwarded to West, the religion department chair.[17]

In a letter published in the *Banner*, Pullias described accusations of modernism as "unsubstantiated," "discredited," and "generally outdated." Pullias's eloquent defense did not convince the *Banner* that Pepperdine College was free of modernism, as it had long since decided to the contrary. When Ralph Wilburn hosted a conclave of biblical instructors to discuss the achievements of the World Council of Churches, a modernist innovation, the editors considered themselves vindicated.[18]

Warnings of Danger

Wolfe's criticisms and Cogdill's charges of heresy and modernism, however, were small potatoes compared to the denunciations of O. L. Castleberry, a Los Angeles-area Church of Christ minister and a participant in the Long Beach conference. Castleberry believed the welfare of the church was "endangered" by George Pepperdine College, and his long list of reasons were published in *The Bible Banner* in March 1948:

- the faculty was theologically unsound;

- the college cooperated with religious denominations, permitting them to worship on campus with musical instruments;
- in chapel, sports announcements consumed more time than gospel teaching;
- the student newspaper and handbook recommended entertainment unfit for Christians;
- a class in folk dancing was taught at the college;
- ballet performances were offered on campus;
- the college scheduled social occasions on the Lord's Day;
- women did not adorn themselves in modest apparel;
- the school sanctioned "mixed bathing" at the beach; and
- Pullias had prevented Otis Gatewood, a renowned Church of Christ missionary, from organizing students to do personal evangelism work on campus.[19]

According to Castleberry, all of these matters had been presented to Dean Pullias for redress, but he had summarily dismissed them, which led Castleberry to go public with his concerns. Appended to his letter were the signatures of ministers Otis Gatewood, Roy Palmer (Long Beach), Homer Hailey, Roy Tidwell (Santa Ana), and Glenn Wallace, all well-known evangelists among Churches of Christ.[20]

Castleberry's charges provoked President Tiner. In his opinion, Castleberry was not a qualified or rational critic as he had spent no more than two months on the campus. Tiner addressed each of Castleberry's charges but in dismissive language and tone. He was clearly tired of his "brethren" challenging the college's Christian commitment.[21]

Tiner's response outraged Castleberry, and he repeated his charges and admonished readers to be guided by them in determining the truth about George Pepperdine College.[22] Castleberry no doubt felt vindicated when Luther Blackmon reported in the next issue of *The Banner* that Tiner had participated in an interdenominational Easter service, which mainstream Churches of Christ considered "a heathen affair, decorated in the pageantry of Romanism." That kind of acceptance of error would "eventually corrupt the doctrine of the church of God," Blackmon said. Since the college was financially independent, the church's only defense was to warn Christians what to expect if they sent their children to Pepperdine.[23]

Going on Offense

As the *Bible Banner* and others challenged Pepperdine's Christian credentials, the college's leadership set out to demonstrate that it warranted the confidence of the church. One such step was establishing the annual Bible lectures in 1943. Under the direction of W. B. West, the lectures attracted as many as 100 Church of Christ preachers and leaders.[24] The college also began hosting the Christian Youth Festival in spring 1947, annually drawing 400 to 500 young people from Churches of Christ to campus.[25]

In addition, President Tiner, Dean Pullias, members of the faculty, and even George Pepperdine himself, contributed articles to church-related journals other than the *Banner*.[26] Most often these appeared in *The Firm Foundation*, a publication from Austin, Texas, whose editor, G. H. P. Showalter, had come to the defense of the college in face of the withering attacks by Foy Wallace.[27]

The *Bulletin George Pepperdine College* published in May 1949 was another attempt to demonstrate that the administration and faculty valued the college's relationship with Churches of Christ. Titled "The Church and Sound Doctrine," it was a collection of twelve presentations made by faculty members to the 7th Annual Biblical Forum and Lectureship. It addressed Christian fundamentals (Pullias), the deity and miracles of Jesus (Wilburn), the inspiration of scripture and the second coming of Christ (Ruby), who is a Christian (Hubert Derrick), and what is a Christian College (George Pepperdine). The published papers formed a tapestry of erudition, thoughtful reflection, wise application, deep conviction, and abundant faith. Nothing in the collection suggested heresy or corruption. Of particular note was George Pepperdine's essay on the Christian college.

> My idea of a college is that it shall be a private institution giving students standardized work in the liberal arts in a Christian environment. . . . Such a college is not a church or a seminary. It cannot be handled as a church. It is not under the control of the church, it is not an auxiliary of the church, or an extension of the church, but it is an extension of the work of the home. . . .
>
> Such a school is a private academic, educational institution with a department where religious subjects are taught. . . . The Bible does not authorize the establishment of any Christian institution other than the church and the home. All so-called Christian colleges are only academic educational institutions with some degree of Christian influence and characteristics. . . . Even the most Christian of colleges can only be ten percent Christian, because 90% of the teaching is on subjects other than religion. . . .
>
> The greatest service *as a College* is to provide excellent educational facilities in an environment that will strengthen and further develop Christian faith.[28]

Pepperdine noted that many people had opinions about how the college should be run and that all the opinions were based upon the judgment of some person. It was not imperative, he argued, "that every citizen in a community or the nation be a Christian in order to call it a Christian community or a Christian nation." In that sense, "Christian" was a relative term, and it was in the same sense that the word was applied to George Pepperdine College.[29]

In other words, the college did not have to meet the *Banner's* definition of a Christian college to be Christian, only the definition of God-fearing men like George Pepperdine, Hugh Tiner, and E. V. Pullias.

Critics Not Appeased

The critics of the college, however, did not buy Pepperdine's defense. In March 1951, Yater Tant editorialized in the *Gospel Guardian* that Pepperdine College had embraced the modernism of Karl Barth and Emil Brunner and had become a menace and threat "to simple New Testament Christianity."[30] To that extent, George Pepperdine had been betrayed by those whom he had trusted, especially Pullias.

Tant had a particular disdain for the dean, whom he blamed for Pepperdine College becoming "a thorn in the flesh and a constant reproach and embarrassment to the faithful Christians in California who know of her liberalism and her compromise with sectarianism."[31] Pullias considered Tant's editorials libelous and told him so in articles that Tant published in the *Guardian*.[32] George Pepperdine pretty much agreed, although he did not confront Tant directly.

Instead, he prepared a lengthy article on the college's accomplishments during its fifteen-year history. He pointed out that forty-nine faculty members attended Churches of Christ and that thirty of those preached or did other church leadership work. He was proud that the Christian environment at GPC had led some students to commit their lives to Christ through baptism and encouraged others to enter full-time church work. All had studied the Bible, and many had prepared themselves for service in business and the professions. And he was proud that the number of Church of Christ congregations in California had increased from approximately ten in 1916 to more than 200 in 1952.[33]

Pepperdine's listing of accomplishments simply evoked deep feelings of sadness and regret in Tant because "noble and worthy" George Pepperdine had been betrayed by his associates. It also pained Tant to have to point out the "very serious danger which Pepperdine College present[ed] to the church of our Lord," specifically the "liberalistic, modernistic attitude" that "contaminated the minds of Christian young people attending there."[34]

Battles Inflict Casualties on Faculty, Administration

The modernism wars, especially the effort to refute Tant and the *Bible Banner*, took their toll upon George Pepperdine College. In early 1951, Ralph Wilburn, a lightning rod for the entire conflict, resigned from the faculty, whether on his own volition or under pressure is not certain. According to the ever-watchful *Gospel Guardian*, Wilburn was pressured because he had rightly become an embarrassment to the administration. Its editor could think of a dozen young gospel preachers with high promise who studied under Wilburn at Pepperdine College and subsequently had chosen not to preach or came to preach "a halting, uncertain, crippled, and emasculated gospel." Wilburn accepted a position at Phillips University in Enid, Oklahoma, a Disciples of Christ school.[35]

After nine years at GPC, W. B. West also resigned as professor and chair of the religion department, although certainly not under pressure. He took a similar position at Harding College in Arkansas, expressing his dissatisfaction with the lack of support he received from Tiner and Pullias and being held responsible for the presence of modernism within the faculty. He was also excited about the opportunity to create a graduate program in religion at Harding.[36] Losing West was a blow to GPC's standing with Churches of Christ, for it was interpreted in many quarters as evidence of ever-weakening ties with the church.

President Tiner was aware of the perceptions, which were evident in enrollment of Church of Christ students at the college. Between fall 1947 and fall 1951, it had decreased in absolute terms from 371 to 153, and from 24 percent of the student body to 15 percent. Attendance at the annual lectureship had decreased to no more than fifty people during the day and 250 at evening lectures.[37] These were clearly reasons for concern, given George Pepperdine's desire to serve young men and women who were members of Churches of Christ.

"Christian College Dilemmas"

Tiner was also frustrated by the perceptions, which became evident in the manuscript of an article he prepared, "Christian College Dilemmas." Tiner noted that historically there were two extreme viewpoints regarding church schools among Churches of Christ, one insisting that they be supported and controlled by the church and the other holding that the church should neither support nor attempt to control the college. He said, however, that a third viewpoint was emerging, which held the church was not to support the college but nonetheless should control it. Tiner saw the third viewpoint as the root of the conflict facing George Pepperdine College and other higher education institutions affiliated with the Churches of Christ.[38]

Tiner reminded his readers that George Pepperdine had established the college named in his honor with the clear understanding that it would be separate from the church. It would emphasize Christian living and fundamental Christian faith, but it would be a private enterprise, not connected with any church, and would not solicit contributions from the churches. The dilemma confronting GPC was profound: "How much more like the church must we make the college so that it will qualify as a Christian college," he asked? "Must the church support, control and direct [all of] its activities?"[39]

In Tiner's view, colleges should be neither church-supported nor church-controlled. Rather, they were to be independent institutions under the direction of Christian people. Their fundamental responsibilities were to offer the best academic training possible to prepare youths for usefulness in today's competitive world, and to preserve and increase the faith of young people so that they would be able to take their place in the Lord's Kingdom through the provision of a Christian atmosphere in the college. "The college cannot be the church, nor should it take over the function of the church," Tiner concluded.[40]

Signs of Weakening Ties between Church, College

Given the punishment Yater Tant and others meted out upon George Pepperdine College, President Tiner and Dean Pullias despaired of ever pleasing the opinion makers in Churches of Christ. This was apparent in the college catalog for 1953–1954 when they eliminated introductory material that had noted George Pepperdine's and the board's membership in Churches of Christ and the policy of the college to select its faculty from members of that church.[41] No mention of Churches of Christ returned until 1956, when the catalog noted that Pepperdine was "a private Christian college operated by members of the Church of Christ although not organically connected with or subject to any church."[42] There was absolutely no reference to hiring practices, nor would there ever be again.

Unwilling to extend themselves further to please the brethren, Tiner and Pullias gave little attention to the religion department after West, a first-class administrator and scholar, departed for Harding. To replace him, Tiner and Pullias chose Joseph W. White, who had minimal academic credentials. White was a Pepperdine College alumnus who held an MA from the University of Southern California. He was a good man and a preacher in Santa Monica, but within the Churches of Christ, White was considered a lightweight and a poor substitute for West. Some suspected White had been chosen for the position because he was unlikely to stand up to the president and dean.[43]

Another sign of the weakening ties between the college administration and the church came through a series of exchanges between Tiner and B.C.

Goodpasture, the editor of the *Gospel Advocate*. In May 1955, Goodpasture requested from Tiner a copy of his mailing list of Church of Christ members so that he could circulate a centennial edition of the *Advocate*. Surprisingly, Tiner told Goodpasture that he had no such list.[44] Later that summer, Goodpasture ran an article in the centennial edition on colleges serving Churches of Christ but did not include Pepperdine College. He later explained that Tiner had ignored his letter requesting information on the college. Goodpasture, as a consequence, had ignored Pepperdine.[45]

Lovell's Efforts to Renew Relationship

Jimmy Lovell, who had joined the board in 1950 with the avowed purpose of returning Pepperdine College to the mainstream of Churches of Christ, feared that President Tiner no longer considered a relationship between the college and Churches of Christ as particularly important and was disengaging from the institutional church. Lovell was particularly concerned about what was going on in the religion department, believing that the faculty was no longer teaching New Testament Christianity.[46] Clearly, he had been reading the articles of his friend, Yater Tant.

Strengthening the religion department was only one of Lovell's suggestions as to how the college might recapture its Church of Christ constituency.

E. V. Pullias served as dean and professor of psychology of George Pepperdine College between 1939 and 1957. He became the target of critics who questioned the college's commitment to the Churches of Christ and was forced out when Norvel Young took over as Pepperdine president.

In 1952 he also recommended to the board that President Tiner and his staff organize a Citizens Council on Christian Education, with all members being from Churches of Christ. Such an organization, he felt, would draw church folks back within the orbit of the college, and it might even lead to gifts.[47] Much to Lovell's chagrin, the plan "died in its tracks." He reluctantly came to fear that Tiner and Pullias did not want the college to reach out to a Church of Christ constituency.[48]

Lovell also recommended other changes that he thought would appeal to the college's Church of Christ base. Among these were firm policies that students caught drinking on campus would be expelled, that neither men nor women would be allowed to smoke, and that the faculty would not include Catholics. Tiner and Pullias did not welcome Lovell's suggestions.[49]

Lovell's most formative recommendation was that the board of trustees be more involved in the life of the college. As a general rule, the board never scrutinized the information supplied by Tiner and Pullias, who had been reporting no problems on the horizon, excepting perhaps financial ones, that the two of them could not handle. They had not even told the trustees about the failure of the Western College Association to accredit the institution in 1951.

Lovell believed this cavalier treatment of the board would continue so long as George Pepperdine remained chair. The gracious personality of the founder and his deep esteem for Hugh Tiner made it difficult for him to ask hard questions. For that reason, Lovell had a long and painful conversation with George and Helen Pepperdine, finally persuading both that it would be in the best interest of the college if Pepperdine resigned as chair of the trustees in favor of Don Miller, one of the original trustees. Probably with a bit of sadness, Pepperdine consented to the change and submitted his resignation as chair in March 1956. Publicly, he attributed his resignation to his advanced age of 70 years.[50]

Concerns about Tiner

Lovell eventually became deeply concerned about Tiner's actions and attitude both at the college and in the Vermont Avenue church where Lovell and Tiner both served in leadership. His concerns led Lovell to make inquiries of some of the staff who worked for Tiner, where he picked up evidence pointing to an extramarital affair. Lovell kept this conclusion to himself for several months, then shared his conclusions with Miller, the new chair of the college board of trustees.[51]

Miller was shocked, and like Lovell, reluctant to believe what the evidence seemed to suggest. In search of irrefutable facts, they followed Tiner to a house in San Diego one Saturday evening in July 1956. Early Sunday morning, after having spent the night in their car, Miller and Lovell knocked on the door of the house and asked the woman who responded to see President Tiner. He came to the door, at which point, the three men, all of whom were embarrassed, retreated to the car for a painful conversation.[52]

After hearing Tiner admit the obvious, Lovell and Miller pleaded with him to terminate the relationship, confess his error, and ask for the forgiveness of his wife and God. At that point, they were clearly more concerned about him than they were about George Pepperdine College. Tiner did make some effort to repair his relationship with his wife, but he was reluctant to admit his error in even a contrived public setting. Lovell and Miller had told him directly that he must repent and confess or resign as president. But he did neither.[53]

Early in August, Miller told George and Helen Pepperdine about Tiner's indiscretion. They were heartbroken, and poured out their surprise, disappointment, and concern in a conversation that went deep into the night. Whether they had an independent conversation with Tiner is unknown, but it is clear that they supported Tiner's August 10 request for a year's leave of absence. Tiner asked for that leave "to engage in some type of activity which might prove to be of value to the College."[54]

Lovell did all he could to help Tiner get his personal life back together. He arranged for Bob Smith, a Rotary friend of Tiner's, a Houston oilman, a member of the college's president's council, and subsequently a regent for SMU, to find a consulting project for Tiner. Furthermore, he and his wife accompanied Tiner and his wife to New Jersey for a pleasant holiday hosted by Clinton Davidson. Tiner, however, made no serious change in his habits. Nor was he noticeably absent from the campus, or at least no more than usual. He continued to work with the president's council and to meet regularly with the board of trustees.[55]

For Lovell, Tiner's response was inappropriate. He was willing to give Tiner time to get his life back in order; indeed, he was willing to make sacrifices to help that happen. He had even resigned as an elder of the Vermont Avenue congregation so he could conscientiously avoid telling what he knew about Tiner. But by December 1956, Lovell had reached the end of his patience and willingness to sacrifice. Tiner had engaged in infidelity, drunk intoxicating beverages, and deliberately forsaken worship services, he declared. Lovell wanted some acknowledgment of that and a pledge to repent and reform, at the least in a private meeting of the board, after which Tiner could return to the presidency of the college and presumably the full faith and fellowship of the church.[56]

Tiner Takes Leave

For two months, President Tiner waffled. Lovell was pleased when Tiner asked permission of the board to exercise his leave of absence immediately at a called meeting at the home of George and Helen Pepperdine on March 9, 1957. The board approved the request, granting a leave that would continue until the expiration of Tiner's contract at the end of August, with the possibility of compensation for another six months depending upon his acceptance of employment elsewhere "or [on] other personal factors."[57]

Clearly Tiner's petition for a leave of absence was not spontaneous. The trustees expected it, perhaps even demanded it. And they had made plans, probably with the help of Pullias, for successor leadership. Accordingly, the trustees appointed a three-member "President's Committee," made up of R. Carroll Cannon, dean of students; Lonnie T. Vanderveer, professor of education; and James D. Young, professor of speech, to carry on the legal responsibilities of Tiner's office. Those three, along with L. C. Houser and Pullias, would serve as the administrative leadership of the college.

Three days later, Tiner announced his leave of absence and the administrative changes at a called faculty meeting. Since Dean Pullias had carried a large part of the responsibility for the operation of the college, the president told his colleagues, "I don't see how my leave will affect the operations on the Campus very much."[58]

His response was naïve, of course. Somehow he seemed to believe that an extended leave would be the end of the matter. But it was not. Critics, especially church leaders, saw it as an opportunity to secure new leadership for George Pepperdine College and to reestablish it as a real Christian school in the bosom of Churches of Christ. They wanted to seize the opening as quickly as possible.

CHAPTER 7

SEARCHING FOR RESCUERS

E ven though President Tiner was officially on a leave because of ill health, the George Pepperdine College board of trustees did not act like they expected him to get well. As early as December 27, 1956, Jimmy Lovell made discreet inquiries of M. Norvel Young about becoming president of Pepperdine and of Batsell Barrett Baxter about becoming dean. Young, a former teacher at GPC, was then the minister of the Broadway Church of Christ in Lubbock, Texas, the largest congregation in the fellowship. Baxter, also a former GPC teacher and son of the first Pepperdine president, was serving as chair of the Bible department at David Lipscomb College in Nashville.

"As you boys well know," Lovell wrote, "there is a lack of confidence on the part of our brethren in the present administration." He thought it was time to make "some changes."[1] Both Young and Baxter acted surprised and indicated they were entrenched in their current jobs, but neither completely rejected the prospect.[2]

When Lovell shared this response with the board, other members called to encourage Young to consider coming to GPC. George Pepperdine and Don Miller cornered Young at the Abilene Christian College Lectureship and told him, "If you don't come, we will lose the school."[3]

Young agreed to visit, and the trustees informed the five-person president's committee—the college leadership group—that they were inviting Young to campus for informal conversations on March 28. The committee encouraged caution, suggesting the trustees wait longer to replace President Tiner, who had not even resigned at that point. Above all, they wanted to be sure the faculty was given a voice in the selection of a new president.[4]

But the board was less concerned about discussing selection procedures than in conveying its concern regarding college administrative practices and shortcomings, particularly the loss of church constituency support and the failure of Tiner and Pullias to disclose the college's loss of accreditation in 1951. Under the circumstances, the trustees believed, it would be appropriate for them to authorize the immediate appointment of a new president as well as a new dean.[5]

Dean Pullias witnessed the exchange between the board and the committee and later recorded in his journal that the faculty committee's defense of him was one of the "finest occasions" of his life, "for it revealed the deep integrity of the men with whom I am working." Like his faculty colleagues, Pullias was acutely suspicious of the trustees' intentions.[6]

Varying Views on Leadership Change

News of possible leadership changes circulated widely in the college community, especially among alumni. Many were apprehensive of any change, while others, like Logan and Harry Robert Fox, endorsed the idea. As alumni and former Church of Christ missionaries to Japan, the Fox brothers loved the college and considered Dean Pullias an esteemed mentor and personal friend. However, in separate letters to Don Miller and Norvel Young, they called for significant change at Pepperdine.[7] It troubled them that President Tiner and Dean Pullias had pushed the college to embrace a "cut-flower" Christianity that was not rooted in "church" and "doctrine."[8]

Harry Robert called for "an honest recognition that 'we' are heirs not only of the church of the first century but also of the 'Restoration Movement' of the 19th century." Thus any school founded and operated by members of Churches of Christ was obliged to unashamedly identify with it.[9]

The Fox brothers were enthusiastic about the possibility of Norvel Young as president. According to Harry Robert, Young possessed five indispensable characteristics: academic competence, abundant church experience, executive ability, past experience on the faculty of the college, and a genuine love for both the church and the college. If the opportunity to install him was "muffed," said Fox, the future of the school would be irrevocably decided; it might still be a fine school, but it would not serve the church.[10]

Both brothers, despite their respect and affection for Dean Pullias, also urged the board to replace him. And, as men of integrity dealing with the teacher who taught them integrity, each brother wrote directly to Pullias asking him to resign for the good of the college.[11]

Tiner Steps Aside

The board of trustees met with Norvel and Helen Young in the home of Don Miller on April 11, 1957. No record of the discussion survives, although there must have been conversation regarding the general status of the college, its relationship with the Churches of Christ, and its current challenges.[12]

The board recognized the awkwardness of talking with a prospective new president when the incumbent had not resigned and knew that hiring a president without faculty input might endanger its accreditation—to say nothing of its relationship with the faculty. To avoid further embarrassment, the trustees commissioned George and Helen Pepperdine to fly to Wenatchee, Washington, where President Tiner was preaching a sermon series for the local Church of Christ, and request his resignation. It was a difficult assignment; for more than twenty years they had shared hopes, dreams, and disappointments with Tiner. On Sunday, April 14, 1957, they sadly confronted their friend and requested his formal resignation. Tiner gave it to them on the spot.

The Pepperdines carried his letter back to the trustees in Los Angeles. Two days later, and with the president's committee in attendance, the board accepted the resignation. After Dean Pullias and other members of the president's committee had withdrawn, George and Helen Pepperdine moved that the board invite M. Norvel Young to fill the office of president of GPC. Their motion carried unanimously.[13]

The news of Tiner's resignation circulated on campus immediately, and the next day after chapel, George Pepperdine personally conveyed the news. Don Miller issued a statement declaring that the board would be looking for a president with "the ability to relate the college closely to the California educational and business community and to the Christian ideals originally defined for it by the founder." Miller did not reveal that the board already had offered the presidency to Norvel Young.[14]

Hugh Tiner never fully explained to the college community why he resigned. In a letter published in the *Graphic* and the *Alumni Voice*, he did reflect upon the good things that had happened at the school in the previous twenty years, especially the development of the "Pepperdine spirit."[15] Almost immediately, Tiner relocated to San Diego, where he became active in civic work.

In 1960, he unsuccessfully ran as a Democrat for the California State Assembly.[16] Five years later, Governor Pat Brown appointed him to serve on the State Board of Funeral Directors and Embalmers.[17] In time, he reconciled fully with his wife, and in 1965 began preaching for the La Mesa congregation in San Diego County. From 1970 until his death in 1981 he was minister of the Uptown Church of Christ in Long Beach. In 1977 he was named to the board of regents of Pepperdine University, and served there for the remainder of his life.[18]

Young Ponders Decision

Meanwhile, Norvel Young struggled with whether to accept the trustees' offer. For months, leaders of Churches of Christ had implored him to embrace the position as the Apostle Paul had embraced the "Macedonian call." Only he, Young was told, could restore GPC to its original mission and save it for Churches of Christ.[19]

But others told Young he would be foolish to leave his position as minister of the world's largest Church of Christ congregation for an uncertain future at GPC. Among these was his mother. Moving to Los Angeles was "not a good step for *many reasons*," she advised him, largely because of the college's precarious financial status, which would mean that all the dreams Young had for the school "just couldn't come true."[20]

Helen and Norvel Young debated the move, listing reasons for and against going to Los Angeles. They found ten reasons not to go:

- the work in Lubbock was enjoyable;
- they had influence in the community;
- they loved West Texas people;
- Billy Mattox, Helen's brother, needed them to help promote Lubbock Christian College;
- Pepperdine was far from home;
- the Los Angeles environment might impact the children;
- the work might strain Norvel's health;
- the influential and conservative *Gospel Guardian* limited the potential of California Churches of Christ;
- they would have to raise a lot of money; and
- the college faculty objected to external leadership.[21]

The Youngs also found nine reasons they should go:

- the work in Lubbock was in good shape;
- details of their current work were becoming wearisome;
- the West Texas field was confining;
- critics of their work in Lubbock were beginning to emerge;
- the challenge of a college presidency was attractive;
- the vestment of authority would provide opportunity to accomplish more;
- they could help raise the spiritual level on the West Coast;
- the GPC board needed their support; and
- Los Angeles could facilitate their personal growth.[22]

As the Youngs listed their pros and cons, members of the college faculty were also weighing the positives and negatives of Young becoming president. For many, the negatives far outweighed the positives. James Young, a professor of speech and a member of the president's committee, said the Youngs should not come because Tiner's successor should come from within the college. He held that turning GPC into a Church of Christ school like Harding or Abilene Christian would be a disaster.

Woodrow Whitten, chair and professor of social science, agreed. Such a "shift in policy," he wrote, would "1) cost the College its dearly won accreditation, 2) cause students, new and old, to stay away from enrollment by the hundreds, 3) demoralize the faculty, 4) make almost impossible the situation of the new president, and 5) set the College back many years." Whitten denied that the current college administration was "dean dominated," noting the presence of a full-fledged faculty organization and a lively chapter of the American Association of University Professors (AAUP), and believed that major shifts of policy should be avoided *"at all costs."*[23]

Young's Vision for Change

Of course, Young *was* planning for major policy and personnel changes if he took the position. He envisioned an administrative team with strong academic credentials whose loyalty to "Christ and the Bible" was unquestioned and who would bring the college into a creative relationship with members of Churches of Christ. The new team would include a president, a dean, a vice president of development, and a head of the religion department. He also saw a board of trustees with three or four new members, some of whom would reside outside the Los Angeles area, and a large advisory board of twenty-five or thirty who would support the new administrative team.[24]

Every administrative and faculty position, Young believed, should be filled by faithful members of Churches of Christ, excepting those positions already held by nonmembers of the church. Young expected to emphasize recruiting young people from Church of Christ homes and planned to have the college, rather than the Vermont Avenue congregation, assume some responsibility for spiritual development, sponsoring evening devotionals and Christian training classes in addition to daily chapel. Moreover, Young planned to appoint an academic who was a well-known churchman as chair of the religion department and increase the number of Bible units required for graduation from eight to fifteen.[25]

The change advocated by Young that most disturbed the college faculty and staff was his idea that E. V. Pullias must step aside as dean and perhaps even from his faculty position. Because of the withering attacks by Foy

Wallace Jr., Roy Cogdill, and Yater Tant, Pullias was widely assumed to be the evil genius behind Pepperdine's presumed advocacy of biblical liberalism and theological modernism.

Although Pullias had been prolific in publishing in Church of Christ journals, he was more often ridiculed for his big words than applauded for his insights. Pullias's definition of "Christian environment" was vague and ahistorical, according to Harry Robert Fox.[26] At the very least, declared Reuel Lemmons, his views had "not been in harmony with the views of brethren generally."[27]

Jimmy Lovell had come to the same conclusion, although reluctantly. He and Pullias served together as elders at the Vermont Avenue church, and he loved "Doc" as he loved few men. But more than once Lovell had fallen under Pullias's "spell," and had come to feel that Pullias had used him "as no man on this earth ha[d] ever used him."[28] It had also been reported to Lovell that ex-faculty considered Pullias unfair, untruthful, a schemer, and domineering despite a posture of humility. Lovell came to conclude that the dean had "had GPC tied hand and foot for years" and that the college would "never move ahead with him on our campus."[29]

Pullias Fights for His Job

Pullias was aware of the pressures mounting against him. He had felt them before, but Tiner had previously served as his buffer from the critics. In return, he had shielded Tiner when questions arose about the president's absences from campus. Pullias wrote in his journal: "These are among the most difficult days of my life. The college to which I have given the major portion of my energy . . . is in danger of total disintegration. . . . My enemies flourish and encircle me; the friends I may have seemed to have are hard pressed and may have forsaken."[30]

At Young's urging, the board of trustees on April 28, 1957, asked Pullias to resign as dean and perhaps even as professor of psychology, so that a new president could appoint his own dean. Pullias did not take the request well. He tapped his longtime friend Jimmy Lovell, on the chest with his forefinger and said, "To me you are just another man," forever ending their recently troubled friendship.[31] Moreover, Pullias threatened to resort to legal means to retain his professorship.[32]

Subsequently, Pullias wrote to Don Miller, chair of the board, to confess his difficulty in understanding why Miller was so deeply displeased with him as dean. Pullias noted that he loved the college and had given it his best for twenty years. Given the forces arrayed against him, Pullias was prepared to resign as dean but not as a professor of psychology. But he requested that the transition be worked out by the board and the president's committee in a way that would not damage his professional reputation.[33]

The president's committee soon learned that Pullias had been asked to resign. Within a week, Woodrow Whitten called a meeting of Church of Christ faculty members at his home; twenty-two of them signed a petition demanding that Pullias be retained as dean and his tenure as a professor be recognized.[34] Wade Ruby, one of the school's founding faculty members, presented the petition to the board on May 2.

The petitioners reminded the board that virtually all of them had sacrificed financially to teach at the college and said it was only "right and proper" that the board "work in close communication with the faculty in the selection of a new President." In summary, the petitioners saw no justification for a change in the operations of the college. They apparently were not concerned about the economic circumstances of the college or the wishes of its founder.[35]

Trustees, Faculty Skirmish

On the advice of the president's committee, the board scrapped plans to meet with the faculty but wrote a letter dated May 7, 1957, denying campus rumors that a complete change of direction of the school was planned, that many heads would roll, and that faculty and students who were not members of the Church of Christ would be ousted. On the contrary, the trustees declared that academic accomplishments of the college would be preserved and improved, that relationships with educational and business communities would continue, and that the institution would rededicate itself to the spiritual and religious ideals expressed by its founder.[36]

Faculty members need not fear they would be ousted because of religious affiliation, the board wrote. But it would continue to be board policy to recruit new faculty who were members of Churches of Christ if they were academically prepared and personally acceptable. The college expected to continue to receive student entrance applications from current sources; there was no intention that GPC would build a student body made up 100 percent of Church of Christ students, but the board did express a desire for an increased percentage.[37]

Regarding the president selection, the trustees reminded the faculty of the institution's bylaws, which gave them the power to appoint the president of the college, as well as its professors, tutors, and other officers. Those officials were to hold office at the pleasure of the trustees. In the board's opinion, its substantial powers had never been abused during the college's twenty-year history. The trustees also affirmed that the president's committee would continue to serve until replaced by a new president.[38]

Contrary to the board's expectations, its May 7 letter was never read formally to the faculty. The letter did circulate, however, and it did aggravate. An unsigned letter charged that the board letter exposed the trustees' fundamental philosophy that they were the "sole policy-determining body" of the institution and that faculty and staff had "no part" in it. It also noted that academic tenure was "meaningless" if the board could hire and fire at will.[39]

If faculty members were concerned about Pullias's future, so too were many alumni. On May 10, the dean had written to alumni to inform them of Tiner's resignation.[40] Within days, the board received scores of alumni letters supporting Pullias in the dean's position.[41]

Pressure on Pullias Intensifies

Faculty petitions and alumni letters notwithstanding, the trustees were more and more inclined to force Pullias to leave the college completely and told him so in a May 28 meeting.[42] Pullias responded that he believed he had another fifteen good years as a professor and that he might resign as dean under specific conditions but did not want the board to press him too far. If the board forced him out without meeting his conditions, he made clear he would bring legal action.[43]

The board knew that the president's committee and many of the Church of Christ faculty supported Pullias and wanted no change in the dean's office.[44] Trustees, however, were so confident that Pullias would resign as dean that both Don Miller and George Pepperdine had talked with J. P. Sanders, current dean at David Lipscomb College and former head of the Pepperdine religion department, about becoming GPC dean. Indeed, Young had made it clear that he would not come to Pepperdine as president unless Sanders accompanied him as dean. Sanders, however, was quite happy at Lipscomb and had no intention of leaving Tennessee. He would need to be sold on the idea of moving to California. That was why Miller and George Pepperdine had phoned him.[45]

That was also why Young and Reuel Lemmons, the editor of the *Firm Foundation,* flew to Nashville to explain that the call to GPC was really a call from God to reclaim the school for "New Testament Christianity" and the Churches of Christ. "Only once in a lifetime does a man have an opportunity to do a job such as that presented the new Dean of Pepperdine College," Lemmons told him. He urged Sanders to make the personal sacrifices necessary "for the sake of the cause of Christ and for the sake of the thousands in the West who might otherwise be lost."[46] By late May, Sanders was ready to accept the call to Pepperdine. But there was one problem; Dean Pullias had not resigned.

Young, Sanders Make Entrance Plans; Pullias Declines to Exit

On June 10, Trustee Robert Jones flew to Nashville to brief both Sanders and Young, who was in Tennessee to discuss developments at Pepperdine with

Sanders. There was no question that Pullias would soon resign as dean, Jones reported; the only question was whether he would also resign from the faculty. Given Pullias's reputation among Churches of Christ, the trustees, Young, and Sanders all favored his full resignation—although there were fears that forcing Pullias to resign from both positions would induce a rebellion within the faculty.

Nonetheless, Young and Sanders committed themselves to assuming leadership of GPC by August 1, presuming that Pullias did resign his deanship and that his role thereafter was satisfactorily resolved.[47] Jones hurried back to Los Angeles to share this good news with trustee colleagues.

In the meantime, the president's committee had met again with the board of trustees and reiterated their desire that Pullias remain as dean. Since the board received the request graciously, the committee assumed no permanent decision had been made.[48]

Simultaneously, Woodrow Whitten, president of the college's AAUP chapter, requested a personal meeting with Norvel Young. He wanted Young to know that, if he accepted the presidency, he would be stepping into a volatile situation that could result in loss of accreditation, wholesale faculty resignations, and massive student withdrawals.[49]

Wade Ruby, the beloved professor of English and minister of the Hollywood Church of Christ, said essentially the same thing to Young. Ruby had high praise for Pullias and believed he would adjust to any change that gave him "dignity and status." The faculty would object to any other course, Ruby warned, as unchristian and academically unacceptable.[50]

When Jones returned from Nashville, the trustees prepared a final offer that Jones delivered to Pullias and the president's committee on June 18. They proposed as one option that the dean resign, accept a year's sabbatical, return to the college as a professor of psychology, and receive further appointments depending upon whether he was able to cooperate with the new administration. As option two, the trustees proposed the same steps absent the sabbatical. Neither Pullias nor the committee found either proposal acceptable, because they did not agree to the timing of the resignation. Pullias preferred at least one more year in his leadership role, with a transition that would not jeopardize his professional reputation. Since the board and the dean could not agree on an exit strategy, Pullias declined to step aside as dean.[51]

Pullias as Symbol

As central as Pullias was to the tension between the board and the faculty, the dean was more of a symbol of the dispute than its cause. The fundamental issues were the parameters of faculty governance and the exercise of

Christian mission. According to an essay by Whitten, the trustees, pressured by external powers, were attempting through the appointment of a new president to alter the nature and character of the institution. In his view, GPC had never been organically connected with any church, with Whitten interpreting "church" as a denomination as opposed to a congregation of Churches of Christ. Nonetheless, the college had a definite Christian character, as was evident in its sizable church membership among faculty, staff, students, and alumni; its inclusion of Bible in the curriculum; and in activities such as daily chapel. Moreover, like Churches of Christ, it prided itself on being nondenominational and nonsectarian.

But, said Whitten, the religious position of the college was actually ambiguous, and it shared a basic dilemma faced by the entire Church of Christ brotherhood: the *ideal* of universal, nonsectarian Christianity and the *actuality* of denominational, sometimes sectarian behaviors. The gulf between the nondenominational ideals and the denominational practices had widened rather than narrowed in the Church of Christ brotherhood in recent years, Whitten asserted.[52]

The dilemma was now being played out on the Pepperdine campus. The trustees and their allies were proposing a course in keeping with what Whitten called the "'middle road' of the 'Church of Christ' denomination." This would permit brotherhood policy to be college policy, with Pepperdine coming along with other "Christian colleges" simply to serve the "middle of the road" segment of the denominationalized Church of Christ. Markers of this approach were a president whose primary dedication was to Churches of Christ, the replacement of the dean and a few of his faculty supporters, institution of a revised admission policy that screened out non-Church of Christ members, the revision of the curriculum, and many changes in campus activities. Such changes "if undertaken suddenly," Whitten predicted, would undermine the academic standing and accreditation of the institution and produce strong resistance and near chaos on the parts of the faculty, student body, and alumni.[53]

Alternate Paths Proposed

As an alternative, Whitten proposed maintaining the present course. This would mean "a gradual realignment of institutional policy" to the extent that it recognized "the denominational character of the Church of Christ" but strove "to eliminate the bigotry and self-righteousness, and spiritual pride" that had crept into the church.

This approach would "promote sound scholarship and seek to enhance the fine academic standing already achieved while striving to gain wider brotherhood acceptance of the institution." According to Whitten, this course involved an effort to keep alive the ideal of nondenominational, nonsectarian Christianity. Admittedly, it would close some doors for the college but open many others.[54]

However, Whitten actually preferred another option, although he granted it was unrealistic. He would prefer to see GPC associate itself with "forward-looking Christian people of many communions and become a Christian liberal-arts university dedicated to serv[ing] ... the advancement of the church universal—the Kingdom of God on earth." He based this option on the belief that sectarian Christianity had no lasting contribution to make to the modern world. This approach was what Logan Fox had labeled "church-less Christianity."[55]

It is unclear how widely Whitten's essay circulated or how much its tenets were embraced, but it is certain that he spoke for the president's committee, Dean Pullias, and a substantial number of the faculty. His essay clarified just how those groups embraced Christian mission and church connectedness and what the future would have been for GPC under their leadership.

It also demonstrates why members of the board of trustees concluded that President Tiner and Dean Pullias were not fulfilling the wishes of the founder in their administration of the college. And it confirmed that the alarm bell sounded over the years by Pullias's many critics within Churches of Christ was not totally false. Clearly, the dean and his friends intended for the relationship between the college and church to diminish.

Final Days for Pullias

Norvel Young was well aware that changing the leadership at GPC would affect the soul of the institution, and one of the reasons he was willing to return to Los Angeles was to bring the college back into the orbit of the institutional church. He understood that objective to be the primary motivation of the board of trustees as well. If so, why was it, Young asked, that Pullias remained in office?

The delays had left him in turmoil, and his frustration focused on Pullias, whose attitude he considered "unChristian and unprofessional." Young found it ironic that the dean resented all efforts on the part of the trustees to pressure him to resign, yet he had no compunction about "threatening legal action and doing all he could to destroy accreditation in case he [was] not allowed to stay."

Young was willing for the board to grant Pullias a yearlong sabbatical after his resignation, but only if the resignation were immediate and the sabbatical was off campus.[56] To facilitate that departure, Young worked with D. Lloyd Nelson, a professor of education at the University of Southern California, a lifelong member of Churches of Christ, a longtime friend of Hugh Tiner, and subsequently a member of Pepperdine University's board of regents, to find a position for Pullias at USC. Those arrangements were completed successfully by mid-June.[57]

As Young was trying to arrange a soft landing for Pullias, the board began to build a case that would warrant firing him. Given the impasse, the board sought out the services of Harold Slane, George Pepperdine's longtime personal attorney. Slane had a private talk with Pullias, apparently a fairly direct one, for the dean signed and submitted a letter of unconditional resignation on June 24.[58] Pullias authorized Slane to deliver the letter to the board if the trustees would first meet with a faculty/staff group; Slane convened the meeting in his office on the evening of June 25.

Faculty in the Dark

In addition to Slane, seven trustees and eleven members of the faculty and staff participated. As Pullias desired, it represented an opportunity for his colleagues to lay their hopes, fears, and recommendations on the table, something they had been unable to accomplish previously. It was immediately apparent they were unaware of the plans that had been made to bring in Young and Sanders. Many of their recommendations, therefore, seemed to come from a time warp. They repeated the mantra that the forced resignation of Pullias would have devastating effects on the college.[59]

They also emphasized the importance of selecting a president and dean from current faculty and recommended an immediate adoption of a tenure policy. They wanted a general salary increase, two representatives on the board of trustees, a continuation of the current structure of faculty governance, and conversion of the president's home into a student union. The board responded positively on the spot, passing a resolution approving the principle of tenure and committing themselves to work collaboratively with the new college administration as well as a new faculty policy committee.[60]

Sometime after 11:30 p.m., Slane called a halt to the meeting. By then it was apparent to everyone that the board of trustees would not be swayed from asking Pullias to resign the deanship immediately, so the faculty/staff committee agreed very reluctantly that the dean would step aside. Slane then produced Dean Pullias's letter of resignation effective as of August 1, 1957, which ended the combined meeting.

Trustees Act Quickly

In a separate gathering, the board of trustees accepted Pullias's resignation unanimously and then authorized immediate telephone calls to Norvel Young in Lubbock and J. P. Sanders in Nashville to invite both to Los Angeles to discuss the presidency and deanship of GPC. Those calls pulled both men from restless sleep.[61]

Young and Sanders caught planes for Los Angeles immediately. Two days later, they were meeting with the trustees to finalize their appointments. Young agreed to a compensation package of $10,000 per year, a car, and $2,600 in travel allowance. Sanders agreed to $8,000 in salary and $3,400 per year in travel expenses.[62]

Reuel Lemmons declared the installation of the new regime at GPC as

one of the most significant events of this generation, so far as the church is concerned. . . . The strong position GPC could have occupied in the history of the growth of the church on the West Coast has been denied it, because the aims and purposes of the past administration differed widely from what most brethren thought that the aim and purpose of a Christian college should be.

But that problem was now solved, Lemmons wrote, and the much-desired support should be forthcoming.[63] And George Pepperdine himself added: "We are confident that [the Young and Sanders team] will lead our college to greater success, both academically and in improved service to all the Churches of Christ on the west coast."[64]

This victory had come, wrote Jimmy Lovell, because of Hugh Tiner's "sin." There was little doubt in his mind that the board of trustees could never have made the leadership change had Tiner not "run into trouble." Lovell expected little trouble regarding the leadership transition from the faculty and staff naysayers, and thought only three or four might leave. Indeed, he believed that God had called the trustees and the new leadership team "to a new land."[65]

Pullias Steps Away

All of this was painful for E. V. Pullias, although it was in concert with his personal expectations for life in general. Excepting for some high points, he confided to his journal, life overall had been "deeply unsatisfying."[66] It remained that way in the immediate aftermath of his resignation as dean. He grappled with how to give up personal power he had held for eighteen years and how to transfer his responsibilities without seriously damaging the work that had been done at the college.

Even more of a challenge, he confessed, was how to deal with his pride. "Doubtless I have loved this college too much," he wrote. "Perhaps I have identified myself with it in a prideful, self-centered way." Suffering, he concluded, "is the means of growth."[67] That being his measure, Pullias did a lot of growing in 1957. In addition to the turmoil at GPC, his oldest son, John, drowned in a tragic accident; his father died unexpectedly; and his youngest son endured a chronic learning dysfunction.[68]

Dean Pullias did take advantage of his promised sabbatical. He also reluctantly accepted a position on the USC education faculty beginning September 1, 1958. He embarked upon a very successful career as teacher and scholar of the principles and values of higher education and continued to work with the LA County Board of Education, an appointment he held for thirty years. Even more significantly, Pullias remained an elder at the Vermont Avenue Church of Christ for the rest of his life, serving at one point alongside Norvel Young. He retired from USC in 1977, and is still honored there annually with the Earl V. Pullias Lectureship in Higher Education. In 1986, after a thirty-year absence, he accepted an invitation to help commemorate the centennial of George Pepperdine's birthday at a gathering on the university's Malibu campus.[69] Pullias died in 1994.

Actions in Hindsight

Nearly forty years after the fact, Don Miller faulted the board for the way it handled Pullias's resignation. There was legitimate concern about the dean taking the college away from the Church of Christ, but "in its inexperience,"

A banker by profession and an active member of Churches of Christ, Donald Miller was an original member of the board of trustees of George Pepperdine College, serving as chair of the board from 1956 until 1970. He played an influential role in convincing Norvel Young to come to Pepperdine College.

he remembered, the board reacted badly, alienating and injuring some highly respected educators. Unlike the faculty, the trustees could not see that it was in danger of being boxed in by editors who had more influence than elders.

Miller blamed poor guidance, presumably from attorney Slane, and said the board erred in not bringing the faculty into the presidential selection process and in asking Pullias to resign. The latter almost led to the termination of the school, Miller believed.[70]

Miller was most likely correct in his criticism of the way the matters were handled; however, he appeared to have forgotten that Norvel Young and J. P. Sanders would not have come to Pepperdine if Pullias had remained as dean. And their absence would also have dramatically changed the history of the school.

NEW HORIZONS—AND SOME DARK CLOUDS 1957–1971

~

CHAPTER 8

INTO A NEW LAND

M. Norvel Young began his presidency at George Pepperdine College in 1957, during an era of dramatic cultural and political change in the United States. The Soviet Union's Sputnik I launched a space race that was really just a new chapter in the Cold War that would pit Americans against the Soviets in Cuba, Europe, and Vietnam over the next decade. Passage of the Civil Rights Act of 1957 was a prelude to momentous events in Little Rock, Selma, Memphis, Chicago, and Los Angeles. Jimmy Lovell did not have this volatile national landscape in mind when he spoke of Pepperdine's leaders having been called to take a "new land," but it would nonetheless be descriptive of Norvel Young's leadership challenges at the GPC campus.

The college was in crisis when Young assumed the presidency in July 1957. It was locally recognized as a small, independent, liberal arts college with a good sports program that educated students in a Christian environment. However, its relationship with the sponsoring Churches of Christ had been strained by the former leadership and by campus teachings and activities that many church members found deeply offensive.[1] These ranged from the taint of theological modernism in the religion department,[2] to the choreographed steps of short-skirted "Choraliers" (a student performance group),[3] to poorly attended chapel services. The critics were certain that the college experience at GPC was corroding students' faith and that the school was not a legitimate Christian college in the fashion of Abilene Christian College or Harding College.[4]

GPC's financial status was also in crisis. Net assets aggregated just under $3 million, including an endowment of $666,582.[5] In five of the six previous years, the college had operated at a deficit, with the shortfall paid from endowment assets.[6] The annual operating budget was $1.2 million, with tuition and fees generating some 60 percent of the income. The endowment supplied no more than 2.3 percent, or $28,000, of the total budget. Thus, for the budget to balance there had to be significant annual, unrestricted gifts of at least $125,000 per year.[7] Those kinds of gifts had been few and far between.

The Vermont Avenue campus was as picturesque as it had been twenty years earlier, but the beauty was deceiving. Necessary maintenance for the aging buildings had been deferred. Living space on campus was inadequate, and the married student housing in Normandie Village was decaying. Likewise, teaching space was insufficient, especially in science fields. Indeed, the Western College Association (WCA) accrediting team in 1954 had declared that a new science building was a must.

At least 1,078 students matriculated at the Vermont Avenue campus in 1957. Some 14.6 percent of them identified with Churches of Christ; almost as many claimed membership in Baptist churches. The most popular majors were business administration and education; one of the least popular was religion. Judging from the college's flexible admission standards, student academic credentials were not distinctive.[8]

GPC received mixed reviews regarding its academic program. It had a solid reputation within the Los Angeles United School District (LAUSD), but

M. Norvel Young was the third president of Pepperdine College, answering a call from the board of trustees in 1957 and remaining in the position until 1970. Young renewed Pepperdine's relationship with the Churches of Christ, and his tireless efforts to raise friends and funds for the college ensured its survival through rocky times and a new campus in Malibu.

the college was frequently criticized by WCA accrediting teams. In 1953–54, for example, the visitors had been critical of the college's general education program, the lack of bachelor of science degree programs, inadequate facilities for science education, a catalog listing courses that were never taught, advertisement of degree programs that had no students, disarray of student records, unacceptable faculty salary levels, and the absence of a tenure policy.[9]

Even under such conditions, the fifty-three full-time faculty members at GPC were well-qualified, with almost 68 percent having either a doctorate or sixty graduate credits in their field of expertise. They thought of themselves as teachers as opposed to scholars, however, and were badly divided regarding what kind of Christian school GPC should be, especially the nature of its relationship with Churches of Christ. A good third of the faculty was threatening to resign in protest of the treatment of former dean E. V. Pullias, who had been forced out of the college by the trustees.

Given the challenging circumstances, why did Young accept the presidency? He told friends and supporters it was because of the challenge. The West Coast was increasing in population and power, and the church was growing there. Thousands of Christian families needed a Christian college to help train their sons and daughters, he said. Young saw an opportunity to provide them "the very best in Christian education," which meant maintaining or increasing the "high academic standing of the college" while also reviving the confidence and financial support of faithful Christians around the world.[10]

Renewing Relationship with Churches of Christ

President Young's foremost item on his action list was to position GPC so that its relationship with Churches of Christ, as opposed to generic Christianity, would be unquestioned. He believed the Church of Christ constituency would be the best source of additional students and unrestricted gifts, two items the school needed to survive. He appealed to the faithful as soon as he arrived in Los Angeles, telling *Time Magazine* he wanted to build a faculty with 100 percent of its members from Churches of Christ.[11] He told the *Los Angeles Times* that he envisioned doubling enrollment to 2,000 students, with half being commuter students.[12] He obviously envisioned much of the student population increase coming from Church of Christ families.

Young was also appealing to that Church of Christ constituency when he formally announced plans to strengthen the on-campus Christian environment, promising to build up the religion department, introduce a more rigorous chapel program, provide a Christian guidance program, create more frequent devotional opportunities, and introduce evening hymn-sings on the central plaza.[13] Dean J. P. Sanders said, "It is our purpose to provide the best academic training in the Liberal Arts in a distinctly Christian environment in order to aid the student in preparing himself for a life of service to humanity and of loyalty and devotion to Christ as Lord."[14]

An Enthusiastic Response

The initial outreaches by Young and Sanders were welcomed by West Coast church folks, and more than 1,000 of them, along with college alumni and students, attended an August 16, 1957, reception in their honor on the college campus. George Pepperdine considered the response "a real vote of confidence on the part of the people of the church in this area."[15]

For most of the fall, Young and Sanders preached two and three times each week at various area Churches of Christ, and they followed their outreach with action.[16] The president cancelled the cheerleader summer camps, pledged to recruit a student body with 50 to 60 percent of its members from Churches of Christ, and set out to assure the centrality of the Bible to the curriculum.[17] As a "sign of progress at Pepperdine," Young and Sanders announced the appointment of Frank Pack as chair of the religion department. The coming of Pack, the head of the Bible department at Abilene Christian and a highly regarded biblical scholar in Churches of Christ, was deemed a sure indication of the school's commitment to its religious heritage.[18]

Young also launched a carefully crafted publicity campaign in the pages of nationally circulated church journals like the *Firm Foundation*, the *Christian Chronicle*, and the *Gospel Advocate*. Notices and ad copy emphasized a heightening of interest in chapel, dormitory devotionals, Christian women's classes, the Timothy Club, and weekly campus hymn-sings.[19]

A Rise in Percentages

The campaign was part of an orchestrated effort to recruit Church of Christ students to the college, and it was effective, especially after George Hill, a recruit from Oklahoma Christian College, became director of admissions in the spring of 1961.[20] Within a year of Hill's appointment as many as 45 percent of the undergraduate class declared themselves to be members of the church. The Church of Christ population reportedly reached 50 percent of all the undergraduates in 1967.[21] Part of that enrollment came from students transferring from Church of Christ-related junior colleges to take advantage of one-half tuition academic scholarships.[22]

President Young was also eager to increase the percentage of the faculty and staff who were members of Churches of Christ, and he met with some success in this area also, partly because a number of openings were created when disgruntled faculty members resigned. By 1959, 78 percent of the fifty-one full-time members of the faculty identified with Churches of Christ. That increased to 83 percent by 1962, but slipped to 77 percent by 1969 when full-time faculty totaled ninety. Young took pride in reporting that two-thirds or more of the faculty who were church members were actively "preaching the Gospel in the pulpits of Southern California," while others were servings as elders and deacons.[23]

Young's administration also organized events that brought Church of Christ members to campus. Beginning in 1960, the school hosted an Annual Youth Forum. In its second year, the forum featured Pat Boone, world-renowned recording artist, film star, and best-selling author who had been baptized by Norvel Young and was a lifelong member of Churches of Christ.[24] Beginning in the late 1950s, Boone often contributed his celebrity to promote Pepperdine's status, and he even contributed some of his royalties from *Twixt Twelve and Twenty*, his wildly popular advice book for teenagers, to the school.

The college also offered the Church of Christ faithful an array of services, including a mission training program that subsequently became an MA degree in missions.[25] In 1963, the school organized Teen Associates of Pepperdine (TAP) primarily from the church constituency, with dues of $1.50 per year.[26] Two years later, Pepperdine organized a Christian Education Workshop that ran for several years and began hosting summer seminars featuring notable church leaders in 1968.[27] Professor Wyatt Jones and his colleagues in the department of education organized workshops for Sunday School teachers and church leaders between 1966 and 1971.[28]

Young also worked hard to ensure campus matters would not provide unnecessary "insults" to Churches of Christ members. For example, he nixed as inappropriate professor of home economics Louise Ashby's suggestion of surveying Pepperdine female students about their use of birth control pills. He did not want to know—nor did he want the church to know—whether Ashby was correct in her hypothesis that 40 to 60 percent did use birth control.[29]

New Supporting Groups

To better mobilize the church constituency, President Young looked to the board of counselors. Organized initially as the board of advisors under the initiative of Jimmy Lovell in August 1957, the fifty men were all leaders within the church, and many were from outside California. Young kept members well-informed so that they could help represent and defend the college in church circles.[30]

Another important church support group was Associated Women for Pepperdine, better known as AWP. It was organized in the home of Helen Young in the spring of 1958 with seven women. By 1964 there were 2,500 members across California and Arizona, and in its first decade, AWP raised $300,000 for campus improvements and $250,000 in scholarships.[31]

What AWP was to women, the shorter-lived board of development was to men. Organized in 1958 and chaired initially by Ken Davidson, the board involved several hundred Church of Christ men from California who assisted with the Living Endowment Association for Pepperdine and other projects, promoted attendance at Pepperdine church-related events, and helped recruit Church of Christ students.[32]

As hard as the Young administration worked to reach out to its church constituency, it always retained some ambivalence, which grew as it became apparent that the external dollars necessary to run the school were not likely to come from Churches of Christ members. Accordingly, the association of the school with the church, although never denied, was not always emphasized in official publications. When and how to show the cross, as it were, remained a conundrum in the life of the college through Young's presidency and long after. Because Pepperdine would have to depend upon non-Church of Christ students and friends to survive institutionally and financially, the Church of Christ markers would have to appear only in subtle form from time to time.

On the whole, this concentrated outreach to the Church of Christ faithful was well received and made Young something of a folk hero within that faith tradition.[33] That Young and Sanders were winning the favor of the brethren was clearly evident in March 1958, the first Bible lectureship under the new regime. More than 2,500 attended, as many as 25 times more than had participated in the lectures of just a few years before.[34] That number increased to 10,000 in 1962, the year of George Pepperdine's death, and remained above 7,000 for the rest of the decade. The Pepperdine lectures became one of the best-attended events offered by Churches of Christ anywhere in the world.[35]

Faculty Prove Harder to Satisfy

With the community of faith largely behind him, Young turned his attention to the faculty. Thanks to Woodrow Whitten, he was well aware that his administration faced opposition there. On his first day on campus, Young wrote to all faculty members, complimenting them on the contributions they had made to the college over the years, speaking warmly of the work of President Tiner and Dean Pullias, pledging himself to "preserve every valid gain of the first twenty years," and promising to build an even greater Pepperdine in the future with their cooperation.[36]

Early on, Young believed that this effort to build bridges to the alienated faculty had improved morale in all but eight to ten cases.[37] Thus, in his address to the faculty in September, he did not back away from his declared and board-mandated intention to move closer to the church constituency. But he did reassure his skeptical colleagues that, despite his statement in *Time Magazine,* he would respect a faculty person's rights and tenure regardless of church affiliation. He also declared that all students would be welcome regardless of their faith.[38]

Judging from a resolution passed by a majority of the faculty in the immediate aftermath of Young's speech, his reassurances did not relieve their anxiety. In strengthening ties with the church, the resolution contended, the president was doing something not intended by the founder. The idea of a nonsectarian liberal arts Christian college had proved sound over the years, the dissenters believed, and the school had achieved full accreditation, graduated loyal alumni, and instituted an effective governance system under the leadership of the former president and dean. The critical faculty proposed that the new administration hang large photographs or paintings of Tiner and Pullias, prepared at faculty expense, in a prominent section of the college library.[39]

The wife of the third president of Pepperdine College, Helen Young for many was the personification of Christian servanthood. In 1958, she founded the Associated Women for Pepperdine, a support group for the college, and she was frequently by her husband's side in his friend-raising/money-raising efforts.

Christian Visions Clash

Clearly, the issue at play in faculty dissent was less about GPC as a Christian college than as a college related to Churches of Christ. Director of Public Relations Robert O. Young insisted that Churches of Christ were "nothing more than another denomination ruled by the 'brethren' rather than a divine institution ruled by the Word of God."[40] Unlike many of the church's faithful, Robert Young doubted the possibility of reconstructing a contemporary church on a New Testament pattern.[41]

In sum, Robert Young and other staff and faculty members felt that reattaching GPC to a denominational Church of Christ would retard its growth and damage its Christian witness. By February 1, 1958, the director of admissions, the head of the education department, Robert Young, and a few professors had resigned.[42] Within two weeks, other notable members of the faculty joined them, including Woodrow Whitten, the dean and associate dean of students, the heads of several academic divisions, the head librarian, and the chief business officer.[43]

It's hard to know just how many faculty and staff members actually resigned. At one time, President Young counted fifteen teachers and two adjuncts, while Woodrow Whitten later tallied twenty-one, including seven administrative heads, seven department heads, and five full-time faculty. Young told the *Los Angeles Times* that the faculty members had accepted better-paying positions elsewhere and that each left with a handshake. In the *Times* two days later, Whitten attributed the exodus to the "professional irresponsibility" of the board of trustees in making key personnel decisions without consulting the faculty.[44]

In the opinion of S. H. Hall, the venerable minister at Arcadia who taught Bible at the college, Whitten deserved to be terminated for challenging the veracity of the president in the public press. It was more than suspicious to Hall that the resignations occurred just as the college was preparing for the program reviews necessary for the WCA accreditation visit, scheduled for January 1959. To have the chairs resign en masse when they did bespoke of malice rather than woundedness, he believed.[45]

Whitten defended his actions and confirmed that a document recording the history of recent administrative changes at Pepperdine was being prepared by a committee of the AAUP local chapter, of which he was president. The document would be a factual account of recent events that would faithfully register the points of view of the trustees, administration and "preacherhood," Whitten said, but also recount the dissenting perspective of a sizable proportion of the faculty. Should the accrediting committee recommend probationary status, it would not be as a consequence of the report but of the events themselves, Whitten told Hall.

Whitten completed the AAUP report on May 26, 1958. Twenty-four pages long plus appendices, it supplied a chronology of events leading to the resignations of President Tiner and Dean Pullias and the appointment of President Young and Dean Sanders. Although it reflected no knowledge of the real circumstances of Tiner's and Pullias's resignations, the document was surprisingly accurate in its recitation of the facts of the case.[46]

Whitten quickly filed copies of his report with the board of trustees and the college administration. Copies were also accepted by the WCA accrediting team that visited the campus in early 1959 even though Whitten was no longer associated with Pepperdine and the local AAUP chapter, operating free of Whitten's influence, had disavowed its earlier support of the document. The trustees were then compelled to prepare and file a response that detailed events as they remembered them. The board's analysis and the repudiation of Whitten's document by the remaining members of the AAUP chapter mitigated the report's charges that the leadership transition had violated the principles of tenure and academic freedom as advocated by AAUP.[47]

Finding Replacements

As evident by the large number of resignations and the continued debates, nerves were raw and feelings hurt among the GPC faculty. Dozens of men and women had made considerable personal sacrifices to create a notable liberal arts college that functioned in a Christian atmosphere but without connection to an organized church. They felt their vision had been repudiated and their life's work disassembled by the coming of Young and Sanders.

While trying to smooth those hurt feelings, Sanders and Young were also working diligently to recruit competent faculty and staff to replace the ones who resigned. Almost all—if not all—of these new hires were members of Churches of Christ, but they were also well-qualified in their academic fields, perhaps even more qualified than the people they replaced, or so opined the WCA accrediting team that visited the campus in January 1959.[48]

Leading George Pepperdine College into a "new land" was no easy task for Norvel Young. Upon assuming office, his chief priority had been to gain the approbation of the school's Church of Christ constituency, and that initiative did meet with a measure of success.

Young also wanted to reach some accommodation with faculty and staff sympathetic to the previous regime. Although that turned out to be more of a challenge than he had anticipated, the recovery time was fairly rapid as he was able to quickly replace faculty and staff who resigned.

There was more to do, however, if the new land were to be conquered.

CHAPTER 9

TAKING CHARGE

On October 21, 1958, George Pepperdine College hosted the world premiere of the film *Twenty-one Years*. The film, subtitled *A Color Motion Picture of Student Life at Pepperdine*, was written, narrated, produced, directed, and scored by GPC alumni who saw the need to do something for the college.

The film was produced with the blessing of the Pepperdine administration but without financing from the school. Dick Meltved and Joe Orlando, both former scholarship students, raised the $5,000 necessary to produce the film, which featured on-camera interviews with George Pepperdine and footage of the campus, students, and programs.[1]

The film was deemed an appropriate context for a presidential inauguration. Thus, Norvel Young was formally inaugurated as the third president of George Pepperdine College in the college auditorium on Friday, November 21, 1958, about sixteen months after he had first taken office. At least 1,000 people attended, including representatives of 168 national learned societies and higher education institutions, faculty, staff, students, alumni, church members, and friends.[2]

President Young titled his address for the occasion "Forward with Faith." He announced his complete support for the historic purposes of GPC: to help the student develop a wise, spiritually centered character, cultivate a vocational skill, and become an effective citizen in a democratic society. For his own presidency, however, he proposed to repackage those objectives into two: the pursuit of academic excellence and the cultivation of Christian values in living. "A Christian college," he declared, "should by its very nature place a premium on excellence in every field." Moreover, it should be interested "in fundamental values and attitudes" and acknowledge that each student was "made in the image of God and capable of full development" physically, socially, intellectually, and spiritually.[3]

To achieve academic excellence and instill Christian values, Young proposed six specific actions:

1. hold and attract qualified teachers who were dedicated to the "distinctive values of Christian education";

2. add to the campus a new science building and student center that would accommodate 2,000 students by 1970 and launch a $3 million development campaign to pay for them and for other improvements;

3. triple the size of the endowment;

4. raise admission standards and strengthen the recruiting program;

5. continually evaluate the offerings and work of the college; and

6. conduct a well-rounded program of wholesome extra-curricular activities designed to cultivate the social, physical, and spiritual potentialities of Pepperdine's students.

Young's plan of action was clear and even bold, but it was not original. The WCA accrediting committee in 1954 had recommended pretty much the same steps.[4]

Eyes on the Prize: Reaccreditation

Like his inaugural speech, almost every action Young took was made with an eye toward the upcoming WCA accrediting visit. The legitimacy of GPC as an institution of higher education, Christian or not, depended upon a positive review. For that reason, President Young and Dean Sanders made the WCA evaluation of 1954 their primary road map for the first two years of their administration. Based on WCA recommendations, they got board approval for salary increases up to $1,200 per year for full professors. The board also approved, apparently with some reluctance, a modest tenure policy. In response to WCA criticisms, the new administration also set up a graduate studies committee to coordinate post-baccalaureate degree programs, attempted to address grade inflation in the undergraduate program, and announced higher admission standards.[5]

It was one thing to set a course based on the 1954 accreditation report; it was much harder to prepare program reviews for a WCA team scheduled to visit in January 1959, particularly after so many departmental chairs had resigned. For that reason, President Young and the board of trustees stayed in close contact with the executive secretary of WCA, Dean Mitchell P. Briggs at California State College, Fresno.[6]

Young and Sanders also turned to Russel Squire, a member of the founding GPC faculty, as the ideal person to coordinate the curriculum review required by WCA and by the California State Department of Education. The two agencies typically ran their reviews simultaneously.[7]

As Squire coordinated the on-campus preparation, President Young solicited the counsel of external consultants, including Glen S. Dumke, president of San Francisco State College and the WCA. Young specifically wanted advice on how to deal with the faculty dissent that threatened to color the entire review process. As a way of marginalizing the negative AAUP report prepared by Woodrow Whitten, Dumke recommended making it available to each member of the visiting committee and having board chairman Don Miller available for questions. He also told Young it was acceptable for GPC to maintain a predominance of Church of Christ members on the faculty but said the accrediting team "would look with disfavor upon everyone being of the same faith."[8]

Young also turned to Harding College President George Benson for advice. Benson noted that educators looked at things differently and recommended that Young keep Dean Sanders near his side during the WCA visit. Sanders spoke the language of educators and understood the academic emphasis. Benson expected the accreditors to examine matters of tenure and academic freedom and encouraged Young to be prepared to answer questions in those areas. Rather than have twenty answers, however, Benson told Young to focus on only the four best answers. It was not a matter of misleading anyone, Benson said, but merely trying to focus attention on the right points.[9]

President Young submitted the college's self-study to the WCA and California State Department of Education on December 1, 1958, and teams from both agencies visited the campus in January 1959.[10] The WCA submitted a written report the next month. The report concluded that the recent campus unpleasantness had not permanently impaired the college's teaching effectiveness and noted with approval the recent development of an official tenure policy, improved faculty salaries, creation of a fund-raising office and campaign, and the plan for a new science building and expanded student housing. The report was critical, however, of the pattern of deficit financing and an endowment that did not grow despite major gifts.[11] The team also expressed concern over admission standards, lack of focus in general education, and a library with less than minimal holdings.[12]

To the disappointment of President Young, the WCA committee recommended reaccreditation for only two years rather than the normal five. The committee justified its decision by saying that Pepperdine was "in a sense a new college because of the unusual number of resignations . . . during the past year or two." And it said only time would tell whether the "off-campus forces," apparently referring to Churches of Christ editors and preachers, would dissipate or whether the new administration could master its major problems, particularly the financial challenges.[13] Young recognized the reality of those concerns, but the two-year term was a bitter pill as it meant the whole, lengthy process would have to be done again in less than twenty-four months.[14] Perhaps unfairly, but likely with some justification, he attributed the outcome to the influence of former Dean E. V. Pullias, who sat on the WCA board of standards.[15]

The team from the California State Board of Education reaccredited the colleges' education programs, although it had some of the same concerns. Was there real interest in an education training program at George Pepperdine College, the team asked, when only 60 of 1,000 students pursued credentials and when effective programming was difficult to arrange in some secondary programs because there were so few candidates? Like the WCA, the state board reaccredited for only two years.[16]

Progress Made—And Rewarded

The 1959 accrediting teams had no more than left the campus than the faculty and staff at the college began preparing for the visits scheduled for December 5–6, 1960. When the WCA visitors arrived, the committee noted some real improvements. The board of trustees had been expanded, the college operated with a balanced budget thanks to a development office that had raised $357,000 from 2,800 people, and the unrest generated by a new presidential administration had calmed. The general education curriculum had improved, library materials were reasonably adequate, and the social science curriculum was tighter.

The visiting team was critical of lower-than-typical tuition rates, continued low faculty salaries, heavy teaching loads, too few faculty with advanced degrees, sloppy recordkeeping, inexperienced administrators in charge of student personnel, and an "astonishingly low" number of graduate students in religion. Yet the committee believed that the college had "turned the corner" and recommended reaccreditation for five years, with an interim report after three.[17] The team from the California State Board of Education identified essentially the same strengths and weaknesses.[18]

Shortly after the WCA and California State Board of Education reviews were finished, GPC was visited by a team from the Northwest Association of Secondary and Higher Schools, the college's original accrediting agency. The visitors were mostly impressed by what they saw and commented on the balance achieved between strictly academic work and "that which [was] plainly church related," with the social science program reviewer speaking appreciatively of the faculty's "spirit of selfless dedication to God and Christ Our Lord."

But the NASHS team also had some telling criticisms and cautions. It observed that the GPC students did not have a "highly developed library habit"; that the music department had not achieved its potential; that there was little independent, objective research among the faculty; and that business department faculty salaries were annually $1,000 to $1,200 less than those paid at similar institutions. Some of the criticism stung, but the GPC administration found the NASHS review mostly encouraging.[19]

With George Pepperdine College thoroughly and fully accredited, President Young and his colleagues could devote their time to implementing specific programs and policies. In order to carry out his vision for Pepperdine, Young depended upon his administrative team, particularly J. P. Sanders, William J. Teague, J. C. Moore, Howard A. White, W. Pence Dacus, and Jennings Davis Jr. He did not find an expanded board of trustees especially helpful, however, especially when it came to addressing one of the college's most pressing problems, how to finance its operations.[20]

CHAPTER 10

CREATING A NEW BRAND CELEBRATING FREEDOM AND FREE MARKETS

"**M**illions Left to Right Wingers," headlined the *New York Times* on May 4, 1966.[1] The story explained that Dallas B. Lewis, the Los Angeles manufacturer of Dr. Ross's Dog and Cat Food who had died on April 25, had left money to the John Birch Society, the Defenders of American Liberty, and Pepperdine College. Pepperdine would receive $1 million provided it "honored Dan Smoot with a doctorate degree" during Lewis's lifetime or within six months after his death.[2]

Smoot was a former FBI agent and an ultraconservative political activist based in Dallas. He published the *Dan Smoot Report* that circulated among 33,000 subscribers and broadcast television and radio programs that reached sixteen million people in thirty states. Smoot's special concern was communist infiltration of American politics and society.[3]

D. B. Lewis, a longtime member of the president's board of George Pepperdine College, was thrilled by Norvel Young's initiatives to brand the school as a politically conservative, stridently anticommunist advocate of the free market and limited government. It was no surprise to anyone at GPC that Lewis made granting an honorary doctorate to Smoot a condition for a $1 million bequest.[4]

Although in desperate need of capital funds, President Young rejected the inheritance within twenty-four hours as faculty petitioned him to decline the bequest and the *Graphic* expressed fear of the school being charged with political extremism.[5] Young justified his decision because "the academic process preclude[d] awarding a degree based upon the contingency of any gift."[6] The president called Smoot to tell him there was nothing personal about the decision, and Smoot noted he would not have accepted a bought degree.[7]

The decision not to accept the $1 million inheritance brought Pepperdine national attention. National columnists such as Russell Kirk praised GPC's administrators as "imaginative and responsible conservatives" who could not be bought, and Walter Winchell congratulated them for generating "billions in good will publicity."[8] In similar fashion, church editor Reuel Lemmons commended Young and the college "on having the courage and character to choose between a principle and a million dollars."[9]

An unexpected compliment came from the Chemical Workers Union, Local 97, in Fresno, California. The local launched a national campaign among American labor unions to get one million members and friends to send one dollar each to GPC to replace the money rejected from the radical right.[10] Just how much money the effort generated is unknown, although taking any money from labor unions would have been difficult to explain to the business elite who supported Pepperdine in 1966.

Fighting Deficits

One of Norvel Young's most daunting—and persistent—tasks was to manage the college finances. Deficits prevailed in all but one of the five years prior to his taking charge and continued during his first year. He was resolved, however, that it would not happen again. Thanks to careful management and creative accounting, it did not.

It helped that Young presided over more generous budgets going forward. Operating income for the 1957–1958 academic year totaled only $1,144,715, for example, whereas in Young's last year as president, 1969–1970, it totaled $6,222,561, a 444 percent increase. Income from tuition grew in those years from $615,000 to $4.4 million, an increase of 620 percent. Endowment income grew modestly, from $34,637 to $75,000. But gift income increased dramatically, from $167,000 to a high of $817,583 in 1968–1969. Expenditures for instruction also increased 609 percent, from $362,000 to $2.5 million. In all, the annual operating budget was more tuition-dependent at the end of Young's presidency than at the beginning, but a larger percentage of the budget went for instruction, from 29 percent to 41 percent.[11]

Whatever its source or however it was allocated, the college budget could not balance without an infusion of external funds. President Young came to California believing that the faithful from Churches of Christ would supply some of the needs, but he never assumed they would provide all. He knew it would be necessary to receive help from the larger Southern California community, although he did not know exactly how to reach that constituency.

The president's initial efforts to organize an effective fund-raising program was notably ineffective. So Young turned for help to the John Price Jones

Company (JPJC) of New York City, the leading fund-raising consultant in university and college circles. In January 1960, the firm issued a forty-three-page report that suggested how GPC could conduct a successful development campaign.[12]

According to JPJC, one of Pepperdine's advantages was its church relationship, which was unique in Southern California, where Protestant denominations typically did not operate institutions of higher education. Thus GPC should embrace its Christian mission and denominational tie "boldly . . . publicly. . . . proudly." The consultants also noted that the God-centeredness of the college augmented rather than overshadowed American principles and citizenship.[13]

But there were also unfavorable factors, including a "shockingly inaccurate grapevine" that perpetuated a myth that Pepperdine held extreme views in religion and politics and that it was dominated by Texans and the decentralized structure of Churches of Christ, which made it difficult to secure group financial support. The neighborhood surrounding the college was no longer an asset, given demographic changes, and "George Pepperdine College" as a name was less advantageous to fund-raising advantage than "Pepperdine College."[14]

Giving Up Football

One of JPJC's more controversial recommendations was that the school should keep its struggling football program. During the Young administration, all of Pepperdine's sports programs were competitive except football. The Waves won just one football game in 1958 and only two in 1959, and this continuing ineffectiveness and the precariousness of the college's financial condition had led to many debates about the wisdom of retaining the program.[15] Alumni and students argued strongly in favor of continuing the sport, while the faculty, administration, and board of trustees were less sold on it, mainly because of its price tag. The cost of the football program totaled 43 percent of the athletic budget and 5 percent of the annual college budget.[16]

In 1960, Pence Dacus was hired as the new coach, but even with additional scholarships, he could not reverse the football team's fortunes.[17] The team won only one game and lost nine in each of the 1960 and 1961 seasons. In a 1961 poll, more than half of the faculty favored dropping football, a vote no doubt influenced by reports that retaining the sport would mean a tuition increase.[18] In contrast, various alumni continued their vigorous defense of football, citing it as a way to perpetuate Pepperdine's "victorious spirit." According to former cheerleader Bob Pratt, the school was about to lose something precious, something that was worth a lot of money.[19]

The board of trustees seriously considered a proposal advocated by alumni that the football team should compete in a conference made up of small, private colleges. But after analyzing economic factors, the trustees in 1961 elected to drop the program by a vote of six to two. Coach Dacus accepted the decision with good grace. He would return to the college in the years to come, but football would not.[20]

Pursuing Excellence—and Funds

Another recommendation from the JPJC consultants was that the college make fundamental preparations before launching a major initiative. And this was another recommendation that the school chose to ignore as Young and his team had already announced a $3 million "Pursuit of Excellence" capital campaign, a five-year initiative that would pay for additional residential space and a new science building. Clearly, that kind of money would not come from the church constituency. But how could a small, independent, Christian liberal-arts college with a particularistic theology develop an affluent constituency in Los Angeles?

Young turned for help to George Benson, president of Harding College in Searcy, Arkansas, and longtime friend of George Pepperdine and his college. He had successfully developed a national constituency for Harding among businessmen committed to individual freedom, the private enterprise system, and anticommunism. When Benson came to address the president's board in fall 1958, he modeled the way to champion those issues to the Los Angeles community.[21] Each student educated by George Pepperdine College, he said, was one California taxpayers did not have to educate. Since 1937, he reasoned, GPC had saved the state multiple millions of dollars, while providing a benefit to the entire community. The college thus deserved the support of concerned citizens.

It was an analysis that Young would embrace and use over and over again, and it gained some traction within the Los Angeles business establishment.[22] Young believed private, independent, Christian liberal arts colleges played an important role in American society—preserving the critical values of individual and corporate freedom. It followed that business and industrial enterprises would support such colleges.[23] So Young crafted a series of initiatives demonstrating the college's commitment to individualism, capitalism, and Americanism.[24]

Freedom Forums

With the president's board as organizer and host, Young launched the college's first Freedom Forum in June 1959 to awaken "Americans to the dangers of Communism and collectivism."[25] Meeting over two days, the forum featured Benson and other high-profile speakers who addressed the danger of international communism and lauded free enterprise. The event showcased George

Pepperdine College as a champion of American values and enabled the college to announce that it had embarked on a $3 million development program.

Through 1971, Pepperdine College hosted thirteen more Freedom Forums, with essentially the same format. The participant list reads like a who's who of the conservative political and economic establishment of the 1960s, including U.S. Senators Barry Goldwater, Frank Lausche, and Robert Dole, Professor Russell Kirk, Supreme Court Justice Charles Whittaker, columnist William F. Buckley, economist Milton Friedman, and General Omar Bradley. Forum III was probably the most successful in terms of audience, with 1,000 individuals attending the luncheon addressed by Senator Goldwater and another 500,000 watching on television.[26]

In the 1960s, the "Pepperdine College Forum," shaped what residents of the Los Angeles area knew about the school,[27] giving them the idea that the school had a "heart of a lion" commitment to personal liberty and private enterprise.[28] Its Christian mission was acknowledged but not emphasized. According to President Young, the forum helped "Pepperdine College reach . . . many of its potential donors," including the celebrated industrialist Morris Pendleton, whose admiration of the forums resulted in many significant gifts for Pepperdine College.[29]

Declaration of Independence

Because the college badly needed an additional women's dormitory, the Young administration investigated borrowing funds from private lenders and from a federal government program. In 1959, however, both avenues were rejected as the college chose to raise the necessary $300,000 by selling bonds bearing 6 percent interest to its many friends. Once announced, the sale went rapidly, with ninety-seven individuals buying the bonds in amounts of anywhere from $100 to $50,000.[30]

On February 12, 1960, at the groundbreaking ceremony for the dorm, President Young gave the financing program a dramatic twist. In a broadside titled a "Declaration of Independence," he reported that the trustees of the college had rejected government loans to finance construction because they believed in "personal initiative, decentralization of government, [and] personal integrity" and opposed "the growing trend toward collectivism." Instead the college advocated "the conservative economic principles of private ownership of property, an open market, and the total freedom which was envisioned by our founding leaders and which [was] guaranteed in the Constitution of the United States."[31]

The "Declaration of Independence" brought a lot of national attention to Young and George Pepperdine College. It served as a pretext for a speech titled

"Education without Federal Aid" that Young delivered to the San Diego Freedom Forum on January 20, 1961. He said, "Pepperdine College had turned its back on Federal financing because it hoped that it could by so doing 'light a candle' in the encircling gloom of increasing Federal intervention."[32] His speech was subsequently republished in the *Congressional Record*,[33] *Vital Speeches* magazine,[34] and *Congressional Action*, a publication of the U.S. Chamber of Commerce.[35]

President Young took a lot of pride in the fact that the college was only one of fourteen accredited institutions of higher education in the United States that had not accepted federal funds for construction.[36] But the college did not turn down all federal assistance, gladly accepting funds through the National Defense Student Loan program.[37]

Neither was the college faculty organization ready for the college to resist all federal funding. In February 1966 faculty members urged the administration to actively solicit research funds from the federal government, encourage various departments to formulate programs designed to attract government support, and keep them informed of any new legislation regarding additional funds. The recommendation was actually endorsed by the board of trustees, with some limits. Moreover, the board also indicated it had an open mind on federal aid such as grants for libraries and other educational projects.[38]

By 1966, therefore, Pepperdine's much vaunted declaration of independence was fading in its institutional memory. Within a few years, the college was accepting substantial grants from the U.S. Department of Justice to underwrite its police education program and funds from the U.S. Department of Housing and Urban Development to fund a Model Neighborhood program. As President Young then put it regarding federal aid: "We'd like to paddle our own canoe as long as it's feasible—but we don't plan to commit academic suicide."[39]

Films, Lectures, and Books

Another tool the college used to project a pro-American image to the business elite was its "Crisis for Americans" film project. Championed by Vice President Bill Teague, the series was intended to demonstrate that national defense was the greatest need facing the United States and that a strong economy reinforced by a vital educational system was the bulwark of the nation's defense against foreign ideologies that sought to destroy the United States. The project envisioned a series of thirteen Hollywood-produced films and an initial budget of $280,000.[40] The first in the series, "Communist Accent on Youth," was released in spring 1961 and endorsed by actor John Wayne.

Three more films followed over the next four years, with all focusing on various aspects of the communist threat to the American Way of life. The films were purchased by universities and school districts nationwide and broadcast by commercial and noncommercial television stations. They also attracted interest from officials in western Europe. Eight hundred prints of the first three films were circulated, and the viewing audience exceeded 1.5 million people, without even counting television audiences.[41]

Despite the interest, the Young administration terminated the "Crisis for Americans" series after the fourth film. The project had raised the national visibility of Pepperdine College, but it had been both labor- and capital-intensive. Benefits no longer justified the costs.[42]

To complement the film program, the Young administration organized a speaker's bureau of six college faculty and staff members. In the early 1960s, bureau speakers reached as many as 1,000 people each week at churches, civic clubs, school groups, and professional organizations, enhancing Pepperdine College's visibility in Southern California.[43]

College officials also commissioned the publication of *The Roots of American Order*, a trade book authored by Russell Kirk, a historian, political theorist, moralist, and social and literary critic whose 1953 book, *The Conservative Mind*, shaped the conservative movement in the United States. Thirty-nine donors contributed $46,000 through Pepperdine to help finance *The Roots of American Order*, which was published in 1974. Front material announced that Pepperdine University was sponsoring the book as its contribution toward celebrating the bicentennial of the Declaration of Independence.[44] Although not well received by members of the academy, the book went through three editions and generated $20,000 royalties for Pepperdine in its first year after publication.[45]

The Freedom Forum, film series, speakers bureau, book deal with Kirk, and Young's "Declaration of Independence" all demonstrate the willingness of President Young to build a Pepperdine College brand that would impress Southern California's wealthy business elite. Members of that group, he believed, could help fund the operational budget and a campaign for Pepperdine's capital projects. Judging from the number of participants and contributors, Young was right.

CHAPTER 11

BURNISHING
THE BRAND

Russell Kirk's book and the "Crisis for Americans" film projects did not meet the full expectations of the Young administration as brand-building exercises. Nonetheless, both burnished the pro-American, traditional Christian trademark the college was attempting to promote. So too did a loose collection of activities and programs dubbed the National Citizenship Program (NCP) that included opinion pieces in county newspapers, a national radio show, and teacher training programs. The cumulative effect of the branding efforts worked to convince some of California's financial elite that Pepperdine College was unique in its commitment to the American Way and was thus worthy of substantial support, including the construction of a second campus.

One such financial elite attracted by Pepperdine's efforts was William Robertson Coe, an English-born insurance magnate turned philanthropist. Coe was concerned that young Americans were not receiving adequate instruction in U.S. history or the nation's core values. Accordingly, Coe bequeathed money to allow colleges to provide summer refresher courses for high school teachers that would support "a positive and affirmative method" of meeting the threat of communism, socialism, totalitarianism, and similar ideologies. Among the institutions selected to participate in the program were Yale, Stanford, and Tulane Universities and a few smaller private colleges, including Pepperdine.[1]

The Coe Foundation and a seed grant from the Pepperdine president's board funded the college's first American Studies program beginning in summer 1960. Initially, the Pepperdine program served fifty high school teachers from across the United States, a number that soon doubled. Teachers were able to take two courses for graduate credit in U.S.-related history, religion, speech, and education. The program continued at least through 1974, reaching well over 1,000 public and private high school teachers in those years. Many of the participants returned to Pepperdine to complete their master's degrees at their own expense.[2]

An integral part of the American studies program at Pepperdine College was the Taft Institute for Government. Founded in 1961, the institute was designed to expand and improve political participation in the United States. It specifically focused on improving civics education for kindergarteners through high schoolers, utilizing college/school community workshops that provided teachers with the latest political science research, innovative pedagogy, and interaction with political practitioners. Pepperdine offered its first institute in the summer of 1965, enrolling a class of twenty-five local teachers, who were able to get six units of graduate credit in contemporary American politics over a six-week summer session. The Taft Institute brought a wide array of California politicians to campus, both Republicans and Democrats. Like the Coe Fellows program, the Taft Institute lasted until at least 1974, and both enhanced Pepperdine College's reputation as a champion of American ideals and principles.[3]

Victories for NCP

Championing traditional American values and the free-market economy was no charade to President Young or Vice President Teague; they held those ideals dearly. But making Pepperdine College a vehicle for the fight was less about promoting those values than it was about capturing the imagination, sympathy, and support of the nation's business elite, whose approval could be translated into unrestricted gifts and capital improvements. Judged on that basis, the NCP had both victories and disappointments.

The earliest victory came from the Freedom Foundation of Valley Forge, Pennsylvania. On the basis of a booklet titled "The Pepperdine Story" (which has been lost), the foundation in 1962 awarded Pepperdine College the Thomas Jefferson Medal and a $500 cash stipend for its exemplary campaign in behalf of American values and for its academic effort to "energize free men" to fight communist oppression.[4]

Another victory was the support found in the columns of the Los Angeles newspapers, such as national columnist Morrie Ryskind's "Through Rose-Colored Glasses," which was published in the *Los Angeles Times* on April 5, 1961. Ryskind observed "What makes it [Pepperdine] newsworthy is that it is an oasis of non-conformity in an academic desert of monolithic liberalism. The faculty believes strongly in both the eternal verities exemplified by the Ten Commandments and the basic concepts of individual freedom as proclaimed in the Declaration of Independence and our Constitution."[5] Moreover, in an age of unrest and protest, Ryskind was amazed that there was so little turbulence on the campus of Pepperdine College.[6] President Young could not have been happier with Ryskind's remarks.

Still another victory was the increased level of support that came from the president's board, which Young made central to his campaign for financial support of the college by recruiting stronger leadership. He selected as chair James Smith, executive vice president of the 7-Up Bottling Company, and, after 1965, George W. Elkins, one of Southern California's most successful realtors. Under Smith and Elkins, the board sponsored the Freedom Forum and helped underwrite the Coe Fellowship program. Individual members supported the film projects, purchased Pepperdine construction bonds, pledged gifts in capital campaigns, and even paid the college's annual dues to the Jonathan Club. This kind of support testifies to Young's success in capturing the attention of corporate America.[7]

Scaife and Seaver Change Future of Pepperdine

Among those were men who would become two of Pepperdine University's most generous contributors: Richard Scaife and Frank Roger Seaver. Richard Mellon Scaife was one of the heirs to the Mellon banking, oil (Gulf) and aluminum (Alcoa) fortune. Teague arranged an interview in July 1961 with the thirty-year-old Scaife, who made a gift of stock to help fund the college's film series by early 1962.[8]

Within three years, Scaife had accepted an appointment to the president's board, been honored by college alumni, given $75,000 to purchase frontage property on Vermont Avenue, and pledged $120,000 for general expenses. In 1967, he contributed $50,000 toward a journalism building on the Vermont campus. Two years later he gave $1.15 million to fund the center for international business and permit faculty salary increases of 11 percent. Through 1970, he would give $3.4 million for construction of the Malibu campus.[9] Young firmly believed Scaife's support was a blessing from God.[10] And he was willing to go to great lengths to cultivate Scaife's support of Pepperdine.[11]

While Scaife was a member of the president's board, Frank Roger Seaver was not. A native of Pomona and a graduate of its college, Frank Seaver began his professional career as an attorney, achieving distinction as the author of the Los Angeles City charter and as legal counselor of the notable oilman Edward L. Doheny. In 1927, he organized his own company known as Hydril, which found success as a manufacturer of oil field equipment, particularly of the "blowout preventer." An educational philanthropist, he served on the governing boards of Pomona College and Loyola University and made major gifts to the University of Southern California and the Pilgrim School of the Los Angeles Congregational Church.[12]

Seaver first became interested in Pepperdine College through NCP. In 1961, Young and Henry Salvatori, a longtime member of the president's board, visited Seaver in his office to sell him on supporting the anticommunist film series. Seaver was so impressed with the presentation that he wrote a check for $7,500 on the spot. He was even more impressed when he and 1,000 other people attended the Freedom Forum addressed by his good friend U.S. Senator Goldwater. Thereafter, his interest in NCP only increased, and he included Pepperdine College in his will, with astounding consequences for its future. Before he died in October 1964, Frank Seaver had given the college $26,360; before her death, his widow had given the college more than $160 million.[13]

A John Birch Academy?

But NCP also had the potential for mischief. In March 1961, the research department of the California Teachers Association (CTA) issued a report on "The Pattern of Attack on Public Education in California by the John Birch Society and Similar Groups." The report named three institutions of higher education that lent support to the society: Harding College, Orange Coast College, and Pepperdine College.[14] That Pepperdine could be considered as a virtual academy for the John Birch Society came as a shock to the Young administration. After a quick investigation, it rejected the notion out of hand and challenged the CTA's conclusion.[15] The organization quickly retracted its charge, but without mentioning Pepperdine College or Harding College by name.[16]

Despite the retraction, in the eyes of many, excommunication from the educational establishment had been achieved.[17] The faculty members were greatly concerned at how the Pepperdine College brand was perceived at large. Members did not want their institution to be seen as politically—or religiously—sectarian. Like academicians elsewhere, most tended to the middle of the political spectrum with a slight tilt toward the left and a preference for the domestic agenda of Democrats. The NCP, with its emphasis upon limited government, individual freedom, and anticommunism, was politically right of center—sometimes far right—and preferred the Republican agenda if not the Libertarian stance. Because the Young administration hosted most NCP events off campus, members of the faculty seldom confronted the face of the program. When they did, they were less than charitable, especially the history and social sciences faculty.

Many on the faculty were embarrassed and horrified by the allegations regarding the John Birch society and largely blamed Vice President Teague for the accusation. Dean Howard White, a New Deal Democrat sympathized with the concerns of his faculty colleagues; nevertheless, he regretted that they had singled out Teague. From his perspective, the real issue was not Teague's promotion of the NCP, but the question of whether the college's emphasis was to be political or Christian. In his mind, it had to be the latter, a position that he held for the duration of his life.[18]

Neither President Young nor members of his administration disagreed with White's view, but they also believed that Pepperdine's chances at future success traveled in direct proportion to how well the college represented the political and economic interests of the well-to-do business community.[19] (White gave more support to that view as his responsibilities at the college grew.)

Faculty skepticism of the NCP and its political agenda continued for the duration of the Young administration. That distrust partly explains the 1966 faculty campaign to accept federal financial grants for construction and academic programs, the enthusiastic welcome given to presidential candidate Hubert Humphrey in 1968, and why fifteen members of the faculty and administration formed a club to support Tom Bradley's candidacy for mayor of Los Angeles.[20] It also demonstrates why the Young administration went to great lengths to justify awarding an honorary doctorate to Governor Ronald Reagan in 1970.[21]

Most Pepperdine College faculty did not openly object to the NCP, if they knew about it at all, but only a few actively supported it. Communication professor Fred Casmir was one of those. Casmir was a German by birth, a member of the Hitler Jungen during World War II, a Christian convert in the postwar era, and an immigrant to the United States. After undergraduate and graduate work, he joined the Pepperdine faculty in 1956. Casmir and like-minded colleagues welcomed a variety of Republican candidates and office holders to the Vermont campus.[22] The on-campus support for the NCP also helped explain the strength of the Young Republican organization and the general support of the United States war effort in Vietnam.

Although it came close to being synonymous with Pepperdine College's brand in the off-campus community, the NCP was never conceived to be an end in itself. It was primarily a means of finding resources to develop the campus, first on Vermont Avenue and then in Malibu. Measured in those terms, the NCP was a success, although not an unqualified one. Pepperdine College had been deeply engaged with America's builders since 1952, honoring them at annual recognition banquets and publishing a magazine in their interest. Young wanted all of this nurturing to give birth to a brick-and-mortar science building, but a science building for the Vermont Avenue campus never materialized, despite several ground-breakings.

After 1957 there were not many waking hours in Norvel Young's day when he was not thinking about the financial needs of Pepperdine College and how to burnish the brand he had so diligently tried to create. His intensive labor led to balanced budgets and national headlines for Pepperdine College.

Simultaneously, President Young and his colleagues were attempting to assure the college's continued academic creditability.

CHAPTER 12

BUILDING AN
ACADEMIC REPUTATION

Norvel Young understood that a new brand for George Pepperdine College must include academic distinction. He also understood that the keys to academic credibility were quality faculty and programs, which had been on his mind when he and Dean Sanders set out to replace the twenty-one faculty and staff members who resigned in 1958. Young and Sanders needed to find replacements who were academically qualified, committed to Christian education, active members of Churches of Christ, and supportive of the administration. According to the Western College Association, the first wave of recruits met those criteria and more.

A second wave of hires through 1965 continued to meet Young's high standards. Among this group were James Atkinson, professor of English and advisor of international students; Douglas Dean, professor of biology and skeptic of biological evolution; Norman Hatch, professor of music and director of choirs; Warren Kilday, professor of chemistry; John McClung, professor of history, tennis coach, and director of housing; Carl Mitchell, psychologist and chair of the religion department; Frank Pack, professor of religion and dean of graduate studies; Stephen Sale, professor of history; and Wayne Wright, professor of physical education, coach, and subsequently director of athletics. All were stalwart teachers, males, and members of Churches of Christ who would spend most of their careers at Pepperdine.

A third wave of recruits arrived in the final five years of Young's presidency, many of whom would also compile lengthy service records. These included Royce Clark, professor of religion; David Gibson, professor of philosophy; Norman Hughes, professor of biology and subsequently dean of Seaver College; Herbert Luft, professor of history and director of the Year-in-Europe program; Edward Rockey, professor of communication; Donald Sime, professor of religion and eventually dean of the School of Business Administration; and Morris Womack, professor of speech.

Given the emphasis upon hiring Church of Christ faculty members, President Young and Dean Sanders were not opposed to recruiting prospects from other colleges affiliated with the Churches of Christ. Young liked to say that there was no competition between lighthouses, but there was when it came to hiring faculty. On several occasions, Young reminded his counterparts in Abilene or Nashville of the church's desperate need for education specialists on the West Coast. President Benson of Harding College could not be appeased, however, and he refused to modify contractual obligations of at least one member of his faculty who had an interest in joining the Pepperdine family.[1]

Sometimes, however, sister institutions were more than happy to allow members of their faculty to move to Pepperdine. Such was the case of James Atteberry, a professor of English at Harding for sixteen years, whose opinions did not always mesh with the administration's. President Cliff Ganus nonetheless spoke highly of Atteberry as a teacher and scholar to Pepperdine officials. Atteberry's hiring initiated a chain of events that brought Atteberry and his wife, Ruth, Jere Yates, James Penrod, Richard Indermill, and Kenneth Perrin from Harding to Pepperdine in 1969. Yates, Penrod, and Indermill taught in the new School of Business and Management; Atteberry became professor of English and Perrin professor of mathematics. President Young later had some second thoughts about the transaction but determined to live by Atteberry's contract.[2]

Atteberry was the ultimate replacement for a legendary figure in the English faculty, Wade Ruby, who had died a few years earlier. As noted in previous chapters, Ruby was a charter member of the George Pepperdine College faculty, the first person to coach basketball, baseball, debate, and the Forest Lawn essay competitors. For fourteen years he also ministered to the Hollywood Church of Christ. But his campus celebrity status came primarily from his hobby as a television quiz show participant. His most notable success was on "Twenty-One," where he won $67,000 over four weeks in 1958.[3] When the case of Charles Van Doren showed that program to be rigged, Ruby insisted that his success had been because of his own efforts.

Unfortunately, Ruby suffered from a heart condition that would disable him from time to time, forcing him to seek shelter at a roadside park or motel if he had an attack while driving. On March 21, 1966, he took refuge in a motel where he died at age 58. His adoring students, faculty colleagues, and church friends went into mourning as Ruby was buried in his hometown of Camden, Arkansas.[4]

Not-So-Happy Hires

Not all appointments by the Young administration developed as expected. Gilbert Richardson joined the faculty in 1964; a Churches of Christ member, he came to Pepperdine as an ABD (all but dissertation) candidate in political science from American University with specialties in Latin America and Russian affairs. When it became evident that Richardson was not actively pursuing his doctorate, Dean Sanders told him continued employment was contingent on completion of his PhD.

Richardson went into an attack mode, arguing that Pepperdine College had lost its way as a private, liberal arts, Christian school and charging that the college preferred interdenominational appointments rather than ones from Churches of Christ, forcing out loyal churchmen. Richardson also charged that the college was taking federal money through the back door while publicly refusing it and argued that liberals in the administration caused President Young to unnecessarily reject D. B. Lewis's $1 million bequest. Richardson told Sanders that he would take his case to the churches unless he received another contract.[5]

Since neither Sanders nor Young wanted to disturb the goodwill they had built among the churches or the Los Angeles business elite, they tried to work with Richardson to assist him in completing his doctorate. Instead, the professor demanded that the history and political science departments be divided and that he be named chair of political science. When Sanders declined to meet his demand, Richardson sent his threatened letter to the leaderships of various Church of Christ congregations in California and to the editors of denominational journals that circulated in the state. The Young administration followed with a letter to hundreds of church leaders categorically and specifically denying the charges in Richardson's letter.[6]

Gilbert Richardson served on the Pepperdine faculty for only three years, yet his situation created a stir among college officials because his criticism challenged the core brand they were working so hard to establish. Richardson proclaimed that Pepperdine was not what it said it was. He would not be the last to make such a charge, nor would the Young administration be the last to deny such accusations.

Pepperdine Faculty Criteria

The Young administration believed Pepperdine College's brand required certain criteria for all full-time faculty members: they must hold or be working on a doctorate in their teaching field, and they must embrace the college's mission to prepare students for lives of usefulness on a foundation of Christian character and faith.[7] "If our goals were solely secular," Sanders had said, "then there would be no purpose for there to be a Pepperdine College. Unless we have something distinctive to offer, then we have no reason for existing."[8]

According to Fred Casmir, an influential faculty leader who also actively supported Young's NCP, the brand also required Christian faculty members to demand excellence, to pursue truth, and to appreciate a democratic society.[9] In the spirit of *en loco parentis*, moreover, Pepperdine faculty members in the 1960s were expected to have office hours five days a week, regularly attend daily chapel, and exhibit upstanding Christian deportment at all times, which included no smoking.[10]

But recruiting and retaining qualified faculty also required that they be paid a livable wage, something that accrediting teams doubted existed at the college through the 1950s. From the very first, President Young committed his administration to addressing the matter of faculty salaries. In his initial year (1957–1958), he raised actual salaries by $1,200 for professors, $600 for associates, $300 for assistants, and $200 for instructors, raising the average salary for all faculty members to about $5,000.[11]

However, even after healthy salary increases of almost 83 percent during the Young presidency, Pepperdine still compensated its faculty far less than did its peer institutions.[12] Pepperdine's average salary in 1964–1965 was nearly $7,000, which was $3,000 to $4,000 less than those at Loyola Marymount and Occidental respectively. It would take another five years for Pepperdine to reach the 1964 levels of Loyola and Occidental: $11,000 for professors, $10,000 for associates, $8,500 for assistants, and $6,800 for instructors.

The Young administration used several strategies to increase faculty salaries, including increasing tuition, which rose from $17 to $50 per unit, almost 300 percent, between 1957 and 1970. Another strategy was to increase the student-teacher ratio. More than anything else, Young sought to increase revenues by increasing the number of students enrolled in the college. He reached his goal of 2,000 students on the Vermont Avenue campus by 1969, a 100 percent increase over the number enrolled when he came in 1957. The financial situation was helped even more by the 5,365 part-time students taking courses in off-campus locations.

To retain faculty, the Young administration provided an increasingly attractive benefits program, building upon medical and life insurance and retirement alternatives introduced by the Tiner administration. To that Young added housing, tuition, and sabbatical leave benefits. By 1965, the college was helping faculty purchase houses near campus; two years later, full-tuition benefits were extended to the unmarried children of faculty, staff, and trustees. And by 1970, the college offered sabbatical leaves to full-time faculty interested in completing research or writing projects.[13]

The Birth of Faculty Research

Most faculty members devoted virtually all of their time to teaching and coun-seling, although research and writing took root during the Young administra-tion. The addition of more faculty members with doctoral degrees nurtured the growing interest in research, as did the addition of new master's degree programs, the enrollment of a substantial contingent of graduate students, and the organization of a formal College of Graduate Studies. The realization that research activities could attract external money to the faculty, particu-larly from the federal government, gave those endeavors economic value in the eyes of the administration.[14]

In early 1966, members of the faculty recommended that the Pepperdine administration create a faculty research committee to encourage research among the faculty, publish a digest of research undertaken, reduce teaching loads for researchers, organize a research center with a secretary, and search for research funds. Much to the horror of members like Gilbert Richardson,

J. P. Sanders served as dean of George Pepperdine College between 1957 and 1970, arriving with Norvel Young and working to boost the academic and Christian cre-dentials of the school. Subsequently, he served as president of Columbia Christian College and as professor of religion at Seaver College.

the faculty also recommended that the administration solicit funds from the federal government. The board of trustees approved the recommendation, so long as no single faculty person devoted more than 10 percent of her or his time and received no more than $2,500 from the college for research.[15]

Later in 1966, the trustees authorized organization of the Pepperdine Research Institute, a nonprofit institute that would be chartered independently of the college with its own board of directors "to do contract research for both government and industry." In 1967, the first year of operation, the institute operated from two houses on 78th Street and brought in $100,000 in contracts. Nearly 80 percent of that came from one contract with the U.S. Air Force on strategic planning.

Despite some leadership difficulties, the institute demonstrated that Pepperdine faculty increasingly saw research activity as integral to their professional life. It also allowed faculty to accept government contracts under the aegis of an entity other than the college.[16]

Tenure—Finally

Little was more influential in attracting and retaining faculty, however, than the assurance of tenure, which brought both academic freedom and economic security. Under pressure from WCA accrediting teams and to pacify faculty wounded by the change in administration, the Pepperdine board of trustees adopted the college's first formal tenure policy in November 1958.[17]

The policy was designed to promote faculty stability and to assure members that their service to the college would "stand or fall on the quality of work done, and that as long as competent, cooperative service [was] rendered each [would] be protected in his position." It granted faculty members the traditional freedom of research and teaching and stipulated that freedom of thought and speech was the lifeblood of an institution of higher learning. But it also cautioned that "irresponsible and thoughtless use of freedom" could destroy the source from which it flowed.[18]

The new policy granted tenure to assistant professors beginning in the sixth year of full-time employment, associate professors at the beginning of the fourth year, and professors with the third year. It also generously granted tenure to instructors with their ninth year of full employment. As a whole, then, the decision to grant tenure was largely a question of time rather than quality in teaching or research.

Once granted, tenure could be terminated only for cause. What constituted cause, however, was broadly defined. It included neglect of duty, dishonesty, moral delinquency or turpitude, professional incompetence or incapacity, misconduct which caused injury or brought discredit to the college, serious or continuous disharmony with the institution's policies, and "activity knowingly or willfully directed toward the violent overthrow of either the Government of the United States or any of its constituent parts." Tenure could also be terminated in the face of *bona fide* financial exigency, or "if demand for particular courses [was] not sufficient to economically justify the continuance of such courses."[19]

The inexact definition of causes for termination concerned WCA accreditors and AAUP staff, but they were pleased that Pepperdine College at least had a tenure policy, which had not been true before Norvel Young assumed the presidency.

Faculty Governance

If Pepperdine's tenure policy was ambiguous, so too was the role of faculty in the governance of the institution. The *Faculty Handbook* declared that "Pepperdine College encourage[d] wide participation of the faculty in all of its educational processes."[20] To achieve that level of participation, the college depended upon twenty-six faculty and administrative committees in 1964–1965. These included the all-powerful administrative committee, chaired by the president; the departmental council responsible for academic decisions, chaired by Sanders; the graduate academic council; the professional problems committee; and the religious life committee. Some committees met weekly, some periodically, and some only on call.[21]

In addition to committees, the entire faculty met once a month, convened by an elected chairperson. Some members considered this meeting all-important if the faculty were to have any significant influence in shaping the direction of the college. However, the administration did not recognize the independent faculty organization as a governing partner, so concerned faculty members sometimes turned to Pepperdine's AAUP chapter, organized just prior to the administrative crisis of 1957. The chapter continued to function as a formal faculty organization through the Young presidency and into the 1970s. Among those who served as presidents were Joseph White, Loyd Frashier, Fred Casmir, Jack Scott, Wyatt Jones, and Grover Goyne.[22]

A "Useful" Education

When Norvel Young assumed leadership of Pepperdine College, he did not articulate any strong academic goals other than maintaining the excellence of the programs in place. A faculty committee said Pepperdine should educate the whole person (physical, mental, social, and spiritual), promote freedom and democracy, and develop in each student an appreciation of free enterprise and capitalism.[23] The general education curriculum expected to deliver upon those objectives did not change much during the Young presidency although the number of major fields did increase from sixteen to twenty-four for the BA degree and from five to thirteen for the BS.[24]

Because of George Pepperdine's emphasis upon a "useful" education, the college had always offered "practical" courses that led to vocational degrees. During the Tiner presidency, most students pursued majors in business administration, teacher education, physical education, or psychology. Religion, fine arts, and the humanities—excluding history—struggled for majors.

The focus on vocationalism accelerated during the Young administration. Among the new degree programs were corrections, engineering administration, health, police management, recreation, social welfare, and technical management. In 1965 Pepperdine officials "nationally pioneered" the technical management degree, partly in response to recommendations by businessmen active in the president's board or the America's Builders network. A curriculum in engineering, business administration, and liberal arts, mixed with on-the-job training prepared students to work in technical, business and human relations areas.[25]

Curriculum expansion, however, was even greater in the graduate program. Master's degree fields grew from four (psychology, religion, social science, and speech) to twelve (business administration, corrections, education, educational psychology, English, history, mathematics, psychology, religion, sociology, speech, and speech therapy).[26] Graduate students increased from no more than 50 to 300.[27] With pressure from WCA, Pepperdine officials coordinated the different degree programs first through a graduate studies committee chaired by a director and then by a program administered by a dean. Howard White had initial responsibility, which he relinquished to Frank Pack in 1967.[28]

Requirements for admission to the graduate program did not change during the Young presidency: an undergraduate GPA of C+ and an "acceptable score" on the Graduate Record Exam (GRE). Graduation required thirty units of course work, a GPA of at least a B, and either a comprehensive examination, a thesis or research project, or a proficiency in reading a foreign language (added in 1963).[29]

Significant expansion also took place in the teacher credential program. By 1964, Pepperdine was authorized by the state to recommend the standard credential in both elementary and certain secondary fields, a status pursued since the founding of the college. By 1970, a full credential required a bachelor's degree plus a fifth year of college work. Graduates of Pepperdine's teaching program were so coveted by the Los Angeles School District that it assigned a full-time coordinator to the college in an attempt to hire graduates for its classrooms.[30]

Raising Admission Standards

Both the Young administration and WCA accrediting teams favored higher academic requirements for admission into Pepperdine College. In published requirements, Pepperdine College welcomed students with high school degrees who had at least ten units of A or B grades, or "acceptable scholarship" in a college preparatory program, or a "very good scholastic record" in a non-preparatory program, or an "acceptable score" on the Scholastic Aptitude Test (SAT). Transfer students required at least a C average in all college work; applicants to the graduate program required a C-plus average in all course work or a B in major work. These modest requirements remained essentially the same during the course of the Young administration.[31]

Pepperdine's fairly ambiguous admission standards were not uncommon for similar tuition-dependent colleges; however, Pepperdine College did not take all applicants. In the 1958–1959 school year, for example, 23 percent of 454 applications were rejected, and an average of 25 percent were rejected in 1966 and 1967. Those rates far exceeded rejection rates at Abilene Christian (2 percent), Oklahoma Christian (2 percent), and Harding College (7 percent); compared favorably with Chapman (17 percent), Loyola (25 percent), and Redlands (26 percent); and looked anemic against Occidental (59 percent) and Pomona (65 percent).[32]

SAT scores for admitted classes improved very little during the Young administration. In 1962, verbal and math scores averaged 935; four years later they were 953—below Loyola by 170 points, Redlands by 207 points, Occidental by 322 points, and Pomona by 377 points. And they would not improve in the near term, largely because Pepperdine's admission office accepted students with an 800 SAT average, presumably in response to the changing demographic of the college's immediate neighborhood.[33]

Academic Excellence and Retention Rates

The academic excellence to which President Young was committed may have found more traction in the classroom than in the admission office. In 1959, Fred Casmir advised Dean Sanders to enforce higher academic standards in all classwork.[34] It was not quite clear what he meant, but more than likely it had to do with what was later called "grade inflation."[35] The push for higher standards led President Young to terminate the forum art series, and evidence of grade inflation caused the California State Department of Education to defer accreditation of special credentials in secondary education in 1964.[36] Young also objected to faculty members using identical standardized tests term after term, a practice that he believed encouraged students to cheat, and to emphasize facts at the expense of analysis and critical thinking.[37]

The Young administration assumed there was a relationship between academic excellence and student retention, which was a problem at Pepperdine. Some 276 freshmen enrolled in GPC in fall 1959, but only 199 matriculated as sophomores, a retention rate of only 72 percent (compared to 90 percent in 2010).[38] How many of those 199 went on to complete their degrees three to four years thereafter was not recorded, but probably no more than 55 to 60 percent (compared to 78 percent in 2010). The dropout rate was of considerable concern to administration and faculty alike. Not only did it consume precious financial resources, it also raised questions about the legitimacy of the education offered at Pepperdine College.

To gain insight to the retention puzzle, Fred Casmir undertook a lengthy study of the student body in 1964. He found that students were more disappointed by the lack of social life, the emphasis placed upon spiritual transformation, and the general costs of tuition rather than academic standards that were too difficult or too easy.[39]

Dean of Students Jennings Davis and Associate Dean Lucille Todd attributed dropouts and other forms of student unrest to the fact that students simply did not understand that Pepperdine offered academic excellence in a Christian atmosphere. If they were fully aware of that objective, Davis and Todd believed, they would settle in and complete their degree.[40] Thereafter, the academic and Christian objectives of the college were announced again and again—at pre-orientation sessions at Camp Tanda near Lake Arrowhead, at on-campus orientation sessions, in catalog copy, and in special communications. But retention rates continued low, and dropout rates remained high.[41]

Introducing the Trimester

In part to address this situation, President Young championed adoption of a trimester academic schedule, which provided year-round education, dividing the academic year into three consecutive sixteen-week terms between September and August.[42] In early 1962, Young appointed a committee chaired by Professor Ladis Kovach to study the feasibility of the trimester schedule for Pepperdine.

According to Kovach, the trimester system had nothing but advantages. Among them was year-round education that would enable a student to graduate in as little as two years and nine months. The scheme also enabled students to get a faster start on graduate studies and would lower their overall expenses. It also enabled the college to better utilize its own facilities and provided an additional income opportunity to faculty.[43]

Pepperdine College pioneered the trimester system on the West Coast, launching it in September 1963. Its version was unique, but its interest in year-round education was not. The regents of the University of California were already discussing a similar system and three years later would implement a quarter system.[44]

For all their bravado, Pepperdine officials were not altogether certain the trimester adoption would work. The acid test would be the strength of the enrollment in the third trimester—the summer months. In June 1964, President Young and his colleagues watched with relief as third-term enrollment reached 751 full-time students, almost 60 percent of the fall enrollment. Revenues for the first nine months increased nearly 23 percent, and the revenues from summer school, which continued to operate, were yet to come.[45]

The trimester system remained the schedule of choice at Pepperdine until 1989, when Seaver College reverted to a semester system with summer blocks.

Five More Years

In November 1965, an accrediting team from the Western Association of Schools and Colleges (WASC, which had been WCA until 1962) visited Pepperdine College. It noted the new trimester system, the professionalization of the faculty, the development of a tenure system, and the emergence of a strong graduate program, among other transformations. The visitors acknowledged those changes as positive and made modest recommendations for further change. President Young conveyed those suggestions to the board of trustees and joyfully reported that the team had recommended reaccreditation for another five years.[46]

CHAPTER 13

DEVELOPING INTERNATIONAL PROGRAMS

To President Young, WASC reaccreditation in 1965 confirmed that Pepperdine College was making progress in its quest for academic respectability. As the visiting team recognized, students were better qualified, faculty salaries were higher, the curriculum was broader, expectations of students were greater, an innovative trimester system was in place, and an impressive array of summer programs was offered. Young could also point to Pepperdine's growing interest in international education as further evidence of academic respectability.

Even before 1962, when the Young administration launched its Year-in-Europe program, George Pepperdine College had a long tradition of offering summer educational travel programs, mostly to Europe.[1] President Young was an enthusiastic world traveler, and he was encouraged by Controller J. C. Moore, a post-World War II missionary in Germany, to create a full-year academic program in Western Europe for junior and senior students. Convinced that such a program would broaden students' educational experience and enhance the college's prestige, the board of trustees endorsed the concept in October 1962.[2]

To select a site for the program, Young turned to Moore and Howard White who chose Heidelberg, Germany, a grand medieval town on the Neckar River that was home to a world-renowned university established in 1386. Pepperdine students would have the option of taking classes in English, most from college faculty at Amerika Haus, a cultural center and library sponsored by the German and the United States governments. Male students would stay in one small hotel and female students in another; all could worship at the Gemeinde Christi, a Church of Christ congregation serving both German national and U.S. military families. Tuition costs would not differ from those in Los Angeles. White, Moore, their families, and thirty-six students launched Pepperdine's Year-in-Europe program in fall 1963.[3]

One of the memorable moments of the first year occurred in November when the Pepperdine students were attending a Chopin concert on the campus of the University of Heidelberg. At the conclusion of the concert, the pianist returned and powerfully played Chopin's "Funeral March" as an encore. He then stood and announced that President John F. Kennedy had been killed in Dallas.[4]

A Permanent Home for a Popular Program

The Heidelberg program quickly became one of the identifying distinctives of Pepperdine College. Forty-three students participated in the program's second year, and student interest continued to increase, making Young eager to secure permanent Heidelberg facilities. When William Banowsky, then minister of the Broadway Church of Christ in Lubbock, suggested a joint venture between his congregation and Pepperdine, Young pursued the opportunity vigorously.

Banowsky reported to Young that the church was considering something like an American Bible chair—institutions situated adjacent to public colleges and universities where students would receive theological training while taking traditional collegiate work at the local institution. Young primarily wanted a permanent building for the Pepperdine Heidelberg program, but was also interested in training young German men for ministry. He was able to accomplish both goals.

In October 1965, Pepperdine purchased a stately mansion on Griambergweg, just steps from the Heidelberg castle, for $115,000. To make the purchase, the college accepted a $75,000 loan from the German Mission Fund as administered by the Broadway church, to be repaid over ten years at 2 percent interest. The payments would be made in tuition scholarships given to young Germans who would enroll in Pepperdine courses offered through what would be known as the Bibelschule.[5]

Pepperdine's students held a Halloween party in the newly acquired house on October 29, 1965, which seemed appropriate as the house needed substantial refurbishment. The cost of the repairs, furniture for forty-two student occupants, realtor's fees, and state taxes added $35,000 to the purchase price, for a grand total of $150,000. One-half of that would come as a "loan" from the Broadway church with the rest financed through German banks.

The student body moved into the remodeled facility in August 1966.[6] Pepperdine appointed H. Glenn Boyd, a former Church of Christ missionary, as the first resident director of the program. He remained in that position until 1973, when Herbert Luft succeeded him. In December 1969, the property was named in honor of J. C. Moore, who had died unexpectedly the previous July. Moore Haus has been the annual destination of Pepperdine students interested in a study-abroad experience since that time.[7]

Building a Bibelschule

Although the Year-in-Europe program was successful on many levels, the Young administration made little progress organizing the envisioned Bibelschule, which had no champion within the Pepperdine community until Herbert Luft joined the Heidelberg faculty in 1967. A German by birth, Luft had taken both his BA and MA degrees from Pepperdine College, and he preached regularly in Churches of Christ in Heidelberg and Bruchsal.

Luft, Boyd, and German minister Reiner Kallus conceived a two-year academic program, with students taking the same courses as Pepperdine religion majors and being treated as regular students. German preachers and American missionaries with academic degrees, among them Ludwig Klinke, Jack McKinney, Gottfried Reichel, and Jaro Schubert, would receive small stipends and travel expenses to teach classes in German at the Heidelberg Gemeinde Christi building. The school would enroll eight to twelve students, both men and women, who would live near the church building. Tuition and rent would be free, paid by Pepperdine and credited to the Broadway church loan. Boyd would assume administrative responsibility for the Bibelschule along with the Year-in-Europe program.[8]

The visionary plans remained mostly on paper until 1968 when Dr. J. B. McCorkle, an elder in the Lubbock church, visited Heidelberg and discovered that a training facility for German nationals was little more than a pipe dream. He expressed his dismay and reminded Pepperdine administrators that the Broadway church had loaned the money to purchase Moore Haus under the assumption that German preachers would be trained. Thereafter, Pepperdine officials made recruiting potential students a priority, tasking Luft "to drive to every church in Germany" and encourage young people to enroll in the Bibelschule. After two years of recruiting and advising, Luft enrolled seven students in classes that began in September 1970.[9]

Ensuring students would receive regular academic credit from Pepperdine enabled the college to insist upon a strong academic program and prevent the Bibelschule from slipping into a glorified Sunday School. The academic credit could also be transferred to other U.S. higher education institutions. One student, Hans Rollman, actually completed his BA degree from Pepperdine without leaving Heidelberg, then took an MA at Vanderbilt, and a PhD from McMasters in Canada, going on to a faculty appointment at the University of Newfoundland with a specialty in the history of the Stone–Campbell movement. Others received only a "Zertifikat" of completion of a theological course of study. But the certificate and the academic units from an accredited institution ultimately led the German government to recognize the Bibelschule as a "seminary" for Churches of Christ, exempting enrolled students from the military draft.[10]

Excepting the years 1978 and 1979, the Bibelschule operated through 1988. By that time, approximately seventy-five young men and women had completed the program and Pepperdine had "paid back" the $75,000 plus interest borrowed from the Broadway Church of Christ. Broadway efforts to raise money for students' tuition and living expenses kept the school operating for a short time after the Pepperdine loan was paid off. But new students were always difficult to find, a telling commentary on the declining status of German Christianity.

By the end of the twentieth century, few outside the Bibelschule's small cadre of faculty and the seventy-plus students who had studied there remembered much about the program. The accomplishments of its graduates, if nothing else,

Herbert Luft joined Pepperdine's Heidelberg program in 1967, where he also played a pivotal role in establishing the Bibelschule. Luft served as the university's executive vice president under Howard A. White in the 1980s and subsequently as vice president of international programs and professor of history at Seaver College.

demands more.[11] As Howard White wrote in 1977: "In the years I have spent at Pepperdine, we have not done anything that has been more pleasurable to me than the Year-in-Europe program, and the best part of it is the Bibelschule. I truly believe it does more good than any other one thing we have."[12]

International Business Studies

Another internationally oriented program begun during the Young presidency was the Center for Advanced Studies in International Business, subsequently the Center for International Business (CIB). Late in the 1960s, Pepperdine College administrators envisioned a center where scholars and practitioners could conduct studies that would directly benefit business, industry, and labor in the United States, allowing the college to render greater service to the community that supplied much of its operating dollars and capital improvements. In early 1969, Richard Scaife, one of the heirs to the Mellon banking fortune, directed the family-run Allegheny Foundation of Pittsburgh, to give $1.5 million to Pepperdine College to finance the center's operations.

Scaife preferred a center that would research national defense issues but told President Young to "use the funds in such a way as to help put Pepperdine College on the map."[13] With the approval of the board of trustees, Young sought to do just that.[14] "Los Angeles with its booming port and international air terminals . . . [was] one of our nation's great gateways to the worldwide industrial thrust," he told the *Herald-Examiner.* Pepperdine College with its new center would "contribute to the international outreach of [the] industrial revolution."[15]

Young chose Arthur Peterson, former president of the Thunderbird Graduate School of International Business, to direct the new center. Late in 1969, Peterson opened offices in the Los Angeles Hilton Hotel and directed research, conferences, training programs, and international forecasts related to business and foreign trade. The CIB had its own charter and board of directors and thus was not directly related to Pepperdine College but described itself as "an affiliate."[16]

Richard C. King, former CEO of a medical electronics firm and a faculty member at Occidental College, succeeded Peterson as director in January 1971. Seeking greater visibility for the CIB, he moved its headquarters to the Los Angeles World Trade Center and facilitated the acquisition of a specialized world trade library in San Francisco valued at $150,000.

Under King's leadership, the CIB established a satellite office in Honolulu headed by Rear Admiral Lloyd R. Vasey (USN Retired). In both places, the work focused on conferences and executive briefings, preparation of international analyses, and publication of books, directories, and studies. At its peak, the CIB employed eight full-time economists, political analysts, and market research specialists. Research was its principal activity, with emphasis on the Pacific Basin and Latin America. The nature of its work did not change when King resigned to take a leadership role in the World Trade Center and David Reagan assumed responsibilities in fall 1974; controversy followed and the CIB was shut down a few years later.[17]

The Center for International Business, the Year-in-Europe program, and the Heidelberg Bibelschule all reflected that Pepperdine College had arrived at a place where it could experiment as an educational institution. Only one of the three programs proved viable over the long term, but all spoke of academic imagination, an international orientation, and serious attention to the Christian mission. They also demonstrated that the Young administration had moved past the crisis of its beginning and was eager to position Pepperdine as a citizen of the world.

CHAPTER 14

CULTIVATING CHRISTIAN MISSION ON A CHANGING CAMPUS

Like most dimensions of George Pepperdine College during the Norvel Young presidency, the student body was in constant transition—in terms of numbers, residency status, demographics, and church membership status. All aspects played a role in the university's ever-evolving views of its Christian mission and the student body's support of that mission.

In 1960, just under 1,200 students enrolled in the college, and almost all were registered for classes on the Vermont Avenue campus. By the end of the decade, 2,100 students, both undergraduate and graduate, matriculated the Los Angeles campus, while another 5,400 took classes for extension credit at off-campus centers throughout California and adjacent states. In 1960, 75 percent of the enrolled students were considered full-time, and 43 percent lived on campus. By 1970, some 71 percent were full-time, but only 23 percent lived in student housing.

Early in his administration, President Young had envisioned a student body made up of a strong majority of members of Churches of Christ. In 1960, the number of Churches of Christ students reached about 50 percent, a considerable increase over what it had been during the Tiner/Pullias years.[1] That percentage, however, was reached only once again in the decade, in 1967. Generally, students associated with Churches of Christ numbered between 35 percent to 40 percent of the undergraduate student body on the Vermont Avenue campus, although the percentage was higher in residence halls.

Although gender diversity in the student body declined in the 1960s—from 1.3 to 2.2 males per female—ethnic diversity increased dramatically. Judging from yearbooks and newspaper reports, Pepperdine College was largely homogeneous ethnically at the beginning of the decade. By 1969, however, African

Americans constituted almost 17 percent of the Vermont Avenue campus student body. According to a report by the federal government, that percentage was among the highest in the nation for schools similar to Pepperdine, and far exceeded neighboring UCLA (2.24 percent), USC (2.18 percent), and LMU (1.66 percent). Sister church schools—Harding, Abilene Christian, and David Lipscomb—had lower percentages than LMU.

That enrollment, of course, reflected the changing demographics of the neighborhood surrounding the Vermont campus, which had become predominantly African American. Thus, when eligible young men and women in the neighborhood contemplated a place to attend college, Pepperdine was the logical choice. A similar rationale applied to black students from other neighborhoods: where better to attend college than at an institution nestled into African American neighborhoods?[2]

The changes in the makeup of the student body led to increasing tension within the student body stemming from how Pepperdine's Christian mission and its allegiance to the American Way played itself out in the curriculum and co-curriculum. Because the Young administration's expectations for the institutionalization of the American Way were implicit rather than explicit, the student body responded positively to most of them, even winning national recognition for its support of American troops in Vietnam.

Pushing Against the Boundaries

But many students were less amenable to the standards enforced as part of the college's Christian mission. The Tiner administration had set the parameters for student behavior; those did not change significantly during the Young presidency, even as the broader college atmospheres across the nation changed radically.

The college continued its prohibition on alcohol and social dancing in the 1960s, with drinking or possession of alcohol of any type, "either on campus or off campus," being dismissible offenses. Although school-sponsored social events both on and off campus remained "danceless," the majority of students saw dancing as healthy and wholesome and wanted the restrictions removed.[3]

Regulations that men could smoke on campus but women could not, in place since 1937, remained unchanged as well, although there was more dissent. The student board resolved on an eight-to-seven vote that women be permitted to smoke within their on-campus rooms just as men were. The Young administration and the board of trustees rejected the petition, but enforcement of the smoking restrictions were so lax that many male and female students continued to smoke wherever they wished, even in the classrooms.[4]

Pepperdine students also found the visitation ban between male and female students in the residence halls troublesome. Led by president Ron Woolfolk, the student government let it be known that they considered the visitation policy a limitation of freedom and an insult to the moral integrity of Pepperdine students. In the fall trimester of 1970, it called for an end to the no-visitation policy and sent a survey to parents and incoming freshmen about the issue; parent responses overwhelmingly favored some degree of limited visitation. College administrators and the board of trustees denied efforts to change the restrictions.[5]

Dress Code Blues

Pepperdine students were expected to be "appropriately dressed and well groomed at all times." School attire included skirts, sweaters, cotton blouses, and flats for women; and shirts, sports shirts or T-shirts with dress or cotton slacks with shirt tails tucked in for men. Church attire consisted of wool dresses, suits, heels, gloves and hats for women, and suits, dress shirts, and ties for men.[6]

Most Pepperdine College students embraced the long arm of the dress code, but some lived with it only fitfully, especially as the 1960s came to an end. According to one report, not until 1969 did women students gain the prerogative of wearing pants to class.[7]

Female members of the faculty were sympathetic with the student resistance to the dress code. Fearing reaction from his church constituency, Norvel Young insisted that women faculty attire themselves in dresses. In 1972, a petition was sent to Young claiming that the policy was outdated, that pantsuits were decent, and that the policy discriminated against women since there was no similar dress policy for men on the staff or faculty. It was signed by thirty-two members of the faculty, including leaders like Warren Jones, Frank Pack, and Loyd Frashier. Executive Vice President Howard White agreed, saying, there were "so many important places where we must take a stand that we lose a good many points [with the faculty] when we take a stand on this kind of issue." Thereafter, the dress policy softened.[8]

Fighting the Chapel Battles

Insofar as aggravations to the students were concerned, dress codes, dancing restrictions, drinking prohibitions, and smoking curtailments were minor when compared to chapel and race matters. The college offered daily chapel services, but it was mandatory for everyone only on Monday and for freshmen and transfer students on Friday also.[9] Beginning in fall 1966, the college required chapel on Monday and Wednesday for everyone and Monday,

Wednesday, and Friday for freshmen.[10] Attendance, however, was not good.[11] Four years later, the mandatory requirement was reduced to one of five chapels per week, with assigned seating.

Dividing students into five chapel groups had less to do with spiritual growth than with containing the more "militant element" of the student body who occasionally used chapel to send a message. Perhaps partially for that reason, dissatisfaction with compulsory chapel remained high.[12]

As in the Tiner years, in the 1960s, the content of chapel consisted of two parts: fifteen minutes of prayer, hymn singing, and scripture reading, followed by thirty minutes for an inspirational message or commentary on a current event. Many students complained that being forced to listen to political rants impinged on their personal freedom.[13] Dean Jennings Davis tended to agree and won the administration's support of a policy that exempted students from programs by "special interest" groups. The result of this, however, was a mass exodus from "special interest" chapel following the devotional.[14]

For reasons relating to doctrinal exclusiveness, only students who were members of Churches of Christ led chapel services, a practice that had prevailed since 1940. Some non-Church of Christ students found the practice offensive and demeaning.[15] It confirmed their suspicions that school officials separated the student body into two groups: those who counted and those who did not.[16]

More concerning was that many Church of Christ students seemed to do the same, easily putting themselves into the "those-who-counted" group. Dean Davis noted sadly many Church of Christ students felt "uncomfortable worshipping with people of other churches." He and other members of the Young administration were troubled by this exclusivist attitude; Davis advocated voluntary chapel, recommended speakers from other faith traditions, and proposed alternative chapel formats.[17] The board of trustees, however, could not be persuaded to open chapel leadership to students who were not members of Churches of Christ.[18]

By 1970, mandatory chapel was a source of great discontent on the Vermont Avenue campus. According to *Graphic* editor Kenny Waters, an ever-growing group of students was calling for the "abolition" of chapel altogether.[19]

Not the Typical 1960s Campus Culture

Pepperdine College was not unaffected by the student ferment occurring on college campuses nationwide in the 1960s. Students took note of these events but were less interested in their political objectives than in how the protests were conducted. Students raising their voices and working together could foster political and social change, even if the Pepperdine causes were quality of campus life and mandatory chapel attendance.[20]

Generally, Pepperdine's student body held conservative political views. According to Barry Goldwater, the campus was "an oasis of non-conformity in an academic desert of monolithic liberalism." But, said *Graphic* editor Tal Campbell, this was primarily because most students held part-time jobs and did not have time to raise a "futile riot." Campbell also asserted that it was a mistake to assume that "conservative administrative policy ... [was] dogma for the classroom" and insisted that "a generally more objective political education" was available at Pepperdine than in a school "regulated by governmental politicos."[21]

Few—if any—Pepperdine students were left-wing on the political spectrum, but some were sympathetic to religious tolerance issues, the Free Speech movement, civil rights groups, and Vietnam war opponents. In 1968, 1,000 of them enthusiastically received Democratic presidential candidate Hubert H. Humphrey.[22]

Students and the administration occasionally clashed over the choice of speakers for events, with the administration in 1969 vetoing the choice of Donald Kalish, professor of philosophy at UCLA and prominent Vietnam war critic, as a graduation banquet speaker. At the same time, the Young administration also refused to give permission to invite well-known radical Angela Davis to campus to engage in a dialogue with freshmen and sophomore students. One student, "TCB," wrote that the refusal demonstrated that pedagogical and spiritual objectives at the college took second place to those of money.[23]

The denial, however, spoke more to the special circumstances then prevalent on the Vermont Avenue campus than to issues of censorship. Racial tension was white hot, and the Young administration feared that a speech by Davis would fan the fire into an inferno. There was reason to be concerned.

CHAPTER 15

RACIAL TENSIONS AND
A CAMPUS TRAGEDY

Pepperdine College could never afford to ignore racial concerns after August 11, 1965. On that day, in the Watts neighborhood of south central Los Angeles, white motorcycle patrolman Lee W. Minikus arrested African American Marquette Frye for driving while intoxicated. Within an hour, an angry crowd of several hundred people began stoning cars and threatening police.

The unrest lasted all night, with riots intensifying and spreading the next day, prompting city officials to ask for help from the California National Guard. By August 15, the presence of 13,900 guardsmen had quelled the rioting and restored order—but by that time thirty-four people had been killed, some 1,000 injured, 4,000 arrested, and nearly 1,000 businesses and buildings had been damaged, destroyed, or looted. The riots were blamed for more than $40 million in damage.[1]

The Watts community lay some three miles south and east of Pepperdine College's Vermont Avenue campus. The destruction associated with the rioting did not reach the college, but it was close enough that people on campus could smell the smoke of burning buildings. Some Pepperdine histories have reported that California Governor Pat Brown bivouacked 400 National Guardsmen in the Pepperdine dormitories and placed machine gunners on top of campus buildings along 79th Street.[2] However, an official list of all duty posts makes no reference to any guard encampment on the Pepperdine campus. And in a 1976 article, *Los Angeles Times* journalist William Trombley specifically denied that troops bivouacked on the Vermont Avenue campus.[3] The campus did fall within the curfew zone but was not directly affected otherwise.

President Young was on his way to Washington, D.C. when the riots began, and he put Vice President Bill Teague in charge of the campus. As the violence escalated, Teague closed the school and sent students and Young's family off campus. When he returned to Los Angeles several days later, President Young quickly recognized that Pepperdine College would never again be the same.

Growing Racial Diversity, Growing Racial Tensions

As noted in the previous chapter, the community surrounding the Pepperdine campus had changed by 1965. Dominated by middle-class, white families when the college opened in 1937, the neighborhood had become a community of hard-working but less affluent African Americans.[4] Pepperdine College welcomed a large number of students from this community, enrolling more students of color than comparable Southern California institutions. The rich ethnic mix of students on the campus brought greater sensitivity to racial issues, both before and after the Watts riots.

The college celebrated its first National Negro History Week in February 1967.[5] In the wake of that event, black students began meeting as an unofficial group, and they helped organize the college's second observance of National Negro History Week the following year, creating an agenda that produced some tensions but no major incidents.[6]

On April 4, 1968, the student body grieved with Americans nationwide over the assassination of Martin Luther King Jr. There were memorial services both on and off campus, including one at a South Los Angeles Church of Christ that involved some 1,500 people, black and white.[7] Discussions sparked by King's death and the memorial services prompted college administrators to pledge to recruit black faculty, to organize and offer a black history course (taught by African American Beulah Marks), to experiment with admission standards for promising black students, to review on campus *The Autobiography of Malcolm X*, to involve more black students in college chapel series, and to charter the Association for Black Students (ABS) as a student organization.[8]

Subsequently, Dean of Students Jennings Davis helped organize an off-campus program for young adults known as "Operation Brotherhood," to promote racial harmony in Churches of Christ and at Pepperdine College. Students worshipping with the Vermont Avenue and Normandie Avenue Churches of Christ hosted the meeting. John Allen Chalk, a white radio/TV evangelist from Texas, and Zebedee Bishop, a black minister from Detroit, addressed the audience.[9]

Dean Davis was notably critical of the college and the church regarding race matters, describing instances when the school had been racially insensitive in matters of hiring, conversation, and fraternity and sorority processes. Equally insensitive, Davis believed, was the "known influence on campus" of SPONGE—Society for the Prevention of Negroes Getting Everything. Other faculty insisted that SPONGE was more of an attitude than an organization, but that interpretation hardly satisfied black students.[10]

Particularly offensive to the black students was Pepperdine's tradition of auctioning off the services of the homecoming court, both female and male, with the winning bidder able to use the "slave" to do ironing, edit papers, run errands, and clean rooms.[11] The associated student board, where black students were well represented, abolished the tradition. But black students were offended that the college allowed a Red Cross bloodmobile that separated blood from black and white students to visit campus.[12]

Objections to ABS Activities

On the other hand, the Young administration and many white students took serious objection to a chapel speaker sponsored by the ABS. Walter Bremond, member of the Black Congress who worked for the U.S. Civil Rights Commission, was a known activist on racial issues. The college administrative committee approved an invitation for Bremond to speak at chapel in December 1968 with assurances that his remarks would not be "inflammatory" or "embarrass us." But in a provocative speech, Bremond reportedly said black students should own, operate, and control the Vermont Avenue campus. When Bremond referenced Los Angeles police as "murdering pigs," at least twenty students walked out.[13]

In November 1968, tension on campus heightened when *Graphic* editor Ron Stump and several staff members appeared at an ABS meeting. According to Stump, he and his team were called racists, asked to leave, and threatened with bodily harm. Stump chose to suspend publication of the November 21 issue of the *Graphic*. An anonymous caller leaked news of the conflict to the *Los Angeles Times;* its subsequent story also circulated on local television and radio stations, exacerbating campus tensions.[14]

African American students considered Stump's suspension an insult and responded by publishing flyers which accused the *Graphic* of having a history of attacking and defaming black students. The student writers found no fault with the Christian principles of Pepperdine but noted that "commitment without implementation" was no more than "intent without action."

According to a flyer titled, "So You've Said It Loud/You're Black And You're Proud. Prove It!!!," the long-term goal was a student body of "harmony and love" who resided "under the glorious canopy of Brotherhood."[15] Black students followed up the flyer with periodic issues of the *Black Graphic*, beginning on November 25, 1968. The first edition called for a boycott of chapel and lamented that black students were "part of a racist institution with little or no voice."[16]

Trustees Concern Grows

Publicly, the administration did not seem overly concerned by what appeared to be an escalation of racial tensions. At the December 17, 1968, board of trustees meeting, Dean J. P. Sanders said most African American students were at Pepperdine because they wanted an education, but he did believe "outside" sources were feeding them information designed to create unrest. Sanders assured the trustees that the real problem was between the black students and the *Graphic*, not between the students and the college.[17]

The trustees, however, believed the situation was far more serious than the dean implied. They were especially disturbed that the college had approved a "black militant," meaning Bremond, to speak in chapel. The trustees tended to blame the incident on the dean of students and members of the social science faculty, whose basic philosophy on political and economic issues was contrary to the administration's perspective. Retaining those faculty and staff, noted trustee Robert Jones, meant the college was not keeping the faith with its business donors.[18]

Death Shatters Efforts for Unity

Even in the face of the campus incidents and greater student unrest nationally, the Young administration clearly believed the Pepperdine campus would remain calm and unified. Faculty and students observed Negro History Week in February 1969 without incident, and prospects for on-campus harmony seemed good.[19]

All of that dissipated, however, with the tragic shooting death of Larry Kimmons on March 12, 1969. Kimmons was a fifteen-year-old African American who lived near campus and attended Washington High School. He and his friends often played basketball in the college gym, although apparently not frequently enough to know that the campus closed all but essential services on Wednesday evenings so students could attend midweek worship services. March 12 was a Wednesday, and the college gym was closed. However, Kimmons and his friends—accounts vary as to the number but there were at least five—lingered on the campus.

Charlie Lane, the campus security officer and a popular figure on campus, encountered the group in front of the gym while patrolling in his car. A sixty-year-old Englishman who had been a Pepperdine employee for twelve years, Lane asked the young men what their business was. When they said they wanted to play basketball, Lane told them what they already knew: it was Wednesday evening and the gym was closed. He also told them they should leave the campus. Presumably, Lane then went to determine if the gym would reopen that evening.

For their part, the teens bypassed the road to the only open campus gate and moved north toward the nine-foot, locked gate on Budlong Avenue. About 9 p.m., Lane encountered them again just west of Marilyn Hall and asked again what they were doing. This time he got out of his patrol car, opened the trunk, took out a shotgun, and placed it on the hood of the car.

Witness reports differed as to whether the teens resisted—either verbally or physically. All witnesses agreed, however, that Lane stepped back to the car, took the shotgun from the hood, and pointed it at Kimmons. Those same witnesses disagreed again about whether a struggle followed, but all acknowledged that the confrontation ended with Lane pulling the trigger and shooting Kimmons in the chest. Lane said it was an accident; the *Black Graphic* said it was "cold-blooded murder on a Christian campus." The teenager was pronounced dead at Morningside Hospital, and Charlie Lane was charged with manslaughter.[20]

A native of Tennessee, Jennings Davis Jr. served as dean of students during tumultuous years on Pepperdine's Los Angeles campus. An outspoken advocate for racial and social justice, Davis chose not to move to Malibu, staying to teach on the Los Angeles campus and subsequently for SBM and GSEP.

Community Reacts to the Slaying

The extent of the tragedy for the Kimmons family and the Pepperdine community was immediately apparent. President Young, whose home was a few yards away, was called to the scene, as was Kimmons' mother, whose home was just off campus. After the police had arrived and the ambulance had taken Kimmons to the hospital, Young, campus physician William Allen, and Vice President William S. Banowsky went to the Kimmons home to convey the college's deepest sympathy and offer any help they could.

Although in great distress, the family received the Pepperdine representatives graciously. Their attitude would soon change to one of enmity, possibly because of the influence of outside militants, but more probably because of the family's great sense of loss.[21]

The next morning, President Young called a community-wide meeting in Friendship Hall on the Los Angeles campus. To neighbors, faculty, staff, and students, he read the official police bulletin describing the events of the night before. Then he followed with his own statement, expressing regret for the incident, condolences to the Kimmons family, and the determination of the college to be proactive in addressing any issue arising from the tragedy.

Members of the ABS had been galvanized into action by the death, and—likely with encouragement of representatives of the Black Panthers, a radical African American group with offices no more than a mile away—they demanded a hearing with Young. Thus, the meeting adjourned to the campus auditorium, where a number of African Americans from the community were present. ABS leader Russell Coe presented a list of nine "demands" to President Young, ranging from keeping Charlie Lane away from campus, to keeping Los Angeles police off campus, to providing scholarships for Larry Kimmons's siblings, to offering compensation for his mother. The black students believed Young accepted all the requests, and they ended the meeting with a prayer.[22]

The Pepperdine administration suspended classes until the following Monday, pledged to meet all funeral expenses for Larry Kimmons, agreed to work with the ABS to produce flyers about the response to the tragedy, promised to use its influence to attempt to postpone the induction of Larry's older brother, James, into the U.S. Army, and pledged to provide scholarships to Pepperdine College for all Larry's siblings. Young described these as actions on the part of a Christian college in response to the tragic death of Larry Kimmons rather than as accessions to the "demands" of the ABS.[23] Public relation consultants had strongly recommended this parsing of words, which was in keeping with the advice of Los Angeles Police Department Chief Thomas Ruddell.[24]

On Friday morning, March 14, the ABS submitted a list of twelve new "demands." The organization had broadened its focus from the Kimmons incident to other matters related to racial tensions. They now asked the college to hire African American faculty and staff with the "approval," "recommendation," "consultation," or "advisement" of the ABS. The students wanted security officers disarmed and input into the hiring of new ones. They wanted a black track coach and the number of African Americans in administrative and staff positions to mirror the ratio of black students. ABS demanded the dismissal of particular white faculty and staff members they charged as being racist and the expulsion of the campus leader of SPONGE, whose very existence was doubted by most administrators.[25]

Board, Faculty View Student Concerns Differently

At a board of trustees meeting held that afternoon at the Los Angeles Athletic Club, Vice President Banowsky provided an update, including the latest student demands. Student Affairs Dean Davis reported that much of the unrest on campus was due to irritants which should have been corrected long before. He had identified, coincidentally, twelve steps for the administration in the 1968 fall trimester. These included hiring black faculty and staff, implementing racial sensitivity training for current faculty, appointing an African American to the board of trustees, hiring black guidance and admission counselors, appointing a director of community relations, providing better training for security officers, and removing any employee who demonstrated racist or prejudiced attitudes.[26]

The trustees clearly listened to Banowsky and Davis but appeared more concerned about handling the crises than resolving underlying issues. They were largely dismissive of the ABS demands and Davis's concerns—stating implicitly and explicitly that solving racial problems should be reserved for the church, not the college. Said H. E. Acklin and Robert Jones: "We should not follow the lead of some who would expend their energies in the missionary approach to solving the racial problems of the nation and, at the same time, lose sight of the fact that our primary purpose and goal is education in a Christian liberal arts college environment."

The board did determine unanimously to stand firmly behind Charlie Lane, and Acklin assumed personal responsibility for paying Lane's legal fees. In October 1969, Lane pleaded *nolo contendere* to manslaughter charges, was convicted of a misdemeanor and granted probation the next month, which he served for a year. In September 1970, he changed his plea to not guilty, which was accepted, and he was released from all penalties. College administrators then found Lane a position at Columbia Christian College in Portland.[27]

A faculty ad hoc committee organized shortly after the shooting was far more responsive to the concerns of the black students. In a report a few months after the incident, it agreed there needed to be more black faculty on campus and black student representation on selected committees. It saw no reason that ABS members could not screen security officer applicants, although screening of faculty candidates seemed problematic. The committee recommended that the college disarm security guards completely and move quickly to implement a black studies program.

The committee claimed no knowledge of SPONGE, however, and stipulated that no student should be dismissed for religious or political beliefs. It also opposed racial quotas in hiring staff but agreed there should be more blacks on staff, that unfair employment practices should be eliminated, and that certain loans should be distributed equitably among ethnic groups. The committee believed hiring a black assistant track coach with ABS approval was reasonable and recommended that five of fifteen graduate assistantships should be awarded to black students. The committee was not enthusiastic about the idea of firing particular faculty and staff members but recommended that black students and Dean Sanders should meet with specific individuals to try to resolve differences.[28]

Student Unrest Continues

The weekend following the shooting was relatively calm on campus and in the community. On Sunday, the 26th Annual Pepperdine College Bible Lectures opened at the Inglewood Church of Christ; before an audience of 400, Vice President Banowsky gave the opening lecture, a moving and courageous address on race matters.

That afternoon, President Young learned that the ABS was organizing a mass rally on campus for the next morning, when school was supposed to reopen. School officials deemed the rally as potentially "inflammatory" and closed the campus through Wednesday, ostensibly not to compete with the funeral arrangements for Larry Kimmons, but actually to exclude "off campus forces" they believed were radicalizing ABS members.[29]

On Monday evening, six ABS students met with Young and Banowsky to discuss their set of twelve demands. The administration and black activists found common ground on some issues, but the *Black Graphic* reported that Banowsky insisted neither group use the language of "demands and concessions."[30]

Fearing a public relations disaster that could jeopardize the future of the college, Young and Banowsky had been advised by their consultants not to agree to any student demands without first reviewing them with the board of trustees.[31] However, both the faculty student affairs committee and the ABS encouraged the administration to compromise and accommodate.[32]

President Young held a press conference at the Biltmore Hotel in Los Angeles on Tuesday afternoon, March 18, the day Larry Kimmons was buried. He announced the college would reopen the next day and reported that provisions made for the Kimmons family had been prompted by the "spontaneous sympathy of students and faculty" rather than student demands.[33]

The *Black Graphic* was not happy with the president's handling of the situation and was especially galled to hear Young say that "we are not conceding to any demands" of black students. Its writers interpreted his public words as an effort to protect his standing with the rich while working with them in private. In other words, the *Black Graphic* lamented, African American students should be satisfied with "meat under the table."[34]

Returning to Class, Resuming Efforts to Improve

Classes resumed on Wednesday, March 19, one week after the Kimmons tragedy. President Young addressed the chapel assembly, reliving some of the week's events. Some black students got up and walked out, unhappy with the resolution of their grievances.

"It comes back to racism, dollars, and cents," wrote EKT in the *Black Graphic*. "Pepperdine has cost us a valuable life, intimidation, insults, thousands of dollars, pain, sorrow, and unnumbered slaps in the face."[35]

The *Black Graphic* was a strident, articulate, but minority voice on the Vermont Avenue campus. Most African American students were not ready to convict Pepperdine College of being a "racist institution with a religious façade."[36] Instead, like Jennings Davis, they saw some evidence that the school was awakening to the challenges of its unique social environment. They pointed to Young's creation of an ad hoc faculty–student committee to address interracial problems. They also noted that the college was increasingly involved in the surrounding community. Clearly, Pepperdine was trying to be sensitive to the challenges of its urban environment, according to these students.[37]

In another step in that direction, Young had announced the intention to create a College of Urban Affairs that would offer undergraduate programs in education, social work, and community-type consulting. He envisioned it as a new focus for the Vermont Avenue campus, with the liberal arts programs eventually transitioning to the recently publicized campus being built in Malibu.

Young's announcement about the College of Urban Affairs was made to a selected church constituency, including Hubert G. Locke, African American minister of the Conant Avenue Church of Christ in Detroit and one of the more distinguished ministers and intellectuals in Churches of Christ. Locke told Young he presumed the "highest of motives" in assigning an urban mission to the Vermont Avenue campus and in creating a second Pepperdine campus in Malibu with a liberal arts and Christian mission focus, but he wanted assurances that "faculty members of both races will be teaching on both campuses"— in essence that Pepperdine would "make every effort possible to prevent the Los Angeles campus from becoming a ghetto college serving a ghetto community."[38]

Six months after the Kimmons shooting, President Young appointed Calvin Bowers as dean of ethnic studies at the Vermont Avenue campus. An African American and a Church of Christ minister, Bowers was a Tennessee native who had earned a master's degree from Pepperdine College in 1960. He was a thoughtful moderate on racial issues who had the confidence and respect of his faculty colleagues and both black and white students.[39] He was joined on the full-time faculty by four other African Americans: Willie Davis in physical education, Norman Cottman in business, Bill Satterfield in business, and Carroll Pitts in religion; about ten more African Americans were added to the adjunct faculty.[40]

Clearly, the Young administration was responding to the black student population, even if it rejected the idea of conceding to "demands." In response, rumors sprang up that the college had gone too far, allowing black students to veto faculty choices and approve selections for security positions. Young denied those rumors but acknowledged that ABS members did have a role in selecting candidates for both positions. When it came to race matters, he wrote, "We have sought to work with our students in the spirit of the Golden Rule."[41]

Most criticism of the role black students played in campus matters seemed to be based on rumors passed on by certain members of the faculty and student body. Banowsky said those rumors reflected the "fear" and "racism" prevalent on the campus.[42] Although he did not have it in mind at the time, Banowsky's words provided an appropriate epitaph for the entire Larry Kimmons tragedy.

CHAPTER 16

RACIAL TENSIONS PERSIST

lthough many of Pepperdine's African American students acknowledged the college's responses to the tragedy of Larry Kimmons, most thought the efforts did not go far enough. Whatever the college might do, said one black student, the fact remained that it was "a racist institution with a religious façade."[1]

During the 1969–1970 academic year, racial issues were at the center of controversies involving student government funding and an assistant track coach.[2] On December 5, 1969, a group of black students led by Ron Wright, a transfer student from Oklahoma Christian, dramatically entered a faculty meeting to reassert their grievances. Within days, President Young responded to each issue and appointed Deans J. P. Sanders, Howard White, Frank Pack, Jennings Davis, Calvin Bowers, and Don Sime to meet periodically with representatives of Pepperdine's black students.[3]

Young's words (or concessions, as some critics charged) were not oil sufficient to smooth troubled waters. In chapel the following day, black candidates for student government offices made campaign speeches that were "vulgar and contemptuous" and stoked racial fires. Young apologized to the faculty and proposed that the faculty's student affairs committee investigate the chapel incident and "either obtain an apology from [the responsible] students or place them on disciplinary probation, or both."

The president agreed that change was appropriate but believed it should "come out of reasoned discussion and in a spirit of good will, not out of fear of violence or profane rhetoric." He planned to move forward with his "eyes fixed on the great ideals of Christian education . . . with fairness, academic excellence and compassion, but with firmness too, in the right as God gives us to see the right."[4]

Pepperdine was moving forward with some of its promises, almost doubling the number of black faculty to nine by the fall of 1970. Of 214 staff members, thirty were black. The percentage of African Americans in the student body remained high, some 22 percent of the total 2,430 students, and they received some 31 percent of the scholarship funds available.[5]

The Malibu Quandry

The on-campus racial tension was an increasing source of embarrassment to President Young and the Pepperdine administrative team because they were at that time seeking millions of dollars to build a new campus in Malibu. The administration had been giving serious thought to establishing a second campus in the Los Angeles suburbs since the early 1960s. The idea began receiving more attention after the Watts riots, and in 1966 a formal committee was established to investigate ways and means to expand the Los Angeles campus. Fairly quickly, the committee came to doubt the viability of the urban campus, given the demographic and economic changes taking place in the surrounding neighborhood. According to the chair of the committee, Don Darnell, Pepperdine College would not survive if its operations were limited to south central Los Angeles.[6]

As alternative sites, the committee evaluated forty different locations. In time, it identified three sites with dramatic potential: 188 acres in Calabasas offered by Southern California Edison Company, 250 acres in Westlake Village offered by the American Hawaiian Company, and 138 acres in Malibu offered by the Marblehead Land Company, which was owned by the prominent Adamson family. Ambivalent about all of the sites, a lukewarm Pepperdine College board of trustees finally agreed with President Norvel Young and Vice President William S. Banowsky that "a college built at Malibu would forever have an edge in distinctiveness on the weight of location alone."[7]

On October 7, 1968, President Young publicly announced that Pepperdine College had accepted the Adamson family's gift of "rare property." It would give the school, he said, "an opportunity to plan and build, from the ground up, a unique campus in which the traditional liberal arts program [would] be undergirded by the latest learning facilities and techniques." Of course, the Malibu location would also enable the school to free itself from the growing quagmire of urban Los Angeles. However, the Young administration insisted that Pepperdine would not abandon its historic campus but would repurpose it to better address the educational challenges of inner-city America.[8]

Immediately, Young and Banowsky launched a major initiative to raise money to build the Malibu campus. That effort brought substantial pledges from Richard Scaife, the Pittsburgh heir of the Mellon fortune, and Blanche

Seaver, the widow of oil tycoon Frank R. Seaver.[9] Pepperdine's administrators chose internationally acclaimed architect William L. Pereira as the chief designer of the new campus. The prospects for the facility created such a buzz among LA's elite that they eagerly accepted invitations to attend the "Birth of a College" gala on February 9, 1970. Three thousand donor prospects distributed to two different venues saw sketches of the new campus, heard pop star Pat Boone sing "God Bless America," and listened to Governor Ronald Reagan praise the value of private higher education in general and Pepperdine College in particular.[10] Attendees were so impressed with what they saw and heard that they pledged hundreds of thousands of dollars on the spot; millions were pledged in the wake of the gala.

The success of the undertaking convinced many that plans for the new campus at Malibu prospered because of the blessings of the Almighty. Too much money had been raised to discount the possibility. For others, however, cosmic forces were not involved. The opening of the suburban campus was

Calvin Bowers served the university as dean of ethnic studies at the Los Angeles campus in the 1960s and 1970s and led a number of efforts to mediate racial tensions on that campus. Later, he served as the university's first equal opportunity officer and as professor of communication at the Malibu campus.

nothing more than a concerted effort of the college to escape the trials and trauma of the inner city, even to turn its back on its Christian mission. To them, Pepperdine was not engaging its multiethnic and lower-income neighborhood in the decision to expand to Malibu. Instead, it was participating in "white flight" to the affluent suburbs.[11]

Strikes, Fires, and a Shutdown

The latter helped explain the public outrage ignited by the nonrenewal of Ron Ellerbe's employment contract. An African American alumnus, Ellerbe worked in the school's public relations office. Black students and faculty interpreted the nonrenewal of his contract as an arbitrary firing of one of their own.[12] President Young appointed a committee of two black and two white faculty members to investigate the charges. That committee, a student committee, and Ellerbe himself subsequently said there was no evidence of racist motivations in the decision, although most agreed the termination was handled badly.[13]

But the explanations did not placate African American students already deeply alienated from the college. On Monday morning, December 7, 1970, a large group invaded the classrooms of the Academic Life Building shouting "strike" and threatening a full-scale student strike if demands were not met.[14] Two days later, at least 100 students disrupted chapel services. At a rally in the quadrangle later that same day, one student loudly declared, "The administration will either acquiesce to our demands or we will throw their asses out the window and burn the buildings down." That evening unidentified groups of students started small fires in the Fine Arts Building, Baxter Hall, and the Business Administration Building, all of which were quickly contained by the Los Angeles Fire Department. A much larger fire was set the next morning in the college auditorium, with destruction of property in excess of $50,000.[15]

About 7 a.m. on Thursday, December 10, an estimated fifty students occupied the Academic Life Building. After ordering all personnel to leave the building, they chained and padlocked exit doors from the outside. Almost immediately, Pepperdine authorities sought a legal injunction against the strikers, but it was delayed on technical grounds until December 16. Simultaneously, some forty uniformed members of the Los Angeles Police Department took up positions around the building.[16]

The Young administration was horrified by the thought of police officers storming a Pepperdine College building. Not only was there a possibility of physical injury and property damage, but such a scene could send a message to the college's business and politically conservative donors that it could not control its own house. Meeting in the president's home within eyesight of the

Academic Life Building, the administrative team "frantically" mulled over options and called an emergency faculty meeting. As Helen Young remembered, many of the faculty and staff members, especially those from the student affairs office, were sympathetic to the strikers, and she was mystified that conscientious Christian people could see things so differently.[17] Late that afternoon, Pepperdine officials decided that someone must confront the students.

Banowsky has recounted that the role fell to him because Helen Young feared for her husband's life. So, with Oly Tegner, the head of the department of education, Banowsky walked out of the president's home, across the quad, and to the 79th Street steps of the Academic Life Building.[18] According to newspaper reports, he told the strikers: "You've got to disperse within five minutes. Every student who does not will be immediately suspended and the Los Angeles Police Department is standing by to disperse you." According to newspaper accounts, within seconds the students began leaving the doorways.[19]

In a brief news conference, Banowsky referred to the strike as a "fabricated incident" and suggested it was "simply another chapter in student-administration confrontations." To him it was significant that Pepperdine's location in the center of a black neighborhood made it "vulnerable" to a "small group of extremists" and outside agitators.[20] The next day, Friday, Banowsky announced that no criminal charges would be filed against the strikers. Pepperdine would handle them just as it had handled the disturbance itself—firmly and within the institution.[21]

Consequences of Banowsky Approach

Banowsky's approach to student dissent served him and the institution well. Wrote Allen Hoffenblum, area director for the Republican Central Committee of Los Angeles County: "I'm most impressed with the manner in which you're handling the disturbance on your campus. Your mixture of firmness with empathy to legitimate problems is most commendable."[22] Indeed, Banowsky later wrote, "Madison Avenue could not have promoted as much good will as provided by that improvised confrontation." That was certainly true for him personally. Shortly thereafter, he was "overwhelmed with speech invitations, elected to twelve corporate boards, given [his] own weekly newspaper column and half-hour KNBC-TV talk show, and Governor Reagan named [him] the Republican National Committeeman from California."[23]

However, despite the positive reactions, the crisis also led to negative consequences. Enrollment in the winter trimester decreased by 8 to 10 percent from the previous year's level. Young attributed that attrition in large part to the bad publicity generated by "our disturbances." Mixed with a struggling national economy, he informed the faculty, the decline in enrollment placed the university "in the tightest economic bind we have been in since the first year I became president." He announced that there would have to be some notable internal changes, including increasing teacher to student ratios from the prevailing 1:11 to something like 1:25, the ratio at Abilene Christian.[24]

In a letter, Vice President Howard White notified all faculty members that their contracts might not be renewed for the forthcoming academic year. White assured his teaching staff, however, that all rights of tenure would be respected.[25]

Black Faculty Air Grievances

Disruptive personnel changes were avoided in 1971 as the Young administration acted with great fiscal prudence. But race and associated issues continued to infuse virtually every dimension of life on the Vermont Avenue campus. During the student lockout, a group of Pepperdine's black faculty and professional staff pointed out that black administrators and department heads had less authority than did their white counterparts; did not control departmental budgets; were subordinate to administrators with less experience; were excluded from decision-making committees, meetings, and conferences; and had difficulty accessing college facilities, resources, or supplies.

The college's black faculty strongly recommended rapid development of the new College of Urban Affairs, organization of a fund-raising program geared to the needs of the Los Angeles campus (as opposed to the Malibu campus), and a re-evaluation of attitudes toward blacks at Pepperdine—beginning with the college president.[26]

Young was willing to listen and act on some faculty and student complaints but not all. Put differently, Young conceded that the students had more legitimate requests than illegitimate ones, but in many ways, the student lockout of December 1970 was a turning point for Pepperdine College, especially as it related to leadership.[27]

Passing the Torch

By that time, Norvel Young had served as president for thirteen long and stressful years. The Kimmons incident, the future of the Los Angeles campus, the selection of a second campus at Malibu, and the need to raise millions of dollars for both had taken its toll. When a group of black students invaded his home and surrounded the family car with his wife and children in it, Young was overwhelmed.[28] It became apparent that he needed help, from someone who would embrace the dream, pick up the torch, and press on; from someone who was younger, more dynamic, self-confident, decisive, even fearless.

For Young, that was Bill Banowsky, who had rejoined his team as executive vice president in June 1968—having served as assistant dean of students between 1959 and 1963. Banowsky immediately made a mark in Southern California as a public speaker and debater and in the Pepperdine community as a visionary, a defender of Christian mission, and a superb fund-raiser. Young had made him chancellor of the Malibu campus in May 1970, seven months before Banowsky delivered the ultimatum to student protestors.

In January 1971, William Slater Banowsky was named president and chief executive officer as the institution was simultaneously renamed "Pepperdine University."[29] Banowsky will always be remembered for his role in creating the Malibu campus, which will be discussed in much more depth in following chapters, but in 1971, the administration had not given up on the idea—and the ideals—of an urban campus.

CHAPTER 17

THE INNER-CITY
CAMPUS

Although clearly excited about the prospects of a second campus at Malibu, the Pepperdine College board of trustees insisted it had no plans to abandon the historic campus in Los Angeles. In fact, the faculty and administration were developing elaborate and innovative ideas to refine and refocus academic curriculum and other programs so that the campus could better respond to the needs of the inner city.[1]

On October 31, 1969, a few months before the "Birth of a College" gala, the board announced that the Vermont Avenue campus would continue to be the "hub of the total operation" of Pepperdine College and would house the central administration, one of two colleges of arts and sciences, the School of Business and Management, and various graduate and teacher-training programs. Even as construction began on the Malibu campus, President Norvel Young and Vice President Bill Banowsky repeatedly reaffirmed the board's intention to transform the Los Angeles campus into a uniquely urban institution.

In January 1970, for example, Young assured college faculty that Malibu campus donors were "very interested in seeing [the Los Angeles] programs continue." Young and Banowsky would deliver similar assurances to multiple audiences in the coming months and years, but as the Malibu hills gave birth to a gleaming new campus their message grew less and less persuasive.

Still, a majority of Pepperdine's faculty, staff, and students did find reassurance in the words of Young and Banowsky and were excited by the prospect of creating a new kind of institution. The idea that the Los Angeles campus would be dedicated to serving the needs of an inner-city population had captured their imagination, heightened their sense of Christian mission, and unleashed their repressed liberal political instincts.

A Challenging Role

Banowsky asked Jack Scott, a religion professor, part-time Church of Christ preacher, and faculty leader committed to an inner-city outreach, to serve as provost of the Los Angeles campus beginning September 1, 1971. Scott gladly accepted the challenge. A Texas native with degrees from Abilene Christian College, Yale University, and Claremont Graduate School, Scott had come to Pepperdine College in 1962 and had developed into such an influential faculty leader that Banowsky worried whether he could tear himself away from the "faculty club" to join the "administrative club." Helen Pepperdine and other political conservatives were more worried about Scott's political views.[2]

Scott's first year as provost was not an easy one in part because the central administration and a group of students who had been recruited to be pioneers on the Malibu campus were on the Los Angeles campus. Because of their presence, Scott had difficulty winning recognition as the leader of anything, particularly an innovative initiative to the inner city. In September 1972, the departure of students and faculty for Malibu relieved both congestion and ambiguity, but challenges continued.

Foremost was that freshman enrollment on the Los Angeles campus declined so steeply that Scott's superiors did not want to authorize a dean for arts and sciences. Eventually, wanting to boost Scott's morale and demonstrate commitment to the Vermont Avenue campus, the administration agreed to appoint English department chair Grover Goyne as dean.

Another challenge was the displeasure Helen Pepperdine openly expressed about Scott's leadership and the direction of the Los Angeles campus. In her judgment, the fields of religion and home economics had been deemphasized so that ethnic studies could be made compulsory. Because Scott and Dean of Students Jennings Davis promoted change, flexibility, and inclusivity, Pepperdine blamed the deterioration of the campus on their leadership. She was also put out with Banowsky for letting it all happen.[3]

Because of Helen Pepperdine's status as wife of the founder and as member of the board of trustees, Norvel Young, as chair of the trustees, could hardly ignore her complaints. On November 18, 1972, he devoted a meeting to discuss them. After complaining that the administration kept the board "inactive, uninformed, and uninvolved," Helen Pepperdine expressed her reservations about the leadership and future of the Los Angeles campus. Trustee George Evans took exception to her complaints, characterizing the university's leadership as "superhuman" and the "best he ha[d] ever seen." Robert Jones agreed with Evans, insisting that leadership had nothing to do with what was happening on Vermont Avenue. There, he said, "we were 'whipped before we started'" because of the kind of students available. In his view, the university should be getting out of Los Angeles as soon as possible.[4]

Bill Banowsky, also a trustee, agreed with Jones. In his judgment, the failure of the college in Los Angeles dated back to the Watts riots of 1965. Thereafter, he believed, the administration had been unable to raise capital funds, the school had lost the moral support of the church, and the percentage of students from Churches of Christ had declined. Support for the campus mission—from both the Churches of Christ and the surrounding neighborhood—had eroded even further following Larry Kimmons's death in 1969, in Banowsky's view. He reminded his fellow trustees that at a December 1969 meeting at La Costa, California, the school's leadership had agreed the college had failed in Los Angeles and that the institution must place its emphasis on Malibu.

The story might have been different, Banowsky asserted, had the Churches of Christ stepped forward to support the Malibu initiative. They had not, however, forcing the Pepperdine leadership to turn to other constituencies for students and construction funds. Banowsky refused to apologize for reaching out to others, even at the risk of offending Helen Pepperdine, who *was* very offended that Banowsky used the word "failed" to describe the institution established and nourished by her husband.[5]

Frustrated and disappointed by the lack of institutional support being given to reinvent the Los Angeles campus, Scott resigned as provost effective January 8, 1973, to become dean of instruction at Orange Coast College, a community college in Costa Mesa, California. Scott later went on to serve as president of Cypress College and Pasadena City College, a senator in the California State legislature, and the chancellor of the California community college system. He never completely severed ties with Pepperdine, however, and in time would serve on the university's board of trustees.[6]

"Harvard in the Ghetto"

The administration in time appointed Professor James Wilburn to replace Scott, and he began his service as provost in February 1973.[7] Wilburn had taken his bachelor's degree from Abilene Christian College, master's degree from Midwestern University in Wichita Falls, Texas, and his PhD in history from UCLA. Along the way, he ministered to Churches of Christ in Wisconsin, produced evangelistic film strips, and directed the Church of Christ Bible Chair at Midwestern. In 1970 he joined Pepperdine as an assistant professor of history attached to the Malibu campus, producing two pilot seminars, "Sources of Racial Attitudes in America" and "Poverty in America," and an interdisciplinary module, "American Ideals and Institutions."

Although a registered Democrat, Wilburn had also assisted Banowsky in leading the campaign in Los Angeles County to re-elect Richard Nixon in 1972. Described by Banowsky as "a people person, with a wonderful touch in human relations," Wilburn saw leadership at the Los Angeles campus as an exciting and timely opportunity. Urban campuses, he believed, were becoming "the vortex of educational dynamism." Wilburn believed Pepperdine University could contribute to the success of urban America, and thus to the larger fabric of civilization, by creating a "Harvard in the Ghetto."[8] Taking up residence in the "presidential mansion" on Budlong Avenue, Wilburn found the work challenging, exhilarating, rewarding, disappointing, and all-consuming.

Because Scott, Wilburn, and Goyne were deeply committed to the inner-city mission of the Los Angeles campus, their selection to leadership was intended to underscore the central administration's commitment to its roots and urban setting. So too was the decision to construct a new learning center. In April 1970, Young and Banowsky had persuaded Blanche Seaver to give $250,000 for that purpose. The new center, they said, would "signal to the community, to our students, to the world, that we are serious about our commitment to this campus." Seaver was quoted as saying: "I am making my investments in the future of the Malibu college only on the condition that Pepperdine College will always remain in its present location."[9]

The Frank Rogers Seaver Learning Center was built in the first ten months of 1971. Adjacent to the library, the center contained a small auditorium; faculty offices; class, seminar, and conference rooms; and an audiovisual laboratory. At the dedication ceremonies on October 30, 1971, Assistant Secretary of Transportation Benjamin Davis delivered a message of encouragement to the university and of appreciation to Blanche Seaver.[10]

The euphoria of opening the first major academic structure on the Los Angeles campus in decades turned to gloom almost on the spot, however. Some fifteen black students, led by Rod Wright (subsequently a California state assemblyman and senator), took it as an opportunity to protest again the death of Larry Kimmons, specifically that his name was not mentioned during the dedication ceremonies. Much to the displeasure of the student senate, ten of the protesters were suspended, including Wright and James Kimmons, Larry's brother. But the protestors achieved one of their goals: on December 10, 1971, university officials hung a portrait of Larry Kimmons with an explanatory plaque on the library wall.[11]

A Vision for an Urban Campus

Jack Scott probably best described Pepperdine's hopes for the urban campus in his inaugural address as provost in October 1971. The Los Angeles campus would, he said, "relate positively to its urban environment" in a multiplicity of ways but especially in its curriculum, offering degrees in urban studies, social psychology, and medical technology. It would also strive to relate learning in the classroom to everyday experiences via something then called "cooperative education" and today labeled "internships."

The idea was to eagerly grasp and learn from the city, Scott said, "rather than shrinking from it in fear."[12] And it would all be done in the context of a Christian world view. For Scott, there was "nothing more needed . . . nothing more relevant, than Christian education in an urban culture."[13]

Actually, Scott was giving a rationale for a change that had already happened on the Los Angeles campus. As early as 1969—in the wake of Larry Kimmons's death—Pepperdine College had organized an ethnic studies department and degree program headed by Calvin Bowers. And in late March 1971, President Banowsky had created a task force to define the educational role of "Pepperdine University, Los Angeles," much as another task force had defined the role of the "Pepperdine University, Malibu." Scott chaired the Los Angeles task force, which included Bowers, Goyne, Olaf Tegner, Glenn Rollins, and Willie Davis.[14] For six months the committee studied, polled, and made inquiries.

Its September 1971 final report recommended that the Los Angeles campus discontinue thirteen majors, including art, chemistry, Greek, home economics, and recreation. In their place, according to the proposal would be new majors that were interdisciplinary and urban-oriented. The committee also recommended a very flexible contract major and a broad-based general studies major, the latter with minimal general education requirements and no specific degree requirements other than twenty-one units in English, mathematics and sciences, social sciences, and humanities. Altogether, the committee envisioned a Los Angeles campus curriculum of thirty undergraduate liberal arts majors, seven teaching credential programs, and fourteen graduate programs in nine departments and two professional schools (business and education).[15]

One of the task force's most radical recommendations was a 20 percent reduction in GE units required for graduation. Goyne said the task force believed "in greater freedom for the student," and Scott said students should not have to take "education like medicine."[16] Executive Vice President Howard White disagreed with both but consented to live with the proposed GE and other curricular changes because of "expediency and political exigencies."[17] The central administration approved the curricular recommendations with only minor changes.[18]

Opportunities and Obligations

With the task force report at hand, the faculty and administration of the Los Angeles campus moved resolutely to implement "community centered programs" that would serve the needs of the inner city. The location of the campus near Watts defined both "its opportunities and its obligations." One obligation was to arrange cooperative programs (internships) with community organizations, businesses, government, and charitable foundations that would respond to the needs of the urban environment. Connections were made through its Center for Urban Affairs, which also offered programs in urban studies, ethnic studies, legal studies, corrections, public management, and an associate of arts degree in computer technology. Opportunities provided at the graduate level included master's degrees in corrections, urban planning and development, public administration, and urban school teaching.

The Center for Urban Affairs also sponsored new courses concerned with women, ethnic groups, the supernatural, marriage styles and other issues. These were not uncommon topics on college campuses in the 1970s, but they incited strident criticism from a faction of Pepperdine's church-related constituency. Professor Larry Keene's scholarly examinations of the occult and gay marriage proved particularly troubling for many.[19]

Virtually all of the programs and courses initiated during this time period on the LA campus responded to a particular need or market in the inner city, and most of them relied to some degree on federal funding. Given Norvel Young's previous renunciation of federal funds and Bill Banowsky's frequently expressed reservations about the heavy hand of the government bureaucracy, it was remarkable that the administration and faculty of the Los Angeles campus so aggressively pursued federal grant money. The change of heart may have been due in part to the national transition from the Kennedy/Johnson to the Nixon/Ford administrations, but primarily it was a desperate need for operational dollars. Precious little funding other than federal money was available for inner-city educational programs in south central Los Angeles.[20]

Focusing on Community-Centered Programs

Faculty and administrators on the LA campus participated in a wide variety of academic and community-centered programs from the late 1960s onward. These included a two-year associate degree in technology offered jointly with Telco Institute of Urban Technology, a nearby trade school, and supported by an $113,000 grant from the Fund for the Improvement of Post-Secondary Education, a federal government agency.[21]

Another highly popular program was the master's of public administration (MPA), which was designed for fully employed adults working for public-oriented agencies and offered via five weekend tutorials. Because of its format, WASC often accused the MPA of lacking academic rigor, but it had strong defenders, especially in the Los Angeles Police Department (LAPD). Of its first 138 alumni, thirty-four worked for LAPD, including Bernard Parks, subsequently the chief of LAPD and a member of the Los Angeles City Council. One of Pepperdine's most distinguished teachers and scholars, Lyle Knowles, was deeply committed to the MPA.[22]

Much of the popularity of the MPA and related undergraduate and graduate programs was due to support received through the Law Enforcement Education Program (LEEP). One of President Lyndon Johnson's Great Society programs, LEEP supported criminal justice employees seeking collegiate credit or academic degrees. Pepperdine became involved in the program in 1972, and within three years was allocating nearly $700,000 per year to some 420 students, the second-largest program in the nation. At one time, LEEP income represented between 3 and 4 percent of the university's total revenue. Although LEEP regional officials were often critical of Pepperdine's management, they continued to fund the program through 1976.[23]

Another notable community-centered program was the University Year for Action (UYA). Envisioned as a "domestic Peace Corps," UYA was a federally-funded program designed to provide volunteers to antipoverty groups, and it made grants to educational institutions like Pepperdine to recruit, train, support, and provide academic credit for students who completed a full-time internship for a year. Pepperdine received its first grant in the fall 1971.[24] Some sixty students a term enrolled in the program, interning for a full year at organizations with social service missions while receiving monthly stipends and earning college credit. Although the program clearly fit in the campus's stated desire to address the challenges of the inner city, some faculty members contested the amount of credit offered and criticized the standard of academic work required. In 1976, Pepperdine phased out its UYA program.[25]

Another well-publicized federal initiative was the model neighborhood program, which aimed to place high school seniors from an inner-city neighborhood in an office of their choice for five weeks during the summer. Students who completed the program received ten units of collegiate credit. In 1972, the Los Angeles campus recruited its first class of seventy students from five district high schools. The 700 credit units generated by the program provided much-needed revenue for the campus while also giving minority students a glimpse of alternative futures.[26]

However, the Pepperdine-sponsored model neighborhood program, which was coordinated by Cookye Williams, a recent alumna, never lived up to its predicted potential, in part because it was poorly financed at the federal level. There was also serious conflict within the Pepperdine staff, and Hispanic partisans charged Pepperdine with discrimination because most of its selected participants were African American. Pepperdine's administrators sought to calm some of that criticism by appointing Israel Rodriguez to represent and recruit for Pepperdine in the Hispanic community. (Rodriguez did just that for nearly thirty-five years, first as an admission counselor, then as financial aid director, and finally as director of Hispanic affairs for Seaver College.)[27]

Glass Sculpting, Grandparents, and Grants

One of Pepperdine's most original but largely forgotten federally-financed outreaches to the inner city was a glass-sculpting program. Funded by the National Advisory Council on Vocational Rehabilitation (NACVR), the program aimed to rehabilitate the hard-core unemployed, specifically the "desperate and angry young Blacks of the area," by teaching them a fruitful vocation. Pepperdine expected to do that by providing instruction in glass sculpting.

Englishman John Burton, a self-taught glass sculptor, instigated the program. A philosopher and author, Burton believed firmly that "creative playfulness" would help unemployed workers support themselves by producing art that had value in the marketplace. In 1969, the Young administration provided space and equipment for a studio; NACVR approved a $25,000 pilot grant; and Burton created a course that Pepperdine could offer for college credit—the first for studio glass sculptors in the United States.[28]

Burton's program was well received and became the subject of a critically acclaimed film, "Harvest of Creative Hands," which was widely distributed to PBS stations.[29] However, in 1973, federal funding for the program ended. The college supported it for another trimester, but the university's chronic shortage of funds prompted Pepperdine to phase out the program permanently in January 1974.[30]

Another Great Society innovation was the foster grandparent program, which the Los Angeles campus became a part of in 1972 when it received an annual grant of $277,003 renewable after five years. The idea was to recruit low-income senior citizens to serve as mentors and tutors for inner-city youth who were physically and mentally handicapped. In addition to providing office space for the program, Pepperdine administrators recruited some 100 foster grandparents to pair with clients of the Spastic Children's Foundation of Los Angeles. Pepperdine continued a loose connection with the foster grandparent organization throughout the twentieth century by hosting the annual recognition banquet.[31]

With additional federal dollars, Pepperdine launched other urban outreach programs, including the National Summer Youth Sports Program first offered in 1970, which allowed local youths from the immediate neighborhood of the campus to participate in organized sports activities. The university reached over 2,135 inner-city youths during the program's first seven years.[32]

A National Endowment for the Humanities (NEH) grant titled "Career Options in the Humanities" was another federally funded program designed to address issues of employment in the inner city. Dean Goyne believed the disciplines in the humanities had much to offer when it came to preparing inner-city youths for jobs. The NEH awarded the university a planning grant to produce a resource and curriculum guide that would place the humanities at the center of any solution to alleviate the problems of urban America.

The guide and the proposal for a "Job Strategies Workshop" so captured the imagination of NEH officials that they contemplated awarding the Los Angeles campus a full multiyear grant in the amount of $250,000 to $300,000. Goyne and his colleagues also used the concept as the basis of multimillion dollar proposals to the U.S. Department of Education's Aid to Developing Institutions Program. The larger grants did not materialize, however, partly because federal officers were not satisfied with Pepperdine's answers to questions about an ongoing California State Attorney General's investigation of the university's executive payroll.[33]

Other federally sponsored initiatives included an on-campus Veteran's Resource Center that provided counseling and tutoring services and served some 200 Vietnam vets in 1973.[34] The Los Angeles campus also sponsored Upward Bound, a program designed to better prepare at-risk populations for higher education. Despite strong external reviews, this program operated for only two years (1974–1976). The campus also hosted an acclaimed Head Start program, one of only a few actually sheltered on a university campus. Less successful was the Adult Basic Education Specialist Teacher Training Institute funded in the amount of $65,000 in 1971.[35]

Christian Service Opportunities

While the Los Angeles campus was reaching out to the federal government to fund most of its community-centered programs, it drew upon its own resources to establish avenues of Christian service for both faculty and students. One of these involved New Urban Dimension, an organization of Los Angeles campus faculty and staff who established a halfway house on Orchard Street for six parolees.[36]

Another was Kairos House, located in Watts some two miles from campus, that aimed to teach Jesus's love by providing food, clothing, tutoring, juvenile guidance, homemaking, and some vocational skills. It was formed in 1968 with African American faculty and staff (Calvin Bowers, Bill Satterfield, Herb Crosby, Carroll Pitts, and John Green) acting as an independent board of directors. It served an average of forty youngsters of all ages six days a week; two of those days were devoted to academic training and the rest to crafts. Participants then sold the craft products they made, earning $6 to $13 per week. The program continued through the mid-1970s.[37]

At the suggestion of J. C. Moore, students as early as 1966 organized the Lighthouse ministry of the Vermont Avenue Church of Christ. A staff of twelve students offered Bible classes, reading tutorials, and recreational programs for neighborhood youths. The program was especially active between 1971 and 1973 when James Parker and Mike Plaisance served as directors, but waning interest and budget cuts closed the program in the fall of 1973.[38]

Other collaborative, nongovernmental efforts served the surrounding community. The college, for example, provided library space for the Victor Gruen Center for Environmental Planning, an energy education resource for city planners and teachers from 1975 to 1980.[39] The Los Angeles campus also hosted the Institute for Urban Development, funded in part by a Ford Foundation grant, with the objective of better preparing entrepreneurs for success in the inner city. It also housed the Los Angeles Christian School, a ministry of the Normandie Avenue Church of Christ, on property near the campus.

In 1974, the sociology department established an early-childhood program that cared for both Pepperdine and community children. Subsequently, the campus contemplated—but didn't follow through with—an alliance with civil rights leader Jesse Jackson's PUSH (People United to Save Humanity). Although no formal alliance emerged, Jackson did help dedicate the School of Education's Reading Center, spoke at the graduation exercises of the School of Professional Studies, and had lunch at the chancellor's home. Blanche Seaver was not pleased by Jackson's Pepperdine activities.[40]

Although often criticized when their efforts fell short for various reasons, Scott, Wilburn, and Goyne were genuinely committed to serving the educational and social needs of the inner city through Pepperdine's urban campus. In pursuit of that objective, they adopted a new curriculum and instituted community-centered programming. Many of the initiatives were funded by the federal government, but other programs were funded privately and had roots in Christian compassion. The curriculum and multitude of programs affirms that in the early 1970s Pepperdine University did take seriously its vision of multiple campuses—urban, suburban, and international—and that the Vermont Avenue campus was expected to serve the inner city. The university was continually reminded, however, that it was one thing to commit the Los Angeles campus to serve the inner city but quite another to make that happen.

CHAPTER 18

DEMISE OF THE "HARVARD OF THE GHETTO"

The community programs initiated on the Los Angeles campus, both curricular and extra-curricular, federally funded and privately supported, were calculated efforts to address the special problems of the inner city and fulfill Pepperdine's oft-repeated pledge not to abandon the urban community. That resolve remained high long after the university opened its Malibu campus in the fall of 1972, and LA Campus Provost James Wilburn spoke honestly of transforming the Vermont Avenue campus into "the Harvard of the Ghetto." But that determination was frequently put to the test by matters that had little to do with good intentions, curriculum, or community-centered programming.

One thorny issue was the question of how faculty tenure would work in the context of a multi-campus institution. Most of Pepperdine's Los Angeles faculty did not want to leave the historic campus or abandon its inner-city mission for the new campus in Malibu. Did tenure protect them in their current position even though the university's limited resources were being distributed over a second campus? In dire circumstances could they transfer their tenure to Malibu? Months of negotiations, board of trustee resolutions, severely hurt feelings, and multiple resolutions by faculty committees at both the Los Angeles and Malibu campuses were required to sort out these questions.

Eventually, the administration agreed that tenure for individual faculty members would be determined by the language in the faculty handbook current at the time of appointment, meaning that the prerogatives in Los Angeles could be extended to Malibu. Those hired after January 1, 1974, however, could work toward tenure only on the campus where they were initially appointed, and according to the language of the relevant faculty handbook.[1]

A Tale of Two Deans

The tenure question was dramatized by the case of Lucille Todd, the much-loved but untenured dean of women and instructor of English who had served at Pepperdine since 1961. Dean Todd embraced a level of tolerance in matters of student discipline and social action that ran counter to the central administration's traditional standards. Needing to do some serious economizing, Executive Vice President Howard White terminated Todd's contract as of fall 1973.

Students and faculty alike protested, even holding a bake sale to raise money to help pay her salary. Dissenters were flabbergasted that a campus of 2,500 students, 40 percent of whom were women, would terminate the position of dean of women, even if fewer than 5 percent of those students lived on campus. The outcry was so extensive that White reversed himself and renewed Todd's annual contract at least through 1979. It was not an issue that Pepperdine officials wanted to come before WASC or in the courts, both of which were possibilities. One of Todd's new duties upon reinstatement was to direct the university's recently inaugurated women's center on 79th Street.[2]

There was no question that Todd's associate, Dean of Students Jennings Davis had tenure. Davis, who had served as dean since 1963, was widely admired for his Christian idealism, generous spirit, student sensitivities, and commitment to the Los Angeles campus. But fellow administrators and some faculty often questioned whether he exercised appropriate levels of leadership in the student affairs office, and they especially questioned his judgment on racial matters. Davis, a Tennessee native, was an outspoken advocate of social justice for black Americans. In March 1973, for example, he had "respectfully" accused the Los Angeles Chamber of Commerce of racism, to which charge the chamber took severe umbrage. As Young and Banowsky were at that time trying to raise $63 million from LA's business elite, the accusation seemed inopportune at best. Simultaneously, Davis chose to teach an elective course on the Jesus Movement, confirming for many in the church constituency that the Pepperdine faculty had gone over to the dark side.

Central administrators debated how to deal best with the tenured and greatly respected dean of students, finally agreeing that he should be exiled to Malibu and that Norvel Young would "bell the cat." Young tried, but Davis would not agree to leave the urban campus for a position in the suburbs. Davis was committed to the inner city, and in the inner city he wanted to stay. And he did, for the remainder of his career, although he resigned his position of dean of students at the same time that Todd was forced out. Thereafter, he taught in the religion department on the LA campus and subsequently for the School of Business and School of Education, retiring around 1992.[3]

Demographics Continue to Shift

Central to the Los Angeles campus in the 1970s was the College of Arts and Sciences, which included the traditional academic departments and offered primarily undergraduate degrees. Nothing was new about the college other than its formal name, which was designed to differentiate it from campus mates SBM and SOE after 1968 and 1971 respectively. As the mission of the Los Angeles campus evolved, the name of the college changed to the School of General Studies and then the School of Professional Studies (SPS).

Enrollment on the Los Angeles campus (excluding continuing education) totaled nearly 2,400 in fall 1972. Over the next six years that number nearly doubled, but little of that increase came from the undergraduate arts and sciences programs. In fact, the number of credit units it sold decreased by some 50 percent between 1975 and 1979. From Vice President White's perspective, if the school sold fewer than 10,000 units per trimester, it should be closed immediately. The college managed to avoid that tipping point for several years, primarily because of the success of its graduate programs.[4]

Not only was the number of enrolled undergraduate students a disappointment; so too was the collegiate readiness of those students. In 1972, entering freshmen scored in the 28th and 26th percentile on the SAT verbal and math exams respectively. The following year, their combined verbal and math mean score was 780 on the SAT, some 150 points below the average score of entering freshmen at Malibu and the national average.[5]

However, the Los Angeles campus enrolled a far more heterogeneous student body than Malibu or similar institutions nationally. In fall 1972, more than 40 percent of the 202 enrolled freshmen were African American, but just 11 percent were members of Churches of Christ. Some 85 to 90 percent of the Los Angeles campus students were commuters, and by 1976 only sixty students were living in residential halls. Of the entire student body, most were part-time, thirty-five years of age or older, and married. Seventy-eight percent were from California, one of the few denominators common to the student body.[6]

The transformation of the campus from residential to commuter impacted both the co-curriculum and the curriculum and the facilities themselves. One of James Wilburn's last acts as LA provost was to close the residence halls and the cafeteria in 1976.[7] Shuttering the last residence hall was not without controversy. Nearly one-half of the rooms had been occupied by African American young men who were part of the Telco program. Since the majority of the occupants were students of color, the NAACP considered the "eviction" racist and characteristic of a university that had no affirmative action program and had given tenure to only one of its thirty-nine black faculty members.[8]

"The Suppressed Oppressed Students of the L.A. Campus" were especially irate. In a letter they threatened to "bomb" Executive Vice President Howard White, his car, and "what's left" of him. According to these students, White had one of two choices, "The Bomb or L.A. campus." He was warned not to ignore their threat. "We're serious, mind you, you f_ creep," the notice concluded.[9] Nevertheless, the residence halls were emptied of all occupants.

Stilling Student Publications

With the demise of the residential community, many of the activities generally associated with campus life disappeared completely. That lack also impacted student publications such as the weekly newspaper, *Inner View*, and the periodically published magazine, *Urbis*. The *Inner View* published its first issue in August 1972 (after the *Graphic* moved to the Malibu campus) and continued for four years. From the beginning, it stridently supported the Los Angeles campus's refocused mission and called to task anyone its writers believed were shirking their duty in achieving that mission. Its criticism of Banowsky, White, and Wilburn, among others, was unrelenting.

The student publications survived an administration effort to discontinue them in fall 1973, but by the time *Inner View* ceased to publish in 1976, it spoke for only a handful of residential students and just a few hundred undergraduates, almost all of whom commuted to campus.

When Pepperdine administrators that year terminated journalism as an academic program on the Los Angeles campus, only a few challenged the decision. One of those was Clint Wilson, faculty advisor for student publications.[10] To him, *Inner View* was "the last flickering hope of an educational ideal at Pepperdine." He charged that administrators were following a higher education philosophy that embodied "the concept of isolation; that the rudiments of college education can best be carried out on a hilltop, far from the less fortunate masses." Sadly, Wilson lamented, over time, "the spirit and excitement at L.A. [had] degenerated into bitterness, frustration and hopelessness."[11]

"All We Need Now Is a Burial Plot"

Journalism and physical education traveled parallel downward paths on the LA campus. When all competitive sports were moved to Malibu in 1972, the PE program had become a mere shadow. Still, PE, chaired by Willie Davis, a star athlete and an alumnus of Pepperdine College, remained a part of the reformed general education program, and intramurals occupied a vibrant role in the co-curriculum. After a six-month study in 1975, Davis proposed a plan to enhance intercollegiate sports on campus.

But the administration quickly rejected Davis's proposal "due to financial difficulties," which, said *Inner View,* had become "a typical Pepperdine slogan." Sadly, opined the newspaper, the death of the sports proposal would lead eventually to the death of the inner-city campus. "All we need now is a burial plot."[12]

The *Inner View* was not the only critic. The faculty association said the action validated "further a lack of concern regarding the needs of this campus." In June 1975, students organized an on-campus demonstration, "shouting bloody murder," and conducting a mock trial, but all to no avail. Within a year, the Los Angeles campus leadership dropped PE from general education requirements, closed the department, and removed all training equipment "lest it be stolen."[13]

Changes in Christian Atmosphere

From the beginning of George Pepperdine College, both administration and faculty boasted of a campus atmosphere that was distinctly Christian. That tradition deteriorated perceptibly in the 1970s. Policies ensuring "modest" dress were abandoned; restrictions against smoking were mostly ignored. Business students reportedly began drinking on campus with the permission of the dean, so long as it was not done in the presence of undergraduate students. Restrictions for residence halls disappeared, and profane and blasphemous language became commonplace.

Of course, chapel expectations changed as well, with the administration eliminating the mandatory chapel requirement beginning September 1973. It continued to offer chapel daily for twenty minutes during the 10 o'clock hour, but it also began to schedule classes and even administrative receptions during that time.

Provost Wilburn and his colleagues attributed this "drift" from tradition, as characterized by the *Graphic* at Malibu, to the fact that the student body was almost wholly commuter in nature and already exempt from chapel. Longtime professor of religion Michio Nagai thought those rationalizations were nonsense and resigned as director of chapel services in protest. A Japanese American who had spent World War II in a Colorado internment camp, Nagai eventually concluded that the de-emphasis of chapel represented a de-emphasis of Pepperdine's historic Christian focus and relationship with Churches of Christ. In March 1976 Nagai resigned from the faculty, saying he found it "increasingly difficult to . . . work within the framework of service to the church with the changing situation . . . at Pepperdine." He had been at the university for twenty-seven years.[14]

Several of Nagai's colleagues had the same fears, including Calvin Bowers and Carroll Pitts. From their points of view, the role of religion on the Los

Angeles campus had become "questionable." Pitts did not think the Christian point of view was being taught in most subjects, even in Bible courses, and some students voiced similar complaints.[15] When the SOE began scheduling classes on Sunday morning within sight of the Vermont Avenue Church of Christ, worshippers there wondered about the authenticity of Pepperdine's commitment to Christian education.[16]

Even so, others saw evidence of renewal of the Christian mission. They pointed to Campus Advance, an evangelistic program sponsored by the Crenshaw Church of Christ. Campus Advance was Pepperdine's answer to Campus Crusade, then a lively evangelical Christian influence on college campuses across the United States, and to the more radical Jesus Movement that claimed access to the gifts of the Holy Spirit. Interest in Campus Advance, however, had diminished dramatically following the opening of the suburban campus in Malibu.[17]

Chancellor Young also pointed to the Kairos House and Lighthouse programs, which were discussed in the previous chapter. There, in the midst of Watts, Pepperdine students and faculty mentors were teaching Bible classes and conducting clinics in reading and mathematics. In addition, students in the Mission Club and the Christian Action Club prepared themselves for evangelistic outreaches, both foreign and domestic, and reached out to international students enrolled on the Los Angeles campus.[18]

Persistent Racial Tensions

The racial tension that had characterized the campus after the shooting death of Larry Kimmons and other incidents lingered through the 1970s. Two incidents reflect the atmosphere. One, a "hate sheet" circulated in 1970 by the Black Student Union advocated "getting guns and starting to shoot."[19] The other, two years later, was a widely publicized threat, presumably by the politically radical Symbionese Liberation Army (SLA), delivered in an envelope holding a .22-caliber bullet to a Berkeley, California, radio station. The note demanded that Pepperdine turn its Los Angeles campus over to the black community for protective custody or be responsible for compromising the safety of Patricia Hearst, who had been kidnapped by the SLA. The SLA document was eventually judged a hoax, but the incident clearly illustrated that the university's standing in the black community was problematic.[20]

A series of on-campus incidents also illustrated that point. Among those were occurrences of arson, burglary, bomb threats, and physical and sexual assaults, some by individuals and others by gangs. These attacks were usually blamed on people coming from the "ghetto," although a series of arson fires initially attributed to black troublemakers was actually set by a white youth. Chief of Security Woody Morrison said faculty and staff sometimes encouraged theft by leaving their keys and pocketbooks unattended. That was clearly not the case in July 1977, however, when a black youth took $1,800 from the Los Angeles campus's cashier's office at gunpoint.[21]

Provost Wilburn and other administrators worked diligently to quiet some of the racial tension that existed both on and off campus. They doubled the size of the unarmed security force, staffed it with African Americans, and kept it on duty 24/7. They recruited and hired black alumni as staff workers and made a special effort to recruit and appoint African Americans to faculty positions.[22] Wilburn also recruited an Urban Board made up of some notable African American civic leaders, including Jesse Jackson, jazz musician Lionel Hampton, and Los Angeles mayor Tom Bradley.[23] Despite such genuine efforts, Pepperdine simply could not placate its critics, which included the NAACP, its neighbors, and some of its own faculty and employees.

A School of Professional Studies

Soon after Wilburn assumed office as provost, he organized a Master Plan Committee for the Los Angeles campus and charged it to review the report prepared only two years earlier. In April 1974, the committee published a 175-page report recommending, among other things, a revamping of home economics, reinstatement of journalism as a major, organization of a School of Psychology, master's degrees in social work and urban planning and development, and utilization of cooperative education pedagogies in the liberal arts. The report also noted the many areas where the Los Angeles campus was already involved in areas of urban outreach.[24]

Wilburn submitted the master plan to his Urban Board for further review in mid-1974. He had organized the twenty-five-member board specifically for that purpose, choosing men and women who were committed to the inner city, were respected by its residents, and could help him raise significant funds for the urban campus. Wilburn expected the board to complete its task in four meetings over thirteen months. The Urban Board reflected insightfully on the master plan but offered no major epiphany or even a small commitment of financial support. Its solution to the problems of the inner city seemed to be to attract more federal money.[25]

Faculty Propose Radical Shift

Discouraged by the response, Wilburn pretty much gave up on his "Harvard of the Ghetto" idea. In October 1975, he took the entire Los Angeles faculty to Griswold Inn in Claremont, California, and over three days asked them to propose appropriate solutions for the campus after looking closely at enrollment trends, programmatic prospects, and student interests. After examining the data, the faculty proposed that the university concentrate liberal arts education in Malibu and professional education in Los Angeles.

Subsequently, a seven-person task force recommended phasing out the College of Arts and Sciences and replacing it with a School of Professional Studies.[26] The re-formed school would be comprised of a set of liberal arts classes offered at times and places convenient to working adults. Those classes would lead to a bachelor's degree in one of five divisions: liberal studies, general studies, public affairs, sociology, and psychology. The abolition of most liberal arts programs was attributed to the changing demographic at the Los Angeles campus.[27] The University Academic Council approved most of the recommendations of the task force, effective September, 1976.[28]

According to Provost Wilburn, the recommendation of his faculty was designed to close down the Los Angeles campus with as little personal pain as possible. The proposal gave members of the faculty and staff several options, allowing some of them to transfer to Malibu while others could leave college teaching and launch new careers immediately. Still others could transition into the new School of Professional Studies, buying a year or two to find another position.[29]

Although academic programming went through some immediate changes, several years passed before the campus actually closed. In 1976, Wilburn resigned his position to assume the vice presidency of university affairs. Dean Goyne remained as chief executive officer of the LA campus until 1979. Linda Salter, professor of mathematics, chair of the general studies division and assistant dean of instruction, succeeded Goyne, serving as dean of the school until 1980, when she resigned to accept a position at Grossmont Community College.[30] John Watson, chair of the master's degree program in human resource management, followed Salter as acting dean, serving there a year, then joining the Malibu management team as an assistant vice president. Nancy Hoisman replaced Watson as acting dean until the School of Professional Studies closed in 1982.[31]

Campus for Sale

As early as 1971, Vice President of Development Donald Bibbero had proposed that the university sell the thirty-three acres as quickly as possible. Neither President Banowsky nor Chancellor Young embraced that position, but Banowsky's actions often suggested he did not anticipate that Pepperdine University would be a longtime tenant of its inner-city campus. In February 1974, for example, he ordered that a valuable tapestry and other items of artistic or aesthetic value exhibited in Los Angeles be transported to a safe place in

Malibu. Two years later, he directed that the bleachers on the baseball field in Los Angeles be transported to the field in Malibu.[32]

It was obvious to County Supervisor Kenny Hahn that Pepperdine administrators were "just waiting to unload the Los Angeles campus."[33] It became even more obvious when administrators leased the presidential mansion and the home economics building to a Christian ministry, "ReJoyce with Jesus," just to keep them from being vandalized.[34]

In January 1976, African American leaders of South Los Angeles Churches of Christ, including Calvin Bowers and Carroll Pitts, asked the university to gift them with the western half of the campus property, including the gym, athletic fields, and Normandie Street frontage. They wanted to utilize the land and facilities for a Christian grade school associated with the Southwest Church of Christ (subsequently the Normandie church), which had been George Pepperdine's home congregation. Although the proposal appealed to Howard White and others, it did not make good economic sense for the university. Thus it was declined.[35]

In early 1978 the city of Los Angeles offered $2.6 million for 15.6 acres of land that the city would convert into a regional park.[36] Although the transaction was jointly announced by Mayor Tom Bradley and President Bill Banowsky, city officials delayed the deal and then reduced its offer to $1.7 million, which President Howard White rejected.[37]

In the meantime, other parties expressed interest in the property. Eventually, the university accepted a proposal from Watt Industries of Santa Monica, which offered just under $1 million for the western four acres of the campus that fronted Normandie Street. Watt intended to build apartment housing for middle- to low-income families. The deal closed in October 1980.[38]

Proposals to purchase the remaining twenty-eight acres of the urban campus materialized in 1980 and 1981. Among these was one from the Crenshaw Christian Center, led by the magnetic Fred Price. With a membership of 8,000 and Sunday morning attendance of 4,000, the center had outgrown its facilities on Crenshaw Boulevard in Inglewood. It was looking for space to house administrative offices, social services, classrooms, and to build an extraordinarily large auditorium, or "faith dome." In April 1981, Price offered $14 million for the property, tendering $2.5 million in cash and $11.5 in seller's notes. For three years, or until the notes were paid, the university could lease 162,000 square feet of building space for $1 per year.[39]

A more lucrative offer from Grace Christian Schools, sponsored by the Gharah Educational Foundation, came just days after the Crenshaw Christian Center proposal had been placed in escrow. That deal had been hurried because the City of Los Angeles, which still wanted the property west of Budlong Avenue, threatened to condemn the tract and thus acquire it for a lesser sum unless the Crenshaw offer materialized forthwith. The need for a deal to forestall condemnation proceedings took precedence over the possibility of a higher selling price, so Pepperdine officials chose not to try to vacate the escrow account.[40]

Regardless of the city's threats, some African American Church of Christ preachers in South Los Angeles were righteously indignant that Pepperdine was negotiating with the Crenshaw Christian Center at all. Did they realize that the center was not a "church of Christ"; that Price brainwashed his congregants like Jim Jones; that he believed in divine healing and speaking in tongues; and that the facility would cripple the work of the Vermont Avenue Church of Christ? Surely, the preachers argued, George Pepperdine would be very disappointed with this fate for the campus he built to further the work of Churches of Christ. The preachers proposed to pay $13 million, with the majority financed by the seller, in order to reconstitute the campus as a K–12 educational facility administered by members of Churches of Christ.[41]

However, given the city's threat, Pepperdine officials felt they had to work with the only financially sound proposal then on the table: the one from the Crenshaw Christian Center. Accordingly, the university transferred title of its Los Angeles campus to Fred Price and the Crenshaw Christian Center on June 22, 1981.[42]

A month after the transfer of title, the Los Angeles City Council declared July 25, 1981, as "Pepperdine Day." At least 1,000 alumni, faculty, staff, and friends converged for a "last hurrah" on the beautiful campus of historic George Pepperdine College. After an alfresco lunch, Oly Tegner, dean of the Graduate School of Education, Jim McGoldrick, associate dean and professor at the School of Law, and Kenton Anderson, dean of the School of Business and Management, rolled up their pants, waded through the fountain, and ceremoniously lifted a freshly painted "Dolores" from the pedestal where she had proudly stood for some forty years. Gently carried to the edge of the fountain, she was then transported to Malibu and a new home at Seaver College.[43]

Although graduate classes would continue on the campus for one more year, the removal of Dolores to the suburbs effectively symbolized the end of Pepperdine's inner-city campus. Its ambition of becoming the Harvard of the Ghetto or a lighthouse to south-central Los Angeles had died aborning. The effort had been valiant, but the outcomes were disappointing.

The demise of the Los Angeles campus did not, however, mean the end of George Pepperdine's dream to prepare men and women to live lives of "usefulness" in a competitive world. In addition to the young people who were being taught in his name at a gleaming campus in Malibu, students had been learning in programs operating under the Pepperdine umbrella in far-flung corners of the world. The institution that he had opened on the Vermont Avenue campus now included a School of Law, a School of Business and Management, and a Graduate School of Education. Those programs will be the focus of the next section of this book.

AN EXPANDING
UNIVERSITY
1966–2000

CHAPTER 19

A UNIVERSITY WITHOUT WALLS

B y action of the board of trustees, Pepperdine *College* became Pepperdine *University* on January 1, 1971. The Norvel Young administration considered that transition a logical development as opposed to an audacious claim. Even while most attention had been focused on the Vermont Avenue campus, the institution had grown from that single campus to one that also included campuses in Heidelberg, Orange County, and Malibu, and from offering only bachelor's degrees in the liberal arts to also offering professional graduate degrees in business, education, and law. As William Banowsky assumed the presidency, the new name was announced with great pride, the reservations of WASC accreditors notwithstanding.

One of the college's earliest steps toward university status was a continuing education program, which was born in 1959 when Professor Paul Buckley offered to deliver a class for twenty-seven Corona, California, school teachers at their workplace. President Young saw in Buckley's innovation the potential to enlarge the influence of the school and develop new revenue streams, so he persuaded Rex Johnston to leave his presidency at Ohio Valley Christian College and join Pepperdine that year as professor of education and chairman of continuing education. Johnston set in motion a series of events that would eventually lead to the 1969 launch of the free-standing School of Continuing Education (SCE) under founding dean Pence Dacus—giving Pepperdine its first reason to think of itself as a "university without walls."

Delivering Learning in Far-Flung Places

The concept of delivering educational programs to students where they lived was not new in higher education, but it was not widely employed in Southern California. Pepperdine College took advantage of this absence, primarily among teachers seeking to upgrade their credentials, but also to anyone seeking intellectual stimulation.

In the early years of the continuing education program, each enrolled student could take up to nine credit units per trimester, and classes of at least ten students were scheduled for late afternoons, evenings, and Saturdays in various off-campus locations, with accelerated courses offered during summer terms. Because overhead expenses were modest, tuition charges per unit were about 40 percent of those on the Los Angeles campus, but all tuition had to be paid upon enrollment. At first, only a limited number of courses taken through continuing education could be applied toward standard Pepperdine degrees.[1]

The continuing education offerings, especially under the SCE, were strongly entrepreneurial. If a deep interest was detected in child psychology, social science teaching methods, or the history of surfing, the continuing education program quickly created a class, enrolled students, and hired an adjunct teacher, usually in that order. In organizing classes and recruiting students, SCE sometimes used the services of third-party contractors, who worked for a commission.[2] Initially, the continuing education program did not grant degrees but offered coursework that could apply toward degree programs on the Vermont Avenue campus. After 1963, courses began to be offered at "resident centers" in Southern California—including Glendale and Anaheim—and eventually SCE developed centers along the southeast coast of the United States and the Pacific Rim. Most such centers were on military bases, and no tuition discounts applied for credits earned there.[3]

Fairly quickly, other Pepperdine College departments and schools saw the potential for such off-campus programs: those in Southern California could act as a feeder to on-campus curriculums, while the more distant programs could generate a revenue stream that could help fund the home campus. Thus, the School of Business and Management (SBM), the School of Education (SOE), and even the School of General Studies (later called the School of Professional Studies), all on the Los Angeles campus, launched their own off-campus programming, sometimes in cooperation with one of the continuing education centers but often separate from them.

Sometimes SCE and one or more of the other schools were offering courses and programs in the same location. Sometimes the courses and degrees were virtually identical, much to the confusion of prospective students, WASC visiting teams, and future historians.

Some of SCE's programs were reminiscent of those George Pepperdine College had offered for extension credit during the Tiner administration. In 1970, for example, SCE sent groups to Sweden, Germany, Denmark, Finland, Russia, Norway, and Hawaii.[4] In cooperation with Michael Cousteau, son of famed ocean explorer Jacques Yves Cousteau, SCE offered "Project Ocean

Search" to eighty-four high school students in 1977.[5] Like many other U.S. institutions of higher education, SCE also gave continuing education credit for courses delivered via educational television, including courses on metrics, aerospace, classical theater, and communication.[6]

Maximizing a Revenue Stream

In 1968, Hillery Motsinger replaced Dacus at SCE and doubled the number of students taking courses over the next four years. By then some 5,000 part-time students pursued 107 different academic programs at 129 locations in four western states. Those students generated 22.4 percent of all credit units sold by Pepperdine, producing a revenue stream of nearly $2 million.[7] In 1972, Motsinger resigned and was replaced by Robert Gordon, who led SCE as it expanded its programs to military bases along the East Coast and Pacific Basin, generating as many as 30,000 credit units per year by 1975.[8] Such results far exceeded Young's original expectations for the continuing education program.[9]

Dacus's most dramatic contribution to the continuing education program was to deliver on-site training in management fields, with degree options, to businesses in Southern California, providing such a program for Northrop Corporation and the American Savings and Loan Institute as early as 1967.[10] The model would be extremely important to the School of Business as it sought a creative method to deliver its new MBA degree.

Dacus also approached military bases, proposing to bring to Edwards Air Force Base a one-year master of arts in education (MAE) program composed of six, five-unit courses, each of which would meet for two months over three 20-hour weekends. Whether Edwards AFB accepted the proposal is unclear, but in 1971 Schofield Barracks, the U.S. Army base northwest of Honolulu, began offering both the MAE through Pepperdine's School of Education and the MBA through the School of Business and Management.[11] The army was quite pleased with the Pepperdine program, which also included classes at Tripler Army Medical Center, and it graduated 179 men and women in the first two years.[12]

Partnership Targets Military Market

But the high praise came only with the help of Pepperdine outsiders as Dacus and subsequent deans looked to educational brokers to help make the programs work. Beginning July 1, 1974, Rockport Management Corporation (RMC) of Washington, D.C., and Pepperdine University entered into a five-year contract authorizing the corporation to represent Pepperdine in establishing undergraduate and graduate degree programs on military bases around the world. Rockport representatives went from one military base to another, recruiting students, and identifying classroom space. All Pepperdine personnel had to do was appoint a director, employ faculty, teach the classes, maintain academic records, bill the United States government, and grant degrees. Rockport received a 20 percent commission on tuition revenue generated due to its services, a sum Pepperdine later came to consider a "financial sacrifice" for the university.[13]

The contract envisioned that RMC would focus its attention on marketing the degree programs. However, its management spent the first three months of the contract designing the concepts and content of the bachelor's degrees in human resources management and administration and working on master's degrees in human resources management, administration, planning and public administration, and counseling. Some Pepperdine faculty helped, but the bulk of planning, writing, and printing textual materials was executed by Rockport personnel. RMC was even involved in identifying, interviewing, and briefing prospective instructors and hiring staff.[14]

Within sixteen months, the partnership between Pepperdine and Rockport had established programs at forty-one locations in fifteen states, the District of Columbia, Guam, Japan, Okinawa, and Philippines.[15] In total there were some seventy-two degree programs involving more than 1,000 students.[16] With few exceptions, base commanders were pleased with the programs. Pepperdine had done an "absolutely superior job," said one Marine Corps officer, "in helping us launch what has become the most complete off-duty education program available anywhere in the Marine Corps . . . perhaps anywhere in the military service."[17]

The university was also pleased with the programs. In the 1975–1976 academic year, the contracts with RMC and Continuing Education Corporation, a marketing firm that served SBM, produced over 14 percent of the total credits sold by the university. Between 1974 and 1976, Rockport alone generated tuition in the amount of $3.1 million, an impressive result even though 26 percent of the amount was in arrears.[18]

Others in higher education were not so pleased. States where the military bases were located often complained about Pepperdine offering degree programs without the state's approval, condemning the practice as "academic colonization."[19] WASC was even more critical, and Executive Secretary Kay Andersen was certain that broker-delivered and/or off-campus credits were tainted almost by definition.[20] More than once, Pepperdine Executive Vice President Howard White was called to defend the military base program and use of contractors before national higher education audiences. He always reassured skeptics that the brokers had no control over the programs and in "no sense directed or controlled the academic activities" on the bases.[21]

Although the military base program had its genesis in the SCE, the school and the program had different missions. SCE provided "continuing education" credit for professionals and intellectual stimulation for lifelong learners, while the base program helped military personnel earn standard collegiate degrees. In recognition of that distinction, Pepperdine declared each base a "resident center" and gathered them into a separate administrative unit known as the Center for Innovative Education (CIE). According to White, CIE was "one of Pepperdine's most valuable assets."[22]

The Fifth Campus

Meanwhile, in early 1974, Dacus, now the vice president for special programs, had won approval for establishing the Orange Center on 17th Street in Santa Ana, California.[23] Dacus envisioned transforming the facility, which was initially just one of many SCE centers, into a free-standing "Fifth Campus, joining Pepperdine's campuses in Los Angeles, Malibu, Heidelberg, and the nearby Law School."

On its own grounds, in its own building and with an independent academic council, the "Orange Campus" housed the School of Continuing Education, the Center for Innovative Education, and a robust residential degree program. A true believer in Pepperdine as a "university without walls," Dacus saw the Fifth Campus as a way to reach Orange County students, to concentrate on completion degree programs articulated with community colleges, and to focus on nonresidential special programs and degrees. He also thought the Orange campus could serve as an antidote to decreasing enrollments at the Los Angeles campus and provide a means to cooperate more fully with Pepperdine's fledgling Law School, which was also located in Santa Ana.[24]

With the approval of the administration and the new University Academic Council, Dacus, Dean Gordon and Associate Dean Lyndell Cheeves immediately offered a full-service collegiate curriculum minus the first two years of the baccalaureate degree. From Dacus's perspective, Pepperdine could not meet the needs of Orange County with cookie-cutter extension programs out of Los Angeles and Malibu. The county needed its own tailor-made programs that would "remain subordinate" to Pepperdine's "basic Christian liberal education approach."[25]

Concerns over Orange Programs

Although Pepperdine's central administration seemed pleased by the Orange Center operations, concerns were growing about some of its practices. Howard White had anxieties about the academic quality of some of the programs, and he received more than a few critical letters about practices that were unacceptable academically and professionally. Dean Gordon sadly confirmed they were occurring.[26]

Lloyd Nelson, chair of the Pepperdine University board of trustees, was also concerned. A longtime professor of higher education at USC, White believed the SCE at Orange had such a bad reputation among professional educators in the area that it needed to hire a public relations firm to upgrade its image.[27]

The School of Business and Management on the Los Angeles campus also had reservations. Because all courses at Orange and other SCE centers were offered for full, resident credit, they automatically satisfied degree requirements on all of Pepperdine's campuses. In almost every case, courses at the SCE centers were offered with a community assistance grant of 25 percent. MBA students on the Los Angeles campus drove to Santa Ana to take the cheaper courses, which were then posted to their Pepperdine transcript as resident credit and applicable to their graduate program. Less because of money than the principle, this practice caused considerable consternation for James Wilburn, the Los Angeles campus provost, and SBM Dean Don Sime.[28]

The deans of Pepperdine's graduate and professional schools insisted upon controlling their own degree programs and were particularly offended that the Orange Center offered bachelor degree-completion and graduate programs with "questionable quality controls" that competed with the degrees presented at the Los Angeles campus. For that reason, SBM and the Graduate School of Education (GSE) insisted upon taking control of the bachelor's degree in administration and master's degrees in administration, education, and public policy administration, which were degrees the CIE offered primarily in resident centers, particularly the military bases.

Pressured by the University Academic Council, the administration accepted the realignment in early 1975 although Dacus argued that the takeover would cost $1 million annually in revenue and the goodwill of military officials. As soon as the realignment was approved, SBM announced it would merge the rogue degrees into its standard programs.[29] That decision, as Dacus predicted, created considerable consternation on the military bases, and SBM agreed to permit currently enrolled students to complete their degrees.[30]

In the internecine controversy between the Orange Center and the Los Angeles campus, the central administration generally sided with Orange. Both Norvel Young and William Banowsky considered Dacus a gifted promoter, loyal supporter, and dedicated churchman—the kind of person Pepperdine needed to survive as a Christian institution. Dean Grover Goyne of the College of General Studies (later the School of Professional Studies) at Los Angeles was a solid leader, but he lacked sparkle; and Deans Sime and Oly Tegner were considered too territorial.[31]

Orange Campus Idea Quashed

The central administration urged a compromise whereby Dacus would over-see the marketing of the business programs and SBM would vouch for their academic quality. Young told Dacus, more in the language of affection than reality, that he could avoid further controversy if he would just find a donor to fund the Fifth Campus in Orange County. In that case, Pepperdine could name it "Dacus College" and be done with interdepartmental bickering.[32]

There is no evidence that Dacus took his mentor seriously, for he pro-posed as an alternative "Pepperdine University–Orange Campus." "Center," he said, "conveyed the foul odor of an extension program and therefore limited enrollment." Orange Campus would put the program on the same basis as Pepperdine University–Los Angeles and Pepperdine University–Malibu.

While Young was receptive to the proposal, Howard White was not. If word of a new "campus," got to Kay Andersen and WASC, White feared it would trig-ger another full-fledged accreditation review.[33] Less convinced about the rosy future of the Santa Ana facility than Young and Banowsky, White thought Dacus would do well to focus on military bases and special programs—not the liberal arts. As it was, White told Banowsky, the payroll and overhead for the Orange Center scared "the wits" out of him. When a 1976 management study by the McKenzie group confirmed White's fears, the notion of a full-fledged campus in Orange County died aborning.[34]

The tussle with SBM and the diminished prospect for a real Fifth Campus disappointed Dacus. He resigned in 1975 and returned to Texas.[35]

Orange Center Folded into LA Campus

Dacus's departure provided an opportunity for the university to decide just what to do with the Orange Center, the CIE, and the SCE. When Dean Gordon suffered an incapacitating stroke in mid-1976, administrative competence of the Fifth Campus deteriorated to the extent that Howard White was ready "to make a clean sweep" and "start over."[36]

In August 1976, White noted that for nearly two decades extension courses and continuing education had been a vital part of Pepperdine's operations but said there had been a steady decline in the total activity of SCE in the past two or three years.[37] He was ready to merge the Orange Center and its schools with the School of General Studies on the Los Angeles campus, fearing a com-prehensive investigation by WASC if Pepperdine did not quickly get its off-campus house in order.[38] "Unless we can soon demonstrate that we are more concerned with quality than with ease of obtaining degrees, we may find a very special investigating team looking at all our work," he cautioned.[39]

President Banowsky agreed that consolidating the work of the Orange Center with the School of General Studies was a prudent step and announced the reorganization effective November 1, 1976. As quickly as possible, all support operations at Orange would merge into comparable offices on the Los Angeles campus; simultaneously, administrators used the occasion to evaluate all Orange programs. If they did not return 50 percent of their revenues to the central administration, they were scheduled for closure.

The School of Continuing Education met a similar fate, although on different grounds. Over the years, its classes and programs had endured much disparagement, with some criticism coming from public school superintendents who found they were paying teachers higher salaries because of questionable credentials earned through SCE courses. One angry principal charged "fraud" and characterized the SCE as a "credit mill."[40] Administrators proposed folding continuing education programs into Pepperdine's School of Education (SOE), but Dean Olaf Tegner rejected the suggestion because he believed SCE had little credibility in the educational community.

Reluctantly, the university acted to close SCE on August 31, 1976. Tegner reorganized salvageable programs and incorporated them into SOE's Center for Professional Development. The decision and act were consonant with President Banowsky's declaration that Pepperdine's future was "better not bigger."[41]

Slow Demise of Military Base Program

The Orange campus consolidation impacted the legendary military program administered by the CIE.[42] By this time, the programming and support functions associated with military bases had become sources of considerable grief to the university. WASC leaders and education officials in other states questioned the program's quality. University officials and Rockport Management argued over its profitability. Base commanders had grown frustrated with operational problems.

The contract with Rockport meant that the program could not be discontinued until 1979, but the contract was modified so that Rockport would halt all recruiting activities and render no further services to the university—although it continued to collect commissions on students previously recruited. By July 1978, Pepperdine could report that all undergraduate and some graduate programs on cooperating military bases had been discontinued.[43]

But the changes did not much impress WASC's visiting committee that year. Members continued to think of off-campus education programs as completely problematic, using language that President White considered "spurious and founded on prejudice rather than information."[44] Academic Vice President John

D. Nicks Jr. was more inclined to agree with the WASC position, however, and he worked systematically to terminate Pepperdine's involvement with any military base program, questioning the program's profitability as well as its quality.

Because of his determination, Pepperdine offered its last such course in March 1981.[45] Between 1975 and 1981, the program had served some fifty-four bases and enrolled multiple thousands of military personnel. Of those who matriculated, at least 2,960 graduated with a baccalaureate or master's degree, generally in human resources management.[46]

Christian Mission Outside the Walls?

The CIE, SCE, the Orange Center and other opportunities for expansion that were seriously explored but rejected in the 1970s all flowed naturally from Pepperdine University's values of individual initiative, free-market economy, and the American Way. Those enterprises, however, had little to do with the Christian objectives of the university's founder.

Other than Pence Dacus's rationale for creating new schools of business and education at Orange, there is no evidence that Christian mission—much less the relationship of Churches of Christ to that mission—ever came up for discussion in matters of program or classroom objectives. Certainly, it was not mentioned to any extent in published material. Experimental and innovative programing was all about receipts and cash flow and had little to do with the noble vision of a university without walls or a cosmic call to Christian distinctiveness. The same was true of the School of Business and Management.

CHAPTER 20

THE RISE OF THE SCHOOL OF BUSINESS AND MANAGEMENT, 1966–1982

From the beginning of George Pepperdine College, the most popular academic major was business administration, a discipline that its founder had defined as "useful education." President Young had no intention of changing that curriculum orientation, despite his rhetoric about the value of small, Christian liberal arts schools. Moreover, providing useful—or practical—academic programs could help win the favor of the Los Angeles business elite, whose patronage the school needed to survive financially.[1]

In early 1964, Young's administrative team recruited D. John van de Water, director of the executive program at UCLA's Graduate School of Management and subsequently chair of the National Labor Relations Board, to help Pepperdine organize a graduate business management curriculum leading to the MBA. Given a lack of enthusiasm from the undergraduate faculty, Young and van de Water set up a separate program at the graduate level, although it was still nested in the business and economics department, with someone from outside as chair.[2]

For that position, Young chose Donald R. Sime in 1968. Sime had taken both his BA and MA degrees from George Pepperdine College, and then a BD from Princeton and PhD from the University of Chicago. After several years at Harding College, he joined the Pepperdine faculty in 1966 as professor of religion. Sime had considerable training in self-actualization theory, environmental learning, counseling, group dynamics, and organizational behaviors. Because of Sime's training; his personal characteristics of patience, persistence, tolerance, and creativity; and his commitment to Churches of Christ, Young saw him as an ideal leader for the business program. Thus, he "stuck his neck out" and appointed a professor of religion as chair of the department of business and economics.[3]

Creating Two MBA Tracks

Meanwhile, the MBA program had accepted its first students in fall 1966, with two distinct plans being offerred. Plan I was traditional, requiring thirty units of graduate classwork capped by written and oral comprehensive examinations. Plan II was distinguished by flexibility and a tutorial format, assuming that students would be fully employed and responsible for their own learning. Those admitted to the program had to have acceptable undergraduate work although no degree was necessary, five years of business or professional experience, a potential for management and administration, and a strong motivation for completing the program.[4]

In the first year, more students enrolled in Plan I than Plan II.[5] Quickly, however, Plan II proved far more attractive. By fall 1969, 110 students filled nine sections, each of which followed the same curriculum of three trimesters of academic work. The first trimester focused on behavioral concepts; the second on quantitative issues; and the third on organizational theory, policy, and management practices. Students had to submit a master's project or thesis. There were no formal written examinations, and student progress was recorded on a pass/fail basis. The faculty delivered the Plan II curriculum in one calendar year, with classes meeting on each weekend from Friday evening through Sunday afternoon.

The weekend courses were initially limited to the Vermont Avenue campus, but following the model Pence Dacus had introduced to continuing education, the business faculty soon offered Plan II at multiple off-campus sites, including Edison Company, Lockheed, and North American Rockwell in Southern California.[6] Other collaborators included Western Airlines, Kaiser, Burroughs, Dean Witter, Flying Tigers Lines, Xerox, and General Dynamics.[7] With the help of Rockport, the marketing firm described in the previous chapter, Plan II was also packaged for easy delivery to U.S. military sites.[8]

A Separate Business School

Upon his selection as chair, Sime began promoting an existing proposal to turn the Pepperdine business department into a full-fledged School of Business Administration. A formal business school was needed, Sime and other faculty said, because of the dynamic growth of business education and because UCLA and USC had such schools.

In addition, Pepperdine's undergraduate and graduate business education programs could not be properly accredited by the American Association of Collegiate Schools of Business (AACSB) unless they were reorganized as a free-standing school. For business educators, AACSB accreditation was the ultimate seal of approval. The proposed school would include a dean, an assistant dean for the graduate division, another one for the undergraduate division, and a director of the management center.[9] The college board of trustees enthusiastically adopted the proposal on December 17, 1968.[10]

Entrepreneurial Spirit Leads to Innovative Programs

Under Sime's leadership, the School of Business (it became the School of Business and Management after 1971) exhibited a decided entrepreneurial spirit—as evidenced by its MBA programs offered at various sites for fully employed students. Competing institutions offered only on-campus instruction of full-time students.

Entrepreneurialism also explained the development of the Presidential Key Executive program (PKE). In collaboration with the Continuing Education Corporation (CEC), a for-profit firm from Orange County, SBM faculty members Thomas Dudley and Wayne Strom distilled the MBA II content to five weekend

Donald R. Sime in 1968 became the founding dean of the School of Business and Management, serving in that position for a decade. Under his leadership, the school demonstrated a decided entrepreneurial spirit, creating many innovative programs, including several for fully employed students.

sessions a trimester. They then offered the program to presidents and executives with at least ten years of experience who led firms with assets of at least $1 million. Classes met at the students' business offices. Some 68 percent of the program relied on leveraged credit—out-of-classroom experiences—yet it still required four trimesters over two years to complete the program.[11]

With Dudley as instructor, the first PKE program was piloted to nine California students beginning January 1971. The program was a resounding success, and over the next thirty years, 1,364 executives earned MBA degrees in 104 sections of the PKE program.[12]

In the early 1970s the MBA III was created. The curriculum consisted of twelve different three-unit classes and was designed primarily for working adults who lived more than four hours' flying time from Los Angeles. Each course in the program, which mainly served members of U.S. military bases, required five weeks to complete. Local instructors taught the first three weeks, while an SBM professor taught the last two, which were divided into eleven intensive preparation and participation sessions. It took approximately sixteen months to complete the degree.[13]

The willingness to engage in creative curriculum development also led to unique and timely undergraduate degree programs on the Los Angeles campus. In April 1969, SBM began offering a bachelor's degree in public management in cooperation with the Los Angeles Police Department to train police for leadership positions. A $27,000 grant from the Law Enforcement Education Program initially helped fund this curriculum. The highly successful program became the prototype for a five-year effort supported by a $900,000 grant from the federal government. That subsidy created no small amount of indigestion for the Young administration given its general view that taking such money was somehow unAmerican.[14]

Beginning in 1970, the business school also offered a bachelor's degree in administrative science, which was available on the Los Angeles campus but was primarily aimed at individuals on military posts.[15] The school also offered a series of innovative noncredit programs, most of which were presented through the Pepperdine Management Center, organized in 1966 and subsequently known as the Executive Management Training Program. One such program was a ten-week supervisor training program for Southern California Edison Company designed to teach over 3,000 employees in classes of twenty-five each for a fee of $275,000. Another was a series of executive conferences opened and closed by two-day live-in seminars at Lake Arrowhead, with six on-campus Monday evening sessions in between. Topics ranged from "human and technical development" to the challenge of a growing labor movement. Management guru Peter Drucker lectured at some of those conferences.[16]

Success on Many Levels

By the end of the Young administration, the School of Business and Management was a success story when measured in enrollments and credit units sold. In the winter trimester of 1968, SBM generated 1,000 credit units; four years later that number had increased tenfold, representing 18 percent of the total credit units (53,806) sold by the entire university.[17] By 1975 that percentage had increased to 24.5, exceeded only by Seaver College's 27.7 percent.[18] Put differently, in a decade, SBM more than doubled its enrollment, both undergraduate and graduate, as measured in credit units sold.

Revenue from SBM rose steadily for the first half of the 1970s, reaching a high of $6 million in fiscal 1975–1976, but dipping sharply after that. Although SBM's net return to the university was significant, it did not match that of Seaver College after the middle point of the decade. In addition, by the mid-1970s, SBM also accounted for an increasing amount of students who took classes but did not pay their tuition bills.

SBM's remarkable success was also reflected in the number of faculty it employed. In fall 1970, there were twenty-three full-time faculty members, and that number more than doubled over the next dozen years. The same was true of part-time faculty, who numbered fifty-one by 1982, and who almost always taught as many or more units than did full-time faculty. The full-time teaching load for the business faculty was twelve undergraduate or nine graduate units, whereas it was fourteen units across the board for all other academic programs, the law school excepted.[19]

Influential Leadership

In the vibrant environment of SBM, the steadiest hand on the administrative wheel was Associate Dean Ruth Atteberry, who joined SBM as a temporary employee in 1969. That temporary status turned into a nineteen-year appointment as associate dean, with Atteberry serving under five deans. Without her, according to James Wilburn, "there would have been no way SBM—or even Pepperdine—would be what it later became. She helped build the school from just a few hundred students to the largest business school in the western United States."[20] Her legacy also includes a written history of SBM's first thirty years.[21]

Strongly endorsed by Chancellor Young, Sime accepted the position of vice president of university affairs in December 1973. He served in that capacity only briefly, although he wore the title "vice president" for a number of years while also retaining his title as dean. It is unclear why he continued to hold both positions, although perhaps it was to block challengers like David Reagan, a Harvard-educated, former president of Houston Community College, and Church of Christ member, who coveted the deanship.

Sime instead made Curtis W. "Duke" Page, professor of behavioral sciences, his associate dean. Page assumed essentially all of the dean's duties, leaving Reagan as the unhappy head of the Center for International Business. Sime's appointment of Page turned out to be unfortunate, however, as Page had no appreciation of the university's Christian mission or the need for personal Christian deportment.[22]

A Troublesome Sense of Independence

SBM's entrepreneurial spirit helped explain its rise to prominence, but it was also the source of a great deal of grief for the university's central administration. Because of their success in the educational marketplace, SBM's leaders were quite confident they needed nothing from the university other than freedom to do as they pleased. In an era of what Howard White described as "salutary neglect," Sime and his successors were usually allowed to do just that. The entirety of the imposing Business Administration Building on the Los Angeles campus was assigned to the new school in 1969, and the business faculty soon expanded into much of Marilyn Hall, elegantly remodeling both spaces to give them the essence of a corporate headquarters.

Concluding that the light blue paint applied to the exterior walls of Los Angeles campus buildings was "unprofessional and distasteful," SBM leaders in early 1973 sandblasted the old paint from the business building and repainted it gray. After the job was completed, SBM leaders were reminded that the buildings were "Pepperdine Blue" because of the preferences of Helen Pepperdine, the founder's wife. However, other buildings were soon sandblasted and painted with the same color of gray.[23]

SBM's sense of independence manifested itself in matters other than paint color. Rather than participate in commencement ceremonies on the Los Angeles campus that included undergraduates and graduates from all schools, SBM leaderships insisted on organizing its own, exclusive ceremony. The central administration granted that request in 1974.[24] Sime and his colleagues also argued that the business faculty alone should select candidates for the honorary doctorate given at business school graduation exercises and insisted on designing their own diploma, another request granted by the administration, although no other faculty had that option.[25]

SBM had a habit of acting first and asking permission—or forgiveness—later, which is illustrated by its MBA III program and how it played out on military bases. Because much of the program's "seat" time was concentrated into the last two weeks of the five-week course, the U.S. Office of Veterans Affairs, which paid most of the tuition charges, expressed serious reservations about the program's academic integrity. It then became clear that SBM had launched the program without first checking with anyone—neither the VA nor the Pepperdine administration. With timely political pressure, Pepperdine administrators escaped disaster, but White concluded that such SBM behavior was a *modus operandi* rather than an exception.[26]

When the university board of trustees voted to raise the tuition rate in fall 1974, certain parties at SBM announced that the rates would apply only to new students. At some cost to the university, President Banowsky accepted the interpretation, but with considerable muttering about "business school people . . . definitely 'playing games' with us."[27]

Dean Sime and his associates also insisted upon setting the salary scales at SBM, granting their faculty higher salaries and benefits than faculty in other schools received.[28] That advantage was necessary, Sime argued, to attain AACSB accreditation, higher enrollments, an accomplished alumni, faculty research and publication, and executive patronage.[29] SBM also allowed faculty to complete their contractual obligation of nine units by teaching weekends only and then paid them overtime wages to teach on week-day evenings. In that way, most SBM faculty during the mid-1970s earned annual salaries of $30,000 to $40,000, whereas liberal arts faculty salaries ranged from $14,000 to $18,000.[30] In addition, because SBM faculty taught only on weekends and evenings, they often held full-time corporate jobs or did extensive consulting. Their situation was so remunerative that few wanted to teach in the full-time MBA program when it subsequently opened in Malibu.[31]

In early 1974, Malibu campus Provost Jerry Hudson told President Banowsky that SBM higher pay scales and lighter teaching loads generated "extreme hostility" among his faculty colleagues. Banowsky agreed that the differentials in salaries were "shockingly high" and contributed to "one of our most serious morale problems," but he did little more than lament the circumstance.[32]

SBM administrators especially demonstrated their independence when it came to sharing revenues with the central administration. SBM leadership claimed increasing revenues as their own, to be invested in additional faculty, higher salaries, larger expense accounts, better facilities, and more student services. University administrators, on the other hand, claimed a substantial percentage to pay for physical facilities, central administrative services, and maintenance of the Pepperdine brand. SBM argued for no less than a 60/40 percent split (so-called E/R, or expenses-to-revenue ratio), with the school taking the higher amount. The Pepperdine administration and some trustees thought that split left far too little for the university, leading to acrimonious debates and negotiations.[33] However, SBM retained its preferred percentage split through 1981.[34]

SBM in Malibu

SBM's sense of independence also explained its view of undergraduate business education. Sime and his colleagues believed that SBM would never be a *real* school unless it offered undergraduate programs. Indeed, the AACSB insisted that every approved school of business needed both undergraduate and graduate programs. For that reason, Sime fought to keep the undergraduate department of business at the Los Angeles campus as an integral part of the free-standing SBM, offering a traditional bachelor's degree in administration as well as the innovative completion programs already discussed.

Incorporating the Malibu campus into the SBM orbit was more difficult. Malibu had been defined as an undergraduate, liberal arts program, and no business major or courses were offered on the campus during its inaugural year. Student interest and marketing potential, however, prompted SBM to add those the next year, and Sime appointed Jere Yates as coordinator and then assistant dean for the Malibu campus.

An experienced office manager from Harding College, Ruth Atteberry joined the staff of Pepperdine's School of Business and Management in 1969 as a temporary employee. Upon her retirement, twenty years later, she had earned the rank of associate dean, an MBA degree from SBM, a doctorate from GSEP, and the gratitude of her colleagues for managing the school with effectiveness and grace.

Mixing business and liberal arts education at Malibu was like mixing oil and water.[35] General education requirements in the first two years totaled sixty-four units, which left no room for the twenty-four units of specialized, lower-division courses required for the bachelor of science in administration degree. Sime and his colleagues argued that SBM should select and even teach its own general education courses and control every aspect of its baccalaureate program.[36] This proposal, along with the disparity in faculty salaries, created substantial heat on the Malibu campus between Hudson and White on the one hand and Sime and Yates on the other, with Banowsky and Young in the middle.[37] White was particularly offended at "the conniving, underhanded manner" in which he thought SBM operated.[38]

An accommodation slowly emerged. Initially, Banowsky stipulated that SBM could control its major courses but not the general education requirements.[39] Then he declared that SBM as well as the Graduate School of Education would be professional schools only and that all undergraduate business and education students would be considered part of the liberal arts colleges, as they were at UCLA.[40]

Beginning in 1977, Academic Vice President John Nicks arranged for the business administration program at Malibu to merge into the liberal arts college as a distinct division, with its faculty reporting to the dean of Seaver College and its students subject to the Seaver general education curriculum. Salaries of the business division faculty remained higher than those of the liberal arts faculty, but that was moderated by a college stipends committee. Thanks largely to Nicks, oil and water did emulsify—a bit.[41]

Questioning SBM Success Story

Traditional academics, including the accreditors of WASC, found the incredible success of SBM hard to explain.[42] Critics contributed it to the lack of academic standards, pointing to its minimal admission requirements and nominal program requirements.[43] They complained about SBM's use of private companies to recruit students and cited the lack of classroom rigor.[44]

Professor John McCloskey justified SBM programs by saying they were intended to produce effective managers and not "academic degreed men."[45] Atteberry recorded that some of the reports or business plans submitted by students as final projects were "works of genius" that proved "astonishingly successful."[46]

Aside from WASC concerns, the criticism most often heard was that SBM virtually ignored the Christian mission of Pepperdine University. The first bulletin announcing the Pepperdine School of Business did note that the college was rooted in Christian principles and stressed the unique feature of Christian education, which the bulletin identified as completeness.[47]

Although Sime possessed outstanding credentials as a Christian educator and stalwart Church of Christ member, none of those seemed to carry over into recruiting students, hiring faculty, or constructing curriculum, particularly in graduate programs. Indeed, in the rapid growth of the MBA programs and the realities of the marketplace, Pepperdine's distinctive Christian mission was diluted or forgotten altogether.[48] In its undergraduate curriculum, for example, SBM substituted ethics classes for religion classes and a course on the Book of Mormon as an alternative to a study of the New Testament. These substitutions, said Howard White, were "contrary to the expressed wishes of our founder and statements in our charter."[49]

SBM leaders exhibited the same nonchalant attitude toward the school's relationship to Churches of Christ, making no effort to reach out to that constituency, especially when it came to hiring faculty. Of the dozens of faculty he hired during his deanship, Sime appointed only two who were members of Churches of Christ. SBM did not ignore ethical content in its graduate curriculum, but the philosophical context for ethical behavior was secular rather than Christian. The approach was not different from what students would have found at UCLA.

Unusual Faculty Cohesion

In evaluating SBM's success, commentators tended to ignore one of its hallmark characteristics: a behavioral workshop designed to foster empathy and understanding in the workplace that kicked off virtually every program. Critics thought the workshops were too touchy-feely and irrelevant in the real world of hard-nosed business. But participants spoke of these sessions as being life-changing and the most valuable experience of the program. Because teaching faculty always participated in these workshops, their sensitivity to class members far exceeded that of the traditional college professor.

That experience may explain why university administrators believed SBM faculty members had a stronger sense of cohesion than did the liberal arts faculty. They were "an essentially satisfied and engaged faculty, with no apparent need for a formal faculty structure," which helped explain why they felt no need for traditional academic tenure, so long as "due process" was exercised.[50]

SBM faculty were eager to preserve their unique working environment and reacted sharply when they saw it threatened. When Sime summarily dismissed a faculty member in 1977, his peers demanded an investigation and concluded that the dean had acted in an "authoritarian, closed" manner. The investigative committee recommended redress for the faculty member and adoption of a tenure policy, which was enacted a few years later.[51]

Passing the Torch

Don Sime retired as dean of the School of Business Administration in 1978. Without Sime, Pepperdine Provost Steven Lemley would insist two decades later, there would have been no school of business; and without the school of business, there would have been no Pepperdine University.[52]

Kenton L. Anderson succeeded Sime as dean. An Indiana University graduate, he had joined Pepperdine in 1969 as professor of management and chair of the department and was one of the architects and subsequent champions of the MBA II program. But Anderson's educational philosophy and practice had little or nothing to do with the Christian mission of the university; indeed, he seemed to get pleasure from telling SBM audiences that he did not belong to any church.[53]

During Anderson's four-year tenure as dean, enrollments increased by some 25 percent, making SBM the third-largest MBA program in the nation and the largest west of Chicago. Nonetheless, WASC criticism was unrelenting, prompting serious revamping of instruction, curriculum, and location of SBM programs.[54] Admission standards were upgraded; units required for graduation increased by 50 percent; the quality of adjunct teachers improved. SBM completely deleveraged the MBA II degree, requiring a 20 percent increase in full-time faculty, and folded its different MBA degrees into one—tailoring it for emerging, middle, and top managers.

Most significantly, SBM terminated all programs that were not campus- or center-based (Irvine, Culver City, Encino), meaning it no longer held classes in motel rooms, church basements, corporate lunchrooms, or military bases. The result was a more traditional MBA, the type mandated by AACSB. WASC applauded the changes.[55]

Anderson resigned as dean of the school in June 1982, having launched much of the revamping of the SBM programs. Leadership had been stressful, and he yearned to return to the classroom. His successor would take SBM to an even higher level of success and respect.[56]

CHAPTER 21

SCHOOL OF BUSINESS AND MANAGEMENT II, 1982–2000

I n 1982 when Kenton Anderson resigned as dean, the School of Business and Management faculty expected to be involved in selecting his successor. They wanted to ensure that the new dean would have "substantial experience in business," be known "nationally" as a business leader, have faculty experience, and preferably hold a doctorate. There was nothing on their priority list about the Christian mission of Pepperdine University.[1]

However, for Howard White, Pepperdine president since 1978, the priority was a dean with a Christian orientation—and preferably membership in Churches of Christ. After an unsuccessful attempt to woo Carl Stem, dean of the School of Business at Texas Tech University, for the job, White turned to James Wilburn.

Former provost of Pepperdine's Los Angeles campus and current vice president for university affairs, Wilburn was an experienced and reflective administrator with a Rolodex full of names of Southern California's intellectual and corporate elite. He was also a lifelong member of Churches of Christ. Wilburn had tired of fund-raising and was looking for another professional opportunity so had enrolled in SBM's PKE program. Before Wilburn had completed his thesis, White and Executive Vice President Herbert Luft approached him about the dean's position. He was thrilled by the possibility.

While most university administrators and much of the faculty considered SBM the "black sheep" of the Pepperdine family, Wilburn thought of it as a "sleeping giant."[2] In his judgment, the creativity and entrepreneurial spirit of SBM's faculty was at that very moment shaping the future of business education in the United States, especially as it related to fully-employed managers. Wilburn accepted President White's offer if he could get faculty support.[3] He sought to bolster that process by completing his MBA thesis and ensuring the support of Anderson and SBM Associate Dean Ruth Atteberry. After a faculty review committee approval, White introduced Wilburn as SBM's new dean at the commencement ceremony in August 1982.

Cultivating Values

Wilburn met with the school's faculty and expressed his desire to raise the profile of SBM within the Pepperdine family and beyond. As initial steps, he proposed that business ethics permeate the MBA curriculum and be taught in every course.[4] Wilburn also proposed a new mission statement that would speak of the school's "Judeo-Christian" tradition. Wilburn was looking for support from the school's powerful personnel committee, which was dominated by senior faculty members of Jewish heritage and faith. He believed committee members would be more supportive of his aggressive agenda of a "values-centered education" if he expressed appreciation for the Jewish roots of Pepperdine's community of faith. His effort to extend the Christian heritage to include related faith traditions became part of the woof and warp of Pepperdine's self-definition for the next several decades.[5]

For Wilburn, the university's Christian heritage had far more significance than mere tradition; he believed the values it inspired preserved "the efficiency and productivity of free institutions" and nurtured "the inner moral self-restraint which [made] economic freedom compassionate and serving." A free society in general and free enterprise in specific were dependent on the value of personal integrity, Wilburn argued.[6] Elsewhere, he noted that he wanted the school "to be an advocate for infusing capitalism with an inner moral sense of responsibility and excitement."[7]

In his judgment, the governmental deregulation of the Reagan era was not practical without "some well-springs of self-control, self-regulation, and self-discipline." Americans did not have a right to "get the government off [their] backs," he argued, if they did not possess an "inner moral gyroscope." He claimed Pepperdine's School of Business and Management was distinctive because it tried to develop that gyroscope.[8] Observers of the business scene in Southern California rightly saw Wilburn as "representative of the Pepperdine nexus of conservative politics, laissez-faire economics and spiritual values."[9]

SBM's 1984 strategic plan, clearly the product of Wilburn's hand, elaborated on the theme of values-centered education, even identifying those values as Christian. As such, the school could bring "a powerful force to the world of business education" because it understood that "faith [was] not a way of looking at certain things, but a certain way of looking at everything."[10] The language of values continued to characterize SBM's description of itself, although the emphasis on "Christian" values became less pronounced. In an abbreviated mission statement adopted in 1987, the school's leadership spoke of equipping managers "to create, maintain, and lead productive and *humane* [italics mine] organizations in a rapidly-changing global environment."[11] The 1988 version of SBM's strategic plan spoke of four "integrating values" that tied eight degree programs together: human relationships, global competitiveness, innovation and entrepreneurship, and managing technology. The list of values did not include any mention of Christian values.

Elsewhere, however, Wilburn wrote of SBM combining these basic values "with the deep spiritual roots of the Judeo-Christian tradition," a process he defined as "truly a sacred calling."[12] A combination of the sacred and the profane may have been Wilburn's aspiration, but it was not for most of his colleagues. As important to them as values-centered education may have been, even more important was that their programs be "student focused, academically respected, business partnered, team operated, innovatively driven, quality conscious, selective and inclusive, fiscally responsible, and service oriented."[13]

Joining Pepperdine in 1970, James R. Wilburn served as provost of the Los Angeles campus, vice president of university affairs, dean of the School of Business and Management, and founding dean of the School of Public Policy. He developed a strategic plan for SBM that concentrated on delivering values-centered education.

SBM had committed itself to be a "high quality provider of applied academic programs" and "a partner" with business enterprises in the development and implementation of those programs. That commitment meant it would not employ a classical research model of business education (as advocated by AACSB), but neither would it embrace a model based primarily on its cash-generating potential (as encouraged by some in the central administration).[14]

From the beginning of his tenure as dean, Wilburn also pushed for SBM to become an actor on the global stage. He proposed doing that through hosting conferences in Asia and Europe and also by improving the quality of SBM's academic programs, emphasizing the school's unique strengths and attracting nationally known business scholars—some at or near retirement age—to teach at the school. The dean would also establish and support a new journal in international business, endow several chairs or professorships, and send professors abroad to better equip them to make the MBA curriculum more international.[15]

Maintaining Enrollment, Quality, Profitability

SBM's student body numbered 2,600 when Wilburn became dean in fall 1982, which was 400 students more than five years earlier. Wilburn did not view this level of growth as an unequivocal blessing, for it generally meant more expense than profit.[16] Thus, Wilburn and his administrative team maintained a fall student headcount of between 2,600 and 2,700 through the 1980s and 1990s. During those years, the student body became far more diverse, with the gender distribution moving from a male to female ratio of 2.35:1 to 1.64:1. Ethnically, the white population decreased from 76 to 65 percent, while the number of African American students increased from 3.8 percent to 6 percent and Asians from 4.4 percent to 10.1 percent. More students claimed a Jewish, Mormon, Presbyterian, Methodist, Episcopalian, Lutheran, or Catholic heritage than membership in Churches of Christ.[17]

Maintaining SBM enrollments was a constant challenge. Initially, the school had no competition in its programming for fully-employed MBA students. Pepperdine virtually invented the method of delivering the degree on nights and weekends at the student's place of business, at least in Southern California. But other schools soon developed programs of their own. To maintain market share, SBM began to advertise its academic programs, initially in print media and then on radio. Advertising was expensive but also deemed effective. "Without advertising," concluded SBM leadership, "we would not have the students, and therefore, we would not have a program."[18]

Wilburn hoped to pay for SBM's advertising and academic upgrades by adjusting the E/R (expense/revenue) rate so that 60 percent of SBM's revenue stayed with the school. It had been at that rate in earlier years and was at the 57 percent rate when he came to office in 1982. By fiscal year 1985, however, it was at 53 percent, a level that distressed Wilburn.[19]

President White readily admitted that SBM had been "a most productive cow that we have milked repeatedly." In his opinion, however, the university had "fed the cow fairly well and [had] provided her [with] an environment that [had] enabled her to flourish." Although White sympathized with Wilburn and worked to adjust the E/R ratio more to the favor of SBM, it did not change much. In FY 1997, it was 56 percent.[20]

Perhaps that accounts for Professor Richard Rierdan's 1988 assessment of the SBM and Pepperdine University relationship. "Our greatest internal weakness is the lack of interest that Malibu has historically taken in the school of business faculty," he insisted. "I can't imagine any other faculty doing as much with as little as we have been given." In his view, it was always everything for Seaver College and nothing for SBM, indicative of a sense of persecution that frequently colored the discourse between the school of business and the central administration.[21]

Creating and Strengthening Degree Programs

When it came to SBM's curriculum, Wilburn championed both old and new degree programs. Even in the face of WASC criticism and a lack of interest of his own faculty, Wilburn saw great value in the bachelor's degree in management, ensuring that it survived into the twenty-first century.[22]

An alumnus and advocate of the PKE program, Wilburn increased the length of the program from twelve to twenty months, with one entire trimester devoted to a basic area of study. Wilburn frequently taught the capstone course, developing personal relationships that lasted for decades. Some alumni also became generous donors to the school and to the university.[23]

Wilburn and his colleagues also developed five new academic programs during his deanship. One of these was the Executive MBA, a hybrid program blending elements of the PKE with the MBA II program and requiring an overseas experience. Another was the master's of science in technology management, launched with the support of Arnold Beckman and the input of Cal Tech faculty in 1989. Much to Wilburn's disappointment, the degree did not survive his retirement as dean in 1994, but a $6 million gift from Beckman helped fund the new business school building on the Malibu campus. A third new endeavor was the joint MBA/JD degree, a five-year program involving the SBM and the School of Law.[24]

A fourth Wilburn program initiative was the full-time residential MBA program on the Malibu campus. The university had long contemplated a "traditional" MBA for recent college graduates, believing it would bring SBM closer to the mission and direction of the university. It also represented a new income stream and an opportunity for the business community to identify with the Malibu campus.[25] How it would impact Christian mission was not publicly discussed. The concept was approved by the University Academic Council on November 15, 1985. Classes would be held in trailers recently vacated by personnel moving to the new Thornton Administrative Center.[26]

Neither SBM nor the Seaver College business division faculty was wildly enthusiastic about a Malibu residential program, which would require SBM faculty to teach during the day and preempt the Seaver faculty from initiating its own MBA program. To create a curriculum, recruit a class, and find a faculty Wilburn looked to John Nicks and Wayne Strom, appointing Strom to direct the program.[27] Strom and Nicks found their first class of thirty by trolling among students who had taken the GMAT test too late to be considered by other schools. Ten were flown from the East Coast to Santa Barbara for an all-expenses-paid, three-day recruiting trip. Nine of the ten became members of the first class.[28] Wilburn made a conscious attempt to find Church of Christ faculty for the residential program, but his efforts bore no fruit.[29]

The alpha year (1986–1987) of the residential program was difficult. It was particularly troublesome to find SBM faculty willing to teach at Malibu, and the physical facilities were inadequate for an academic program.[30] In face of this general unpreparedness, the students came "to the point of rebellion" and declared in a petition that they would be unable "to recommend this program to anyone, not to mention our close friends."[31]

The students tended to blame the "central administration" rather than SBM's leadership, and Pepperdine President David Davenport was taken aback by the criticism. Now was not the time, he told Strom, to draw lines between SBM and the university. What was needed was a team approach to solving the problem; Strom, of course, agreed and would work sensitively to "see this one through."[32] The program survived the rocky start and continued to operate into the twentieth-first century as a central piece to SBM's Malibu curriculum. Strom held the position of director through the first year, to be followed by Robert Thomas, the former vice president for administrative affairs at Pepperdine, Jack McManus, and Stanley Mann.

Wilburn's fifth and favorite new program was SBM's most demanding— the master of international business (MIB). Having taught in Heidelberg, done a thesis on international education, and been invited by Baron Edmond de Rothschild to launch a series of annual conferences on international strategic alliances, Wilburn frequently asserted that business was no longer domestic or international, but only global. With faculty committee assistance, in 1989 he inaugurated an MIB that called for one full year of courses in Malibu and a second year in one of two partner business schools in Germany or France. Its distinctive was a strong language emphasis with a lab in Malibu that rivaled the well-known Monterey, California, program that trained CIA and military intelligence operatives.[33]

Looking for a Home

As dean, Wilburn relocated the central offices of SBM twice. Although the scene was pretty well set during Kenton Anderson's deanship, the actual move to "Pepperdine University Plaza" at 3415 Sepulveda Boulevard did not take place until Wilburn became dean. David Murdock, owner of Dole Food Company, Sherwood Country Club, and recipient of an honorary doctorate from Pepperdine University, owned the property. Murdock promised Wilburn that if the university leased his office building, he would make a significant gift to the proposed new facilities for SBM at Malibu. Murdock never made the gift, and five years later when the lease expired, the university did not give second thought to moving.[34]

Eager to demonstrate permanency both to WASC and SBM, university officials purchased an equity position in a more commodious property in Culver City at 400 Corporate Pointe in January 1988. Fifteen years later (December 2003) it moved to the Howard Hughes Center, also with a Sepulveda Boulevard address. Meanwhile, the university also took equity positions in educational centers in Encino, Irvine, and Long Beach (1988).[35]

During his twelve years as dean, Wilburn spent almost every day scanning the social and economic landscape of Southern California and beyond for potential donors to build an SBM campus at Malibu. Even before he began his tenure, he had identified a promontory high above Seaver College where he intended for the university to construct a business building. He calculated it would take $6 million but later realized that Los Angeles County and California Coastal Commission regulations would make it far more expensive.

He was not reluctant to ask for gifts, and he quickly got them from Fred Hartley of the Forest Lawn Corporation, the Keck Foundation, Baron Edmond de Rothschild, and Arnold Beckman. But not until the late 1990s did construction begin and not until 2002 was the building completed. In the meantime, university administrators had diverted to Seaver College some of the money Wilburn had raised, and other gifts depreciated, losing as much as one-half of their purchasing power. Major gifts from Rothschild; John Drescher, who owned a city block in Santa Monica; Luella Ulrich, who gave her Malibu property on a bluff overlooking the ocean; and George Graziadio, banker and builder, allowed the creation of an on-campus presence for SBM.[36]

A Russian Connection

Probably Wilburn's most interesting connection made in behalf of SBM was with Baron Edmond de Rothschild of Paris, Geneva, Zurich, and Rome. Wilburn arranged for Rothschild's son's admission into Seaver College and then promptly asked the Baron to serve as a member of the capital campaign committee for SBM. Rothschild agreed and made major pledges toward Wilburn's envisioned new building.[37]

Rothschild also suggested that the two of them cooperate in hosting an annual conference in Geneva, Switzerland. The baron would invite ten to fifteen influential European business leaders and Wilburn would invite a similar number of senior American business leaders to discuss concerns of mutual interest and economic development. The first such conference, held in 1985, was titled "Building International Strategic Alliances," and included eighty senior executives from fifty companies in nine European nations, Japan, and the United States.[38] Similar conferences occurred on three subsequent occasions, with the help of Price-Waterhouse Company, at Rothschild's ski resort in the French Alps village of Megeve.

These conferences opened a large number of doors for Pepperdine and enhanced the university's profile in Europe as well as America. That profile partly explains Pepperdine's involvement in Russia following the collapse of the Soviet Union in 1989. During a visit to Moscow the following year, Wilburn engaged in informal conversation about free enterprise and the future of the state of Russia. Subsequently, he was asked to organize a committee of American business leaders to consult with Russian businessmen on challenges they expected to face. In time, he was appointed as chairman of the U.S. Committee to Assist Russian Reform and directed to work closely with the Russian Committee on Privatization. Wilburn found his work "inspirational" and "exciting," for he felt he was witnessing "the birth of a nation."[39]

A $2 million grant from the United States Department of State to the Committee to Assist Russian Reform permitted Wilburn to bring 100 general directors of manufacturing entities from Moscow to Los Angeles for a two-week crash-course on international business. SBM faculty taught them how to develop strategic business plans, acquainted them with supply-side economics (through the lectures of Art Laffer, author of the famous Laffer curve), and introduced them to venture capitalists from the Silicon Valley and elsewhere.[40]

Changing of the Guard

Toward the end of Wilburn's deanship, SBM confronted serious financial challenges due to declining enrollment in its fully-employed programs.

Pepperdine compensated by cutting expenses, starting new programs, opening a new center in Long Beach, diversifying marketing, opening programs in the San Francisco area, and reinitiating radio advertising and more aggressive print ads.[41]

There was no stated relationship between the challenges confronting SBM and Wilburn's decision to resign as dean in 1994, but he had felt the burden of the office for several years and longed to return to the classroom. His ambition to settle in as a tenured professor of business, however, was never fully realized: two years into his "retirement," President Davenport asked him to serve as the founding dean of the new School of Public Policy, which he began in mid-1996.

The search for a permanent replacement at SBM ended in 1996 when Otis Baskin, who had an undergraduate degree from Oklahoma Christian University and a PhD from the University of Texas at Austin, accepted the position. Baskin had held teaching and administrative positions at several colleges and universities, had written an acclaimed book on public relations, and was a lifelong member of Churches of Christ.[42]

Baskin saw SBM as an emerging school whose quality was not widely recognized, and he sought to change that by earning AACSB accreditation. With the cooperation of President Davenport, he hired thirty-one PhD-qualified faculty, which increased the number of full-time faculty to seventy-six and raised the percentage of all full-time faculty to sixty. Special efforts were made to recruit better students for the fully employed MBA programs, resulting in a reduction of attrition rates from 50 percent (the national average) to just 7 percent. Baskin and his colleagues also formed strategic alliances with nineteen quality business schools outside the United States and saw GMAT entrance scores for the full-time MBA program in Malibu increase by 120 points.[43]

After four years and a three-volume self-study, the external recognition that Baskin sought for SBM came when AACSB granted accreditation in 2000. Pepperdine's educational centers, a focus on employed students, and active participation in the practice of business had once been viewed as negative features but were now considered positives. Accreditation—along with international recognition of the executive program—set Pepperdine apart from the crowd.

The position was affirmed by a *Business Week Magazine* ranking placing the SBM Executive program number eleven worldwide, number one in teaching ethics, and number four in teaching business strategy. Simultaneously, *U.S. News & World Report* ranked Pepperdine number fourteen in part-time MBA programs and number seventeen in executive programs. To Baskin, all of this external recognition resulted from the perceptible improvement of educational quality.[44]

These developments pleased George L. Graziadio Jr., cofounder of Imperial Bank and a mover and shaker in Southern California's business community. Graziadio was a warm friend of Norvel Young, who introduced him to Baskin in August 1995. Graziadio and Baskin bonded almost immediately. By January of the following year, Graziadio had promised to endow the school with a gift of $15 million, pledged to help raise another $10 million to fund construction of an executive center, and promised to help build a 100-member board of visitors to advocate for the school in Southern California.

In recognition of his contributions, Pepperdine University named the school of business the "Graziadio School of Business and Management" (GSBM) in 1996. Graziadio took satisfaction in the name change and the AACSB accreditation, but he did not live to see the dedication of the complex that would house the "Graziadio School" on the Malibu campus.[45]

But, at his passing, he was well aware that his patronage assured the perpetuation of a school that sought to educate the whole person within the context of the "founding values of the university," served business practitioners and their employers through instructional excellence and a global orientation, enrolled some 2,600 students, and had graduated nearly 25,000 alumni. All of that must have been gratifying to George Graziadio.[46]

CHAPTER 22

MAKING OF THE SCHOOL OF EDUCATION, 1971–1981

From the founding of George Pepperdine College, both education and psychology were major fields of study. They were organized into a single department until they were separated in 1951. Lonnie T. Vanderveer, who did his graduate work in Oklahoma and Texas, chaired the department of education until 1957 when he resigned from the faculty to protest the dismissal of E. V. Pullias as dean of the college. Olaf Tegner replaced him as chair of the department.

Tegner was a fixture at George Pepperdine College from the moment he set foot on the campus as a freshman in 1939 until his death in 2005. After graduating from GPC, Tegner took a commission in the U.S. Navy, but he returned to campus in 1944 soon after receiving a medical discharge. Tegner returned to help edit *On The Beam* for Pepperdine servicemen and to found the Pepperdine alumni association, serving as director and president for the next twenty years. He also worked as graduate manager of athletics, coordinated all the school's publications, and managed Normandie Village. Simultaneously, he earned a master's degree in history at Pepperdine and one in education at USC. By 1956, he had completed his doctorate in educational administration at USC and was teaching in the education department at GPC.

President Norvel Young asked Tegner to take leadership of the department after Vanderveer resigned in 1957. Tegner served as chair until January 1, 1971, when Young upgraded the department into a full-fledged School of Education (SOE) and named Tegner as the dean.[1] The reorganization was designed to lend credence to Pepperdine's declaration that it was more than just a college of departments and was instead a real university with colleges and multiple campuses.

Much of the success of Pepperdine's educational programming, before and after SOE was organized, was due to Oly Tegner's leadership. According to a 2006 doctoral study by Olivia Yates, he was a man of humility, integrity, sincerity, respectfulness, and an active moral compass. He was personable, optimistic, witty, and sensitive to the needs of others. Bill Banowsky said Tegner was "always building, and always supporting." In short, concluded Yates, the dean had all the attributes of a genuine "servant leader."[2] Norvel Young considered Tegner "a Renaissance man . . . the epitome of the kind of product Pepperdine sought to produce."[3]

Shared Values—Not Definitions

Tegner's personal qualities were very much rooted in his upbringing as the child of Salvation Army ministers. During the Great Depression, he helped his mother prepare daily meals for 150 people, an experience that made him deeply sensitive to the needs of others. He easily aligned himself with George Pepperdine's Christian vision for his college. But not entirely.[4]

Tegner was never quite comfortable with the school's relationship with Churches of Christ. His ambivalence was not directed toward the Churches of Christ in particular, but against any religious denomination. In describing Pepperdine University in SOE publications, he noted only that the university was founded upon "the Christian Ethic."[5]

When it came to hiring faculty, Tegner cared very little about where— or whether—candidates went to church. By 1980, 64 percent of his school's faculty identified their church membership either as "Undeclared" or "Protestant." During most of Tegner's tenure as dean, there was never more than a single member of Churches of Christ on his faculty. The dean did work diligently to appoint those who had "shared values," but those "values" were so poorly defined that at least one longtime SOE faculty member announced that Pepperdine was not a Christian university, at least outside of Malibu.[6]

The Pepperdine administration permitted Tegner to construct a thriving School of Education connected to the rest of the university by ambiguous "shared values," as it had also done with the School of Business and Management. Indeed, after 1968, it was widely acknowledged that George Pepperdine's dream of Christian liberal arts education would live on in Malibu but the application would be less obvious elsewhere in the institution. Beyond Malibu, the criterion of success would be revenue, then academic excellence, and then mission. Vice President Howard White rued the dimming of Christian mission and relationship with Churches of Christ, but he was willing to make the sacrifice if the professional/graduate schools generated revenue to support the campus in Malibu.

Tegner and Young had been friends since 1957, and Tegner had supported Young's appointment to the presidency. Thereafter, the two became as close as brothers. They and their families traveled the world together, conspired to improve Pepperdine together, spurred each other on to good works, and shared their faith. On one trip to Israel, Young baptized Tegner in the Jordan River. When it came to building a SOE, therefore, few second guessed the dean, assuming whatever he did had the blessing of Norvel Young.[7]

Delivering Education, Credentials

According to its *Faculty Handbook*, the new, free-standing SOE had four major objectives: preparing educators, fostering research, providing expertise, and improving humankind.[8] It offered bachelor's and master's degrees as well as a broad range of teaching credentials, which after 1971 were offered at various off-campus sites. Tegner also wanted SOE programs on the new Malibu campus, not because he wished to create an education empire, he said, but to provide bachelor programs that would feed the graduate programs on the Los Angeles campus.

The liberal arts faculty at Malibu did not agree and believed Tegner's insistence on oversight was an effort to subvert the essence of the new campus with "shared" rather than Christian values. Fearful of outright civil war between faculties, in 1978 President Banowsky put an end to the bickering by assigning it a new name, "Graduate School of Education" (GSE), and limiting its programming to professional and graduate education. Seaver College would offer the undergraduate and credentialing programs in teacher education. Simultaneously, Banowsky abolished the independent graduate school of which Frank Pack had served as dean for several years.[9]

Given changes in state credentialing requirements, the focus on graduate education made sense. According to a new state law passed in 1970, prospective teachers had to major in the subject matter in which they expected to teach; consequently, the professional education courses taught on the Los Angeles campus for undergraduate majors had become largely superfluous. The student body there dwindled, and the university reallocated its resources to Malibu.

Stanford University had modeled a way to deal with this problem, creating a program that took degreed students from any accredited school, gave them required teacher education subjects, arranged student teacher experiences, and facilitated the credentialing process. Its program was fully accredited by both the National Council for Accrediting Teacher Education (NCATE) and WASC. California embraced the Stanford model in Ryan Act of 1970;

thereafter, prospective teachers in California had to complete a fifth-year program that resulted in a master's degree and a teaching credential.

Senior staff at the California Commission on Teacher Preparation and Licensing (CTC) recommended that Pepperdine create a stand-alone graduate school of education offering MA degrees in education plus a teacher credential packaged as a fifth-year program. Tegner's eagerness to comply accounted for the creation of the independent SOE in 1971 and the GSE in 1978.[10]

Of course, the graduate program in education had been a principal focus of the university since 1956 when the department of education offered its first master's degree.[11] The MA in education was directed toward prospective teachers who wished to meet requirements for a credential or for educational workers who wished to qualify for a master's degree only. By 1973, SOE also offered MS degrees in school management and administration and in school business management.[12]

Subsequently, it offered an MS in education and an MA in urban school teaching. Tegner and his colleagues delivered the latter over three trimesters at inner-city school buildings with classes offered in the evenings and on weekends—one of the first to offer programs in that way. It was not uncommon for SOE to have six master's programs going simultaneously.[13]

Pepperdine's First Doctoral Degrees

SOE's most notable milestone in graduate education was the approval and implementation of Pepperdine's first doctoral degree, the EdD—doctor of education—in institutional management in fall 1976. Pepperdine's version of the degree emphasized human relations, administrative theory and organizational development, research methods and technology, and values and educational philosophy. It was a six-trimester program with three courses per trimester and required a dissertation but not languages. A practitioner rather than a research degree, the program was designed to accommodate forty students at a time.[14]

When the first class of students got to the dissertation stage in 1978, faculty members proved reluctant to serve on dissertation and comprehensive exam committees, as directing dissertations and reading doctoral exams was a time-consuming commitment on top of full teaching schedules. In-service training for the entire faculty, additional stipends, and course-release time solved most of these problems. GSE graduated its first EdD class in 1979, with degrees going to four students.[15]

By then it also offered a second EdD program in community college administration, structured in large part by Irving R. Melbo, former dean of education at USC and visiting distinguished professor in education at Pepperdine. The first in the United States with an emphasis upon community college administration, the new degree launched under the direction of Lamar Johnson in 1977.[16]

Tegner and his education colleagues saw the doctoral degrees as evidence of institutional excellence.[17] They also celebrated being selected to host a chapter of Phi Delta Kappa, the premiere professional association for educators, in 1977.[18] An even more significant landmark was establishment of the Julian A. Virtue Chair, named in honor of the chairman of the board of Virco Manufacturing Company. The purpose of the chair was to "disseminate knowledge and understanding of the American economic system throughout the structure of the country's public and private educational system." Melbo held the chair initially, while Richard E. Ferraro, a member of the Los Angeles Board of Education, directed the teacher workshops and seminars associated with it.[19]

A Chair from the Shah

Another indicator of excellence, at least in the eyes of Norvel Young, was creation of the Her Royal Majesty, Empress Farah of Iran Chair in education established by the Shah of Iran in 1978. Aware that the Shah had used Iranian petrodollars to inaugurate relationships with several United States universities, Young and his Pepperdine colleagues in 1977 submitted an audacious proposal to the Iranian consulate in San Francisco and the embassy in Washington, D.C. The proposal envisioned a $1 million gift from the Iranian government to endow a chair in international education at SOE and eight scholarships for Iranian graduate students.

Pepperdine would honor the royal family by naming the chair after Her Majesty and continue to serve the more than forty Iranian students already enrolled at Pepperdine University. University officials asked for the privilege of presenting the proposal to the Shah himself and awarding him with an honorary doctorate of law. To everyone's relief—and surprise—the Iranian Embassy agreed to arrange the presentations.[20]

In April, Young, Banowsky, Tegner, Richard Seaver and their wives, flew to Tehran. In appropriate ceremonies, they solemnly bestowed the doctorate upon his Royal Majesty, the Shah of Iran. Simultaneously, the delegation brought up the matter of a $1 million endowed chair and scholarships. The Shah accepted the proposal on the spot, with details to be worked out over the next several weeks through the offices of the National Iranian Oil Company.[21]

Chancellor Young and his colleagues immediately announced the establishment of the chair and appointed Melbo, then the occupant of the Julian A. Virtue chair, to hold the new position. But no check came. Accordingly, Young scheduled a trip to Tehran to deliver a Doctorate of Humane Letters to Empress Farah on October 10, 1977. In private ceremonies, Young praised Her Royal Majesty for being "instrumental in increasing opportunities for women" to participate fully "in the life of [her] nation."[22] He also brought up the matter of the $1 million endowment, whereupon the Shah said he would take care of the matter immediately.[23]

But still the money did not come, and perhaps for good reason. Young had barely left Tehran when demonstrations in opposition to the royal regime broke out. As resistance increased over the next year, most Americans would have presumed promises by the Shah for a cash outlay were null and void. But not Chancellor Young. In September, he wrote the Iranian ambassador to refresh his memory and remind him that the chair had been created, announced, and filled, and that Pepperdine had admitted more than 100 Iranian students to its various programs in Los Angeles.

The letter was effective. On September 12, 1978, Ambassador Ardeshir Zahedi wrote a $1 million check to Pepperdine University. Four months later, the Shah and his family fled into exile.[24]

In July 1980, the Shah died. Many around the world did not mourn his passing, but the Pepperdine University leadership did. Young wrote to his widow, then in Cairo, extolling His Majesty's "wise leadership and his many humanitarian advances" and predicting he would be remembered "as an eminent world leader."[25] The words were a bit hyperbolic, written while Iranian revolutionaries held fifty-two Americans as hostages. But for Young they were heartfelt; he did not forget friends who gave Pepperdine University $1 million.

GSE announced the establishment of a chair in the name of Her Royal Majesty, Empress Farah of Iran in its 1978–1979 bulletin.[26] The following year, the bulletin noted that Dr. B. Lamar Johnson, rather than Melbo, had been named to occupy the chair. Emeritus professor of education at UCLA, Johnson was known as the father of the California community college system, for extensive work with the U.S. Agency for International Development (USAID), and for helping GSE implement its doctorate in community college administration.[27] Reference to the chair was dropped from the 1980–1981 bulletin," but the 1981–1982 bulletin carried language identical to that in the 1979 bulletin.[28]

The catalog for the 1982–1983 academic year spoke of "The Farah Diba Pahlavi Chair in Education," but the next mention was as a scholarship fund in the 1984–1985 Graduate School of Education and Psychology catalog.[29] No allusion to "The Farah Diba Pahlavi Chair in Education," either as an academic position or as a scholarship fund, appeared in future catalogs. Chancellor Young probably never forgot the Shah of Iran, but Pepperdine University seems to have done so.

Off-Campus Offerings

As noted in previous chapters, Pepperdine began delivering off-campus education courses at multiple locations early in Young's presidency, and the dramatic growth of those programs eventually led to the creation of the School for Continuing Education (SCE). SCE's work, as noted previously, was something of an embarrassment to Dean Tegner, who apparently believed the SCE program delivered too much academic credit for too little work.[30]

At the same time, Tegner was quite open to off-campus programs that offered standard academic fare, were taught by regular faculty members, and resulted in recognized degrees, specifically an MA in education. Forming a Center for Professional Development (CPD) within the confines of his own school, Tegner and his colleagues offered just such a program in Hawaii, first for teachers in Hilo, and then to U.S. Army personnel on Oahu beginning in January 1971. The army program was an immediate success, enrolling thirty in its first class and 471 in one class two years later, and netting $25,000 in profit the first year.[31] Such a positive response encouraged SOE to replicate its Hawaiian program at military bases at El Toro, Yuma, San Diego, and Subic Bay in the Philippines. Subsequently it would open "residential" centers at Irvine and Sherman Oaks. What made CPD programs distinctive from those of SCE, Tegner believed, was that they used regular faculty and delivered a curriculum at the convenience of fully-employed students.[32]

Tegner may have been comfortable with SOE's off-campus programs, but WASC was not. Executive Director Kay Andersen was suspicious of any external degree program.[33] In addition, the 1974 WASC reaccrediting team was especially critical of the close relationship between SOE and the Los Angeles Unified School District (LAUSD), which maintained liaisons on the Pepperdine campus. The team's report characterized Pepperdine as little more than "a small Los Angeles City Teacher's College" and virtually accused it of selling degrees.

SOE administrators were quite sure that the WASC visitors had in their report "neither exercised objectivity nor pursued factual data."[34] Executive Vice President White was outraged by the "grossly inaccurate and insulting statements" about SOE, which he considered as offering one of the university's "strongest programs." He attributed the "break-down of objectivity" to the prejudicial remarks of one member of the visiting team who was an administrator at a nearby university. White's vigorous defense did not clear the record, but it did encourage the senior commission to overlook the report and grant Pepperdine accreditation for another five years.[35]

Twenty-four months later, a three-person visiting team from WASC found SOE a "very alive place" and "an on-the-move group" that demonstrated "a healthy and vigorous interest in the inner city community of Los Angeles." It did have reservations about the EdD degree, but the concerns were ultimately addressed and the degree was approved.[36]

Meanwhile, Dean Tegner remained highly suspicious of the work of Pepperdine's School for Continuing Education. In 1976, when a stroke incapacitated its dean, Robert Gordon, leaving the school without leadership, Tegner proposed that SCE merge with his school's Center for Professional Development.[37]

Given the specter of NCATE accreditation and WASC's continuing reservations about off-campus programs, especially those designed for the military,[38] Pepperdine's central administration accepted Tegner's proposal. The results were dramatic, but not for the better. The merging of SEC with CPD simply did not generate "the action" anticipated. Headcounts for SOE as a whole plummeted from 1,500 in fall 1976 to 540 in fall 1979.[39]

During Dean Tegner's leadership, which stretched from 1971 to 1983, the Graduate School of Education enjoyed growth in the number of faculty (by 28 percent) and number of students served (by 11 percent), but not in the number of credit units sold. Those declined by 27 percent, thanks to higher expectations of off-campus academic programs—military and domestic—and changing credential requirements.[40]

As a percentage of the university's general budget, the impact of SOE was modest. Just how much revenue each of the schools generated was closely held information, but judging from the fact that SOE matriculated some 12.5 percent of the total student body in 1983, it probably generated no more than 10 percent of total revenue. Its contribution to overhead expenses was virtually nil.[41] SOE spent 100 percent of its revenue, while Seaver College returned nearly 38 percent, the law school some 37 percent, and SBM almost 47 percent. In short, SOE throughout most of the 1970s and 1980s was essentially a service operation to the teaching profession in Southern California.

CHAPTER 23

THE GRADUATE SCHOOL OF EDUCATION AND PSYCHOLOGY, 1981–2000

One of Olaf Tegner's notable achievements as dean was to facilitate the 1981 integration of the Department of Psychology into the Graduate School of Education to form the Graduate School of Education and Psychology (GSEP). That move, in a way, was an echo of the original organization at George Pepperdine College, where education and psychology had been joined in a single department until 1951.

That year, Dean E. V. Pullias, a psychologist, championed a separation of the two programs in part to facilitate a master's degree in general psychology, GPC's second.[1] Everett L. Shostrom, subsequently an acclaimed author, film producer, and researcher, chaired the department at that time, heading a faculty of six.[2] Shostrom introduced a master's degree that de-emphasized empirical, data-driven studies in favor of applied learning, perhaps the first such degree program in the United States.[3] In 1954, he resigned from the faculty and was eventually replaced by Robert E. Holland, a mild-mannered gentleman and Churches of Christ member, whose service to the university extended from 1957 to 1977.[4]

Growth of the Psychology Program

Holland envisioned a larger role for Pepperdine's department of psychology, and in 1960 proposed the inauguration of a clinical doctorate. President Young concluded the proposal was premature, but he did support new master's degrees. By 1965, psychology offered four graduate degrees. In both graduate and undergraduate programs, Holland promoted a humanistic emphasis and believed that Pepperdine's philosophy of training and mental health delivery services had developed "through a Christian commitment and environment." Thus, the school emphasized training practitioners as "whole person[s]" who were "well-integrated . . . up and above their training."[5]

In 1973, one year after Pepperdine opened the Malibu campus, Holland again floated the idea of offering a doctorate, this time a PhD in psychology. Although most undergraduate majors had moved to Malibu, his department remained one of the strongest on the Los Angeles campus, primarily because of its programs in educational psychology.

With Pepperdine in an expansive mode, the central administration welcomed the prospect of a doctorate. WASC was also encouraging but stipulated a doctoral degree had to be offered in a separate school of psychology. Jerry Hudson, provost of the Malibu campus, objected to such a move because he did not want an additional school claiming sovereignty over undergraduates at Malibu. Consequently, Holland's proposal languished.[6]

He renewed the idea for a clinical doctorate in psychology two years later, and the University Academic Council (UAC) tentatively approved his proposal, which included the establishment of a free-standing school of psychology.[7] Vice President White, however, was less enthusiastic, believing such a school would have little more than paper prestige.[8] Deans Norman Hughes at Malibu and Grover Goyne at Los Angeles also objected, fearing diminishment of the psychology major on their campuses.[9] Their concerns plus a serious limitation of resources caused the central administration to again table Holland's proposal.[10]

After two decades of leadership, and wearied by the doctoral wars, Robert Holland retired as chair of the psychology division in 1977. He left a legacy of a growing and respected program that served 500 students in several Southern California locations.[11] Holland's replacement, Dianna L. Solar, emphasized professional programs in marriage, family, and child counseling, coordinating them with new master's degrees in child clinical psychology and ministerial counseling psychology.[12] In 1980, Solar resigned and was replaced by L. James Hedstrom, who had been a Pepperdine undergraduate and the first to enroll in the university's master's degree program.

The Birth of GSEP

Hedstrom launched his term as chair just as Pepperdine administrators implemented plans to close the Los Angeles campus. Consolidation and relocation were in order, and no one in the university was better at consolidating than Dean Tegner. He may not have proposed but he certainly did not resist the administrative suggestion that the education program accept the entire psychology program as an equal partner in a new Graduate School of Education and Psychology. Herbert Luft suggested the GSEP acronym.

Simultaneously, the new school, along with the School of Business and Management, would leave Pepperdine's original campus for more suitable quarters elsewhere in West Los Angeles. There was some trepidation about the merger on the part of the full-time psychology faculty, who were outnumbered seven to one by the education faculty. But the new school was forged in 1981, although not officially launched until March the next year.

Psychology brought to GSEP some 350 students enrolled in two major programs: a traditional master's program and a series of block courses designed to upgrade professional credentials. Tegner served as founding dean; Hedstrom served as associate dean for psychology, and Jerry Novotney served as associate dean for education. The central administration relocated GSEP's offices, classrooms, and clinics to multistory facilities on Sepulveda Boulevard in 1982.[13]

The psychology students bolstered the financial position of the school, but general revenues from tuition continued to fall well below expectations. Indeed, the school was operating at a $1.2 million deficit if the cost of central services were included. This compared with a $549,000 profit for SBM and a $2.4 million profit for Seaver College. Administrators attributed the poor performance to GSEP's location on the Los Angeles campus and factors that restricted the demand for public school teachers.[14]

Tegner Surrenders Reins

Pepperdine's leadership pushed to address issues that would improve the school's reputation and make it more competitive. WASC visitors had identified some problems, including limited library resources, lack of rigor in admissions and student expectation, and poor graduation rates. Tegner was concerned about signs of grade inflation; President White was embarrassed by a low pass rate on the basic test required of all prospective teachers; and Vice President Luft saw an anemic commitment to the Christian mission of the university.[15]

In the interest of improving the school, Tegner came to demand more of his faculty colleagues, losing patience with those who missed faculty meetings, failed to fulfill committee responsibilities, and treated doctoral candidates and their programs too casually. He insisted that his colleagues keep office hours and meet all classes as scheduled, and his demands were not always appreciated.[16] If certain members of the GSEP faculty had issues with Dean Tegner, so too did some members of the central administration. The dean was a "most valuable man," President Banowsky had written, "but he would be worth even more if he always worked within the system."[17]

Tegner retired as dean in 1983 at the age of sixty-five. He had presided tirelessly over the development of a well-respected school, first of education and then education and psychology, but he was weary of the second-guessing of his leadership. However, he continued to serve his alma mater as vice president for educational relations until his death in 2005.[18]

Academic Vice President William Phillips appointed William B. Adrian as the second dean of GSEP in 1983. A native Californian and a lifelong member of Churches of Christ, Adrian served only two years as GSEP dean, being chosen to serve as executive vice president of the university in 1985. That position soon morphed into the role of university provost, a post that he held until 1993.[19]

At Long Last, a Doctorate Program in Psychology

In his short stint at as dean of GSEP, Adrian helped implement the psychology faculty's decades-long desire to award a doctorate. After soliciting advice from Dr. Paul Clement, a Pepperdine alumnus and training director of the Fuller Clinical Psychology Program, Adrian and Hedstrom proposed to offer the PsyD, or doctor of psychology, which was a professional or clinical degree, rather than the PhD, an academic or research degree. Clement also envisioned a counseling clinic with a Christian philosophy.

In due time, the university's academic councils and central administration approved the program, as did WASC. GSEP announced the PsyD program, recruited students, and admitted its first class of twenty-five (selected from eighty applicants) in September 1986. Steve Brown served as the program's first director. Two years later, a counseling clinic was founded, making its services available on an ability-to-pay basis. Robert deMayo was the first full-time director.

Nineteen students from the first class of PsyDs completed all requirements and graduated in 1990, passing the state written exam at a 78 percent rate, as compared to a 52 percent average. That year, the American Psychological Association accredited Pepperdine's PsyD program, and then reaccredited it in 1993 and again in 1998.[20]

Growth of a School

From 1983 until 2000, enrollments at GSEP more than doubled. In fall 1982, the headcount totaled 793; the skilled marketing of James Woodrow helped it increase to 1,573 by fall 1993, and it remained at that level through the rest of the decade. In the early years, more than 60 percent of those students were in psychology programs; the percentages reversed by 2000. The number of graduates grew annually from 500 to 800 through 1993, and then slipped back to just over 500 by 2000.

Due to a doubling of tuition rates between 1985 and 1999, revenues grew as well, from $2.5 million in FY 84 to $16.4 million in FY 99, and GSEP's expenses to revenue ratio increasingly benefited the university.[21] By the end of the century, GSEP was making a substantial contribution to the university's overhead.

The number of full-time faculty increased from twenty-two in 1985 to fifty-four in 1999, of which 60 to 75 percent were tenured. During the same period, part-time faculty increased from thirty-nine to ninety-nine, with some 20 percent listed as racial or ethnic minorities. Judging from a faculty survey conducted in October 1999, the GSEP faculty's interests were no different than those at a state-supported school, and little concern was expressed about the university's Christian mission.[22]

Nick Stinnett served as dean of GSEP between 1985 and 1987. On his watch, enrollments in the division of education increased by 30 percent, due in part to new linkages with Southern California school districts. Scholarly publications increased; the education division was certified to offer a leading professional credential; and the school hosted an international conference on family strength featuring Art Linkletter, Pat Boone, Joyce Brothers, and John Robinson.[23]

Replacing Stinnett was Nancy Magnusson, the first woman appointed to lead one of Pepperdine's core schools. She held that position until 1999, when she resigned to accept the directorship of Pepperdine's London Program. Subsequently, she returned to the university as senior vice president for planning, information, and technology.

During Magnusson's administration, GSEP strengthened and increased almost all of its programs and faculty. Over the years, WASC had been critical of GSEP's EdD in institutional management program because of the school's virtual open admission policy, high dropout rate, questionable comprehensive exams, and subpar dissertations. Magnusson's administration made improvements in these areas and increased graduation rates, especially among minority students. During Magnusson's term, African Americans earned nearly 15 percent of the doctorates awarded, one of the strongest records in the nation.[24]

Describing a Vision

As part of the overall strategic planning process initiated by the Davenport administration, and thanks to the leadership of Dean Magnusson, GSEP wrote perhaps its most comprehensive strategic plan in 1995. According to the plan, the vision of GSEP was to

> create a vital academic community composed of adult students, fulltime and adjunct faculties, staff, alumni and community representatives, in which knowledge and critical thinking, professional

competence, compassion for the individual and commitment to the community [were] pursued eagerly and valued highly.

The document identified GSEP's distinctives as its spiritual mission, its teaching strategies that combined adult learning and professional training, its community involvement through professional preparation, and its use of technology as a tool for learning.[25]

For the first time in its strategic planning, GSEP tried to come to grips with the Christian mission of Pepperdine University and the institution's historic ties with Churches of Christ. At the school, the plan stipulated, students learned ethical decision-making by combining the values of the university with their profession's codes of ethics. The challenge to the faculty was "to hold in two hands the ties to the Churches of Christ and its values, and a focus on the customer/student possessing a wide array of religious and spiritual interests." Such a challenge, the plan asserted, produced "tension and ambiguity that, when contained appropriately, yield openness, healthy diversity, and meaningful spiritual activity."[26]

Nancy Magnusson joined Seaver College as an assistant professor of psychology in 1979. She subsequently served as associate dean of Seaver College and then as dean of the Graduate School of Education and Psychology, the first woman appointed to lead one of Pepperdine's core schools. During her term, the school strengthened its programs and graduation rates and created a comprehensive strategic plan.

Although multifaceted in its approach to the university's Christian mission, the strategic plan asserted, "GSEP's history and culture reflect the values of Christianity—care-giving, respect for the individual and service to the community." The historical relationship with Churches of Christ, it insisted, was evident in the school's current demography, as nearly 2.5 percent of the students, 15 percent of tenure-track faculty, and 19 percent of the staff were members of the church. The faculty and staff included elders, deacons, and a board member of the Associated Women of Pepperdine (AWP).[27]

GSEP's relationship with Churches of Christ, the plan argued, was also evident in the establishment of the M. Norvel and Helen Young Chair in Family Life, approved in 1985 and filled by Professor of Psychology Dennis Lowe six years later. It was the dream of the Youngs that the chair would strengthen families in Churches of Christ.[28] To implement that dream, Lowe, with the strong support of Dean Magnusson and President Davenport, established the Center for the Family in 1996. Under Lowe's direction and Sara Jackson's administration, the center offered practical seminars for marriage enrichment and parenting and training for churches, professionals, and lay leaders.[29]

Magnusson resigned as dean after twelve years of service. She left behind colleagues and friends who held her in high regard. Jack McManus, who had served for a time as associate dean and had made GSEP a national leader in educational technology, considered her "the best leader I . . . ever had."[30] McManus served as interim dean of GSEP from 1999 to 2001, making way for Margaret Weber in 2001.

McManus greatly influenced the content and structure of GSEP's revised strategic plan submitted to WASC in 2000. Notably, the plan envisioned a more public link with the mission of the university, a more integral role for classroom technology, and a professional school that was more mission-driven and market-sensitive.[31] It was up to Weber to implement the plan, but at the dawn of the twenty-first century, the Graduate School of Education and Psychology was clearly more comfortable with George Pepperdine's vision of Christian education than it had been at any time in its history.

CHAPTER 24

THE SCHOOL OF LAW, 1969–1980

As Pepperdine University expanded to include a School of Continuing Education, a School of Business and Management, a Graduate School of Education and Psychology, and international programs, it also added a School of Law when it took over a struggling young program in Orange County.

In 1964, a group of lawyers and civic-minded entrepreneurs had organized the Orange University, College of Law in Santa Ana, Orange County, California. Offering a four-year curriculum of evening classes only, the school had attracted 238 students by 1968. The school, however, struggled financially, lacked full-time leadership, and was unaccredited. College trustees believed the future of the law school depended upon establishing a relationship with a recognized institution of higher education.

Ed DiLoreto, a California industrialist who served as chair of the governing board, was a longtime friend of Pepperdine College and admirer of its National Citizenship Program. He proposed to Vice President Bill Teague that the college assume management of the College of Law. There would be no cost to Pepperdine unless it wanted to purchase the facility being used for classrooms.[1]

Pepperdine College trustees were divided over the wisdom of the move, although Teague, then between campaigns for the U.S. Congress in Orange County, strongly supported the idea. He believed adding such a school would give the college a strong presence in Orange County, an increasingly important suburb of Los Angeles as well as a bastion of conservative politics. Physical quarters for the school could provide space for some of the Pepperdine's continuing education classes, a School of Law would be additional justification for university status, and the acquisition would enable the college to be a "pioneer" in Christian education in the legal field. Trustee Helen Pepperdine, however, was quite positive that "Christian" and "law school" were contradictory concepts. Moreover, she did not want the college founded by her husband to become so big that it would lose its Christian identity.[2]

The Pepperdine College administration and the majority of trustees decided that the positives outweighed the negatives and finalized the acquisition of the school on May 6, 1969. Pepperdine agreed to accept responsibility for the school, seek accreditation, and keep it in Orange County in perpetuity.[3] The sitting dean, the Honorable Vincent S. Dalsimer, agreed to continue in his position for at least another year, and the school's library, furniture, and fixtures were moved into new quarters in Santa Ana.[4] That fall, the first trimester under Pepperdine management, 237 students registered for the evening classes.[5]

Looking for Leaders

Meanwhile, President Young was searching for a permanent leadership team. He tried to interest John Allen Chalk, a noted Church of Christ minister and televangelist in Abilene to serve as the chief external officer and fund-raiser. Chalk recommended Ronald Phillips, an Abilene Christian College graduate with a law degree from the University of Texas, to be dean. Chalk and Phillips came together for an on-campus interview in April 1970, and Young offered them permanent positions on the spot. Chalk eventually declined the offer, but Phillips accepted, becoming dean as of fall trimester 1970. He would serve in that capacity for twenty-eight years and be a driving force in shaping the School of Law into a nationally recognized institution.[6]

As the Young administration was selecting leadership for the new law school, it also welcomed visits from examiners of the California State Bar Association, which granted the school a two-year provisional state bar accreditation as of July 1, 1970, making the Pepperdine College School of Law (SOL) the only accredited legal education program in Orange County.[7] It boldly opened a full-time day program that offered students a chance to earn the juris doctor (JD) in three years. In fall 1970, that program attracted thirty-four students; 219 continued in the night school program.[8]

President Young formally inaugurated Ron Phillips as dean before an audience of 500 at the Disneyland Hotel on November 2, 1970. The occasion called for only brief comments of acceptance and a pledge to develop "a superior quality law school, where students can learn in a Christian environment" from the new dean. He then stepped aside for an address by Richard Kleindienst, then deputy attorney general of the United States, who delivered stimulating remarks titled "The Attack Against Crime—A Program for the Seventies."[9] It was an impressive event, the first in a long sequence of law school banquets that would bring U.S. Supreme Court judges, noted lawyers, and eminent commentators to speak to Pepperdine students, faculty, and friends.

Under Phillips's steady hand, the law school seeds took root and grew. For the 1971–1972 first-year class, 452 students applied but only 338 were accepted, including 120 full-time students. Phillips added five full-time professors: Wadieh H. Shibley, Judge E. Guirado, Charles Nelson, James McGoldrick, and General Duane L. Faw. Moreover, the library grew from 4,000 to 21,000 volumes by 1972, although 60,000 were needed to meet American Bar Association (ABA) accreditation standards.[10] Despite continued concerns about the limited number of qualified applicants and the minimal size of the law school library, the ABA in August 1972 granted provisional approval, subject to annual re-inspections for up to five years, during which time full approval had to be achieved.[11]

ABA approval was immediately reflected in increased enrollments. In 1973–1974, matriculation in both the evening and day divisions increased by 40 percent. Dean Phillips did not want to enroll more than 600 students for fear of jeopardizing final ABA approval, noting that only eight ABA-approved schools enrolled more than 600. University administrators, however, were too worried about the school's financial challenges to consider limiting enrollment, and in 1975–1976, Pepperdine's law school enrolled 664 students. Not surprisingly, the undergraduate grade point averages and Law School Aptitude Test (LSAT) scores remained low, as did the bar pass rate.[12]

Serious Commitment to Christian Mission

Pepperdine's SOL took seriously its announced commitment to create a Christian climate in which students could complete their legal studies. Dean Phillips, for example, owned the Christian mission publicly in speeches and printed materials. "The philosophy of the School," one of his documents declared, "is to train men and women for the practice of law . . . through a program of academic excellence in a Christian environment." The standards of conduct in such an environment were "commensurate with the Judeo-Christian faith."[13]

More subtle was his declaration that the school believed the practice of law was a "social art" that carried with it a "social trust." Hence, legal skills could best be taught in an environment that also taught "moral responsibilities." Pepperdine was not a religious institution, Phillips said, but its policies began by recognizing there is "a higher order of Being than man himself."[14]

Phillips also consciously tried to hire faculty willing to contribute to a learning environment of academic excellence and Christian values. In the spirit of George Pepperdine's own vision for his college, Phillips went to great lengths to find excellent faculty—and students—who were also members of Churches of Christ.[15]

Making the Malibu Leap

By August 1973, the law school had outgrown its Santa Ana accommodations and moved to a commercial building in Anaheim. Known fondly as the Pepperdome, the three-story campus included a swimming pool, two roof-top tennis courts and a spacious cafeteria. Some detractors called it the "Mickey Mouse law school," partly because the Matterhorn ride at Disneyland was visible from the building.[16] These quarters were only temporary, however, and Pepperdine was actively exploring options for building a campus in Orange County.[17]

Phillips and his colleagues strongly supported keeping the law school in Santa Ana because: (1) Pepperdine had made a commitment to keep the school in Orange County; (2) it was the only ABA-approved school in the region; (3) the

A Texan with degrees from Abilene Christian and the University of Texas School of Law, Ronald E. Phillips became the first full-time dean of the Pepperdine School of Law in 1970. He served in that capacity until 1997. During his administration, the law school grew from a night school with part-time students in Orange County to a fully accredited and highly respected institution on the Malibu campus.

county provided a pool of well-qualified students; (4) housing and abundant clinical opportunities were available for students; and (5) Pepperdine had a virtual monopoly in legal education in Orange County.[18]

However, in April 1975, Phillips told Pepperdine trustees that his position had changed. He now believed it would be better to move SOL to Malibu because: (1) the ABA would not accredit the law school until it had a permanent location; (2) there had been no success in finding an appropriate piece of land in Orange County or a donor to help underwrite construction; (3) the ABA preferred the law school to be located near other components of the university, especially the liberal arts undergraduate school; (4) legal educators believed a law school could not be truly first-rate unless it was on a university campus; and (5) Pepperdine fund-raisers believed they could more effectively raise funds for the law school if it were presented as part of the Malibu campus.[19]

Moreover, Phillips argued, the educational environment had changed substantially in the past six years, for both Orange County and Pepperdine. The need now was for a "prestige" law school, and the school was most likely to have the greatest long-range impact in Malibu. Of course, it also helped that Odell McConnell had offered a gift of $1 million toward a new building if the law school moved to Malibu, a million dollars that subsequently turned into two million.[20]

Phillips and his colleagues were well aware that the 1969 agreement committed Pepperdine to operate a school in Orange County in perpetuity. The college board of trustees, however, read that provision to mean a night school— and only so long as there was a demand. Several signers of the agreement for Orange Law School agreed with that interpretation. Therefore, on April 19, 1975, the day before the formal dedication of Seaver College, Pepperdine trustees adopted a resolution mandating the relocation of the SOL to Malibu by fall 1977. The night school at Orange County would continue through 1978–1979, or until enrolled evening students had an opportunity to complete their degrees.[21]

Executive Vice President Howard White initially had serious reservations about moving the law school to Malibu. A flourishing law school there, he said, would always have a large proportion of students who did not "share our commitment to close relations with the Churches of Christ" and would likely dilute "the spiritual atmosphere we wish to maintain in Malibu."[22]

But Phillips and his faculty colleagues did not believe the law school would be a corrosive influence on Pepperdine's Christian environment or mission and took pains to demonstrate it. And according to American Association of Law Schools visitors, they did so successfully. In 1978, the visiting team noted that Pepperdine SOL had "a long tradition of educating its students to be sensitive to high human values, and [that] its entire academic program approache[d] value questions head-on without embarrassment and in a fashion which the students find to be most helpful to them." The team found the "sense of honor and maturity" among Pepperdine students "extraordinary" and believed that the school was to be "commended for cultivating these fine attributes."[23]

University officials broke ground for the Odell McConnell Law Center on the Malibu campus on May 22, 1976, during the law school's spring graduation, moved from Orange County to Malibu for the occasion. U.S. Supreme Court Justice Harry Blackmun was the primary speaker, and he and McConnell were both given honorary degrees.[24]

It took two years and $12 million to construct Phase I of the 77,000 square-foot Odell McConnell Law Center and the adjacent student housing complex, the George Page Apartments.[25] The center was not quite complete when students arrived in fall 1978, and for several weeks they attended classes in Seaver College buildings.[26] On January 12, 1979, SOL hosted its first major conference: an address by Ronald Reagan on the future of the United States in world affairs, moderated by Professor Gerald Turner.[27]

The formal dedication of the law center did not occur until November 17, 1979. Staged before an audience of some 2,000, including delegates from forty-nine schools of law, the ceremonies bore witness to a "miracle," said benefactor Odell McConnell. Associate Justice of the U.S. Supreme Court William Rehnquist delivered the dedicatory address, affirming that institutions like Pepperdine University School of Law played a vital role in the perpetuation of the rule of law in the nation.[28]

Growing in Numbers and Reputation

Among those factors driving the expansion and relocation of the SOL was the growth of its student body. The full-time program began with thirty-four students in fall 1970. By 1977, the last full year in Orange County, the law school enrolled 564 full-time students and only forty-nine part-time students. Some 1,700 applicants from thirty different states competed for 214 first-year seats; by 1992, there were 3,500 applications for 245 places. As admissions became more selective, the student body's academic credentials improved. The students were also more diverse geographically, if not in gender or ethnicity.

The same was true of the rate of Pepperdine graduates passing the California state bar examination. In fall 1972, that rate was an embarrassing 51 percent.[29] But the percentage improved dramatically and was up to 72.3 in 1977, a rate about equal to other accredited law schools in the state.[30]

Students enjoyed a much enlarged full-time faculty, whose number increased from zero to 21 between 1969 and 1976. Students also had the advantage of a much improved library, moot court competition, a law review, and the student bar association. Students even published their own newspaper, *The*

Pepperdine Advocate. Some so identified with the legal profession that they felt free to sue, or threaten to sue, if the university actually levied tuition increases announced in 1973. And the threat apparently worked, for the university rolled back hikes in tuition for some students enrolled in the night school.[31]

The ABA gave Pepperdine's law school provisional approval in August 1972. The ABA re-inspection team saw few serious deficiencies in 1975, although it remarked negatively on modest faculty salaries, inexperienced teachers, marginally prepared entering students, and a budget that was 90 percent tuition dependent. However, the team was particularly impressed with Dean Phillips's "outstanding devotion and achievement" and the marked improvement in support from the central administration, especially President Banowsky. The visitors recommended the ABA's full approval, which was granted in July.[32]

Accreditation Caps Achievements

Three years later, the law school petitioned for membership in the American Association of Law Schools (AALS), an accrediting agency with higher standards than the ABA. A consultant revealed that the major stumbling blocks to membership related to the "perennial root problem of finance." Pepperdine faculty's teaching load was heavy—above six units per semester—and its salaries were inadequate, ranking fourteenth among California's fifteen schools of law. The consultant also felt scholarship funds were inadequate, which limited enrollment of ethnic minorities.[33]

The matter of salaries had been a trial for Dean Phillips from the beginning of his tenure. ABA visitors almost always noted that salaries at Pepperdine, both faculty and dean, were near the median of the national scale, but Phillips was quick to point out that average nationally meant "well-behind" regionally.[34] Substantial tuition increases funded major salary increments beginning in 1977, including raises of 7 to 19 percent for law school faculty and dean.[35]

Also troubling to Dean Phillips and the accrediting agencies was how the law school and the central administration related on matters of budget. When the School of Law was acquired, the ultimate objective of any Pepperdine expansion was to generate revenue that would contribute to the bottom line. The central administration expected the new School of Law to make its contribution as well—not the 50 percent of net as asked of SBM, but at least 20 percent. The ABA accreditors, however, would have nothing of it. The School of Law was not to be a profit center for Pepperdine University. They understood the need to pay a modest amount for direct overhead, but were quite comfortable with a budget that set aside only 4 percent for such costs. With the much coveted approval for the AALS on the line, President Banowsky could only agree—at least in principle.[36]

The four-member AALS visitation team reviewed Pepperdine's law school over four days in April 1978. Overall, the AALS visitors were impressed with what they found, but the AALS governing body concluded that membership was premature because too much "was still in process," particularly the McConnell Law Center.[37] On a subsequent visit in late 1979, AALS visitors found the SOL had its house in order and recommended full membership for Pepperdine University in AALS, which was endorsed by the governing body in January 1980.[38]

Endorsement by the AALS was a milestone, capping the transformation of the Pepperdine University School of Law from a struggling evening school in rented facilities in Orange County to a reputable day school in an impressive law center situated on a majestic campus in Malibu. And unlike other professional schools within the university, the School of Law embraced quality education within a Christian environment. Clearly, AALS affirmation confirmed the reality: the Pepperdine law school had survived its infancy and was well on its way to adulthood.

CHAPTER 25

THE ODELL McCONNELL LAW CENTER, 1980-2000

lthough the American Association of Law Schools (AALS) was positive in its evaluation of the Pepperdine School of Law in 1980, the American Bar Association (ABA) was less enthusiastic when it visited the next year. It was impressed with the new facilities at Malibu, but the ABA accrediting team thought the SOL was still short on space, and it was unhappy with faculty salary levels, student financial aid amounts, support for the library, and graduates' first-time bar pass rates. The ABA did not change the SOL's official accreditation status, but it did ask for a report on the school's progress before July 1983.[1]

Dean Phillips provided the requested report, noting that in the previous three years the law school faculty had received salary increases of 10, 20, and 16 percent, and would get an 8 percent raise in 1983–1984. Phillips also reported that the university had pledged $6 million to construct Phase II of the Law Center and assured the ABA that a faculty committee was studying the bar passing issue, although he acknowledged that the student/faculty ratio remained a problem at thirty to one. Accreditors declared that ratio "unacceptable," recommended that the ABA continue to monitor the SOL, and asked for a progress report by December 15, 1985.[2]

Phillips and his colleagues worked diligently to address the ABA's reservations. Above all else, they recruited students with better academic predictors. Phillips also worked to recruit professors who were excellent teachers, serious scholars, and compatible with the school's Christian mission.[3]

Some of the problems the accreditors had identified were chronic, and most were tied to limited finances. As a private school under twenty years old, the SOL was wholly dependent upon tuition. To pay higher salaries or enhance the library required the administration to increase tuition, enroll more students, or both. Through Howard White's presidency and beyond, the school did both. Enrollment went from 550 in 1979 to 637 in 1983, to 700 after 1988. Tuition per credit unit went from $119 in 1978, to $274 in 1983, to $545 in 1990, and $915 in 2000.

The combination of higher tuition and additional students increased revenue substantially, and the SOL's annual budget tripled between 1979 and 2000, from $3.5 million $10.8 million. The central administration insisted that part of the revenue be utilized to pay for overhead institutional expenses, including capital debt, building and grounds maintenance, computer systems, and registrar functions. Just how much was always in dispute, of course. Dean Phillips wanted to spend all the SOL revenue internally, noting that a 100 percent expense to revenue ratio (E/R) was not uncommon in top law schools.

As long as the law school was in Orange County, Pepperdine officials reluctantly approved a 95 percent E/R ratio. They were less sympathetic after the law school moved to the Malibu campus where general overhead expenses were substantial. After several sharp disagreements with the dean and stern reminders from the ABA and AALS, the Davenport administration continued the 95 percent ratio, but only within the context of budgeted expenses and revenues. Revenues beyond those that were budgeted, the president insisted, would be divided according to a ratio more favorable to the central administration. "If the American Bar Association, AALS, the faculty and others could not understand [why], I would be very disappointed," he said.[4] GSEP had a similar E/R ratio, but Seaver College kept only 63 percent of its tuition revenue while SBM kept just 53 percent.[5]

Since Phillips saw so little possibility that the E/R ratio would be increased in the SOL's favor, he campaigned to utilize most funds raised through the Law Center's development efforts. Primarily for that reason that he organized a School of Law Board of Visitors composed of an impressive group of alumni, honored jurists, distinguished attorneys, and well-wishers in January 1982. Within three years, members of the board included many local and national luminaries, including Justice of the California Court of Appeals Armand Arabian; alumnus and Los Angeles City Attorney (later mayor) James K. Hahn; Justice of the U.S. Supreme Court William H. Rehnquist; and William French Smith, former U.S. attorney general.[6]

Phillips wanted the board to advise the SOL on a variety of matters, but he also expected it to financially support some of the school's initiatives in excellence. In 1983, the board realized some of Phillips's expectations when member Leonard Straus gave $1.5 million to fund a professorship.[7] Similar endowments were created in the years that followed.[8]

Raising the Bar

Separate from the finance issue were the concerns regarding poor California bar examination passing rates, which had been raised by both the ABA and AALS. In 1977, only 72 percent of Pepperdine first-time takers had passed, whereas the pass rates for the University of Pacific, USC, and Loyola were 91, 81, and 77 percent, respectively.[9] The Pepperdine rate decreased to 55.3 percent in 1980 but improved to 62.4 percent in 1982. Phillips pointed out that the average passing rate for all ABA-approved schools in California was only 47.2 percent in 1982, and he noted that Pepperdine was one of only six schools that had improved its scores.[10]

Meanwhile, a law school faculty committee chaired by Associate Dean James McGoldrick concluded there were only two ways to increase the rate: require higher GPAs for graduation or enroll students with better LSAT scores. The committee, Phillips, and the university administration agreed to pursue the second option.[11]

The new approach did not affect the results of the bar exam in 1986, however, when the pass rate for Pepperdine's SOL dropped to 48.1 percent. However, bar pass rates improved to 62.1 percent in 1987 and 85 percent in 1990, a level retained and exceeded through the 1990s. Even so, the law school pass rate rarely rose above the bottom five of the sixteen approved ABA schools on the California bar examination.[12] Phillips and his colleagues liked to point out that almost 50 percent of Pepperdine's students were from out of state and had no trouble passing the bar exam in their home states.

Expressions of Christian Mission

If finances and bar pass rate were red flags for accreditation committees and other critics, so too was the McConnell Law Center's subtle emphasis of Pepperdine's Christian mission. Since Ron Phillips became dean in 1970, he had always claimed the broader Christian mission of Pepperdine University as the mission of the law school as well, an emphasis reflected in his statements, hiring, and recruiting. His insistence on keeping the faith had caused him and the school some grief, and one member of the AALS accrediting committee had even (erroneously) hypothesized that a school serious about its Christian mission could not gain full membership in the organization.[13]

Like others at Pepperdine, Phillips could be restrained when it came to articulating the Christian mission of the law school. In 1983, any reference to Christianity was dropped from the school's application form. President Howard White wanted to know why, especially as WASC had been impressed by how the Law Center exercised its influence for Christianity.[14] Phillips reported that a query regarding Christianity on the application form had scared away "hundreds of students whom we would very much have liked to have had."[15]

In practice, Christian mission at the Law Center manifested itself less as a restriction than as an affirmation. Unlike Seaver College, there were no chapel requirements or restraints on alcohol in off-campus housing. (Alcohol restrictions remained at the on-campus Page Apartments as President White was unwilling "under any circumstances to permit alcoholic beverages in any on-campus resident hall."[16])

In an effort to affirm Christian faith and practice, Dean Phillips sponsored a midweek Bible study in his on-campus home, encouraged an active Christian Legal Society among students, and sought a critical mass of faculty who were members of Churches of Christ. That ratio in 1977 reached 36 percent, compared to 54 percent for Seaver College. Moreover, all faculty were free to speak of their Christian faith, and some lent their talents in support of Christian legal causes, all of which helped create a clear Christian ethos at the Law Center. The school's approach to Christian mission was criticized by some students who claimed it hurt the school's esteem in the community, but most embraced—or at least accepted—the atmosphere.

Moving Ahead—and Abroad

Once established on the Malibu campus in a commodious new building, the SOL, like the university as a whole, was eager to demonstrate that it offered an educational program worthy of its dramatic setting. Partly for that reason, Associate Dean McGoldrick envisioned a semester-abroad experience in London, and in fall 1981 arranged for Pepperdine students to take courses in international law at Regency College in cooperation with the American Foreign Institute and AALS approval. In addition to classes, student would undertake internships at various London locations and live in rooms leased at Beaufort Gardens in Knightsbridge.

Students were enthusiastic about the opportunity, and some thirteen signed up for the inaugural program; Professor Charles Nelson served as faculty mentor. Pepperdine was second only to Notre Dame in launching an American law school program in London.[17]

In spring 1984, Seaver College launched its own year-abroad program in London, and Colleen Graffy, a Seaver College alumna, became director of the Seaver program and coordinator of the law school program. Eager to centralize administration of the two programs, Graffy identified and the university in 1987 purchased an elegant and historic property at 56 Prince's Gate that was large enough to house at least forty undergraduates and provide classroom space for both programs. Although there were some tensions caused by merging the two programs in one facility, the London program continued to be very popular with law students, with some referring to it as Pepperdine's "secret treasure."[18]

Once in the field of global programming, the SOL moved to expand its offerings beyond just London. Over time it came to offer exchange programs in Augsburg, Germany; Copenhagen, Denmark; and Seoul, South Korea. It also established a strong externship program in Washington, D.C., with an international law emphasis. Students participating in one of the exchanges and taking fourteen units in prescribed and electives courses also qualified for a Certificate in International and Comparative Law.[19]

On-Campus Curriculum Enrichment

In its new Malibu facilities, the SOL continued to emphasize advocacy and clinical programs as an academic enrichment opportunity, with second- and third-year students receiving academic credit for fieldwork and classroom components. Most notable of the clinical programs was the Legal Aid and Family Law Clinic at the Union Rescue Mission in downtown Los Angeles, which afforded students the opportunity to help the homeless and the poor of the inner city.

The Vincent S. Dalsimer intra-school moot court competition occurred each spring with the final round scheduled for the day of the annual law school dinner. Typically, the bench for the final round included some of the most distinguished jurists in the United States, usually in town to address the dinner. These included U.S. Supreme Court justices Sandra Day O'Connor, Byron White, Clarence Thomas, Ruth Bader Ginsberg, and John Roberts. With that level of judging, it was no wonder that Pepperdine's moot court teams historically did extremely well in national appellate competitions.

Little put the Law Center on the map more than the distinguished jurists, attorneys, and policymakers who made the university a regular port of call. In addition to addressing the annual law school dinner and presiding over moot court competitions, they also came to give special lectures and teach classes and short courses. William Rehnquist was teaching a Pepperdine class in constitutional law when Dean Phillips notified him that the U.S. Senate had approved him as chief justice of the Supreme Court in 1986.[20] Given Pepperdine University's propensity to favor advocates of academic excellence, Christian mission, and American free enterprise, it is not especially surprising to note that speakers and other visitors were often known for conservative political agendas.

In 1973, Dean Phillips inaugurated the practice of appointing a recognized legal scholar or teacher as a visiting distinguished professor. The first such professor was Frederick I. Moreau, a legal scholar from Kansas. Subsequent visitors included Kenneth York of UCLA, Charles Galrin of SMU, Milton Copeland from University of Arkansas, Stanley Henderson from the University of Virginia, Douglas Kmiec of Notre Dame, and Kenneth Starr, Solicitor General of the United States. After 1983 the scholars were known as D. & L. Straus Distinguished Visiting Professors.

Establishing Institutes, Reputation

The reputation of the SOL was also enhanced by the addition of academic institutes designed to promote education, research, and training in a specialized field. Foremost of these was the Institute for Dispute Resolution, one of the first such programs in the American West and a manifestation of arguably "the most important social experiment in our time," according to Dean Derek Bok of the Harvard Law School. In fall 1986, the institute opened with L. Randolph Lowry as founding director. A Seaver alumnus and protégé of former Seaver College Provost Jerry Hudson, Lowry was also a lifelong member of the Churches of Christ.[21]

The purpose of the institute, as Lowry saw it, was to teach students how to resolve disputes without the burdens of litigation by using strategies focused on reconciliation, mediation, negotiation, arbitration, mini-trials, and judicial settlement. He also saw it as an opportunity to reach out to individual Christians, churches, and Christian ministries through the Institute's periodic workshops for professionals in the field, including those from nonprofit and church groups.

Through the SOL, the institute offered, in addition to certificates, a master's degree in dispute resolution beginning in 1995, the first of its kind to be offered through an ABA/AALS approved law school. Leonard and Dorothy Straus, longtime supporters of Pepperdine University, were so impressed with its work that they endowed the institute the following year.[22] The newly named D. & L. Straus Institute of Dispute Resolution in 1997 was ranked by *U.S. News & World Report* as number three it its field. That ranking climbed to number one in 1998 and again in 2004 and 2006, a position it held for the next nine consecutive years.

At different times, the SOL established other institutes and centers. In the early 1980s, it joined with the Los Angeles County Bar Association and the *Los Angeles Daily Journal* and its owner, Robert Work, to establish the Ira Sherman Center for Ethical Awareness. Professor Gregory L. Ogden directed the center, whose first project was to publish 10,000 copies of a research manual on legal ethics for members of the county bar. Early in the twenty-first century, the Nootbaar Institute subsumed the work of the Sherman center.[23]

Late in the 1980s, Professor of Juvenile Law William Haney organized the Center for Community Development and Training. Legendary for their sacrificial service to at-risk youth, Haney and his wife spent much of their time working in probation camps, prison facilities, and community centers across the gang-torn territory of south-central Los Angeles. His law students—150 each year—presented lectures to offenders at youth correction facilities and prisons and volunteered as reserve deputy probation officers. Through Haney's work, Pepperdine earned a reputation as a school that cared about young people who were in trouble.[24]

Recognizing Progress and a Lifelong Achievement

The need for additional space at the law center had been a theme of accreditors since 1982, and Dean Phillips never ceased to remind the central administration of that worry. His persistence paid off when $6 million was included in the $100 million Wave of Excellence Campaign (1984–1989) to complete construction of Phase II of the law center. Plans called for 43,000 additional square feet, which included library expansion, three new seminar rooms, two new classrooms, a trial court room, a student recreation center, and additional faculty offices, with most of the new space below ground.

Construction began in 1990 and ended in 1992. The new facilities were dedicated on September 16, 1992, by ninety-year-old Louis Nizer, noted author and one of the foremost trial lawyers of the twentieth century.[25]

With additional space, increased scholarly activity by the faculty, and improved bar pass rates, the ABA/AALS accreditation visit in October 1995 resulted in the very best report the Pepperdine University School of Law had ever received. The visiting team concluded that the Law Center had made laudable progress in the field of legal scholarship; in diversifying its student body, faculty, and professional staff; in its strong commitment to greater student aid; and its "dramatic advancement" on the California bar examination. It also noted with favor the Straus Institute for Dispute Resolution, the London program, and the Center for Community Development and Training.[26]

The site-visit team concluded that SOL remained "a values-centered, quality-oriented institution of higher learning," producing graduates who had "the potential to be outstanding lawyers" and making "substantial progress toward contributing positively to the advancement of legal thought and knowledge." Much of this was due to the leadership of Dean Phillips, the report concluded, noting that "The School's commitment to the development of moral character as well as intellectual ability [was] inspired by the example he set."[27]

President Davenport told Dean Phillips that the report was "as good as any I have ever seen and better than one could reasonably expect anywhere. It is a fine tribute to your leadership, and I would certainly be feeling good about the validation of my work, if I were you."[28]

And clearly Dean Phillips did interpret it as a commentary on his life's work. He had presided over developing the Pepperdine University School of Law from a struggling night school with part-time students in Orange County into an institution of full-time students attending classes in spacious and elegant quarters overlooking the Pacific Ocean. The quality of students and faculty had improved dramatically.[29]

His record, however, was not fully appreciated by the community of legal educators—or even all within the Pepperdine community. Prior to the 1995 accreditation report, critics began arguing that it was time for new leadership at the SOL. Dean Phillips had already served four times longer than most law school deans. The really good professors, one critic wrote to Davenport in 1992, had left and been replaced by "uninspired types who will obey [the dean's] orders."[30] Some members of the central administration had also wearied of the dean's inflexibility on certain issues, and one senior faculty member even charged him with being a poor leader in handling personnel issues and having violated Christian ideals. Phillips in turn called upon his critic to repent for circulating untruths.[31]

With no termination date on his contract as dean, Phillips ignored early calls to step aside. In due time, however, Phillips—like all Pepperdine deans—was placed on a five-year contract. At the termination of his contract in 1997, Phillips announced his retirement from the deanship, although he would continue to serve as Pepperdine vice chancellor and dean emeritus, focusing on raising money for the McConnell Law Center.

An administrator for a quarter of a century, Phillips knew the value of tenacity and had learned not to put much credence in the murmurs of critics. Still, censure clearly tired and hurt him, especially as he was coping with the recent death of his beloved wife, Jamie. But Phillips was confident his legacy would be strong: a School of Law not judged by a flawed ranking system but by the values it placed on "the quality of people's lives."

Under New Leadership

After Phillips's announcement, Provost Steven Lemley launched a national search to select a new SOL dean. Three of thirty-five serious candidates made the final cut: Professor Richardson Lynn, longtime associate dean of the Pepperdine School of Law; Professor Douglas Kmiec from Notre Dame University School of Law and visiting distinguished professor at Pepperdine; and Kenneth Starr, formerly a U.S. Court of Appeals judge, U.S. solicitor general, distinguished visiting professor of law at Pepperdine, and currently the independent counsel investigating President Bill Clinton's Whitewater business dealings. President Davenport offered Starr the position in February 1997. He also offered him the post as the founding dean of the new School of Public Policy.

Although still involved in the Clinton investigation, Starr accepted both Pepperdine positions offered by Davenport beginning August 1, 1997. The initial reaction on campus and in the local community was positive. Starr's appointment, said Dean Phillips, would get people "to look more closely at us."[32]

The decision was not well received in other quarters, however. Political partisans believed Starr had not finished his investigative job. His resignation would reduce "the credibility of the investigation," said the *Washington Post*. The outcry was so great that Starr decided to stay on the job until it was over. Pepperdine administrators accepted his decision and announced they would keep the deanships open until he was ready to assume them.[33]

Neither Starr nor university officials anticipated that the wait would be very long. In the meantime, journalists made much of the fact that Richard M. Scaife, a life regent and generous friend of Pepperdine with a reputation of supporting conservative political causes, had made a $1.1 million gift to start up the new School of Public Policy. Journalists thought they smelled a right-wing conspiracy, forgetting that Scaife had been critical of Starr's work as special prosecutor.[34]

Neither Scaife nor any other donor, Provost Lemley insisted, had influenced the selection of Starr as dean. Some critics refused to believe it, but most of those did not recognize the quality of Pepperdine's law school nor understand that the university and Starr had a connection that transcended politics and economics: his father was a Church of Christ minister, Starr had attended Harding College, and he and his extended family remained closely connected with the church.[35]

Starr remained committed in his pledge to Pepperdine, but ending the investigation proved difficult to do, especially after details of the affair between President Clinton and Monica Lewinsky were publicized in January 1998.[36] He sadly withdrew as dean designate of both the Pepperdine University School of Law and School of Public Policy in April 1998.[37]

Associate Dean Richardson Lynn then accepted a five-year appointment as permanent dean. As dean, Lynn had three goals: continue to graduate competent, honest, and ethical lawyers; get faculty more involved in scholarship; and identify more financial resources and thus increase the endowment. To achieve those goals, he began improving the school's brand as an academically excellent institution. Among other things, Lynn turned the *Pepperdine Law Quarterly* into the glossy *Pepperdine Law Magazine* and fostered the school's hosting of more scholarly journals.[38]

Under Lynn's leadership the school organized the Wm. Matthew Bryne, Jr., Judicial Clerkship Institute and the Institute for Entrepreneurship and Technology Law and established the Legal Aid Clinic at Union Rescue Mission. Lynn also continued to emphasize the advocacy programming that produced winning moot court teams and invited Supreme Court Justice Ruth Bader Ginsberg, who had a more liberal reputation than most of the justices Pepperdine typically invited to campus, to preside over the annual competition.[39]

Lynn paid for his initiatives with money that once had gone to discount tuition as he had discovered that the Law Center was giving away more in tuition discount scholarships than any law school in the country. Over time he learned that gradually reducing scholarship aid while moving up in the rankings did not hurt admissions at all, and it laid the basis for the school's subsequent move into higher national rankings.[40]

For unknown reasons, President Andrew Benton and Provost Darryl Tippens chose not to renew Lynn's contract as dean, appointing Charles Nelson as interim dean for the 2003–2004 academic year. After another national search, Starr was again chosen dean of the SOL, a position he filled between 2004 and 2010, a term beyond the limits of this book.

The Pepperdine University School of Law had its genesis in 1969 when the university incorporated the Orange University College of Law in Santa Ana, California. Over the next three decades, primarily under the leadership of Dean Ron Phillips, the law school transformed from a night school with part-time students to a fully accredited institution with multiple innovative programs and a reputation as a leader in Christian legal education. All things considered, the transformation was truly remarkable, bolstering the idea that miracles were happening in Malibu.

BUILDING A
SUBURBAN CAMPUS
1966–1975

CHAPTER 26

CHOOSING A SECOND CAMPUS: WHITE FLIGHT OR COSMIC CALL?

Well before the Watts Riots in August 1965, the Young administration was considering the possibility of establishing a second campus somewhere in the Los Angeles suburbs. The decision-makers calculated that the growth potential of the Vermont Avenue campus was limited because it was too expensive to expand in that area. The University of Southern California might be able to afford to grow there, but Pepperdine College could not.[1]

A subcommittee was established to study the feasibility of suburban expansion, but the administration cautioned its members against a "careless discussion" of the matter. They did not want "to create any alarm or panic among donors, prospective students or patrons of the college, or our own student body and faculty."[2] After the Watts riots, the administration approached the possibility of a second campus with greater passion.

In January 1966, three years before Larry Kimmons was killed on campus and almost five years before the student lockout, the board of trustees appointed a committee from among members of the president's board. Its primary charge was to investigate ways and means of expanding the Los Angeles campus.[3] Early on, the committee concluded that buying property adjacent to the campus would be more expensive than establishing a second campus in the suburbs. Committee members even came to doubt the viability of the Vermont Avenue campus, given the demographic and economic changes taking place in the neighborhood.[4] Committee chair Don Darnell was certain that Pepperdine College's survival as an institution depended upon it leaving south central Los Angeles.[5]

For most of 1966 and much of 1967, the site selection committee (Darnell, Richard Ralphs, Walter Knott, Bryant Essick, Morris Pendleton, and Don Warren) evaluated as many as forty sites.[6] They rated the properties according to nine criteria, including whether the site would: come to the college as a complete gift; facilitate a distinctive institution that would attract gifts; have a good climate; require extraordinary development costs; and offer job opportunities for students.[7]

Only three of the forty sites were given serious and detailed consideration. As previously noted these were:

- Calabasas, 188 acres at the northwest corner of the Ventura Freeway and Las Virgenes Road, offered by Southern California Edison Company;
- Westlake Village, as many as 250 acres at the northwest corner of Lindero Canyon Road and Thousand Oaks Boulevard, offered by John Notter and the American Hawaiian Company; and
- Malibu, 138 acres on the northwest corner of Pacific Coast and Malibu Canyon highways offered by the Adamson family and the Marblehead Land Company).[8]

President Young secured the services of the Robert Johnston Company (RJC) of Los Angeles to assist the selection committee in the summer of 1966. The company was charged to assess Calabasas, the first option to become available, as a possible site for a new campus, as well as the overall feasibility of moving ahead with an expansion program. After review, the consultants reported that Pepperdine College should indeed expand to a second campus and organize a development campaign to pay for it. They also recommended the Calabasas site but cautioned that in the Calabasas community—as in the entire San Fernando Valley—the idea of a neighboring liberal arts college campus generated more curiosity than promises of money to help build.[9]

Fund-Raising Makeover

Whether Pepperdine were to try to expand at Calabasas or elsewhere, RJC recommended it take a new approach to fund-raising. Above all else, the college should restructure its development office, which RJC considered to be in shambles because Vice President Bill Teague was preoccupied with running for U.S. Representative. Release Teague, the company suggested, and appoint a new director of development. Given the circumstances, Young agreed.[10]

As a viable candidate for Teague's position, the consultants proposed J. Dan Benefiel, one of their own vice presidents. Benefiel knew the mechanics of raising money, had deep roots in the Stone–Campbell religious tradition, and was a lifelong friend of Ronald Reagan. Young quickly embraced Benefiel and dispatched Teague to Orange County to run the new law school. Consequently, Benefiel played a significant role early in the fund-raising campaign that produced the Malibu Miracle, the phrase eventually used to describe the series of events that came together in unexpected ways to produce a stunning campus on the edge of the Pacific Ocean.[11]

In the makeover of the development office, Young also designated J. C. Moore Sr. as vice president for planning to handle deferred giving, removing him from his longtime role as manager of the college's financial affairs. It was a terrific disappointment for Moore, who had been at Young's side for twenty years, and he soon resigned to take the presidency of Columbia Christian College in Portland, Oregon. Before he could leave for his new position, however, Moore died from a heart attack.[12]

As Benefiel joined the development team, so too did Charles Runnels. A Texas native and a U.S. Navy veteran, Runnels was an alumnus of Stephen F. Austin University in Nacogdoches, Texas; Columbia University in New York; and the University of Houston School of Law. He had come to Los Angeles in 1961 in a role with Tenneco Inc. of Houston, and took a "visiting executive" role with Pepperdine in 1967. In 1969, Runnels resigned his executive position with Tenneco and threw "his lot" with Pepperdine full-time as a liaison with the business community. He began as first vice president for business relations, became vice chancellor in 1971, and chancellor on December 31, 1984. Runnels, a longtime elder in both the Inglewood and Culver Palms Churches of Christ in Los Angeles, proved particularly adept at working with the captains of industry who comprised the president's board. And when it came to cultivating Blanche Seaver, only Bill Banowsky would be as influential.[13]

Larry Hornbaker also joined the development team in 1969, shortly after he and Walter Burch completed a successful $12.6 million capital campaign for Abilene Christian College. Hornbaker served Pepperdine for most of the next forty years in various capacities, from administration to fund-raising.[14] His colleagues recognized him as a genuine servant leader, and Howard White described him as "knowledgeable, tactful, diplomatic, and indefatigable."[15]

RJC strongly encouraged Pepperdine College to create a master plan that would establish a "case"—academically, culturally, physically, and financially—for the development of the college. The document would also describe the college's current role in higher education and its value to society. Such a statement was important, the consultants said, because funds no longer flowed to colleges with a "need" but to those with a purposeful plan. To draw attention to the plan, the consultants recommended that the college publish and distribute periodically a series of presidential statements relating the larger issues of the day to Pepperdine's philosophy, purposes, and practices.[16]

Bicameral Board?

RJC also recommended creating a separate, nonprofit Pepperdine corporation to carry out the fund-raising activities of the college. The college's board of trustees would select the directors of the new corporation from the president's board whose members were known for their community influence and financial power rather than their membership in Churches of Christ. Pepperdine's affiliated religious body, the report observed, "lack[ed] both the numbers (in California) and the wealth to finance this quantum advance." Indeed, RJC noted that the religious affiliation would "handicap" the college in "competing for strong volunteer leadership with colleges such as Pomona and Occidental." The directors of the new corporation would share responsibility for the policy and operations of the school with the trustees but primarily assume the task of raising funds and developing the college financially.[17]

The report further recommended that fund-raising become the responsibility of volunteers, supported by a professional staff. In the college's current alignment, the responsibility for financing the growth of Pepperdine was lodged nowhere and thus gravitated to the principal administrators.[18] Finally, RJC recommended a $5 million to $6 million campaign for the first phase of establishing a new campus. If someone were to give 25 percent of that amount, it would be appropriate to name the campus after them.[19]

President Young welcomed the recommendations. For some time, he had struggled with how best to involve the business elite who served on the president's board. To expect them to give large sums of money to the college without giving them some voice in its governance seemed illogical. However, George Pepperdine had founded the school upon the assumption that a board of trustees of committed Churches of Christ members would anchor and preserve the Christian mission of the college. A man who had dedicated his presidency to preserving Pepperdine's church relationship, Young had reservations about a second board, but he saw it as preferable to diluting the religious orientation of the board of trustees. And the U.S. Congress, after all, was a bicameral institution.

The Pepperdine board of trustees was more skeptical than its president.[20] The idea of having two boards with governing responsibilities was difficult to embrace when one of them would be composed of influential businessmen with no understanding of Churches of Christ. Even Vice President Teague was cool to the idea.[21]

These qualms notwithstanding, under President Young's urging, the trustees unanimously authorized creation of a "Pepperdine College Board of Governors" in November 1966, some fifteen months after the Watts riots.[22] But the board never materialized. In addition to being a divisive proposal, the idea seemed to run afoul of a California state law that prohibited nonprofit corporations from operating under two governing boards. Restructuring the college board of trustees would await the presidency of William S. Banowsky.[23]

Making Its Case Statement

The Young administration also found it difficult to produce a Pepperdine master plan as recommended by RJC. Such a plan required input from the faculty, who were divided on the merits of opening a second campus, so the administration determined to produce a "case statement" for the second campus with little faculty input. Young appointed a thirteen-person committee chaired by Dan Benefiel to draft a statement that would cultivate excitement for a second campus in the suburbs. The committee found the task far more challenging than anticipated, and after a year, a suitable document was still inchoate.[24]

In late 1967, President Young turned to longtime church friend, publicist, and fund-raiser Walter Burch to draft an appropriate document. A native Texan, Burch was then living in West Islip, New York, as part of a church-planting effort. He expected to extract a case statement from six "conviction papers" that he would write but publish over Norvel Young's signature. He titled those essays "Education and the Nourishment of Hope," "Higher Education Is Becoming Sectarian," "The Resurgence of Idealism," "The Decline of Law," "The Recovery of Moral Purpose," and "Seven Concerns of Pepperdine College." The specific concerns identified in the last essay related to ultimate values, intellectual development, universal views, moral standards, local educational needs, American ideals, and prudent administration.[25]

Integral to Burch's planned case statement was a credo he expected to title "Pepperdine College Affirms." It was to be a brief but sweeping statement of the fundamental principles upon which the college stood, from the existence of God, to the pursuit of truth, to the quality of student conduct. Burch had finished his first draft of the affirmations statement by November 1967, but Benefiel thought it sounded too "unctuous" and passed it along to Billie Silvey, a talented writer and niece of Helen Young, to soften its tone. Silvey did refine some of the language, but the case and affirmation statements were still in process when Bill Banowsky joined the Pepperdine administration in June 1968.[26]

Among Banowsky's earliest assignments was to transform Burch's work into a document that would justify opening a second campus in the Los Angeles suburbs.[27] In just over six months, he submitted a final copy of the case statement, "The Affirming College, A Case for the Dual Campus Concept of Pepperdine College." The document had three parts: "The Nation's Problem: A Value Vacuum," "Pepperdine's Answer: The Affirmation of Values," and "Pepperdine's Future: The Advancement of Values Through a Two-Campus Structure." Using some of Burch's analysis, the document argued that decadence and erosion within society and turmoil and frustration within higher education hindered social and economic progress, cast ominous shadows over the future, shamed the present, and belittled the nation's past. In this time of crisis, higher education was more of a problem than a solution, little more than "a concept without perspective or discernible direction."[28]

According to Banowsky, Pepperdine College represented an alternative. In its own distinctive way, it sought "to make a significant contribution to the overall betterment of society" and to maintain and propagate "a desirable society perspective." The aim of Pepperdine was to produce graduates who were "totally educated individuals": positive, constructive, well-adjusted, dedicated, aware, competent, learned, sophisticated, and God-fearing. The college, therefore, was distinctive, and its plans to expand to a second campus in the suburbs of Los Angeles deserved the patronage of patriotic men and women who feared for the future of their nation and city.

The Significance of the "Affirming College"

The final version of the case statement also incorporated Banowsky's rendition of the "Affirms Statement," with an additional declaration that Pepperdine enjoyed the fruits of the free-enterprise system and accepted the obligation "to preserve and improve it." That clause would disappear, and Banowsky would over time modify other language before the statement was chiseled in stone.

Few documents in the history of Pepperdine University were as formative as the "Affirming College." Heretofore no one had given such a full explanation of the institution's *raison d'etre* other than vocational preparation and commitment to Christian mission. This document, however, declared that there was something dramatically cosmic about the university's work. Not only did that work speak to the existence of God and the reality of absolute truth, but it positioned education in all of its fullness—the liberal arts, disciplined student conduct, an atmosphere of order and authority, and even the free-enterprise system—as part of the divine process. The world might undergo great convulsions because of secularism and materialism, but a "complete" education that began with the quest for God and ended in the preservation of the American Way had the power to overcome those forces. That was the mission of Pepperdine College; that was its purpose for building a second campus. It would build something that would last "forever," employing the image of John Ruskin, building with such purpose and faithfulness that future generations would take grateful notice that their fathers had laid the stones for them.[29]

The notion that Pepperdine College was an antidote to a world that had rejected God, abandoned traditional values, and turned its back on American political and economic ideals was not new. That had been the message of Norvel

Young to his church constituency and to the Los Angeles elite in the late 1950s and early 1960s. But thanks to Walter Burch and Bill Banowsky, the "Affirming College" was a far more sophisticated and nuanced statement of why Pepperdine merited the attention of wealthy and patriotic donors. With significant emendations, as in the case of the Affirms statement, it became the principal theme of official publications, Associates dinners, and major campaigns, as well as unofficial statements well into the twenty-first century. Specifically, Pepperdine University merited the attention and support of its many publics because its commitment to traditional values, to the American Way, and to academic excellence made it the ideal antidote to a world run amok.

However, the idea that there was something cosmic about Pepperdine building another campus beyond the influences of south central Los Angeles did not sit well with all observers—or even with everyone in the Pepperdine community. Cathy Meeks, one of the student protesters at the Vermont Avenue campus, said building the second campus "was a way to escape from a community too difficult to deal with," and people needed "to stop calling themselves Christian and doing that."

Ten years after the protest, Meeks reflected that "It's O.K. if you can't hack it and you want to run, but don't tell me that you represent the Nazarene when you're running. Because Jesus would give you the power you need to face a changing community."[30] Just as critical of the hypothesis was Candace Denise Jones, a graduate student in history at Seaver College almost three decades after the move to Malibu. In her 2003 master's thesis she argued that the motivation for a second campus was nothing more than "white flight" from the inner city rather than some miraculous call to greatness.[31]

Setting Sights on New Site

As Burch and Banowsky were creating a case for a second Pepperdine campus, the anticipated site of that campus changed dramatically. In October 1967, accountant George Evans, a member of the Pepperdine College board of trustees, informed the site selection committee that the Adamson family in Malibu might be open to granting land for Pepperdine's suburban campus. The Adamsons, clients of Evans, owned the Marblehead Land Company. In partnership with Alcoa, the Pennsylvania company of Mellon/Scaife family, the Adamsons expected to develop several thousand acres of rural Malibu, with one of its features being an institution of higher education. Thanks to Evans, in November the Adamsons made a fairly firm offer of 138 acres as a building site.[32]

In late December, with Charles Runnels now acting as coordinator, members of the site committee met in the Los Angeles office of William Pereira, a noted architect engaged by the Adamsons to develop a master plan for Malibu.

Pereira reviewed topographical maps and briefed the committee on the broad outlines of the project. Members left his office and drove directly to Malibu. They were immediately impressed with the advantages of the general location: ocean view, rural setting, temperate climate, absence of smog, mountain atmosphere, and the value of "Malibu" as a national brand.

For the committee and President Young, those factors outweighed the disadvantages of considerable site preparation expenses. Besides, the Malibu property had so captured the imagination of two of Pepperdine's most generous donors that they promised additional contributions to help with those costs. Specifically, Blanche Seaver, widow of Frank R. Seaver, offered to donate 164 acres she owned in Palos Verdes to that end, and Richard Scaife agreed to make a contribution of $500,000 in stock.[33]

The campus selection process was further complicated in February 1968 when the developers of Westlake Village laid before the trustees another attractive option: 250 acres of prime real estate at the intersection of Lindero Canyon Road and Thousand Oaks Boulevard. The offer generated considerable enthusiasm among members of the site selection committee as well as the board of trustees. It had easy access to utilities and sewers, was just off the Ventura Freeway, and was near the population centers of the San Fernando and Conejo Valleys. But committee members were not impressed with plans for an industrial park adjacent to the property, the hilly terrain, the cost of site preparation, the smoggy climate, and the hot summers.[34]

Westlake versus Malibu

From March on, the Darnell selection committee considered only Malibu and Westlake. For unknown reasons, the early interest in Calabasas had vanished. Over the next several months, most members of Pepperdine's extended community registered an opinion regarding the merits or disadvantages of the sites. At the request of trustee Orbin V. Melton, an executive in the Walt Disney Company, the consultants who had located Disney World in Orlando, Florida, prepared a comparative survey of Westlake and Malibu as a college site. The Disney consultants concluded that Westlake was better, primarily because of the excessive costs of site preparation at Malibu, and the growth potential of the Highway 101 corridor.[35] Architects from Weldon Becket Company, also Disney consultants, concluded similarly.

The Brooks Foundation from Santa Barbara, an educational consultant, was just as bullish on Westlake, although its specialists did acknowledge that students would prefer the Malibu site. Helen Pepperdine and trustee Arnold Sallaberry agreed with the consultants, but for different reasons. They felt that Malibu was too closely identified with materialism, a value inimical to a Christian college.[36]

Trustee Robert Jones also supported the Westlake proposal, in part because of his antipathy toward those who supported Malibu, specifically members of the president's board. Jones believed that board and its site selection committee were exercising prerogatives which belonged to the board of trustees. Jones was also fairly critical of President Young for making decisions he thought should have deferred to the board of trustees, even implying that the trustees met irregularly just so the president could make decisions without interference.[37]

Trustee Melton did not share Jones's criticisms of the board or the president, and he tilted toward Malibu even after his preferred consultants recommended the contrary. He took it upon himself to visit the two sites on June 18, 1968. What he found did not impress him. Even after a great deal of work, the Westlake site could not possibly be good for anything except "raising goats," he concluded. Malibu was equally uninviting. Melton thus concluded that Pepperdine should not accept either offer and could get far superior sites. "We should take our hat," he wrote to Don Miller, "put it on our head and out of our hand, because we have a great deal to offer." Still, Melton would favor Westlake without reservations if the developers would grant a more attractive site. On the other hand, if he had to make a decision between the two properties "as is," he said he would support Malibu.[38]

Given the consultants' recommendations favoring Westlake, the antipathy of some trustees toward Malibu, and ambivalence of other trustees toward both sites, it was not surprising that the Pepperdine College board of trustees came to favor Westlake. On June 24, 1968, following formal presentation by principals from both Westlake and Malibu, in a meeting attended by ten of the fifteen trustees, they voted unanimously to finalize an agreement for the Westlake property, presuming that the college could build on plateaus rather than in valleys, construct an additional access road, and locate more favorable construction locations. Since there was no assurance that the Westlake developers would grant those concessions, however, the trustees also wanted to keep the door to Malibu open.[39]

A Case for Distinctiveness

President Young, however, much preferred the Malibu location and had been working to bolster its standing.[40] To do so persuasively he had turned to Bill Banowsky, even while Banowsky was still preaching in Lubbock. As the president expected, the young preacher delivered a brilliant, tightly argued justification for Malibu.

Pepperdine College's *raison d'etre* was distinctiveness, he wrote, in a document that circulated probably only to the site-selection committee, president's board, and the board of trustees. That extra something was:

- the school's "bold Christian claims undergirding all academic work";
- its emphasis upon human values in a mechanized society;
- its nonsectarian stance;
- its efforts to create a truly spiritual campus atmosphere;
- its personal attention to individual students;
- its ability to maintain basic American ideals "tempered by a dynamic willingness to change and experiment"; and
- its "independence from state, federal, church, or political control."

When it came to competing with USC, UCLA, Occidental, or even El Camino College, distinctive education was Pepperdine's "only hope."[41]

And when it came to maintaining distinctiveness, he argued, campus location was important. Indeed, "to an operation like ours, mere location can make the difference between mediocrity or excellence, between success and failure." The Westlake site was a splendid one, Banowsky wrote, but it was "seriously *lacking in distinctiveness*." A great master plan featured lakes, golf courses, and imposing homes, but Westlake's destiny was to be "a self-contained little city without distinctive or dynamic ties with Los Angeles." It was the kind of place the state of California would choose to put one of its neighborhood junior colleges, he wrote.[42]

On the other hand, there would always be *"only one Malibu."* According to Banowsky, "A college built at Malibu would forever have an edge in distinctiveness on the weight of location alone." That was because of Malibu's unique ties with Los Angeles, its distinctive reputation, its beauty and aesthetic qualities, its climate, the changelessness of its environment, and its appeal to discriminating students, faculty, and donors. Banowsky concluded that "Malibu has that intangible something which distinguishes it from more ordinary sites [such] as Westlake." Above all, "Malibu [had] the capacity to excite," he concluded.[43]

Turning toward Malibu

Banowsky's analysis clearly had an impact on the naysayers. Even more important, however, the Westlake developers declined to modify their offer, whereas the developers of Malibu did. The Adamson family agreed to grant the college clear title to the 138 acres earlier than anticipated and to sell it four adjacent parcels of land totaling 58.7 acres for $388,000. The amended offer assured a tract of land sufficient for a first-class campus in Malibu. That development, the continued encouragement from Young, and the likelihood of a

Malibu recommendation from the site selection committee prompted a dramatic reversal of opinion within the board of trustees. In a straw poll taken on July 30, 1968, a preference for Malibu was expressed by eight of the trustees (H. E. Acklin, Lipscomb Crothers, Austin Ellmore, George Evans, James Lovell, Orbin Melton, Donald Miller, and Clarence Shattuck), while Westlake was favored by three (Robert P. Jones, Helen Pepperdine, and Arnold Sallaberry).[44]

Simultaneously, the site selection committee formally recommended Malibu as the location of Pepperdine's second campus to the president's board, where many members were concerned about the additional cost of preparing the site.[45] Site Committee Chair Darnell presented the facts and figures, followed by a strong appeal from Young in which he declared that the distinctiveness of the Malibu site would excite students, faculty, and potential donors more than the Westlake option. After some debate, the president's board voted unanimously to recommend the Malibu property to the board of trustees.

Following the vote, Young revealed that certain friends of the college were so pleased with the decision that they had already donated $500,000 toward the development of the Malibu campus. Young was referring to Richard Scaife, although he did not mention him by name. "I wish you could have been there and seen the smiles of genuine joy on the faces of all of our President's board members," Young wrote to Scaife. "We took a picture of those present, and all of us left, floating about six inches off the ground."[46]

Within weeks, Scaife would send a check covering the pledged amount plus $800,000 more—a total of $1.35 million. According to Young, it was "the largest single check ever received by the college and the largest gift that [had] been made in its thirty-one years since the original gifts of the founder." He was understandably overwhelmed, but not speechless. "I wish that the critics of our capitalistic system could really know some of the benefits that flow from the generosity of families like yours. . . . If all of those who have helped create the wealth of our country would be as responsible and as wise as you in the distribution of its fruits, this country would flower as we have never dreamed." That Scaife may have been acting out of self-interest—the successful development of Malibu was to the financial advantage of one of his family's companies—did not seem to occur to Young.[47]

On August 13, the board of trustees, with only five of the fifteen members present, accepted the recommendation of the president's board that Malibu be the site of Pepperdine College's second campus. They then decided to withhold approval until some provisions in the Adamson letter of offer were refined. Final agreement came on the evening of October 2, 1968.[48]

Announcing a Rare Gift

Five days later and five months before the shooting of Larry Kimmons on the Los Angeles campus, President Young made the dramatic announcement at a press conference in the Los Angeles Statler-Hilton Hotel. He thanked the Adamsons for the "gift of rare property" that would enable Pepperdine College to create a new multi-campus concept, with one campus designed to advance the college's traditional liberal arts role and the other to address the educational challenges of the inner city.

Because the Malibu area was not presently served by a four-year college "and because of the rare beauty and aesthetic qualities of ... Malibu, the location would give Pepperdine an opportunity to plan and build, from the ground up, a unique campus in which the traditional liberal arts program [was] undergirded by the latest learning facilities and techniques."[49] Simultaneously, Pepperdine would commit its Los Angeles campus to urban educational programs, an emphasis especially appropriate for a school with Christian mission.[50]

Merritt H. Adamson responded for the family. He and his two sisters were fulfilling the destiny of the property by donating it to Pepperdine College for construction of a four-year coeducational and residential facility. The 138 acres were, after all, in the heart of the original Spanish Land Grant, Rancho Malibu Topanga Sequit, made by the king of Spain in 1804 to Don Jose Bartolome Tapia, a Spanish soldier. Twenty-two miles long, Rancho Malibu had been owned by the Rindge-Adamson family since 1891, when it was purchased by Frederick H. Rindge, a Harvard graduate, supporter of higher education, and founder of the nationally famous Rindge Manual Training School in Cambridge, Massachusetts.

Rindge had transformed the Malibu property into a productive ranch. Following his untimely death in 1905, his widow and three children continued to occupy and operate Rancho Malibu.[51] To pay operating costs, property taxes, and fight a legal battle to prevent construction of a railroad and highway through the ranch, the family organized the Marblehead Land Company to lease prized beach property in 1927. Some of the leases went to Hollywood notables. Nine years later, in the midst of the Great Depression, the company had to take voluntary bankruptcy, and bondholders subdivided and sold the most desirable sites. In 1951, the family, then dominated by Rhoda Rindge Adamson, regained control of what was left of the ranch. It was her son and two daughters who donated the 138 acres to Pepperdine.[52]

President Young promised the Adamson family and the friends of Pepperdine College that the Malibu campus would be ready for students in fall 1971. Just two years away, it seemed like an unrealistic date given the money to be raised, campus to be built, curriculum to be created, faculty to be chosen, and student body to be recruited. And it was an overly optimistic projection date—but only by one year. In September 1972, almost miraculously, a new Pepperdine campus did open in the Malibu hills.

CHAPTER 27

THE MIRACLE WORKERS:
THOSE WHO GAVE

I n 1968 William Banowsky and Norvel Young considered the recently
acquired Malibu site as "the planet's most beautiful blank canvas." To bring
forth a new campus from it, however, would require some miracle workers—planners, architects, contractors, and committed friends with money.

Young and Banowsky were of one mind that the principal planner must
be "an unsurpassed master artist." They initially disagreed about whether
the role should be filled by William Pereira or Charles Luckman, former partners who had together and separately created many high-profile projects.[1]
Banowsky favored Pereira, who had been featured in *Time Magazine* and was
widely respected among LA's rich and famous for his good looks, expensive
cars, reclusive proclivities, and eccentric genius.[2] In time, Young conceded to
the wishes of his colleague and was able to do so without alienating Luckman.[3]

Birth of a College Gala

In late 1968 Pereira and his associates set to work developing drawings for the
founding circle of buildings at the Malibu site.[4] There was no time to waste
because Pepperdine administrators anticipated presenting the plans to the
Los Angeles community at a black-tie gala scheduled at the Century Plaza
Hotel for February 9, 1970. Leonard Firestone, president of Firestone Tire and
Rubber Company, had agreed to chair the committee planning the occasion,
and California Governor Ronald Reagan had agreed to address it, embracing
his role as "bait" to get an audience. The college anticipated bestowing an honorary doctorate of law upon the governor at that time, an honor not fully supported by some of Pepperdine's students and faculty.[5]

For its "Birth of a College" celebration, Pepperdine University sent out
elegant invitations to 10,000 of its more prosperous and socially prominent
supporters. Both Governor Reagan and President Richard Nixon followed

with something akin to personal notes encouraging attendance. The invitation listed a veritable who's who of California's business and artistic elite as members of the sponsoring and dinner committees. Acceptance rates were so high that a second ballroom at the Beverly Hilton Hotel was reserved for the same evening.[6]

At the appointed time, both venues filled with an average of 1,500 invited guests. Blanche Seaver led the pledge of allegiance; Pat Boone led the national anthem; County Supervisor Kenneth Hahn led the invocation; Jeb Magruder extended greetings from President Nixon; and Richard Mellon Scaife presented Governor Reagan with his doctoral degree. The governor spoke to both groups, declaring that private colleges like Pepperdine were "the bulwark of freedom" and saved taxpayers of California over $200 million each year.

Vice President Banowsky followed with comments focused on the purpose of the evening: raising money for the new campus at Malibu (with nearly $10 million of the required $25 million still needed), introducing the campus's anticipated innovative interdisciplinary curriculum, and unveiling the new master plan for the campus. The latter was especially well received. The color images of red-roofed, white-sided, and sharp-edged Mediterranean buildings set in the Malibu hills above the Pacific Ocean simply awed the two audiences. And that feeling lingered for several months, bringing more than $2 million in new pledges of support.[7]

Executive Vice President Howard White considered February 9, 1970, "as one of the finest nights in the history of Pepperdine College." More important to him than the prospect of additional funds was the chance "to tell our story to so many people who have the most of both means and influence." In White's judgment, "Pepperdine College, will, from this day forward, be better known and much more appreciated by the community leaders of California." And this had been done even though "we made very clear our Christian commitment as well as our desire for academic excellence in person-centered teaching." White was compelled to "thank the Lord for this marvelous expression of interest in Christian education."[8]

Blanche Ebert Seaver

The Birth of a College event was a smashing success and brought donors and prospective donors closer to Pepperdine College than ever before. This was particularly true of Blanche Seaver. Her husband, Frank R. Seaver, as already noted, had supported Pepperdine College in many small ways during his life and had made it a minor beneficiary of his will when he passed away in 1964. These gestures endeared the college to his widow and were the beginning of a relationship that lasted for the duration of her 102-year life and resulted in gifts of more than $160 million to the college.

The youngest of ten children of Norwegian immigrants, Blanche Ebert was born in Chicago in September 1891. By the age of six, knowledgeable musicians recognized her as a child prodigy, a reputation confirmed when she began teaching music at the fabled Hull House founded by Jane Addams. She made her first visit to California at the age of twenty-one and moved permanently to Los Angeles in 1915. In addition to training myriad musicians in her own studio, she published two dozen songs during her lifetime, and the Philadelphia symphony orchestra performed her arrangement of "Battle Hymn of the Republic" in 1919.

But Blanche's career plans changed when she married Frank R. Seaver a day after her twenty-fifth birthday. For the next forty-eight years, she devoted herself to Frank, and after his death, to his memory, never failing to remember his birthday or visit his grave site. During his life, Frank reciprocated her love and loyalty. "You want to stay married?" Frank supposedly asked his nephew. "Then do what your wife wants." He followed his own advice.[9]

In 1933, Frank purchased a company that manufactured heavy oil drilling machinery, blowout preventers, and threads for oil piping. He renamed it Hydril, abandoned the heavy production, and concentrated on the specialty items. The company eventually produced thousands of patented parts used in oil field equipment, most notably the Hydril blowout preventer. By 1970 there was no oil field in the world that did not lease its preventers from Hydril.[10]

Like George and Helen Pepperdine, the Seavers never thought of wealth as a luxury to enjoy personally. Early in their marriage they founded an orphanage in Mexico City. In 1956, Frank gave $1 million to his alma mater, Pomona College, and subsequent gifts totaling more than $7.5 million allowed Pomona to build one of the finest science centers in higher education. Frank Seaver made equally impressive gifts to USC and to the First Congregational Church of Los Angeles, where he was a longtime member.

Blanche Seaver was active in many charitable, cultural, and civic affairs in Los Angeles. In 1960, she was elected to the board of trustees of USC, only the third woman to sit as a member of that august board. After Frank's death in 1964, she was elected to membership on the board of trustees of Pomona College; in 1968, she was named a member of the president's board of Pepperdine College and in 1976 as a member of the university board of regents.[11]

Blanche Seaver was very much impressed that her "dear husband" had included Pepperdine College in his will and therefore gladly accepted Norvel Young's invitations to attend Pepperdine programs and social gatherings. She liked what she saw and heard, especially the college's Christian witness, demand for responsible student conduct, strong sense of patriotism, and support of Republican Party principles, particularly the free-market economy. Indeed, her response was so positive that in October 1967 Norvel Young, Bill Teague, and Henry Salvatori, presented her with a formal proposal for a $4 million gift to build the suburban campus then envisioned at Calabasas. Seaver was impressed with the proposal, in part because it was in concert with her husband's dictum: "If you want to do something for the future of your country do something for the youth, for they are the future of the country." At the same time, she did not yet have enough confidence either in the college or herself to make that large a commitment.[12]

Blanche and Banowsky

Within two years, that attitude would change, thanks to William S. Banowsky. The seventy-seven-year-old widow met the thirty-one-year-old Pepperdine vice president in late November 1967. The bond between the two was almost instant: the middle-class-born, Midwest-raised, spiritual, sentimental, and

Blanche Ebert Seaver was Pepperdine University's most generous benefactor, eventually donating more than $160 million to the school. Her support of Pepperdine, which eventually led to the creation of Frank R. Seaver College of Arts, Letters, and Sciences, was her way of creating a permanent memorial to her husband, who died in 1964.

grandmotherly Blanche and the middle-class-born, Southwest-raised, spiritual, dashing, and son-like Bill. Each knew what the other was thinking, and—judging from extant letters between the two—they could even communicate in code. Their affection for each other was genuine, and their sense of connectedness, or family, was strong.

For more than four years, a day seldom passed when the two did not speak, and they spent more evenings than not in the company of each other. Banowsky's wife and four sons and Seaver's sister, Mabel Marks, were often present too—at concerts, exhibits, or political functions. The ultimate objective, of course, was to encourage Seaver to gift or bequeath the remainder of her estate for the development of Pepperdine's campus at Malibu.[13]

Blanche Seaver was not an easy soul to cultivate. She had high expectations of her escorts. In her company, they were expected to wear an American flag lapel pin, be happy patriots of the United States, and speak glowingly of the free-enterprise system. They were to use six-cent stamps with the emblem of the American flag rather than the profile of President Franklin D. Roosevelt. They were to take her telephone calls, read her messages, and complete her study assignments. (She regularly sent Banowsky a packet of political and economic treatises and directed him to read and report on them. He generally turned the material over to an assistant to do the reading while he did the reporting.)[14]

Her escorts were not to drink alcohol at her table, and were expected to turn their wine glasses upside down. Neither were they to leave food on their plates—or on hers. To prevent waste she expected her escorts to finish the entrées on her plate that she did not eat. They were also to be skeptical of labor leaders, Jews, and African Americans. She was "furious," for example, when Pepperdine gave honorary doctorates to Los Angeles Mayor Tom Bradley, jazz musician Lionel Hampton, and Rabbi Juda Glasner, being placated only by the fact that the degrees were extended on the Los Angeles campus rather than at Malibu. According to Banowsky, Blanche Seaver was "absolutely unpredictable" when it came to politics and personal preference.[15]

When Sir Anthony of the Knightly Order of St. Brigitte failed to treat her with the measure of respect she thought she deserved, she severed relations with the organization, returning ribbons, decorations, and files. Upon her recommendation, Bill Banowsky and Norvel Young did the same thing. She had lower opinions of Richard Nixon and Henry Kissinger than she did of Sir Anthony. Like her husband, Blanche Seaver once held Nixon in high esteem, but his political moderation eventually disgusted her, and his support of Kissinger, whose foreign policy she considered irresponsible and disloyal, only compounded her contempt. President Ford made her black list when he pardoned Nixon.[16]

Seaver's distaste for Ford was apparent in September 1975 when the president came to the Malibu campus to dedicate the Brock House and Firestone Fieldhouse. He stopped first at the Brock House lawn to greet distinguished guests. Going from table to table, he eventually made his way to where Blanche Seaver sat; she turned her back toward the president. Witnessing what had happened from his seat next to Seaver, John Wayne rose to his feet, heartily greeted the president, and ushered him to the next table.

When he heard about the incident, President Banowsky, whose political career was at the moment hanging in the balance, was livid. He confronted Seaver, chastised her soundly with some unchristian words, and walked away. Seaver was completely undone and demanded that Charles Runnels take her home immediately, insisting that she wanted nothing to do with Banowsky or Pepperdine ever again. Runnels and his wife did take her home, but they spent the next two hours praying with her, trying to calm her enough that she would rethink her determination to sever her ties with Pepperdine. In time she did, thanks to Charles and Amy Jo Runnels.[17]

Blanche Seaver almost always listened to her heart. It was because of her good and generous heart that she offered to pay the tuition of some of the Banowsky and Runnels children to elite private schools and to make both Banowsky and Young beneficiaries of her will.[18] Above all, her good heart prompted her to explore the faith tradition of her Pepperdine friends, to attend the Inglewood Church of Christ, and, with Bill Banowsky officiating, accept baptism by immersion at the age of 86.[19]

Frank R. Seaver College

Several years before her baptism, on November 29, 1969, the day after Thanksgiving, Blanche Seaver had dinner in the home of Shirley and Pat Boone in Beverly Hills. Also attending were Gay and Bill Banowsky, Helen and Norvel Young, and Bill and Peggy Teague. After dinner, Pat Boone sang "Just for Today," Seaver's well-known composition, and then Norvel Young presented Seaver with a twenty-four-page proposal requesting an $8 million gift that would make "Seaver College at Malibu" a reality.

Most of the document described the philanthropic highlights of Frank Roger Seaver's life of service, with emphasis upon his growing interest in the work of Pepperdine College. Implicit to that description was that Blanche Seaver could now finish the work of her husband by underwriting the construction of a new campus devoted to academic excellence, God, the American Way, and the free-market economy.[20] Such an opportunity Blanche Seaver was prepared to accept.

She had already signaled her willingness to make major gifts to support construction of the Malibu campus. The earliest of these had come around the flagpole on the future site of the campus when she had pledged to give thirty acres of land at Palos Verdes in support of construction and to make the Malibu campus her number one priority. It was a pledge that netted some $3.1 million for the college, just the first installment on millions of dollars in gifts for the Malibu campus in years to come.[21]

Young and Banowsky desired to announce the establishment of the "Frank R. Seaver College, Pepperdine University" at the "Birth of the College" dinner in 1970. However, Richard Seaver did not want Blanche to attach his Uncle Frank's name or invest his fortune until it was clearer that the college would survive its birth. In his judgment, that should not be done until suitable fund-raising goals ($24 million) had been met and there were reasonable assurances that the Malibu campus would become a reality.[22]

So "Frank R. Seaver College, Pepperdine University" remained a secret for another five years even as the grounds and buildings rose from the Malibu hills. Blanche Seaver made one generous gift after another for the Malibu campus and a $250,000 gift to fund a Seaver Learning Center at the Los Angeles campus, presumably to signal that Pepperdine was "serious about our commitment to the urban campus."[23] In October 1971, even before the Malibu campus opened, she signed a will that bequeathed most of her personal assets (valued at $7.7 million in May 1972) to the "Blanche Ebert Seaver Trust for Frank R. Seaver College."[24] All parties eventually agreed to a second will, signed in 1973, that incorporated features to better protect both Seaver and the college trust.[25] Two years later, with the future of the Malibu campus more certain, the university officially dedicated the liberal arts undergraduate college as "Frank R. Seaver College, Pepperdine University."[26]

More Miracle Raisers

Blanche Seaver was the largest donor by far of those who helped make the Malibu Miracle campus a reality. But there were others who also made significant and timely gifts; the most important of these was Richard Mellon Scaife (1932–2014) of western Pennsylvania, who also had a residence and business interests—including sixteen newspapers—in California. Through family foundations, Scaife controlled some $400 to $500 million in assets.

His gifts to Pepperdine totaled more than $9 million through 1978; they were frequently unrestricted, although at times they funded specific projects or actions. Among the latter were the Center for International Business, the site preparation of the Malibu campus, additional acres for the central campus, and fees for consultants to evaluate university management practices. As important as Scaife's dollars were to Pepperdine, equally important was the way his support legitimated gifts from other donors.[27]

Excepting one significant gift to the new School of Public Policy in the mid-1990s, Scaife's support of Pepperdine University pretty much ended in 1978 at the beginning of the presidency of Howard A. White. His significant gifts were remembered by a small plaque embedded on a wall that overlooked "Scaife Terrace and Bridge" just west of Towne Square.

Though not to the same extent as Blanche Seaver and Richard Scaife, other notable Southern Californians helped make the Malibu Miracle a reality. Among these were John C. (1888–1973) and Alice Tyler (1913–1993). A native of South Dakota and a veteran of World War I, John Tyler was the founder of Farmers Insurance Company. In October 1971, the Tylers pledged $2.5 million to the university to underwrite the construction of the student center on the Malibu campus.[28] When John died in 1973, however, his widow challenged the will to exclude Pepperdine. After protracted legal maneuvers, she lost in court, and when she died in 1993, the university received $35 million from her estate. Meanwhile, Blanche Seaver supplied the money to complete the *Tyler Campus Center.*[29]

Morris B. Pendleton (1901–1985) was another major contributor. A native of California and a graduate of Pomona College, Pendleton's first and last job was with Plomb Tool Company, subsequently the Pendleton Tool Company. His generosity to Pepperdine included a gymnasium at the Los Angeles campus and the Pendleton Learning Center and the Pendleton Computer Science Center at Malibu, where he also established a fund that would enable faculty to entertain students and bring the American Humanics program to Seaver College.[30]

Charles S. Payson (1898–1985) was a native of Maine; his wife, Joan Whitney Payson (1903–1975), was a native of New York and heir to the Whitney banking fortune. The family came to Pepperdine's attention when their son, John Payson, transferred from Bowdoin College in Maine, where he had had a less than stellar freshman year, to Pepperdine College in 1963. Under the tutelage of Wade Ruby and James Smythe, young Payson blossomed into an exceptional student of English literature, graduating with honors three years later. His parents were so grateful that they accepted Young's and Banowsky's proposal for the family to help fund the new library at the Malibu campus with a $1.5 million lead gift.[31]

Another major contributor to the Malibu campus was Fritz Huntsinger (1899–1986), a German native who had immigrated to the U.S. and settled in Ventura, California, in the 1920s. Starting there as a janitor in a machine shop, within ten years, he owned his own tool company, which eventually became a part of the number one supplier of oil field production equipment. A personal friend of George Pepperdine, Huntsinger joined the university board in 1958 and actively supported the board's freedom forum and great issues series. He contributed $2.6 million in cash to pay for the Huntsinger Academic Complex, one of the critical first buildings on the Malibu campus, and also donated the 800-pound, six-foot-tall teak carving of the American eagle (sculpted in Thailand) that was placed in Payson Library. For Huntsinger, who would go on to serve as a university regent on the expanded board in 1976, the eagle symbolized freedom and all that was good about America.[32]

George W. Elkins Sr. (1899–1993) contributed with gifts to help construct the central auditorium on the campus. Raised on a ranch in New Mexico, Elkins migrated to Beverly Hills, California, in 1921 to begin a career in real estate. He was one of the developers of the shopping center on Rodeo Drive, one of the principal owners of the Beverly Hills Hotel, a trustee of the Los Angeles Zoo, and one of the founders of the Economic Roundtable of Los Angeles.[33]

Jerene Appleby Harnish (1893–1980) gave some $5 million to Pepperdine during her lifetime or through her estate. Through her Ontario, California, newspaper and her radio stations, Harnish was a strident voice in defense of the American Way, Republican politics, and the free-market economy. Harnish agreed to fund with a $1 million gift the Appleby Center for American Studies, essentially a classroom building; in 1979 she made a $2.1 million gift for the School of Law library and a house in the Malibu Meadows addition as a residence for the university vice president..[34]

A Pennsylvania native, Benjamin Dwight Phillips (1885–1968) and his wife, Mildred Welshimer Phillips (died 1983), came into the Pepperdine orbit not because of politics but because of the school's ties to the Stone–Campbell movement. Although the Phillips family had supported many educational institutions in the Stone–Campbell religious tradition, such as Bethany College and Phillips University, they had never supported an institution associated with noninstrumental Churches of Christ. Banowsky, however, cultivated a relationship with the family emphasizing Pepperdine's deep roots within the Stone–Campbell movement.[35] The Phillips family gift of just under a million dollars funded the signature, 125-foot theme tower gracing the entrance to the Malibu campus.[36]

Through their family foundation, John and Beverly Stauffer helped make possible the Malibu campus chapel. John Stauffer (1898–1972), of John Stauffer Chemical Company, and Beverly M. Stauffer (1904–1982) had come to appreciate Pepperdine College's citizenship education program and its strong Christian mission. A strongly committed Catholic, Beverly Stauffer volunteered to cover most of the costs to build what she fondly designated "the little chapel on the hill" on the Malibu campus. However, she would never quite understand why President Banowsky did not authorize weekly Mass in the chapel.[37]

Leonard Firestone (1907–1996), was son of the founder of the Firestone Tire and Rubber Company. Firestone had served on Pepperdine's president's board since 1955 and chaired the sponsoring committee for the Birth of a College gala. He was such a good friend of Pepperdine that Bill Banowsky and James Wilburn offered to name the Los Angeles campus after him for a contribution of only $4 million. Firestone declined but agreed to a $1 million gift to help construct a field house at Malibu.[38]

Margaret Brock (1904–1997), heir to a commercial jewelry fortune, had a minor acquaintance with Pepperdine before 1970 because of its program recognizing American builders. A high-profile Republican fund-raiser and activist, she liked what she saw and heard at the Birth of a College gala and eventually agreed to a $325,000 gift to build the house overlooking campus that would serve as the official residence of the university president. The result was the imposing 9,000 square-foot Brock House, completed in 1973 and dedicated in September 1975. As a regent of the college, Brock later endowed student scholarships at the law school and gave historic beachfront property to the university.[39]

Nebraska-born George C. Page (1901–2000) hitchhiked to Los Angeles, arriving in 1917, a year later than George Pepperdine. Working first as a busboy and soda jerk, he saved enough money to found Mission Pak, a company that distributed oranges and other fruit to regions of the nation enshrouded in cold weather. A noted philanthropist, he funded multiple buildings in the area, including the George C. Page Museum at the La Brea Tar Pits in Los Angeles. In 1978, Page gifted two residence halls for students at the Pepperdine School of Law in Malibu, and subsequently gave his home to the university.[40]

A native of Texas, Charles B. Thornton (1913–1981) helped found Litton Industries in Beverly Hills in 1953. The quintessential entrepreneur, Thornton was famous for saying "I can't stand useless leisure." He gave a lead gift to enable construction of the $10 million central administration building on the Malibu campus that now bears his name. His wife, Flora, would later serve on the university's board of regents.[41]

Standing with Pepperdine Principles

Through the first two construction phases of the Malibu campus, from 1970 to 1978, Pepperdine's miracle-working friends gave some $64 million. What accounted for their generosity? It was not just because they were friends of Frank Seaver, energized for the Pepperdine project by Blanche Seaver. And it was more than merely a vote in favor of a college campus that presumably had escaped the unrest apparent on other campuses in the 1960s and 1970s.

Bill Banowsky was probably right when he said donors gave "because they like what we stand for at Pepperdine. They believe in our principles."[42] Those principles, of course, included reverence for God, but even more important was belief in the free-market economy, in the American (as opposed to the communist) Way, in limited government, and the capitalistic system. Over time, those Pepperdine principles had been conveyed via the American Builders recognition nights choreographed by Jimmy Lovell, and reinforced in the Freedom Forums, anticommunist films, Great Issues Series, and curriculum packages sponsored by the institution but largely financed by the president's board.

Along with the rising tide of political and religious conservatism in the California Sun Belt, these highly visible programs made Pepperdine University, with its dynamic leadership, a likely antidote to all that was wrong with higher education nationally and a stimulus to attaining all that it promised. To the university's miracle workers, the future belonged to the young... rightly trained.

They considered Pepperdine to be a good place to train them.

CHAPTER 28

The Miracle
Takes Form

W hen Pepperdine University dedicated the Malibu campus in May
1970, it was in the wake of 230 American colleges and universities
shutting their doors to protest the invasion of Cambodia by U.S.
troops and the deaths of four Kent State University students. The uproar suggested to many Americans that radical leftists were in control of the nation's
college campuses.[1] In stark contrast, the dedication ceremony at Malibu was
set in a strong patriotic context that featured the Pledge of Allegiance, lively
marches from a U.S. Navy band, and the presentation by a Navy color guard
of a fifteen-by-twenty-five foot American flag donated by the Santa Monica
Rotary Club.[2]

To an audience of thousands that included thirty-nine delegates from
other academic institutions, David Lawrence, editor of the *U.S. News & World
Report* magazine, spoke on "The Role of Private Colleges in Today's World."
Schools like Pepperdine, he argued, best served society by developing within
their students a strong moral force, presumably something state schools could
not do because of their need to keep state separate from church. Moral force
was the greatest means of achieving peace that man could develop, for it could
strengthen nations and bring people together.[3]

For two years prior to the dedication, Young and Banowsky had been
feverishly raising money to cover construction costs. Pereira's master plan
called for construction in two phases. Phase I began with site work and construction of three complexes: the academic center, the science center, and the
campus center. Residence halls were also included. The initial cost estimate in
November 1969 for Phase I was $18.5 million. Additional structures—includ-
ing the theme tower, chapel, field house, president's home, provost's home,
and additional residence halls—landscaping, amphitheater seating, furniture, equipment, and change of work orders, increased that amount by 30

percent to $24.6 million within a year and by 30 percent more to $32 million by April 1973.[4] Thanks especially to Blanche Seaver and Richard Scaife, and to an effective fund-raising team that reached out to other donors, $22 million of that amount was in the bank or firmly pledged by December 1970.[5] By January 1973, $34.6 million was raised or pledged.

Not all of that amount was liquid, as it included assets like real estate and end-of-life bequests. By April 1973, to meet ongoing expenses the university had borrowed $6.1 million, all of which was due in January 1974. If administrators sold every asset they could, they would still be $2.1 million short. Indeed, cash was so scarce that they had to borrow from the operations budget and mortgage parts of the Los Angeles campus and the Seaver Trust to pay construction invoices.[6] And things did not get better. As the construction program moved into Phase II, with costs of another $31 million, the debt went from $6 million plus to $15.6 million by 1976.[7] Of course, managing the debt and construction costs required severe budgetary restrictions that minimized the prospect of faculty and staff salary increases.

Implementing the Master Plan

With remarkable support from its friends and bankers, after 1970 Pepperdine University turned its attention to implementing the master plan as crafted by Pereira and Associates. Central to the plan was the clustering of academic buildings on a low hilltop "in much the same way the medieval hilltop towns of Italy were built." Presumably there were two advantages to this scheme: it drew together the various buildings, which further fostered the interdisciplinary academic approach adopted for the Malibu campus, and it left most of the site undeveloped, which enhanced the natural atmosphere of the campus.[8]

Before site preparation could begin, the property had to be surveyed for possible sites of Native American habitation. In 1970 a team from the UCLA Archaeological Survey reconnoitered the property and made one excavation, a rock shelter at the mouth of Winter Canyon (located just above the Seaver Drive point of entry and no longer visible) which exposed thirteenth-century remains of intertidal shellfish, pelagic fishes, sea and land mammals, birds, plants, and stone and bone tools. The crew catalogued some 597 artifacts, which they turned over to Pepperdine in August 1971.[9]

William J. Moran Company of Alhambra, California, won the construction contract, working along with the Pereira company under the general direction of Typodynamics, a consulting firm Pepperdine hired to act as its agent in dealing with the technical aspects of design and construction.[10] All major decisions were made on a team basis with the university having the final say and ultimate responsibility. Jerry Hudson, provost and dean of the Malibu campus, represented the university. By edict of President Banowsky, all phases of the construction work were to go through Hudson, "every single detail."[11]

Site preparation was in full swing by August 1970.[12] Construction followed quickly thereafter, and by July 1972, most of the work on the three major components of Phase I was completed, including the 66,000 square-foot academic complex, 50,000 square-foot Murchison Science Center, 300-seat auditorium, and the 50,000 square-foot student center.[13]

Breaking Ground and Dedicating Buildings

For each complex, the university hosted elaborate groundbreaking and dedicatory ceremonies. On April 13, 1971, for example, officials honored the sponsors of the academic complex, the Huntsinger, Payson, and Pendleton families. With 500 people in attendance, those ceremonies featured the first pouring of concrete and an address by Wernher von Braun, the father of the American space program.[14]

The university hosted an even more memorable groundbreaking ceremony for the John and Alice Tyler Campus Center on October 14, 1971. As world-famous heart surgeon Michael DeBakey, a personal friend of the Tylers, concluded his dedicatory address to an audience of 200, four skydivers with smoke trailing floated to an adjacent landing.[15]

Buildings designated as part of the science center were dedicated individually. On October 31, 1971, the groundbreaking for Elkins Auditorium featured Herbert Stine, chair of President Nixon's Council of Economic Advisers. About five months later, on April 24, 1972, a ceremony featuring S. I. Hayakawa, the controversial president of San Francisco State College, dedicated the Jerene Appleby Harnish American Studies Center, then only 60 percent completed. The ceremony concluded without incident, although university authorities had received a bomb threat earlier in the day.[16]

On January 28, 1973, after the Malibu campus opened, the university dedicated the John Stauffer Laboratory. Celebrity conductor Lawrence Welk, member of the university's president's board, introduced the principal speaker, U.S. Senator Barry Goldwater. Goldwater told the 2,500 attendees that Pepperdine, as a Christian college, was "catching on" to its responsibility to support democracy, free enterprise, and Americanism. The faculty advisory committee and much of the faculty were appalled by the senator's message and considered it an embarrassment to the academic image of the university.[17] The center as a whole was dedicated again on April 28, 1974. Edward Teller, the father of the hydrogen bomb, spoke and was recognized by the university with an honorary doctorate.[18]

Theme Tower Becomes Lightning Rod
for Controversy

Most of the construction and dedications of Phase I structures were without controversy, but not the Phillips Theme Tower. Bill Banowsky envisioned a large cross on the campus that would signal Pepperdine's commitment to its Christian mission. This idea was a fairly radical dream for a preacher or school associated with Churches of Christ, which eschewed "graven images." Pereira, a man of faith himself, liked the idea of a theme tower; however, he preferred an obelisk. According to Banowsky, the two ultimately compromised on a 125-foot obelisk that embedded the image of the cross and could be lighted from the interior. It would be located at the entry to the campus.[19]

Pereira drew up the plans in early 1972, and the Phillips family agreed to fund the tower. In March, the California Regional Planning Commission publicly endorsed the plans, but significant opposition to the tower developed within the Malibu community.[20] According to attorney Alvin Kaufer, the president of the Malibu Homeowners' Association, not only would the tower degrade the natural landscape, but "it would impose Pepperdine's religious beliefs on the community." Altogether, he added, "From an environmental, aesthetic, religious and social viewpoint, the 'tower' [was] an unfortunate choice."[21]

Despite the strong opposition, Banowsky proceeded with building plans. In this case, as with the entire campus construction, he had the cooperation of the Los Angeles County bureaucracy, which—prior to authorization of the California Coastal Commission in late 1972—approved hundreds of construction permits to facilitate the Malibu Miracle. A groundbreaking ceremony, with the Phillips family present, was held on April 12, 1972. Moreover, Banowsky authorized contractors to raise the steel superstructure of the tower over the weekend beginning May 26, 1972. Neither deed was well received in Malibu, and the critics sued the university.[22]

For more than six months, all work on the tower ceased, and the superstructure began to rust.[23] The campus opened with the tower only half completed. In Banowsky's mind, that sent the wrong message about the mission and stability of the school. In March 1973, the president later recalled, he attended a community meeting in the Malibu Civic Center to address some of the unresolved issues. After two hours of heated exchange, someone asked whether he would agree not to light the cross at night if the litigation were dropped. Banowsky immediately said "yes," but presumably with one caveat: "during my presidency." With that understanding, legal action was withdrawn, stucco was added to the superstructure, and the tower was completed by September 1973. The following May, the Phillips Theme Tower was dedicated as "a symbol of Pepperdine University's commitment to the restoration of New Testament Christianity."[24]

In his published memoirs, Banowsky insisted that neither he nor the university ever agreed that the tower would never be lighted, saying only that he promised it was to be dark for his presidency only. It is not clear, however, that he made that caveat apparent to his Malibu critics. For example, to the president of the homeowners association Banowsky wrote: "I am able to report that steps have been taken to preclude any arrangements for lighting the tower in any way. This means that we will not illuminate the cross, neither will we light the tower itself in any way whatsoever." The phrase, "during my presidency," was not included.[25]

In fact, the cross in the tower was lighted during Banowsky's presidency, specifically during the Christmas season 1977, with permission from County Supervisor Kenneth Hahn.[26] The lights continued to glow into the early years of Howard White's presidency. According to Larry Hornbaker, the Los Angeles County board of supervisors agreed not to enforce the conditional use permit that turned off the lights so long as no Malibu citizen complained. Surprisingly, none did officially until the 1980 Christmas season, when they threatened to bring suit against the county.[27] Pepperdine administrators turned the lights off, and they have stayed off, despite periodic student efforts to get them turned back on.[28]

Stained Glass and Winds of Complaint

Like the Phillips Theme Tower, the Beverly Stauffer "Little Chapel on the Hill" also had a difficult birth. With the insistence of Beverly Stauffer, the university chose Robert and Bette Donovan of Burbank, California, to design and cut the glass windows. The artists chose the "Tree of Life" as the governing theme for their work, which culminated with an image of the Book of Life, or the Bible, in the upper center of the south front. To prepare sufficient glass for 3,000 square feet of window space took thirteen months, twenty-eight workers, and 125 colors of hand-blown, stained glass from a company in Milton, West Virginia. The results were the largest expanse of glass windows west of the Mississippi River.[29]

The Tree of Life design, even with input from Helen Young, drew considerable criticism. Some did not understand why the artists placed a book where there should have been a cross. Rather than reflect historic opposition within Churches of Christ to graven images, it seemed to reflect a perceived propensity to "bibliolatry." Banowsky objected on artistic grounds, saying the color and design created "a garish, psychedelic scene" that unjustifiably blocked the view of the ocean.[30] Still others objected on engineering grounds. The glass was designed to withstand winds of only twenty miles per hour, when the construction code demanded it to withstand winds up to eighty miles per hour.[31]

The Donovans finished their glass work but left it without a final signature until 1995, after most of the controversy had died down. On November 4, 1973, a year after the Malibu campus opened, the university staged a two-phase dedication ceremony for the chapel. The first phase occurred at the chapel itself, where Norvel Young recognized Stauffer's generosity and ecumenism, the university choir sang, Bill Banowsky spoke, Jerry Hudson prayed, and Monsignor Hawks described the chapel as part of the commerce between heaven and earth. Phase two of the ceremony occurred in the student center before an audience of Protestant ministers and Catholic nuns; Lawrence Welk conducted the national anthem, and Dr. Karl A. Menninger spoke on "Sin and Crime."

The university immediately incorporated the chapel into the life of the community, including granting permission for the Malibu Church of Christ to worship there each Sunday. But questions persisted regarding the soundness of the windows, and in February 1974 and January 1975 high winds blew out some of the panes. Not until the windows were glazed with a second plate of clear glass were they considered capable of weathering Malibu's natural elements.[32]

Field House, Campus Housing

University officials expected the Firestone Fieldhouse to be ready when the Malibu campus opened, but it was not. Construction was delayed because classrooms, laboratories, library, student center, and residence halls had been given priority.[33] Work began on the $2.5 million facility in early 1972, and it was completed in October 1973. Because Leonard Firestone was in Belgium for an ambassadorial appointment, dedication of the building was deferred.[34]

As Moran Construction was completing the field house, it was also constructing Brock House, a home for the president. Situated on a hill overlooking the center of the campus, the 9,000 square-foot house had two levels, with the bottom level designed as family quarters and the top level dedicated to official use, with large dining and reception areas as well as the president's office. Gay Banowsky, an accomplished artist, left an imprint upon many of the architectural details of the $410,000 house. The Banowskys moved into the new official residence in February 1973, and the garage became space for the presidential office staff.

Simultaneously, Jerry Hudson, his wife, and four daughters took up residence in a house constructed for the provost of the Malibu campus. The single level, U-shaped structure sat on a knoll overlooking Winter Canyon and the Pacific Ocean adjacent to the Brock House. The Hudsons occupied the house until 1975 when they left for Hamline University in Minnesota. Thereafter, it became a girls' residence hall, staff offices, and then again the residence for the university provost, William Adrian, in 1986. The structure was dedicated as the Wilma Day Mallmann House on October 8, 1982. Mallmann (1893–1987) donated $118,000 to renovate the provost's house; subsequently, she established a trust that funded a significant scholarship and bequeathed to the university a collection of 209 rare fans.[35]

An even more critical aspect of Phase I construction was completion of sixteen student housing units; ten of these wood-framed, stucco-covered, box-like structures were completed just before the campus opened in September 1972. Moran completed six additional units between 1972 and 1973. All but one were named after donors or friends of donors.[36]

Seaver College—Officially

Of all the dedication ceremonies conducted during the campus construction, two were particularly meaningful. Both were in 1975. On April 20, the Pepperdine community celebrated naming the Malibu campus as the "Frank R. Seaver College." The chosen date was a perfect Malibu day, bright, clear, and cool. Officials staged the campus dedication ceremony in the Fouch Amphitheater before U.S. Senator George Murphy and delegates from sixty-two institutions.

Governor Ronald Reagan spoke glowingly of the work of Frank Seaver, self-described as a "plain old duffer who kept his nose to the grindstone," and Blanche Seaver, whose prayer was not for tomorrow's needs but to "be kind in word and deed, Just for Today." He also spoke of the advantages of capitalism over socialism, the most visible proof of which were the lives and work of Frank and Blanche Seaver, which now included the establishment of the Frank R. Seaver College of Liberal Arts.[37]

Banowsky followed with his dedicatory remarks, "The Spirit of Purpose," in which he defined Seaver College as "the cornerstone of the University," committed as it was to teaching rather than research and to discovering ultimate truth while also keeping pace with change.[38] President Banowsky grandly dedicated the school "to the glory of God and the service of mankind."[39]

Not everyone was happy about the name of the school changing from "Pepperdine University, Malibu" to "Frank R. Seaver College." George Pepperdine College alums saw it as proof that the university's administration intended to separate the school from its roots. And judging from comments in the *Graphic,* many Seaver students felt the same way.[40]

Presidential Celebration

The second notable dedication in 1975 celebrated the completion of Firestone Fieldhouse and marked the conclusion of Phase I construction. Early in April 1975, Banowsky invited President Gerald Ford to visit the Malibu campus, deliver an address, and use the opportunity to dedicate Firestone Fieldhouse and Brock House. Banowsky noted that Pepperdine's supporters, who had donated $40 million to the university, constituted the Republican elite in the state who supported the national party; unstated but obvious was that Banowsky was serving as national committeeman from California, had ambitions to be a Republican senatorial candidate, and deserved some special considerations. Through back channels, Banowsky even agreed to write the president's address.[41]

Just when the Ford White House accepted the invitation is unclear, although probably after July. In that month, Banowsky would declare his support of President Ford for re-election (rather than Ronald Reagan), and the president would float Banowsky's name before Congress as a candidate for undersecretary of the Department of the Interior. It seems doubtful that any of those considerations would have taken place had Ford already accepted or rejected the invitation to speak at Pepperdine. Rather, Ford's acceptance seems more like a response of thanks to Banowsky for his public support and as salve for the insult the Pepperdine president had suffered at the hands of the press and members of the U.S. Congress when his name had been mentioned for the Interior Department position. Ford owed Banowsky a favor, actually many favors, and he agreed to speak on the Malibu campus on September 20, 1975.

Preparing for the first visit of a sitting United States president was no small task, and it taxed limited resources. In addition to interacting with the White House and Secret Service staff, Pepperdine officials had to secure and manicure the campus, generate an audience of about 15,000 people, furnish the proper amount of seating, accommodate 150 television and newspaper representatives, and arrange an appropriate ceremonial program. Preparatory costs ran as high as $60,000, not including some $70,000 to construct retaining walls and stairs beneath the bridge just above the fieldhouse parking lot.[42]

And if that kind of planning did not tax the university's resources sufficiently, two personal tragedies virtually depleted them. On the Monday before Ford's Saturday appearance, Professor Charles Wilks, a young, dynamic mathematician who cherished the Christian mission of the institution, was killed in a motorcycle crash on Tyler Drive near Firestone Fieldhouse.[43]

Even more taxing was the car wreck of Chancellor Norvel Young on the Tuesday before President Ford's Saturday visit. On that day, driving while intoxicated, Young rear-ended a car on Pacific Coast Highway, killing two elderly women. White House Chief of Staff Donald Rumsfeld suggested that Ford's visit be aborted, but Banowsky was able to convince them to the contrary. As scheduled, on Saturday, September 20, the presidential helicopter delivered Gerald Ford to the Malibu campus for his three-hour visit.

President Banowsky greeted President Ford at the temporary helipad on the baseball diamond. After responding to Ford's inquiries and condolences regarding Young's accident, Banowsky whisked him by car to the Brock House where Ford greeted "Mrs. Republican" Margaret Brock and dedicated the two-year-old house she had gifted to the university.[44] At the brunch that followed on the back lawn of the Brock House, the President greeted a group of distinguished guests for an hour, then donned an academic gown and rushed to Firestone Fieldhouse for the dedicatory ceremonies.

Meanwhile, approximately 18,000 spectators, including ninety-six delegates from colleges and universities, assembled in bleachers raised on the ocean side of the southern entryway to the field house. Pat Boone opened the program with the "Star Spangled Banner," and John Wayne led the "Pledge of Allegiance." The Seaver College choir sang "Sweet, Sweet Spirit" as a new Pepperdine flag designed by Gay Banowsky and Peter Munselle unfurled in the ocean breeze. Richard Seaver and Leonard K. Firestone followed with brief remarks. After receiving an honorary doctorate from the university, President Ford then effectively delivered "The Vital Role of Independent Education in America's Future," remarks prepared for him by Banowsky. Ceremonies ended with a prayer by Reuel Lemmons, and President Ford rushed back to the helipad and lifted off to make his next appointment.[45]

Had the presidential trip justified the investment of countless hours of staff time and expenditure of at least $120,000, especially when a $900,000 note was due and the university had no money to pay it? Judging from the correspondence received, most associated with Pepperdine believed it did. A handful complained about wet paint on the bleachers, while a few others objected to inadequate parking. But most thought it was a triumphant, even magical occasion. For them, "sun kissed, ocean washed, mountain guarded and island girded" Pepperdine (which is how Norvel Young had described the Malibu campus) had received local acclaim and international publicity, not just for its setting but also for its academic programs, Christian environment, defense of the American Way, and support of the free-enterprise system.[46]

Phase II and Beyond

The university had completed most of the Phase I construction of the Malibu campus by mid-1974 and were simultaneously making plans for Phase II construction projects. Among structures envisioned were a fine arts complex, an administration building, a law school building, married student housing, six additional dormitories, a swimming pool, and a baseball field. Envisioned too were facilities for the School of Business and Management, the Fifield Religious Studies Center, a sewage treatment plant, and a boulevard just below the chapel. Costs were set at another $32 million, making the total cost for Phase I and II construction approximately $63 million.

For all practical purposes, Phase II construction began with the breaking of ground for the fine arts complex, a 25,000 square-foot structure known as the Founder's Building, in November 1977. Smothers Theatre, one of the two major components, was a 500-seat facility built with a gift from Frances D. Smothers (1886–1977), who had a lifelong interest in promoting the theater and student actors.[47] The second major component of the Founder's Building was the music wing, which provided three levels of practice and performance rooms as well as offices. Its costs were covered by other donor gifts and construction bonds.

A California native, Frank Roger Seaver founded his own company, Hydril, which found phenomenal success as a manufacturer of oil-field equipment. He was well-known for his educational philanthropy to Southern California schools, which included a bequest to George Pepperdine College to support its civic education program. His widow became Pepperdine's largest benefactor, and Frank R. Seaver College of Arts, Letters, and Sciences is named in his honor.

A crucial aspect of the athletic facilities at the Malibu campus was a swimming pool. Gifts came slowly until Blanche Seaver agreed to support the project if the pool were named in honor of Raleigh Runnels, the young son of Charles Runnels who had succumbed to melanoma. With her support, the pool was funded, constructed, and operational by September 1975.[48]

Already a generous supporter of student scholarships, Eddy D. Field (1903–1994) saw to the construction of a first-class baseball facility, gifting the university with property that sold for $171,000. The university broke ground for the Eddy D. Field Baseball Stadium on May 20, 1977. It took another thirty-six months to finish the complex, to the great frustration of Field. He was persuaded, nevertheless, to gift another $600,000 for an office, physical training, and reception facility, which later became Helen Field Heritage Hall, in honor of his wife. The university dedicated the Field Baseball Stadium on March 30, 1980. Helen Field Heritage Hall was dedicated in July 1983 and would soon be used as a reception center for the 1984 Olympics.[49]

In addition to buildings, the university poured considerable resources and energy into landscaping the campus, even launching a "Trees for Pepperdine" campaign.[50] To help pay for a project initially estimated to cost $200,000 but which escalated to more than seven times that much, officials focused their fund-raising efforts on trees while also planting grasses, wildflowers, shrubs, and trees. "Only God can make a tree," one Pepperdine brochure exclaimed, "but you can plant a tree at Pepperdine Malibu."

The campaign was only marginally successful, but there were some significant highlights. William Palmer of Hollywood donated a fifty-six-year-old coral tree to the cause in November 1972. Transporting it to campus had to be done at night by truck via Pacific Coast Highway, under a special order by Governor Reagan, as local officials did not want to divert traffic to accommodate the expanse of the tree. After an eight-hour journey, the tree was placed at the Malibu Canyon entryway to the campus, which it guarded for another two decades or more.[51]

A decade of construction had given life to the Malibu Miracle. It had transformed a bare Malibu hillside into a gleaming campus of Mediterranean-style buildings surrounded by plantings of pine and eucalyptus trees. The transformation required visionary leadership, gifted architects, skilled contractors, and talented craftsmen. It also cost $63 million.

But the finished product was so striking that only a few thought it had not been worth the cost.

CHAPTER 29

EDUCATION BEGINS AT THE MALIBU CAMPUS

W ith its location determined and some buildings constructed, Pepperdine University, Malibu, opened for business on September 6, 1972. Chancellor Young and President Banowsky, of course, had been most visible in conceiving of the campus and getting it built. Others assumed the responsibility for making it operational as an educational institution.

Foremost among the academic administrators was Howard A. White, who had answered Norvel Young's "Macedonian call" and moved to George Pepperdine College in 1958. His superiors quickly observed his administrative talents—especially his mastery of detail and systematic decisions—and made him chair of the social science department, then dean of the graduate program, then dean of the undergraduate program, and then executive vice president and chief operations officer. After 1971, White was the "inside" president, responsible for all internal operations of the university, from academic programs to business operations. Excepting construction matters, there was not much that did not first go by White. He managed to stay on top of his work even through the illness and death of his wife in January 1973.[1]

While White's responsibilities were university-wide, Jerry Hudson's centered on the Malibu campus. Hudson, a Tennessee native, took his BA in history at David Lipscomb College, where he was a student of Howard White, and in whose footsteps he followed by completing MA and PhD degrees in history at Tulane. Upon White's strong recommendation, he joined the Pepperdine faculty in 1962, proved himself to be a superior teacher, and was an early faculty participant in the college's Heidelberg program. Like White, Hudson also preached regularly, first at Westchester and then at Culver City Churches of Christ.[2]

In 1969, Vice President Banowsky told Hudson he was considering him for a "key position" on the Malibu campus, but he wanted three assurances:

(1) that Hudson would recognize the importance of Pepperdine's Church of Christ connection; (2) that Hudson would understand the importance of the business community's connection; and (3) that Hudson would find a positive alternative to faculty tenure on the Malibu campus. Although deeply engaged in finalizing the interdisciplinary curriculum for Malibu—a process that literally turned his hair gray—Hudson apparently gave Banowsky the right answers. In 1971, President Banowsky appointed Hudson provost and dean of the Malibu campus.

Hudson accepted the position but jokingly told Banowsky that he expected to become Pepperdine president when Banowsky became governor of California. Taking over in Malibu, Hudson distinguished himself as manager of the $32 million Phase I construction budget and implementer of an innovative academic curriculum while winning the respect of most of the faculty, the student body, and the general public.[3]

But Hudson was only half joking about succeeding Banowsky as Pepperdine's president. When Banowsky waffled over running for public office and needled Hudson about privileging faculty over administration and the arts and science disciplines over business administration, the provost resigned in 1975 to accept the presidency of Hamline University in St. Paul, Minnesota.[4] Howard White lamented Hudson's departure, for he considered him as an exceptional administrator who was without any identifiable "weaknesses or shortcomings . . . in character, personality and ability."[5] After Norvel Young's traffic collision, Pepperdine's board of trustees tried to call Hudson back to Malibu as president of the university (with Banowsky to assume the role as chancellor). But Hudson had been at Hamline for no more than a year, and it seemed unprofessional to terminate his contract with so little cause. Eight years later upon the retirement of Howard White as president of Pepperdine, Hudson would have accepted such an appointment, but the board would choose not to offer him the position a second time.[6]

The divisional chairpersons, all with terminal degrees and all members of Churches of Christ, reported to Hudson. He appointed one of them, John D. Nicks Jr., as assistant dean during the second year of operation of the Malibu campus. Two years later, Norman Hughes, then chair of the natural science division, succeeded Nicks. When Hudson resigned, Hughes became the first full-time dean of the Malibu campus. Hughes had joined the Pepperdine faculty in 1970, one of those selected specifically to help implement an interdisciplinary curriculum prepared for the Malibu campus. Thoughtful, deliberate, mission sensitive, gentle yet an articulate spokesperson for his faculty colleagues, Hughes served as dean until 1983, when he returned to the classroom.

While Hudson and Hughes managed the academic side of the Malibu campus, Robert "Bob" Thomas was the dean of student affairs with responsibilities for student life beyond the classroom. Thomas felt that because the Malibu campus was entirely new, it should be making its own traditions separate and apart from the Los Angeles campus. As Robert Fraley, director of admissions, remembered: "There was no precedent, no tradition, no pattern to follow; everyone was a new student."[7]

Devising a New Kind of Curriculum

The academic curriculum to be employed at Malibu was under consideration immediately after the Adamson family deeded their 138 acres to Pepperdine College. Administrators, donors, and architects generally agreed that the campus's mission and curriculum would determine the tangibles of its design and buildings, so President Young appointed a committee initially made up of administrators to create an innovative liberal arts curriculum worthy of a residential campus at Malibu.[8]

The committee on facilities and curriculum had its first meeting on October 18, 1968, co-chaired by newly arrived Executive Vice President Banowsky, and Pence Dacus, dean of continuing education. To serve with them, Young appointed Jerry Hudson, Jack Scott, Donald Sime, and Olaf Tegner. Young and Dean J. P. Sanders were ex-officio members, while Mabel Bean was to serve as secretary. Young charged the committee to consider new techniques and practical concepts of Christian education in proposing a curriculum—and to keep their deliberations secret.[9]

In the midst of the committee's deliberations, Banowsky made some notable adjustments. He renamed the group the "Malibu Curriculum Planning Committee," selected Dacus as the official chair and added J. C. Moore and faculty members Loyd Frashier and Tom Dudley. Through the remainder of 1968 and into the spring of 1969, the committee worked diligently. All members read extensively in the literature of experimental higher education, paying special attention to Franklin Patterson's and Charles Longworth's study of Hampshire College, *The Making of a College: Plans for a New Departure in Higher Education* (1966). The committee also interviewed experts in the field, including John Goodlad of UCLA and E. V. Pullias, former Pepperdine dean who was now at USC, and visited at least ten colleges with reputations for creative, interdisciplinary educational practices.[10] Committee members also circulated extensive questionnaires to the college community.[11]

At the end of April 1969, the committee submitted its "Progress Report and Initial Recommendations" first to the academic council and then to the faculty of Pepperdine College. It envisioned an undergraduate liberal arts campus at Malibu that would help students understand the basic ideas that unified all knowledge. To achieve this objective, the committee proposed an integrated, interdisciplinary curriculum that avoided the usual departmental organization and instead was organized around four major academic divisions: humanities, social sciences, natural sciences, and communications.

In each of these areas, students would take four-unit courses delivered in one of four different modes: traditional discipline-integrated lectures; "continuous progress," which was a type of self-paced instruction; small seminars; and field work or independent study. Graduation would require thirty-two courses, divided evenly between lower- and upper-division classes. Students would major in one of the four broad categories of knowledge but would also emphasize a particular discipline within that category. Thus, a student's transcript would read: "Major–Humanities; Emphasis–Religion." Supporting the interdisciplinary curriculum would be a resources center that would provide the tools to facilitate individual student learning.[12]

Unenthusiastic Faculty Response

This grand vision of a cutting-edge academic program was not well received by many Pepperdine College faculty members. They were deeply troubled by the de-emphasis of the traditional disciplines and disappointed that departmental chairs stood to lose standing at Malibu. Some of these faculty members organized their own "Malibu Campus Curriculum Review Committee." Assisted by Arlie Hoover, Wyatt Jones chaired the committee. Other members included Herman Wilson, Fred Casmir, Douglas Dean, Paul Randolph, and Wayne Wright.

The faculty committee believed new curriculum plans for Malibu should have proceeded through normal faculty channels and wanted time to review the ideas thoroughly and prepare an alternate proposal. President Young consented to their request and authorized a very small budget for the committee, but insisted that the group rename itself "The Faculty Committee for the Formulation of an Alternative to the Proposal for Curriculum and Organizational Reform at Malibu." Moreover, he required the committee to complete its work in three weeks so that the architect could get to work.[13] Banowsky found the entire situation "ludicrous" and evidence that the faculty and even the administration would never accept the recommendation of any committee advocating curriculum reform.[14]

As the faculty committee was undertaking its independent study, the administratively appointed academic council sanctioned the work of the Malibu curriculum planning committee, embracing the premise that the suburban campus would offer something other than a duplication of the Los Angeles campus program.[15]

The original Malibu curriculum planning committee tried—mostly in vain—to calm faculty fears. It insisted that

- physical facilities, rather than the academic program, would limit the number of faculty and students at Malibu;
- the new curriculum would have no bearing on faculty tenure and would not prevent students from majoring in a particular discipline;
- religion as a field of study would not be de-emphasized;
- faculty would not be forced to teach interdisciplinary courses;
- the committee had carefully coordinated its work with WASC staff so that the proposed curriculum did not threaten accreditation; and
- its proposal was nothing more than a recommendation to the administration, trustees, and faculty, who were free to reject it.[16]

Faculty Committee Offers Alternate Vision

Working diligently for three weeks, the Jones-chaired faculty review committee completed its work in late July. Its thirty-six-page final report not only identified multiple reasons to rethink the proposed curriculum but also recommended that Pepperdine College re-examine its plan to expand to Malibu. The report asserted that the school's decision to move from a black neighborhood into an affluent suburb was not motivated by Christian ideals; that relegating the Vermont campus to lower-income students undermined that campus's academic standards; and that expansion endangered the financial sufficiency of the college at large. Moreover, the proposed new curriculum reflected the administration's lack of respect for the faculty, which had not been consulted. It was a classic example of "expansion without representation."[17]

The faculty committee did like some of the curriculum proposals, including the interdisciplinarity of the first two years of instruction, the preference for the liberal arts, and the interest in team teaching. But there was more that it disliked, including

- broad-based "majors" such as "natural science" with disciplines like "biology" listed only as an "emphasis";
- no religion division and that courses both in the Old and New Testaments would be taught by "machines": tape-recorded lectures that could be accessed at any time;
- the fact that the proposed curriculum package would eliminate most commuter and transfer students; and
- the idea that disciplined-focused departments had been abandoned but their functions retained.

In conclusion, the committee reminded the administration that interdisciplinary curriculums elsewhere had suffered a student dropout rate of as much as 65 percent.[18]

Forging Ahead

Both the faculty review committee and the Malibu curriculum committee presented oral and written reports to a formal meeting of the faculty on July 30, 1969. After some discussion, the faculty voted to accept the interdisciplinary curriculum proposal. Banowsky was thrilled with the faculty's "impressive vote" for "the new, highly innovative, exciting, creative, dynamic, forward-looking interdisciplinary curriculum"; President Young rejoiced that the faculty rose above the parochial interests of seventeen sitting department chairs and the unfounded concern that the college would abandon its Vermont Avenue campus.[19]

A week later, Pence Dacus and Wyatt Jones briefed the board of trustees on the advantages and disadvantages of an interdisciplinary curriculum at Malibu. Dacus championed the administration-preferred plan. Jones countered with the proposal that privileged the prevailing departmental structure and traditional majors. The board was respectful but hardly impressed with the faculty's counterproposal. All but one, who abstained, voted in favor of the interdisciplinary approach. Only six of the twelve members were present and voting, however.[20]

Having received approval of the faculty and the board of trustees, the struggle over the curriculum came to an end. Banowsky had every reason to take pride in the accomplishment. Discharging the Malibu curriculum planning committee members, he wrote, "I do not need to tell you how significant—perhaps even historic—your work may have been in creating the exciting new curriculum plans."[21]

Banowsky at that point in time was less concerned about the curriculum's historic impact on students and faculty than on its immediate significance for the architecture of the campus. Now Pereira and his team could work concretely on designs and drawings that would facilitate interdisciplinarity, namely close clustering of buildings, a common laboratory, no more than one large lecture hall, classrooms holding fewer than twenty students.

Meanwhile, administrators and faculty were at pains to provide a clear rationale for the interdisciplinary curriculum and area-based majors. According to Jack Scott, the unique approach was premised upon the fundamental assumption that valueless education was folly, that knowledge was related rather than fragmented, and that an integrated curriculum prepared students for a future where specialized knowledge (discipline) was quickly obsolete.[22] "The mere accumulation of fragmented information," he asserted, did not constitute "education of the whole person."[23] Norman Hughes noted that the new Malibu curriculum would be unique in requiring students to assume a large responsibility for their own learning in self-paced courses, large interdisciplinary lecture courses, and small seminars.[24]

It was one thing to frame a rationale and envision elements of a "radical" curriculum, but it was another to actually implement that radical curriculum. As evidenced by the faculty review committee report, a substantial number of faculty members were suspicious of any sweeping change. In addition, most were committed to particular intellectual disciplines and did not look kindly on proposals to dilute them. So the administration compromised to accommodate them and other constituencies. By September 1971, officials had modified the intended curriculum so that the Malibu campus would open with twenty-five traditional majors grouped into six rather than four divisions—adding religion and fine arts to the original proposal of humanities, social science, natural science, and communication divisions.[25]

Faculty criticism had prompted the addition of a division in religion. Graduate Dean and Professor of Religion Frank Pack lamented, for example, that there was not a single course planned on the book of Acts or the New Testament church; that there was more of an emphasis upon theology than biblical doctrine; that there was only one course devoted to the Old Testament; and that there was no course concerning the work of the local church. Such deficiencies were unacceptable for a school that stood in the tradition of the Stone–Campbell movement and wished to train students for both the pastoral and teaching ministry.[26] Not wanting to offend its church constituency, the central administration agreed.

Rounding Up a Faculty

With the campus under construction, leadership in place, and the curriculum constructed, the Pepperdine administrators began steps to assemble a faculty for Malibu. In doing so they looked for qualified liberal arts scholars, preferably with doctorates or the equivalent, who valued interdisciplinary studies, embraced a flexible pedagogy, cherished the free-enterprise system, supported the American Way, treasured Christian service, and worshiped with Churches of Christ.

In addition, the perfect professor at Malibu was also to exhibit certain behavioral characteristics, including

- professional involvement;
- attendance at mandatory and most voluntary chapel assemblies;

- attendance at all formal university functions (graduations, convocations, dedications, student receptions) and as frequently as possible at informal functions (athletic events, plays, and lectures); and
- spending forty hours every week on campus in preparation, classroom, and student consultation time.

The ideal professor would also eat in the cafeteria as much as possible; make Pepperdine his or her only professional occupation; assist the dean of student affairs in rigorously enforcing all campus rules and regulations; and be sensitive to involvement in the Malibu community.[27] The ideal faculty member, therefore, would be significantly different from faculty who served in most of the educational institutions in the United States. To find all of that in one person was no easy task, especially if traditional tenure was not to be offered. A tenure-less campus was especially important to business elites and Pepperdine friends like Morris Pendleton, who attributed much of the turmoil on university campuses in the late 1960s to the ranting of tenured professors.[28]

The Pepperdine administration rightly assumed it would be difficult to find the desired qualities among the current faculty on the Los Angeles campus, where most members questioned the desirability—or even rationality—of opening a campus at Malibu, not to mention the idea of an interdisciplinary curriculum. Thus, university officials looked beyond the LA campus to assemble the Malibu faculty. Among those recruited were Tony Ash (religion), Royce Clark (religion), David Gibson (philosophy), James R. Greer (psychology), Cora Sue Harris (history), Stewart Hudson (communication), Norman Hughes (biology), Richard T. Hughes (religion), Steven Lemley (communication), Lawrence McCommas (music), Stephen McHargue II (political science), John D. Nicks Jr. (social science), George Poole (physical education), Edward Rockey (communication), Robert Thomas (student affairs), and Ronald Tyler (religion).

Pepperdine's administrative team soon discovered, however, that it could not assemble a full faculty for Malibu separate and apart from the one in Los Angeles. It had neither sufficient economic resources to employ two separate faculties nor a large enough pool of suitable candidates. So certain Los Angeles faculty who seemed to meet the Malibu criteria were invited to relocate. Among those who accepted the invitation were James Atteberry (English), Fred Casmir (communication), Douglas Dean (biology), Loyd Frashier (chemistry), Walter Glass (physical education), Clarence Haflinger (music), Arlie Hoover (history), Wyatt Jones (psychology), Warren Kilday (chemistry), John McClung (history), Carl Mitchell (psychology/religion), Frank Pack (religion), Kenneth Perrin (math), Stephen Sale (history), James Smythe (English), William Stivers (Spanish), Eugene White (art), Morris Womack (communication), and Wayne

Wright (physical education). As it turned out, some 60 percent of the first Malibu faculty had prior service in Los Angeles.[29]

Incorporating Los Angeles faculty into the Malibu program generated its own set of problems. Not all were enthusiastic about the new curriculum; not all were sympathetic with the business elite who had funded the Malibu miracle; not all were excited about the leadership of Banowsky and Young. On the other hand, all were tired of the financial sacrifices required of faculty who taught at Pepperdine. And all cherished the tenure they had earned by their service at Pepperdine-Los Angeles, and insisted that their tenure follow them to Pepperdine, Malibu. Any suggestion to the contrary generally radicalized the faculty and provoked an angry response from the AAUP chapters on both campuses. Therefore, despite the prejudices of the business elite who built the Malibu campus and the administration's preference to initiate a tenure alternative, the practice of recognizing and awarding tenure to Pepperdine faculty continued.[30]

Finding Students

While Pepperdine officials were enlisting faculty and staff for Malibu, they were also recruiting students. In keeping with the plan to make Malibu a liberal arts college that took seriously its Christian mission and relationship with Churches of Christ, President Banowsky and Chancellor Young at first envisioned a student body with 75 percent from Churches of Christ, a figure that was later modified to 60 percent.[31] To recruit this number, Banowsky turned to Silas Shotwell, a childhood friend from Fort Worth, a rising star in Churches of Christ, and a preacher in Albuquerque. He told Shotwell that Pepperdine needed someone to recruit Christian students for the Malibu campus "like USC recruits football players." Shotwell agreed to serve as special assistant to the president if he could bring some friends from Albuquerque, specifically graphic artist Bill Henegar and secretary Christa Winegeart. He also persuaded Banowsky to hire "Big Don" Williams, the youth minister at the Broadway Church of Christ in Lubbock, as one who could relate directly to prospective Church of Christ students.[32]

Renaming his office the "Department of Church Services," Shotwell and his staff launched a nationwide campaign that included ten large youth rallies in major cities with heavy density of members of Churches of Christ. One of the first was the Thanksgiving Youth Festival on the site of the new campus. The event included a rally at Knott's Berry Farm theme park and gatherings under tents in Malibu; more than 500 California youth attended, beginning a tradition that continued into the twenty-first century. At other youth gatherings across the country, popular preachers spoke, student subsidies were offered, and a media blitz was launched. In the year before the Malibu campus opened, Pepperdine spent three times as much money recruiting, most of it aimed at Church of Christ students, as it had spent five years earlier.[33]

The results of the effort were mostly disappointing. Only forty of the 147 students—28 percent—assembled in 1971 as the Malibu pilot program were members of Churches of Christ. That percentage was almost the same the next year when the Malibu campus opened with 866 students. Banowsky prophesied that the percentage would never be as high again and would "very slowly, but steadily decrease."[34]

As it turned out, the decrease was not all that slow. Five years later, only 10 percent of the Malibu student body and less than 5 percent of Los Angeles campus students claimed membership in Churches of Christ. By that time, the division of church relations had closed, Silas Shotwell had been terminated, advertisements had been canceled, and tuition had been raised.[35] Bill Henegar was transferred to university affairs, and Don Williams was reassigned to admissions. President Banowsky had concluded that recruitment efforts among Churches of Christ were not cost-effective and that the church constituency was not sold on the Malibu Miracle.[36]

More gratifying than the yield of church-related students was the harvest of students with stronger academic credentials. The 147-member pilot class had GPAs and standardized test scores that were significantly better than national norms.[37] But, as with the percentage of Church of Christ members, the numbers declined rather quickly, dipping under national averages in only a few years.[38]

Given the targeted recruiting campaign, the demographic of Malibu's first class was a bit of a surprise. Eighty-two percent, or 711, of enrolled students were from California, while only eight students were from the heartland of Churches of Christ—Texas, Tennessee, Oklahoma, and Arkansas. Fifty-three percent were males. Only 3.6 percent of the class was African American, compared to 18 percent on the Los Angeles campus.[39] Clearly, the demographic profile of the initial classes was not as diverse as preferred.

The social and political profile of the student body was more diverse than expected, however. In fall 1975 the *Graphic* editors administered a poll that compared a cohort from Oklahoma Christian College to 130 Seaver students. They found that 61 percent of Seaver students opposed the death penalty, while 62 percent of OCC students favored it. Only 49 percent of Seaver students attended church once each week, 50 percent used alcohol, and only 45 percent thought premarital sex was wrong. On the other hand, 100 percent of the OCC cohort attended church weekly, no more than 5 percent used alcohol, and 83 percent thought premarital sex was wrong. The *Graphic* also found there were almost as many Democrats as Republicans on the Malibu campus.

Obviously, the Malibu student body had a different world view than that of a comparable student body of a Church of Christ school elsewhere.[40]

Gratitude Amid Chaos

The Malibu campus opened on September 6, 1972, only days after the campus had been connected to sewer facilities and only hours after it had been connected to natural gas. In the ten residence halls there was no hot water, no toilet seats, no showers heads, and no desk carrels. Three students shared each room. Construction crews had not made roofs leak-proof, nor paved the main parking lot, nor concreted sidewalks, although they had managed to erect a chain link fence between women's and men's residence halls. "Everywhere" there were "snakes, mice, and ants."[41]

Nevertheless, there was a sense that the Malibu pioneers were experiencing something very special, with "every tree . . . planted, every slab of concrete poured and every lamp pole erected."[42] Despite the chaos, virtually all faculty, students, and staff saw the launching of the Malibu campus as answer to prayer. No one expressed this better than Norvel Young. On September 25, 1972, at an assembly of students in Elkins Auditorium, he spoke of the moment as the "fruition of a dream," one that he had pursued for more than a decade. For him the Malibu campus was confirmation of Jesus's words in the gospel of Matthew, that "If you have faith as a grain of mustard seed, you will say to this mountain, 'move' and it will move." It was indeed true that the Malibu hills had actually been moved to make way for the campus.

However, many students did not retain those feelings of gratitude in the months to come, even though Dean of Student Life Robert Thomas and his team worked diligently to accommodate their physical and social needs. In addition to construction inconveniences, the students complained chronically that there was nothing to do on campus, especially on the weekends. Furthermore, there were the irritations of mandatory chapel, the ban on dancing, the restriction of visitation hours for the opposite sex in residence halls, and the limitation of lighting to save electrical costs.[43]

The first trimester of the inaugural year of the Malibu campus constituted four months of blues for the student life office. By all accounts, circumstances improved in the second trimester, but many students still found it less than satisfactory: as many as one-half of them did not come back for a second year.[44]

Those Malibu students who dropped out or transferred elsewhere were quickly replaced by an efficient admission's office, and the undergraduate student body almost doubled between 1972 and 1975, from 858 to 1,592. By 1978, it had reached nearly 2,200.[45] Having no published minimum academic standards for admission helped recruitment, but that fact also explained why the attrition rate between the freshman and sophomore years was so high; at times, 45 percent of all undergraduates were new to the campus. To get further insight to the attrition, the admission office surveyed forty non-returning students in fall 1974. Responses revealed that students came to Pepperdine-Malibu because of its location, spiritual emphasis, academic reputation, and small size. They left because of financial reasons, their personal academic circumstances, an inadequate social life, and too much emphasis on religion.

Innovative Curriculum in Practice

When the Malibu campus opened in September 1972, its liberal arts curriculum was offered by six divisions. Soon, Pepperdine's School of Education and School of Business and Management were also offering undergraduate programs at Malibu, with the liberal arts faculty managing general education courses and the professional school faculty controlling major courses.[46] In 1974, the largest divisions were social science, communication, and natural sciences, with the most popular majors being biology, education, communication, and business administration. Religion was the smallest division.[47]

A preference for professional as opposed to liberal arts degrees, a preference that dated back to the founding of George Pepperdine College, became a consistent characteristic of the Malibu campus. That helped explain the 1978 fusion of the fine arts division with the humanities division and the creation of a stand-alone business administration division, which soon became one of Seaver College's largest. The undergraduate education program was incorporated into the social science division.[48]

The innovative interdisciplinary curriculum designed by the Malibu planning committee made its mark on the campus. One of the more noble experiments was the "continuous progress" (self-paced) courses, which included English composition, created by Ed Rockey; "Biblical Knowledge," created by Paul Watson; and "American Ideals and Institutions," created by Jim Wilburn. As inventive and modern as these courses may have been, they soon went the way of most self-paced courses in other educational institutions across the country—more than 60 percent of enrolled students failed to finish them. More enduring were the traditional but discipline-integrated introductory courses such as "Man in Science" by Norman Hughes; "Western Heritage" I and II by Grover Goyne; and "Man in Society" by John Nicks and Robert Gilliam. These courses served the general education curriculum until Seaver College adopted a new GE program in 1986.[49]

From the beginning of the Malibu campus, administrators wanted to fight the fragmentation of knowledge by de-emphasizing disciplines and majors. They began in Malibu offering major work in only twenty-six fields of study.

But they could not hold the line, and the number had increased to thirty-nine within six years. The number of majors offered held fairly steady in the years to come, however. At the seventy-fifth anniversary year in 2012, it totaled only forty-three.

The university leadership assumed from the beginning that the Malibu campus would be primarily undergraduate, but a graduate program in education began within a year. Eight additional graduate degrees were soon offered, only five of which were in the liberal arts: American studies, communication theory, English, history, and religion. The number of master's degrees increased by one when community/clinical psychology was added in 1984. Unlike their colleagues at other institutions, the liberal arts faculty at Malibu never got very excited about graduate education. Indeed, some programs such as psychology, English, and history would drop their master's degrees eventually.[50]

In early April 1973, the Malibu campus graduated its first class in the Wilshire Ebell Theater on 8th Street in Los Angeles. With his usual flair and humor, Bob Hope delivered the traditional commencement address. Along with ninety-two MA or MBA graduates and an honorary doctorate, nine received bachelor's degrees, something of a marvel in that the campus offered freshman and sophomore classes almost exclusively. Clearly these nine had taken most of their credits on the Los Angeles campus.[51] In subsequent years, more and more graduates had taken their course work at Malibu. In 1974, those numbered 136; in 1977, they totaled 307; and in 1980, they numbered 443.

Academic Criticisms and Accreditation Troubles

Students who walked across the stage to get their diplomas represented tangible evidence of the success of the educational process at Malibu. But detractors noted that in 1973–1974 some 13.6 percent of the entire student body made the dean's list with a 3.2 GPA or better, and a "whopping" 9.6 percent earned a 4.0 GPA.[52] President Banowsky counseled his colleagues about the danger of "academic mediocrity."[53] But rather than dealing directly with grade inflation, the faculty merely raised the bar for honors.[54]

The 1973 edition of *College Rater*, an early version of *U.S. News & World Report's* annual evaluation of colleges and universities, expressed sobering reservations about Pepperdine University's academic reputation. On a list that evaluated 470 privately supported institutions in seven categories, the *Rater* ranked Pepperdine as 443, awarding it only 413 points out of a possible 1,142, fewer than any California college and fewer than David Lipscomb and Abilene Christian Colleges. Pepperdine's weaknesses, according to *Rater*, were low admission standards, an inadequate number of books in the library, inadequate faculty salaries, and too many faculty members without doctorates.[55]

This report provided a portrait of Pepperdine far different than the one Banowsky and Young had painted for the wealthy elite who had paid for the Malibu campus. Banowsky was outraged, complaining to the publisher that the ratings were "irresponsible and blatantly inaccurate" and based upon "fragmentary and terribly dated" information. He was also upset that the *Rater* viewed Pepperdine University as a whole, making no distinction between the campus in Los Angeles and the campus in Malibu.[56]

Banowsky frequently complained that evaluators judged Pepperdine University as a whole on the basis of the performance of the Los Angeles campus. In December 1970, WASC even questioned whether the school was worthy of the "university" designation, which it would bestow upon itself the next month. WASC pointed to problems in academics and other areas, saying faculty did not have effective input to meaningful decision-making; college salaries were inadequate; the library's budget was insufficient; student personnel services were in turmoil; and the quality of Pepperdine's growing off-campus program, especially in Hawaii, was problematic.[57]

However, Banowsky was convinced that WASC's negative impression of Pepperdine came primarily from what visitors had observed on the Los Angeles campus, and he insisted that WASC evaluate Los Angeles and Malibu as two distinct colleges when it conducted its 1974 evaluation. That wish, he insisted, was wholly appropriate for a "multi-versity" like Pepperdine.[58]

To the surprise of some, the accrediting agency consented to the request. The strategy, however, did not result in a better review. The WASC visitors still found fault for the same reasons mentioned above. The accreditors also complained about the lack of an organizational structure that unified the various elements of the institution, the absence of a university-wide academic structure, and the privileging of donors over faculty members. Furthermore, the visitors remained skeptical of Pepperdine's 1971 decision to call itself a university.[59]

The preliminary report of the WASC visiting team deeply offended Pepperdine administrators and faculty.[60] Banowsky was "disappointed" and "alarmed" by the report's "harshness of . . . language" and lack of objectivity. He was especially troubled by charges that the university was little more than an "educational brokerage" in its off-campus programs, that it was composed of "tight and secret enclaves," that there was a "lack of coordination of academic policy," and that an "uncoordinated plurality of activities [did] not add up to a university." Moreover, the report spoke of a "disgruntled faculty" and "inadequate salaries," questioned whether "educational quality" prevailed, and charged Pepperdine as being little more than "a small Los Angeles City Teacher's College."[61]

The president's unofficial and official responses resulted in only minimal changes in the language of WASC's final report, which remained stern and accusatory. Banowsky's outcry, however, may have shaped the accreditation decision of the agency's senior commission. Rather than issue any sanctions, it accredited both Pepperdine University-Los Angeles and Pepperdine University-Malibu separately, requested a progress report in two years, and scheduled a comprehensive review of both campuses in spring 1979. In other words, Pepperdine won reaccreditation for another five years, a victory that Banowsky joyfully reported to the board of trustees in September 1974.[62]

Executive Vice President Howard White filed the university's two-year interim report with WASC in April 1976. He noted that President Banowsky, under the authority of a new forty-member board of regents had made considerable progress in addressing concerns about the university's operating structure. The president now delegated responsibility for day-to-day operations of the university to White, and finance issues to Warren M. Dillard, vice president of finance. The deans for each of the six schools reported to the executive vice president. University Information Services managed a computerized data processing system that handled all student records.[63]

With pride, White also pointed to the formation of a University Academic Council (UAC) in October 1974. As executive vice president, he chaired the council, which was responsible for establishing common academic policies for all components of the university, approving all new degree programs, and reviewing existing ones.[64]

Polishing Pepperdine's Academic Reputation

The *College Rater* incident and the 1974 WASC review forced Pepperdine to focus on raising the school's academic profile. The unresolved issue was how best to do it. In one high-priority initiative, university officials inaugurated a visiting professor program for distinguished scholars beginning in 1975. It was promoted in a brochure touting Pepperdine as "an emerging institution" and then featured the four distinguished academics who were casting their lot with Pepperdine.[65]

Included among these was Edward Teller, well-known for his research in nuclear and molecular physics. He joined the Malibu faculty in academic year 1975–1976, as the Distinguished Visiting Professor of the Arthur Spitzer Chair of Science and Technology.[66] Because of their support of nuclear armaments during the Cold War, both Teller and Spitzer were much admired among Pepperdine's conservative supporters.

Nobel laureate Willard Libby also joined the Pepperdine faculty as distinguished visiting professor in 1975. Libby, longtime professor of chemistry at UCLA, was known for his discovery of radiocarbon dating. At Seaver College, his assignment was to establish a pre-environmental curriculum that would feed graduates into UCLA graduate programs.[67]

Historian Keith Berwick also accepted an appointment as a distinguished visiting professor. Berwick, well known for his scholarly work in the Revolutionary era of American history, had taught at UCLA, Claremont, and USC and also been awarded four Emmys for television broadcasting.

The fourth distinguished professor was Irving Melbo. Dean emeritus of the USC School of Education, Melbo was legendary in the Los Angeles educational community for his work with community colleges. Unlike the other visiting professors, he was attached to Pepperdine's School of Education, and his service extended to more than one year. Indeed, Pepperdine made him the first recipient of the Julian A. Virtue Chair in Economics Education and a founder of the Julian A. Virtue Institute of Economics Education, which, among other things, offered summer seminars and classes for Los Angeles teachers.[68]

Melbo was the only participant in the visiting professor program to give Pepperdine more than the use of a distinguished name and perhaps a lecture or two, which is all they were really expected to do. In 1975, Pepperdine was looking for instant credibility as a legitimate academic institution, and claiming a relationship with distinguished scholars was a step in that direction. It was even more beneficial, especially for elite donors, that those scholars opposed communism, embraced free enterprise, and revered the American Way.

Other programs were also designed to demonstrate academic respectability. The long-running Taft and Coe American studies programs for teachers were restructured and offered on the Malibu campus through 1975, when the programs ended due to lack of funding.[69] The final program involved thirty-one teachers and an impressive array of guest speakers.[70]

To enrich its curriculum and attract more students, the Malibu campus added American Humanics as a program and youth agency administration as a major in 1974. Founders intended the program to train workers for leadership positions in nonprofit youth services like Boy Scouts, YMCA, and Girl Scouts. Pepperdine's program was the first on the West Coast, and administrators expected it to bring fifty additional students to Malibu. The program was never that successful, but it was sufficiently institutionalized to survive into the twenty-first century.[71]

Pepperdine administrators also considered offering a full-fledged equestrian program on its Malibu campus, even dreaming of creating the "west coast center for equestrian education."[72] The plans for an equestrian program did not work out as envisioned, however. Complaints from Malibu neighbors and a lukewarm reaction from donors prompted the university to drop its plans for an equine studies major in 1976, although it offered an equestrian PE alternative through the remainder of the century.[73]

It was one thing to build Pepperdine University's Malibu campus, it was another thing to operate it as an educational institution. The process that began well before the campus opened in September 1972 involved selecting new leaders, constructing an innovative curriculum, selecting appropriate faculty, and recruiting a student body. Once the new campus opened, the process of education began. Thereafter it was largely a matter of adapting the real to the imagined and compromising the theoretical with the practical, all the while projecting a positive image of Pepperdine University. The birth pangs were real, but by 1975 most of them were in the past.

The expansion of a small inner-city college into a multifaceted university with programs around the world and a shiny new campus in the Malibu hills could not have occurred without dynamic—and frequently controversial—leadership. We consider now a few of those leaders and their most significant decisions and actions.

AMBITIOUS LEADERSHIP, SWIRLING CONTROVERSIES 1968–1978

CHAPTER 30

PRESIDENTIAL POLITICS

After five years as minister of the Broadway Church of Christ in Lubbock, Texas, thirty-two-year-old William S. Banowsky returned to Pepperdine College as executive vice president on June 1, 1968. President Norvel Young believed that the college was at a critical point and needed Banowsky's brand of "dynamic leadership." The vice president's primary responsibilities would be to raise funds for the new Malibu campus. Young confessed that he could "hardly wait" until Banowsky moved to Los Angeles and got started.[1]

The relationship between the president and his new associate was unique. The two had first met on the campus of David Lipscomb College in Nashville in 1958 when Banowsky was a graduating senior with a degree in speech communication. Young was impressed with the Texan's striking good looks, personal warmth, self-confidence, candidness, intelligence, and mastery of public speaking, and he immediately tried to recruit him for a position at George Pepperdine College. After completing a master's degree at the University of New Mexico, Banowsky accepted the invitation, moving to Los Angeles as associate dean of students in 1959. Simultaneously, he began work on his doctorate in communication at the University of Southern California. When he completed that degree in 1964, he resigned to become pulpit minister of the Broadway Church of Christ in Lubbock, never expecting to return to Los Angeles.

Young had other ideas, however, and he regularly consulted with Banowsky regarding issues confronting Pepperdine. Most important, he looked to Banowsky to construct the decisive argument to locate a new campus at Malibu.[2]

The bond between Young and Banowsky was much like a father-son, or older brother-younger brother relationship. There was a deep love and a strong sense of loyalty between the two. Young took pains to promote Banowsky's career and took pride in his accomplishments. But like most fathers or elder brothers, he was at times mystified by some of the younger man's ambitions, especially in the political arena.

Banowsky considered Young a "big person" who had bestowed extraordinary measures of time, energy, and love on him; but he was perplexed when Young held firmly to values and traditions that Banowsky considered antiquated—especially his all-encompassing relationship with Churches of Christ.[3] But the remarkable partnership between the two was never more evident than it was after Young's 1975 car accident that took the lives of two women. Banowsky rushed to Young's side, where he pretty much remained for the next three years. "His battle is my battle," he wrote of Young at the time, and "I want him to win."[4]

An Impressive First Impression

Bill Banowsky, his wife, Gay, and their four young sons joined the Pepperdine College family the first week of June 1968 and quickly made an impression on the college and Southern California. Two days after the June 8 assassination of Robert Kennedy in Los Angeles, Banowsky addressed the weekly meeting of Rotary Club of Los Angeles. In a stirring address titled "The Abuse of Freedom," he posited that the nation's rising tide of violence was due in part to the misapplication of the idea of freedom. American society had recklessly flung off its restraints, leaving it like a ship without a compass or a rudder.

The solution, Banowsky said, would come from embracing individual responsibility and a clear application of law and order. The Rotarians gave him a standing ovation. Morris Pendleton, a member of the Pepperdine president's council and a personal friend of George Pepperdine, enjoyed the speech so much that he paid to reproduce and circulate thousands of copies of it.[5] The address was also broadcast by radio station KNX to a listening audience of millions. Thereafter, Banowsky received hundreds of invitations to deliver that and other speeches to countless audiences. He accepted a goodly number of those invitations, resulting in name recognition for himself, honorariums to supplement his income, and a widespread conviction that Pepperdine College had dynamic and safe leadership that championed both conservative Christian values and the American Way.

Six months later, in January 1969, Banowsky had a similar triumph in Santa Barbara, California, this time with the help of a public relations firm. Arranged by Campus Advance, a ministry associated with Churches of Christ operating at the University of California, Banowsky met former Anglican bishop James Pike to debate sexual standards associated with the so-called new morality. The brash and traditional vice president did more than just hold his own against the wily, liberal bishop; but the presence of "left-wing" agitators forestalled a complete victory—or so Norvel Young reported to Blanche Seaver. Nevertheless, Banowsky had done himself and the school "quite a bit of good" from a public relations perspective.[6]

In April 1969, Banowsky had one more high-profile public debate, this one at Ball State University in Muncie, Indiana. His opponent was Professor Joseph Fletcher, author of the much-read *Situation Ethics* (1966), and the topic was moral relativity. Banowsky affirmed the existence of moral absolutism; Fletcher denied it. If applause was the measure, Banowsky won the debate, reported the *Muncie Star*.[7] Although other opportunities regularly presented themselves, the Indiana debate was Banowsky's last in a public forum setting. He had achieved what he intended: standing as an advocate for absolute values in the defense of family, faith, and homeland—not only for himself but also for Pepperdine College.

Rocketing Up the Ladder

Banowsky had returned to Pepperdine as executive vice president of the college at large. With the acquisition of the Malibu property soon after, President Young changed his title within a few months to executive vice president of the Malibu campus.[8] Always eager to increase the level of Banowsky's responsibility, Young altered his title again to chancellor of the Malibu campus in September 1969. Young was mimicking the organizational structure of the University of California, where a chancellor presided over each campus.[9]

But he was also responding to his joy at working with Banowsky, a delight not shared by all. Religion Professor Fred Davis and an unnamed trustee, for example, thought Banowsky was far too young and "phony" to have such a responsible position.[10] But the criticism did not faze Young, and on February 10, 1970, he resigned as president and chief executive officer of Pepperdine University, effective January 1, 1971, so that Banowsky could take over the positions. At the same time, Donald Miller resigned as chair of the board of trustees so that Young could take on that role, which he did, serving as president and chair until January 1. On that date, Banowsky became president; Young became chancellor of the university (remaining chair of the board of trustees); and the trustees appointed Howard A. White as executive vice president and chief operating officer. White's appointment was meant to relieve Banowsky of most day-to-day administrative matters.[11]

And the plan worked perfectly. One of Banowsky's faculty colleagues estimated that the new president spent no more than 10 to 15 percent of his time on internal university matters. Curriculum, personnel, and construction issues associated with the Malibu campus were referred to Provost Jerry

Hudson. Banowsky delegated similar duties on the Los Angeles campus first to Provost Jack Scott and then to Provost James Wilburn, both of whom reported to White. As CEO, White had direct supervision of the university's business offices. From time to time, President Banowsky did interest himself in some details of the university's daily activities, such as the failure to conserve energy on the Malibu campus, the inadequacy of chapel singing, the question of students dancing, and the issue of faculty salaries. But altogether, much to the chagrin of the *Graphic*, he was pretty much invisible on campus.[12]

Raising His Off-Campus Profile

As the trustees desired, the majority of Banowsky's time was devoted to raising money to construct the Malibu campus. Since success in that realm depended upon enhancing the public profile of Pepperdine College, every speech or TV appearance made; every breakfast, lunch, dinner, banquet, ceremony or concert attended; every column written, or interview given contributed to the larger effort.[13] Banowsky in the 1970s took on the responsibilities of a weekly show on KNBC-TV, tri-weekly columns in the Los Angeles *Herald Tribune*, and a monthly column in *Newsweek* magazine.[14] In 1972, he sought and received membership in the the Los Angeles Country Club and the Bohemian Club, a prestigious men's club in San Francisco.

With the encouragement of Ronald Reagan, Banowsky agreed to chair the Los Angeles County Campaign to Re-elect Richard Nixon in 1972, even though major Malibu donors George Elkins and Blanche Seaver disapproved. (Elkins thought the position would distract Banowsky from his university responsibilities; Seaver disapproved of Nixon.) And a year later he accepted the non-salaried position as the Republican national committeeman for California.[15] In short, Banowsky was never off duty.

Fortunately, Banowsky had support in these Malibu friend-raising/ money-raising endeavors. His wife, Gay, was a constant and elegant companion, despite raising four sons and teaching art classes at Pepperdine. Helen and Norvel Young were dedicated and tireless partners. Charles and Amy Jo Runnels, Larry and Carole Hornbaker, and Bob and Peggie Bales became increasingly involved. James Wilburn took leave from the university to assume the heaviest burdens of the Nixon re-election campaign as Banowsky's paid assistant. And a host of ghost writers prepared material for the TV shows and print-media columns; many of the writers were compensated directly by the university.[16] Public relations consultants won Banowsky appointments to prestigious boards and made news of his schedule.[17] Still, even knowing that Banowsky had such help, the number of events attended, presentations made, columns formulated, letters written, and hours "on duty" were stunning.

As President Banowsky worked to enhance the standing of Pepperdine University in the Los Angeles community, he added considerable luster to his own image. Many friends came to believe he was hiding his candle under a bushel—wasting his talent as president of a small, struggling Christian college. Surely he could make a bigger and better contribution on a much larger platform, as president of an established state university or in an elected political office.

Although he had signed a five-year contract with Pepperdine beginning January 1, 1972, Banowsky soon explored the idea of replacing S. I. Hayakawa as president of San Francisco State University. Although encouraged by Glenn Dumke, chancellor of the California State University system, Banowsky subsequently withdrew from consideration, in part because he had no desire to be grilled by the SFU faculty and in part because Malibu donors like Morris Pendleton said he should have his "head examined" if he pursued the position. Wait ten to fifteen years, Pendleton wrote, and you will have an opportunity

William S. Banowsky became Pepperdine University's fourth president in 1971, serving in that role until 1978. He presided over some of the most significant changes in Pepperdine history, including the opening of the Malibu campus and the restructuring of the university's governing structure.

to go to Harvard. Banowsky told Governor Ronald Reagan that he rejected the idea of going to SFU because the state system was so bureaucratized and because he had determined to make a political contribution within the Republican structure—"to fight rather than switch," as he told television newsman Tom Brokaw.[18]

Testing Political Waters

Banowsky had always found the possibility of public office seductive. As early as 1970, he had contemplated running for the U.S. House of Representatives in West Los Angeles, but he took Blanche Seaver's advice not to pursue that option.[19] Following his participation in President Nixon's 1972 re-election campaign, he sought a suitable appointment in Washington, D.C. When no fitting offer was forthcoming, Banowsky determined to take a "sabbatical" from politics.[20]

It was not much of a sabbatical. In June 1973, Banowsky agreed to serve as Republican national committeeman from California. That position placed him near the pinnacle of the Republican establishment in the Golden State, but it also swept him up in a storm of controversy. First, he went on record in support of Ronald Reagan to replace Spiro Agnew as Nixon's vice president.[21] As the Watergate scandal gained momentum, Banowsky urged President Nixon not to resign, speaking as a national committeeman and a university president.[22] Within nine months, however, he reversed himself and joined with other California Republican leaders to call for Nixon's resignation, charging that the administration had perverted essential American freedoms.[23]

Meanwhile, Banowsky assessed his chances as a Republican candidate for the U.S. Senate seat held by Democrat Alan Cranston. In mid-1973, he commissioned a professional survey of voters in Los Angeles and Orange counties. The results of that survey were discouraging. The poll showed Banowsky likely to get only 3 percent of the vote in a Republican primary against two likely candidates and only 18% of the vote in a general election against Cranston.[24] The president of Pepperdine University quickly announced he would not be a candidate for the U.S. Senate from California.[25]

Looking at Lubbock

And if he were not to be a candidate for public office in California, then should he even be a university president in California, Banowsky asked himself? Perhaps he should go back to Texas where his unique blend of piety and politics would be more welcome. At Pepperdine University he encountered schizophrenia between secular and sacred values, a willingness to be in the world but not content to be entirely of it. That duality wrought within Banowsky, wrote friend and mentor Darrel Rickard, a "battle . . . far greater than I realized" and involved him "in things that my conscience would have difficulty accepting."[26] The struggle had left him with a "fatigued state of mind," concluded minister William E. Young.[27]

To put that struggle behind him, to bridge the dichotomy, Banowsky seriously considered accepting the presidency of Lubbock Christian College in the summer of 1973. There, in the bosom of Church of Christ brethren, he could find the philosophical consistency that would bring him peace of mind.[28] It also offered him a new locale should the political bug ever bite again.[29] Indeed, the discussion with LCC was so serious that Chancellor Young believed Banowsky would accept the offer as of January 1, 1974. Howard White disagreed, writing in his journal there was about as much chance that Banowsky would go to Lubbock as that White himself would open a house of prostitution.[30]

Young believed Banowsky's consideration of the Lubbock offer arose from "frightening" changes he had noticed in his younger colleague dating back to early 1972. It seemed Banowsky had moved left of center on almost everything, from university governance, to student conduct, to national politics. Young had actually begun to think he and Banowsky had grown so far apart that they were pulling against each other and that "divorce" was the only solution. Banowsky had about "done all he can do for us," Young wrote sadly.[31]

In the end, of course, Banowsky did not go back to Texas. Rather, he bargained with Young and the board of trustees for new working conditions. He thought he could find "deep satisfaction" and make a long-term commitment to Pepperdine if he were permitted to devote his full energies to an academy committed to "open and free spirit of inquiry" whether the subject was scientific, political, or religious, and he pointed to Harvard, Vanderbilt, and USC as models. In other words, Banowsky wanted to secularize the university, but he could not do that against the "will and judgment" of Norvel and Helen Young, whose "deepest commitment," Banowsky understood, was "to save Pepperdine for the church."[32]

Thus, he proposed something of a compromise: if Young would agree to his longtime desire to "open" the university board of trustees to nonmembers of Churches of Christ, the thirty-eight-year-old Banowsky would commit to leading an "open" Pepperdine until he was forty-five. He saw only minimal consequences in the short run: there would be tension but no major severing of ties with Churches of Christ, and there would be no immediate change in the university's "basic political and business conservative approach." Sooner or later, however, ties with the church would be broken and a less conservative political-economic stance adopted. Banowsky saw no alternative. "Pepperdine will either go under or else go open."[33]

There may have been additional reasons for Banowsky's decision to remain in California. If *Los Angeles Times* reporter John Dreyfuss got it right,

Richard Scaife and Blanche Seaver, Pepperdine's two largest active donors, told the president to stay in both his university post and as the California Republican national committeeman.[34] Banowsky obviously took their advice, re-engaged with the university, and quickly returned to the center of California Republican politics, where he continued to gain attention and stature. In July 1974, *Time Magazine* declared him to be one of the 200 faces of the future.[35] His name was widely mentioned as a Republican candidate for the U.S. Senate seat held by Democrat John Tunney, and Banowsky was expected to decide whether to run by late March 1975.

Investigation Tarnishes Image, Reputation

Widespread public notice of a long-festering Pepperdine University problem, however, predetermined his course. As will be discussed in more detail in the next chapter, George Pepperdine College alumnus Trent Devenney had concluded that his alma mater, and especially Banowsky, had deserted the true faith of the American Way and the free-market economy.[36] Devenney got little traction until he revealed that Banowsky, Young, and two other Pepperdine administrators paid themselves undeclared retirement benefits in cash—a revelation that got the attention of the California attorney general.

In October 1974, after a two-year review and an untold number of legal briefs, the attorney general found Banowsky and Young had done nothing that warranted charges but much that was imprudent. Even so, the matter received little public attention until March 12, 1975, when the *Sacramento Bee* broke the story of the attorney general's investigation with a sensational lead revealing the secret account that enhanced four administrative salaries. The *Bee* published a follow-up account in June based upon a confidential preliminary draft of the attorney general's staff report prepared fourteen months earlier. The article marveled that the attorney general's office had not initiated either criminal or civil action against Banowsky and others, implying that the attorney general, Republican Evelle Younger, had given special consideration to the Republican national committeeman and potential senatorial candidate, William S. Banowsky.[37]

In May 1975, given all of the negative publicity associated with the attorney general's investigation, Banowsky decided he would not be a candidate for the Senate. He attributed his decision to a "scurrilous, right-wing political attack" and to an executive pay system for which he was not responsible. The consequence was the loss of a "potential political career." But he said he was at peace with the development. In a letter widely circulated to the university community and his political friends, he noted that "Ultimate questions, as opposed to immediate ones, intrigue [him] most." Thus, "A school is a better place than a congress to address the ultimate questions. And a school like Pepperdine, dedicated ... to mankind's spiritual search," could address those questions best. Presumably, he was pleased to continue as president of Pepperdine University inasmuch as he accepted a new five-year contract.[38]

Tilting Toward Washington

Yet the political bug still itched. Gerald Ford had succeeded Richard Nixon as president in August 1974, and he moved quickly to ensure he would receive the Republican nomination for president in 1976. On July 9, 1975, if not earlier, one of Ford's operatives called Banowsky, still the Republican national committee- man, and asked him to declare publicly with forty other notable Californians that he would support the president's bid for election. Banowsky agreed to do so, although apparently without giving much thought to Ford's potential primary opponents. Later that evening, he received what he has described as one of the "saddest phone calls in his life." Former California Governor Ronald Reagan was calling to ask Banowsky to endorse him for the presidential nomi- nation. Banowsky had to tell the man who had given so much of his time to promoting Pepperdine that he had pledged support to Gerald Ford. It was four years before Reagan and Banowsky would talk again.[39]

However much he may have regretted endorsing Ford, Banowsky intended to use that decision to his and the university's benefit. Just days later, on July 21, he was on his way to Washington, D.C., to consider an appointment as under- secretary of the Interior Department. In the process, he learned that a nomina- tion and confirmation process would likely be long and complex. Clearly some saw Banowsky as little more than "a fund-raiser" for Reagan who had "no back- ground whatever for a high post in the Interior Department," as the *New York Times* would subsequently state. His choice, the *Times* concluded, "was plainly dictated by the desire of Mr. Ford's political advisors to undercut the President's only serious rival [Reagan] for next year's Republican party nomination."[40]

Embarrassed by the presumption that he was being used to sidetrack Reagan's quest for the presidency, Banowsky suddenly canceled his remain- ing appointments, caught a plane to California, and announced he was not a candidate for any government position. Indeed, Banowsky said, his work at Pepperdine was "deeply gratifying," and he took "pride of authorship" in every tree planted, each building built, every faculty member hired, and every stu- dent enrolled.[41]

But the "real" reason for the change of heart had little to do with his grati- fying work at Pepperdine. In the midst of negotiations in Washington, he had called the Internal Revenue Service office in Los Angeles to check on an income tax audit launched in the wake of the California attorney general's investigation. He was told there were still "serious" unanswered questions over some expense accounts. Although Banowsky's tax returns were eventually deemed acceptable, he did not want revelations about his write-offs publicized at Senate hearings.[42]

Still, Banowsky was puzzled by his reception in Washington. For enlightenment he turned to political insider Horace Busby, a shrewd Texan with roots in Churches of Christ who had worked in the White House during the Lyndon Johnson administration. In Busby's opinion, Republican moderates had ganged up to oppose Banowsky not because of his identification as a conservative right-winger but because of his history as a "fundamentalist" preacher. If Banowsky wanted to pursue a political career, Busby advised, he should drop out of sight and reincarnate himself with a more appropriate image. Three years later Banowsky would act upon the advice and move to Oklahoma, where, in due time, he would seek the Republican nomination for U.S. Senator.[43]

Politics and Pepperdine

Although the endorsement of Ford's presidential campaign failed to benefit Banowsky personally, it proved to be advantageous for Pepperdine University. On September 20, 1975, President Ford arrived on the Malibu campus to help dedicate the Firestone Fieldhouse and the Brock House. Despite the pall cast by Norvel Young's collision four days earlier that had taken two lives, the event was a smashing public success. Indeed, 18,000 Southern Californians assembled to hear Ford hymn the praises of private liberal arts colleges that sought truth in the context of the American Way and Christian mission. Surely the presidential visit was a direct dividend to the university for Banowsky's lengthy involvement in Republican politics.[44]

Not all thought Banowsky's political activities were an unequivocal blessing for the university. According to David Reagan, director of Pepperdine's Center for International Business, President Banowsky's political activities brought more negatives than positives for Pepperdine. Greater visibility and a network of wealthy friends were clearly positives, but Banowsky's indecision about running for office obscured the focus of the university's nature and role.

According to Reagan, no one could answer authoritatively the question, "Just what the hell is Pepperdine University?" A Christian school? An academy for the Republican right? Was it closed or open in its quest for truth? No one knew, Reagan argued, because leadership seemed more concerned with political winds than educational pursuits. His advice to Banowsky was either to "fish or cut bait": be a politician or an educator. Either decision would make the university stronger. But Banowsky attributed any indecision to "his hesitation to take on the agonizing implications of our church relationship versus our academic expectations." Clearly those issues lingered, but in the fall of 1975, he had never been happier in his work or more optimistic about his tenure with Pepperdine—or so he said. Partly for that reason, he found it possible to resign as the California co-chair of the Republican national committee.[45] Also a factor in his decision was the need to manage the administrative, political, and financial consequences of Norvel Young's collision and forced retirement from the university.

Of course, Banowsky did not lose his interest in politics completely. With the help of ghostwriters, especially Sheri Keyser, he continued to publish thrice-weekly columns in the *Los Angeles Herald Examiner.*[46] He invited political friends like Dick Cheney and John B. Connally to be his guest at Bohemian Club functions.[47] He even reached out to left-of-center politicians like Governor Jerry Brown, with intermediary John Marin describing Banowsky as a "liberal" who at his "dynamic center" was "sensitive to the winds of change" that stirred "our increasingly non-partisan masses."[48]

And after nearly eight years as president and "profound feelings of love and attachment," Banowsky resigned his position at Pepperdine to accept a similar assignment at the University of Oklahoma beginning October 1, 1978. He was forty-three.[49] At Pepperdine, he had pretty much accomplished his priorities: building a $63 million campus at Malibu, opening the university to secular influences, and revising the charter and bylaws to include non-Church of Christ regents. By mid-1978, for organizational and budgetary reasons, the university was on a course of consolidation rather than expansion. Never content with routine, Banowsky needed a new challenge. Moreover, he longed for an environment where he "would not have to mesh a deeply conservative religious background with the realities of the modern world."[50]

The University of Oklahoma, an esteemed public institution in the state his grandparents had helped pioneer, offered that possibility. Moreover, it could provide options for reviving his political interests. Because going to Oklahoma was like going home to Texas, he wrote Richard Scaife, it would give him "a tremendous power base . . . to speak out on the issues and have an important national impact for the things in which we believe." Clearly, being president at OU would "provide interesting possibilities for even more important national opportunities in the future."[51] In other words, Oklahoma represented a palette from which Banowsky could begin to paint another version of his stymied political career.

CHAPTER 31

THE TRENT
DEVENNEY AFFAIR

Born in 1941, Trent Devenney grew up in Bakersfield, California, and matriculated its schools through junior college. In 1961, after attending Pepperdine's Freedom Forum featuring U.S. Senator Barry Goldwater, he determined to complete a baccalaureate degree at George Pepperdine College in Los Angeles. He had concluded that the school clearly championed the American Way and supported the free-market economy, characteristics he considered non-negotiable in the selection of a college.

In the application process, Devenney revealed that he was raised in the Congregational church but found it too liberal and was attending St. Francis Catholic church. He submitted three personal references; two were very favorable, but one characterized him as an unhappy and immature boy who complained about his teachers, made ridiculous arguments, and was unable to see two sides to a given issue. For a student-hungry school, however, such negative comments were hardly sufficient to deny admission. Thus, Devenney joined the student body at George Pepperdine College as a junior history major in fall 1961.[1]

At the college, Devenney was an average student. In his first year he served on *The Graphic* staff, authoring articles that revealed his strong conservative political philosophy. He was also very active in Young Republicans and was elected state president of the conservative splinter of the organization he helped establish. He graduated from Pepperdine in 1964 and Hastings Law School in San Francisco in 1969, and by fall 1973, was a deputy in the Los Angeles city attorney's office.[2]

From there, Devenney had frequent occasions to observe what was happening at his alma mater, and he did not like what he thought he saw. He was concerned about the racial tensions, liberal professors, and the urban emphasis. Above all, Devenney was unhappy because he believed the administration in its day-to-day operations was violating the conservative political and economic principles it preached when soliciting gifts from the Los Angeles business community. Nothing galled Devenney quite so much as the fact that President Young once made national headlines by rejecting federal aid, only to stand in line later for whatever federal grant was available. Equally troubling was the "hypocrisy" of Young and Banowsky in acceding to the actual demands of campus black militants while announcing that they would never negotiate under duress. From Devenney's point of view, both Young and Banowsky, but especially Banowsky, were "opportunists" whose political conservatism was "phony."[3]

Yet, despite what appeared to be lack of conviction, Banowsky's political career was skyrocketing, thanks in part to help from Governor Ronald Reagan. That was all too much for a Goldwater Republican, a true believer who viewed compromise as a sin—or at least a weakness. From Devenney's perspective, Banowsky was the worst kind of hypocrite and needed to be exposed.

Doyle Swain felt the same way. A lifelong member of Churches of Christ, Swain had left a position at Harding College to join the Pepperdine College staff in 1961. At Pepperdine, he served first as director of civic affairs, playing a major role in organizing the award-winning national citizenship program. He also served as assistant director of the Center for International Business. A gifted writer, Swain contributed to the *American Builders* magazine, composed public relations pieces, wrote speeches, and even agreed to ghostwrite an article for Banowsky to be published in the *Southwestern University Law Review.*[4]

Like Devenney, Swain was a true believer in Christianity, conservative political principles, and the free-market economy. He was certain that Pepperdine University was drifting from its first love, and he wrote Blanche Seaver that there was no academic freedom for the only two conservative professors at Pepperdine: Professor of Communication Fred Casmir and Professor of Biology Douglas Dean.[5] Swain and Devenney became fast friends when they met in the fall of 1961. How closely they stayed in touch when the younger man was in law school is unclear, but they certainly re-established their friendship after Devenney returned to Los Angeles.[6]

Reporting on Pepperdine's "Improper Practices"

In 1972, Devenny made an extensive study of the academic, social, and religious life of Pepperdine University and subsequently produced two lengthy "white papers." The first, 167 pages long, was titled "Pepperdine Project, Preliminary Report No. 1, R/D No. 2" and dated January 20, 1973. Although his name was not attached, Devenney authored the document. In this "report," he blamed Young and Banowsky for racial tensions on the Los Angeles campus between 1968 and 1972, insisting they sold out to liberal, collectivist militants.

He charged liberal Howard White with recruiting and hiring known trouble-makers from Harding College and said the creation of the ethnic studies program and department of urban affairs demonstrated that Pepperdine administrators had embraced curricular "relevance" rather than maintaining the study of the demonstrated truths of Western civilization.[7]

Devenney's principal source for discerning the errors of Pepperdine College were the columns of *The Graphic* published between 1968 and 1972. He quoted the issues of the student newspaper so liberally that it was as if he had the bound copies in front of him. Several years later when librarians microfilmed file copies of *The Graphic*, the 1968–1972 volumes were missing. If Devenney borrowed the university library's copies, he forgot to return them.

Doyle Swain wrote the second white paper, "The Odyssey of Pepperdine University," which was fifty-nine pages long and dated March 19, 1973. Its purpose, Devenney wrote, was to summarize the circumstances at Pepperdine and serve as an introduction to the first paper. By bringing to light administrator's "improper practices, hypocritical methods and techniques," wrote the authors, perhaps the university could be returned to "the path marked out for it by its founder." If not, then the authors were prepared to take their case "to donors, patrons, the public at large, or others who may honestly, but mistakenly, believe that Pepperdine is faithful to the image it has perpetuated for itself."[8]

In these documents, Devenney and Swain had much to say about the sins of Young and Banowsky. The college solicited funds from patriotic businessmen to produce anticommunist films but never showed them on campus. The college claimed to support academic freedom, but conservative professors were made to feel unwelcome. The institution claimed strong religious ties, but the Bible was no longer the core of the curriculum. Presumably the college stood for traditional values, but it recruited faculty and students known for dissidence and disruption.[9]

To the presumed hypocrisy, Devenney and Swain added malfeasance and dishonesty. Grant money given by wealthy patriots, even Frank R. Seaver himself, for anticommunist films had been diverted to other projects. All members of the board of trustees, including Young, his wife, and Banowsky breached trust and integrity to manipulate the university to their personal advantage. Banowsky's courting of elderly, wealthy, influential, and socially prominent women like Blanche Seaver bordered on the unethical, especially when he also courted liberal males like Seniel Ostrow, a Malibu neighbor and president of Sealy Mattress Company. Banowsky and Young, moreover, promised the school's wealthy supporters that the new campus in Malibu would not offer tenure to its faculty but promptly reneged on the pledge.[10]

In "The Odyssey of Pepperdine University," Swain claimed he and Devenney had no desire to destroy the college but did want some changes. These included governance changes, including the resignation of Norvel and Helen Young and William Banowsky from the board of trustees. They also wanted Bill Banowsky to resign from the presidency, blaming him for "the vast deterioration that ha[d] occurred in the character of Pepperdine as an educational institution during the last five years or so."[11]

The addition of heavy references to the Christian mission of Pepperdine University in the second white paper suggested the influence of Swain and the enlargement of the circle of dissenters. Welcomed to the ranks were Archie Luper of Ventura, California, and Ira Y. Rice Jr., of San Francisco. Both were Church of Christ members, and Rice was a preacher who edited *Contending for the Faith*, a monthly journal that rarely lacked some caustic words about the "drifting" at Pepperdine.[12] Rice and Luper joined the group with the announced objective of keeping the school Christian and within the orbit of Churches of Christ.[13]

Explosive Insider Information

Sometime in April 1973, after the two white papers had been drafted, Bill Robertson joined the dissenters. The university's chief accountant from May 1967 to June 1972, he was an able and dedicated employee who had been terminated, probably unjustifiably, because of a personality conflict. Still smarting from the circumstances of his firing, Robertson shared some explosive information with Swain and Devenney, telling them about a Pepperdine account called "University Planning Consultants (UPC)." Since 1966, board of trustee chair Don Miller had annually submitted an invoice to pay the consultants some $40,000. President Young then approved the invoice, a check would be cut and promptly returned to the president's office. What the invoices did not show, Robertson reported, was that Young subsequently cashed the check at a local bank without a signature endorsement. Swain and Devenney were absolutely convinced that the administration was engaged in criminal fraud.[14]

Armed with such evidence, Devenney took his case systematically to some of the university's stronger supporters. There is no evidence that he got much of a hearing until he visited with Gordon Del Faro. Owner of R. & R. Tools in North Hollywood, Del Faro had been a consistent but not a heavy donor, having given no more than $9,100 between 1966 and 1972. Del Faro cast his lot with the dissenters and thereafter was the "client" in whose name Devenney acted.[15] His motivation was essentially pragmatic, however: he wanted to prevent the dynamic President Banowsky from "competing with sound conservative politicians" in the future.[16]

Devenney then took his case to the university's most faithful and generous supporters: Helen Pepperdine, Appleby Harnish, Blanche Seaver, and Richard Scaife. Helen Pepperdine gave him a hearing, and perhaps even encouragement, and she also shared Devenney's white papers with Young and Banowsky, who had not seen them previously. After considering the documents, Helen Pepperdine concluded that the charges "were irresponsible and without sufficient basis in fact," and she chastised Devenney for stirring up trouble.[17]

Harnish, a successful newspaper publisher in Los Angeles County and an outspoken advocate of right-wing politics, also listened to Devenney initially but terminated correspondence with him after she satisfied herself that university development officers did not receive finder's fees.[18] Devenney also approached Blanche Seaver, but with even less success.[19] Apparently Devenney was unable to speak directly to Scaife, and his one-sided correspondence with officers of the Scaife Family Trusts made little impact.[20]

Pepperdine released Swain as an employee in September 1973, a few months after the release of his white paper. Young could never quite understand why Swain had chosen to join with Devenney.[21] Banowsky might be more moderate than true believers preferred, but he was hardly a traitor to conservative political values or Christianity.[22]

The State Weighs In

Devenney asked in April 1973 to take his case to the university's board of trustees, but Young declined his request.[23] At that point, the dissenters took a fateful step and submitted all their documentation to the California attorney general, insisting it warranted a full investigation of the university's administration, which was clearly guilty of hypocrisy, malfeasance, and fraud.[24]

Aware that Devenney had taken this action, President Banowsky asked to have breakfast with Evelle Younger, the attorney general. They met as fellow Republicans, one an elected official and the other the national committeeman of the party. No minutes of the meeting have been found, but the two clearly did agree on an immediate course of action. At the end of breakfast, Banowsky formally asked Younger to undertake an official inquiry of administrative practices at the university. Should anyone ask, the request was not made under the duress of the Devenney charges but because the university wanted to manage its dynamic growth more effectively. Indeed, the university was engaged in the process of updating its charter and bylaws and would welcome input from the attorney general.[25]

The state inquiry began almost immediately, managed by Deputy Attorney General Arthur Tapper and executed by investigator John F. Fiscus, who was in residence at the university for three months beginning June 11, 1973.[26] The attorney general's office mulled data gathered by Fiscus and Devenney for an additional seven months, finally issuing an interim report on April 4, 1974. Written largely by Tapper, the document identified three areas of concern.

1. President Banowsky and Chancellor Young appeared to dominate and control the university's financial affairs because of the antiquated structure of the board of trustees and their membership on it.

2. Banowsky and Young had received "improper payments" through the UPC account despite presumed authorization from the board.

3. The president and chancellor, along with members of the trustee's executive committee Robert P. Jones and George A. Evans engaged for their own profit in business and financial activities tied to Pepperdine and to each other, including the selection and development of the Malibu campus.

Thus, Tapper concluded, "for many years Pepperdine and several of its fiduciaries [had] operated in a manner contrary to law." Of specific concern were the financial interrelationship of the four trustees and their ability to exercise their legal responsibilities toward Pepperdine. Tapper saw evidence that the trustees had made speculative investments involving real estate and banking in behalf of the university but to their own advantage.[27]

Pepperdine administrators read the report in two different ways. Norvel Young told trustee Jimmy Lovell that the attorney general had not "found anything out of line" but had to make recommendations of some kind to rationalize all the time and effort his office had taken on the investigation.[28] But other administrators thought the interim report was something of a bombshell that seemed to affirm the biases and assumptions of Devenney. Clearly the university's effort to shape the initial product had failed. Banowsky and Young would not want the interim report to circulate, especially within the faculty.[29]

The University Responds

Tapper expected Pepperdine attorneys to respond to the interim report with corrections, additional information, and solutions, and they turned in fifty-six pages of vigorous responses seven weeks later on May 29, 1974. Counsel admitted that the Pepperdine charter and bylaws were indeed antiquated but said Banowsky and the Youngs had taken seats on the board precisely because they were so dated and participation of the trustees was so haphazard. University administrators had already launched an effort to update the bylaws and secure additional members for the board of trustees, and in the meantime, the Youngs and Banowsky deemed it appropriate to resign from the board.[30]

The university's counsel saw no conflict of interest between the investments of some of the trustees and the school. He denied any collusion between
Trustee George Evans and the Adamson family—his client—to defraud the
school via some agreement with Alcoa, developer of Malibu Estates and one
of the companies controlled by the Scaife interests. As evidence, he noted that
the Malibu site was first suggested by Ken Ross, a Pepperdine alumnus and
Malibu resident—not Evans.[31]

As for the "University Planning Consultants," wrote counsel, it was a
misguided attempt to disguise the amount of executive compensation. The
board of trustees in 1966 had authorized annual and lump-sum payments for
retirement purposes to key administrators—originally Young and Bill Teague
with Banowsky and Charles Runnels added later. The executive committee of
the board, which had the responsibility for setting the administrative salaries, established the UPC as a way to disguise the additional payments from
inquiring eyes, particularly those of the faculty. The scheme was problematic
and impolitic but not illegal. Moreover, the total amount paid to the administrators was in keeping with executive salaries from comparable Southern
California institutions. Nonetheless, this method of paying executives raised
suspicions, so President Banowsky had already replaced it with a more open
executive payroll, counsel reported.[32]

When it came to real estate speculation, counsel could only admit that it
had occurred. Involved were board members Robert Jones and George Evans,
Young, Banowsky, and Andrew Rawn, executive officer of Typodynamics, the
construction management firm for the Malibu campus. None of the transactions, or deals, however, involved university assets or compromised public
trust—with one exception. That involved property near Riverside, California,
in which Jones and Young had invested jointly but then given a portion to the
university. Since it had worked to the advantage of the university and occurred
after the fact, it hardly represented a conflict of interest. Counsel did agree,
however, that the speculation on a parcel of land in Malibu (Vista del Malibu) by
Young, Banowsky, and Andrew Rawn was probably imprudent, given the company's consulting role in the construction of the campus. That being the case,
Young would buy Banowsky's interest in the parcel and then donate the whole
to the university to support student scholarships.[33] Unspoken in the arrangement was Young's desire to preempt any demand from the attorney general
that Young and Banowsky reimburse the university for money paid through
the UPC account.[34]

The attorney general's office took no final action on its Pepperdine investigation until October 1974.[35] By then the university, with eight additional
trustees, an amended charter, and new bylaws on the drawing board, had put
its governance system in order; eyebrow-raising executive pay procedures

had been mended; and it had been demonstrated that real estate speculation involving Pepperdine administrators and members of the board did not involve university assets nor infringe public trust. Given those developments, Attorney General Younger was ready to close the case that had lingered in his office for eighteen months. Following an exchange of letters of understanding on October 30, 1974, the matter was officially put "to rest."[36]

But not quite. As the state of California completed its investigation, the federal government began another. Agents of the Exempt Division of the Internal Revenue Service arrived to audit accounts of the university and its administrators. Their requests required hundreds of employee hours to fill, and were particularly demanding of Banowsky. But they uncovered only minor infractions, and—like the attorney general of California—the IRS eventually found the university and its administrators guilty only of sloppy bookkeeping.[37]

Pepperdine in the Papers

Throughout the state and federal investigations, the Los Angeles and Malibu faculties had only a partial understanding of the issues, despite—or perhaps because of—the fact that Banowsky had briefed the Malibu faculty on the investigation on February 20, 1974.[38] In general, the faculty response at that time was remarkably temperate. That all changed, however, on March 12, 1975, when Denny Walsh, the *Sacramento Bee* Pulitzer Prize-winning journalist, broke the story of the attorney general's investigation with a salacious lead about a $77,500 "secret" account that enhanced the salaries of Banowsky, Young, Runnels, and Teague. But the story focused on Banowsky, the Republican national committeeman and a prospective candidate for the U.S. Senate, and Walsh reported that the attorney general's office said the practice was so questionable that legal action was appropriate.[39]

How Walsh came to write the story was never made clear. He did have lengthy conversations with Trent Devenney, who believed the Republican attorney general had whitewashed the investigation to favor Banowsky.[40] Yet it might have been brought to Walsh's attention by others who merely had political axes to grind. Supporters of William A. Norris, the Democratic candidate for attorney general were looking for issues that would challenge the integrity of Younger, the incumbent. Since the Pepperdine case ended without even a reprimand, Norris could charge that Younger was either soft on crime and/or valued his Republican ties to Banowsky above justice.[41] Or Walsh might have been tipped to the story by Goldwater Republicans who did not see Banowsky as a suitable Republican candidate for the U.S. Senate and were eager to expose him as a fraud and cheat.[42]

The day after the *Bee* story, the *Los Angeles Times* published its own version, as did most state newspapers over the next several days, including the *Graphic* and *Inner View*.[43] The story also made national headlines in the *Chronicle of Higher Education*.[44] Although President Banowsky had presumably informed the faculty about the investigation in the spring of 1974, they were surprised when the story broke in newspapers a year later.[45]

Individuals and faculty groups sent letters of censure, especially disturbed by what was widely described as a "slush fund" for the secret use of the administration. Evidence that their president and chancellor received funds in addition to their "regular" salaries—whether for retirement or not—angered them. The American Association of University Professors (AAUP) chapter on the Malibu campus met "in a mood of moral indignation," declared faculty leader Ola Barnett.[46] Members of the faculty had worked for less than minimum salaries, forgone raises, and skimped on supplies—and all the while their leaders had grown "fat" on surreptitious payments to themselves.[47]

A "Concerned Faculty Member" from the Los Angeles campus wrote the president: "Here's hoping we can look forward to your early retirement and replacement with a Christian as concerned with faculty welfare as furthering his own political ambitions."[48] Carl Mitchell, chair of the religion division, feared that keeping salaries secret meant the university was neither upholding the highest ethical norms nor affirming trust and good faith within the community.[49] A "Concerned Pepperdine Supporter" from Malibu wrote Banowsky that "The current scandal is a great personal tragedy for both [you and Dr. Young]. Please do not convert it into a tragedy for the University by dragging out the inevitability of your resignations."[50]

The story also grabbed the attention of preachers and lay members of Churches of Christ. Archie Luper announced that Young and Banowsky needed to repent and pay back any money received through the UPC. He wanted Don Miller and Reuel Lemmons to repent as well, the latter for refusing to point out Young's and Banowsky's "sinful activities" at Pepperdine. Ira Rice Jr. was less interested in the soul-welfare of the Pepperdine leadership than in exposing them. To be sure, Rice and Luper represented only the conservative fringe of the Church of Christ fellowship, but their criticisms stung nonetheless.[51]

Banowsky Counterattacks

Given the negative reaction to the newspaper accounts both on and off campus, Banowsky recognized the need for a public relations counterattack. Although it appeared under the name of student editor Neva Hash, he wrote a lengthy *Graphic* article titled "Pepperdine critics exposed." In it he named all of the dissenters who had teamed up to damage the reputation of the university and denied that Pepperdine had abandoned its principles.[52] He also carefully crafted a memorandum to the faculty and staff—signed by the chair of the board Don Miller—that sought to explain the context of the mysterious retirement account, denied the existence of any "secret fund" for executive pay, declared the board of trustees' full approval of the payments, and emphasized that the attorney general had found "nothing improper in the conduct of the institution."[53] A similar letter went to the editors of newspapers in Sacramento, Fresno, and Modesto.[54]

Banowsky also spoke to the Los Angeles and Malibu faculties. The meetings were heated, and the one on March 20 at Los Angeles was the "most hostile" meeting he had ever attended. It started with 400 people; four hours later seventy people were still there. It was a shouting match, with students taking the lead, protesting everything from lack of carpets to the absence of a van. At Malibu, most of the criticism came from Church of Christ faculty (Carl Mitchell, Fred Casmir, and Bill Stivers) who had recently signed a petition asking for closer relations with the church. Banowsky spared them no scorn, equating Churches of Christ with the narrow views of Ira Rice and promising that he would push to widen the gap with the church constituency. He directed some of his denunciations toward the AAUP, reminding members that he had advised the faculty a year earlier of the attorney general's investigation. If AAUP was going to excoriate him for moral failure, why did it wait a year, he asked?[55]

The *Fresno Bee* published Miller's letter in full under the title "Pepperdine Replies," but an appended "Editor's Note" took exception to the substance of the letter. According to the deputy state attorney general, the *Bee* argued, the minutes of the board reflected "no express and explicit authorization of the secret payments," nor had Pepperdine authorities actually initiated the inquiry, something that had been done by Pepperdine critics.[56]

In the meantime, Denny Walsh somehow got access to one of the very limited copies of the attorney general's interim report released fourteen months earlier. He exposed it to the public in another column in the *Bee* on June 16, 1975. Gleefully, he noted that according to the report four trustees of Pepperdine University had operated for many years "'in a manner contrary to law.'" And despite these violations, Walsh wrote, "the attorney general's office initiated neither criminal nor civil action." In a gesture of objectivity, Walsh dutifully noted that Pepperdine's lawyer, James Crowley of Latham & Watkins, considered the attorney general's interim report as "outrageous" and "irresponsible."[57]

Faculty Furious, Frustrated

The combined impact of Walsh's two articles was significant in all quarters, but especially within the faculty at Malibu. The knowledge of Banowsky's "secret slush fund" made it difficult for members to accept the announcement that there would be no salary increases in the upcoming 1976–1977 academic year. They were furious but had been unsuccessful in registering their complaint with the president or regents. In frustration or as the "last act of desperation," the Malibu faculty called a boycott for Lincoln's birthday, February 12, 1976. On that day 90 percent of faculty canceled classes but not office hours.[58] They also sent a delegation to confront the president at his Brock House office, directing it to make a strong case for salary increases. Banowsky apparently listened to and even commiserated with the petitioners, but he promised no relief. Instead, so the story goes, he instructed the faculty representatives to end their demonstration and reminded them that if they did not cease and desist he could replace them overnight. Banowsky always denied that such a confrontation ever occurred, yet he took perverse pleasure that the story circulated so widely and for so long.[59]

But the faculty's efforts were not in vain. Despite announced intentions to the contrary, President Banowsky and the new board of regents managed to find money to fund salary increases of 3 percent in 1976–1977 and 9 percent in 1977–1978. Banowsky denied any relationship between the salary increments and the faculty boycott. Rather, he attributed the increases to an improved cash flow in the university's financial situation.[60]

But an alienated faculty combined with a tarnished public image was not a recipe for institutional success. Ever sensitive to how others saw him and the university, President Banowsky took a bold step in an attempt to repair that image, inviting William Trombley, one of the *Los Angeles Times's* foremost reporters, to visit the university's campuses and freely write about what he saw. Trombley accepted the invitation and wrote a lengthy story published in the *Times* on April 18, 1976. It was a well-written, perceptive, and objective piece of journalism that recounted the attorney general's investigation, assessed faculty discontent, and measured the growth of the university.[61]

Given what might have been said, Pepperdine could rejoice in Trombley's report. Said President Banowsky, who considered the piece a fairly balanced profile: "I can remember when tiny Pepperdine College couldn't have gotten a paragraph in the *Los Angeles Times*. Now we merit an entire section."[62]

Although Norvel Young's car wreck and President Gerald Ford's visit pushed the Trent Devenney affair off the front burner, the heat did not soon dissipate.[63] The incident helped foster the first significant revision of the university's original governing documents. It included an enlargement of the board of trustees—soon renamed the board of regents—that also included members who were not from Churches of Christ and the adoption of an appropriate system of executive compensation. The negative publicity of the attorney general's investigation surely influenced President Banowsky to decide not to run for political office in California—and may even have speeded his departure for Oklahoma.

In part because of the Devenney incident, the Pepperdine faculty at Malibu and also at Los Angeles found their voices, insisting on a more equitable division of the university's resources. Finally, the Devenney reports, along with the participation of Luper and Rice, exacerbated the historical tension between Pepperdine University and Churches of Christ. But it did not cause a complete rift.

When Devenney wanted the two churchmen to join in a legal action against the university, both declined. Brothers, they said, did not take brothers to court, which was more than Devenney could comprehend. The Church of Christ brothers, he lashed out, all looked like flimflam men to him, virtual collaborators with those who had no concern for business morals and ethics. "I don't think you people are going to do one damn thing," he concluded.[64]

Devenney was right. And the relationship between the university and the church lived on.

CHAPTER 32

CHANCELLOR YOUNG'S STRUGGLE

C hancellor Norvel Young and Larry Hornbaker, Pepperdine University's vice president for administration, chatted after church services on Sunday, September 14, 1975. They spoke again the next evening by telephone. The conversation on both occasions revolved around the university's serious financial condition. The good news was that the U.S. Veterans Administration was sending Pepperdine $750,000 to cover tuition costs for enrolled veterans. The bad news was that the money had not arrived and there were bank notes, big utility bills, and monthly salaries to pay. It was a classic case of a "cash crunch," Hornbaker lamented. The balance sheet actually looked good, but accounts receivable totaled nearly $5 million, and conversion of non-cash gifts into cash had proved difficult. The university needed $900,000 in cash immediately, and Hornbaker had not been able to find it or find anyone willing to lend it.[1]

Young commiserated with his younger colleague, inquired whether this or that option had been checked, and encouraged him to keep looking for a short-term loan. In the aftermath of Hornbaker's conversations, Young was overwhelmed. This was not the only bad news he had received recently. Earlier on Monday, he had learned of a tragic motorcycle accident on the Malibu campus that claimed the life of Charles Wilks, a vibrant young math professor who had recently transferred from the Los Angeles campus and whose family Young had known for almost a lifetime. A few days earlier he had learned that the upcoming visit of President Gerald Ford would cost the university an additional $200,000 at the very time there was not enough money in the checking account even to pay salaries. And, of course, reminders of the Trent Devenney-inspired attorney general investigation of the Pepperdine leadership were still cropping up in state newspapers.[2]

Equally unsettling was the interminable debate between himself and President Banowsky on whether to open the governing board of the university beyond Church of Christ members. Just as troubling was the ceaseless flow of condemnation from some of his Church of Christ brethren regarding the soundness of Pepperdine as a Christian college. All of these pressures were compounded by a heart attack and two strokes Young had suffered in the previous six years.[3]

Hornbaker's Monday evening conversation left Young on the verge of despair. For a bit of relief, he later reported, he did something "completely out of character." More in character would have been an afternoon sail on a catamaran such as Young had recently described in *Guidepost* magazine. That particular respite had nearly cost him his life. This avenue of relief did too.[4]

Instead of heading for the ocean, Young drove across Pacific Coast Highway from his beach-front home to the Market Basket store and bought a fifth of vodka. Although he described this act as out of character, it had been a long time since Young was the teetotaler he had been raised to be—that status had ended even before 1969, when a physician recommended a glass of wine to relieve some of his physical and emotional stress.[5] Thereafter, Young had been known to release a lot of stress at the "shrine of Bacchus" during gatherings at the Bohemian Club, a men's club that met annually near San Francisco.[6]

After returning to his home, Young drank three-fourths of the vodka bottle before going to bed. He slept only fitfully, however, awaking before dawn. With pressure unrelieved, he had a cup of decaffeinated coffee, one-half milligram of Coumadin and thirty milligrams of Enderol—both prescription medications for his heart condition—for breakfast. About 10:30 a.m. he had another 30 milligrams of Enderol and one capsule of Librium—a prescription antianxiety medication. The chancellor also finished off the "few ounces" of vodka left in the bottle, mixed with Fresca. He then showered, shaved, and dressed for a luncheon appointment at the California Club in downtown Los Angeles.[7]

At 11:45 a.m., Young turned his car onto Pacific Coast Highway (PCH) and drove east. Twenty minutes later, near the intersection of Coastline Drive and PCH—what is now the entrance to the Getty Villa—he rear-ended a Ford Falcon carrying three women. The Falcon's gas tank burst into flame. The two elderly women in the back seat died, one at the scene. The driver, a daughter of one of the women who was killed, survived. A bystander rescued Young from his car, or he might also have perished there.[8]

In less than an hour, officials notified Helen Young of the car crash involving her husband. She immediately called Bill Banowsky, who at that moment was finalizing some details of President Ford's imminent visit. Banowsky dropped everything and rushed to Young's side, rendering pastoral and administrative care—deciding how to inform faculty, staff, boards, and donors; how to handle the press; whom to select as an attorney—that forever endeared him to the heart of both Young and his wife.[9]

Outpouring of Sympathy and Condemnation

The story made a big splash in the media, both secular and religious. Immediately, the Youngs began to hear from both friends and critics, near and far. Now was the time for "compassion," wrote president's board member Fritz Huntsinger, for such a tragedy "could befall any of us at any time."[10] Parishioners of Our Lady of Malibu Catholic church lifted up the chancellor and his wife in prayer during Mass.[11] Prentice Meador, a young Church of Christ minister, saw in the accident an opportunity to "demonstrate to the world the church's forgiveness" and urged the Pepperdine board of trustees to retain Young as chancellor.[12]

A host of notables rose to express their support and confidence, including actor and businessman Gene Autry, construction magnate Stephen D. Bechtel Sr., minister and attorney John Allen Chalk, Loyola Marymount University President Charles S. Casassa S.J., former U.S. Army General Omar Bradley, spiritual leader Norman Vincent Peale, Pastor Robert Schuller, Catholic church Cardinal James Francis McIntyre, pop star Pat Boone, and television personality Art Linkletter. Each would write as a character witness for Young at the time of his sentencing.[13]

Not all were so supportive, however. Blanche Seaver, a committed teetotaler, had little compassion for Young when she learned he had been drinking in "secret" for more than six years. That it was under "doctor's orders" made little difference to her.[14] A woman from Sherman, Texas, observed that Young had mixed with the proud and rich to the extent that he had tragically become one of them "rather than the servant of Christ."[15] A male correspondent thought Young's behavior was inexcusable and warranted his immediate termination as chancellor, criticizing university officials for not having "guts enough to suspend a drunk from your midst."[16]

Surprisingly, one of Young's harshest and most vocal church critics, Ventura restaurateur Archie Luper, rushed to the chancellor's side in the hospital, wept with him, and urged him to repent. When Young acknowledged his wrong, Luper embraced him as if he were the prodigal son who had been lost but now was found. Thereafter, he was hesitant to leave Young's bedside.[17]

A month after the accident, Helen and Norvel Young met with the Pepperdine board of trustees at its quarterly meeting. Upon advice of legal counsel, they chose to speak about the accident only in vague generalities and to supply each member with a copy of a "bland letter," to use Chair Don Miller's words, that Helen Young had recently circulated to Churches of Christ faithful. Following that brief comment, the Youngs stayed to participate in board discussion on various agenda items as if nothing had happened, leaving only when the executive committee convened.

Very concerned, Miller wrote fellow trustee Jimmy Lovell that he "had the feeling that Norvel intend[ed] to carry right on, putting it all aside." In the executive committee meeting, Miller proposed that the university grant Young a leave of absence so he could concentrate on healing and preparing a defense. Three of the trustees disagreed, thinking such an act would drive Young to drink. So Miller called fellow trustee Reuel Lemmons, one of Young's close friends, who said he would encourage the chancellor to accept the leave offer. Young subsequently took a leave of absence, which the judge would later demand as well.[18]

Young's Day(s) in Court

Young's first court hearings took place in October 1975. By the end of the month, the prosecution dropped all charges but involuntary manslaughter. Young pled guilty and asked no special favors by way of plea negotiation.[19] Judge Pearce Young (no relation to the chancellor), delayed sentencing until January, pending court and parole hearings. The hearings were notable for their sober reflection on the life and career of Norvel Young. The question that participants struggled to answer was how a man of Young's character, practice, and beliefs could behave in such a way.

Bill Banowsky was probably the most effective expositor. In meetings in the judge's chambers, he attributed Young's behavior to anxiety generated by having to live with one foot in two worlds. Banowsky had used such language more than once to describe his own dilemma, and it was so compelling that Young came to use it himself.[20] His downfall was not alcohol, the chancellor testified during his probation hearing, but stress stemming from his effort to balance the sectarian demands of Church of Christ fundamentalists with the educational realities of academic freedom, among other things. "This dual life," he would tell the judge, "this need to be two different people . . . has torn at my soul for many years."[21] It was "increasingly difficult," he said, "to accept the simplistic assumptions of the hell-fire and brimstone fundamentalism which most preachers in this church teach."[22]

Young had been subject to this kind of ambivalence for years, as is clear in his writings where he criticizes the "bibliolatry" and "Phariseeism" of some of his brethren and his own indecision in exposing it.[23] For fifteen years he had struggled to preserve the university's relationship with Churches of Christ despite the reluctance of church leaders to embrace Pepperdine as one of their own. The rejection had been part of his stress-induced heart arrhythmia requiring an extensive hospital stay in 1969, and it had led him to doubt doctrinal positions of mainstream Churches of Christ, everything from the verbally inspired word of God, to creationism, to salvation of Church of Christ members only.[24]

Judge Young was sympathetic. In January 1976, he rendered a bold but controversial decision for a felony offense. Among other things, he ignored two prior DUI convictions, one in 1961 in Dallas and another in 1969 in Los Angeles. The judge then sentenced the chancellor to four years of probation, the first year of which would be served in the county jail. He fined him $2,000, suspended his driver's license, and directed him not to consume alcoholic beverages or visit places where they were sold. Judge Young stayed incarceration for six months with the understanding that the chancellor would sever all official relationships with Pepperdine University and pursue serious public service as a way of making restitution for his crime and determining whether the prison term would be further stayed. The judge approved as a public service option Young's proposal to pursue a research project in collaboration with the University of Southern California's Safety Center on the connection between stress on the "high-effective" performer, alcohol, and traffic accidents.[25]

Judge Young well knew that his sentence was the stuff of controversy. It had been one of his most difficult sentences ever, he confessed, and he pronounced it with "full awareness" that not all members of the general public would agree with his decision to require no jail time. What made the case unique for the judge was that the defendant admitted his guilt and that the surviving victim had requested the defendant not be punished beyond the grief he had already experienced. The judge saw the case as a Shakespearean tragedy. He believed that for "this intelligent, sensitive and compassionate man" the tragedy was "not the disgrace he ... suffered as a leader of his church and of his university," but that in "one terrible moment he took the lives of two innocent people, who, if they had survived, would be 'praying for him.'"[26]

Deputy District Attorney Robert Altman disagreed with Judge Young. He conceded Chancellor Young's contributions to society, his fragile physical condition, situational pressure, and his demonstrated remorse. Nonetheless, he said, "Dr. Young has [not] recognized the drinking problem he does have," and "I personally feel, that when a person has a previous conviction [and drives] while highly intoxicated and, as a result ... causes the death of two people, I think such a person should go to jail."[27]

Ben Bycel, an officer of the American Civil Liberties Union (ACLU), also had reservations about the sentence. He wondered if the decision would have been the same if Young had been poor and lowly. He tended to think not and considered the decision a case of "real, if unequal justice." Judge Young, of course, took exception, arguing publicly that equal justice did not necessarily mean equal sentencing.[28]

Moving Forward

Whether or not the sentence should have included jail time, Chancellor Young moved swiftly to execute the terms of his sentence. Upon his request, the board of trustees granted him an unpaid leave of absence as chancellor through July 31, 1976. The board also insisted that there be no surreptitious communication with him, a restriction trustee Morris Pendleton wanted scrupulously observed lest someone might say that Young was "chiseling on the sentence."[29]

After July, Young's leave of absence status continued with court-approved modifications that allowed trustees to authorize Young as a "consultant" to the Pepperdine president "for fund-raising, development and such other functions as may be assigned to him." He would receive $3,000 per month plus use of the beach-front Adamson house, for which the university paid the state $1,000 per month.[30] In 1978, Young returned to the administration as chancellor with all restrictions lifted.

Young also moved quickly to begin his work at the USC Safety Center. Working with Professor John J. Dreher, funding from USC, and endorsement of the California Highway Patrol, he launched a scholarly study of physical and behavioral stress and some of its effects on people. Following a year of Young's careful research, his findings were ultimately published by Pepperdine University Press in 1978 as *Poison Stress Is a Killer: A Monograph on Physical and Behavioral Stress and Some of its Effects on Modern Man.* His work also became the basis of a diversionary program used by the Los Angeles Municipal Court for as many as 1,000 drunk-driving offenders each month.[31]

In addition to the book, Young also shared his results with thousands via at least 100 public addresses and workshops. His lectures on alcohol abuse were widely acclaimed for approaching the subject rationally yet personally.[32]

Almost daily Young reached out to his church constituency. In December 1975, he addressed the University Church of Christ, which he had once served as an elder. "I have sinned against God," he said, and also against the two women who died, the one who was injured, the church, Pepperdine University, and his associates. He confessed that his "use of alcohol was involved in this accident." He reported that he had asked God for forgiveness, which he believed had been granted, and now asked for the church's forgiveness and prayers. He assured the church that he was not addicted "to the regular use of alcohol," and that with God's help he would "never use alcohol again in any form." The Malibu church elders considered the statement "courageous, candid, and forthright," willingly forgave him, and joined in prayer in his behalf. They believed God would use Young's talents "to do much more for Christ's cause in the future."[33]

The report of the public confession was thereafter widely printed in church periodicals.[34] Young followed with dozens if not hundreds of sermonic confessions throughout California and in the heartland of Churches of Christ. The forgiveness that Young sought was granted, at least by the church at large.[35]

Young had a harder time explaining to the church the statements he and Bill Banowsky had made at his probation hearing: that the church's fundamentalist rigidity had warped his soul and helped drive him to drink. Harvey Childress, minister of the Pacific Beach Church of Christ in San Diego, wrote that church members in his area were confused that Young said part of his stress stemmed from the fundamentalism of Churches of Christ and "the hell and damnation preaching" of some of his brethren. Childress invited Young to come to San Diego and "clear this up so that we know what you mean, and can forget it and go on with our work for the Lord together."[36]

Young described his answer as an unfortunate response that did not mean what it appeared to mean. Prepared with the help of his attorney and others, he said, his statement had tried to convey to the court some of the pain he had experienced via the "extremist attacks" from Trent Devenney and Ira Rice. In doing so, however, Young said he had used words "which were ill-chosen," causing some to question his "loyalty to the church to which I have given most of my life and in whose fellowship I intend to work the remainder of my life." He assured them of his foundational beliefs and his continuing commitment to Churches of Christ.[37]

Officers of the court watched Young carefully during his first year of probation. The sentence of one year in the county jail was deferred for six months, and then again for another six months to January 1977; after a probation hearing, it was lifted altogether. The court was impressed that Young had done more than necessary to fulfill the requirements of the sentence. The judge was impressed with Young's book and the program to be used in the courts with DUI transgressions and so removed the prospect of any jail time—but not the three additional years of probation.

Thomas Pike, an executive with Fluor Corporation, was jubilant. "A courageous and compassionate judge had the wisdom to depart from traditional punitive sentencing, which paved the way for the constructive and dramatic outcome of this personal rehabilitation and restitution," he wrote. In his judgment, "The interests of justice and society have surely been much better served by this enlightened action of the Court. . . . God is good! Sweet are the uses of adversity!" he exclaimed.[38]

The families of the two women who died in the fiery crash in September 1975 were forgiving toward Chancellor Young but believed some restitution was appropriate. In 1976, they brought suit in civil court for several hundred thousand dollars; in mid-1977 the suit was settled out of court for $167,000.

The university's insurance carrier paid all but $15,000, which was to be paid by Young. The university loaned the $15,000 to the cash-strapped chancellor, who repaid the sum over the next two years, although with credit and a tax deduction for a life membership in the Pepperdine University Associates.[39]

Pepperdine Feels the Impact

A traumatic event for Young personally, his wreck also profoundly affected Pepperdine University. Its image of gleaming prosperity, well-endowed by the wealthy elite of Southern California, was considerably tarnished. The public tended to read the "cash flow" problems that had so disquieted Young as evidence of portending "bankruptcy."[40] For a time, Pepperdine administrators had to reassure potential donors as well as lenders that the university's finances were actually quite sound.

The financial wake of the Young accident may also explain why administrators looked to a government agency like the California Educational Facilities Authority (CEFA) rather than private institutions to finance construction of the fine arts complex and the law school building in 1977. Applying for those funds would force the university to define its Christian mission much more narrowly.

Despite Young's many sermons and articles, part of his church constituency remained unconvinced that he was really repentant and that Pepperdine University was really a Christian school. Surely that was true of Ira Rice, Young's longtime nemesis at *Contending for the Faith*; but it was also true of longtime friend and self-proclaimed guardian of the faith, James G. Bales. A professor of religion at Harding College, Bales pointed to Young's use of alcohol and Pepperdine's addition of non-Church of Christ members to its board of regents to make the case that Young and Banowsky were traitors to George Pepperdine's vision for the college.[41]

Young had long challenged Bill Banowsky's assumption that adding non-Church of Christ members to the board of trustees would be more positive than negative, and he alone had blocked Banowsky's efforts to do so. After the crash, however, Young was absent from the seat of power for almost two years. During this period, the board of trustees with only members of the Churches of Christ morphed into the board of regents, that began with 40 percent non-Church of Christ members, a percentage that soon grew to 49 percent. What Howard White had predicted just days after the accident had materialized: "This is the end of an era for Pepperdine. This will end Norvel's influence in the inner circles. . . . I think the chances are very strong that Bill will now secularize the school, adding gradually to the Trustees various ones who are not members of the church."[42]

Little did White know that Young was actually complicit in the dramatic change. In the wake of the wreck, he had written to his younger protégé, "You have been a wonderful and loyal friend through this difficult time and I want to tell you again how much Helen and I appreciate it. If there is anything else I can do to help on the Board meeting for the 17th, let me know. I want to support you as I indicated in the hospital that I would and as I have been doing."[43]

Young's accident also elevated the university into the folklore of Malibu. In late 1976, about a year after Young's crash, the Eagles rock group released the fabulously popular *Hotel California* album. The album's final song, "The Last Resort," refers to a woman coming west with hopes and dreams to chilly winds that blow through the canyons to Malibu, where pretty people play and rich men put up ugly boxes that "Jesus people" buy and then call it paradise. The lyrics speak of satisfying "endless needs" and justifying "bloody deeds, in the name of destiny and the name of God" and then celebrating those deeds on Sunday morning.[44]

Almost immediately, mythologizers associated the song with Pepperdine and Young's fatal wreck, claiming that one of the women killed was a Pepperdine student. Although none of it was true and the songwriter has denied connections, the myths have lingered for forty years. Composer Don Henley, a born-again Christian, said in a 1987 interview: "The gist of the song was that when we find something good, we destroy it by our presence—by the very fact that man is the only animal on earth that is capable of destroying his environment." On another occasion, he said the song was primarily a commentary of "how the West was lost." He made no reference to either Pepperdine or its chancellor.[45]

Rebuilt Reputations, Expanded Expectations

Another fact made clear after Young's crash was that the faculty honored the chancellor as one of the founding fathers of the renewed and reborn Pepperdine University. Members rushed to his side to support him and his family in the wake of the accident and were deeply troubled by the status of his mental and physical health. Few, if any, viewed the accident as a pretext for Young's complete retirement, and a goodly number, if not most, wanted him to resume administrative responsibilities but in a less-prominent role.[46] Thereafter, for the most part, faculty members regarded Young as a statesman, an institutional treasure who should be nurtured rather than criticized. When Young returned to full duty in 1978, he was warmly welcomed by his faculty colleagues.

Ultimately, the tragedy of September 16, 1975, produced a level of institutional maturity heretofore unknown at Pepperdine. Vice President James

Wilburn tried to speak to that transformation some two years after the accident. In the immediate wake of the event, he said, each week brought new insights into the nature of the institution, "most underscoring the fact that it had matured greatly," and had gained confidence in "its newly found urbanity and broadened sense of humanity." Pepperdine University was not the same school in 1977 that it had been twenty-four months earlier. It was, Wilburn wrote:

> no longer perceived as a fundamentalist outpost, a kind of Western buckle on the Bible belt, more wedded to doctrine than to concern for human agony and human growth. Nor was it a faceless sprawling political organization, like many secular state universities. Rather it ha[d] attained an image of an institution mature enough and large enough to overcome one man's tragedy. . . . In a traumatic experience, [it had] discovered strength, stability, friends, financial backing and community support, which no one could have foretold until its metal was tested by fire.[47]

CHAPTER 33

ON BEING BETTER, NOT BIGGER

The late 1960s and early 1970s were years of political and social turmoil in the United States as the country dealt with the Vietnam War, civil rights demonstrations, political scandals, horrific murders, and assassinations of high-profile figures. For Pepperdine University, ironically, they were not so much years of turmoil as years of dramatic growth.

The watchwords were "bigger and better." This was most evident, of course, in the construction of the Malibu campus, but it was also apparent in the establishment of the first year-in-Europe program; the development of the schools of law, business and management, education, and continuing education; and the founding of the Orange Center, the Center for International Business, and the Center for Innovative Education, which was primarily the military base program. In those days of expansion, Pepperdine was like the old British Empire—the sun never set on its degree programs.

The evidence of growth was apparent in enrollment and financial figures. The number of students who matriculated, excluding off-campus programs such as those on military bases and provided by extension, grew from 1,247 in 1967–1968 to 8,591 in 1975–1976, an increase of almost 700 percent. In the same period, operational budgets increased from $4.4 million to $38.6 million, and gross assets rose from $7.7 million to $26.6 million.[1] The growth was so dramatic that the university, with its "mom and pop" business model, had serious difficulty meeting demands for such basic services as finance, admission, registrar, and student information.[2] It lacked the effective administrative policies, procedures, and practices necessary to manage a large and complex organization.

One major structural problem arose because the various schools and centers of the university tended to see themselves as administrative islands. With some exceptions, they duplicated central services, especially those related to student information and financial accounts, and each felt quite free to contact vendors independently.[3] As a general rule, the different schools discounted central authority and resisted most attempts to institute uniform policies. A major study conducted in late 1975, to no one's surprise, concluded that Seaver College was most in compliance with central administration policies whereas the School of Business and Management was least.[4]

Overworked and Understaffed

It did not help matters that the central administration was spare and overworked. Through 1975, at least, President Banowsky had no interest in the operational details of the university—they bored him. Plus, he was preoccupied with raising money for the Malibu campus and with his personal ambition to hold an elected political office. When circumstances caused him to shelve his political ambitions, Banowsky announced he would devote all his time to managing the university, a decision that cheered his colleagues. "For the first time," wrote Executive Vice President Howard White, the president was "taking a realistic view of our situation."[5]

Up to that point, Banowsky had pretty much left the day-to-day management of the university to White. By 1975, twenty-one offices reported directly to White. Almost everything except development matters came across his desk, including accrediting activities, student transcripts, campus security, and athletics. He readily admitted that his responsibilities were too many, too complex, and too varied for one person and that the arrangement triggered bad judgments, hasty decisions, and poor personnel choices.[6] Indeed, White pointed to the finance office, which was in chaos because he had made poor choices for director.[7]

Unhappy students, military base commanders, clients like Northrop Corporation, and most units of the university agreed with White that the finance office was in shambles. According to David Reagan, who took over as the head of the Center for International Business in 1974, its procedures were antiquated and its personnel were unqualified. He could not believe, for example, that the budgeting process began only three to four months before the onset of the fiscal year. Even more unbelievable was the inability to get an up-to-date financial report and the apparent need of every administrative unit to keep a second set of account books. It was obvious to Reagan that the university had grown too fast and that it needed to pause until infrastructure offices could catch up.[8]

When major donor and regent-to-be Richard Scaife offered to fund a professional study of management structures and processes at Pepperdine, the administration readily accepted. Scaife wanted to determine whether any further investment in Pepperdine was warranted, while the university's management welcomed plausible solutions to its operational problems. McKinsey and Company, an East Coast-based firm with Los Angeles offices, was chosen to conduct a study into every part of the university's operation.[9]

In May 1976 McKinsey's initial report identified the university's assets and challenges. Its assets included

- a unique emphasis upon Christian values and free-enterprise business principles;
- a strong and highly entrepreneurial management;
- a non-bureaucratized institution that allowed immediate response in decision-making;
- an unusual ability of top management to raise capital funds; and
- a family-oriented organization willing to make personal sacrifices.

Some of the institution's larger challenges were

- how best to express its concern for conservative economics and Christian values;
- whether to expand or consolidate educational offerings;
- how to improve academic quality; and
- the requirement of key personnel to be members of Churches of Christ.

The single most immediate challenge identified by the study was a need to establish an organizational structure that would enable the university to respond efficiently to its growing needs.[10]

The consultants had several recommendations for solving the university's organizational challenges. They recommended

- organizing the new board of regents into eight standing committees, including an executive committee;
- reducing the number of managers reporting directly to the chief operating officer;
- placing all development activities under a vice president for university affairs; and
- making major changes in the areas of financial management and control, registration and student records, electronic data processing, personnel administration, and scheduled maintenance of facilities at Malibu.[11]

Changes Start at the Top

The McKinsey report was remarkably influential, particularly regarding the structure of Pepperdine's administrative hierarchy.[12] It initially recommended a chancellor/chief executive officer (CEO) who would report to the board of regents, a president/chief administrative officer (CAO) who would report to the chancellor, and four vice presidents—for academic affairs, finance, administrative services, and student services—who would report to the president. A vice president for development would report to the chancellor, and a general counsel would report to the president.

The board of regents liked the proposed structure and acted to fill the senior positions even before the report was formally presented. Norvel Young, on leave because of his legal penalties, was not expected to rejoin the university at his previous level of responsibility, so the board approved President Banowsky for the chancellor position. To be president and CAO, it selected Jerry Hudson, the former provost of the Malibu campus, who had left Pepperdine less than a year earlier to assume the presidency of Hamline University in Minnesota. The regents assumed Hudson would be delighted to return as Pepperdine's new president.[13]

Although Howard White had long functioned as the chief operating officer of the university, the regent's planned appointments left the "old" executive vice president—in terms of tenure and age—without a portfolio. His former duties had all been allocated to the president and four new vice presidents. White had become the scapegoat for the administrative troubles that plagued the university.[14]

This turn of events hurt White's pride, particularly because he had hardly been consulted during the course of the study. Change itself was not the problem, he insisted, but the manner in which it might be made. "There are many kinds of reorganization that I could accept," he wrote, "but I would like them to be accomplished in a manner that does not appear to be a cold decision of a management group that worked eight weeks." White welcomed Jerry Hudson's coming as chief administrative officer but wanted to have input on certain issues before sweeping changes were made. "I do not think it is immodest for me to say that I have a more complete view of the internal workings of this University than any other one person." In his attempt to serve the university, White believed he had followed in the path of J. C. Moore, Pepperdine's longtime business officer, who had "kept accepting more and more personal responsibility with no suitable employment of individuals to whom he could delegate responsibility for lesser matters." Despite his years of service, White wrote, "on the advice of a management consulting team Mr. Moore was pushed aside, [and] his health and his heart were broken."[15] Moore had died of a heart attack in 1969, shortly after resigning from Pepperdine to become president of Columbia Christian College.

Not So Different After All

As it turned out, what the McKinsey report envisioned and what actually happened were different things. Jerry Hudson determined not to accept the regent's offer of the presidency, and Norvel Young made it clear he eventually wanted to return as chancellor.[16] Given those developments, Bill Banowsky chose to retain the status quo whereby he would continue to serve as president, occupied primarily by external issues (fund-raising), along with a strong executive vice president who would be responsible for internal affairs.

However, he eagerly embraced the McKinsey recommendations for the appointment of vice presidents who would report to White and make his management responsibilities more realistic. The "McKinsey babies" were John Nicks as vice president for academic affairs; Robert "Bob" Thomas as vice president for administrative services; Warren Dillard as vice president for finance; and Mike O'Neal as vice president and legal counsel. The new organizational structure provided a pattern of operation that survived well into the twenty-first century.

Scaife and his colleagues in Pittsburgh were generally pleased with the administrative realignment but not with the people chosen for the new positions. Richard Larry, the director of one of Scaife's foundations, had suggested that Banowsky not limit his search for vice presidents to members of Churches of Christ, and Scaife was not happy when Banowsky ignored that advice.[17] Speaking specifically of Nicks and Thomas, Scaife said he did not doubt they were "fine individuals," but was concerned that they had been chosen without "good, across-the-board search procedures" and that they lacked the seasoning and "authoritative experience required." He was concerned that Nicks's PhD was in educational administration rather than in a discipline like psychology or religion and that Thomas held a doctorate in education rather than in physics or math. We share the McKinsey view, Scaife concluded, that the university has an unfortunate "tendency toward hiring and promoting individuals who do not bring sufficient relevant experience to their jobs, and therefore, must learn their professions on the job."[18]

President Banowsky did not much like working with Scaife's lieutenants and identified two problems regarding their advice to Pepperdine University. First, he said, they usually did not know what they were talking about; and, second, Scaife was not giving the millions he had given in previous years. Indeed, in the previous two years he had given "virtually nothing." Nonetheless, the "Scaife connection" was vital to the university, especially since Scaife and Richard Seaver had formed a close alliance. Thus, Banowsky went to great lengths to justify his decision to keep White as executive vice president, at least for the short term. White, he wrote, was responsible for many of the assets of the university developed over the previous eight years, including a 581 percent increase in enrollment, a 611 percent increase in operational budget, and an 820 percent increase in net assets.[19]

White had taken care of interior issues, Banowsky wrote, while the president and the chancellor had tended to exterior matters. He had demonstrated serious judgment weaknesses in some personnel choices and in failure to delegate authority, but his strengths were enormous: a keen intelligence; a highly practical, hard-headed mind; an ability to say no; respect from senior officials and deans; and spiritual leadership. In addition, White worked seven days a week with no social or recreational life, simply commuting from his home to his office early each morning and returning late each night; and he showed tremendous loyalty, never failing to execute any directive given to him. Because of those attributes, Banowsky concluded that White was the only suitable candidate to be executive vice president and determined that he would appoint him to the office by administrative action instead of undertaking a national search.[20]

Robert Thomas served as the first dean of students of the Malibu campus in 1972. After 1976, he held appointments as vice president for administration and director of the on-campus MBA program.

The Scaife interests accepted Banowsky's decision regarding White, but they were never happy with it. Indeed, they declined to do much of anything else for the university thereafter. Their coolness was painfully obvious during White's presidency, which would not have occurred had Banowsky permitted him to be sacrificed as the scapegoat of the McKinsey report.

A Time to Consolidate

In the spirit of "better rather than bigger," a core principle of the McKinsey group, Pepperdine management moved quickly to consolidate its operations in the mid-1970s. At the Los Angeles campus, as already noted, it terminated the liberal arts program and emphasized professional degrees, both undergraduate and graduate.[21] It also incorporated the many programs of the Orange Center into those on the Los Angeles campus, eliminating twenty-eight staff positions and saving hundreds of thousands of dollars.[22] Curtailing the work of the Center for Innovative Education meant initially closing activities on all military bases outside of California and Hawaii and all bases within a few years.[23]

Consolidation also meant establishing greater control over the university's finance office. For many years, it had been the source of great grief for students, administrators, and vendors.[24] In June 1975, President Banowsky appointed Warren Dillard as vice president for finance, a position emphasized in the McKinsey report, and asked him to get hold of the nuts and bolts of the finance office as quickly as possible. To the delight of administrators but the consternation of students, especially those in the off-campus programs, he had collected $1 million worth of accounts receivable within a year.[25]

The McKinsey study also influenced the structure and function of Pepperdine's development activities. For at least a decade, an office of development headed by a vice president had existed at Pepperdine. It had functioned narrowly, however, hosting the Freedom Forum, identifying and nurturing prospective givers, encouraging alumni, and managing special events. It was more in the business of friend-raising than fund-raising, a task left to Banowsky, Young, and Runnels.

The consultants believed that some of the development office's biggest activities actually distracted time and resources from the central purpose of raising capital funds and operational dollars. One such event was the Tyler Ecology Award, a $150,000 prize endowed by John C. and Alice Tyler, who envisioned an annual prize that would recognize the contributions of scholars to the science of ecology. The Tylers named Pepperdine University as the facilitator, but the university had little to do with the award other than providing a suitable setting for it to be bestowed.[26] The initial award gala in 1974 was a high-profile event that attracted much-appreciated attention for Pepperdine, but by the end of the decade, the development office found it less and less advantageous to use its resources to promote the award announcement.[27]

The McKinsey consultants also had reservations about the *Battle of the Network Stars*, an ABC made-for-television athletic competition on the Malibu campus between ten TV personalities from each of three major networks. Events included a 440-yard run, bicycle race, swim relay, double tennis matches, obstacle course race, and golf putting. Actual competition initially occurred on October 24 and 25, 1976, and aired on November 13 that year as a two-hour, prime-time special hosted by sportscaster Howard Cosell.[28] It was a successful production for ABC Sports (35 million viewers), and it was especially successful for Pepperdine University. ABC paid $3,000 for the use of the campus, and the broadcast gave millions of people around the world a view of the sparkling Seaver College campus, nestled between the mountains and the ocean in fabled Malibu. That view was enough to prompt many young viewers, even those with strong SAT scores, to send an application for admission.[29]

The *Battle of the Network Stars* continued an association with Pepperdine through 1988, introducing Pepperdine to many Americans.[30] The production produced challenges year in and year out, however. In the tents and production areas, for example, workers and contestants smoked and drank freely, and at least one churchman complained about the "lewdness" of the participants.[31] Overall, however, Pepperdine administrators concluded that the *Battle of the Network Stars* had far more pluses than minuses for the institution.

But from the point of view of the McKinsey consultants, the network stars' competition and the Tyler Ecology Award were more about publicity than about serious fund-raising. Raising money was something other than an event—it was a sustained effort to identify and cultivate prospective donors. They recommended creation of a well-staffed office devoted just to development/advancement and the appointment of a vice president to lead it. With Norvel Young still on leave and the burden of fund-raising largely on his shoulders, President Banowsky quickly agreed. On May 1, 1976, he appointed as the new vice president of development James Wilburn, who had just resigned as provost of the Los Angeles campus.

Launching the Associates

Given the mission of the revamped office and the financial difficulties of the university, Wilburn's appointment was fortuitous. He immediately set out to organize a staff, which included Bob Bales, Annette Fuchs, Claudia Arnold, Bill Henegar, and Patricia Yomantas, that would help the university find a dependable source of annual revenue. As his first major effort, Wilburn chose to organize a group of supporters known as Associates, who would pay $1,000 annually to be members of the group.[32]

To mark the fortieth anniversary of Pepperdine, Wilburn, his team, and President Banowsky wanted to launch an Associates program with 250 "civic, business and cultural leaders who represent[ed] the backbone of the university's future." The annual membership gift of $1,000 from those leaders, Banowsky wrote to David Packard, would "help maintain the educational and economic principles for which we stand."[33] As the speaker for the first meeting on February 9, 1977, the development staff recruited Nobel Laureate economist Milton Friedman, who agreed to speak on "The Future of Capitalism," a subject particularly suitable for the audience Wilburn hoped to recruit.

Wilburn and Banowsky agreed that recruiting 250 members would make the Associates program a success, but the astonishingly positive response convinced Banowsky that the program could be "a money machine."[34] By early January, Wilburn had reached the 250 membership goal, and Banowsky pressured Wilburn and his team to recruit another 150 members by the date of the dinner. They were successful, enrolling what came to be known as the "Founding Four Hundred."[35] "The out-pouring of support," Banowsky wrote in the event's program, surpassed "our most optimistic expectations!"[36]

The audience in the packed ballroom of the Beverly Wilshire Hotel heard Friedman speak boldly in defense of free enterprise and the American Way. He also complimented Pepperdine University "and especially the Associates, for your ability not only to survive but to flourish in an educational world increasingly dominated by government institutions." "Unless this trend can be contained, or even better reversed, by the continued existence and growth of private institutions like Pepperdine University and my own University of Chicago," Friedman warned, "our free society will be in mortal danger."[37]

According to historian Darren Dochuk, those who made up the Founding 400 left the banquet recommitted to the principles of the free market. That commitment soon manifested itself in a successful campaign to limit state taxation, Proposition 13, and in the election of Ronald Reagan as president of the United States three years later. Dochuk saw a direct connection between those electoral victories and the Founding 400. Probably a bit of a stretch, his conclusion nonetheless acknowledges the social, economic, and political power of the women and men who formed Pepperdine's first group of Associates. Among them were old friends like Leonard Firestone, Charles Thornton, Walter Knott, and Ronald Reagan. New friends included Armand Hammer, John Olin, Joseph Coors, William Ahmanson, Walter Annenberg, Richard DeVos, and Will and Ariel Durant.[38]

When the Founding 400 and their guests arrived at the Beverly Wilshire Hotel, they encountered picketers who carried signs protesting Friedman's free-market views as applied in Chile.[39] Afterward, one of Pepperdine's senior administrators expressed deep disappointment that the entire event was celebrated on a Wednesday evening—a traditional midweek church night—that the cost was excessive, that alcohol was served, and that the Christian goals of the university were not mentioned. In fact, noted the critic, Friedman did not even know that Pepperdine had a Christian mission.[40]

Criticism notwithstanding, Banowsky and Wilburn considered the Associates program a resounding success. The power elite that now identified with Pepperdine augured well for the future, and the infusion of $400,000 unrestricted operational dollars went a long way toward resolving the university's perpetual cash-flow problem.

That the Associates program had long-range potential was again apparent at the second annual dinner, when economist John Kenneth Galbraith and journalist William F. Buckley debated whether the federal government should regulate the price of oil and natural gas. Their speeches were later broadcast on PBS. Six hundred "Charter" Associates and 200 guests attended the affair, which was chaired by motion picture icon John Wayne. Within two years, the number of Associates reached 1,000, generating an annual unrestricted income of $1 million.[41]

Magazines and Computers

In response to the McKinsey report's recommendation to create a professional office of university affairs, Wilburn also launched a full-color magazine in summer 1977. Expected to replace *Pepperdine News* and *Alumni Voice*, the new publication was to feature what President Banowsky termed the essence of the university: its people. Gracing the cover of the first issue was an image of Leonard Firestone, who had gifted the university with a field house and chaired the first Associates dinner. Inside were stories on the Founding 400, the John and Alice Tyler Ecology Award, and the dedication of the Eddy D. Field Baseball Stadium. Although there were pages devoted to alumni, faculty, and student notes, judging from cover photos and feature stories, Pepperdine's people clearly were its donors.[42]

The McKinsey consultants also encouraged an update of the university's data processing infrastructure. They recommended installation of a single, mainframe computer, a $600,000 Sperry 9060 UNIVAC, an idea supported by the University Computer Systems Committee.[43] Of course, the 9060 UNIVAC was a sizeable machine that needed special temperature and humidity controls. President Banowsky was able to prevail upon Morris Pendleton and his wife to underwrite one-half of the construction costs of a Computer Science Center on the Malibu campus, which opened in July 1977 with the UNIVAC in place.[44]

However, the real challenge was getting software to work as it was designed. Although a day or two later than projected, the new system did produce accurate fall term class rosters and student statements for the entire university, something of a first for Pepperdine.[45] By January 1978, the administrative systems of the university were improving, in part due to new personnel but primarily because of the computer.[46]

Still, like many of his administrative colleagues, Banowsky had serious reservations about the computer center and its work. Because of the "horrendous costs," the "scores of people" hired, and continuing complaints, he saw it as the "number one" concern in the operation of Pepperdine University. It was frustrating to him, he confessed, to be "at the complete mercy of something of enormous expense and of great importance to the institution, for which [he had to rely] upon the judgment of experts." He sent a memo sharing his doubts with Larry Craft, vice president for university systems.[47]

Craft had joined the Pepperdine staff two years earlier to solve the data processing issues in the registrar's office via the introduction of computer technology. His success was so striking that he was quickly promoted to vice president and assigned the task of computerizing the entire university. Craft acknowledged the president's frustrations over the expenditures, but he and his colleagues were doing good work, Craft insisted. "I believe we operate, after only 16 months of experience in this new environment, at a level which would impress and surprise 'experts' inside the institution or out."[48]

Coming to grips with an inefficient data processing operation was an administrative challenge required of a maturing educational institution interested in becoming "better rather than bigger." The same was true of issues regarding organizational structure, undisciplined educational programs, and a distracted development team. The marvel was that the Banowsky administration addressed them at all, given its preoccupations with building the Malibu campus, the president's political career, the chancellor's car accident, the California attorney general's investigation. As it came to grips with the turmoil on the business side, the administration also had to face problems on the academic side—particularly its relationship with its faculty.

CHAPTER 34

FACULTY FIGHT
FOR RESPECT, FAIR
TREATMENT

T he academic enterprise on the Malibu campus confronted troubling challenges, and one of the root causes was the faculty's sense
of alienation from the Malibu Miracle. According to Professor of
Communication Fred Casmir, the alienation stemmed from the administration's lack of respect for the faculty.[1] As he judged it, the leadership did not
value the faculty; it did not treat the faculty professionally; and it did not
share governance with the faculty.

And apparently, Casmir was right. Forty years later, in a letter to the
author, Bill Banowsky recalled his days as Pepperdine president: "I *deliberately* took the faculty *on* because more than half of them opposed the move [to
Malibu] and most of them were academically mediocre" with an unimpres-
sive publication record.[2]

To better channel its communication with the administration, the Seaver
faculty, following the example of the Los Angeles campus faculty, formed a
chapter of the American Association of University Professors (AAUP) in the
year after the Malibu campus opened.[3] The chapter's thirty-five members constituted 67 percent of the full-time faculty. Early leaders of this organization
included Kenneth Perrin (math), Ola Barnett (psychology), David Gibson (philosophy), and Wyatt Jones (education).[4]

In addition to AAUP, a faculty advisory committee (FAC) also promoted
the interests of faculty members at Malibu, as did a similar committee at Los
Angeles. Administrators always defined FAC as the voice of the faculty. At
Malibu, early leaders of the organization included John Nicks (psychology),
James Smythe (English), Stephen Sale (history), and Stephen McHargue (politi-
cal science).

Both AAUP and FAC members were concerned about political, social, religious, professional, and economic issues. At Malibu, a priority was increasing the level of faculty participation in governing the school. Among other things, the faculty wanted to have the right to vote on the selection of division chairs.[5] Citing AAUP guidelines, it also argued that it should have primary responsibility for determining the appointment, reappointment, promotion, granting of tenure, and dismissal of faculty colleagues and that faculty should participate in determining policies governing pay increases.[6] From President Banowsky's point of view, these desires meant the faculty had forgotten that its primary role in the institution was to teach—not administrate.

Issues of Politics, Gender, and Race

As on the Los Angeles campus, the Malibu faculty often took exception to the administration's emphasis on conservative political values, the free-market economy, and the American Way. That was apparent in a rebuke that James Smythe and the FAC delivered to Larry McCommas, the chair of the Malibu music department. McCommas's choral ensemble often sang Fred Waring's patriotic piece that opened with "Where, O where but in America, can you sing true freedom's song." For Smythe and his colleagues, the song was an embarrassment because of its idealized nature, particularly the segment concerning "Dixie." The song may have appealed to Pepperdine's conservative constituencies, said Smythe, but it sent the wrong message about the progressive spirit of the faculty. McCommas found it ironic that of the 10,000 persons who had heard the ensemble in twenty-one appearances no one showed less "appreciation and patriotism" for its work than the Seaver faculty committee. So far as is known, however, he dropped the song from the choir's repertoire.[7]

Members of the Seaver faculty were also concerned about gender discrimination. Most vocal was Ola Barnett, who was active in the National Organization for Women (NOW). Disquieting to Barnett and her colleagues was a presumed inequity in salaries between men and women, the lack of affirmative action in recruiting female faculty and staff, the limitations placed by Churches of Christ on women in worship services, the male-oriented nature of career-day programs, and the university's lack of a consciousness-raising educational program on the matter of gender discrimination.

Both President Banowsky and Executive Vice President White met with Barnett and her colleagues on several occasions, trying to demonstrate evidence of equal treatment and gender equality and reminding them that Seaver College utilized a gender-blind salary scale and promotion criteria.[8] They noted that a woman directed student publications, headed the library, and served as assistant dean in the School of Business and Management.

There was a robust athletic program for women, and President Banowsky, like his patron, Blanche Seaver, publicly supported the Equal Rights Amendment (ERA) to the U.S. constitution, despite opposition from some of the university's most prominent financial supporters.[9]

NOW supporters were heartened by some steps Seaver College had taken to be more gender inclusive, especially when it came to salary. But the number of female faculty remained a disappointment. In 1979, both the university and Seaver College faculties included only 19 percent women on the average. Yet even here, there were encouraging signs: at Seaver 35 percent of assistant professors were female, in contrast to less than 1 percent of the professors.[10]

The situation was less hopeful when it came to race. There was a total absence of African Americans on the Malibu campus faculty in its early days. This lack was deeply concerning not only to some faculty members, but also to President Banowsky. When Provost Hudson was assembling the Malibu faculty, Banowsky encouraged him to include persons of color, not wanting it to appear that Pepperdine was creating a "white, conservative, church of Christ-oriented campus."[11]

Hudson found it difficult, however, to entice African Americans to join the Malibu faculty, even from the several dozen who worked at Los Angeles. From their point of view, Pepperdine had neglected and ignored the urban campus, jeopardizing the job security of the black faculty and staff at Los Angeles. To take a position in Malibu was to join the enemy. Moreover, the Black Faculty-Staff Association, chaired by Professor of Sociology Josephine Yelder, believed that Pepperdine University was in violation of Title VII of the 1964 Civil Rights Act and the Equal Employment Opportunity (EEO) Act of 1972 as it was not providing equal employment opportunity for minorities or women.[12]

Program for Affirmative Action

In the late 1960s, much of the racial tension on Pepperdine's Los Angeles campus was played out within the context of federal executive orders and the Civil Rights Act. The measures required schools, particularly those with federal contracts valued at more than $50,000, to take affirmative action to overcome past discrimination and to encourage "voluntary affirmative action" to attain a diverse student body and work force. Pepperdine officials took pains to demonstrate they did not discriminate on the basis of race, pointing to a student body of 24 percent African Americans, concerted efforts to recruit Hispanics, academic programs supporting ethnic studies, and off-campus programs that embodied the tenets of affirmative action.[13]

By the mid-1970s, however, both racial and gender activists in the university said Pepperdine needed to formulate an affirmative action document describing how it planned to fulfill the intent of the Civil Rights Act. Calvin Bowers, who was chair and subsequently dean of ethnic studies at the Los Angeles campus and a minister at the Figueroa Church of Christ, said he was personally embarrassed that Pepperdine had no written affirmative action program that spoke specifically to the amelioration of racial discrimination. Similarly, Barnett insisted that Pepperdine was beyond the pale of the law because it did not have an affirmative action plan and a full-time employee responsible for enacting the plan.[14]

But Pepperdine was in compliance, insisted White. It "had conscientiously sought to abide by all requirements" of the civil rights and equal opportunity laws, including the development and execution of an affirmative action program. It had consciously tried to recruit minorities and women, begun to post new job openings or opportunities for promotion, and categorized various jobs throughout the university to guarantee equitable compensation. In addition, the university's various faculties had given serious attention to equalizing salaries; and the administration was recording its practices in anticipation of announcing a formalized affirmative action program.[15]

According to legal counsel, the amended Civil Rights Act impacted Pepperdine only narrowly because its programmatic connections with the federal government were limited in both number and amount. Indeed, the university had only one "contract," as opposed to "grant," valued at more than $50,000. Second, the school and comparable institutions had a unique standing before the law. Because they were Christian and church-related, the First Amendment to the U.S. Constitution gave them the right to discriminate in selection of personnel on the basis of faith and practice. All of this meant, the lawyers said, that Pepperdine did not need an official affirmative action *plan* that included hiring quotas and a bureaucracy, but it did need a clearly described *program*, or process, of action. The difference between the two was significant: a *plan* measured, whereby a *program* described.[16]

With the help of counsel, the university did draft a nondiscrimination policy and affirmative action program in March 1976. In its opening paragraph, the document stated boldly that Pepperdine would continue to discriminate in selecting faculty and staff, giving preference to members of Churches of Christ. It claimed that prerogative as a distinct First Amendment right (free exercise of religion), noting that the university was chartered as a Christian institution associated with Churches of Christ. This exception aside, the document declared, it was "the established policy of Pepperdine University to select the most qualified persons available for University positions without regard to race, religious creed, color, national origin, ancestry, physical handicap, age or sex." Pepperdine was also committed to the same policy of nondiscrimination in education, research, and community service, and in its business and personnel policies.[17]

Howard White circulated the draft to the various campus constituencies in April 1976.[18] Although it attracted some criticism for various elements, the criticism eventually subsided, and Bowers even agreed to serve as chair of the university's affirmative action committee.[19]

Pepperdine's administration asserted that it "did not discriminate on the basis of sex ... except when full compliance with the regulations under Title IX would be inconsistent with the specific religious tenets held by the controlling religious organization." Of the latter there were two: that women should not serve in positions of authority or leadership over men in public worship, religious instruction, or in the home, and that God approved sexual relationships only between male and female in holy wedlock. Thus Pepperdine reserved the right to exclude women from religious leadership activities and to take disciplinary action against persons determined by the university to be involved in homosexual relationships or heterosexual relationships outside wedlock.[20]

Given all of the expressed reservations, the school did not adopt final language of the twelve-page "Pepperdine University Policy of Nondiscrimination and Program of Affirmative Action" until June 1977. The general objective of the affirmative action program was "to recruit and hire more women, minorities, and disabled." To achieve that result, it articulated specific administrative practices that were to be implemented by an equal opportunity officer (EOO).[21]

Parts of the program were already operative, and Bowers, a mainstay on the Los Angeles campus since 1969, had taken a part-time EOO position on February 15, 1977, an office he continued to hold after being assigned to the Malibu campus seven months later. Bowers split his time between appointments as professor of communication and EOO. His charge as EOO was to develop and implement "an effective University program of affirmative action," a task he exercised faithfully for twenty-seven years.[22]

High Teaching Loads, Low Wages

Nettlesome to the Seaver faculty was the teaching load requirement of fourteen units—four courses—per trimester. Relative to similar universities, it was a heavy teaching requirement, especially when demanded each trimester. Even more irritating was that colleagues at the School of Business and Management taught only nine units—three courses delivered on weekends—of graduate classes, and twelve units—four courses, also on weekends or nights—of undergraduate classes.[23]

According to some Seaver faculty, the heavy teaching load tended to squelch any ability for research, and Assistant Professor of Religion Richard

Hughes encouraged the administration to reduce teaching loads for those with research projects. The proposal was not received with enthusiasm, even though Chancellor Young did think the university should encourage more research and writing.[24]

Particularly challenging to faculty and administration relationships were issues that related to the financial stability of the institution. Most indicators, from physical appearance of the campuses to the *President's Annual Report,* suggested robust fiscal health after 1968. Annual operational revenue increased from just under $7 million in 1969–1970 to $15.3 million in 1972–1973, the year the Malibu campus opened, to $37.4 million by 1977–1978, Banowsky's last year as president. Revenues grew during that era by nearly 550 percent, with tuition payments constituting the principal source of the revenue, up to 73 percent at the end of the era.[25] During that time, tuition rose from $45 per unit to $121 per unit.

But the outward indicators gave a false impression of fiscal tranquility.[26] Between 1968 and 1978, the university managed to balance its annual operational budget, but most times just barely, and only because administrators were aggressive in obtaining unrestricted gifts. They also had to be direct in reminding colleagues of the relationship between the amount of money that came in and the amount that went out. In that context, the faculty experienced the reality of the budget.

Early in 1971, a 10 percent decline in fulltime equivalent (FTE) students placed the university in its tightest economic bind in fourteen years, according to Norvel Young. The chancellor responded by proposing to eliminate 10 per cent of the full-time faculty and enacting other draconian measures. To make these actions more palatable—and in response to WASC criticism about low faculty wages—Young offered a small salary increase to all remaining faculty except those in SBM.[27]

The faculty took exception to these cost-cutting measures. Even with the raise, said Assistant Professor of English Gary Hart, Pepperdine teachers would remain one of the lowest-paid faculties in the nation. And the Los Angeles faculty expressed dismay that some of their colleagues had not been reappointed, insisting that the action had reduced faculty morale to an all-time low. Equally disappointing was the board of trustee's decision to put a moratorium on granting tenure, which the faculty believed violated principles and guarantees in the faculty handbook and bordered upon racial and gender discrimination. In the eyes of the faculty, financial concerns of the university had trumped their rights and privileges.[28]

Fighting Tenure Battles

Until 1973, the granting of tenure on the Pepperdine University campuses had been almost automatic and was based primarily upon amount of time spent in grade—such as the number of years as an assistant professor. Because there was nothing comparable to tenure in the business world, President Banowsky and some of the wealthy elite who supported the Malibu campus wanted to find an alternative to the tenure process for faculty. Well aware of those attitudes, the faculty generally took tenure-related comments or actions as a presumptive attack on a professional prerogative. They were particularly outraged when Banowsky advocated and the trustees mandated a moratorium on grants of tenure because of financial reasons and limited tenure to the campus where a faculty member had been originally hired.[29] Employing faculty handbook provisions regarding notification dates, the faculty forced the administration to delay implementation of the tenure freeze and then to lift it after two years.[30]

Given the interest in tenure as a resource to be either trimmed or expanded, both the faculty and the administration needed a clearer definition of how tenure could be achieved and lost. Working together, although not always harmoniously, they eventually drafted a new statement on tenure that the trustees approved on December 13, 1973. That document committed Pepperdine University to the principle of academic freedom and stipulated that persons hired before January 1, 1974, would attain tenure under the conditions of the various faculty handbooks in effect at the time of their first employment.[31]

The most important shift in the new policy was to make plain that tenure was not a vested right: under no circumstances would any person appointed to the faculty have a guarantee of tenure. Instead, tenure would be granted on the basis of student evaluations, discharge of professional duties, adherence to professional ethical standards, and personal professional attainments. Five years of teaching service was necessary to qualify an associate professor for tenure application; four years for a full professor. The new statement also described administrative procedures for the advancement and denial of tenure applications.[32]

As it turned out, none of the parties involved—trustees, administration, or faculty—envisioned the 1973 tenure declaration as the final word on the subject as key definitions and issues had been left unresolved. To develop language addressing these issues, Executive Vice President White turned to law firm Latham and Watkins, and on August 2, 1975, presented that firm's draft of a tenure policy to the trustees. The board approved the complicated document unanimously.[33]

Clarifying Tenure Procedures

The new tenure statement embellished the various provisions of university policy, acknowledging a symbiotic relationship between "academic freedom and economic security," and declaring both were "essential for acquiring and maintaining a strong faculty." It defined tenure as the right to continue to be employed in the college or school and field of specialization in which tenure was attained until a defined retirement age and with salary and benefits commensurate with other faculty members. But the statement stipulated three exceptions to this rule: financial exigency, a situation whereby declining enrollments mandated substantial economy; termination for cause, defined as neglect of duty, moral delinquency, misconduct that brought discredit to the university, serious disharmony with the institution's policies, and willful activity to overthrow the government of the United States; and, finally, refusal to move to a new campus, an infraction unique to Pepperdine. The document restated that after January 1, 1974, tenure would not be considered as a vested right and would only be granted on the basis of having met certain objective criteria. The application for tenure was to be submitted first to the divisional chairperson, and from there would proceed to the school's rank, tenure, and promotion (RTP) committee, then to the dean of the college, and finally to the university administration. The tenure application process ended with the board of trustees, which approved or rejected the application.[34]

President Banowsky viewed the adoption of the revised tenure statement as a welcome change. For too long, he was quoted as saying, Pepperdine had been a "Ma and Pa" school that lacked the academic rigor necessary to question "whether a faculty member should be granted a lifetime contract."[35] The revised document suggested that the expectation of rigor was emerging.

The faculties of the university were pleased with the administration's desire to promulgate a tenure policy, but they felt that the 1975 version was still too ambiguous. The Los Angeles faculty, for example, wanted definitions of "reasonably commensurate" salaries, "continuous disharmony," "appropriate action," "requirements for promotion," "reasonable time," and "those who will make the decision." The Seaver College faculty wanted similar clarifications, but they were more concerned with the implications of financial exigency for tenured faculty.[36]

Executive Vice President White also had reservations about the tenure policy. In his opinion, the policy made it "virtually impossible to dismiss faculty members short of commission of felonies, public and obstinate idiocy, or some such thing." He thought the university would need to "establish practical procedures" for evaluating teachers in their first two years so those with substandard ratings could be identified and dismissed. White's recommendation was subsequently folded into the process as "pre-tenure review."[37]

Fighting Salary Battles

From President Banowsky's perspective, the possibility of an unbalanced budget trumped faculty arguments for academic freedom and personal economic security. He was more concerned about faculty demands for a corrective salary increase of 20 percent than he was about their demands for tenure reform. The AAUP leadership continued to argue that the faculties at Malibu and Los Angeles were two of the poorest paid in Southern California, even though tuition had increased 27 percent and student-faculty ratio by 50 percent in the previous two years. They also argued that there was a relationship between attracting and keeping good faculty and attracting and keeping good students, that low faculty salaries contradicted the prestige image the university wished to project, and that the priority given to bricks and mortar demoralized long-suffering faculty.[38]

Faculty arguments notwithstanding, Banowsky and his administrative colleagues elected not to award any salary increase for the academic year 1973–1974. The faculty reacted with outrage that White said was more intense than he had seen in his fifteen years at Pepperdine.[39] Ken Perrin and his AAUP and FAC colleagues quickly asked for reconsideration, arguing that financial circumstances of the university were much brighter than initially envisioned. Enrollment at the Malibu campus had increased by 40 percent, and an improved cash flow meant the institution had not been forced to borrow money at the end of the fiscal year. Given those developments, they thought a salary adjustment was due, and could be accomplished without raising tuition further. Without such an adjustment, they feared that the organization of a faculty union would be seen as a necessary option.[40]

Banowsky stoutly maintained that salary increases for the 1973–1974 fiscal year were not possible. He did hold out hope for raises the next year, but not much. Rather, Banowsky intended to win concessions on salaries by offering a more faculty-friendly tenure policy.[41] And he did. At the December 1973 meeting where the trustees adopted the improved tenure policy, they also announced an 8.3 percent salary increase for full-time faculty beginning the next fall.[42]

Faculty members were not happy with the size of the increase, and some did launch a serious conversation about organizing the faculty into a union. Others, however, saw the increase as realistic, especially in light of the revised tenure policy, just as Banowsky had hoped. But Norvel Young feared the administration might have been too clever. There was no way to cover the cost of a salary increase, even a modest one, without raising tuition. And if the faculty had its way, there would be subsequent raises and the need to increase tuition again. To avoid that necessity, Young recommended that Banowsky assign someone to circulate the prospect of faculty layoffs and "other counter information" to temper the demands for further increase.[43]

But the demands did not go away; they just got more militant. Members of the liberal arts faculties at both Malibu and Los Angeles complained that their salaries were not only low but they were even inequitable within the university. Along with a sympathetic Vice President White, they pointed out that the median salary of faculty at SBM was $31,000 and that five members of its faculty made in excess of $40,000 annually, thanks to weekend courses taught as an overload.[44] The highest paid Seaver faculty member, on the other hand, made a bit more than $17,000 for two trimesters.[45]

Belt Tightening Amid Cash-Flow Crisis

The 1975–1976 period was one of Pepperdine's best. Seaver College launched its inaugural year on a spectacular new campus. In an unexcelled public relations coup, President Gerald Ford helicoptered in to bless the campus. The university launched its women's sports program as well as a men's aquatics program. And a more precisely defined tenure statement was adopted.

Yet the 1975–1976 period was also one of Pepperdine's worst, particularly fiscally. Not only was it dealing with the fallout of Norvel Young's crash, the university was also dealing with a revenue shortfall of $2.4 million. Thanks in part to "window dressing" events like the presidential visit, said Trustee Don Miller, the university was in a "financial bind" and unable to pay its current bills. He held Banowsky and Young responsible and "told them off explicitly."[46] The *Inner View* also held the pair responsible, writing: "Pepperdine has not been taught into bankruptcy by the faculty and it has not been studied into financial straits by the students. Rather, it has been administered into difficulty. Yet, those suffering the most because of administrative ineptitude are the students and the faculty."[47]

The administration, in turn, attributed the "austere financial climate" to a national economic crisis and a "cash flow" problem. Pepperdine had valuable property it had not been able to sell to the university's advantage, and it had a large amount of accounts receivable, primarily some $5 million in student debts. To overcome the cash-flow problem, the university had been forced to borrow heavily, and now those loans were coming due. To meet payments required draconian austerity measures, the prospect of which, claimed Chancellor Young, had driven him to the bottle.

In November 1975, Banowsky instituted a total hiring freeze, and the university laid off thirty staffers and ordered cutbacks in intercollegiate sports and realignments in liberal arts programs in Los Angeles, impacting twenty-two teachers and staff. Administrators announced another tenure freeze and less generous tuition discounts for family members. And they delayed plans to construct an on-campus law school. Banowsky pleaded with staff to conserve electricity on the Seaver campus by turning off some of the 268 lights that burned each night.[48]

Banowsky even resorted to personal appeals in an attempt to win the cooperation of some of his administrative colleagues. On a note regarding payment of back rent to the World Trade Center, Banowsky scrawled a hand-written note to SBM Dean Don Sime:

> I wish there were some way I could convince you . . . and all of your colleagues of the grave seriousness of our cash flow problem. It genuinely threatens the *very survival* of the University. Isn't there some way you could help me by cutting 10% to 15% out of the Business School expenses?[49]

Such appeals obviously had some impact, for the university overcame most of its deficit by cutting $1 million from academic support and $1.8 million from scholarships. It even ended the fiscal year with a $280,000 favorable variance.[50] The university also found ways to enhance payouts from the university's endowment, taking actions that brought no immediate relief but eventually brought in a greater annual return.[51]

Acts of "Desperation"

To preempt a call for an even more substantial increase, Banowsky announced a 3 percent salary raise for the fiscal year 1976–1977 and hinted of another increase the following year. Seaver faculty were more than disappointed— they were insulted. The FAC demanded detailed salary information regarding various schools. Unhappy faculty revived talk about forming a union and demanding collective bargaining. The AAUP chapter proclaimed a Day of Fasting and Prayer.[52]

Unlike some of his administrative colleagues, Howard White took such talk very seriously. As two ways to oil the troubled waters, he suggested that the university give faculty members with married children tuition benefits and appoint a committee to participate in informal bargaining.[53] The Seaver faculty welcomed the gesture, but that and a 3 percent raise were just not enough.

Year after year, the faculties of Pepperdine University had been denied meaningful pay increases. Consequently their salaries compared unfavorably to colleagues teaching at places such as Loyola Marymount University.

There, for two semesters (nine months) professors received total compensation of $23,600, associates received $18,200, and assistants received $14,600. At Pepperdine, for two trimesters (eight months), professors received $15,300, associates averaged $13,100, and assistants received $11,500. The disparity in salary meant that most Pepperdine faculty had to teach the summer trimester, take on an overload, or even accept outside employment to make ends meet. Consequently, said historian Stephen Sale, "we have a lot of exhausted faculty members," and "you just don't achieve excellence when you're overworked and underpaid."[54] Like many of his colleagues, Sale agreed with the editors of the *Graphic,* who had criticized Pepperdine's administrators for not putting first things first: that is the academic enterprise ahead of raising funds to build a spectacular campus.[55]

Most faculty believed salaries were so low because of the financial costs of the Malibu Miracle. Others pointed to the $500,000 annually invested in the NCAA Division I athletic program, which many believed was a foolish extravagance for an institution perpetually strapped for cash. Administrators, Ken Perrin said, thought it more important to compete with UCLA in basketball than with Biola University in math. Perrin and some faculty colleagues were convinced that if Seaver College competed at NCAA Division II or NAIA levels there would be money for adequate salaries.[56]

Perhaps nothing fostered more faculty outrage than the public revelation of how four chief administrators had received "retirement benefits" between 1966 and 1973 through a dummy account. Banowsky had reported the practice to the faculty, but downplayed it by saying the state attorney general had found the procedure was not illegal and dismissing the topic by saying the practice had been discontinued.[57] But when further details came to light in a March 1975 *Sacramento Bee* article, faculty rage boiled over.[58]

With frustrations deep-seated and widespread, 90 percent of the Seaver faculty suspended their classes as a protest over faculty treatment on February 12, 1976. As already noted, it was something less than a full-fledged strike: participating faculty remained in their offices but chose not to teach that particular day. For Goldwater Republicans like Stephen Sale, one of the faculty leaders, it was so close to being a strike that it made him uncomfortable. That he would even participate—much less lead such a protest—demonstrated just how disenchanted he was with Pepperdine's administrators. For him the strike was "the last act of desperation."[59]

Faculty participants wanted it known that they were protesting more than just salary issues; they were seeking administrative recognition of faculty members as professional persons, respect for the faculty's professional judgments, and restoration of administrative credibility. As AAUP President

Stephen McHargue lamented, there was "just plain disbelief on the part of the faculty" when it came to administrative pronouncements.[60]

The Seaver College faculty association renewed its interest in collective bargaining, undertaking a study of advantages and disadvantages of forming a faculty union. For an institution long associated with free-market advocates, the prospect of collective bargaining was a matter of regret to both administration and faculty. Perrin, who had led the study, opposed it. Loyd Frashier was not all that enthusiastic either, but given the "gross discrepancies" between salaries in Seaver College and other Pepperdine schools he did not see much of an alternative. Carl Mitchell feared unionization would polarize the faculty and negatively impact prospective donors. Fred Casmir, who only a few years earlier had run for U.S. Congress as a conservative Republican, favored the faculty initiative. In his view, the administration disregarded the faculty's request for equitable salaries because it believed that "Christians should make sacrifices." That attitude, Casmir said, was "hard [for the faculty] to take as Christians and as professionals."[61]

Making an Impact

The atypical assertiveness of the Seaver faculty led to positive consequences. Within a month of the strike, the board of trustees approved a faculty salary increase that would average 8 percent and a staff increase of 6 percent for the year 1975–1976. The trustees tarnished that victory by authorizing another two-year moratorium on tenure, but the "freeze" lasted for less than a year, and the board granted additional raises in the next two fiscal years.[62]

Although the combined salary increases of 19.3 percent over three years were substantial, they barely improved Pepperdine's standing in AAUP rankings. Based upon 1976–1977 figures, Seaver College faculty salaries ranked in the twentieth percentile of all universities and colleges reporting. The average faculty salary at Pomona College was $11,000 higher; at Pasadena City College it was $10,000 more, and $4,000 more at the University of Pacific.[63]

Convinced that more needed to be done, the five-member Seaver College FAC entered into negotiations for an acceptable salary package with a Howard White-led administrative team. Both groups agreed to a 6 percent across the board increase for all university faculty members beginning 1977–1978. To acknowledge inequities in salary levels between schools, they also proposed an additional 9 percent increase for Seaver faculty and 6 to 9 percent more the following year. The negotiating parties also agreed to a reduction in teaching load at Seaver from fourteen to twelve units per term. The salary package also committed the Seaver faculty to stop trying to organize a union under the auspices of the National Labor Relations Board (NLRB). Instead, the administration would look to the FAC as the faculty's official negotiating body.[64]

The Seaver faculty accepted the higher salary/lower teaching load package in a unanimous vote in November 1976. The new board of regents adopted the package the following month. Vice President White rejoiced that Seaver College was able to "start concentrating on people rather than buildings."[65] With combined salary increases between 34.3 and 43.3 percent, the Pepperdine faculty was willing to rejoice as well. Many would have also witnessed to the value of a good old-fashioned strike/protest and to the support of WASC accreditors, who had criticized the inadequate salaries in both 1970 and 1974.

By November 1977, the financial crisis of the previous years had lessened. Vice Chancellor Runnels reported to the American Association of Independent and Private Colleges and Universities that Pepperdine University was in a strong financial condition. In the previous year, the school had been able to retire all of its short-term debts, improve its endowment, and handle its long-term debt comfortably. It, moreover, enjoyed an A-rating in the bond market and had been able to sell a $7.5 million CEFA bond issue easily.[66] He might have added that all of this had been possible even as the university raised annual salaries by $500,000. Altogether it was a notable accomplishment, but the strained relationships between administration and faculty did not heal overnight. Nor did the affiliation with the university's church constituency.

NAVIGATING CHURCH CONNECTIONS 1970–1985

CHAPTER 35

NURTURING THE CHURCH RELATIONSHIP

D elivering the May 1970 dedicatory address for the Malibu campus, William S. Banowsky spoke profoundly about "a spirit of place." It was his first effort to articulate publicly the vision and educational philosophy propelling the expansion of Pepperdine University to a suburban campus. Noting that college campuses around the nation were wracked by students protesting the Vietnam war, Banowsky asked why the nation seemed to be coming apart. Humankind had started the twentieth century with such confidence in the "efficacy of education," but after seventy years had no answers to the "same, ancient human problems." Given this sad reality why build another educational center in beautiful Malibu, Banowsky asked? Because, he answered, Pepperdine's new suburban campus would address the central human questions of the day differently.[1]

Fundamental to the Pepperdine way was pedagogy both values-centered and person-centered. Elsewhere, education was conducted in a values vacuum, a state of detached neutrality that privileged mere "facts," leading to life conclusions bereft of meaning. The ministry of teaching on the new Malibu campus would combat this sterility by bringing together a community of scholars who "unashamedly" embraced Christian values as eternal truths. Moreover, these values would flow not just from a deep personal faith of the faculty but also from the "fraternal relationship" with Churches of Christ, ties that Pepperdine intended to "strengthen, not loosen." The Malibu campus would also "focus personal attention upon each student as an individual" rather than as a statistic, emulating Jesus's teaching that one person was of greater worth than the combined material world.[2]

What Pepperdine University hoped to create in the Malibu hills, Banowsky declared, was "a spirit of place": a location where minds would be opened, lives would be changed, and lasting relationships would be formed. Embodying the "soul" of the campus, those endeavors were of deepest concern to Banowsky. It was why the Malibu campus would "look not at the things that are seen, but at the things that are unseen; for the things that are seen are temporal, but the things that are unseen are eternal."[3]

Affirming Mission, Purpose

That there was something eternal about Pepperdine University's mission was not a new thought for Banowsky. In his 1968 case statement for a second campus, described in chapter 26, he had included a declaration on what Pepperdine affirmed as its fundamental mission. The so-called "Affirms Statement" spoke of truth as eternal and touched on student conduct and responsibilities, social order, the value of a liberal arts education, and the benefits of free enterprise.[4] University officials published a much-revised version in the 1973–1974 Malibu campus catalog.[5] Banowsky tinkered with the document for several years until he came up with language he liked better, which was published in the 1978–1979 Seaver College catalog. Barely changed over the next 40 years, the 1978 edition was a notable rearticulation of the values- and person-centered educational distinctive that Banowsky advocated in his "Spirit of Place" speech.[6]

> Pepperdine University Affirms
> That God is, and
> That He is revealed uniquely in Christ.
> That the educational process
> cannot, with impunity,
> be divorced from the divine process.
> That the student, as a person of infinite dignity,
> is the heart of the educational enterprise.
> That the quality of student life
> is a valid concern of the University.
> That truth, having nothing to fear from investigation,
> should be pursued relentlessly in every discipline.
> That religious commitment, which is no excuse for mediocrity,
> demands the highest standards of academic excellence.
> [That freedom, whether spiritual, intellectual,
> or economic, is indivisible (*added in 1980*).]
> That knowledge makes a claim calling,
> in return, for a life of service.

In an address titled "A Spirit of Purpose" delivered for the dedication of the Frank R. Seaver College of Liberal Arts on April 20, 1975, Banowsky elaborated on the distinctive qualities of the Malibu campus. It was small; it was residential; its faculty devoted itself to the "ministry of teaching" and had the highest

standards of personal conduct; it was a community of scholars with distinctive spiritual beliefs; it affirmed that ultimate truth actually existed although
its own vision of that truth was limited; and it rejoiced in being dedicated to the
glory of God and the service of mankind. As such, the president declared, Seaver
College was the "cornerstone" of Pepperdine University's institutional life.[7]

No administrator at Pepperdine would have disagreed with Banowsky's
assumption that the qualities that made the new Malibu campus distinctive
were somehow rooted in the university's relationship with Churches of Christ.
Norvel Young, for example, credited the church relationship for Pepperdine's
regulated social environment, which contrasted with the "moral jungle" on
state college campuses. He also credited it for the school's friendly relationship with the business establishment, embrace of the free-enterprise system,
and championship of the American Way.[8]

The Malibu campus provost, Jerry Hudson, blanched at making a cozy
relationship with the business community a distinctive of church-related
education, but he too embraced values- and person-centeredness as part of
the equation. He also added academic quality, believing that mediocrity was
"inherently un-Christian." To him academic excellence was deeply Christian
and when delivered "in a context of an affirming faith" was a mark of distinction indeed.[9]

Hudson's view was strikingly parallel to that of a predecessor at George
Pepperdine College, E. V. Pullias. The former dean had come to hold that there
was no conflict between academic excellence and Christian commitment but
that demonstrating as much was "the most significant problem of our time."[10]
Moreover, quality Christian education was impossible without a very close
relationship with a particular church or denomination. relationship. Lacking
such a relationship, a school would drift "toward a colorless, often impotent
religious position which manifest[ed] itself in a weak commitment in all
areas, including behavior."[11]

Howard White accepted values-centeredness, person-centeredness, and
academic excellence as qualities emanating from a church relationship, and
he also added "spiritual liveliness." Stemming from a basic commitment to
Jesus Christ, spiritual liveliness provided a unifying intellectual principle
that contrasted the academic anarchy of "neutralism, scientism, relativism,
materialism, and secularism" in modern education. At Seaver College, that
special spiritual energy imbued everything from required religion courses, to
mandatory chapel, to restrictions on drugs and alcohol, to training of preachers and missionaries, to the integration of faith into the various disciplines.
White was no sectarian and was "more concerned about loyalty to Christ than
keeping some kind of connection" with Churches of Christ, but he strongly
believed there was "no such thing as being Christian" without a connection

to "the body—the church."[12] And for Pepperdine that meant connection with Churches of Christ.

Defending the Church Connection

President Banowsky was surprised when an early draft of the 1976 McKinsey report recommended severing the traditional relationship with Churches of Christ, prompting him to write an eloquent defense of the university's historic attachment.[13] Although the church provided very little financial support, he argued, "it was a part of the soul of the institution." From it came "the university's general conservative stance on social, moral, ethical, political, economic, and academic issues." Continued contact with the church was important, "not in pursuit of some sectarian cause, but as the cornerstone of the institution's heritage."[14] Banowsky's defense was so persuasive that most of the language critical of the Church of Christ connection was eliminated from the final McKinsey report.[15]

The relationship with Churches of Christ offered tangible financial benefits beyond nurturing the soul of the university. The formal connection with Churches of Christ gave faculty and staff who were church members special standing before the U.S. Internal Revenue Service. For doctrinal reasons, they were recognized as "ministers" within the tax code and allowed to claim ministerial housing allowances as income tax deductions, a financial break that partially mitigated their inadequate university salaries.

To protect this benefit, Howard White argued strongly in favor of a clear and forceful articulation of the historic ties with Churches of Christ, not only in the bylaws of the university, but in minutes of the regents, the student handbook, in college catalogs, and university publications. Without that recognition, agencies of the U.S. government could conceivably pronounce that a relationship with the church was false and withdraw ministerial housing allowances and the school's ability to discriminate in hiring practices on the basis of religious considerations. It could even disqualify the university from competing for federal grants.[16]

To demonstrate that the university valued a close relationship with Churches of Christ, the Banowsky administration embraced policies that touched all elements of the institution. Students were expected to follow the disciplined lifestyles of a traditional Christian college. That included, among other things, attending chapel, taking courses in religion, not consuming alcohol, not dancing on campus, and adhering to visitation limits in residence halls. The administration also stipulated that divorced students were unwelcome.[17]

Faculty and the Church

The church connection also had implications for faculty and staff. The presumption was that all senior administrators would be active members of Churches of Christ.[18] The expectation was the same for faculty; if they were not associated with Churches of Christ, they were expected to be an active member of some community of Christian faith. It was widely accepted, even when it came to granting tenure,[19] that there was "no such thing as an at-large Christian."[20] At Malibu, 83 percent of faculty members and 100 percent of senior administrators and division chairs were associated with Churches of Christ in fall 1974.[21]

However, limiting faculty across the university to Christian churchgoers was problematic because the rapid expansion of graduate and extension programs had not been designed to purvey Christian ethics and lifestyles. For those programs, accommodation to the church-connection preference was deemed permissible since they acted as revenue generators for the liberal arts at Malibu.[22]

To illustrate further that the university honored its church connection, the Banowsky administration and its successors invested significant resources in the religion faculty on the Malibu campus. In schools connected with the Churches of Christ, it was an accepted principle that the second-most important person on campus—trailing only the president—was the chair of the religion department. That principle was not always the operational standard on Pepperdine's Los Angeles campus, but it was expected to be true on the Malibu campus. For that reason, the administration named notable churchmen as religion division chairpersons. Anthony "Tony" Ash (1972–1975), a widely known minister and scholar recruited from Abilene Christian College, was the first. He was followed by

- Carl Mitchell (1975–1980), a Pepperdine College alumnus and trained marriage and family counselor;
- Frank Pack (1980–1983), a much-respected scholar and teacher, from Abilene;
- Carroll Osburn (1983–1986), who held the doctorate from University of St. Andrews in Scotland and would spend most of his academic career at Abilene Christian;
- Tom Olbricht (1986–1995), celebrated teacher, scholar, and author, also from Abilene; and
- Rick Marrs (1995–2004), a Johns Hopkins-trained Old Testament scholar.

In addition, a group of teacher–scholars enhanced the profile of the Pepperdine University religion division among Churches of Christ. Foremost of these was Jerry Rushford, minister and church historian, who joined the faculty in 1978 and soon made his mark as director of the Bible Lectures. Royce Clark was respected as an independent thinker, and Richard Hughes was a resolute advocate for academic scholarship. Later twentieth-century additions to the faculty included Randy Chesnutt, Ron Highfield, Ira Jolivet Jr., Daniel Rodriguez, and Tim Willis, all serious scholars with a deep commitment to Churches of Christ.[23]

A Church of Christ in Malibu

Another demonstration of the university's desire to remain faithful to its relationship with the Churches of Christ came in the form of a campus congregation. The Malibu Church of Christ had organized on April 5, 1970, well before work had begun on the new Malibu campus. Charles Runnels and Banowsky had hoped an established Church of Christ congregation like the one at Westchester or Inglewood would plant a new congregation at Malibu under the leadership of its elders. Instead, independent of any other group, five to six families began gathering for worship services in the Los Angeles County Court House on Civic Center Way in Malibu.

The small congregation called Ed Rockey to preach and Jere Yates to lead the singing. Pioneers in the congregation included the families of Bill Banowsky, Bob Gilliam, Walter Glass, Grover Goyne, Jerry Hudson, Norman Hughes, Richard Hughes, John Nicks, Kenneth Perrin, and Norvel Young.[24] When the campus opened in 1972, the Malibu church moved its services to Elkins Auditorium and subsequently to Stauffer Chapel. Some were disappointed by the move because they wanted the congregation to focus on *Malibu* instead of the university.

As an agent of the university's Christian mission, the Malibu church played an increasingly significant role. After Ed Rockey, it provided a pulpit for Tony Ash (1972–75), and for faculty members including Robert Douglas (1975–78), Jerry Rushford (1978–81), David Davenport (1982–83; 84–85), Carroll Osburn (1983–84), and John Free (1984–85). Not until 1985 did the congregation hire its first full-time preaching minister, Dan Anders, who filled that role until ill health forced him to resign in 1998. Ken Durham served as minister between 1998 and 2011. The campus church gave some financial support to the Bibelschule in Heidelberg, Germany. But most important, it offered formal worship opportunities where students could witness and experience the power and promise of Christian community, with a Church of Christ world view.

Pepperdine officials saw the Malibu church as the only consciously denominational witness on campus. At other Church of Christ-related colleges, doctrinal messages came through religion classes, chapel services, and personal testimony in the classroom. At Pepperdine, however, students and some faculty resented such messages, which they considered attempts by the minority to inflict its will on the majority. Rather than give up on evangelism, Pepperdine administrators looked to the Malibu church to witness Church of Christ doctrine to Seaver students.[25]

But the small congregation was not prepared for that responsibility. Not only were its members divided as to mission (the town or the gown), but its resources were limited. How could the congregation maintain an evangelistic witness on the campus when it could not even afford a full-time minister? To help, Pepperdine officials first looked to the Santa Barbara Church of Christ, which supported a ministry known as Campus Advance at the nearby University of California.

In 1977, with organizational support from Rick Rowland, Pepperdine's new aquatics coach, and financial support from the university and Regent George Evans, the Santa Barbara church sent Craig and Patti Bowman as full-time coworkers to organize a campus ministry on the Seaver campus. The following year, the Malibu church assumed responsibility for their work, while inviting other California congregations to join in covering costs. The Malibu church, renamed the "University Church of Christ" in 1978, continued to supervise campus ministry into the twenty-first century, although the ministry's role over time would change from evangelistic to pastoral.[26]

The first campus ministers, Craig and Patti Bowman, served jointly from 1977–1980. They were succeeded by David Ladd and David Pippen (1980–1981), Don Crawford (1981–1982), Tom Reynolds (1982–1984), Pat Iseke (1984–1985), Scott Lambert and Hung Le (1985), Dave McMahon (1985–1987), Scott Lambert (1987–2005), LaJuana Gill (1990–1997), and Linda Truschke (1998-).[27]

The campus ministers focused on the spiritual development of the entire student body, not just students from Churches of Christ. They provided weekly Bible studies, off-campus retreats, mission workshops, and small-group gatherings, in addition to Sunday school and regular worship services. They also offered full-time mission opportunities through SHARE, a local program that sent students as missionaries to Brazil (Steve and Corleen Parmelee) and Germany (Rick Cupp). Three-fourths of the university church's budget went to support these missions, the Heidelberg Bibelschule, and LA inner-city mission points. Commitment to evangelism was so palpable in campus ministry that forty-five baptisms per year were not uncommon.[28]

Tending to Church Relations

To illustrate further the university's connectedness to the Church of Christ, administrators crafted programs specifically for its benefit. Foremost of these, of course, was the annual Bible lectureship. In 1971, the university launched the chancellor's council, designed to be to the church community what the president's board was to the business community. Subsequently, Silas Shotwell and "Big Don" Williams traveled widely in California and created the Thanksgiving Youth Festival to share the news that Pepperdine was a safe haven that offered a distinctive education for Church of Christ students.[29]

In 1977 the university formally reconstituted an office of church relations with Carl Mitchell as its director. It was responsible for all university outreaches to the churches, including the Bible Lectures, youth fest, mission workshops, family referral services, choral tours, the Heidelberg Bibelschule, and the off-campus MA program in religion. In fall 1977, the university's net cost of its church programming totaled $60,000, which seemed a disproportionate sum given the demands on the budget.[30] The following year, President Banowsky downsized the church relations office and put it under the supervision of the dean of Seaver College.[31]

Church Community Remains Skeptical, Critical

Despite the Banowsky administration's conscious nurturing of the church relationship, many church leaders remained skeptical of the university's claim that it was a *real* Christian school. What worried them, they said, were aberrant student and administrative behaviors. Pepperdine students smoked, danced, and drank alcohol, the church folk believed. They dressed immodestly, with women wearing shorts and pant suits. Presumably, President Banowsky belonged to a wine-tasting club and condoned dancing and consumption of alcohol at university-sponsored galas. After his car wreck, Norvel Young was liberally criticized for taking to the bottle in times of stress.[32]

Church critics were convinced that senior administrators had abandoned patterns of traditional conduct expected of Christian colleges. In their judgment, chapel was no longer a priority at the school, liberal visitation hours in residence halls promoted promiscuity, and the professional schools hired faculty and staff who were not members of Churches of Christ. The graduate schools scheduled classes and the undergraduate schools scheduled athletic events on Sundays.[33]

Some of the criticism had roots in theological concerns.[34] Church leaders complained that the university, influenced by black revolutionaries and white atheists, had hired theological liberals as teachers who questioned the inspiration of scripture and that the Bible was the source of "all truth."[35] They noted that three of those teachers were on the founding editorial board of *Mission Magazine,* a journal published and read by the more progressive Church of Christ members.[36] They charged that all but two teachers of science believed in biological evolution and that some religion department professors even skipped teaching the first eleven chapters of Genesis.[37] Moreover, some notable critics added, Pepperdine officials purveyed religious "error" by permitting Pentecostals to host a Jesus Music Festival, campus speakers to offer "altar calls," the choir to sing "Ave Maria," students to raise money for the Salvation Army, and Catholic priests to dedicate Stauffer Chapel.[38]

Ira Rice Jr., editor of the San Francisco-based *Contending for the Faith*, declared that Pepperdine University was known in California "as the greatest, single source of error being infiltrated among the churches."[39] Randy Mayeux, a young Church of Christ preacher and leader of the university's chancellor's council, said he could no longer defend Pepperdine or recommend it to young people.[40]

Alumnus and minister Dave Schulze believed both Pepperdine and the church would be better off if the two divorced. "Pep's spiritual mission," he wrote, had for years been "largely superficial and shamefully hypocritical."[41] And Mary Alice Richards wanted to retrieve her bonds purchased in the 1960s, insisting she could not support a school that was not "genuinely Christian."[42]

Questions from Inside

Not all doubts and criticisms came from outside Pepperdine. Howard White, the ultimate insider, recorded in his journal that neither Young nor Banowsky was "seriously concerned about New Testament Christianity." Banowsky was an "agnostic" who felt comfortable with most of the Christian ethical tradition, White conjectured, and Young found the historic ideals of Churches of Christ problematic but for some reason—friends, wife, mother—wanted to keep Pepperdine close to the church.[43]

Others within the university also thought they saw evidence that the university's Christian commitment was less than genuine. Professor William Green, who began teaching in the religion department following his retirement from a distinguished career at the University of California-Berkeley in 1962, believed the college had forgotten its founder's foremost goal: to save souls through biblical teaching and "sound doctrine."[44] In February 1975, twenty-four of his Malibu colleagues expressed their concerns that Pepperdine had become "so secularized" that it was impossible "to relate meaningfully . . . to our constituency in churches of Christ."[45]

And the initial dinner for the Pepperdine University Associates sparked criticism from inside and outside the university. The wife of a member of the board of trustees wrote to Banowsky to complain that it had been inappropriate to invite Rabbi Edgar Magnin to give the invocation at that 1977 event. Surely someone "more in keeping with the claims of the school" and "a believer in Jesus Christ" could have been chosen, she said. "To fail to honor Jesus Christ's name initially at this affair appeared to me to be a cop out."[46]

President Banowsky was defensive in his response. "Edgar," he wrote, was regarded as the "number one invocateur" at such occasions, having prayed at the inaugurations of Presidents Nixon and Eisenhower. Pepperdine University was a school not a church, and the occasion was a banquet and not a religious service, he reminded his correspondent. Banowsky also acknowledged that others had criticized his selection of Norvel Young, an alcoholic, to give the dismissal prayer, and of Pat Boone, a disfellowshiped member of the Inglewood Church of Christ, to sing the national anthem. All of this criticism left him with great heartache, he concluded. Clearly there were a "number of very dedicated people whose vision of what Pepperdine never was and certainly never will be hinders the vision of those of us who want the University to become better at what it is."[47]

That "heartache" would lead Banowsky to fight for changes in the Church of Christ relationship in university governance and administration.

CHAPTER 36

LIMITING THE CHURCH RELATIONSHIP

Although the Banowsky administration often eloquently defended the university's relationship with Churches of Christ as necessary and fruitful, early on it concluded that the relationship had limits. As the president saw it, the university had "grown to the very edge of the brotherhood" and stood "with one foot in and one out." In his mind that had been a source of greatness, but it was also "the source of schizophrenia."[1]

It would be easier, he wrote, "to be either a Bible college, on the one hand, or an utterly secular university on the other." To combine spiritual commitment with academic openness was "to tread the narrow edge of unrelieved intellectual tension." But, he claimed it was "a more exciting path than either the emptiness of mere secularity or the sterility of fundamentalist simplicity."[2] His actions, however, did not always demonstrate his excitement at the difficulties along the path.

Despite publicly equating the soul of the university to the Church of Christ relationship, Banowsky was not convinced that all Pepperdine faculty, even those at Seaver College, had to be members of the church. Early in the history of the Malibu campus, he told Provost Jerry Hudson and then subsequently Academic Vice President John Nicks to hire faculty who were not members of Churches of Christ, a directive that he seems not to have shared with Howard White, although White clearly knew about it.[3] Simultaneously, Banowsky made sure Pepperdine University described itself in college guidebooks and directories as "non-denominational" as opposed to being affiliated with Churches of Christ.

Finessing for Funding

The university was also willing to place limits on its relationship with Churches of Christ when it came to financing construction of the Malibu campus. In 1977 a possible source of funds was the California Educational Facilities Authority (CEFA), a state agency that sold bonds to underwrite capital improvements for educational institutions that did not—among other things—discriminate on the basis of religion.[4] Of course, Pepperdine did discriminate on the basis of religion in its personnel, admission, academic, and student life policies.

To enhance Pepperdine's chances for CEFA funding, the Los Angeles legal firm of O'Melveny and Myers suggested revising any descriptive language that suggested a sectarian spirit prevailed at Pepperdine. They found problematic language in the Seaver College bulletin that spoke of a "distinctive Christian flavor" in classes and activities and that described the "Introduction to the Bible" course as a record of God's action in history. Equally questionable was language in the law school catalog that implied a connection between the school and the church.[5]

Not all of the law firm's recommended revisions were accepted, but at Seaver College "chapel" did become "convocation," and religion faculty did sign statements requiring appropriate academic standards when teaching introductory Bible courses. University administrators also consented not to hold religious services in buildings constructed with CEFA funds, specifically the law school and the new fine arts building. These concessions assured the university of CEFA funding.[6] They also demonstrated the limits of the university's relationship with Churches of Christ.

Chancellor's Council Discounted

So too did the work of the chancellor's council, which Norvel Young had organized in 1971 to improve communication between the school and the churches. In 1974, with the encouragement of Young, some staff support, and the reported approval of Banowsky, council members organized a task force that was to help the university "identify its purposes and goals and evaluate its spiritual life."

Robert Scott, a minister who had been trained in social science methodology, was selected as chair. During 1974, 1975, and 1976, he and student David Ogilbee hosted twelve different assessment meetings on and off campus. By February 1977, Scott had drawn only one tentative conclusion: the university would never be a Christian school unless it was "led by administrators and served by faculty and staff who demonstrate Jesus Christ is Lord in all they do." The implication of the interim report, of course, was that Pepperdine lacked such a demonstration; thus, Banowsky did not want to see the full report. It would be "in no way helpful to what we are doing," he told Regent Ken Ross. Instead, "it was a completely sectarian effort that asked a lot of Mickey Mouse questions of the wrong kind of people and came up with a set of do's and don'ts which they wished to enforce upon all of us."[7] He told Young to "forever kill" the study, for it "just pushes us further out to sea."[8]

Banowsky's reaction disappointed members of the council. David Malone, the minister of the Church of Christ at La Mesa, California, resigned in protest in February 1977. The *raison d'être* of the university, he said, was not Christian education but survival. "Its means are its ends, namely to insure the life of Pepperdine before any other concern."[9]

Despite Banowsky's reservations, Scott did complete the report in fall 1977. The 135-page document was particularly concerned about "how members of the university community could work together to affirm a Christian life-style and a Christian philosophy of education in a more nearly desirable manner." That was possible, the report concluded, only if

1. a Christian philosophy of education integrated and synthesized the isolated fragments of knowledge;
2. a Christian faculty taught liberal arts courses within the framework of Christian philosophy;
3. a daily chapel experience was offered; and
4. student moral behavior was in harmony with the godly life.

In other words, quoting Elton Trueblood, "Christian emphasis, in order to be real, [had to] be something integral rather than something added."[10]

A Board Overhaul

Banowsky did not find the report very helpful as he had come to believe what Pepperdine needed was not a closer relationship with Churches of Christ but a more limited one.[11] This was especially true of the university's governing board. By George Pepperdine's preference, membership on the board of trustees was limited to members of Churches of Christ. Over the years, trustees had served the institution with honor, but none of them were individuals of great wealth capable of funding a $63 million campus in Malibu. Donors who had made the campus possible, such as Richard Scaife, Blanche Seaver, Morris Pendleton, and Leonard Firestone, were ineligible to serve on the governing board because they were not Church of Christ members. In Banowsky's mind, the church membership requirement was an unnecessary limitation and a serious impediment to the perpetuation of the university into the twenty-first century.

On the other hand, Howard White and others believed changing the requirement would be a dramatic step toward the secularization of the university. The church ties, White believed, were foundational to the school maintaining its Christian mission, and he pointed to Harvard and Yale, USC and Occidental, where severing of ties with sponsoring denominations was the first step in the secularization of the institution. In his judgment, adding trustees who were not members of Churches of Christ would be "one of the greatest mistakes ever" made. Norvel and Helen Young held positions somewhere in between, desperately wanting to retain ties to Churches of Christ but also to incorporate into the governance system business leaders of means who were not members of the church.[12]

The board of trustees had been under fire for various reasons since the mid-1960s. In addition to not having the wealth Banowsky and Young desired, many of them had little administrative experience, and their often spotty attendance at board meetings seemed to show a lack of commitment. At most meetings barely a quorum attended. Between August 1968 and August 1973, two members missed 100 percent of those meetings, five missed 87 percent or more, and three missed between 48 and 86 percent.[13] Howard White observed that most members of the board could not "administer themselves out of paper sacks," although they were "fine" people.[14]

Convinced that change was necessary, President Banowsky had attorneys with the firm of Latham and Watkins review university bylaws. They told him what he wanted the board to hear: the bylaws were out of date and in need of "extensive revisions."[15] The office of the California attorney general concurred.

Partly to respond to criticism, the board of trustees added nine new members in July 1974 and July 1975, bringing the total number to twenty-four. These included D. Lloyd Nelson; T. A. Rogers; John D. Katch; Evelyn Clark; Orbin Melton; Kenneth Ross Jr.; Thomas G. Bost; Joe R. Barnett; and Jack Alan Scott. All were members of Churches of Christ.[16]

A direct consequence of the attorney general's investigation (discussed in previous chapters) was the March 1975 amendment and restatement of the university's bylaws and articles of incorporation. With prior approval of the attorney general's office, the updated documents called for as many as thirty trustees, all of whom would be members of Churches of Christ. They stipulated bimonthly meetings; defined the responsibilities of the executive committee; reserved to the board itself the responsibility of approving executive compensation; limited the terms of trustees to two five-year appointments; and created a nonvoting position of "life trustee," should she want it, for Helen Pepperdine. They also established a nonvoting office of "Trustee Emeritus"; created "action" and "study" committees; defined the role of chancellor, who would be the senior policy officer of the university and responsible to the board of trustees; and mandated that all senior administrative employees were to report all annual income above $250, a provision that President Banowsky "seriously" questioned.[17]

Push for Opening Board Continues

Banowsky did not believe the amended and restated bylaws and articles of incorporation were adequate—or final. He continued to agitate for a board that would include men and women of means who might also be from a religious tradition other than Churches of Christ.[18] Under Banowsky's prodding, Richard Scaife's encouragement, and Latham and Watkins's coaching, a trustee subcommittee of Robert Jones, Lloyd Nelson, and Thomas Bost undertook a lengthy and careful study of previous plans for expansion of the board. In December 1975, just months after Chancellor Young's car crash, the subcommittee offered its own expansion proposal. It recommended

- enlarging the board from twenty-four to forty members and renaming it board of regents;
- that the chair and "at least" 60 percent of the new board (twenty-four members) be members of Churches of Christ and known as "trustees";
- that all Church of Christ members would constitute a religious standards committee (RSC) and be given exclusive power and authority to determine the religious, spiritual, and campus life rules, regulations, and policies of the university; and
- that the RSC would name the president.[19]

The proposal represented a radical shift in Pepperdine's historic form of governance. And it was presented at a dramatic moment in its history: Chancellor Young and his wife, Helen, chose that day to attend their first board meeting since his September crash. After the Youngs retired from the room, the trustees reviewed the desperate financial condition of the university and its immediate cash requirement for $3.6 million while celebrating a gift of a half-million dollars from Blanche Seaver. Thereafter, the board launched a two-hour discussion on the subcommittee's proposal to amend the charter and bylaws to admit non-Church of Christ members to the governing body.[20]

The advocates of the proposal argued that exclusion of non-Church of Christ members from the governing board jeopardized the financial stability of the university. People able to make substantial gifts were less likely to make them unless they had some authority on the governing board of the institution. Proponents introduced a letter from Richard Seaver, Blanche Seaver's nephew, who argued that broadening the base of the board was "critical to the well-being of the university." His endorsement of the proposed bylaws pretty much carried the day. At the end of the debate, Helen Pepperdine moved and Earl Warford seconded the adoption of the proposal. Without further discussion, the board voted unanimously by secret ballot to accept the proposal.[21]

It was a stunning reversal of views for Helen Pepperdine, who had registered a strong objection to admitting non-Church of Christ members to the board only a few months earlier. She would rather stand up against the displeasure of Bill Banowsky, she had said, than face the Lord for opening "the board to non-church members, *especially* for money." But her head had changed, if not her heart.[22]

At Banowsky's suggestion, the chair of the trustees, Don Miller, nominated twelve men, who collectively had given more than $40 million to Pepperdine since 1968, to join the university's governing body. These were George Elkins, Bryant Essick, Leonard Firestone, F. Miles Flint, Fritz Huntsinger, Hulsey S. Lokey, Morris B. Pendleton, Richard Ralphs, Richard Scaife, Richard Seaver, Leonard H. Straus, and John V. Vaughn. All had been members of the university board, and all had been major supporters of the miracle then transpiring at Malibu. Richard Seaver withdrew his name from consideration on the basis of conflict of interest, and the eleven new regents were confirmed simultaneously with the formal adoption of the "Amended Articles of Incorporation and By-laws of the University" on January 17, 1976.[23]

Banowsky Wants More

Despite the extent of changes, Banowsky was not satisfied. "We have greatly strengthened things already by breaking open the sectarian exclusivity," he wrote to Helen and Norvel Young, but in doing so "we have also created a them and us syndrome." The legalized 60/40 percent ratio, he believed, was both "plastic" and "divisive," and he was "determined" to remove "any requirements" for regents to be members of the Churches of Christ.[24]

The climate seemed propitious for still more change. Banowsky acknowledged that the addition of non-Church of Christ members to the governing board had discouraged some church members, but there had been no "blood-letting."[25] From the sidelines, Norvel Young was not so sure. Maintaining an explicit church tie, he told Banowsky, was imperative if the university was to continue its Christian commitment and even its conservative economic stance.[26]

But the reservations of Young, White, and others only solidified Banowsky's resolve. A serendipitous change in the leadership of the regents facilitated his determination. For unknown reasons, chair of the governing body, Robert Jones, resigned his position after little more than a year of service and was replaced by Lloyd D. Nelson.[27] A professor of education administration at USC, Nelson was a lifetime member of Churches of Christ, an Abilene Christian graduate, and an elder in the congregation at Sierra Madre who did not worry that adding non-church members to the board of regents would jeopardize Pepperdine's Christian commitment. He seemed to understand that the school "desperately" needed "financial leaders" who could help "pay for the big … pay raise" just granted the faculty, to quote Banowsky. No wonder the president considered Nelson a "God send."[28]

The new chair did not disappoint, appointing a committee in March 1978 to review the recently amended governing documents. Serving on the committee were Robert Jones, Bill Banowsky, Tom Bost, John Katch, and Hugh Tiner.[29] Banowsky set the agenda, proposing that the ratio of Church of Christ members to non-Church of Christ members on the board be changed from 60–40 to a 51–49 percent ratio—from twenty-four Church of Christ and sixteen non-church members to a ratio of twenty-one to nineteen members. This was necessary, he said, because Church of Christ regents generally did not provide any financial leadership and had left the university "rotting in the ghetto."[30]

Banowsky also proposed other modifications. In his judgment, neither the chair of the board nor a majority of the executive committee needed to be members of Churches of Christ, and he also recommended that the size of the RSC be reduced from all Church of Christ members to just nine. He felt the RSC was a bomb that needed to be defused and believed reducing its size would help do that.[31] Recognizing that his proposals would raise anxiety levels within the school's church constituency, he also recommended that the president of the university be restricted to a member of Churches of Christ.[32]

Banowsky did not get all his wishes. Language restricting the chair of the board and the majority of the executive committee to church members remained unchanged. But the regents approved the other modifications to the charter and bylaws by written ballot June 13, 1978. The final vote was never recorded, probably because it was not unanimous.[33]

Religious Standards Adopted

Although intended to limit the influence of the church, the new charter and bylaws, ironically, unleashed an effort to expand it. The new governing document tasked the RSC, composed of nine of the board's Church of Christ members, to set religious standards for the university. Beginning September 1977, RSC chair Kenneth A. Ross Jr. and a subcommittee set out to articulate "Pepperdine University's religious standards." With the help of consultant Robert Douglas, a member of the Seaver College religion faculty and minister of the University Church of Christ, the subcommittee produced a set of standards related to faculty hiring and a statement of faith to be required of members of the religion faculty.[34]

The June 1978 version of the "Standards and Procedures for Hiring Selection" at Pepperdine University stipulated that all "faculty members at Pepperdine University should be chosen [because they] demonstrate outstanding Christian character and faith." There were only two mandates when it came to Churches of Christ: all who taught in the religion faculty should be members, and chairpersons of other divisions and deans of all schools should seek to fill open positions first with qualified church members. The recommendations did not constitute new policy; they merely committed historic procedures to paper. The proposed confession of faith for the religion faculty, of course, was another thing altogether. Banowsky could hardly bear codifying hiring standards at all, but mandating a confession of faith was more than he could take.

The university, the president insisted, had never had a religious "litmus test" and had never mandated a creedal statement, primarily because it flew in the face of the Church of Christ understanding of the "individual priesthood of believers." A confession of faith affronted human dignity and assaulted "the highest ideal of university education." And it bordered on creedalism and thus violated the Church of Christ's traditional position. He noted that guidelines were already in place regarding admission, the overall purpose of the university, and religious standards for the student body. In his view, nothing further was needed.[35]

Significantly, Howard White did not agree with Banowsky. Not only did he want to strengthen the ties with the church, he wanted internal documents that showed such ties actually existed. In a confidential letter to Reuel Lemmons, editor of the *Firm Foundation,* he spoke highly of Douglas, who had drafted the two-page confession of faith for religion faculty, and said he would welcome a strong statement from the board regarding faculty hiring. Success in that kind of hiring, he said, required strong support from "the very top," suggesting that that kind of support had been lacking.[36]

On July 25, 1978, President Banowsky called a meeting at the Brock house to discuss the "Standards and Procedures for Hiring" document, just weeks before he left for Oklahoma. Included were chair of the regents Lloyd Nelson; dean of Seaver College Norman Hughes; chairpersons Bob Gilliam, Ken Perrin, Gerald Turner; and executive vice president Howard White. The president communicated clearly that he did not like the standards and wanted them withdrawn altogether, and others also expressed their reservations. Nelson, however, indicated that he could hardly tell Ross and the RSC that they could not exercise powers the new university bylaws had granted to them.[37]

Thus on December 11, 1979, the RSC did adopt a statement of "Standards and Procedures for Faculty Selection" after it had labored for more than a year with President Howard White to get a document of some kind. What the RSC adopted gave a general statement on the need for selecting faculty who were qualified both academically and spiritually, concluding that only "persons who demonstrate outstanding Christian character should be chosen and retained as faculty members at Pepperdine University." These persons "should be actively and responsibly involved in local church life." The document prescribed that "all administrators shall conscientiously fill faculty positions with individuals who will contribute to the academic and spiritual excellence of the University." Moreover, all full-time members of the religion faculty were to be members of the Church of Christ but no further statement of faith would be required.[38]

The standards spoke of "a critical mass of faculty sufficient to sustain [the] relationship" with Churches of Christ and charged chairpersons and deans to find "qualified faculty who are members of the Church of Christ." When there were two candidates with equal credentials, preference was to be given to the one who was a Church of Christ member. Those doing the hiring should understand, however, that formal church ties alone were insufficient to meet this requirement, and new faculty should be carefully reviewed after the first year and dismissed if they had not contributed to the Christian mission. The same would be true for those being considered for tenure. The vice president for academic affairs was charged with implementing the hiring standards and procedures, and the RSC expected to play a role in tenure decisions.[39]

Crowning Glory

Although not happy about the action of the RSC, President Banowsky considered changing the bylaws and articles of incorporation as his crowning achievement at the university, ahead even of the miracle at Malibu. The school, he told the *Graphic*, had been "weakly governed" by the old board of trustees but that had all been changed. Banowsky had used his friendship with the California attorney general and the attorney general's investigation of the school to persuade the governing board to admit non-Church of Christ members. Then he had "gone into the courts and changed George Pepperdine's founding charter." It was all part of his long-range plan, he confided, to let more "daylight in[to] the place."[40]

The results of Banowsky's long-range plan had clearly marked the limits of the university's relationship with Churches of Christ.

Jimmy Lovell, the longtime member of Pepperdine's governing body, was not much disturbed by the changes, "as shocking as it may be to some," he said. From his perspective, the university was "far more church related than ever before and far more than Brother Pepperdine ever had in mind." In his view, Churches of Christ had "at least another 50 years to speak for Christ through Pepperdine, [and] what person living or dead could ask for more [given what] the church . . . put in it?"[41] President Banowsky was certain that no one could.

CHAPTER 37

A NEW PRESIDENT RECOMMITS TO THE CHURCH

Williams S. Banowsky accepted the presidency of the University of Oklahoma in August 1978, confident that under his leadership Pepperdine University had achieved a place of distinction on the United States educational map. As evidence he needed only to point to the beautiful campus in Malibu and to the well-endowed Seaver College. Furthermore, the university was strong and stable with growing enrollments, balanced budgets, multiple campuses, worldwide programs, and wealthy friends. Pepperdine's future seemed bright, even limitless. That being the case, he felt free to "repot" himself in Oklahoma.

Banowsky announced his departure to a joint meeting of the board of regents and the university board on August 15, 1978. Just prior to the announcement, he and Lloyd Nelson, chair of the regents, spoke to Howard White privately and asked if he would be willing to serve as interim or acting president, an option that Richard Seaver and selected administrators presumably had already endorsed. Genuinely flattered, White accepted the offer with only one stipulation: permission to leave for a long-planned vacation to Europe the next day. When that was given, the three men returned to the meeting room and announced the decision.[1]

White extracted a promise from Nelson that no decision would be made on how to select a president until he got back from Europe. That agreement, however, did not keep others from making their own recommendations. Nelson preferred a screening process that would include faculty and students, a procedure that White questioned. Professors Ken Perrin and Bob Gilliam asked that Seaver faculty be part of it; the student government association made a similar request. Worried that White's appointment might become something other than "interim," Norvel Young called from Hong Kong to strongly urge White not to go to Europe until the question of presidential succession was decided.[2]

Young's concerns reflected the feelings of donor and regent Richard Scaife, who strongly objected to a "caretaker administration" in general and to Howard White in particular. To Scaife, an interim president represented a serious drift from the "dynamic" leadership and mission of the previous decade, and he viewed as liabilities White's age, inexperience as a fund-raiser, and sensibilities of a New Deal Democrat. Scaife also objected to restricting the presidency and chair of the regents to Church of Christ members, so he was unimpressed with White's denominational connections.[3]

Much to the consternation of Scaife and Norvel Young, as it turned out, White never served as interim president. On his European vacation, he had dinner with Richard Seaver at the Vendome in Baron's Hotel in London. White apparently impressed Seaver with his knowledge of the internal workings of the university, his courtly behavior, and his familiarity with a lengthy wine list. At the end of a three-and-a-half-hour dinner, Seaver encouraged White to think of his presidential appointment as not "necessarily terminating." At that point, White correctly concluded that his future role at the university would be as "president" rather than "interim president." When he returned to California, the board of regents offered him a two-year contract as president, which was extended for another year, then for two more, then for two more— until he retired in 1985.[4]

Through the seven years of his presidency, however, Howard White was continually bedeviled by those who insisted he was serving only until a *real* president could be found. Presumably, that was what Norvel Young regularly conveyed to Scaife, an assurance that White considered an "outrageous departure from the truth." When the "interim" president continued to serve, Scaife terminated his support of the university and snubbed White publicly.[5] Some of White's administrative colleagues also seemed to embrace the untruth about the interim status and, in White's mind, circled him like "vultures," trying to position themselves to be the chosen one when his contract expired.[6]

The Fifth President

Howard A. White was inaugurated as Pepperdine University's fifth president on September 13, 1978, twenty years after he had arrived on campus as a professor of history. Born in 1913 near Florence, Alabama, White matriculated David Lipscomb College at the age of seventeen; two years later (1932) he graduated with honors and as class president, although he stayed a third year to edit the school newspaper.

Between 1933 and 1942, White preached full-time at locations in Mississippi, where he experienced "happy days" and came "to love the people" very much. At the end of that period, he took up regular work at the Carrollton Avenue Church of Christ in New Orleans, under the condition that he could attend Tulane University. For the next twelve years, he served that church and attended Tulane, taking BA, MA, and PhD degrees in history. During that time, he met Maxcine Feltman, the supervisor of women at David Lipscomb College, and they were married in June 1952 on the Lipscomb campus. Six months later, with his doctorate nearly done, the couple moved to Nashville where White taught in the history department at Lipscomb and preached in a succession of area churches.[7]

Norvel Young convinced White to join the Pepperdine faculty as professor and chair of the social science department in June 1958. Over the next thirty years at Pepperdine, White proved to be an astute teacher and accomplished administrator known for his mastery of detail and 24/7 work ethic. He took great pleasure from his job, but nothing gave have him more satisfaction than being the cofounder of Pepperdine's Heidelberg program in 1963 and serving as an elder for the Malibu Church of Christ. On the other hand, nothing produced more sadness than the premature death of his wife, the mother of his two sons, in 1973.[8]

White's inaugural ceremony was notable for its simplicity and sense of history. There was no special gathering of institutional representatives, no elaborate investiture with symbols of academic office. At a regular convocation on September 13, 1978, Pepperdine students watched faculty in academic regalia process to the front of Stauffer Chapel; saw former president Hugh M. Tiner lead the Pledge of Allegiance and former president M. Norvel Young lead the invocation; and heard farewell remarks from former president William S. Banowsky. Subsequently, D. Lloyd Nelson, chair of the board of regents, presided over a brief investiture ceremony, with the symbol of office being a large commemorative coin loaned for the occasion by Blanche Seaver.[9]

Building on Church of Christ Foundation

White then delivered his inaugural address, beginning with generous praise for his predecessor. Banowsky, White said, was a one-of-a-kind leader who could not be replaced and whose name would be illustrious even if Pepperdine and Seaver College lasted a thousand years. His challenge as the next president, he predicted, was to do three things:

1. to distribute the university's resources (people, space, time, books, equipment, repute, and money) to the best advantage;
2. to emphasize academic excellence; and
3. to sustain the institution's distinctive heritage.

In managing that heritage, he recognized the need to "preserve the openness, the freedom, the right to disagree, and to maintain the diversity that belongs in a University." At the same time, White argued that it was desirable to have unity in common goals and purposes. That there would be tension he did not doubt, but he saw that as a healthy sign of life. Finally, his administration would be about values, specifically "individual responsibility, moral absolutes, belief in the American system of free enterprise, and belief in the indivisibility of freedom in the spiritual, intellectual and economic realms."[10]

All of these values, White believed, ultimately rested on a religious foundation bolstered by Pepperdine's historic relationship with Churches of Christ. If that were destroyed, the consequences would be disastrous. White concluded on an optimistic note: "This institution is so strongly established, its friends and supporters are so numerous and dedicated, its human and financial resources are so great, its heritage is so valuable and its distinctive purposes are so needed in our society, that its future with the help of God is bound to be one of glorious achievement."[11]

But White was not quite as confident as he portrayed in the inaugural speech. Needed resources and academic excellence would come, he believed, but he had concerns about Pepperdine University sustaining its Christian heritage. In his mind that relationship had been under serious attack during the Banowsky era, when the president had not given "a fig" about the church connection and even seemed ashamed of it.[12] Consequently, the university was on the verge of becoming just another secular institution of higher education. Howard White did not want that to happen, and he made as the top priority of his administration preserving Pepperdine as a Christian university by maintaining its historic relationship with Churches of Christ.

Crafting a Mission Statement

He began the process by formulating a mission statement for the university, something long encouraged by WASC accreditors.[13] Although Banowsky had crafted a poetic and profound "Affirms" declaration, he had chosen not to draft a statement that gave a common purpose and meaning to the work of the entire institution. Thus, there was no document that conveyed coherently and sensibly Pepperdine's educational philosophy, goals, and objectives. Banowsky had said producing such a document would have required a fistfight with the faculty. White too worried about the response of the faculty, who, he said, could agree on only two things: to raise salaries and hang the dean. But he believed a formal statement of Christian mission acknowledged by the faculty and adopted by the board of regents would contribute to Pepperdine's survival as faith-based university. Eager as he was, it still took him eighteen months and blistering criticism from WASC to get the process started.[14]

With the help of administrative colleagues, the president cobbled together paragraphs from various published documents and program reviews, and in fall 1980 circulated a draft to the faculty, assuring them the document contained no new principles. The response revealed a faculty severely divided and susceptible to the proverbial fistfights predicted by Banowsky. Ruing that reception, White determined not to submit a draft of the document to any faculty or administrative group for independent approval, just further comment. He let the discussion cool for a year and a half while reviewing mission statements of other colleges and universities, then submitted a final draft to the board of regents, which endorsed the mission statement unanimously on September 14, 1982.[15] It had been an exhausting process, but ultimately a productive one.

Howard A. White served Pepperdine University as executive vice president under President Banowsky, then became the institution's fifth president in 1978. He served in that role until 1985, strengthening the university's ties to the Churches of Christ, bolstering its academic achievements, and overseeing campus construction projects even while impressing students with his "personal touch."

Published as a separate booklet, "The Mission of Pepperdine University" described the university as independent, Christian, and dedicated to preparing students for "a life of usefulness" based upon "Christian character and faith." Pepperdine was not a church or religious body, but as an educational institution it had a distinctive heritage and mission, part of which was its commitment to the value of human freedom, whether "expressed in economic, intellectual, or political activity." Moreover, the university was "free of direct ownership and control by an ecclesiastical body" and was governed by a self-perpetuating board of regents, a majority of which had to be members of Churches of Christ.[16]

According to the new mission statement, Seaver College of Letters, Arts, and Sciences was the heart of Pepperdine University's educational life. Its interdisciplinary curriculum sought to unify knowledge around Christian truth. The professional schools were logical extensions of the priorities established in the liberal arts college. Also, faculty members, who were crucial to the mission, must possess the proper academic qualifications to be successful teachers, embrace high ethical and moral standards, accept the institution's Christian values, and be respectful of its heritage. To address the university's educational philosophy, the document presented the well-known "Affirms Statement."[17]

A clear, succinct statement of Pepperdine's educational mission as a Christian university was a welcome development. Not only did it speak to the institution's spiritual roots and purposes, but it offered the "arch of understanding" that was of such interest to WASC accreditors. It did not answer all questions, remaining ambiguous about *why* the Christian distinctive was imperative at the university and just how that would work itself out in real time.

Still, it was clear that for President White and other Pepperdine administrators, faculty, and staff, Christian mission was the university's *raison d'être.* It was expected to permeate every dimension of the university (even the professional schools), from how it did business, to what went on in the classroom, to on-campus social activities. It was a pathway to truth and a means of unifying knowledge in the person of Christ. Presumably, it freed students from prejudice, superstition, unfair discrimination, heartless secularism, and mindless religion; and it represented an alternative to a world that promised little more than nuclear holocaust, moral drift and uncertainty, crime and violence, broken homes, and fractured families.[18] As incomplete and imprecise as it may have been, the new mission statement was an encouraging first step in recommitting the university to its historic relationship with Churches of Christ.

So too was the June 1982 decision of the board of regents to reject the plea of Richard Scaife and Richard Seaver to open the positions of chair of the board of regents and president of the university to non-Church of Christ members. President White objected to the proposal because it would likely sever Pepperdine's relationship with Churches of Christ and make the university susceptible to impositions by government agencies. It would mean, wrote White, that the university could "not discriminate in hiring as we now do," and would allow appointments of individuals "without reference to their character or religious beliefs." It might force the university to appoint "extreme left-wing" teachers, "even Marxists" to the faculty. It took four years (1978–1982) of patient persuasion, the formulation of a position paper titled the "Unique Character and Mission of Pepperdine University," and an informal opinion from the California attorney general, but the regents ultimately rejected the Scaife-Seaver led initiative. The decision heartened White and gave him cause to believe that the church connection was still viable, if not strong.[19]

The Importance of Critical Mass

In the calculus of the Christian university, however, White believed the faculty played the largest role. Only if they modeled Christian mission would it be assured. Knowing the history of higher education in America, President White had concluded that institutions that were once Christian became secular after they severed their relationship with the founding denomination. However, because Churches of Christ had no formal hierarchy, the connection with the university could not be maintained via a convention, synod or diocese. It could be sustained only through individual faculty, staff, and students who were church members and worked and worshipped at the university.[20]

White took some comfort in knowing the new bylaws required the chair of the regents and the president of the university to be members of the Church of Christ, but he was acutely aware that two persons alone could hardly keep the university connected to the church and in pursuit of its Christian mission. More necessary would be a "critical mass" of administrators and faculty who were committed members of the church. Without such a concentration, White believed, Pepperdine's Christian mission was in jeopardy.[21]

White's concern that Pepperdine University have a "critical mass" of Church of Christ faculty members, was supported by the religious standards committee (RSC) of the board of regents.[22] Their "Standards and Procedures for Faculty Selection" document, as already noted, called for legal discrimination in hiring in order to favor Church of Christ candidates. Not wanting to offend faculty who were committed Christians but not Church of Christ members, White and his administrative colleagues chose not to circulate the document widely. Besides, said one administrator, what the RSC wanted was already being done.[23]

But was it? Vice President John Nicks in early 1978 had told regents chair Lloyd Nelson that he was working hard to recruit faculty from Churches of Christ. Two years later he tried to assure White of the same thing. The president was skeptical, however. Between 1976 and 1980, Seaver College had forty-nine opportunities to hire faculty and had chosen Church of Christ members only fifteen times, or 30 percent. Of twenty-two totally new positions, only three had been filled by members of the church. Depending on who did the counting, the percentage of faculty who held membership in Churches of Christ ranged between 55 and 41 percent.[24]

Very concerned by those numbers, the chair of the regents insisted that the administration observe RSC's policy statement regarding faculty selection. White told Nicks, who opposed "creedal tests" for prospective faculty, that henceforth he wanted to interview every candidate being considered for an appointment and have the final say in who was hired. The president had concluded that two more years of Nicks's hiring practices would put the university "hopelessly down the secular road."[25] In the president's view, Nicks "demonstrated repeatedly . . . that he would prefer to diminish rather than strengthen our church relationship."[26]

A Controversial Change

White was certain that Pepperdine University's future as a Christian institution was in jeopardy. He had both admiration and affection for Nicks, but given his hiring record and a devastating 1979 WASC report, he felt it was past time for a change. Making it, however, would be a challenge, for Nicks was well regarded among the faculty, being credited for pay increases, an improved tenure policy, and the demise of the military base program, among other things. Almost from the beginning of his administration, White knew he wanted to replace Nicks with Herbert Luft, head of the program in Heidelberg and director of the Bibelschule. He was an efficient administrator who had supervised an expansion of Moore Haus that had come in under budget and on time. If White had any reservations about Luft as an administrator, they were buried beneath his appreciation for Luft's personal loyalty, remarkable work ethic, commitment to Churches of Christ, and European world view.[27]

White rightly surmised that the faculty outcry would be too great if he tried to simultaneously dismiss Nicks as academic vice president and replace him with Luft. So he chose to first abolish the position of academic vice president, saying the office was no longer needed because of the emergence of strong deans at the school and college levels. Next, he encouraged Nicks to find a position elsewhere in the university, which he did, moving into university development and later to SBM. White then reactivated the position he once held personally, executive vice president, and appointed Luft to it, effective January 1981. He charged Luft with two primary responsibilities: reverse the decline in the number of Church of Christ faculty employed at the university (every dean plus a 60 percent critical mass for Seaver College) and win full accreditation approval from WASC's impending visit. Luft's initial appointment was for only a year.[28]

White got far more faculty opposition to his administrative change than he anticipated. The *Graphic* quoted one faculty member as saying, "I think losing Nicks is an absolute disaster. There's no question he was pressured out. He's tough to deal with and White got tired of fighting him. [White] wanted a 'yes man.'" Dean of Students Stuart Love said he was "seriously reconsidering" his decision to stay at Pepperdine, while his wife, D'Esta, who was Nicks's secretary, said she was looking for another job.[29] Dan Caldwell, assistant professor of political science, who was a Nicks's appointee and head of the faculty organization, objected to the decision on multiple grounds, and said the change would exacerbate the lack of trust between faculty and administration.[30]

The university faculty subsequently adopted a resolution of protest by a vote of 37–23, which represented 38 percent of the entire faculty. It praised Nicks for his contribution to the university and criticized White for acting without faculty input. White, who believed the president should have the authority to make unilateral changes in the central administration, replied that there was no mechanism for formal consultation with the faculty regarding such a move. He noted that Nicks had been chosen as academic vice president without any faculty participation, as had all central administration members and school deans.[31]

Faculty leader Ken Perrin very much regretted the dismissal of Nicks, but he agreed with White that there was no truth to the "vicious rumor" that the president did not have the right to make his own appointments. By March the controversy had cooled, in part because Nicks refused to be drawn into it. President White marked it all up as an "episode in our on-going development."[32]

With Herbert Luft as his executive vice president, President White made significant progress in building "critical masses" of faculty and administrators. Luft successfully employed John Wilson as dean of Seaver College and William Adrian as dean of the Graduate School of Education and Psychology; both met the church qualification. He recruited for dean of Business and Management an internal candidate, James Wilburn, the sitting vice president for university affairs and former Church of Christ minister. To the central administration, White added two lifelong church members, David Davenport as general counsel, and William Phillips as academic vice president. By the time Luft returned to Germany in 1983, all of Pepperdine's deans and most of its central administration were members of Churches of Christ.

Luft also experienced some success in increasing the number of church members on the faculty. University-wide and in absolute terms, the number of Church of Christ faculty increased from forty-five to fifty-seven; at Seaver College from thirty-four to forty-two in absolute terms and from 41 to 46 in percentages. SBM increased from 4.4 to 12.7 percent (from two to six). The number in both the Graduate School of Education and Psychology and the School of Law, however, declined.[33]

Much of the increase in the number of Church of Christ faculty came from recruiting faculty from other Church of Christ schools, which did not always please the other schools.[34] The number of Church of Christ students at Seaver College did not drop, but it did not increase. Still, the presence on campus of administrators, staff, and faculty who were members of Churches of Christ was far more apparent than at any time within the previous decade.

Many church leaders welcomed White's initiative to bring Pepperdine back into the orbit of the church. Randy Mayeux, Long Beach Church of Christ minister, chair of the chancellor's council, and frequent Pepperdine critic, was delighted with the critical mass approach. He wrote to compliment Luft on his integrity and solid commitment to the church, and for "stirring up a lot of dust." [35]

"Part of the Problem"

Not everyone was pleased with the renewed emphasis upon Church of Christ membership as a priority for hiring. Some argued that faculty candidates who were church members were likely to be mediocre in both training and intelligence—true believers but unqualified academics. Recently hired faculty such as Dan Caldwell, Ron Fagan, Nancy Magnusson-Fagan, and Carolyn Vos Strache considered the critical mass approach demeaning. They and others who strongly supported the Christian mission of the university but were not members of Churches of Christ had come to Pepperdine expecting be part of "the solution," only to find out they were considered "part of the problem." As President White told Magnusson-Fagan, if a faculty person was not a member of Churches of Christ at Pepperdine, their faith commitment did not really count within the context of the university. Knowing that White was using the rhetoric of "critical mass" and not delivering a theological judgment did not make his comment any more palatable, then or later.[36]

The sense of being outside of the club troubled Dan Caldwell from the beginning of his tenure at Pepperdine in 1978. In addition to being widely recognized for his work in the field of international relations, Caldwell was a man of faith and much involved in the Presbyterian Church. A year after he joined the Seaver faculty, he asked to be considered as a teacher in the Heidelberg program. The administration received his application but delayed a definitive answer for eighteen months. At that time President White confirmed what had long been rumored: Caldwell would not be considered for the post because he was not a member of a Church of Christ.

White tried to explain why. The university was able to purchase Moore Haus because of the financial help rendered by the Broadway Church of Christ in Lubbock, he told Caldwell. Pepperdine's faculty representative in Heidelberg, therefore, needed to be available to interact with German congregations, a task that required a knowledge of the nuances of Church of Christ doctrine and practice. It was, said White, "a practical consequence of maintaining a strong relationship with Churches of Christ." The Church of Christ faithful thought White's explanation was a clarifying moment in the university's relationship with the church. Caldwell thought it was evidence of discrimination, even though Pepperdine would soon establish programs at other international sites where, as the president had promised him, no requirement for church membership would be instituted.[37]

Restricting visiting faculty at Heidelberg to members of Churches of Christ continued until 1996. In 1989, pressed by Caldwell, Dean of International Programs William Phillips searched the records and found no evidence supporting restriction of visiting faculty to church members.[38] Howard White, by then president emeritus, was dismayed. He agreed that the $125,000 loan from the Broadway church in Lubbock had long since been repaid but believed a "moral obligation" lingered "to operate our program so as to make an educational contribution to the church in the nation that has shown us great hospitality for a quarter of a century." Because his successors had such respect for White, his view restricting the Heidelberg visiting faculty to Church of Christ members prevailed through his life. Thereafter, the policy changed, severing one of the cords that White believed bound Churches of Christ to Pepperdine University.[39]

White's Subtle Pragmatism

Even in the critical mass debate, it was never a matter of "my church right or wrong" for President White. Indeed, it was his practice to edit out references to the church in official publications, saying he did not wish "to speak in sectarian terms," or project a "veneer of religiosity," or "appear to be coercing individuals into any dogmatic position." When this position was interpreted to mean there should be no reference to the church, he ordered that every major publication with a descriptive segment about the university include at a minimum: "Pepperdine University is related to the Churches of Christ, of which the founder, Mr. George Pepperdine, was a lifelong member. The institution is under the control of a self-perpetuating Board of Regents and is free of direct ownership and control by an ecclesiastical body." Such language, which would be included in the new mission statement, properly referenced the church relationship, White believed, but did not "overpower people with it."[40] In other words, it was subtle, but not too subtle.

White had the same pragmatic approach when it came to appointing and retaining members of the faculty. He was aware that the pool of qualified faculty from the Church of Christ had its limits. But he also believed that on those occasions when it was necessary to look at candidates of other faiths, it was the obligation of administrators of a Christian institution "to lead in selecting faculty who [would] at the same time serve Christ and maintain academic quality."[41] In that process, White would not exclude non-Christians, even though the 1981 tenure policy demanded of candidates a "consistent pattern of support of generally accepted Christian values and the mission of the university." Pepperdine, he said, was all about "values rather than theology." For that reason, the Jewish faith of Professor O. J. Krasner at Pepperdine's School of Business and Management in "no way preclude[d] him from obtaining tenure," nor did it "place him in the slightest disadvantage with other applicants for tenure."[42]

Although White spoke frequently about a "critical mass," his official definitions were always ambiguous. As new dean of Seaver College, John Wilson found the ambiguity troubling, and he met with President-elect David Davenport, Vice President for Academic Affairs William B. Phillips, and Provost William Adrian in April 1985 to set more precise parameters. He found consensus within the group that the Seaver dean should be a member of Churches of Christ but that divisional chairpersons, assistant and associate deans, and directors of programs need not be; that academic divisions in Seaver College would strive to have a "critical mass" of 50 percent of the faculty who were members of Churches of Christ; and that "Non-Church of Christ faculty who [were] strongly committed to the mission of Pepperdine [would be] considered valuable members of the Seaver community and indeed be preferred over Church of Christ members who [were] nominal in their spiritual commitments, or [were] cynical or negative toward the institutional church."[43]

But when Wilson wrote to summarize the points of agreement, Davenport objected; in his mind, the meeting had been an informal discussion. He did not disagree with the conclusions, only with the assumption that they had been lifted to the level of policy. Clearly, it was possible to give certain matters too much definition; ambiguity had its advantages when it came to the implications of Christian mission.[44]

Reaching Beyond University Walls

In addition to strengthening church ties within the university, President White was eager to have the university reach out formally to Church of Christ congregations, and he looked to the office of church services, which had been reconstituted under the direction of Carl Mitchell in 1977. Five years later, Jerry Rushford, associate professor of religion and minister of the University church, took charge of the office, a position he held for the next thirty years.[45] He was given supervisory responsibilities for the Thanksgiving Youth Festival, the Heidelberg Bibelschule, the chancellor's council, the Seaver College chorus tour, the off-campus religion MA program, special seminars and workshops, Christian education Sunday, and—of course—the annual Bible lectureship.[46]

Under Rushford's energetic leadership, his office also inaugurated the annual William E. Green Lecture in 1980 and the Thomas F. Staley Lecture in 1981. Rushford also made Christian education Sunday and the Bible Lectures model outreaches to the church. By 1986, on Christian education Sunday, nearly sixty Pepperdine faculty and staff filled some seventy-five different church pulpits throughout Southern California—promoting the spring lectures and the work of Pepperdine University. The lectures themselves grew from 800 attendees to 5,000 annually, with representatives from virtually every state and a dozen or more nations. Little during Rushford's tenure as director was as influential in impacting the faith and practice of Churches of Christ in North America as the Pepperdine lectures. At this work, President White believed, Rushford was little short of a "genius."[47]

Pepperdine University staff and faculty continued to demonstrate a relationship with Churches of Christ in less public settings. Among these was Professor of Law Jim McGoldrick's legal brief in defense of the elders of a congregation in Collinsville, Oklahoma, who had disciplined a congregant for perceived immoral conduct. Known as the Marion Guinn case, it made national headlines, reflected badly upon the discipline practices of Churches of Christ, and ended with a verdict against the church. Most church members, however, thought the elders had acted biblically. Certainly Howard White did, and he was pleased that McGoldrick had acted to support the institutional church, even if the Oklahoma judiciary had not.[48]

President Banowsky had believed that greatness required Pepperdine University to cut its umbilical cord with Churches of Christ. Howard White, on the other hand, insisted that the university's search for distinction required it to retain its Christian mission and its relationship with Churches of Christ. He devoted his entire administration to recommitting the school to its traditional church ties: hammering out a mission statement, winning board approval for a faculty hiring plan that privileged Church of Christ candidates, gaining regent support for bylaws that mandated church membership for the president and chair of the board, embracing critical mass as a basis of hiring faculty, and reinvigorating the office of church relations. His focus on retaining Pepperdine's historic connection with Churches of Christ defined his administration—but did not limit it. During White's presidency, the university also successfully engaged accreditors, focused on academic quality, struggled with governance issues, conducted a successful fund-raising campaign, developed a strong national brand, launched a new campus building program, and experienced a measure of institutional maturation.

INSTITUTIONAL MATURATION 1978–1985

CHAPTER 38

WASC Sets
THE AGENDA

B eyond his desire to recommit the school to its traditional church ties, Howard White had little flexibility in determining the agenda of his administration. That was largely decided by the accreditors from the Western Association of Schools and Colleges (WASC), the first team of which was scheduled to visit in early 1979, only a few months after he took office.

Vice President for Academic Affairs John Nicks and a faculty team had been at work on a reaccreditation report for months. Their 207-page report was filed in November 1978 describing how the university had been thoroughly engaged in "reevaluation" and "consolidation" of its activities since WASC had visited four years earlier. Enrollment had been reduced from 9,000 to 7,000 students; the liberal arts program on the Los Angeles campus had been phased out; off-campus programs had been reduced; nine schools, colleges, and centers had been consolidated into five; faculty members were better paid; student registration and admissions functions had been centralized; student records were better maintained; and a new forty-member board of regents had been constituted.

With the establishment of an all-university academic council, Pepperdine was no longer a *multi*versity but a true *university*. It thus desired accreditation as a single rather than as two distinct institutions, a reversal from what Banowsky had previously deemed necessary. The self-study concluded the university was achieving its goals, had the resources to solve its problems, and had reason to be optimistic.[1]

The twenty-seven-member WASC review team was not so sure. In January and March 1979, it visited Pepperdine's twenty-four campuses and centers, including those in Hawaii. They declared the self-study was "barely adequate to serve the purposes of [the] visitation team" and were confounded that it did not declare the Christian doctrines of "the priesthood of all believers" and the significance of "inherited tradition" relevant to the educational mission. "Rather than finding contemporary expression for these "'free church' ideas," Pepperdine University explained itself in terms indistinguishable from many institutions and organized itself with a greater deference to traditional authority than most.[2]

The accreditors were even less pleased by the response of some university officials, who denied WASC visitors access to pertinent materials and even key administrators.[3] Greatly offended, the accreditors attributed the debacle of the self-study and on-site experience to Nicks and even recommended his dismissal from the university.[4] The academic vice president may have been responsible for local arrangements and the tone of the document, but the content of the self report was the work of multiple faculty committees, who did not have a particularly high regard for the evaluation process.

In its 195-page preliminary report, the visiting team identified twenty-three specific issues that Pepperdine University should address immediately. Among those were formulating a clearer concept of its mission, inducing a greater sense of institutional cohesion, producing accurate financial information, and lowering administrative costs relative to academic programs. The team also expressed concern over the proliferation of degrees at Pepperdine, the lack of a comprehensive policy on tenure, and limited library space. The team also had serious concerns about academic integrity, including low admission standards, grade inflation, and part-time students meeting requirements for a master's degree in a single year. The Human Resources Management (HRM) degree offered by the School of Professional Studies, primarily on military bases, was suspect in all categories. In all, the visitors' preliminary report found little to praise about the execution of Pepperdine's educational mission during the Banowsky years.[5]

In June 1979, the commission agreed to reaffirm the accreditation of the school as a single institution, but it issued "a formal warning," something less than probation, "to underscore the serious nature of the concerns raised." The commission requested a status report detailing how the university was responding to its recommendations by December 1, 1980, and scheduled the next full accreditation visit for late 1982. Put differently, WASC reaccredited Pepperdine, but formally warned that full accreditation was tenuous—for the second time in a decade. In WASC's eyes, the miracle at Malibu was not quite as illustrious as some thought.[6]

Strategic Plans, Policies

Thereafter, the concerns of the accreditors determined the White administration's agenda. As already noted, it took two years and a fistfight with faculty, but a clear statement of what it meant to be a Christian university associated with Churches of Christ was written and eventually adopted by the board of regents in September 1982. Simultaneously, the administration in 1980 launched a university-wide effort to craft a strategic plan to guide the institution over the next decade, appointing a Strategic Planning Guidance Committee (SPGC) with Vice President James I. Penrod as chair. By September, SPGC had identified six broad categories of institutional goals and objectives: academic support, institutional support, instruction, public support, research student services, and Christian environment.[7]

For much of the 1980s, multiple committees worked on the plan, attempting to first establish plans for the different schools—the components of a *multiversity*—and then fashion those strategies into a single plan for the *university*. By the end of the decade, each of the schools and colleges had stand-alone strategic plans. No single plan was ever developed for the university, however. President White avoided the fight he foresaw with faculty by never finalizing and publishing a strategic plan. His successors did much the same thing.[8]

WASC had also found the university wanting when it came to the accessibility of policies and procedures that impacted both faculty and staff. Fortunately, Pepperdine University teams had been at work on such basic documents since 1979. White had established a procedures committee, chaired by his assistant, Shirley Roper, to write up "all policies that [were] necessary to the successful operation of the University." The objective was to institute a larger measure of professionalism and coherence within the institution.[9] By 1981, the committee was able to publish a two-volume "University Policy Manual."[10]

Strengthening Governance Policies

WASC also called for greater faculty and student involvement in the governance of the institution, uniform policies for faculty and staff, and a coherent and comprehensive policy on tenure.[11] WASC correctly ascertained that the university's administration had been reluctant to invite faculty into governance processes except in matters of curriculum. The regents, most of whom were corporate executives, were supposed to choose the president, and the president was to choose the vice presidents. White feared the university could not maintain its "distinctiveness" if the administration abdicated its responsibilities in faculty selection and other matters and became a "rubber stamp" to faculty prerogatives. However, the WASC concerns and the faculty outcry over the demotion of Nicks caused him to rethink the selection process of key administrators.

Accordingly, he tasked faculty leader Dan Caldwell to draft a document that acknowledged a faculty role in interviewing and recommending candidates for the offices of the academic vice president, dean, and division chair, as well as faculty members. Those guidelines were then debated by the different faculty associations and administrative committees, leading to the pioneering "Procedures for the Selection of Specified Personnel and Faculty at Pepperdine University," which White approved in July 1982. More than thirty years later, the guidelines continued to bear witness to the institutional maturation of the university and the power of an accrediting agency.[12]

President White also responded to WASC's concern about governance by creating a Dean's Council in fall 1981. With a membership of the four academic deans (Seaver College, SBM, GSE, and SOL), the council was to meet six times each year to share information, seek greater uniformity in application of university policies, and provide mutual support. It was a meager first step in giving the deans a voice in the governance process.[13]

To improve channels of communication university-wide, White organized an annual management conference at an off-site location for all top and mid-level managers; the first was held in Ojai in October 1980. The administration also reinstituted an all-university faculty retreat that had not gathered since 1971, began the practice of distributing edited minutes of key administrative committees to selected managers, and established *Peptalk*, a weekly newsletter for all employees.[14]

Tenure Revisited

WASC's 1979 visitors had found Pepperdine University's faculty tenure policy as adopted by the board of regents in 1975 "unacceptable." Among other things, it was not uniformly applicable: Seaver College and the School of Law had different tenure policies, while SBM and the SOE relied upon "due process" in personnel decisions. The academic affairs committee of the board of regents agreed with WASC's concerns and told White it would not approve another tenure application until the administration created a policy that described what tenured faculty were actually getting.[15]

Academic Vice President Nicks took on the responsibility of drafting a new university-wide tenure policy. Drawing on an AAUP model, Nicks prepared a first draft for distribution by August 15, 1980, then met with faculty from each of the schools and colleges to determine reaction. Their concerns were familiar: uncertainty about whether tenure was granted by the school or the university; the purpose of five-year reviews for tenured faculty; the process of reappointment; the nature of grievance procedures; the declaration of financial exigency; the meaning of "non-support" of values, principles and policies; and the definition of academic freedom.[16]

Nicks, as recommended by the president, resigned as vice president in early 1981, and White took responsibility for finalizing the new tenure document. He looked to Tom Bost, Mike O'Neal, and David Davenport as his major counselors. Reconciling the diverse interests took "long, weary months" and proved to be the "most tedious" exercise in his long career, White reported. But it resulted in a document that the board of regents approved on September 8, 1981.[17] The faculty approved it the following month.[18]

Applicable to all units of the university—Seaver College and the professional schools—the new tenure policy was notable on several grounds. As in 1975, it defined "tenure" as "the right to continue to be employed by the University in the field of specialization and in the school in which tenure [was] attained." It insisted that tenure was a privilege; it was not automatic nor a matter of time-in-grade. Tenure would replace "due process" in SBM and SOE. Probationary or pre-tenure appointments were not to exceed seven years. Candidates for tenure would be judged on the quality of their performance in four areas: "teaching; service to the community and the institution; scholarly, artistic, or professional achievement; and a consistent pattern of support for generally accepted Christian values and the mission of Pepperdine University."[19]

The new policy also instituted five-year reviews, formalized steps necessary for tenure consideration, articulated areas of evaluation, and described processes to be followed if tenure were denied. Significantly, the statement also better defined the role of faculty in the process of granting or denying tenure, most notably in the formation of the university tenure committee. At the same time, it also made clear that the critical decisions on tenure matters remained within the power of the administration and the board of regents. Much to White's satisfaction, the new policy made support for Christian mission part of the tenure equation. But some of his faculty colleagues found the provision problematic: how could tenure candidates actually quantify their contributions to the value system of the university?[20] Within five years, much to White's chagrin, the language was revised out of the policy, leaving the matter to the individual colleges and schools.

But on the whole, the tenure policy adopted in September 1981 revealed a university whose faculty and administration were learning at least to work with, if not to trust, each other.

Limitations on Academic Freedom?

Although President White was a major player in the new tenure policy, he had some reservations about the relationship between tenure and "academic freedom" in a Christian university. To his mind, "academic freedom [was] the right to inquire, to study, to investigate, and to announce the conclusions of one's research." Administrators had the obligation to stand ready to protect that freedom when it came under attack, as in the case of a faculty person being harassed for a political or scientific perspective. But academic freedom did not supersede the "moral and spiritual commitments [faculty members] made when [they] joined the faculty, [specifically] being supportive of the faith," by which he meant a Christian world view and ties with Churches of Christ.[21]

Should a faculty person's commitment change, White believed that "simple integrity and common decency" demanded that they resign from the university and seek employment where their world views were more compatible. If faculty members overreached academic freedom, White believed administrators should exercise "due process" in seeking removal. To argue that there were "no conditions for removal of faculty short of conviction of a felony [was] to argue that a school [had] no right to maintain its Christian identity."[22]

Dan Caldwell's bid for tenure brought the dilemma of academic freedom and the preservation of Pepperdine University's Christian mission home to President White. With graduate degrees from Tufts and Stanford, Caldwell joined the Seaver College faculty as an assistant professor of international relations as White began his presidency in 1978. A superb but demanding teacher, Caldwell quickly became a spokesperson for faculty prerogatives, first as vice president of Seaver College's AAUP chapter and then as president of the Seaver Faculty Organization (SFO). His championing of various faculty issues and his dismay at not being selected to teach in Heidelberg led President White to conclude that Caldwell was not supportive of Pepperdine's relationship with Churches of Christ.[23]

White called Caldwell to his office on Feb. 8, 1982. Referencing prepared notes, White complimented him for his teaching, scholarship, and his Christian values but told Caldwell that faculty members were expected to be in general harmony with the values of the university and to support its policies. Agitation, both overt and concealed, to get rid of the church connection was a violation of the basic policies of the institution and was both "inappropriate and unacceptable." White pointed out that Pepperdine also had a conservative political orientation and that anyone who could not accept these orientations should perhaps look elsewhere for work.[24]

After telling White that he considered the president's remarks to be a personal attack, Caldwell asked permission to tape-record the remainder of their conversation so it would be available if there were ever litigation. The request shocked White, who had not considered the conversation a confrontation. When the president would not consent, Caldwell then spoke of his three and a half years of support of the university and denied any interest in secularizing Pepperdine. Subsequently, White emphasized that his only "substantive question was whether or not Caldwell was able to support, or at least not actively oppose, the kind of church-related institution" that Pepperdine was. In other words, could Caldwell live with the university's special relationship with Churches of Christ?[25]

From the president's point of view, the question was never answered. Within months, Caldwell requested a two-year leave of absence (from September 1982 to August 1984) to take up a position as associate director of the Center for Foreign Policy at Brown University. At the same time, he asked that his tenure application go forward, a request endorsed by his division chair and dean. Herbert Luft, the new executive vice president, declared his support for the leave and tenure applications if Caldwell would work within the framework of Pepperdine's heritage and abide by its policies. Caldwell responded that he understood the relationship with Churches of Christ and did not oppose it.[26]

All of this posed a major dilemma for President White. When Caldwell's tenure file came to his desk, he had a hard time forgetting that the applicant had talked of suing the university. But White genuinely appreciated Caldwell as a teacher, scholar, and Christian gentleman. He did not want to risk Pepperdine University being seen as sectarian, nor did he want to risk a legal action or a WASC inquiry. So White recommended tenure for Caldwell and his promotion to associate professor at the very time he was starting a two-year, off-campus leave. Tenure, White insisted, was granted on the assumption that Caldwell would accept and work within the university's mission statement, "including its affiliation with the Churches of Christ."[27] Under those circumstances, Caldwell served the university well into the twenty-first century.

Gender, Racial Inequities

As the university responded to WASC's concern about tenure and academic freedom, it also grappled with questions concerning gender issues. Professor of Psychology Ola Barnett had accused the university administration of gender discrimination ever since she joined the faculty in 1970 on the Los Angeles campus. Early on, her issue was salary discrimination, but after Seaver College and the School of Education adopted across-the-board pay scales in 1972, that issue was no longer of concern.[28] Gender ratios remained concerning, however. In 1982, university-wide ratios of men to women were 6:1 (180 FTE) and in Seaver College 4.2:1 (90 FTE). Of even greater concern was the absence of women in the seats of power. Barnett blamed that on two things: the patriarchal traditions of Churches of Christ and the "religious exemption to non-discrimination laws" included in federal statutes.[29]

Nancy Magnusson-Fagan had a slightly different take. She blamed the lack of female administrators at the university to the dearth of professional women in Churches of Christ, common among religious groups with a conservative theology. She noted, however, that when Church of Christ females were unavailable for administrative positions, the university's leaders did not look for women from other faith denominations but hired men who were Church of Christ members. In other words, it was not gender that blocked the professional advancement of Pepperdine women but their religious faith. As Magnusson-Fagan, a non-Church of Christ member at the time, said, "It excludes me from the 'in' group . . . I don't have access."[30]

According to *Graphic* reports, she would not want to "overemphasize it . . . because people have been terrific." Nonetheless, "you have this feeling, when push comes to shove, that you're in the 'out' group." The preference for men as administrators and faculty members at Pepperdine University had much to do with its Christian mission, she added. "There is a strong feeling in the administration that if they loosen up the ranks—if it doesn't stay Church of Christ—then the university will not stay Christian. The intent of that exclusion then is not sexism . . . but the result is."[31]

Director of campus life, a Church of Christ member, and Norvel Young's daughter, Sara Jackson acknowledged the hiring preference given to church members and accepted Magnusson-Fagan's thesis that it was difficult to find church women with experience in higher education. But within Churches of Christ, she insisted, discrimination against women did not exist. Glenda Taylor, assistant director of church services, agreed with Jackson. "No one in the church of Christ," she said, thought women were "second class citizens."[32]

Shirley Roper, President White's executive assistant, concurred but admitted that if a male and a female of equal qualifications were to apply for the position of vice president, the male would be the ultimate choice. "That's just the way it is at Christian schools," Roper explained. "They traditionally choose someone who has a background of ministry." For Professor of English Vicki Myers, church membership was not an issue "in terms of the way her co-workers and higher-ups [had treated] her." But Myers would have agreed with Director of Public Information Patti Yomantas's observation: "Inroads to middle- and upper-management positions at Pepperdine University are rarely paved by women."[33]

Not just men, but white men dominated the university ranks. In 1983, of the fifty-one tenured faculty in Seaver College only two were black, Professors Calvin Bowers and Jo Ann Taylor. University-wide, of the 186 full-time faculty, only six were ethnic or racial minorities. By 1988, that number had increased to thirteen of 209. Given the emphasis upon hiring Church of Christ members, it was not surprising. Across the United States, the preponderance of church members were Caucasian. But other factors contributed. When the Los Angeles campus closed, its concentration of faculty of color had dispersed. Most of the ones who had been invited to join the Malibu faculty chose not to do so. It was a long drive to Malibu, and the welcome was problematic. Besides, they had employment options at locations where they would be enthusiastically received.[34]

From President White's perspective, the maleness and whiteness of the Pepperdine University's administration and faculty had little to do with gender or ethnic discrimination. The fundamental issue was whether the university would be Christian or not, which to him depended upon a relationship with Churches of Christ. The women certainly had the right to raise the issue of discrimination, he said, but they "should understand that by accepting a position here and signing a contract to support our policies that they should regard it as a professional obligation to honor their contract." As he had made clear to Dan Caldwell, White believed that if a faculty person could not be happy with Pepperdine's intention to associate itself with Churches of Christ, they had an obligation to go someplace else, with his blessings.[35]

Academic Coherence, Consolidation

As President White and his administrative team wrestled with the ramifications of institutional cohesion, they also grappled with WASC's anxiety about the lack of academic coherency. Of principal concern was the university's extensive off-campus programming that degreed undergraduate and graduate students in human resources management (HRM). Via the Center for Innovative Education (CIE), as noted elsewhere, Pepperdine offered the degree primarily on military bases in the United States and in the Pacific Ocean. Directed by Robert Gordon, CIE served 1,000 students off and 800 on the Los Angeles and Orange County campuses in 1979. Keeping up with that many students was a major challenge for the university's student and financial record offices, and the challenge was rarely answered effectively. To speak of "administration" at CIE was to make "a frustrating joke," said one of its teachers.[36]

From the beginning of his tenure as academic vice president in 1976, John Nicks had serious reservations about the HRM program. He was critical of its administration, dubious of its academic integrity, and absolutely convinced that the program—and other off-campus programs operated by SBM and GSE—cost the university money. It was primarily as a cost-saving measure, then, that Nicks first pushed to abandon the off-campus courses.

He did not get full attention of his colleagues, especially President White, until the 1979 accrediting team articulated WASC's wrath, describing the HRM degree as without "adequate precedent" and "obviously inferior."[37] It helped, too, that the *New York Times* expressed amazement that the university gave full academic credit to students on military bases for only two long weekends of academic (seat time) work.[38] Consequently, in 1980 Nicks won enough support to order the HRM and other military base programs closed, generating a savings of some $50,000 annually. The following year, he shut down the MBA II and the ME programs in Hawaii, ending a fourteen-year relationship between Pepperdine and the Islands.[39]

Much of WASC's concern over grade inflation at SBM emanated from two undergraduate programs: the bachelor's of science in administrative science (BSAS) and the bachelor's of science in management (BSM). To address the problem, the business school terminated the BSAS degree and did some in-service grade training for faculty in the BSM program.[40] The School of Education made similar attempts regarding grading doctoral student comprehensive exams and assessing doctoral dissertations.[41]

To further satisfy WASC, officials combined the psychology program (400 students) with the education program (550 students) on the Los Angeles campus to create the Graduate School of Education and Psychology (GSEP) as of July 31, 1981. This was done despite psychology's preference to be based at Malibu.[42] Simultaneously, President White and his colleagues also closed the School of Professional Studies and incorporated whatever fragments remained into GSEP.[43]

As noted elsewhere, administrators likewise merged the free-standing School of Continuing Education into GSEP's Center for Professional Development at the Los Angeles campus. Dean Oly Tegner believed the combination would generate additional revenue by increasing enrollment, but his analysis proved wrong, and GSEP's enrollments and revenues continued to plummet.[44] Consequently, GSEP, like SBM, had fewer and fewer classes to schedule on the Los Angeles campus. Nothing the administration had done worked to give the Vermont Street campus administrative viability. That effort and "academic coherency" seemed a contradiction in terms.[45]

President White and his colleagues, as detailed elsewhere, had long entertained the idea of selling the Los Angeles campus. There was a perpetual need for additional money in building out the campus at Malibu, and the academic quality questions associated with the Los Angeles campus seemed to dictate a sale as well. Fred Price and the Crenshaw Christian Center stepped forward to purchase the property for $14.5 million in 1981, and over the next two years, the university vacated the Los Angeles campus and moved to a new "Center" on Sepulveda Boulevard. SBM and GSEP consolidated their previously "off-campus" courses and programs at the Sepulveda location and in other centers to the extent that they satisfied WASC's expectations of what a university with a coherent curriculum looked like.

Return of WASC

Little the university did administratively during the first four years of Howard White's administration was unconnected with WASC, including forcing out Nicks as academic vice president and the appointment of Herbert Luft as executive vice president. White blamed the bad WASC review of 1980 on Nicks and brought in Luft to see that it did not happen again in 1982.[46] Well aware of White's expectation, Luft threw himself into preparing for the accrediting team visit scheduled for November 1982. That meant finalizing initiatives that had been launched in response to the previous visit and preparing a 385-page self-study that detailed the university's progress. The self-study was created with the help of a steering committee led by Loyd Frashier.[47]

Chaired by Robert Thomas of Brigham Young University, the twelve-member WASC reaccrediting team arrived on campus in November 1982, and the visit went extraordinarily well. The team singled out eight positive improvements for special commendation:

- the fund-raising effort, which had "few peers in American higher education";
- the responsiveness of the entire campus community to the recommendations of the last accrediting team;
- the commitment to a full-scale, strategic planning process;
- unusual strides in financial management;
- impressive restructuring of the off-campus programs;
- sensitivity to the present and potential use of computers;
- provision of excellent secular training in an explicitly Christian environment; and
- SBM's innovative response in the field of professional management education.[48]

Judging from the report, Pepperdine's frenetic, campus-wide reaction to WASC's warning in 1980 had paid handsome dividends. As was expected, the team also identified areas where additional improvements were possible. Among other things, the university should consider:

- reducing its number of vice presidents;
- adding additional space to Seaver College;
- imposing policies to govern the outside activities of SBM faculty;
- coordinating the business education curriculum at Seaver College and SBM;
- instituting admission and exit standards at GSEP; and

· giving greater attention to the collections and space needs of Payson Library and to faculty roles in teaching and governance.[49]

President White considered the report "one of the best we have ever had." He took some satisfaction in that faculty respect for the administration was observed to be "substantial, and perhaps even remarkable." And he was pleased that the committee believed faculty quality had not been compromised by the administration's attempts to recruit members of Churches of Christ. White, however, disagreed with the committee's recommendation that faculty should have a greater role in governance. He granted full voice for faculty in academic matters, but believed the university could retain its Christian mission and historic relationship with Churches of Christ only by preserving a limited governance role for faculty—until it was willing "to accept responsibility for its decisions."[50]

WASC's senior commission met in February 1983 and was impressed with the report of its visiting committee. It removed the warning previously given Pepperdine University, reaffirmed accreditation, and scheduled a limited fifth-year visit in the fall of 1987. The 1987 visit would not require a full self-study or a large visiting team. The executive director of WASC was generous in his praise of Vice President Luft. So too was President White. "Without your leadership," he wrote to Luft, "the visit would not have been so successful."[51]

Launching an administration in the wake of William Banowsky's presidency was an extraordinary challenge for Howard White. That challenge, however, did not come from questions about his ability to give direction to the university or to represent it to its various constituencies. He did that well. The real challenge was to address the issues that had led WASC to question Pepperdine University's fitness as a legitimate educational institution in 1979. As it turned out, White did that well, too.

CHAPTER 39

MANAGING FOR EXCELLENCE

oward White and his administrative colleagues employed a distinctive educational philosophy in their management of Pepperdine University. Like President Banowsky, they postulated that there had been an erosion of values in America and that Pepperdine offered an institutional alternative because of its commitment to religious and civic values, full academic freedom, and the highest levels of educational excellence. One nationally recognized consultant concluded that "Pepperdine [did] not seem . . . to carry the image of a religious school. Rather it is seen as a university with religious principles." White welcomed that description because it did "not bring with it the concept of exclusivity" and sectarian narrowness.[1]

As important as the Christian distinctive was to the president, he readily acknowledged that instilling spiritual qualities was only one component of the university's mission. From time to time, he also talked about the free-market economy and the American Way.[2] At all times, however, he mentioned academic excellence. His aim, he wrote, was "to try to prove that it is possible for a university to have a strong Christian orientation and high academic standing."[3] To him, Pepperdine's central quest was to transmit the learning of the ages within the framework of biblical revelation—and do it with distinction.[4] Whether that was possible was an open question. Other private schools had tried and failed. President White wanted to believe it could be done at Pepperdine upon the premise that the "educational process" and the "divine process" were one and the same and that "spiritual commitment" demanded "the highest standards of academic excellence."[5]

White looked to his administrative team to help him achieve that goal, expecting them to be effective administrators and advocates of both academic excellence and Christian mission. If they were not, he encouraged them to find a more favorable atmosphere elsewhere, which was his reasoning for bringing in Herbert Luft to assume the duties of John Nicks in 1981. In the two years that followed, White was pleased by Luft's leadership in garnering a positive WASC review and a greater percentage of Church of Christ faculty members.[6] He also endorsed Luft's credo that "other institutions have history; ours has future," but the president was disappointed by Luft's overall performance.[7] So in June 1983, Luft returned to Germany as dean of European programs with responsibility for those in Heidelberg, London, and eventually Florence.[8]

David Davenport succeeded Luft as executive vice president. Holding degrees from Stanford (BA) and the University of Kansas (JD), Davenport had joined the Pepperdine School of Law faculty in 1981. He was so supportive of excellence in both academics and mission that President White appointed him as the university's legal counsel two years later and, after another year, executive vice president, a position Davenport held until he assumed the presidency in 1985. Other administrative transitions shaped the White presidency. Some longtime Pepperdine administrators, including Larry Craft and Robert Thomas, left to pursue other opportunities; while some incoming newcomers, such as John G. Watson, and Michael F. Adams would significantly impact the university for decades.

Enthusiastic Support, but Signs of Trouble

Chancellor Norvel Young, who had been restored to full duty simultaneously with White's appointment as president, continued to work externally to promote Pepperdine and raise money to help balance the university's operating budget.[9] Although White was genuinely appreciative of all the courtesies Young and his wife, Helen, had extended to him over the years, he never quite trusted the former president's declarations of friendship and support.[10]

And although White fully appreciated that Young's job was to promote Pepperdine and raise money, he often thought it was done at an unnecessarily high price in terms of mission and institutional integrity. He learned in early 1981, for example, that the chancellor was working to open PKE programs in Hong Kong and Taipei, China, at the very time White was trying to curtail Pepperdine's overseas activities in response to criticisms from WASC.[11]

In identifying and harvesting potential sources of support for Pepperdine, Young was open to almost any possibility. On one occasion he entertained the idea of accepting money to endow a university chair that would honor the memory of Chiang Kai-shek, the Nationalist Chinese leader revered in Taiwan. However, Arthur Spitzer, a major Pepperdine donor, thought the chair would be a disaster. "To establish a Chair for a dictator from the right or left is something Pepperdine should avoid," he said. Not wanting to aggravate a generous donor, Young dropped the idea.[12]

President White also feared that Young's practice of conferring Distinguished Diplomas of Honor jeopardized Pepperdine's academic reputation. The chancellor bestowed the diplomas—honors he had created himself—on dignitaries whose affection and admiration he wished to cultivate. The certificates looked very much like the diplomas given for an honorary doctorate and were extended with all the pomp and circumstances of a regular graduation exercise. Young generally chose the recipient, at least early on, without the approval and sometimes even the knowledge of the university's board of regents or administration.

Between 1979 and 1983, Young presented diplomas to Norman Cousins, Seniel Ostrow, a former president of Taiwan, a former prime minister of India, the president of South Korea, the king of Thailand, and the president of the bank of Thailand. White's worst fears were realized when the president of the bank of Thailand noticed he had not received the doctorate he had anticipated and insisted upon a genuine honorary degree. To save the institution from further embarrassment, White and the regents consented to the exchange. Thereafter, Young awarded few distinguished diplomas of honor. How many he extended altogether was not recorded.[13]

Young's effort to develop wealthy constituencies along the Pacific Rim arose from the need to annually raise $2 million to $3 million of unrestricted money to balance the university's operating budget. The stress in Young's office and household was palpable, reminiscent of what had existed in 1975 before his car wreck. To his personal embarrassment, he began using alcohol almost on a daily basis. Facilitated by professional counselor Robert Dorris, five of Young's colleagues (Bost, White, Hornbaker, Runnels, and Adams) confronted him on May 2, 1983. Young consented to check into an addiction recovery clinic, where he agreed to a recovery plan that restricted him to Southern California for six months and required a restructuring of his job to relieve stress.[14] In July 1985, Dorris reported that Young had achieved the "essential goals" set for him.[15] Eighteen months later, the chancellor helped found and sponsor an Alcoholic Anonymous meeting on the Pepperdine campus.[16]

Howard White always gave Young the benefit of the doubt when it came to alcohol addiction. He did so because of Christian charity and because "We need his ability to raise money. I realize that without him, none of us would be there today."[17] But White was also worried about what he perceived as ethical lapses in Young's personal behavior and in his work on behalf of Pepperdine. Fearful that Young's improprieties would tarnish Pepperdine's academic and Christian reputation, White systematically and factually chronicled them, then gathered them into a twelve-page document that he probably shared with the chair of the regents in mid-September 1984.[18] The next month, Chancellor Young announced his retirement as of December 31, 1984. As chancellor emeritus, his duties would be to assist the university in development efforts in the Los Angeles area, rather than in Asia or the Middle East. Longtime vice chancellor Charles Runnels succeeded Young as chancellor.[19]

Help from New Chancellor, Board

Charles Runnels had been part of the Pepperdine administrative team since 1967. By 1985, he had personally recruited 350 of the members of Pepperdine University Associates, brokered many of the largest gifts the university had received, and managed the prestigious university board. He was noted for his energetic service to the university, telling the Pepperdine story both early and late to individuals and groups at the California Club, the Los Angeles Country Club, LA Five Rotary Club, and the Bohemian Club.[20] His work as chancellor and later as chancellor emeritus yielded huge financial dividends for the university; no fund-raiser had a better record.

In addition to a capable administrative team, President White also looked to the board of regents to help him burnish the university's academic standing. He found the two chairs he worked with, D. Lloyd Nelson and Thomas G. Bost, to be men of discretion and sound judgment and was encouraged by the eagerness of the religious standards committee to promulgate standards that privileged Church of Christ candidates in certain situations. He also discovered the regents supported him in his insistence upon administrative prerogatives in university governance and in emphasizing academic excellence.

Beating the Curve on Computer Literacy

One notable effort to cultivate academic excellence came in the form of a campaign for institution-wide computer literacy announced by President White in 1982. The goals were to make faculty, staff, and students familiar with computing, word processing and communication devices, and computer-assisted problem solving by 1984. The university's focus, White announced, "would be less on uses of technology than on technology's impact on the character of liberal education." The university had acquired its first computer in 1970, a small IBM used by SBM. In 1972, Pepperdine joined a consortium sponsored by the National Science Foundation (NSF) which made time-share terminals available to students in each school and college. The university continued to slowly acquire equipment and programs, and by 1981 nearly half of the university's student body in four schools had been exposed to some form of meaningful, hands-on computer experience.[21]

To meet President White's goal of literacy within two years, the university, under the leadership of Vice President James Penrod, devoted significant resources to the effort, offering classes at undergraduate and graduate levels, professional development seminars for faculty and staff, and twelve day-long camps for middle and high school students. Pepperdine also co-hosted computer literacy institutes, publishing the proceedings of the first one in 1983. That same year, IBM selected the university to be one of a dozen participants in an $8 million national computer literacy program, part of which would equip and fund a training center at Pepperdine for thirty high school teachers. Simultaneously, GSEP sponsored a computer fair for 500 local teachers and became a test site for hardware from the CPT Corporation.

That fall the university replaced its old mainframe with a new Sperry 1100/70, expecting cost savings and minimal disruption of operations. When Sperry did not deliver special assistance on conversion, however, the university changed directions and converted to UNIVAC's DMS1100 system, seemingly the quickest and most economical route to integrated packaged software. It also negotiated with Victor Technologies to provide personal

Charles Runnels was arguably the foremost fund-raiser in the history of Pepperdine University. Joining Pepperdine in 1967, Runnels played a key role in winning the favor of Blanche Seaver and other donors while serving in a variety of roles for the university. He succeeded Norvel Young as chancellor in 1985.

microcomputers to students and staff at a substantial discount and with Intecom for a $4 million computerized communication system.[22]

The computer literacy initiative was in keeping not only with Pepperdine's quest for academic excellence, but also with its spirit of entrepreneurialism. It brought national attention to the university and introduced an early awareness of computer technology across campus. But it hardly attained the level of literacy that White expected. The Victor computer arrangement proved to be a disappointment, leaving most of the university's faculty without access to personal/office computers as late as 1986.

"Our rhetoric . . . outpaces reality by a considerable margin," observed Academic Affairs Vice President William Phillips. Noting the strong faculty demand for office computers, he concluded that having a PC outranked "having an office with a window." Phillips strongly encouraged the university to commit to placing a computer workstation on every full-time faculty member's desk "with all deliberate speed." His administrative colleagues heard him, funds were budgeted, and his recommendation became reality by 1988. Thereafter, Pepperdine kept up with or a little ahead of the curve when it came to computer technology and systems.[23]

Front-Runner in International Study

Pepperdine was well ahead of the curve in international study. As previously noted, it had established a Year-in-Europe program in Heidelberg in 1963, the second such American program in Germany. Three years later the academic program moved to Moore Haus near the Heidelberg castle, which served as residence for thirty-five students initially and fifty-four students per term after 1980.[24]

At the urging of Associate Dean James McGoldrick, the Pepperdine School of Law pioneered the university's first academic program in London, England, opening a fall semester program there in 1981, as noted in an earlier chapter.[25] When Herbert Luft returned to Germany in 1983, President White instructed him to prioritize the creation of an undergraduate program in London.[26] Luft and his assistant, Colleen Graffy, managed to establish a program that began in spring 1984, housing forty-three students in the quarters just vacated by the law students at Beaufort Gardens, and offering classes in halls at Imperial College. Psychologist Clarence Hibbs was professor in residence, and Graffy served as director. Initially, Seaver offered its London program only in the spring and summer terms, but student demand was so large that it became a year-round program in 1986.[27]

Having Pepperdine students spread out across London was not an ideal situation, and Graffy was eager to centralize administration of the programs.

She and Luft identified two properties, and after visits by Dean of International Programs William Phillips and Executive Vice President Andrew Benton, the university bought the elegant building at 56 Prince's Gate for $3.15 million in 1987. With 14,000 square feet of space, the estate was large enough to offer rooms and beds for forty Seaver students and classrooms for both Seaver and School of Law students, although the shared space often caused some administrative headaches.[28]

Meanwhile Luft moved to open another program in Florence, Italy, in summer 1985, the last months of Howard White's presidency. It began as a one-trimester program involving twenty students led by Professor of Religion Carl Mitchell and Professor of Art Robert Privitt.[29] Student interest was high enough that it became a year-round program in the 1987–1988 academic years. As in Heidelberg and London, the sophomore-level classes in Florence were tailored to the dramatic location: Italian, fine arts, religion, and history, with field trips to Pisa, Rome, Venice, and other European cities.[30]

Thanks to Edward and Jill Di Loreto and Augustus and Patricia Tagliaferri, the Florence program moved to permanent quarters in 1995 when the university purchased Villa Platoff and Astor Hotel. Rededicated as Villa Di Loreto, the late nineteenth-century villa housed classrooms, a library, staff offices, and a faculty apartment; while the three-story Residenza Tagliaferri provided quarters for fifty-two students.[31]

The three Year-in-Europe programs were minimally coordinated until William Phillips was assigned the responsibilities of dean of international programs in 1987. Over the next two decades, Phillips worked to integrate the programs into the Seaver College academic curriculum and to involve at least 50 percent of the student body in international studies. Over time, he added summer programs to Scotland, Spain, Russia, Japan, France, and Argentina, among others. He helped to upgrade facilities in London and Florence, and to add a Spanish-speaking program in Buenos Aires in 1994 and a French-speaking program shortly after the turn of the century.

The Seaver College international study program also expanded widely in terms of numbers. At the end of White's presidency, around 100 Seaver students participated in one of the programs each year. By the end of Phillip's tenure as dean in 2005, some 500 or more participated, giving Pepperdine one of the three largest programs in the United States in terms of percentage of undergraduate students enrolled. This popularity was due in part to an innovative curriculum package that permitted students in most majors to complete their sophomore year while studying abroad as if they were on the Malibu campus. Also tuition, board, and room costs were the same as those for in-residence students, at least through the twentieth century.

Fortifying the Faculty

President White and his administrative colleagues were eager to attract and retain the finest faculty possible, and so sought both short- and long-range solutions. The short-term solution, borrowed from a practice of the Banowsky era, was to recruit distinguished but retired scholars who would accept limited-term appointments as visitors to the university's faculty. Presumably, the addition of scholars who had made reputations elsewhere would bring immediate academic credibility to Pepperdine at a relatively small cost.

Program participants included B. Lamar Johnson, formerly dean of education at UCLA and widely known for his scholarship on community college administration; Warren Bennis, retired from USC and a pioneer in leadership studies; Glenn S. Dumke, formerly chancellor of the California State University system; Edward Teller, recognized as the father of the hydrogen bomb; Keith Berwick, noted historian, author and television broadcaster; David C. McClellan, a Harvard psychologist known for personality research; Russell Kirk, author and historian noted for his conservative world view; Samuel D. Thurman, a legal ethicist from University of Utah School of Law and former president of AALS; Kenneth H. York, legal scholar from UCLA; and Arthur Laffer, known for advocacy of supply-side economics within the Reagan administration. These and similar scholars taught courses, facilitated workshops, or gave lectures in all four schools at the university. Evidence suggests, however, that they were not widely used as resource persons, even to the point of embarrassment for President White. They were part of the Pepperdine family, but not integral to it.[32]

As it turned out, quick-starting academic reputability proved problematic. In reality, it had to be developed over time, grown rather than bought. The White administration came to understand that the first step on that road was to pay the faculty competitively, something Pepperdine had not done for most of its history. Continual reminders from WASC and a near faculty rebellion in 1976 had loosened the purse strings of the board of regents and the central administration, but not dramatically.[33] Salaries became tangibly better after 1980, however. Ten percent increases in 1980–1981, 12 percent in 1981–1982, and 11 percent in 1982–1983 raised salary levels on the AAUP scale from the twentieth percentile to the ninety-fifth percentile for assistant and associate professors and the eightieth percentile for professors. In 1982–1983, salaries for professor, associate professor and assistant professor ranks averaged $38,600, $29,800, and $24,600 respectively. By 1986, they averaged $46,200, $37,800, and $32,200. When White retired as president, Pepperdine salaries were substantially above those of Occidental, Claremont McKenna, University of Pacific, and Redlands. The fringe benefit package was significantly lower, however.[34]

Although the level of salaries was very competitive, the faculty teaching load was not. During White's tenure, all faculty members taught three trimesters per year, although with varying loads. In the graduate schools, faculty taught two courses per term, or a 2–2–2 load, while in Seaver College the load was three courses in two terms and two in one term, or 3–3–2. At Seaver each course was generally worth four units of credit, so most teachers were teaching thirty-two credit units per year, where at comparable institutions faculty taught eighteen to twenty-four units per year. It was a burdensome assignment if the faculty person did nothing more than teach; it was an onerous assignment if the faculty member wanted to do scholarly research as well.

And yet a surprisingly large number of Seaver faculty did carry out research. Most notable among researchers was the biology faculty—Joseph Williams, Stephen Davis, Gary Tallman, and later Dwayne Simmons—but its members did research with a twist. They generally involved undergraduate students. Research activity began in the summer of 1977 in a combined effort to isolate stomata, minute pores in the epidermis of green plants through which gasses and water passed, from plant leaves. It took two years before another team of students and faculty accomplished the feat and was able to publish the results, with students listed as coauthors. The biology faculty packaged what they had learned about undergraduate research into a grant proposal for the National Science Foundation (NSF) titled "Summer Undergraduate Research-Biology." In 1989, the proposal was funded, and it was re-funded through 2014, bringing select biology undergraduate students from across the nation to the Malibu campus to learn the process and experience the wonder of hands-on scientific research.[35] The legacy of the student-focused research program of the biology faculty was extensive, and it inspired—and continues to inspire— the work of colleagues in other disciplines and departments.

Other university faculty engaged in more traditional research, pursuing a line of inquiry that ultimately resulted in publication. Judging from a bibliography prepared for WASC visitors in 1982, there was more publishing going on than evaluators had assumed. Among the more prolific in Seaver College were Lewis R. Aiken (psychology), Dan Caldwell (political science), Fred Casmir (communication), Michael Collings (English), and Ronald Whittaker (communication). In SBM notable researchers were professors Kurt K. Montamedi, George Reisman, and Robert Wright. Some of the more productive scholars in GSEP were Stephen W. Brown and Gordon Wells (psychology), and Diana B. Hiatt, Chester McCall, and James I. Penrod (education). In the School of Law, Noel Keyes and H. Newcomb Morse were publishing.[36]

Although President White maintained that Pepperdine University was essentially a teaching institution, he recognized the importance of research to the well-being of the teaching enterprise and the academic reputation of the university. For that reason, he had done additional research and writing on his own dissertation and succeeded in publishing it with Louisiana State University Press.[37] As Pepperdine president, he gladly considered funding any proposal that would encourage faculty to pursue formal scholarship, which resulted in released time or reduction of teaching load to free faculty for scholarly activity.[38]

In 1985, he supported Vice President Phillips in financing a research council that funded proposals for sponsored research. The council awarded eight grants initially in the amount of $32,205. By 1987, it had disbursed $168,493 in thirty-seven separate awards, with a third of those going to professional schools.[39] And White was willing to go the extra mile to help faculty who had a track record for genuine scholarship, as in the case of Richard Hughes. Even after Hughes had accepted a position at another school, White agreed for Pepperdine as "institutional liaison" to accept and disperse funds donated to support Hughes's history of Churches of Christ in the United States.[40]

Faculty Morale

Faculty morale at Pepperdine University was a difficult thing to judge in the early 1980s. WASC teams detected some negative feelings in their visits in 1979 and 1982 and tended to attribute them to the lack of communication between administration and faculty over mission, strategic planning, and governance. On a day-to-day basis, however, these and other concerns were muted by substantial pay increases and tangible perks that ranged from use of a private faculty dining room to tuition remission for the children of faculty, which was adopted in 1977.[41]

Moreover, the university had achieved national recognition, being ranked as an institution of note by the *New York Times* and the *U.S. News & World Report* magazine, and gaining recognition as a venue for the *Battle of the Network Stars* and for the Olympics in summer 1984. Paid well, treated well, and working in an institution with a growing favorable reputation, most members of the faculty considered themselves fortunate and were willing to hold their tongues when it came to their administrative nemeses. President White sensed the measure of peace that prevailed on the campus and was grateful.[42]

Bolstering the Library

One mark against Pepperdine's academic reputation, however, came from the library. Early on in the White presidency and under the leadership of librarian Dorothy Moore, the main university library possessed 269,816 volumes distributed between buildings on the Los Angeles campus and the Malibu campus. The library's acquisition budget was $279,850 for books, microfilm, and periodicals. The law school library consisted of 96,667 volumes stacked in 22,679 square feet with an acquisition budget of $289,200. To supplement traditional inter-library loans, the university participated in a regional cooperative. None of this helped circulation, however, which dropped from 77,698 transactions in 1973 to 58,689 in 1978.[43]

In 1979, WASC considered all of this inadequate. Space was the biggest problem, especially in Payson Library. It had been designed to accommodate 300 study stations and 80,000 volumes. Given a student population of 2,100, the library was 220 seats short. All available space was given over to shelving 146,027 volumes. The anticipated incorporation of the Los Angeles collection would make the situation only worse. Moreover, the library was insufficiently staffed, and the librarians were too busy doing nonprofessional duties. Finally, with the exception of the law school library, institutional support for the university's library was inadequate. According to WASC, the university spent only about 2.5 percent of its total educational budget on the library when it should be allocating twice that much.[44]

Under the leadership of Harold Holland, who returned as director in September 1981, library services improved modestly over the next few years. The collections and services grew; Payson Library was named as a government depository.[45] In March 1985 a computerized reference system was inaugurated.[46] Meanwhile, the library on the Los Angeles campus closed, and the university established supporting collections at the different Los Angeles, Sherman Oaks, and Orange County educational centers in Southern California. Most of the energy, however, was poured into planning for an expanded library in Malibu. Renovation began in 1986, doubling square footage from 20,808 to 42,500. The result almost doubled student seating capacity, from 225 to 502, and provided space to increase the size of the collection to 278,000 volumes.[47]

The efforts to bolster the library were just one of many made during the presidency of Howard White, who worked throughout his administration to achieve both academic and mission excellence at Pepperdine. As it turned out, those efforts would also benefit the university as it launched a concerted effort to build prestige among financial supporters, potential students, and the higher education community nationwide. Those constituencies did not necessarily recognize that White's management had left the university more mission centered or academically excellent, but they could not escape the fact that Christian principles pervaded the Malibu campus and that ivy was beginning to grow on its stuccoed walls.

CHAPTER 40

BUILDING PRESTIGE

As President Howard White and his administrative colleagues struggled to promote both academics and mission, they worked simultaneously to build the university's prestige in Southern California and
beyond. Elevating academic quality clearly enhanced Pepperdine's status, but
it did not make headlines in the morning newspapers. Supporters and donors
expected to see the university's name in prominent places, proving it was a
leader in the education community and a celebrant of the American Way.

Most illustrative of the work to boost Pepperdine prestige was the
Associates program. Founded in 1977, as already noted, it was the single most
important public outreach on Pepperdine's public relations agenda. By 1982,
1,000 individuals paid $1,000 a year to be part of the group that journalists
described as the "Who's Who of California elite." The theme of the annual dinner and the choice of speakers set the public relations agenda for the academic
year, to the extent that it even provided the context for the university's annual
report. At the dinner there was generally a passing reference to Pepperdine's
Christian mission, but the greatest attention was paid to an American civil
religion that recognized the patriotic faith of our national fathers. Speakers
included General Alexander Haig (1979), Admiral Thomas H. Moorer (1980),
and Librarian of Congress Daniel Boorstin (1985). At the May 1983 dinner,
Pepperdine conferred an honorary doctorate of law on First Lady Nancy
Reagan. Over 1,200 people attended the event, held in a large, elegantly-dec-
orated tent on the soccer field above the swimming pool, which was reported
worldwide via the *New York Times* and the London *Times*.[1]

Honoring Private Enterprise

For a similar purpose Pepperdine also sponsored an annual Private Enterprise
Award dinner to honor champions of American capitalism. The university, Jim
Wilburn argued, was "a product of the American private enterprise system."

Indeed, "From the profits of Western Auto to those of Hydril, Pepperdine [had] been able to provide an alternative kind of higher education. . . . Its future growth and welfare [was] also tied directly to the ability of the private enterprise system to survive in a healthy condition during the years ahead."[2] The university would do well to dedicate itself to the capitalistic system, as an expression of its spiritual values, Wilburn counseled, and one way to demonstrate that commitment was to honor one of Southern California's economic elite at a gala event. The first such dinner occurred in 1979, honored Arnold O. Beckman, noted chemist, inventor and businessman, and featured nationally recognized Catholic philosopher and journalist Michael Novak. Beckman subsequently gave $6 million to help fund an SBM building on the Malibu campus.

From 1980 through 1985, honorees included Corwin D. Denney, Justin Dart, Fritz Huntsinger, Julian A. Virtue, and Richard K. Eamer. Notable speakers were Donald T. Regan, Norman Vincent Peale, and Jack Kemp. In 1986 Sanford C. Sigoloff, corporate turnaround expert, was honored, and former President Gerald Ford spoke, delivering word-for-word an address prepared for him by Wilburn.[3]

The Private Enterprise Award and dinners were but one part of a larger entity, the Center for American Private Enterprise (CAPE), established in 1977. As envisioned by Vice President Wilburn, other components included an Institute for American Ideals and Institutions, built around a basic course required of all Seaver students; a Corporate Associates Chair of Economics, which would bring nationally known senior lecturers to Pepperdine to speak on the economics of private enterprise; the Julian Virtue Chair in Economic Education, which would teach private enterprise economics to schoolteachers; the Institute of American Citizenship, a one-week, summer institute designed for high school seniors; the Center for Entrepreneurial Studies, which aimed to collect and preserve interviews with men and women whose lives illustrated the essential characteristics of private enterprise; and the Summer Institute for Economic and Political Education, which would provide intensive graduate institutes for teachers from across the nation each summer, perpetuating the expired Coe and Taft programs.[4]

Wilburn was unapologetic about Pepperdine's outreach to corporate America. In the 1981 fiscal year, over 200 corporations supported the university. Those gifts, and others, he said, had obligated the institution to "wield a moral influence on the world of business." It was, Wilburn said, Pepperdine's "deep conviction that the ultimate and lasting value of the American economic system . . . was its deep rootedness in religious faith." The degree to which individuals were guided by moral self-restraint dictated the extent to which they could handle freedom—including economic freedom. "Cut adrift from a deep sense of spiritual commitment, economic freedom [could] ultimately be self-destructive and exploitative." Thus, the university's responsibility was to share that reality with its corporate partners and help them reject "the value-free and secular 'faith' which ... threatened to become our national religion." As mutually enriching forces, Pepperdine and corporate America could create a "powerful union," Wilburn concluded, with CAPE as the agency for that cooperation.[5]

Despite Wilburn's good intentions, CAPE remained little more than the wish of his heart. Only a few corporate funders, including the Keck Foundation, Corwin Denney, and Julian Virtue, saw the advantages to a powerful union for good with Pepperdine. Others supported the Youth Citizenship Seminar, a weeklong, all-expenses-paid introduction to the American Way for high school seniors started on campus in 1978.[6] But CAPE did not seriously stir the imagination of corporate America, even in the midst of the Reagan revolution.

Celebrity Firepower

To gain prestige within the Los Angeles community, Pepperdine was never shy about using the celebrity of public figures. No one reflected this propensity more than Ronald Reagan, who spoke at university functions at least ten times in the 1970s.[7] Members of his administration and political fellow travelers carried on the tradition during the White presidency as speakers and recipients of honorary doctorate degrees. These included William H. Rehnquist, Nancy Reagan, Pete Wilson, Maurice Stans, Daniel J. Boorstin, and Sandra Day O'Connor. The parade of Republican dignitaries was so impressive that the *Thousand Oaks News Chronicle* noted that Harvard got top billing in Washington when the liberals were in power, but Pepperdine got it when the conservatives were in control.[8]

Pepperdine also enlisted Hollywood celebrities in its cause. These included Cary Grant, who gave property to Pepperdine; Charlton Heston, whose wife exhibited her photography on campus and whose daughter attended Seaver College; John Raitt, who gave a benefit performance and subsequently funded a recital hall; and Lawrence Welk and Louis L'Amour, who received honorary doctorates.[9]

The Spotlight of Sports

Little worked more effectively to elevate Pepperdine's prestige than sporting events. As mentioned elsewhere, one of the most visible was the *Battle of the Network Stars*, during which millions of TV viewers got a glimpse of the Malibu campus filled with Hollywood stars and deduced on the spot that Pepperdine was a great university.

The campus made an even more dramatic appearance before a worldwide audience of 2.4 billion people as the venue for water polo in the summer

Olympics in Los Angeles in 1984. The idea of offer Pepperdine's facilities to the Los Angeles Olympic Organizing Committee (LAOOC) had been floated as early as 1977. White seized the suggestion and ran with it after he became president, able to make an impressive appeal because of the virtually new Olympic-size Raleigh Runnels Memorial Pool and its pristine setting.

The LAOOC quickly saw the advantage of the site and approved the Pepperdine proposal. In September 1981, the committee and the university signed documents committing Pepperdine to host the water polo event and to lease to LAOOC the pool, Firestone Fieldhouse, dining facilities, residence halls, and other facilities between July 1 and August 15, 1984. Pepperdine agreed to cancel one summer session so students and faculty would not be on campus; staff were urged to take vacations. Administrators anticipated losing as much as $750,000 in revenue, although the university would get 10 percent of the gate receipts.[10]

President White appointed a Pepperdine Olympic Organizing Committee in April 1982. Chaired by Athletic Director Wayne Wright, the committee included fourteen additional staff and faculty members. Between 1982 and 1984, it prepared for the Olympics by hosting a series of preliminary events, including the U.S. Olympic Academy and the World Cup Water Polo games.[11] Assistant Professor of Physical Education Carolyn Vos Strache arranged for Pepperdine to host the U.S. Olympic Academy VI in June 1982, which promoted knowledge of the Olympics via annual meetings and age-appropriate curriculum for elementary and secondary schools.[12]

Although there were a few sour notes in the university's Olympic preparations, the 1984 August games were a mountaintop high for Pepperdine University when it came to building prestige. Around Raleigh Runnels Memorial Pool, the LAOOC raised 5,000 bleacher seats. It converted Heritage Hall into a VIP lounge and housed 1,700 officials, security forces, and members of the Olympic band in student residence halls. The games were televised around the world. Every water polo match was a sellout.

Over their course, some 100,000 fans visited the Malibu campus without a security problem or even one parking jam. In the wake of the games, the LAOOC painted the athletic offices, resurfaced the Firestone Fieldhouse parking lot, and replaced the grass in the field above the pool. And much to the surprise of everyone, Pepperdine's 10 percent take on the gate receipts netted a profit over all expenses of $285,084. White had been expecting a deficit of some $350,000. No wonder the president would say that it was one of the brightest chapters in the history of the university.[13]

Hosting Soviet, American Authors

When it came to the prestige factor, the 1984 Olympic games served Pepperdine well. In a less dramatic way, so did the American-Soviet Writer's Conference. President Reagan's Department of State had helped develop a literary conference of professional writers as a way to span the breach between the United States and the Soviet Union and to lessen the tensions of the Cold War. Conferences were held on alternate years in the Soviet Union and the United States.[14]

Who introduced the program to Chancellor Norvel Young is unclear—probably friend and former editor of the *Saturday Evening Review of Books*, Norman Cousins—but once he heard about it he moved quickly. In August 1982, with the help of substantial grants from Armand Hammer of Occidental Petroleum and Seniel Ostrow of Sealy Mattress Company, Young organized a delegation of nine U.S. writers to attend the conference scheduled for Kiev, Ukraine. The delegation that accompanied him included Robert Bly, Gwendolyn Brooks, Vera Dunham, Erica Jong, Harrison Salisbury, Arthur Schlesinger Jr., Susan Sontag, Irving Stone, and Studs Terkel, as well as Olaf Tegner.[15]

Writers were promised a Russian translator and passage to go anywhere in the Soviet Union. Erica Jong, for one, took advantage of the opportunity to do some family history in Odessa, an experience that seventeen years later culminated in the book, *Of Blessed Memory* (1997).[16] In closed sessions, the Russian and American conferees shared stories and experiences and lamented that the political landscape had so disrupted professional and personal relationships. Chancellor Young was so inspired by the potential that he extended an invitation to the group to meet at Pepperdine University the next year. The conference accepted his invitation, although it would be two years before the conference assembled on the Malibu campus.[17]

By 1983, the long-running Cold War had heated up because of the Soviet occupation of Afghanistan and its downing of a Korean passenger jet. Even though the conference was endorsed by the Reagan administration, some regents saw it almost as treason to exchange anything but bullets with the Soviets. In light of that attitude, Vice President Michael Adams encouraged a delay—or even cancellation—of the conference.[18]

Chancellor Young delayed the conference until March 1984—just five months before the Olympic games. Eleven Russian authors attended, including Nikolai Fedorenko and poet Ivan Drach. The American delegation included Cousins, Dunham, Stone, Sontag, Jerome Lawrence, Robert Edwin Lee, Wallace Stegner, Daniel Taradash, and Elaine Attais.[19] Although the Soviets stayed in Santa Monica, the conference sessions were held on campus, with interpreters and translations provided via earphones. The conference was closed except to carefully selected invitees, which did not include students.[20] According to the *Los Angeles Times*, Pepperdine went "all out" to host the event.

> The conference went off smoothly in an atmosphere that was at once elegant, bountiful and friendly: meals on campus where participants laughingly toasted each other with sparkling cider and water, and joined hands at Chancellor and Helen Young's home for grace; vans for transportation; simultaneous translation; attention to wishes and whims; entertainment. A trip to the Shubert to see "42nd Street" and meet the cast; Disneyland; the museums. . . . Those at Pepperdine were complimented and thanked profusely by their American and Soviet guests.[21]

The conference went so well that it returned to Malibu in 1992.[22]

National School Safety Center

Pepperdine's quest for prestige helps explain its interest in capitalizing on its relationship with Ronald Reagan after he became president of the United States. Reagan had been a warm friend of the university at least since 1968, and at least twenty-six people associated with Pepperdine (five administrators, eleven board members, two members of the faculty, and eight students) attended Reagan's presidential inauguration ceremony in January 1981. By late 1983, President White had approached the White House about Pepperdine University's hosting the future Reagan presidential library.[23] Although Reagan ultimately located his library in Simi Valley, California, it is clear that a Pepperdine location was considered by the Reagan White House for a time.

The longtime relationship with Ronald Reagan did not pay off in a presidential library, but it did result in the university hosting the National School Safety Center (NSSC). Under the leadership of state Attorney General George Deukmejian, the California Department of Justice had organized the center in 1980. The White House wanted to re-create it at the national level. In late 1983, the White House directed the U.S. departments of justice and education to form the NSSC in partnership with Pepperdine University. Made by the Office of Juvenile Justice and Delinquency Prevention, the two-year, $3.95 million grant was awarded to Pepperdine without competitive bids and on the assumption that George Nicholson, friend of Reagan aide Ed Meese, would be its director and chief counsel. The NSSC opened in Sacramento on June 1, 1984, with Nicholson as its founding director.[24]

The purpose of the center was to focus national attention on cooperative solutions to problems that disrupted the educational process. Its goal was "to promote school safety, improve discipline, increase attendance, and suppress drug traffic and abuse in all our schools" by providing centralized assistance for school boards, educators, law enforcers, lawyers, business leaders, parents, students, and the public. NSSC coordinated a national network of professionals and concerned citizens who were working to create and maintain safe schools, and a thirty-person staff prepared and marketed publications, resource papers, films, and public service announcements addressing current school safety issues. After 1984, it published three times annually *School Safety*, a news journal that kept 50,000 readers informed of best practices in the school safety field. The center staff also provided legal assistance, developed model school safety codes, and maintained a resource center that included more than 50,000 articles, publications, and films.[25]

For an academic institution the size of Pepperdine, NSSC was a major undertaking. Its biennial grant of nearly $4 million was the largest federal grant the university ever received from federal government sources. Housed initially in Sacramento, the administrative relationship with the central campus was more of a charade than a reality. Technically it reported through GSEP and was advised by a board of Pepperdine people. The relationship became more meaningful in 1986 after the headquarters of the program relocated to the new Pepperdine center at Encino and Ronald Stephens, former Pepperdine vice president of administration, replaced Nicholson.[26]

During Stephens's tenure as director, the center reached out to more than 100,000 schools. Its focus was youth violence, child abuse, weapons in schools, gangs, drug traffic and abuse, attendance, bullying, discipline, and more. The center continued to publish training materials, produce training films, serve as a national clearing house, conduct training programs, and provide technical assistance to school districts, law enforcement agencies, and juvenile-serving professionals nationwide. It even offered a master's degree in school safety through GSEP. Over the years, the center produced $17 million in grant funds and revenues to the university, nearly 40 percent of which constituted "overhead." Part of the overhead provided the budget for the council that helped fund faculty research.[27]

With Stephens as director, the NSSC developed into a "very positive and nonpartisan force for schools throughout the country," said Provost William Adrian. It remained part of Pepperdine University until 1999. In that year Pepperdine had appointed Special Counsel Kenneth Starr as dean of the School of Law, an action that President Bill Clinton's partisans in the U.S. Departments of Education and Justice took as an affront. Because it looked doubtful that Pepperdine would receive additional funding for its school safety center, the university made the decision to close the NSSC. All of the center's assets, including endowment accounts, office furnishings, and related resources were turned over to the university. The center itself, however, continued on as an independent entity with Stephens as executive director. He also held the academic chair of school safety at GSEP.[28]

Wave of Excellence

The effort to enhance the university's prestige ran simultaneously with a major fund-raising campaign labeled "Wave of Excellence." With the departure of Bill Banowsky, the White administration feared it would not be able to sustain the remarkable fund-raising efforts of the previous decade. So they hired Los Angeles consultants Brakeley, John Price Jones, Inc. (BJPJ) to investigate the feasibility of a focused campaign over a limited period of time. It found strong support for a capital campaign of $35 million over a five-year period or $100 million over a ten-year period. The case for the campaign rested on the "religious ethic in tandem with the American ethic of free enterprise." Its principal objective would be to raise the academic profile of the university via increased endowments rather than new buildings so that it could compete "with the best in the West."[29]

In its research, BJPJ "detected a nimbus around the Institution that defied definition and eluded quantification, but was none-the-less real." It was impossible, therefore, to convey the "whole story" which was about "a group of people moved forward by a dream, George Pepperdine's originally, that is ... still relevant today and will be even more relevant tomorrow."[30] It was a BJPJ consultant who said that Pepperdine did not "carry the image of a religious school" but of a university with religious principles. The distinction was subtle but important "because the latter perception [did] not bring with it the concept of exclusivity."[31]

The consultants' research did reveal areas that needed improvement, including its academic reputation, which was only modest, something recently affirmed by WASC. "The ivy has not yet grown on the walls," one source had observed. It also noted the obvious, that leadership, meaning President White, was aging. It discerned, too, that some people assumed the university did not need money, given its opulent setting, and noted a lack of volunteers to carry out fund-raising activities plus inadequate coordination and discipline in the fund-raising that took place.[32]

Pepperdine administrators determined to launch a campaign along the lines suggested, which was authorized by the board of regents in December 1981. The capital gifts would build an endowment and establish chairs that would attract outstanding scholars. It would also enable the university to construct an administration building, build a fine arts facility, find homes for SBM and GSEP, complete Phase II construction of the law school, expand the university library, and build a communication building.[33]

President White and Vice President Adams announced "The Wave of Excellence Campaign" at the Associates' dinner on May 8, 1984. A forty-five-page booklet made the case for the campaign (without any reference to an affiliation with Churches of Christ). Rather than $35 million, however, university leaders proclaimed a goal of $100 million to be raised over the next six years, elevating the target because $36 million had already been raised during the silent portion of the campaign. Indeed, in the previous four years, Pepperdine had ranked second nationally in funds raised by coeducational institutions of similar size. Unlike previous fund-raising efforts, the Wave of Excellence campaign depended upon volunteers to make it a success.[34]

The campaign proved successful almost from the beginning. In fiscal year 1986 alone, gifts totaled $20 million, the best fund-raising year ever—surpassing even the halcyon era of Bill Banowsky and Norvel Young.[35]

Balancing Acts

President White understood that keeping Pepperdine on solid financial ground was absolutely essential to the success of any prestige initiative or fund-raising campaign. The first step in demonstrating such solid financial footing required annual budgets where expenses did not exceed revenues. His predecessors had achieved balances in each of the previous twenty years, and he wanted that sequence to continue.

Annual revenues during the White era more than doubled, from $48.7 million to $100 million.[36] Student fees (tuition, board, and room) accounted for 74 to 79 percent of that amount.[37] Fortunately, expenditures did not exceed revenues even with a 14 percent inflation rate and—thanks to the Reagan revolution—a 17 percent decrease in federal aid to higher education. The latter cutback was particularly significant as 65 percent of all Pepperdine students received some kind of financial aid, much of it from or guaranteed by the federal government.[38]

Other negatives also squeezed the university's balance sheet, including dramatically reduced enrollments at GSEP, unpaid tuition bills at SBM, [39] and the extraordinary costs associated with relocating GSEP and SBM to new facilities. Especially problematic for the balance sheet was the unpredictable payout from Hydril stock, which constituted the bulk of the university's endowment.[40]

To counter the negative pressures, the White administration took steps either to increase revenues or to curtail expenses. Between 1978 and 1985, most obviously, it raised tuition rates by 125 percent, or from $131 to $295 per trimester unit. It also increased the amount of its own money distributed as grants or loans. Known as tuition discounting, the practice became one of the cornerstones of Pepperdine's student financial aid program. By fall 1983, 51 percent of the funds awarded came from the university, 37 percent from federal sources, and 9 percent from the state of California.[41]

The White administration also relieved some of the negative pressure on the balance sheet by fixing its accounts receivable system, whittling down the long list of students whose past due bills were collectively millions of dollars in arrears.[42] Bold cuts in expenditures, while creating consternation among the faculty and staff, also helped keep the budget in balance.[43] And White's administration worked out arrangements with Richard Seaver to reduce its holdings of Hydril stock in a transaction that would eventually generate millions of dollars for the university and permit it to diversify its endowment portfolio, making it less vulnerable to the whims of the marketplace.

A Place To Call Home

There was significant new construction during the White presidency, as much as $25 million worth, the most since the opening of the Malibu campus, and all elements added to Pepperdine's growing reputation for a distinctive appearance and focus on campus life. Included were Eddy Field Stadium, Heritage Hall, the Fine Arts Complex, an apartment complex of thirty-six two-bedroom units that would house 140 law students, and an additional complex of seventy-five units that would house 300 Seaver College juniors and seniors (today's Lovernich Apartments).[44]

Perhaps the most dramatic construction on the Malibu campus in the White era was the faculty-staff condominium complex. It was the university's response to a problem that circumscribed its chances of long-term success: the lack of affordable housing in Malibu for both faculty and staff. The problem made it difficult to recruit faculty and to foster casual faculty-student interactions. Less publicly noted, the housing problem limited the size of the campus church, along with its ability to minister to the spiritual needs of students, faculty, and Malibu.

After considering different possibilities, the White administration, with the strong encouragement of Regent Morris Pendleton, determined to construct forty-four faculty-staff condos of varying sizes and values along Baxter Drive and six executive units on Tiner Court.[45] The units would be affordable to faculty and staff because they would be sold at the cost of construction, with the price of land and expense of site preparation absorbed by the university.[46] The work began in 1980 but moved very slowly. The plans included multiple floor levels and many corners; further, the new units were placed on "cut and fill" pads that required placement of deep caissons to stabilize.[47]

After more than a year of frustrating delays and "negligent and defective work" that ranged from the wrong thickness of drywall to twisted and loose framing, the university was forced to fire its original contractors and hire a new company to get the project back on track.[48] The work progressed quickly from there, and the project was acclaimed by the *Wall Street Journal* and on the *NBC Today Show* in the fall of 1981. By February 1982, twelve condos were ready for occupancy; and by June 1982, twenty-two faculty families had moved into the Baxter Drive units. All units were occupied by the end of the year.[49]

President White was thrilled with the project and confident that on-campus housing for faculty would bring students and teachers closer together. He was delighted to learn that within a year, 95 percent of the Baxter Drive residents had entertained students in their homes. The David Davenport family, for example, had as many as 300 students in their home during the year. That was the point of having campus condos, said White. They had not been designed "to provide a haven for faculty away from the students." He told Davenport, "In my opinion, the construction of the faculty and staff residential units on campus has proved to be one of the most beneficial moves the University has made in recent years."[50]

Centralizing Administration

White was almost as enthusiastic about construction of a central administration building. Pepperdine administrators were spread out across the campus: President White's office was on the upper level of Brock House, while his staff worked out of his garage; other administrators worked in Huntsinger, Mallmann House, Adamson Beach House, Tyler Campus Center, and temporary trailers. Staff were squeezed into every nook and cranny, including closets, and overcrowding issues were compounded by the closing of the Los Angeles campus in 1982. On the master plan since 1972, an administrative building became a priority in the Wave of Excellence campaign. Thanks to a major gift by Flora Thornton and to supporting gifts by George Page, Virginia Braun, and Bertie Bettingen, the $10.5 million Charles B. Thornton Administrative Center (TAC) became a reality.[51]

The four-story building contained 85,000 square feet, housing offices, meeting rooms, classrooms, mail room, and lunch room. With Coastal Commission approval, the university broke ground on the new complex on September 24, 1984. In another spotlight event for Pepperdine, Governor George Deukmejian delivered the dedicatory remarks, "in the spirit of Ronald Reagan." Bulldozers broke earth during the last year of the White presidency, but the building was not completed until early in the Davenport administration in mid-1986. By August that year, offices on the bottom two floors were occupied.

An Unexpected Deluge

Also on the first floor of the new administration building were 18,000 books, which had been stored there during the course of a $2 million renovation of

Payson Library.[52] Then on August 2, 1986, during afternoon commencement ceremonies for SBM, a university workman driving a utility truck sheared off a fire hydrant in the main parking lot. The broken hydrant let loose a 60-foot high geyser that sent 4,000 gallons per minute of water down the dirt slope, into the second floor of the library, and through to the new administration building. The Los Angeles County Fire Department arrived within minutes, but it took another forty to find the hydrant's shut-off valve. When the flood finally abated, more than 160,000 gallons of water had soaked the first and second floors of the library and the new Thornton Administrative Center, including 18,000 books.

Once the river was stemmed, the university issued a plea for help. Dean of Admission Bob Fraley had already strung clotheslines throughout his office on the second floor of TAC and hung new student records out to dry. But what about the books? According to one observer, what followed was "one of the most valiant volunteer efforts" on record "as students, faculty, staff and their families, members of the community, and even construction workers all came to [the] rescue." It was

> a sight to behold, as the volunteer brigade shuttled the soggy book cartons from the lower floor [of TAC] to the upper parking lot and spread the thousands of volumes out on the pavement to begin drying them in the sun. We were eventually aided by officials and librarians at the Los Angeles Central Library, who . . . had suffered a similar disaster just a short time earlier. We [also] received immediate assistance from Ralphs Grocery Company, which loaned us a truck to transport nearly 15,000 wet books to a location where they could be freeze-dried and, with luck, salvaged.

Those books did not return to the shelves until 1988.[53]

The Power of Appearances

When it came to cultivating prestige for Pepperdine, little could match the sheer natural beauty of the Malibu campus, and White clearly agreed with his presidential predecessor that the appearance of the campus was one of the university's best assets. As a resident, White was particularly sensitive to the appearance of the grounds. For that reason, he supported turning the space between Pacific Coast Highway and Stauffer Chapel into a grassy meadow, and he delighted in its transformation from random chaparral to a verdant, irrigated park, with two small lakes of reclaimed water, exercise stations, and picnic tables. Because it was done in-house, landscaping the meadow took longer than anticipated and "cost us dearly," said Bob Thomas, but the result seemed worth the wait and expense, and the board of regents designated twenty-five acres of the meadow as Alumni Park in 1979.[54]

As the meadow was under construction, White was busily expanding the boundaries of the Malibu campus itself. In February 1981, he purchased from Alcoa Company 187 acres of land bordering the campus to the north and west for $3.4 million. Seniel Ostrow gave an additional nine acres. The purchase and gift rounded out the size of the campus to 819 acres; subsequent gifts brought the total to 830 acres, the expanse of which remained the same into the twenty-first century. President White, ever the historian, liked to refer to the 187-acre acquisition as his "Louisiana Purchase."[55]

The additional acquisitions, most of which was vertical ground, were thought of as a buffer to urban encroachment, which also proved an effective buffer to natural disasters, such as fires, floods, and earthquakes—all of which buffeted the campus at various times. But the addition of the extra land made Pepperdine's neighbors even more suspicious that the university was planning unbridled—and unsightly—growth. The Malibu community had never particularly welcomed the university, and ill will festered during the so-called "sewage wars," conflict over the expansion of the campus wastewater treatment plant, in the late 1970s and early 1980s.

Battles over wastewater treatment and the university's long range development plans continued for years, involving local residents, Los Angeles County, the California Coastal Commission, the state legislature, and other state and county regulators. Details of those battles are beyond the scope of this book, but it is worth noting that a newly hired assistant vice president, Andrew K. Benton, succeeded in eventually getting the necessary approvals for expansion of the wastewater treatment plant and the university's fifteen-year plan for the build-out of the Malibu campus.

Rising Rankings

The success of White's efforts to attract attention while cultivating a distinctive culture that would increase Pepperdine's prestige level was demonstrated in the rankings of third parties like the *New York Times* and the *U.S. News & World Report*. In January 1982, Pepperdine was mentioned in the *New York Times Selective Guide to Colleges 1982–83*, which reviewed the distinctive characteristics of only 250 out of 3,000 colleges nationwide.

The authors labeled Pepperdine University as one of "the best and most interesting in America," saying Seaver College was "fairly serious about academic pursuits," but with a casual tone. It noted that some critics complained that standards were too low and that the school's environment was too controlled, but it ranked business, communications, computer science, and life sciences as the strongest areas. At first glance, the guide observed, Pepperdine "seems like a partygoer's dream come true . . . Surfers ride perfect waves from dawn to dusk, but few, if any of them are Pepperdine students. This Pacific paradise is actually one of the most conservative schools in Southern California . . . Intellectuals, partiers, social activists, gays and other nonconformist types will not find much company . . . If you attend Pepperdine, you'd better be a Republican." The reviewer concluded, "Pepperdine offers a solid, personalized education in an intimate small town atmosphere, and most students value it as much for its warmth as for its moral rectitude."[56]

The November 28, 1983, issue of *U.S. News & World Report* reinforced the evaluations of the *New York Times.* The magazine placed Pepperdine as fourth in its category of Regional Liberal Arts Colleges west of the Mississippi River. This placement resulted from a poll of 1,308 college presidents. "All of us are justified in feeling very proud that a school so young has attained this kind of national recognition," President White told the board of regents.[57] White was even more proud two years later when *U.S. News* judged Pepperdine number one from 151 comprehensive universities in the Midwest/Far West region.[58]

Pepperdine educators, like those at other colleges and universities, were quick to question the value of annual rankings, which seemed to be more the result of a popularity poll of college presidents than an analysis of educational effectiveness. Nevertheless, Pepperdine's educators seldom hesitated to proclaim where the institution stood in the rankings—if they were at the top or near the top. And Pepperdine was almost always at or near the top when it came to regional comparisons. Beginning in 1987, however, the magazine reclassified Pepperdine as a doctorate-granting national university like Stanford and Harvard, ranked it 151 in that category, and did not list it in the publication. In 1990, *U.S. News* placed the university initially in the second quartile of 200 nationally recognized schools. In 2001 it worked up to the first quartile, ranking forty-nine of the top fifty-one comprehensive universities in the nation. Such a ranking was a remarkable achievement for a school with such a brief history.[59]

By all measures, the Howard White presidency was successful in its efforts to build the prestige and name recognition of the university. Through events ranging from the 1984 Olympic games to the launch of the National School Safety Center, to the Wave of Excellence campaign, and the construction of faculty condos and Alumni Park, Pepperdine's name and reputation were increasingly visible locally, nationally, and internationally. But sustaining Pepperdine University as an institution of higher education with a Christian purpose into the twenty-first century also meant getting control of the financial structures and practices of the university, providing necessary physical facilities, and negotiating with state and county regulatory agencies.

In none of these areas was there unequivocal success, but White ended his administration convinced that progress had been made in each. As further evidence of improvement he would point to developments at Seaver College.

CHAPTER 41

SEAVER COLLEGE
MATURES

During Howard White's seven years as its president, Pepperdine University won acceptance as part of the educational establishment in the United States, as evidenced by various national rankings, including athletic ones. In almost every case, the phenomenon had been fueled by events transforming the undergraduate school, Seaver College. New leadership, better prepared students, revised institutional goals, an enhanced academic profile, and a successful athletic program all helped earn national recognition for Pepperdine's flagship liberal arts college.

Norman Hughes served as Seaver dean for most of White's presidency, resigning to return to the classroom in July 1983. To find a successor, Vice President for Academic Affairs William Phillips coordinated a national search that involved faculty participation, a first for Seaver College. Biblical scholar and archeologist John F. Wilson surfaced as the candidate of choice for the deanship position. Wilson held a bachelor's degree from Harding College and a doctorate from the University of Iowa. He was currently serving on the faculty at Southwest Missouri State University at Springfield, where he had also directed the Church of Christ Bible chair. Over his career, Wilson earned an international reputation for his work on the archaeology of ancient Philippi and Banias. As dean, he became known for his thoughtful articulation of what it meant for Seaver to be a Christian college and for his ability to place the task at hand into a larger context.[1]

Wilson announced early on that his goal was to establish academic excellence at Seaver College. As he judged it, that would require three essentials:

- a superior faculty known for its quality teaching and professional prominence;
- a superior student body recruited for its exceptional abilities, character, promise, GPA, and SAT scores; and

- a superior curriculum characterized by its liberal arts "breadth," and major "depth."

He also identified as a priority the improvement of library resources.[2]

Joining Wilson as associate and assistant deans over the next fifteen years were Reginald C. Westmoreland (communication), Nancy Magnusson-Fagan (psychology), Dwayne Van Rheenen (communication), Donald Shores (communication), Don Thompson (mathematics), Carolyn Vos Strache (leisure sciences), and June P. Palacio (nutrition and food management).

The Seaver dean's office was responsible for academic affairs, but the dean of students was responsible for the co-curriculum of the college, which included supervision of chapel exercises, the Student Government Association (SGA), and the interfraternity council. Serving as dean of students during the White era and beyond were Stuart Love (1979–1982), Mike Armour (1982–1984), and Carl Mitchell (1984–1987).[3] They were followed by Ed Mandrell (1987–1989), D'Esta Love (1989–2001), and Mark Davis (2002-).

Critical to Seaver College accomplishing its mission was the work of the dean of admissions. With the exception of two years, Robert Fraley, a native of Texas and a graduate of Abilene Christian College, was Pepperdine's chief admission officer between 1967 and 1990. Fraley had accomplished the incredibly difficult job of recruiting the Malibu campus's first class in 1972. He continued to fill the campus year after year, during some turbulent times.

Student Profiles

Through the White era, undergraduate enrollments escalated in number—despite calls from both Malibu neighbors, faculty leaders, and the student body for limiting that growth. In 1978, the college had a student headcount of 2,000; that number increased to 2,576 by 1985, despite assurance to the Malibu Township Council that enrollment would be limited to 2,100 full-time equivalent students. The gender distribution remained about the same over that time period: ten males to nine females. The student body color, however, whitened. Between 1983 and 1989, the number of Asian students did increase from 4 percent to 5 percent, but Hispanic students remained at 4 percent, and African American students declined from 4 percent to less than 3 percent.[4]

The number of international students also decreased, from 15 percent to 11 percent. Of the sixty nationalities on campus, the largest number came from Iran, and many of them experienced financial difficulties when the United States froze all Iranian assets as a response to the hostage crisis beginning in 1979.[5] Forty-three percent of Seaver students came from households with income levels above $50,000 per year, while 30 percent came from families with incomes below $20,000.[6] With regard to religious preference, 22 percent of the student body was Catholic. The percentage of students with a Church of Christ preference increased from 11.5 to 14.1.[7]

Seaver College students continued to be politically conservative, like the university's administration. In 1984, when Ronald Reagan was running for re-election, SGA sponsored a voter registration drive that added 265 Republicans but only 20 Democrats to the voter rolls.[8] The conservative influence may help explain why SGA voted down a resolution to honor Martin Luther King Jr. with an appropriate plaque on the basis that existing campus plaques honored only people who had directly helped Pepperdine.[9]

Higher admission standards led to a rise of SAT scores for incoming students. By 1984, the combined SAT score of entering freshmen was 1,044, up 96 points from four years earlier, and more than 100 points above the national average, which was below 900.[10] GPAs from entering freshman also rose, improving from 3.15 in 1981 to 3.26 in 1985. With better students coming in, retention and graduation rates improved dramatically. In 1983, only 51.4 percent of entering freshmen actually graduated from Seaver. Two years later, the rate had increased to 65 percent.[11]

Faculty Participation

The academic structure of Seaver College during the White era remained much as it had been during the Banowsky years. To emphasize interdisciplinary study the college was divided into six divisions: business administration, communication (including English composition and foreign languages), humanities/fine arts, natural science, religion, and social science/teacher education. In 1987, shortly after White's presidency ended, fine arts became a separate seventh division.

The chairs of the various divisions met regularly with the Seaver dean as an administrative council. The principal policy-making body of the college, the Seaver Academic Council (SAC), met monthly to vet and approve all curricular changes. It was composed of the division chairs and elected faculty members from every division.

A once-active AAUP chapter on the Malibu campus became inactive during President White's tenure. What caused its demise is unclear. Certainly a salary scale that rose to the 95th percentile range for all professorial ranks eliminated some of the urgency for such a chapter. So too did a tacit agreement between the faculty and the administration to recognize the Faculty Organization (FO) as the principal vehicle for faculty input into the governance of the college.

All full-time faculty were included in the FO and had the opportunity to elect its leaders. The FO was responsible for finding or electing faculty members for other standing committees, including academic ethics, admissions and scholarship, athletics, buildings and grounds, faculty enrichment, professional problems, stipends, student life, and teacher evaluation.

Matters related to tenure and promotion of faculty were considered and recommended by a faculty-elected rank, tenure, and promotion (RTP) committee. RTP did its work according to policies and procedures laboriously worked out and stipulated in the Seaver College *RTP Manual*.[12] The manual included a statement of the tenure policy that was elaborated in the *Seaver College Handbook*, which also addressed faculty benefits, faculty responsibilities, and services available to it.[13]

Relationship with Faculty

Pepperdine administrators generally understood that the success of any strategic plan or vision depended upon a contented faculty. Early in President White's administration the faculty at Seaver College was hardly contented. It nursed wounds from its salary confrontations with President Banowsky and from its conflicts with White over administrative and faculty hiring policies. But White at heart was a professor who had great respect for his teaching colleagues, and the faculty found it difficult not to reciprocate. Rising salary levels almost certainly contributed to the good feelings, as well.

Of course, White's administration had its share of detractors in Seaver College. One source of irritation was the question of academic freedom, which arose in various situations. In one, White backed an adjunct sociology teacher who invited Tom Hayden, one of the Chicago Nine and a candidate for the state assembly, to speak to her class. He was less tolerant of the same teacher for bringing in representatives of alternative lifestyles—including homosexuals and drug addicts—and instructed that she not be rehired.[14]

From the perspective of some faculty and students, academic freedom was also at issue in the administration's continuing tussle with Seaver's student publications, including both the *Graphic* and *Oasis*. This tension contributed to a confrontation between the *Graphic* staff and Steve Ames, who was appointed as director of student publications for the 1978–1979 academic year. When Ames dramatically relieved all five student editors from their positions,[15] there was a loud outcry from the newspaper fraternity and some Pepperdine faculty and students.[16] But board of regents members and other faculty members supported Ames,[17] and he went on to run a successful publication program at Seaver for the next five years, garnering multiple regional and national awards.[18]

Seaver Strategic Plans

As part of the general effort to develop a university-wide strategic plan, Seaver College began to construct its own plan under the leadership of Dean Norman Hughes and Vice President John Nicks. Planners identified the distinctive qualities and principles that should define the college in the 1980s, believing that its mission was to influence the "development of the whole person: intellectual, spiritual, ethical, emotional and physical." In order to do so, Seaver should provide a values-centered liberal arts education based on the teachings of Christ and foster a campus student life that would maximize those values. It should also emphasize excellence in academic studies whereby students would think logically; learn how to communicate and compute; come to appreciate the cultural heritage of Western civilization; and be made aware of the contemporary world of philosophy, natural science, the arts, literature, and social issues. The curriculum should sensitize students to intellectual and cultural diversity, to complexities and ambiguities, and to Christian principles and values. Clearly, the vision of Seaver College of itself had not changed much since its inception a decade earlier.[19]

Although Hughes and his faculty colleagues invested considerable time and energy in developing a vision for Seaver College, not until the administration of Dean Wilson did a comprehensive plan actually emerge. After multiple versions and four years of painful battles, the college brought forth a document that would guide it into the twenty-first century. According to the new strategic plan, the fundamental mission of the college had not changed, although it was more distinctively codified.

- Seaver was to provide a link between the knowledge and wisdom of the past and the challenges of the future.
- It was to be primarily an undergraduate and residential college, both a liberal arts and a Christian school, whose ties to Churches of Christ called it to a serious commitment to biblical Christianity.
- The Seaver student was to be the heart of the educational enterprise.
- Incoming students should have outstanding records of academic performance, strong moral characters, inquisitive minds, and creative abilities.
- Seaver students should be diverse in economic and social status, geographical origin, racial and cultural heritage, and religious tradition.
- There should be a "significant representation" from Christian backgrounds, with a "significant number" from Churches of Christ.
- Graduating students should leave with an ability to continue their education, to think, to communicate, to appreciate cultural diversity, and to embody moral integrity.
- They should also be eager to serve.[20]

The strategic plan also described the ideal Seaver faculty, which, as a community of scholars, would manifest excellence as teachers. All members should hold the highest appropriate degree in their areas of teaching and research, function as role models as well as academicians, have an inquisitive spirit that manifested a love for learning, be devoted to Christian moral and ethical values, and manifest a sense of servanthood. The Seaver faculty would also be diverse—in age, gender, race, geography, religion, and skill sets. It would, moreover, reflect the university's historic relationship to Churches of Christ as it also recognized the contributions of those who were not members of Churches of Christ but complemented and shared a commitment to the mission of Seaver College.[21]

Familiar Battlegrounds

As evidenced in its strategic plans, Seaver College remained deeply committed to transmitting Christian values to its students, but it often struggled to determine the best ways to convey that commitment. The administration—and some faculty—continued to believe that chapel services should be an integral part of that effort, but the student body continued to find chapel requirements onerous. In 1978, Director of Campus Life Ralph Beck wanted to use the weekly assembly to enhance the spiritual life of the campus and acted to streamline announcements, reserve some services for just congregational singing, and feature speakers who shared only a spiritual message.[22] But Beck's reorientation of chapel was controversial. According to Nicks, it was not broad enough.[23] Professor Ron Fagan protested because devotional services, patterned as they were after practices of Churches of Christ, limited the role of women.[24]

Most students objected to chapel not so much because of its content but because attendance was mandatory. They were eager to secure exemption for off-campus duties.[25] President White was dismayed when he learned that half of the student body was exempt from most chapels. He requested that only a few exceptions be granted, and, moreover, that absolutely no competing academic classes be scheduled during the once-a-week chapel service.[26] This earnestness about chapel prompted one student to remark that he knew Seaver College had religious expectations but he "had no idea that [administrators] took the rules so seriously."[27]

However, the resistance to mandatory chapel and other such rules—particularly those against on-campus dancing and the ones that limited visitation in residence halls—did not mean the student body rejected the Christian mission of Seaver College. Although some students resented the Church of Christ presence on campus, according to *Graphic* reporter Rick Cupp there seemed to be a revival of religious interest on campus in the early 1980s. The symbol of the fish was ubiquitous, many students were baptized, and attendance increased at local churches, including Malibu Presbyterian, the Vineyard, and the University Church of Christ, where some 150 students attended. Led by Jeff Yani, the eighty-member spiritual life committee of the Student Government Association sponsored five activities a week, among them Bible studies, prayer breakfasts, concerts, and outings to Disneyland.[28]

Ensuring Academic Excellence

All discussions of strategic plans for Seaver assumed a level of academic excellence, and achieving those goals required Dean Hughes (and those who followed him) to address course standards, faculty expectations, and grade inflation. Through his encouragements and the work of faculty committees, the college made measurable progress in raising its academic profile during the White administration.[29] Between 1975 and 1980, the overall grade point average (GPA) at Seaver went down from 3.18 to 2.59, which was lower than the national GPA average of 2.75.

The quest for a stronger academic program also focused considerable attention on Seaver College's cherished general education (GE) program, which constituted half of the 128 units required for graduation. The program was designed to provide the curricular "breadth" required to fulfill the objectives of a Christian liberal arts college, while requirements for a particular major provided the "depth." Some faculty wanted to fine-tune the number and distribution of courses; others wanted to increase major requirements at the expense of GE and elective courses; still others wanted to change the delivery of the entire GE program.[30] The role of graduate education at Seaver College raised additional concerns.

President White considered most of these issues to be attempts to weaken Seaver's commitment to the liberal arts. He and other Seaver faculty were convinced that undergraduate students pursuing professional programs like business administration and communication needed the full version of a liberal arts curriculum.[31] Thus, White opposed any proposal to increase major requirements at the expense of general education, including the idea of offering courses with three units of credit rather than four.[32] In fact, White would have preferred that Pepperdine not award a bachelor's degree in any professional or vocational subject.[33] He was just as adamant about narrowing the scope of interdisciplinary courses and expressed pride that during the "permissive" 1960s Pepperdine had not yielded to pressure to dilute, much less delete, the liberal arts.[34] He wanted that same fortitude to prevail in the 1980s.

Interestingly, White also championed small master's degree programs at Seaver College and opposed the July 1984 recommendation from Seaver's academic planning committee for "terminating graduate programs in general ... and applying those resources toward better undergraduate programs." White thought "it would be a serious step backward for Pepperdine University to eliminate all of its MA degree programs at Seaver College. We should be thinking in terms of strengthening them and making them what they ought to be." He did not see great expense associated with graduate education and held that any department that could not award a respectable MA degree was probably not giving a very good bachelor's degree either. Most likely based primarily on the esteem White commanded, his views on graduate education at Seaver College prevailed.

Making Some Changes

Following a national trend, the faculty continued its vigorous conversation on the general education curriculum after John Wilson began his tenure as dean in 1983. Included in the discussion were proposals to lengthen class periods, to reduce course credit from four to three units with faculty teaching four courses rather than three, altering the school calendar (particularly the third trimester), creating an academic advising center staffed by an assistant dean, altering the division structure, and adding computer literacy and foreign language requirements to the curriculum.

The debate over the proposals was so heated that Executive Vice President David Davenport feared for the negative impact on faculty morale. He also feared for the cost of some of the proposed changes, and his recommendation was to delay any decision. He also encouraged the faculty to recognize that colleagues generally draw conclusions based upon emotions rather than facts, to understand that change for the sake of change was not good, and that Seaver College should not be doing things just because other schools were doing them. Pepperdine, he said, was well-known because it did its own thing.[35]

As it turned out, most of the proposed changes wound up being debated and implemented without significant division among the faculty, and noticeable modification was pretty much limited to the GE curriculum. Beginning in 1983, entering freshmen were required to have two years of high school foreign language. Starting in fall 1985, students had to demonstrate computer literacy by completing a module on social and humanistic aspects of computing in an existing course. They also had to demonstrate proficiency in computer problem-solving either by examination or by taking a two-unit introductory course in computer science.

In 1986, GE requirements were more prescriptive, with sixty units of course work selected from ten categories rather than six. The new categories included English composition and literature (eight units); religion (twelve units); Western heritage (twelve units); American heritage (twelve units); behavioral science (twelve units); foreign language (four units); natural science (eight units, with four of those in a laboratory); speech and communication (four units); physical education (four units); computer literacy (zero units). With only a few refinements, the GE curriculum instituted in 1986 remained in place into the twenty-first century.[36]

Great Books, First-Year Seminars, Honors Programs

Also in the mid-1980s, a Great Books program was added to the curriculum. As a field of study, Great Books had been popularized by Professor Mortimer Adler at the University of Chicago.[37] At the encouragement of GSEP Dean William Adrian, President White hosted Adler at the Brock House in December 1984.[38] Adler so inspired Associate Professor of Education Michael Gose that within eighteen months Gose had helped to launch Seaver's own Great Books Colloquium. In the four-trimester program, students read masterworks of Western civilization from Plato to Solzhenitsyn and discussed them in small seminar groups in a spirit of shared inquiry. The personification of liberal education and substituting for part of the GE program, the colloquium attracted student interest immediately.[39] It also attracted external interest: the Fletcher Jones Foundation of Irvine, California, endowed a Great Books chair in 1995. The Seaver College program was one of fewer than a hundred such programs in the United States.

External voices also influenced Seaver to embrace a first-year seminar program. Nationwide, colleges and universities experienced a high dropout rate of freshmen students, which could be at least partially blamed on students' difficulties transitioning from high school to college. To address the root causes of the retention issue, the University of South Carolina launched a series of seminars for new students in 1972. The seminars were designed to build community among a small group of freshmen, expose them to college expectations, and provide them resources for how to learn in college. The seminar proved so popular and promising that a first-year seminar movement soon followed. Seaver College joined the crusade and introduced its seminar program in 1987. Although faculty could not decide whether the primary purpose of the seminar was to introduce students to the college experience or to a particular discipline, students seemed to find the first-year seminar helpful, and retention rates to the sophomore year increased to 98 percent at Seaver College by the end of the twentieth century.[40]

Another example of a growing sense of academic excellence among Seaver's administration and faculty occurred in 1981 when the biology faculty, under the leadership of Joe Williams, adopted an honors program for students that required publishable research. The program was initiated as the faculty attempted to get all biology students involved in a relevant research project, an effort that would subsequently bring national acclaim to the biologists and a National Science Foundation grant to the university.

Excellence in Athletics, Too

For Howard White, the quest for excellence did not stop with the classroom. It extended to the university's athletic program, which he firmly believed was good for the institution. Athletics promoted school spirit, provided wholesome recreation, inspired pride, and enhanced the university's relationships with its higher education peers, he believed.[41] White was Pepperdine's number one sports fan, seldom missing an on-campus game or match, especially water polo, and attending many off-campus competitions as well. He never failed to recap athletic success in his reports to the university board or the board of regents. And he was rankled when the *Los Angeles Times* failed to cover Pepperdine's athletic events. "The *Los Angeles Times* is not a good judge of what is newsworthy, or it is guilty of an arrogant perversity," he said.[42]

White had reason to be proud of the athletes. In October 1984, as the *Graphic* reported, Pepperdine was rated nineteenth in the nation in overall winning percentage (.638) for the 1983–1984 academic year, with seven of its nine teams (men and women) winning top 20 honors. The school's "diminutive program [had] achieved a winning reputation that most schools in Division I would be proud of," the reporter declared, and it had been done on a limited budget.[43] Moreover, four-year rates of graduation among scholarship athletes had improved dramatically, from 67 percent in 1982 to 85 percent in 1984 to 88 percent in 1988. The national graduation rate was just 42 percent.[44]

These kinds of data points, along with impressive won-lost records of individual sports, demonstrate that during Howard White's presidency the goal of the athletic program at Pepperdine was "better, not bigger."

Almost before its time, Pepperdine University had a fully grown and widely recognized athletic program and was well on its way to developing highly respected programs of academic excellence in a maturing Seaver College.

CHAPTER 42

PASSING THE BATON

Given the circumstances of his appointment, Howard White looked for a successor almost from the beginning of his presidency in 1978. That quest stretched out until 1985, longer than he originally anticipated because the board of regents extended his own contract for two or more years at a time.

As early as 1980 White had settled on Harold Hazelip as his personal choice to succeed him. Holding an undergraduate degree from David Lipscomb College and a PhD in religion from the University of Iowa, Hazelip was well known in Churches of Christ as the dean of the Harding Graduate School of Religion in Memphis and as a speaker on the internationally broadcast *Herald of Truth* television program. White corresponded with Hazelip extensively, spoke with him on the telephone, and even hosted him for a quiet visit to the Malibu campus in 1981. He proposed that Hazelip join the Pepperdine administration first as academic vice president or similar office for a year or two. That course would introduce Hazelip to the "Pepperdine way," which was substantially different from the Lipscomb and Harding ways, and allow White to mentor him in negotiating those differences before he assumed the presidency.[1]

Hazelip was interested, but he was not sure that White could execute the succession moves he planned. He did not want to resign his position at Harding in the pursuit of another post that might not materialize. So Hazelip declined White's offer, having concluded that he wanted to be a communicator of the gospel rather than a college administrator. President White was deeply disappointed.[2] Ironically, almost two years later Hazelip reconsidered his decision, but White had to tell him the search had entered a new phase and other candidates had been identified.[3] Not wanting to lose Hazelip's friendship or influence with the churches, White did get him elected to a term on Pepperdine's board of regents simultaneously with former President of the United States Gerald Ford. In 1987, Hazelip was named president of David Lipscomb University, a position he held for ten years.[4]

Long-Running Search Committee

The executive committee of the board of regents in 1982 created a five-person[5] committee—plus Howard White and Norvel Young—and assigned it the responsibility for identifying a suitable successor to the president. Over the next two years, the committee considered at least fifteen individuals.[6] Four surfaced as the most plausible candidates: Hazelip, Jerry Hudson, Terry Johnson, and David Davenport. Of the four, clearly the hungriest for the position was Jerry Hudson, formerly the provost of Seaver College, and the current president of Willamette University in Salem, Oregon. White had assured Hudson that he was very much in the pool in May 1983. White admitted, however, that he had some reservations about his protégé, primarily that he was no longer committed to maintaining the connection of Pepperdine with Churches of Christ. He wanted the next president to pursue that connection actively rather than merely acquiesce to it.[7]

Of the other three likely candidates, Hazelip eliminated himself early on. Terry Johnson, then the president of Oklahoma Christian College, expressed an interest but was happy in his current position. David Davenport had a different response; he was interested. Davenport had joined Pepperdine as a professor at the law school in 1980. He rose to Howard White's attention almost immediately, not only because of his qualities as a teacher but also because of his work as the preaching minister of the University Church of Christ. The president soon appointed Davenport as university counsel, a position he held until 1983. That year, much to the consternation of some of his administrative peers who also had presidential ambitions, White promoted Davenport to replace Herbert Luft as executive vice president.[8]

The Sixth President

Although only in his early thirties, Davenport was well known for his intellect, his thoughtful decisions, his astuteness as an administrator, his grasp of the "big picture" and his sensitivity to the "Pepperdine way." As vice president, he had won the admiration of administrators, faculty, staff, and students, including an endorsement from the Seaver College faculty advisory committee. This support, his administrative experience within the university, and his calling as a preacher impressed the search committee. All Pepperdine presidents after Batsell Baxter had internal experience at the university; all had served as Church of Christ preachers.[9]

On April 11, 1984, the search committee voted to recommend David Davenport to the executive committee of the board of regents as the successor to Howard White. A month later, the executive committee endorsed the recommendation and submitted it to the full board for consideration. On June 12, at a regular meeting of the regents, the board voted to appoint Davenport as the sixth president of Pepperdine University. Davenport would begin his term a year later on April 16, 1985, serving as "President Designate" until then.[10] Thereafter, White would serve as president emeritus, with responsibilities in the area of development, as counsel to the president, and for special assignments.[11] Tom Bost announced the decision of the regents to the university community immediately; White followed with an expression of his enthusiasm for the decision.[12]

In the entire selection process, there had been no formal input from faculty, students, alumni, or community. According to White, the regents were eager to consult with those who had opinions, but they had no intention of giving different interest groups a vote in the final selection. The faculty should be consulted in all important matters, White observed, "but I do not believe that the faculty should have as much authority as some modern educators have advocated" in the selection process. White's view was not unique at Pepperdine. None of the previous five presidents had been selected with formal input from faculty, students, or alumni.[13]

David Davenport officially began his term as president of Pepperdine University in 1985 and served until 2000. A native of Kansas, Davenport became Pepperdine's sixth president when he was thirty-four. He was seen by many as "the very embodiment" of Pepperdine.

Distinctive Accomplishments

Howard White served seven years as president of Pepperdine University. During those years, he later reflected, he had dedicated himself to three basic endeavors: fiscal responsibility and soundness, academic excellence, and preservation of the distinctive heritage of the university. As specific accomplishments, he could have cited a stronger curriculum, thirty-three new faculty, dramatically improved faculty salaries, tighter admission standards, four urban educational centers (West LA, Irvine, Long Beach, and Encino), two doctoral programs, institutional computer literacy, and national recognition. It was notable too that financial (endowment) resources had more than doubled, from $90 million to more than $208 million, and that the university had added 200 acres to its Malibu campus and constructed major facilities costing in excess of $55 million.

Capital improvements included music and theater buildings, 450 student apartments, fifty faculty and staff condominiums, Helen Field Heritage Hall, and Eddy D. Field Baseball Stadium. The Thornton Administrative Center was started but not completed during his presidency. White almost singlehandedly brought the Olympic Games to the Pepperdine campus in 1984. No wonder that Tom Bost, chair of the board of regents, concluded that Pepperdine's financial and academic health was "unparalleled in the University's history."[14] Modestly, White attributed it all to the graciousness of God.[15]

All of this was important, the editors of the *Graphic* readily admitted, but to them it missed the point. President White's real legacy was his "personal touch." He openly communicated with students on formal and casual occasions, addressing them by their first name. He transcended "the stereotype of the stuffy, unapproachable administrator." Moreover, White was a visible president, always mixing with the crowd at sporting events, attending departmental banquets and events, and hosting "Meet the President" nights at the Brock House. The editors urged future administrations to "maintain a philosophy akin to White's very human approach to people."[16]

"Tendency Toward Correctness and Perspicuity"

White's human approach came at considerable personal cost, however. He was on duty, engaged in university business seven days a week. He seldom if ever watched television, although he was a voracious reader, when he could take the time. He felt compelled to check the contents of mass mailings, review graphic designs, police the color of Malibu campus buildings, read minutes of administrative committee meetings, examine plans for graduation exercises, and review the list of those chosen to live in faculty/staff condominiums.

In his extensive correspondence, aided by his facility with dictating machines, White had no tolerance for typographical errors or misspelled words. In "thank you" notes sent from his office, and there was a plethora of them, he had certain "idiosyncrasies" he wanted observed: no contractions, hyphens limited to adjectives only, "Sincerely yours" rather than just "Sincerely," no split infinitives, and use of "eager" rather than "anxious." When he saw these and other errors in the correspondence of his colleagues, he thought he saw evidence of administrators doing sloppy work.

Although he possessed a sense of humor and a hearty laugh, White could also be grumpy, peevish, duplicitous, and a bit paranoid. He grumbled to his staff that he no longer wanted to learn first about actions of the university operations committee in the pages of the *Graphic*. Spotting some errors in a grant proposal, he told Vice President Michael Adams that thereafter he would personally proofread all copy that was sent from Adams's office. When Adams acknowledged White's "tendency toward correctness and perspicuity in language and form," White responded that when he requested that something be done, "it just be done," or that he be given some advance notice and explanation as to why it should not be done.[17]

He wanted the deans of the different colleges to know budget figures for their schools only. He did not want the regents to belong to a national association for fear it would raise questions about how Pepperdine did business. He did not trust the faculty to perpetuate the school's Christian mission.

"Keeper of Its Conscience"

But despite his faults, White was a man of great personal integrity. So far as is known, his name was never associated with any action or connection that might possibly be considered a conflict of interest with the school. He once refused the gift of a fruit basket from a person who was applying for admission into SBM.[18] In his heart of hearts he even had reservations about currying favor with Blanche Seaver for her money only.[19]

In his mind, there was more to being president than completing a "to do" list, being approachable, or being honest. In White's judgment, he told his successor, "the president of the university [was] the keeper of its conscience, the guardian of its heritage, the leader who points the way to change that will show progress but will not violate the basic ideals of the institution." He recommended that David Davenport quote George Pepperdine often, for he had the clearest vision of what he wanted to do with the school.[20]

Future Challenges

Going forward White saw the university confronting four great challenges:

- addressing the growing cost of higher education and the increasing gap between what the university must charge and what the students could pay;
- doing the hard work necessary to build academic excellence;
- retaining what was "uncommon" about Pepperdine, notably its dramatic beauty, emphasis on values-centered education, and commitment to the ideals of American free enterprise; and
- preserving the distinctiveness that grew out of the school's religious commitment to the Churches of Christ.

"To sever its ties with its affiliated church would be to cut its tap root," White often said. The Christian dimension and the value system of Pepperdine University were flowers that could "not bloom apart from its connection with its tap root."[21]

Altogether, White was bullish on the future of the university. The institution remained "so strongly established, its friends and supporters so numerous and dedicated, its human and financial resources so great, its heritage so valuable and its distinctive purposes so needed in our society, that its future with the help of God is bound to be one of glorious achievement."[22]

Howard White served as Pepperdine's fifth president until April 16, 1985. Thereafter he welcomed the opportunity to do things he wanted to do "rather than spending all of my time doing what I think I ought to do." He particularly looked forward to doing some serious traveling, especially to Europe. He moved into one of the condominiums on the executive pad on President's Drive. His friends and former students honored him by partially endowing the Howard A. White Chair in History, the first occupant of which was James L. McDonough. McDonough was a distinguished historian of the American Civil War and a former student of White's.

Because of deteriorating health, White left the employment of the university on August 31, 1987, although it was never announced publicly. He died in 1991 at the age of 78.

COMING OF AGE
1985–2000

~

CHAPTER 43

LIGHTING THE WAY

In 1984, Ronald Reagan credited his presidency with having restored "morning again in America." That same year the Pepperdine University board of regents designated David Davenport as the school's next president. In ceremonies during the spring 1985 Bible lectures, Howard White spiritually invested Davenport as president and declared the selection as one of his presidency's "supreme accomplishments."[1] Then on October 21, 1985, in Firestone Fieldhouse before an audience of 4,000 people that included members of the board of regents, the university board, the faculty, the student body, and representatives from 300 academic institutions, Davenport was formally sworn in as the sixth president of Pepperdine University.[2]

In his inaugural address, Davenport echoed Reagan's imagery of light and darkness. Universities, he said, were in the business of "lighting the way" via the glowing light of reflection, the searching light of discovery, and the guiding light of values. Pepperdine's distinctive mission, he believed, was to combine those three lights into one bright beam that would stream out from Malibu "across the Pacific Ocean toward the twenty-first century."[3] As Davenport told a *Los Angeles Times* reporter, his goal was "to combine [the] traditions of Christian commitment and academic excellence and make Pepperdine a national leader in private education, even if on a list of just one."[4]

Davenport was only thirty-four years old when he assumed the office of president. Like George Pepperdine, he was a native of Kansas, and his childhood had been deeply shaped by dedicated parents who took seriously Christian faith—as Church of Christ members—and capitalism—as bakery owners. He attended Stanford on a debate scholarship, earning a BA degree "with distinction" in international relations. He received his juris doctor degree from the University of Kansas, where he was elected to the Order of the Coif, edited the *Kansas Law Review,* and won national and international awards in moot court competition. During his collegiate years, Davenport had reservations about the Vietnam War and sympathy for liberal social reforms.[5]

He also campaigned for several political candidates and served for two summers as an intern in Washington, D.C., first in the senatorial offices of Robert Dole and later in the executive office of the president of the United States. As an attorney, he practiced in the San Diego law firm of Gray, Cary, Ames & Frye. In 1980, Davenport joined the faculty of the Pepperdine University School of Law and later served for two years as the university's legal counsel. In 1983 he was selected to serve as the university's executive vice president; a year later he was chosen as president-elect.[6]

Over the years, Davenport was always drawn to the ministry. As a young law student, he served as youth minister of the Overland Park Church of Christ near Kansas City. Participating in his group was Sally Nelson, an aspiring graphic artist. The two were married in August 1977. While living in San Diego, Davenport preached first part-time and then full-time at the El Cajon Boulevard Church of Christ. He continued his preaching at the University Church of Christ when he joined the School of Law faculty and then the administration of the university in 1981. He remained a powerful minister of the gospel as president of the university, speaking before lectureship audiences and as a guest in pulpits around the world. In 1992 he even contemplated leaving the presidency to assume a full-time pulpit in Springfield, Missouri.[7]

Foundational Leadership

Like all five Pepperdine University presidents before him, then, David Davenport was a preacher. Choosing a president with that credential was not mere chance; the university highly valued tradition and continuity of leadership, which was also apparent in the foundational leaders who served in the Davenport administration. Foremost among these was Thomas Bost, the chair of the board of regents. A lifelong member of Churches of Christ, Bost joined the Pepperdine board in 1974; six years later he succeeded Lloyd Nelson as chair, a position he held for the duration of Davenport's presidency.[8]

As his executive vice president/provost, Davenport chose William Adrian, who served as provost until June 1993.[9] Steven Lemley succeeded Adrian. His selection followed input from a screening committee that included administrative and faculty representatives, the first such committee at Pepperdine.[10] As his vice president of academic affairs, Davenport retained William Phillips, who would take a leadership role in the flurry of strategic planning that occupied the early years of the Davenport presidency. In 1987, Phillips assumed responsibility for Pepperdine's study abroad programs, a position he held until 2005 when he returned to Seaver as professor of physics.

Davenport also retained Howard White's friend-raising/fund-raising team. That team included Charles Runnels as chancellor, who played an important part in many fund-raising efforts—none more important than maintaining the university's relationship with Blanche Seaver.[11] It also included Michael Adams, who continued as vice president for university affairs until 1989, when he accepted the presidency of Centre College in Danville, Kentucky.[12] Other staff contributors to the fund-raising efforts included George C. "Bob" Bales, Pepperdine's reliable connection with the Hollywood elite; and Larry Hornbaker, first as the university's senior vice president, and then as executive vice chancellor, a position he held until his retirement in 2002. Hornbaker was the glue that held the friend-raising team together.[13]

John G. Watson continued as vice president for student affairs, returning to the classroom in 1992, but then accepting the position of athletic director in 1998. He replaced Wayne Wright, who retired from the athletics position after twenty-one years of notable service.[14] Davenport also retained Mike O'Neal and Andrew K. Benton as key leaders in his administrative team, O'Neal as vice president for business/finance and Benton as Pepperdine's lead legislative and community representative. In 1992, O'Neal became vice chancellor, and Benton became executive vice president.[15]

Most of Davenport's administrative team was in place as he assumed the presidency. Two major players joined subsequently. One, Robert Thomas, had been at Pepperdine until he became president of the University of Montana West at Dillon in 1979. He returned to Pepperdine in 1988 as dean of SBM's residential program on the Malibu campus; a year later, Davenport asked him to serve as vice president for administration, an office he held until he retired in 2002. The other, James Morgan, came on board in fall 1985 as assistant vice president for information systems with the task of making computer literacy a reality on the Pepperdine campus.

As a whole, the leadership team had much in common. Virtually all had previously worked at Pepperdine, received bachelor's degrees from private liberal arts colleges with Christian missions, and immigrated to Southern California from the south central and southeastern United States. After 1992, all but one member of senior management were lawyers. All but three were members of Churches of Christ. All were white, and all in the senior circle were male, although Nancy Magnusson was named dean of GSEP in 1988, the first woman to serve as head of one of Pepperdine's core schools. In short, there was not a lot of gender, social, or ethnic diversity in Davenport's leadership team. Although Pepperdine accomplished much under this leadership team, they were not always perceived as united in the service of academic excellence and Christian mission. From the perspective of one young faculty member, who believed he spoke for many of his faculty colleagues, many of the administrators were "more concerned about their territories or little kingdoms rather than the institution as a whole."[16]

The "Pepperdine Ideal"

By all accounts, Davenport was an effective leader. He was an excellent communicator and at his best as a crisis manager. He analyzed problems thoroughly, and "his solutions were usually ingenious and logical." He had a sense of humor, delegated easily, and supported those who reported to him. He also portrayed an excellent image to the public: a bright, pleasant, Christian family man who had his personal priorities straight, who was not enamored with power and money, and who represented in his own life the "Pepperdine ideal." He was a spiritual role model for students and was committed to Churches of Christ.[17] Said one reporter: Davenport seemed "the very embodiment of the smoothly honed, outward-facing Pepperdine of today: a full head of well-coiffed gray hair, Beverly Hills tasseled loafers, a spacious office full of framed photographs of the likes of Bush and Reagan."[18]

Even his strongest supporters, however, thought Davenport had room for improvement as a leader. One admirer observed that the president tended to approach problems on an ad hoc basis rather than from an idea and goal perspective and on a de novo basis as if each problem was completely new. Others believed he relied too much on "lawyer types" from his own generation who were too quick to dismiss complexity. Because Davenport delegated so much and seemed so reasonable when challenged, friends and foes alike found it difficult to attribute unpopular decisions to him, giving rise to the description "Teflon Dave." The vision for Pepperdine that was clear within Davenport's own mind was not always so clear to others, in part because he valued ambiguity rather than bright lines of delineation. Some charged that he was not sufficiently aggressive in strengthening the ties to Churches of Christ, while others accused him of showing preference for Church of Christ employees.[19]

Like most people, Davenport had some strong preferences. He wanted academic ceremonies completed efficiently without lengthy slide shows or an excessive number of awards. He insisted that no school, particularly the law school, "owned" a particular physical facility to the exclusion of other schools. He did not want his administrative colleagues to make appointments before 9:30 a.m. or after 4 p.m. so that the day's early and late hours could be reserved for administrative meetings. He did not want his associates taking friends and family members to lunch on the university's tab, nor did he want food served in the administrative building other than at lunch time. Like Banowsky and White before him, he wanted the Malibu campus to look good and to be safe, requesting public safety to remove broken-down vehicles and be more diligent in curtailing speeding on campus. He also wanted Seaver College to avoid scheduling classes and games on Wednesday evenings so that students could be free to attend campus ministry events, some of which were at his own home.[20]

Seeking Organizational Efficiency

From the commencement of his presidency, Davenport recognized weakness within the administrative status quo and sought to correct it. Of primary concern was fragmented decision-making and the lack of communication between the different units of the central administration and between the central administration and the various academic units, concerns often identified by WASC. Having read widely in the literature of organizational behavior, he tried to address the issue initially by streamlining the university's committee structure in fall 1986. He combined multiple administrative committees into just three: the provost's cabinet, the university planning committee, and the university budget committee. He also initiated a periodic management briefing session for the university at large.[21] Because the scheme worked effectively, its basic components survived into the twenty-first century.[22]

Davenport did further surgery on the university's administrative structure as of October 1, 1991. His principal objective was to remove "the territorial fences and molecular structures" that continued to characterize Pepperdine's management. Since his personal preference was a hierarchical and pyramid-like organization, his solution was to reconfigure the university's structure from six into three major operating areas: academic to be led by a provost; administrative to be under the direction of an executive vice president; and development, or fund-raising, to be led by an executive vice chancellor. The managers selected to head those areas were William Adrian, Andrew Benton, and Larry Hornbaker, respectively.[23]

Other functions, such as finance and student affairs, were either folded into one of the three basic operating areas or transferred to the individual schools. Seaver College, for example, was given responsibility for its own student recruitment, financial aid, student affairs, and international programs, in addition to its typical concern for academic processes. More importantly, it was also given budgetary responsibility for the college and its services, putting it on the same basis as the professional schools. This "pushing down" of real authority to the schools, however, effectively reduced the office of the provost to little more than chair of a holding company of deans. That reality was probably the deciding factor in Adrian's decision to retire from the position, return to the classroom, and ultimately leave the university.[24]

In addition to a quest for administrative efficiency, Davenport's realignment was also a response to concerns of WASC accreditors, who had long been puzzled by Pepperdine's organizational chart and governance procedures. The realignment also produced savings of at least $1 million annually, especially with the abolition of the university offices of administration, finance, and student affairs. This savings helped the university recover from a $4 million real estate investment in the Malibu Civic Center area that went bad. It also helped establish a $1 million Strategic Initiative Fund (SIF) that Davenport would use to finance non-base budget projects that directly impacted academic or student programs. SIF remained a critical funding source for faculty scholarship into the twenty-first century.[25]

Identifying Two (or Three) Peaks

Unlike most of his presidential predecessors, Davenport had thought deeply about educational theory and practice as it pertained to a university with a Christian mission. In an address to the Seaver College faculty in October 1990, he spoke of the "twin peaks" of a quality educational experience. Via one of the peaks, the university experience transformed students—mind and heart—into "whole persons." Such a transformation involved student learning and faculty caring in ways that were not often apparent in contemporary higher education. The other peak offered an education with Christian values at its center. Thus, a class in corporate law would look different at Pepperdine than would a class in corporate law at the University of Kansas. A "twin peaks" education, Davenport believed, would produce students with renewed minds and transformed natures, as described in Romans 12.[26]

Davenport acknowledged past confusion regarding the character and content of such an education at Pepperdine University. That confusion had been exacerbated by the university's move to hedonistic Malibu.[27] Certain individuals had found the institution guilty of being too religious, while others had found it not religious enough. Some academic programs within the institution ignored Christian mission and Church of Christ heritage, while others, especially at Seaver College, emphasized them. Some individuals deemed themselves disenfranchised because of the university's mission and its roots; others who were committed to that mission and those roots shied away from identifying Pepperdine as a Christian institution.

To make the most of the twin peaks, the president called upon his colleagues to nurture the school's relationship with Churches of Christ as the institution became more fully known as a Christian university. "I believe," he told a faculty audience in language reminiscent of his predecessors, "that if Pepperdine were to disconnect from those roots, that [it] would not continue over the long haul to be a Christian university." In the tree of education that was Pepperdine, the Church of Christ heritage represented the roots, a Christian university known for its spiritual diversity represented the trunk, and a values-centered education represented its fruit. The essence of a Christian university, Davenport declared, was its product, not the "critical mass" of administrators, faculty, and students who were members of Churches of Christ.[28] According to historian Richard Hughes, Davenport was "making room . . . for faculty of all religious persuasions and [encouraging them], regardless of religious orientation to contribute to Pepperdine's Christian mission."[29]

At various times, President Davenport would also emphasize a "third peak," what he called "real world experience" or useful/workplace education. Pedagogies included internships, service learning projects, and servant leadership experiences. To him those were "networks of light" that rounded out quality Christian education. He revisited the theme in the late 1990s, speaking of Pepperdine as a "connective university." The school's purpose was to help students connect multiple dimensions of life: theoretical with the practical, knowledge with service, scholarship with real life, and faith with learning.[30]

Although Davenport always advocated for service learning as a connective tool, after 1992, he seemed to place its value somewhat below his original "twin peaks" of transforming academic experience and Christian values. It troubled him that both academics and church folks—both on and off campus—insisted that academic excellence *and* Christian values were not simultaneous possibilities. In a 1994 address, "Coming of Age," Davenport took issue with the *either/or* approach. Pepperdine, he insisted, was about *both/and.* "Education," he said, was "not merely the dissemination of information for the mind, but it [was] also [about] the formation of a life and even the transformation of the character and values."[31] The quest to unify the two objectives put the university into a class of its own.[32]

Strategic Planning Emphasis

To get a better sense of what the university could and could not do—and also to respond to the constant criticisms of WASC—Davenport made strategic planning central to his administration. Using as beginning points the 1982 mission statement adopted by the board of regents and reviews of academic programs initiated the following year, he insisted that each school and program prepare its own mission statement and strategic plan. Those plans should address three major concerns: the development of excellence in academic programs, the development of a sense of university, and the demonstration of commitment to the university's mission and unique heritage. By late 1990, each of the schools, along with international programs, information resources, Payson library, and student development had adopted mission statements and strategic plans.[33]

Meanwhile, Davenport attempted to develop a coherent strategic plan for the university as a whole. Although various guidelines and goals were adopted in the next few years by strategic planning committees, they did not give birth to the strategic vision that Davenport desired. Accordingly, he directed the university planning committee to open its collective heart and come up with a vision that was radical and compelling, something that Pepperdine alone could do. He suggested it begin with three presumptions:

- that Pepperdine was a Christian university offering a values-centered education;
- that the university had high expectations and aspirations of itself, charted its own course, took risks, pursued opportunities, and could move quickly; and
- that education of the whole student was at the heart of all that was done.[34]

It was a compelling charge. No university-wide strategic plan on how to implement the presumptions emerged, however. As President Banowsky had said, such a plan would have required a fistfight.

New Set of Assumptions

Despite repeated attempts, the best Davenport could get was a new document titled the "University Assumptions for Academic Strategic Planning." Largely facilitated by Provost Steven Lemley, the document explicitly stated the values and descriptive assumptions that should guide Pepperdine's academic planning and decision-making. It contained descriptive segments on academics, the co-curriculum, the spiritual mission of the university, program delivery, and "Initiatives-1997 and beyond" (Drescher Campus, School of Public Policy, Institutes and Centers; Conference Centers; and Special Programs). Subsequently, it also included segments on assessment and adjunct faculty. After circulating the assumptions document to faculty and staff, the university planning committee formally adopted it on October 15, 1997. Thereafter, it was promoted by the university's leadership as a workable substitute for an institutional strategic plan.[35]

In one sense, the assumptions document pulled together the principles and practices embraced by the Davenport administration since 1985. It embraced the twin peaks philosophy of academic excellence and Christian mission, included the third peak of service learning, envisioned a 50 percent participation rate in international programs, and imagined a thriving upper campus at Malibu reserved for graduate education. In another sense, it represented a significant departure from business as usual. The document, for example, went to unusual lengths to describe what it deemed Pepperdine's unique view of teaching and learning: a blending of modern and postmodern educational concepts whereby the scholar/teacher, as a demanding but caring friend, joined students, "person[s] of infinite dignity" and the "heart of the educational enterprise," as truth and knowledge seekers. At Pepperdine, the educational process involved every facet of human personality, body, mind, and spirit.[36]

The document also declared that Pepperdine intended to cooperate with relevant accrediting bodies such as WASC. But there was a limit to that cooperation, and the university vowed to be "fiercely independent" if its mission and educational philosophy were threatened. Additional accreditations, including The American Association of Colleges and Schools of Business (AACSB), would be sought only when it was widely perceived that they would be consistent with the university's mission and of substantial benefit to students.[37]

The assumptions document also declared boldly that the university should plan to demonstrate clearly how students could adopt Pepperdine's Christian values for their own lives. It mandated that all schools—not just Seaver College—should address ways the university's Christian mission could impact students both in and out of the classroom and how faculty and staff could serve as role models consistent with the mission.[38]

Despite President Davenport's aversion to the concept, the document also embraced "critical mass" as a way of maintaining and advancing the university's Christian mission, heritage, and culture. It seemed an appropriate way to satisfy WASC's persistent demand that Pepperdine clarify how its Christian mission intersected with faculty hiring. Framers of the assumptions document held that maintaining a relationship with Churches of Christ via a group of faculty, staff, and student Church of Christ members was necessary to help Pepperdine retain its broader Christian identity. The document then boldly announced the preferred proportion of church faculty members: 60 percent for Seaver College, 30 percent for the School of Law and School of Public Policy, and 25 percent for GSEP and SBM.[39]

Significantly, the assumptions document did not include political and economic values as part of Pepperdine's distinctive values-centered education. Former presidents and some current staff would have easily combined political, economic, and Christian values, making a connection between the free-market economy and the Sermon on the Mount, or discounting any liability in Pepperdine's reputation as a Republican bastion. For Davenport, although a moderate Republican, that reputation was a problem. He took pride that the university had hosted political radical Tom Hayden at least five times and that he publicly contemplated voting for Texas maverick Ross Perot for president rather than George Bush in 1992. However, when Bill Clinton landed the presidential helicopter on the Pepperdine campus in his 1996 re-election campaign, Davenport sent Executive Vice President Andrew Benton to greet him.[40]

"Faith Is Our Fortune"

As the university planning committee was shaping the assumptions document, a spiritual development task force was trying to set clearer parameters of a Pepperdine values-centered education. Launched in 1996 and chaired by Associate Dean of Students Mark Davis, the task force endorsed the 60 percent critical mass figures for Seaver College in its final report, "Faith Is Our Fortune" (1998), and prescribed so much more. Utilizing the twin peaks imagery and a title that mirrored George Pepperdine's biography, the report described the objective of the college as providing first-class academic training in the liberal arts, building in the student a Christ-like life, and demonstrating a love for the church and a passion for the souls of mankind. It reviewed George Pepperdine's vision of his college as having been established to teach religious principles and build character. It defined "spiritual development" as something that happened when an agnostic developed a faith in God or when a thoughtful Christian was equipped for greater service to the kingdom—and all that lay in between.

In the interest of Seaver College continuing to grow in academic excellence and Christian commitment, the task force offered twenty-one recommendations. These included:

- better communicating how the Church of Christ heritage could sustain the life of the mind;
- recognizing that the desired proportion of active Christian students on campus was 65 to 70 percent;
- understanding that a "values-centered education" at Pepperdine meant a "Christ-centered education";
- making provisions for non-Church of Christ ministry groups on the Malibu campus;
- being more intentional in offering principles of the Christian faith in religion classes;
- helping students to integrate a Christian world view into their academic discipline; and
- becoming an affiliate member of the Coalition for Christian Colleges and Universities.

The task force concluded that implementing these and other recommendations could help the university assure the perpetuation of George Pepperdine's founding vision for his school: the building of Christian character and faith in its students.[41]

Purpose, Service, and Leadership

As the spiritual development task force was doing its work, President Davenport and a committee of administrators and faculty, with input from the entire community, were drafting a new statement of institutional mission intended to replace the statement adopted in 1982. It was presented to the board of regents on March 26, 1999; the regents adopted it unanimously after only minimal debate. Designed to clarify the specific content of values-centered education for all constituencies, especially for critics who complained that Pepperdine was a purveyor of secular values, the statement confidently declared that "Pepperdine University is a Christian University committed to the highest standards of academic excellence and Christian values, where students are strengthened for lives of purpose, service, and leadership." Davenport's twin peaks of quality—*both* academic excellence *and* Christian values—had prevailed as a declared mission.[42]

The identification of Pepperdine University as a "Christian" university in a board-approved mission statement culminated a fifteen-year process of re-envisioning the educational philosophy, organizational structure, strategic plans, and basic mission of the institution. The result lighted a distinctive path for the university to follow into the twenty-first century.

CHAPTER 44

SUPPORTING
CHRISTIAN MISSION

E ssential to Pepperdine's future, according to the Davenport administration, was retaining its historic relationship with Churches of Christ.
Over the years, the university had nourished a number of ties that held
it to the Church of Christ, believing those ties would help sustain the university's Christian mission and efforts to offer an excellent values-centered education. The Davenport years brought some innovation into the effort to fulfill
that mission.

On the Malibu campus, one way to nurture the church relationship was
for the university to host a Church of Christ congregation, which it had done
since 1972. That congregation took a quantum leap forward in its institutional
life when it appointed its first full-time minister, Dan Anders, in 1985, the same
year Davenport was inaugurated.[1] During Anders's twelve year ministry, the
congregation grew from 310 to 350 in Sunday morning attendance and from
$2,500 to $5,015 in weekly contributions.[2]

With offices in Tyler Campus Center and Sunday services in Elkins
Auditorium, it was deeply involved in international mission work, especially
in Mexico, but also in local benevolence activity. The congregation flourished
to the extent that university officials considered constructing a joint-use
Christian Center that would house the University Church, the religion graduate program, and a day-care center. The facility died aborning, however. The
possibility of a church building resurfaced in the late 1990s, but lingered as
only a faint possibility by the twenty-first century.[3]

The Role of Women

Like most Churches of Christ, the University congregation limited public worship roles and positions of authority to male members. Pepperdine also limited
women's roles in on-campus worship services, particularly convocation. In an

era and location sensitive to women's roles, this practice drew ire from believing females within the church and in the Pepperdine community at large. The issue was hotly debated for several years in relation to both Pepperdine services and worship services at the University Church of Christ, leading to changes in both locations although several years apart.

When it came to women participating in devotional segments of Seaver College convocation, the central administration initially defended its tradition of exclusion. Vice President John Watson noted that the limited role of women in convo preserved the university's long-term connection with Churches of Christ and hence its Christian mission.[4] But in the face of mounting criticism, especially from the *Graphic*, and after the University Church decided to hire a female campus minister, the Davenport administration agreed to re-evaluate the issue. The president felt strongly that the university was not the church, and was thus not bound to do things as the church did.[5]

Seaver College Dean John Wilson agreed but preferred that any change be incremental and start with women reading scripture, while Dean of Students D'Esta Love was graciously persistent in her support of a larger role for women in convocation.[6] A faculty vote showed widespread support for Love's position, affirming in a lopsided vote (73 to 13) that women should be encouraged to participate "in all religious leadership activities" of the university.[7] The religious standards committee of the board of regents took up the issue in December 1991. Persuaded by the arguments of the Davenport administration and impressed by the faculty support, the committee endorsed a measure authorizing participation of women in devotional settings at university functions, including convocation.[8]

In August 1992, at the first convocation of the academic year, women presented the devotional with Dean Love delivering a historic prayer. Many in the audience shed tears.[9] It was a major milestone in the history of Pepperdine and Churches of Christ—but it was not universally supported. Objectors included "Big" Don Williams, who protested by resigning from his position as assistant director of church services, instructor of religion, and principal recruiter of Church of Christ students. He had served the university for twenty-one years.[10]

The University Church did not alter its own worship practices in regards to women for several more years. However, in response to the climate of concerns and a serious re-evaluation of scripture, the University Church leadership began including women on worship teams and as co-leaders of congregational ministries. After May 1998, women began to participate as communion servers and scripture readers. By 2010, women were included in all church roles except for preaching and serving as elders.[11]

Campus Ministry

The principal outreach of the University Church was Campus Ministry (CM), which had begun in 1977. For well over a decade, it was the only "official" unit on the Malibu campus devoted to the spiritual development of students, but beyond worship services and Sunday Bible classes, it exercised that assignment tentatively, almost one-on-one until 1984. That year, at the suggestion of graduate student Lance Friis, CM organized "Care Group" in the Fireside Room in Tyler Campus Center where students could gather to praise, pray, learn, and fellowship every Wednesday evening. Under the leadership of Scott Lambert, who became the full-time campus minister in 1987, and LaJuana Gill, the first full-time female campus minister of the University Church appointed a few years later, Care Group soon attracted 100 to 115 students weekly, both members and nonmembers of Churches of Christ. By 1990, that number had increased to 200, more than the total number of Church of Christ students enrolled at Seaver College.[12]

CM also began organizing other spiritual life activities during the Davenport years. Annual fall retreats attracted 150 students initially and as many as 250 by the end of the 1990s. It organized outreaches to the Midnight

D'Esta Love served as dean of students from 1989–2001 and helped lead a campaign in the early 1990s to allow women to play a larger role in campus convocation services. In August 1992, she delivered a prayer at the first convocation of the academic year, a devotional led by women, which was a milestone for the university.

496 | Coming of Age 1985–2000

and Union Rescue missions in downtown Los Angeles; sent students to build houses in San Felipe, Mexico; and simulated hunger strikes to generate aid for churches in Croatia and Rwanda. It also welcomed hundreds of students from Church of Christ schools across the United States to World Mission Workshops in 1990 and 1997. In 1990, CM sent its first delegation of fifteen students on a Let's Start Talking (LST) mission to Brussels, Belgium. A similar CM team, composed of Ben Wall, Jeff Cooper, and Jason Hawes, traveled to post-Soviet Union Russia in 1991 and established the first Church of Christ in Moscow.[13] Thereafter, as many as three to five LST groups from Pepperdine University undertook international missions annually into the twenty-first century.[14]

Opening (Some) Religious Doors

Although Seaver College did not formally recognize student organizations that were "denominational" in character, CM was allowed because Churches of Christ thought of themselves as "nondenominational." In addition, CM received substantial university support and was not technically a student or church organization.[15] By the end of the 1990s, however, the reality of Pepperdine's religious diversity prompted the college to review its stance. Thereafter, Catholic, Jewish, and Protestant denominational students were allowed to organize as clubs (Newman, Hillel, and Campus Crusade for Christ), although they did not receive official recognition for a few more years.

The Office of Student Affairs also began providing an array of spiritual services through its spiritual life assistant (SLA) program. By the end of Davenport's presidency, consequently, CM was just one of several groups that ministered to the spiritual needs of Seaver College students.

Although Pepperdine was trying to broaden its Christian outreach, that outreach did not apply to the International Church of Christ (ICOC). Also known as the Crossroads or Boston movement, the ICOC had its genesis in the campus ministry program of the Crossroad Church of Christ in Gainesville, Florida, and came to national attention in Boston in the 1970s. Its evangelistic techniques were so intense that critics of the movement called it a cult. In fall 1993, ABC television's *20/20* program reported on the ICOC and suggested that it and mainline Churches of Christ were one and the same. This assertion raised red flags among some of Pepperdine University's supporters.

Davenport went out of his way to disassociate Pepperdine from the ICOC.[16] He had to repeat those efforts in 1999 when the ICOC tried to plant a congregation in Malibu. The effort failed, however, much to the relief of the Davenport administration.[17]

Nurturing Its Roots

When it came to the Churches of Christ at large, no one in the president's administrative circle wanted to sever those roots; in fact, the university actively worked to support churches, particularly through the office of church relations and the annual Bible Lectures. Under the continued leadership of Jerry Rushford, the Lectures thrived during the Davenport presidency. Attendance reached as high as 5,000, with participants coming from most states and dozens of foreign countries; most returned home with a sense of renewal and contentment that all was right with the spiritual world and Pepperdine University. No college or university related to the Churches of Christ got more positive public relations benefit from its lectureship than Pepperdine, or had more influence on the church because of it.

Equally beneficial in reassuring the church constituency were Christian Education Sundays, coordinated festivals for church youth groups, publication of the *Pacific Church News,* and performances of "Won by One," an a cappella student group formed in 1995 by the Seaver College admission office to help recruit Church of Christ students.[18]

Efforts of the Davenport administration to cultivate an active relationship with Churches of Christ reached all the way to Japan. In 1948, Pepperdine people, both staff and alumni—including E. W. McMillian and Harry Robert Fox—had played a major role in the establishment of Ibaraki Christian College (ICC). The relationship between ICC and Pepperdine continued through the years, although mostly informally. In 1994, Pepperdine located an international program on the ICC campus. That arrangement lasted for only two years, although the program's cancellation reflected primarily on the complicated educational calendar in Japan.[19]

Aiding Financially

Pepperdine also sought to demonstrate its commitment to Churches of Christ through its scholarship and financial aid programs. This was particularly evident in scholarships provided by the Associated Women for Pepperdine (AWP), drawn from a modest endowment and various fund-raising activities. AWP awards were restricted to students who were members of Churches of Christ and were awarded on the basis of need and merit. In the White administration, some seventy-five scholarships averaging $666 in value were given annually.[20]

By reducing the level of the grants, AWP was able to increase the number of awards to 225 beginning in 1993, hoping that the "honor of a scholarship" would attract more Church of Christ students to Seaver College. Simultaneously and according to college's strategic plan, the financial aid office began awarding aid to qualified, need-based students according to stipulated priority groups, the first of which was active Church of Christ members. The other three categories included students from minority groups, students with academic promise, and students with a talent for spiritual leadership. As directed by Seaver's strategic plan, John Wilson and his dean of admissions, Paul Long, were using scholarship funds to *shape* rather than *fill* classes.[21]

The new method of allocating scholarship funds had the desired effect. In 1985, as the Davenport presidency began, only 12.1 percent of the 2,567 Seaver College students were identified with Churches of Christ. In 2000, at the end of his term of service, that number had increased to 20.3 percent of a student body of 2,808, bettering Seaver College's strategic goal.[22]

Faculty Recruitment

Not as successful was the Davenport administration's active recruitment of faculty who were members of Churches of Christ. In 1985, only 69 of 204 faculty members at Pepperdine University, or 33.8 percent, were Church of Christ members. That increased to 39.2 percent by 1994, or 93 of 237. By 1998, it had slipped back to 37.5 percent, or 94 of 251. Some 73 percent of the faculty who were church members taught at Seaver College. Despite that preponderance, Seaver failed to reach its critical mass goal of 60 percent as stipulated in the assumption document, while the School of Law and the School of Public Policy matched or exceeded their goals of 30 percent each. GSEP and GSBM did not achieve their 25 percent goals, with GSEP totaling 21 percent and GSBM equaling only 10 percent.[23]

Meeting the critical mass goals remained difficult in part because administrative directives to recruit and hire Church of Christ faculty members always got pushback. Sometime the pushback was direct. One dean, for example, argued that candidates with Church of Christ religious affiliation were generally unqualified for the particular position being filled. Provost Adrian challenged that argument; from his vantage point he had no evidence that hiring members of Churches of Christ had "compromised" quality.[24]

On other occasions the pushback was indirect. In the hiring process, some argued, faculty preferences should be given preeminence, with faculty members making the final choice on the basis of academic credentials as opposed to church membership. In contrast, President Davenport and his administrative team held that the hiring process should involve *both* administration and faculty and the final appointment should be acceptable to both groups.[25] Another indirect pushback was when faculty argued in favor of a non-Church of Christ candidate in order to increase religious diversity at the university, a status hard to criticize but one that ran counter to critical mass goals.[26]

More disconcerting to Seaver Dean Wilson, however, was when special efforts were made to hire a new faculty member who was a member of Churches of Christ, only to watch as that person later decided church membership was burdensome. The individual had proclaimed membership to get the job but would abandon it later, especially after she or he got tenure.[27]

Creating a Christian Environment

The Davenport administration readily agreed that cultivating Christian-centered values required more than a certain percentage of people with roots in the Churches of Christ. Throughout its history, Pepperdine University had counted upon certain required activities to sustain the desired Christian environment, including chapel/convocation attendance for undergraduates. Weekly convo attendance was required during the Davenport administration, although credit was available through several options. Chapel/convo still opened with prayer, and speakers often had spiritual messages, but it was hardly a worship service.

The desired Christian environment also rested on rules regulating student behaviors, including dress codes, residence hall visitation regulations, prohibition of alcohol on campus or at campus events, restricted areas for smoking, and limits on dancing, to name only a few. These requirements had been weakened before Davenport's presidency, and they softened even further during it, so much so that a national publication described Seaver as being "Bible College lite."[28]

For those who thought deeply about the subject, issues such as dress codes or dancing had little to do with Pepperdine's commitment to Christian values. That was certainly the position of Dean John Wilson of Seaver College, who at a 1988 faculty conference, defined Christian values as "whatever Jesus Christ valued." Of those, he identified three that seemed particularly pertinent to Pepperdine:

1. it was more valuable to be right than rich;
2. it was more valuable to serve than to be served;
3. it was more valuable to love than to win.

After an extended theological discussion of each value, Wilson concluded: "I find myself in an institution which publicly identifies itself, not only with this visionary, uncompromising prophet [Jesus Christ], but even, and specifically, with his values." After a poignant pause, he concluded, "Are we ready for this? Is it really what we want to do?"[29]

He was not quite sure that the university was ready. Clearly the administration did not want it to be a "free-floating 'Christian' school" unattached to

Churches of Christ, Wilson subsequently told the university planning committee. But it was becoming that, if not worse. SBM was virtually secular, and GSEP was diminished if not moribund when it came to Christian mission. Wilson granted that Seaver College was committed to "Christian values," although those values were amorphous. Faculty members were mildly interested but negative toward Churches of Christ.[30]

Some of the faculty most negative toward the church, Wilson held, had been hired between 1977 and 1980 during the tenure of Academic Vice President John Nicks. Those appointees, some of whom who had publicly advocated for ending the Church of Christ relationship, now held influential positions in the governance of Seaver College. Wilson found troubling the idea that Nicks was at that time applying the type of hiring policies responsible for the tension at Seaver at SBM, which, because of strong leadership, public relations skills, and good connections, dominated the image and nature of Pepperdine in the public's opinion. If the circumstances at SBM were uninterrupted, Wilson argued, Christian-centered education will "die with us."[31]

Help from Lilly

Obviously, the Christian university Wilson envisioned required more than chapel attendance, a strict dress code, and faculty role modeling. He agreed with Davenport that it should not be possible to separate academic instruction from a focus on values at a Christian university and that the educational enterprise required an integration of learning and faith in the curriculum and co-curriculum, in the classroom and on the athletic court, in the laboratory as well as the seminar room. If the university's values were to be the values of Jesus Christ, there could be no dichotomy of thought and action.

No one on at Pepperdine was quite sure *how* to combine faith and learning, however. Certainly it was beyond the experiences of most Pepperdine administrators and faculty. Fortunately, the Lilly Endowment in Indianapolis was interested in the mission and health of Christian liberal-arts institutions like Pepperdine. In 1991, it formed a network of such schools to encourage the integration of faith and learning. Thanks to the petitions of Professor of Religion Richard Hughes and Professor of Political Science Stephen Monsma and the interest of Provost Bill Adrian, Pepperdine became a charter member of the Lilly Network.[32]

Out of this came an awareness of other institutions of different denominational traditions that were also seeking to perpetuate their historic missions by combining academic excellence with values-centered instruction. In cooperation with Valparaiso University, the Lilly Foundation sponsored annual conferences of network members to discuss how best to integrate faith and learning on university campuses. Pepperdine representatives attended those conferences faithfully and even replicated them on the Malibu campus.[33]

Thanks to a grant from the Pew Foundation, Hughes and Monsma hosted a national conference on "Christian Primitivism and Modernization" in June 1991. The next year, thanks to a Lilly-funded grant, they hosted a summer seminar for Pepperdine faculty on integrating a Christian world view in the classroom. The teachers were the foremost scholars in the field: George Marsden, then at Duke Divinity School; Nathan Hatch, then at University of Notre Dame; and Nicholas Wolterstorff at Yale.[34]

In 1993, with Hughes and Adrian as principal investigators, Pepperdine won a $440,000 grant over five years from the Lilly Foundation to study "how religious mission and quality academics can be effectively integrated at 14 Christian institutions of higher learning." That grant resulted in six regional conferences on the topic and one widely acclaimed book: *Models for Christian Higher Education: Strategies for Success in the Twenty-First Century* (1997). Pepperdine University was one of the models.[35]

Center for Faith and Learning

Given Pepperdine's growing reputation in the field, the Davenport administration created its own Center for Faith and Learning in 1999. The center's task was to help make the university a national leader in efforts to combine the ideals of Christian faith with the ideals of the academy. It would do so by facilitating on-campus faculty seminars and regional conferences, encouraging faith-based scholarship, and hosting distinguished Christian scholars. To be director of the new center, the university appointed Richard Hughes, who was widely known both on and off campus for advocating that the life of the mind and Christian faith were complementary rather than contradictory, especially when it came to diversity and academic freedom. Moreover, he was convinced that there was much within the heritage of Churches of Christ to sustain the life of the mind. Hughes would report to the provost.[36] The center received a special grant from the Lilly Fellows Program to facilitate a biannual conversation among Lilly Network schools in Southern California, which included California Lutheran University, Loyola Marymount University, and Westmont College, on what it meant to be a church-related educational institution.[37]

As a new century began, therefore, there was a growing consensus that academic excellence and Christian values *did* mix at Pepperdine, a general realization that the school had not fully experienced since E. V. Pullias was dean, if even then. President Davenport's advocacy of twin peaks of Christian education rooted in Churches of Christ faith and practice seemed sustainable.[38]

CHAPTER 45

A RISING REPUTATION

I n 1987, Pepperdine University celebrated its fiftieth anniversary. Led by
Vice President Michael Adams, the Pepperdine administration was eager
to use the moment to review the university's remarkable progress and celebrate its promising future under the slogan, "The spirit of the past; the wave
of the future." A full menu of celebrations and commemorations took place
during 1987, but three were particularly notable.

The first occurred on New Year's Day when the university sponsored a float
in the 98th Tournament of Roses Parade in Pasadena, California. Christened
"Quest for Atlantis" in recognition of Pepperdine's effort to provide a dynamic
environment in which to pursue knowledge, the float included six columns
sculpted into Grecian gods and goddess and was adorned with thirteen variet-
ies of flowers, plus seaweed strands. Six Pepperdine students dressed in the
flowing robes of ancient Greece, stood on the edges of the float.[1]

A fund-raising campaign gathered the $150,000 to pay for the float, and
students, alumni, and friends of the university decorated it.[2] Some students
complained that the float was hardly worth the expense, but others said building the float had induced a "real sense of unity and pride." Seaver student Scott
Honour described the crowd response to the float along the parade route as
"amazing." "In the long run people will remember Pepperdine," he said.[3]

University officials also hosted a "Golden Wave Weekend" on September
19–21, 1987. The weekend began on Saturday evening with a black-tie dinner of
the Pepperdine University Associates at the Beverly Hilton. On Sunday morning, the University Church met for worship services in Firestone Fieldhouse
with Howard White delivering a sermon on "The Christian Heritage of
Pepperdine University." There followed numerous activities, including an old-
fashioned barbecue in Alumni Park, alumni art exhibits, musical acts, and
burial of a time capsule in front of the Thornton Administrative Center to be
opened in September 2037.[4]

On Monday the university hosted a formal convocation in a field house full of students, alumni, and friends. Board of regent's chair Thomas Bost gave the invocation, while former chair Donald Miller, who had been on the podium when Pepperdine College opened, led the Pledge of Allegiance. President Davenport awarded Alumni Medals of Honor to twelve outstanding alumni, the first such recognition in the history of the university.[5] Among these was J. Richard Chase (BA '53, MA '54), the president of Wheaton College, who also delivered an address titled "Hope: The Heart of Education."[6]

Many returned in the afternoon to partake of an intellectual feast offered by members of the faculty, including Professor of Business Jere Yates, Howard A. White Professor of History James L. McDonough, Professor of Education Terence R. Cannings, Professor of Business Paul Foote, Professor of Religion Jerry Rushford, Professor of Communication Fred L. Casmir, and Professor of Law Charles I. Nelson. The Golden Wave Weekend was a clear reminder of the transformation of George Pepperdine College from a small denominational college in south central Los Angeles to a national university with a rising academic reputation. Or, as one newspaper reporter declared: "Pepperdine, once derided by academic snobs as an obscure church school that owed its existence to the generosity of the founder . . . has come of age."[7]

Illustrating that coming of age was the intent of the publication of a commemorative book, *Crest of the Golden Wave*. Jerry Rushford edited the 310-page, coffee-table size volume of narrative and pictures. Former President White wrote the historical narrative that wound its way through five chapters, while Patti Yomantas, then director of foundations and special communications, wrote the biographical essays on each of Pepperdine's six presidents. The book made no claim of being a comprehensive or critical history of the university's first fifty years but was published to help celebrate its progress. Like the sundial, therefore, it counted only Pepperdine's sunny hours.[8]

WASC Comes Back

Notably, the anniversary year coincided with WASC's next scheduled review. The previous visit in 1982 culminated in a report that was about as good as it ever got in the long relationship between WASC and Pepperdine University. Vice President William Phillips assumed responsibility for preparing the self-study for the 1987 visit.

The completed self-study responded thoroughly to the concerns WASC visitors had expressed five years earlier. Space needs at Seaver had been relieved by the remodel of Payson Library and construction of the Thornton Administrative Center, the Stauffer Telecommunications Center, Heritage Hall, and the completion of the music wing of the Fine Arts Center. It would be relieved further by upcoming completion of the Cultural Arts Center. Moreover, substantial revision of general education requirements and additional faculty had strengthened the liberal arts curriculum of Seaver College; admission and exit standards in GSEP had been made more explicit; SBM policies regarding outside activities of full-time faculty had been tightened; and more full-time faculty served the programs offered at the educational centers.[9]

A four-person WASC team visited Pepperdine in December 1987. On the basis of the team's report, the senior commission in February 1988 reaffirmed the accreditation of the university "without reference to any specific stipulation or requirement." But it did raise a substantial number of new concerns that the university should address before the next visiting committee arrived. Among these were the lack of a university-wide vision, a governance model that involved faculty in priority setting and decision-making, and an effective strategic planning process. Concerning to the accreditors were tension between academic quality at Pepperdine and the need for maximum enrollment; variation in faculty load, compensation, and performance evaluation across schools; that the Church of Christ factor in determining appointments was ambiguous and confusing; and that there was an absence of vigor in affirmative action. In the minds of the visitors, laboratory space at Seaver College was inadequate; undergraduate business programs at SBM and Seaver were not coordinated; resources within Seaver were inadequate to meet new general education requirements; Seaver overrelied on "objective test taking" instead of critical writing skills; and admission and exit standards at GSEP needed to be more explicit.[10] WASC's next visit was scheduled for October 1992.[11]

President Davenport appreciated the thoroughness of the report but was concerned about whether it captured the essential nature and spirit of the university, particularly its Christian mission. He recognized, however, that the university needed to improve its processes, especially those relating to strategic planning. In all, the WASC experience confirmed rather than challenged Pepperdine's rising reputation.[12]

Riding an Excellent Wave

So too did the university's $100 million "Wave of Excellence Campaign," the institution's second capital campaign, which had been unveiled in 1984. All funds raised, said campaign coordinator Mike Adams, would work to support the university's objectives: academic excellence, maintenance of a religious and ethical heritage, support of the free enterprise system, a quality faculty with a values-centered world view, an atmosphere of freedom, and a curriculum that educated leaders for tomorrow. All of these goals were matters of immense importance to the economic elite and political conservatives of

Southern California. By the time the campaign was finished in 1989, those donors had given 90 percent of the $138 million raised.[13]

Because of the Wave of Excellence campaign, Pepperdine was judged to be among the top ten most successful universities in fund-raising efforts. Adams found the success remarkable. He wrote President Davenport that "virtually nobody in the country believes we raise the kind of money we do with almost no alumni support and no support from wills and bequests."[14]

The benefits of the campaign were tangible. The university's endowment increased to nearly $80 million, up from $56 million. Gifts from the campaign also paid for the construction of four major buildings. These were the Thornton Administrative Center (TAC), for which dedication ceremonies were held on January 18, 1987;[15] the extensive renovation and expansion of Payson Library, dedicated on April 26, 1987;[16] the John Stauffer Telecommunication building, dedicated on December 1, 1987; and the Cultural Arts Center (CAC), dedicated in November 1991 with a nine-day gala featuring Hollywood celebrities.[17] The campaign also provided funding for purchase of the Prince's Gate property in London in 1987 and partial funding of Phase II of the School of Law (completed in 1992) and permanent facilities for SBM on the Malibu campus, not completed until 2003.[18]

In addition, Wave of Excellence donors funded nine endowed faculty chairs and professorships. Among these were the D. & L. Straus Chair of Law, the Julian Virtue Chair of Economic and Entrepreneurial Education, the Muriel Lipsey Chair of Counseling and Clinical Psychology, the Corwin Denney Chair of Business, the Carl P. Miller Chair of Journalism, the Flora Thornton Chair in Nutrition, and the Howard A. White Chair in History. The campaign also permitted curriculum initiatives, including a focus on volunteerism and service-learning pedagogy in Seaver College, and established eighty new scholarship programs and eleven new loan funds.

To the satisfaction of WASC, Payson library also benefitted from the campaign beyond just a renovated building. The Davenport administration added new facilities for educational media, the university archives, and academic computing. The catalog and checkout system were computerized, and 15,000 books damaged by the broken water main were repaired and returned to their shelves.[19]

Pepperdine University libraries offered patrons a full-text database that faculty, staff, and students could access from offices, residence halls, or homes. By 1995, "Pepperdine TitleWave" provided passage into electronic periodical indexes and 1,425 additional full-text titles. Four years later, librarians counted 565,791 volumes in the university library collection (excluding the law school). The base library budget was up 52 percent, yet that was only 3.29 percent of Pepperdine's total expenditure for educational and general purposes, well below the 6 percent recommended by the Association of College and Research Libraries. Limited budgets mirrored inadequate space and other services at the educational centers, weaknesses that WASC visitors almost always noted. In 2000, they also concluded that Payson Library looked dingy, in part because it continued to use furniture that had come from the old Los Angeles campus.[20]

During the Davenport administration, various forms of technology came to exert a critical force in the life of the university. By 2000, the university provided robust networking and telecommunications infrastructures; production mainframe, mid-range and server systems; a full range of photocopy services; and complete support for specific standard desktop computing platforms. During the summer of 1999, the university migrated to the Windows NT Network Operating System that permitted the exchange of information anywhere in the world via a standard web browser and internet connection. The university was a "wired" institution.[21]

Better Students, More Faculty

By most objective measures, the academic quality of the freshman class improved during the Davenport administration as GPA, SAT, and ACT scores all rose significantly. Between 1985 and 2000, high school GPAs of enrolled freshmen improved from 3.23 to 3.57. Composite SAT scores (verbal and math) rose from 1,032 to 1,200, while ACT scores increased from 23 to 26. The selectivity rate also improved. In 1985, of the 2,507 who applied for admission to Seaver College, 57 percent were admitted with 46 percent of those students actually enrolling. Fifteen years later, of the 5,105 who applied, 36 percent were admitted with 35 percent ultimately enrolling.[22] By 2000, then, the freshman class was better qualified academically, and the admission process was more selective, although the yield rate (those who actually enrolled as compared to admitted students) had softened.[23]

Retention and graduation rates also rose. The one-year retention rate improved from 79.4 percent to 89.3 percent between 1987 and 1999. Five-year graduation rates, however, rose, fell, then rose again: from 64.8 percent for the class entering in 1987 to 72.7 percent for the class entering in 1992, to 65.3 percent for the class entering in 1995. By 2005, those rates reached 81 percent.[24]

The overall number of full-time equivalent student (FTES) remained relatively stable during the Davenport era, with an upward trajectory. University-wide, they totaled 5,825 in fall 1989 and 6,726 in fall 2000, an increase of some 15.6 percent. Seaver College enrollments were also up 15.6 percent, from 2,365 to 2,735. GSEP had a hefty increase of nearly 89 percent, from 759 to 1,360. SBM and the School of Law remained steady with enrollments of some 1,950 and 700 respectively.[25]

In direct response to WASC concerns, faculty numbers, both full- and part-time, increased. In 1989 there were 371 full-time equivalent faculty (FTEF) university-wide. Of that number, Seaver College had 47 percent, although it had just under 41 percent of the total student body. In 2000 there were 474 FTEF across the university, with the proportions of faculty and students unchanged for Seaver College. In 1989, the student/faculty ratio for the university was 15.7 to 1, which improved to 14.1 to 1 by 2000. For the same time period, the ratios for Seaver College decreased from 13.4 to 12.3 to 1. By comparison, at the beginning of the twenty-first century, GSBM had a ratio of 16.8 to 1, GSEP 15 to 1, and the School of Law 16.1 to 1.[26]

As the number of FTEF rose during the Davenport era, so too did economic circumstances of faculty. In 1986, AAUP data ranked total compensation paid to Pepperdine's faculty in the top 5 percent of all comprehensive universities nationwide. With benefits, that amounted to $58,300 annually for full professors, $47,400 for associate professors, and $39,700 for assistant professors. According to Academic Vice President Phillips, however, the salaries appeared higher than they were because of the high cost of living in Southern California. Professor Steven Sale said, "We have a ways to go based on the equity of where we have to live, but I see signs of sincere interest in providing fair salaries from the administration."[27]

Indeed the Davenport administration had a reputation of paying competitive salaries. In 1999 Pepperdine salaries plus benefits remained in the 95th percentile nationally, averaging $112,300 for professors, $93,100 for associate professors, and $77,900 for assistant professors. Of course, these were just an average, with the higher salaries at SBM outweighing the lower salaries of the liberal arts faculty in Seaver College.[28]

Teaching AND Research

More competitive salaries brought higher expectations of the Pepperdine faculty. Throughout its history, Pepperdine's administrators had always favored the primacy of teaching. Early in his administration, contrary to the expectations of WASC, Davenport celebrated Pepperdine's emphasis on teaching rather than research. In his view, one of the "most significant problems in higher education [was] that universities tended to define excellence in terms of research or scholarly contribution to an academic field rather than teaching students."[29] Seaver College Dean John Wilson, an accomplished scholar himself, tended to agree with the president.[30]

Both were delighted when Charles Luckman, architect and friend of the university, funded a substantial cash award to recognize effective teaching beginning 1990. The Charles Luckman Distinguished Teaching Award went to six, then nine faculty: three to five from Seaver College and one to two from each of the other three Pepperdine schools. Recipients were chosen by their peers, and each Luckman fellow received a $3,000 stipend annually for three years. The Luckman program was a noble gesture underscoring Pepperdine's belief in the primacy of teaching, but long-term, it did not work as well as the sponsor had hoped, becoming something of a popularity contest. And it was expensive, some $81,000 a year at its peak. After 1994, the program was terminated, later replaced by the Howard A. White Distinguished Professor program.[31]

Only Provost William Adrian took some exception to the prevailing Pepperdine view of the primacy of teaching. From his perspective, academic scholarship facilitated professional growth of individual faculty; it was the nutrient that kept the plant green. In Adrian's judgment, research was a natural expectation of each faculty person, but—to the disappointment of his faculty colleagues—he did not believe it should be dependent upon released time from classroom responsibilities.[32] Adrian was supported by a vocal minority of Seaver College faculty—and WASC accreditors, who feared overemphasis on teaching at Pepperdine risked intellectual isolation of the institution.[33]

In time Davenport came to see that engaging students in serious research activities was an active-learning pedagogy that was far more effective than a passive-learning methodology facilitated by a "sage on a stage." Following the 1990 publication of Ernest Boyer's *Scholarship Reconsidered*, he came to understand there were different types of academic scholarship, including discovery, the integration of knowledge, the application of knowledge, and study of pedagogical techniques. He also became significantly more supportive when the academic affairs committee of the board of regents was reluctant to grant tenure to faculty candidates who had no scholarly publications.

By 1996, the academic climate at Pepperdine had so changed that the annual faculty conference featured the scholarly activity of the faculty and encouraged more. Moreover, a section defining the different dimensions of scholarship as categorized by Boyer was embedded in the assumption document that was to guide strategic planning in the university. At Seaver College this meant that scholarship came to be required for promotion within the professorial ranks: either one peer-reviewed book or three peer-reviewed papers for promotion to associate and an equal number of additional publications for promotion to professor.[34]

Davenport's change of attitude toward research might have been aided by the National School Safety Center (NSSC) federal grant, which returned first 10 and then 50 percent as an overhead charge. By early 1985 that totaled

$123,000 per annum, with 45 percent going to the university's general fund and 10 percent to academic units. The remaining 45 percent went to the University Research Council to be allocated to faculty performing research and writing proposals that could generate additional overhead. President Davenport insisted that the NSSC overhead funds be used as seed money, as "a base of research funds that will endure for many years, and not be depleted." Organized in the spring of 1985, the University Research Council within two years had funded forty-three separate faculty projects for a total of $168,493. Such funding continued through 1996, although overhead funds were never as abundant as desired. By December 1996, the grant fund budget was in deficit, and seed money was no longer available.[35]

Like his Pepperdine predecessors, Davenport wanted the university to fund its own research as he wanted no contractual obligations to the federal government. He was willing to live with federal government grants like those from the National Science Foundation or to the National School Safety Center, but only fitfully.[36]

During the Davenport years, Pepperdine also made an effort to recruit respected scholars and teachers for senior tenured positions, some of whom were hired to fill the endowed chairs funded by the Wave of Excellence campaign. Other notable appointees included Dwayne Van Rheenen, who joined the Seaver faculty as professor of communication, and Fulbright and Rotary scholar George Neilson, professor of theater. Thomas H. Olbricht, one of the foremost biblical scholars and teachers in Churches of Christ, came as professor and chair of the religion division, an appointment that President Davenport believed was, excepting the presidency, the most important in the university. Dean Wilson called Olbricht's coming a "watershed" moment in the history of Pepperdine, especially in its relationship with Churches of Christ.[37]

The selection of Pepperdine faculty as Fulbright scholars was also an indicator of an improving reputation. In 1986, Robert Wright, professor of organizational theory at the SBM, became the first applicant from Pepperdine to win an appointment as a Fulbright scholar; Wright worked at the New University of Lisbon in Portugal.[38] Roy Adler, professor of marketing at Seaver College, followed Wright; his appointment was also in Lisbon in 1987. Others followed in subsequent years, with all coming from SBM or Seaver. [39]

More Tenure Reviews

Meeting WASC's expectations also meant further attention to faculty tenure issues. At issue were the matters of financial exigency, appeals processes, mandatory retirement, and five-year reviews.[40] The process began just as Davenport was named president-in-waiting in April 1984 and moved at warp speed in comparison to the drafting of the primary tenure policy three years earlier. The board of regents approved the modifications five months later in September.[41] Tenure policies and procedures underwent modest revisions again in 1986.[42]

But from the administration's point of view, the amended tenure policy still retained far too many ambiguities and inconsistencies. General Counsel Gary Hanson and Provost Adrian were particularly sensitive to those uncertainties. Hanson substantially rewrote the university tenure policy in 1991–1992, although he did not plan to make substantive changes. Any material alteration in the policy statement was nothing more than an "attempt to simplify, clarify, and remove the inconsistencies that naturally [arose] when a policy [was] modified piecemeal over the years." The resulting draft had extensive stylistic revisions but few changes that were deemed substantive.[43]

Provost Adrian saw to it that the document drafted by Hanson was widely circulated throughout the university both for discussion and endorsement. The process engendered good feedback as well as ownership. Indeed, one member of the faculty at SBM was "heartened by the serious thought" his colleagues put into the review, "and by the constructive nature of the criticism."[44]

After two years of drafting and review, the Davenport administration submitted the revised tenure statement to the board of regents on June 8, 1993. The document was adopted unanimously. Noticeably different in style, it included important clarifications of the tenure process at the university. For example, it clearly described the tenure review process, which began with the school tenure committee, proceeded to the dean of the school, then to the university tenure committee, on to the university administration (defined as the president and the provost), and finally to both the religious standards and academic affairs committees of the board of regents.

The document also stipulated that all faculty members would normally apply for tenure during their sixth year of service rather than the fifth. The revised tenure statement explained more clearly a formal appeals process, placing the burden of proof on the faculty grievant. Finally, the document also spoke to the circumstances of financial exigency, defining a representative body to be consulted before its declaration and stipulating that non-tenured professors would be terminated before tenured professors.[45]

Remarkably, the 1993 version of the tenure policy stood as the governing statement without revision until 2006. Given all of the heat between faculty and administration that issues of tenure had generated over the years, it was a testimony to the Davenport administration that such equanimity prevailed with the new policy. Surely it spoke to the level of trust that prevailed between the principal players, to the skills of a new generation of leadership, the value of a year-long vetting process, and to a rising level of institutional maturity.

Collaborative and Consultative

According to the norms of higher education as promulgated by WASC, a national reputation required faculty that participated in the governance of the university. The Davenport administration embraced that hypothesis and sought to institute a "collaborative [and] consultative" model of participation. The chosen model was not "faculty governance," but neither was it the administrative paternalism of former years.[46]

Illustrative of the collaborative approach, according to Provost Lemley, was faculty representation on the newly formed University Planning Committee (UPC), a major administrative committee charged to review all strategically allocated resources. He also saw evidence of the new approach when faculty participated prominently in a 1994 search for a new SBM dean, "the first truly national search for a senior administrator." He noted as well that all deans were formally evaluated by their particular faculty beginning 1994–1995 and that faculty helped fashion the tenure statement in 1991–1993.[47]

He could also have mentioned its participation in drafting the assumptions document and different school strategic plans. By 2000 there was strong faculty representation on the university's four primary committees: UPC, University Faculty Committee (UFC), the University Academic Council (UAC), and the University Tenure Committee (UTC).[48]

Reining in Tuition Increases

To meet the expectations not only of WASC, but also of faculty, staff, and students, required the university to have a solid financial basis. Neither educational excellence nor Christian mission would reach fruition without money to pay for it. Under Davenport's leadership, the university's financial resources improved significantly between 1985 and 1999. Not only did the university continue its succession of balanced budgets, but total assets more than tripled during the period, from $252 million to $808 million. Total liabilities went from $68 million to $214 million. Total consolidated revenues increased from $76 million to $213. Consolidated expenses kept pace, increasing from $69 million to $154 million. The market value of endowment funds increased from $59 million to $335 million, while the value of campus property increased more modestly, from $128 million to $184 million. Operating budgets nearly doubled during the Davenport years, from $78 million to $142 million.[49]

At first glance, the financial standing of the university looked strong. Consultants Cambridge Associates of Boston, however, were worried about Pepperdine's rising tuition rates and student charges. Between 1987 and 1990, increases averaged 9 percent, climbing to just below the rates charged by Stanford. The Cambridge group feared that the rising tuition increases were not sustainable; in addition, it predicted that the competition for students, especially in Southern California, would require substantial amounts of financial aid, a further drain on Pepperdine's bottom line.[50]

The consultants were concerned because Pepperdine was "much more tuition-dependent than any other institution in the comparison group." In 1990, they noted, 75 percent of the university's revenue came from tuition, up 10 percent from five years earlier. The more dependent the university was on tuition, the consultants counseled, the "more vulnerable" it was to tuition price competition. To guard against such consequences, Cambridge Associates recommended that Pepperdine diversify its revenue base. The graduate programs had provided significant revenue in the past, but growth in those programs seemed to be slowing. As alternatives, the firm recommended tapping alumni-giving potential and recommended concentrated effort to enlarge the endowment to some $450 million.[51]

Provost Adrian thought the Cambridge study overstated the problems somewhat but supported the study's conclusions overall. As he told his administrative colleagues in early 1990, the problem that dwarfed all others was keeping tuition and other charges down "to a reasonable level." Pepperdine was already one of the most expensive institutions in the country.[52]

Adrian's argument resonated with his colleagues, and the percentage of tuition increases at Pepperdine declined steadily between 1991 and 1999, from 6.88 percent to 4.31 percent. By the end of the Davenport era, tuition, fees, and room and board totaled $31,300 per year, up from $13,375 from 1985, or 43 percent. The four-year cost was $125,000 rather than the $200,000 Adrian had feared.[53] Still, Pepperdine was the fourth most expensive in total costs of any independent school of higher education in California. Average debt per graduate was $21,669, although only 60 percent had any debt.

Defying Classification

The Davenport administration's efforts to burnish Pepperdine's reputation as a distinctive player in the higher education community were reflected by evaluations of external ranking agencies, especially *U.S. News & World Report*. In 1985, the university was first in its class in schools in the Midwest or Far West.[54] In 1987, a reclassification meant that Pepperdine was not even listed in the publication, a disappointment to some administrators and faculty. The absence, according to the university's *Annual Report*, was because "Pepperdine is impossible to categorize. It is unlike any other institution anywhere, and it defies pigeonholing. In some ways, it is out of place on any list except the one it has created for itself."[55]

However, Pepperdine did return to the list in 1990, when it was ranked at the top of the second quartile of 200 national universities.[56] It made the first quartile in 1992 but did not climb that high again until 2001 with a ranking of forty-ninth.[57]

Pepperdine also received positive rankings through the 1990s from the Templeton Foundation, which included the university on its "Honor Roll for Character Building Colleges" and on its "Honor Roll of Free Enterprise Teaching." For the academic year of 1997–1998, it listed Pepperdine as an outstanding example of the best in American higher education. Earlier in the decade, the politically conservative *National Review* had listed Pepperdine among the fifty best liberal arts colleges in the nation.

Seven years into his presidency, David Davenport had every reason to conclude that Pepperdine University was building a solid reputation in independent higher education. Thus, in 1992, when leadership prepared for WASC's reaccreditation visit, the sense that the school was worthy of its rising reputation pervaded the self-study.

CHAPTER 46

MORE ACCREDITATION CHALLENGES, MORE FUND-RAISING SUCCESSES

Under the leadership of Provost William Adrian, Pepperdine University began preparing for the 1992 WASC visit some three years in advance. Kay Andersen, the retired executive director of WASC's senior commission, visited the campus twice as a consultant to discuss new guidelines and procedures for the self-study process. In September 1990, President Davenport appointed a steering committee to coordinate the self-study and accreditation visit. Norman Hughes and I, both Seaver faculty members, cochaired the committee, which was assisted by nine task forces organized according to the different evaluative standards.

Draft reports were complete by July 1991, and in October, a combined faculty and management conference examined the reports, the first time in Pepperdine's history that a self-study for WASC had been openly discussed. After revisions to the documents were made, student groups from each college and the board of regents reviewed the draft and suggested modifications; more revisions were made. In August of 1992, Adrian sent copies of the completed document to WASC.[1]

The self-study first addressed concerns raised by WASC in 1987, noting dramatic improvements in those areas, especially in getting the constituent parts of Pepperdine to think and behave like a *uni*-versity: creating mission statements, implementing strategic plans, and streamlining management, as described in chapter 43.[2] According to the self-study, the university continued to give preference in hiring faculty and administrators to candidates who professed Christian faith, particularly membership in Churches of Christ. Nonetheless, it sought greater cultural diversity via recruitment, enrichment programs and curricular innovations, and had achieved a 4 percent increase—from 14 to 18—of minority representation in the student body although there had been less change within the faculty.[3]

The self-study referenced changes both in physical facilities and academics in the previous five years, including the construction of the Cultural Arts Center and renovation of Payson Library, the addition of ten additional tenure-track faculty at Seaver College (106 in 1986 to 116 in 1991), the conversion of the library's holdings to the Library of Congress classification system, and a decision to keep separate the undergraduate business programs at Seaver and SBM. Seaver College, the report noted, was maintaining academic integrity in Western Heritage classes through critical writing assignments, and GSEP had taken measures to tighten admission and retention requirements.[4]

The WASC team who visited campus October 20–23, 1992, reported that Pepperdine was "an institution of many strengths," including "extraordinary attention to students," achievement of "high levels of student satisfaction with the instructional program," building of "a beautiful and functional campus in a relatively short time," engagement in "strategic planning within the individual academic units," use of educational centers for a "significant program in professional education at the graduate level," and a "challenging general education program."[5]

Negative Tone Overall

But those general compliments aside, the visiting team's report to the senior commission was fairly negative. It expressed misgivings about the lack of consistency in the university's description of its mission and priorities, noting that Pepperdine's religious orientation did not appear in SBM's extensive advertising of its programs. It also asserted that the university's "denominational screen," or the preference given to Church of Christ members, did not serve the hiring and promotion process well.[6]

The visitors were also concerned about the "intellectual rigor and requirement for high student performance" at all schools. They were concerned about the impact of uneven funding on the various schools and critical of the university's heavy reliance on part-time faculty. Seizing upon comments by both President Davenport and Seaver Dean Wilson that downplayed the significance of research, the team feared that the university risked becoming intellectually isolated because of its "very heavy orientation to teaching and slight emphasis on even very broadly conceived scholarship." It thought educational quality had become hostage to the priority given to buildings and facilities of all types.[7]

According to the WASC team, Pepperdine seemed sincere in its wish to improve ethnic diversity, but it detected no sense of urgency in making it happen. And like previous visiting teams, it was critical of Pepperdine's governance system, which it saw as centralized, "top down," and lacking strong faculty influence on major policies and decisions. The team was amazed that senior administrators expressed a conscious preference for an "administrator-run" rather than a "faculty-run" or a "board-run" university.[8]

Finally, the WASC visitors had major concerns about the physical and financial resources of the university. The educational centers were modest and limited in resources when compared to the Malibu facilities. Moreover, focus on an expanding physical plant had limited growth of the endowment. In the team's view, Pepperdine was overextended and undercapitalized, and it did not believe Pepperdine's board of regents was fully aware of potential problems.[9]

Davenport Perplexed, Exasperated

After seeing a draft of the team's final report, President Davenport agreed with some of the report's criticism but found "perplexing" the report's "strong language" about the insufficiency of faculty scholarship, for he believed that there was "significant evidence" of it occurring.[10] He insisted that the ethnic diversity "trend lines" were improving, especially in the student body; while acknowledging that Pepperdine was not attempting to pursue "a faculty governance model" common in many universities, he believed there was more meaningful faculty involvement than the report recognized.[11]

As for the university's finances, Davenport said that "thirty plus years of balanced budgets, the steady building of assets and reserves, the reduction of endowment spending rates, and the recent reallocation of $1 million from management to education [was] indicative of financial strength." And he pledged that the upcoming "Challenged to Lead" campaign would emphasize endowment and academic support.[12]

Regardless of Davenport's response, WASC's senior commission generally accepted the findings of the visiting team. While reaffirming the accreditation of Pepperdine, it scheduled another comprehensive visit for the fall of 1998—in six years rather than the usual eight—and demanded an interim report in November 1995—in two years as opposed to the usual four.[13] The commission said the range and magnitude of the university's challenges justified the accelerated schedule.[14]

Although he had anticipated the commission's decision, President Davenport was nonetheless exasperated. From Davenport's perspective, the WASC experience in 1992 questioned the reality of "institutional autonomy" or "independent" higher education. Many of the accreditors' concerns, he believed, fell within the province and responsibility of individual institutions—not academic accrediting agencies. He liked WASC's premise that assessment of student learning should be the main focus of the review process and that the assessment should be based on a "culture of evidence" collected continuously rather than via a crash program of self-study every few years, but he thought WASC got the purpose of accreditation all wrong.[15]

Davenport believed its purpose was to establish and apply standards of basic academic quality—not to formulate "policies about this and that" following an extraneously conceived social agenda. Thus, Davenport told the *Graphic,* Pepperdine was looking into alternate accrediting methods, including a relationship with the Association of Liberal Arts Colleges.[16]

Leading the Opposition

On March 17, 1994, Davenport expressed his skepticism of accreditation in general and WASC in particular to representatives of twenty primarily independent colleges gathered in his Malibu office. Encouraged by President Thomas Dillon of Thomas Aquinas College in Santa Paula, Davenport had invited representatives from thirty-seven colleges, including Stanford and USC, to discuss WASC's report on the future of self-regulation and a new statement on diversity that had been adopted three weeks earlier despite the opposition of Stanford, USC, and Pepperdine.[17]

For the twenty institutions that sent representatives, passage of the diversity statement represented a loss of institutional independence, while "self-regulation" threatened even more. Was not WASC in the business of *accrediting* rather than *regulating* institutions of higher education, the group asked? To them it was ironic that WASC wished its members to adopt a "culture of evidence" as a means of self-assessment, yet it offered no such evidence that such actions were warranted. For Davenport and like-minded representatives, "self-regulation" represented the potential loss of institutional autonomy via the acts of an overreaching accrediting agency.[18]

No vote was taken in Davenport's office, but there were outcomes to the meeting. First, no one left the gathering thinking Pepperdine was reconciled to an accreditation process that had delivered a stinging rebuke in 1992. Second, the WASC leadership took note and opened its April meeting in Maui to consider some concerns of the dissenters. Davenport sent Provost Steven Lemley to that meeting with instructions to demonstrate "fierce independence," which the provost manifested at the conclusion of his ten-minute address by raising his arm with a clenched fist and shouting, "Resist." Third, in the presence of such restiveness, Stephen Weiner, the executive director who facilitated Pepperdine's 1992 review and initiated discussions on self-regulation and diversity, resigned in 1995. He was subsequently replaced by Ralph Wolff, who initiated two years of meetings of presidents and representatives from a large number of member institutions, public and private, to re-examine accreditation. The result would be an accreditation process more focused on the institutions' own aspirations, supported by evidence-based practices.[19]

Interim Report

Pepperdine on November 8, 1995, filed its mandatory "Third-Year Interim Report," which was masterfully written by Lemley with faculty and regent input. He tried to address the major concerns the senior commission had raised less than two years earlier: academic quality and rigor; the overuse of adjunct faculty; the informality of program review; strategic review and allocation of resources; educational quality vs. brick and mortar; governance procedures; physical and financial resources; and mission.[20]

As he did so, he detailed the trials and triumphs of the Davenport administration during its first decade while admitting some of its challenges. Above all else, Lemley assured WASC, Pepperdine was committed to academic quality broadly defined—including faculty scholarship. He noted that Pepperdine was working to create a "culture of evidence" in Seaver College through standardized freshman surveys and a student portfolio project, reiterated faculty involvement in the university's strategic planning and institutional governance, reported that changing financial circumstances would allow the university to shift emphasis away from buildings, and identified activities which indicated the university was being less subtle about its Christian mission.[21]

In his interim report, the provost also revealed some significant changes that had occurred since 1993, including:

- a new master's degree in dispute resolution at the School of Law;
- a reconfigured and strengthened EdD degree at GSEP;
- slumping enrollments at SBM;
- conceptual interest on the part of President Davenport in service learning as a pedagogy;
- a new provost at the university and a new dean of GSEP;
- a new passive recreation center at Malibu and entirely new facilities in Florence, Italy; and
- new MBA programs offered by SBM in the San Francisco area and Ventura County.[22]

The provost also reported that the number of minority students at Pepperdine had increased from 14.3 percent to 21 percent between 1988 and 1994. Minority faculty had increased from 12 to 21, or from 5.8 percent in 1990 to 8.9 percent in 1994. During the same time period, the number of female faculty had increased 44.1 percent, or from 34 to 49. The figures indicated, Lemley said, a direction and not a destination. Although the state of California was backing away from mandatory affirmative action, President Davenport had announced that Pepperdine would continue to enrich the ethnic, racial, and gender diversity of its faculty because of moral considerations rather than legal ones.[23]

WASC's senior commission was pleased with Lemley's interim report, especially in light of major disruptions from fire, earthquake, and flood the university had recently experienced. The report provided "solid evidence of response" to the commission's "concerns and of vital progress on a number of fronts." Moreover, it agreed that it was appropriate to defer the date of the next comprehensive visit until the "Challenged to Lead" campaign and various academic improvements had more time to bear fruit. Accordingly, it scheduled the next review for fall 2000.[24]

Challenged to Lead

Not surprisingly, even though the Davenport administration questioned WASC's methods and philosophy, it continued to manage the university in light of the accreditation agency's expectations of an academically excellent institution of higher education. Fundamental to that endeavor was generating a revenue stream that would pay for buildings, programs, faculty, and students since it could not all come from tuition and fees but should come from a robust endowment.

Most of the millions raised during the Banowsky and White administrations and the Wave of Excellence campaign had gone into the construction of the Malibu campus. The amount set aside for endowment was deemed inadequate to supplement salaries, underwrite new programs, or provide student scholarships. A campaign dedicated to enlarging the endowment seemed the logical next step, so Davenport turned to the fund-raising team made up of Chancellor Charles Runnels, Executive Vice Chancellor Larry Hornbaker, and Chancellor Emeritus Norvel Young.

As the earlier Wave of Excellence campaign illustrated, Pepperdine was at its best when it came to fund-raising. Under the leadership of Davenport's predecessors, according to one reporter, Pepperdine had consciously reached out to Southern California's Republican elite to help fund its development. The success of that effort and the university's rise to academic respectability paralleled the rise of its Republican constituency to national power. To many, Pepperdine was known as that "party school by the shore" where officials from the Ronald Reagan administration were constantly stopping by to speak. Editor Norman Cousins and President Davenport insisted that this did not mean Pepperdine was right-wing in its politics, but the identification with the Reagan establishment did the university no harm when it came to image management and fund-raising.[25] Indeed, it complemented the principal message of Pepperdine fund-raisers: the university was politically and socially conservative, and it promoted traditional American values, especially the free market, championed the liberal arts, and advocated strong Christian values. Few institutions managed their image better than Pepperdine, one reporter concluded. Television personality and frequent visitor to campus Ben Stein agreed. Compared to Pepperdine's marketing efforts, he said, Columbia and Yale universities were "pathetic" amateurs.[26]

Seeking Campaign Clarity

As the administration prepared to publicly launch the Challenged to Lead campaign, Seaver Dean John Wilson and others advocated for a clearer understanding of where the money would go. Wilson feared the cost of raising the money would consume a disproportionate share of what was raised. Moreover, he wanted the campaign to be associated with the university's strategic plans and to focus on improving what the university was already doing rather than

Steven S. Lemley served as provost of Pepperdine University from 1993 to 2000. Under President Davenport, Lemley facilitated many of the university's attempts at strategic planning and served as the primary liaison with WASC.

creating something new. In other words, he wanted to "finish" Seaver rather than make plans for expansion, as in the creation of a Malibu-based MBA program or a new school of public policy. He also wanted to be sure that any justification for the campaign addressed the kind of university Pepperdine wanted to be and its historic connection with Churches of Christ.[27]

To help make a case for the campaign, President Davenport held a series of meetings at Brock House beginning in 1992. More than 150 friends and alumni participated. The consensus drawn from these meetings was that Pepperdine could provide moral and academic leadership to remedy the many social ills plaguing the nation. Some participants were so enthusiastic that they made pledges to help. Although eager to get started, the Davenport administration delayed announcing the new capital campaign until it had drafted a "case book" identifying the needs of the university and defining how gifts would be strategically allocated. Out of respect for Dean Wilson's point, it also wanted to predetermine the costs of the campaign.

In due time, it was agreed that 60 percent of the gifts would be dedicated to the endowment, student aid, and faculty chairs; 22 percent for new and remodeled physical facilities; 7 percent for faculty/staff incentives, libraries, and other new programs; and 11 percent for unrestricted gifts to balance annual operational budgets during the life of the campaign and for running the campaign. The cost of the campaign beyond normal expenses was set at 1.63 percent of the amount raised, some .37 percent less than the national average. To the disappointment of Wilson, however, the case book had little to say about the university's historic relationship with Churches of Christ, although it did make explicit reference to George Pepperdine's Christian vision for the school.[28]

Campaign Kickoff

The university announced its third capital campaign on the evening of September 17, 1994. An audience of 570 initially gathered around the Raleigh Runnels pool on the Malibu campus for a welcoming reception then moved into Firestone Fieldhouse, which had been regally transformed into a hall encased in blue tapestries and billowing linens punctuated by statuary, trees, and floral arrangements. A thirty-piece orchestra greeted guests. Following a sumptuous banquet and before details of the campaign were revealed, President Davenport delivered his keynote address, "Coming of Age."

After citing some of Pepperdine's more notable accomplishments, he told the audience the university had "successfully progressed through [its] birth period, then through the period of adolescent growth and [had now] come of age." It was something to celebrate, but it was also a time "to decide what kind of university we [will] be." In the history of higher education, he reminded his audience, schools like Pepperdine were born with the twin goals of academic excellence and strong values. Over time they set aside their emphasis upon values. Pepperdine did not want to follow that course, for it believed that it was not an *either/or* choice between excellence and values but a *both/and* choice. The university wanted to provide future leaders of the country with "an opportunity to get the very finest academic experience while also being strongly grounded in values." For Pepperdine, education was more than the mere dissemination of information for the mind; it was also "the formation of a life and even the transformation of the character and values of . . . young people." Davenport concluded his message by inviting members of the audience to join Pepperdine in its quest—which he dramatically announced as "Challenged to Lead."[29]

Larry Hornbaker declared the goal of the new campaign—$300 million. To be sure it was "an ambitious and bold initiative," even a "quantum challenge," but it would "endow Pepperdine at a level consistent with the University's rise to prominence." Hornbaker also introduced those who would chair the campaign steering committee: Jerve M. Jones, Rosemary Raitt, and Charles Runnels. He also announced leaders of other support committees, suggesting the campaign would rely on volunteers more than previously. Nonetheless, it was fairly clear that in the Pepperdine tradition of fund-raising, the bulk of the work would be done by staff rather than alumni and friends.[30]

The Challenged to Lead campaign went smoothly. During its silent phase, which began in 1992, some $101 million had been raised. In the next six months, $31 million dollars more was raised. By 1997, more than 75 percent of the campaign goal had been raised, including $33.2 million from the John and Alice Tyler estate and $51.7 from the Seaver trust, which brought the total given by the Seavers over the years to $160 million. Additional millions came from George Graziadio ($25), the Keck Foundation ($3), Wally Jones (the first alumnus to give a major gift of $1 million or more), and the Fletcher Jones Foundation ($1 million). The university also received gifts of property valued at millions of dollars from John Drescher (seven acres in Santa Monica), Luella Ulrich (Gull's Way), and Milt Drucker/Tom Holland/Harold Tragerman (twenty-four acres of Cottontail Ranch), helping the campaign exceed its $300 million goal by $13 million by 1999.[31]

Declaring Victory

Hoping to raise enough to build a science center, a graduate campus, and a building for communication and business, however, the campaign continued as scheduled into the next year. In 2000, leaders declared victory after having raised a total of $353.1 million, exceeding the original goal by 17 percent.[32]

Contributing to the campaign were 30,128 donors, including 34 percent of the alumni and 74 percent of faculty and staff. And unlike previous campaigns, there had been significant assistance from affinity groups: Seaver Board of Visitors, Center for the Arts Guild, SBM Board of Visitors, School of Public Policy Founder's Cabinet, and Friends of Firenze, among others. Clearly, a journalist was a bit premature in predicting that Pepperdine could no longer count on the support of Southern California's rock-solid conservative entrepreneurs because they were literally dying off. However, the observation that the university would have to rely more on alumni for financial support in the future was more on target.[33]

During the course of the campaign, Pepperdine's endowment fund increased by more than $192 million to a total of $335 million. Capital improvements included seven major building projects: Howard A. White Center (1995), the 280-bed Rockwell Towers (1994), Villa di Loreto and Residenza Tagliaferri in Florence (1998–99), Harilela International Tennis Stadium (1999), Tari Frahm Rokus Field (1998), Keck Science Center, and the Center for Communication and Business (CCB). Finding a principal donor for the communication and business building had long been a challenge; lacking one, $10 million from donors and other sources permitted construction, but at only 60 percent of the size initially envisioned. The result was a three-story building of 36,600 square feet that housed the communication and business divisions of Seaver College as well as the public safety unit of the university. The building was dedicated in 2002 after David Davenport had left office.

Other construction or renovation attributable to the Challenged to Lead campaign included George Page II Apartments (1987), Page Terrace parking lots, Duane Faw Student Lounge at the School of Law, Ralphs-Straus Tennis Pavilion (1993), and expansion of Tyler Campus Center (1998). The campaign also funded site preparation for the 50.4-acre Drescher Graduate Campus in Malibu, which would house programs for the Graziadio School, GSEP, and School of Public Policy.

Products of Campaign Success

Development of a graduate campus in the hills above Seaver College had been a dream of the Davenport administration since the early 1990s. The ability to make the dream a reality was ensured by the success of the Challenged to Lead campaign. Before site preparation and construction could begin, however, the university had to run the permission gauntlet of the California Coastal Commission and Los Angeles County.

That process was well underway by 1997, but actual site preparation did not begin until late in the last year of the Davenport administration.

Occupancy did not occur until 2003. George Graziadio was dismayed by the pace; his motto was "T.N.T." or "Today, Not Tomorrow."[34] But he soon learned that was not the motto of the Coastal Commission, although his subsequent exertion of influence did help move the permitting process along.

Other achievements were new facilities at the Ventura County education center in Westlake Village and a state-of-the-art multimedia center for GSEP at Pepperdine Plaza in Culver City. Important academic developments included funding of thirty-six chairs, professorships, and fellowships; allocation of $28 million in endowed student aid, scholarships, and work-study grants; funding of significant library and technology resources; inauguration of the first master's degree in dispute resolution; offering of a doctoral degree in educational technology; extra funding for an opera program; and the establishment of the new School of Public Policy and its associated institute.[35]

Equally important was the endowment of the Weisman Museum, which had opened to rave reviews with Nora Halpern as director in 1991. Halpern had previously worked as curator of the Frederick R. Weisman art collections in Los Angeles. A philanthropist and art collector, Weisman had made his fortune as president of Hunt Foods and as one of the first distributors of Toyota cars in the United States. Halpern persuaded Weisman to donate part of his collection to Pepperdine and give an additional $1.5 million for operation of the museum. In recognition, the university named the museum after Weisman. Halpern resigned in fall 1994, in the wake of a dispute over censorship, to be replaced by Michael Zakian, who had previously been director of the Palm Springs Desert Museum.[36]

Cultural Enrichment Initiative

Another academic benefit of the Challenged to Lead campaign was a cultural enrichment initiative underwritten by grants from National Medical Enterprises of Santa Monica (NME) and the James Irvine Foundation. The NME $1 million grant (fall 1991) funded a new Cultural Enrichment Center (CEC) directed initially by Connie James that reached out specifically to some twenty-five undergraduate students of color. Named after Richard Eamer, president of NME, the Eamer scholars teamed up with older students, alumni, and business and community leader mentors who provided both social and academic support. The center had a secondary purpose: to help all students become more culturally aware via such events as Rainbowfest, a celebration of the cultural contributions of racially diverse groups on the Seaver campus, and visiting speakers. Among the latter were Maya Angelou in October 1993 and Carlos Fuentes in 1994. With the Black Student Union at Seaver College,

CEC also sponsored activities during Black History Month, and subsequently supported a Martin Luther King Jr. holiday.[37]

The 1992 Irvine Foundation grant of $500,000, the first of three, sought to bolster the university's effort to recruit minority faculty by helping them finish their doctorates with the understanding they would then serve as a member of the faculty for as many years as they had been helped. It was a "grow-our-own" approach to the challenge of securing minority faculty. The first three potential faculty chosen were David Holmes, Mary-Antoinette Smith, and James Taylor. Simultaneously, President Davenport made $50,000 per school available to hire faculty members who were from underrepresented groups. The Irvine grant also enabled the university to bring dozens of diverse speakers for convo appearances.[38]

Over the years, the Davenport administration's cultural enrichment initiative reached thousands of people through multiple venues. Although it surely facilitated racial and ethnic sensitivity, it had only a modest impact on demographics. As President Davenport reported to WASC, between 1993 and 1999 the number of Pepperdine University students from minority groups grew 3 percentage points, from 19.6 percent to 22.6 percent. Thanks to the graduate schools, the total number of underrepresented groups in the student body was more than respectable, and Davenport took considerable pride in the fact that Pepperdine ranked among the top twenty institutions of higher learning granting degrees to black doctoral candidates. But the picture did not look nearly so good for the faculty. Minority faculty members totaled only 6.9 percent of the whole in 1993, increasing to 10.9 percent in 1999.[39]

Mixed Signals from WASC

When WASC initially set the year 2000 as the date of its next visiting team, no one could have known that it would be a remarkable transitional year for Pepperdine University. It marked the end of David Davenport's fifteen years as president and the beginning of Andrew K. Benton's administration. It was also the last of Steven Lemley's seven years as provost, much of which had been devoted to acting as Pepperdine's liaison with WASC. In that capacity, Lemley and his staff, including Associate Provost Norman Fischer, began working in 1998 to organize the necessary self-study. Flora Thornton Professor of Nutrition June Payne Palacio and Professor of Law Charles Nelson served as co-chairs of the faculty steering committee.

Because Pepperdine's 1995 interim report had responded so fully to issues raised by the 1992 visiting team, the WASC staff recommended that Pepperdine focus full attention on the present and future. Therefore, Pepperdine's self-study intentionally concentrated on five primary concerns: expectations for faculty scholarship and research; the use of information and educational technology; the university's Christian mission related to its academic mission; the creation of a culture of assessment; and the encouragement of diversity. Lemley and his team hoped to stimulate a conversation with the WASC visitors that would enable Pepperdine to make progress in those areas.[40]

It did not work out that way, however. When the seven-person visitation team, which was chaired by Thomas E. Corts, president of Samford University in Birmingham, Alabama, arrived on campus in October 2000, it was clear they were planning to focus on the 1992 report—regardless of what the WASC staff had told Lemley. Instead of engaging in the university-wide "strategic conversation" which Lemley and colleagues had planned in close consultation with the staff of WASC, the team seemed to be treating the visit as a check-list inspection.[41]

The approach gave Lemley some sleepless nights as he foresaw severe implications for Pepperdine and WASC if the team's report focused on trivial concerns such as "currency of board minutes and typographical or grammatical errors in dissertations" rather than helping Pepperdine define "culture of assessment," among other weighty matters. Sorrowfully, Pepperdine people would perceive the team's report as yet another "misfire," which would suggest that the visiting team had walked "carelessly" on "fruitful ground that had been intensively and delicately cultivated."[42]

He tried to redirect the visit—even writing a bold but professionally risky letter to Chairman Corts in the early-morning hours before the final exit report was delivered.[43] But his efforts seemed fruitless as the team's predominantly negative report was sprinkled with references to the 1992 report and questions about Pepperdine's Christian mission and ties to the Churches of Christ.[44] It also made specific suggestions for corrections. The board of regents should maintain current, complete minutes. The university should consider regular evaluations of the president and regular self-evaluations of the board of regents, establish a more formalized university-wide faculty voice, enforce quality control measures to eliminate inaccuracies in doctoral dissertations, enhance the collections and consider refurbishment of Payson Library, and place an advocacy voice for student affairs at the executive level.[45]

Final Evaluation Is More Positive

Fortunately, the WASC senior commission was not heavily influenced by the visiting team's negative report. It its letter of affirmation, it commended Pepperdine for a successful transition to a new president and acknowledged the strength of the faculty and expectations for student performance. And it recognized that the university was deeply committed to its students, had a strong sense of community and pride, was well served by an active and engaged board of regents, and aspired to further strengthen and sustain its academic reputation and institutional performance. But like the visiting team, it too saw a need for the university to develop an institution-wide strategic plan and to articulate the Christian mission in ways that could effectively inform decision-making, particularly at the school level.

It also recommended that the regents review the articles of incorporation and bylaws so that they reflected appropriate distinctions between policy and administration and addressed Christian mission and official purpose. As did the visiting team, the senior commission urged the university to develop its own benchmarks and goals for institutional improvement and to more actively involve faculty in the evaluation and assessment processes of student performance.[46]

Despite the criticism of the visiting team and some reservations of its own, the senior commission was on the whole pleased with developments at Pepperdine. It reaffirmed the accreditation of the university for ten years, the longest period in the institution's history. Its reputation as a university of substance was finally confirmed by WASC.

Clearly, Pepperdine University had come of age during the Davenport administration.

CHAPTER 47

LAUNCHING THE SCHOOL
OF PUBLIC POLICY

P resident David Davenport had long held that Pepperdine University was
ripe to open a fifth school. It was not clear to him, however, what kind of
school that should be. As early as 1992, just after a half-year sabbatical,
he asked the senior administrators, academic deans, and select faculty members of the university planning committee for their suggestions. The consensus was that it should be either a school of international studies or public policy. Not sure what to do with that opinion, Davenport asked Provost William
Adrian to take the lead in advancing the conversation. In his view, some
higher education institution would soon build a new school in the American
West in one or both of those areas, and he would "like us to think carefully
about whether we should be pursuing this."[1]

While the University Planning Committee (UPC) was discussing the prospect of a new school, members of the Seaver College political science faculty
led by Professor Stephen Monsma in February 1993 proposed to Adrian that
Pepperdine create a Center for the Christian Study of Public Policy. "Rooted in
the political science and international studies programs of Seaver College," the
proposed center would also tie into the School of Law, GSEP, and SBM in order
to explore "the nature and applications of a Christian worldview in relationship to the world of government and politics." It would operate with a director, educate twelve post-degree fellows, and sponsor biannual conferences.[2]
Although belated in responding to the proposal, Davenport was impressed,
even encouraged, by it, but he did not want to consider options until he had
had time to unfold the initiative he was already working on.[3]

According to one observer, Davenport had long held that Pepperdine
University had promoted a conservative world view—economically, politically,
socially, philosophically—to wealthy supporters but never really delivered on
that world view with demonstrable programs or products. This was especially

the case in Seaver College, where the political science faculty often favored liberal public policies. The president believed that Pepperdine's response over the years had lacked integrity and that to restore veracity, the university should move boldly toward implementing a program with a more conservative orientation.[4]

A Ronald Reagan School?

By mid-1993, Davenport was envisioning a School for Public Policy at Pepperdine named for Ronald Reagan. The proposed school would offer a master's degree in public policy (MPP), a joint degree with the law school, and possibly a practitioner-based doctoral degree. The approach to the field would be interdisciplinary, and the new school would serve 200 full-time students. Davenport bounced the idea off Lodwrick M. Cook, CEO of Arco, longtime friend of former President Reagan and member of the Pepperdine University board of regents. Davenport noted that both Ronald and Nancy Reagan held honorary doctorates from the university, that Pepperdine was now ranked by *U.S. News & World Report* in the top quartile of colleges and universities, that the proposed school would work closely with Reagan's projected presidential library, and that Pepperdine would raise its own endowments. The university needed only the endorsement of the Reagan foundation and the Reagan family to make it a reality by fall 1994. Much to Davenport's delight, Cook exhibited real interest in the proposal.[5]

As it turned out, the school was not to bear Reagan's name. Why is unclear. The Reagans themselves certainly held Pepperdine in high regard, but their advisors may have worried about the university's ability to implement a School of Public Policy worthy of the Reagan name. It was a relatively small school with limited resources. The Davenport administration was deeply disappointed, but continued with its plans. It would have a new school with or without the Reagan name.

Proposal Moves Forward

In the meantime, President Davenport and his colleagues were hard at work completing their full proposal. First, George C. Heider, an American Council on Education (ACE) fellow delegated to Davenport's office for the year, made a careful study of twelve existing public policy graduate programs, then drafted a document that described the proposed school, its programs, and requirements.[6] Students would follow one of four academic tracks: economics, American politics, international relations, and regional/local policy. Each track would require a thesis, a project, and an internship. Full-time students would follow a two-year sequence of courses (forty-eight units) and graduate with a masters of public policy degree; mid-career students already serving in fields of public service would follow a three-semester sequence of courses (thirty-six units) and graduate with a masters of arts in public policy.[7]

Elsewhere it was stated that Pepperdine's distinctive contribution to public policy education would come from the study of the founding principles of "freedom, order, democracy, the free market" and limited government. The development of the school could be justified by the "conviction that there [was] a need ... for leaders who [were] educated in an environment of fundamental values like faith, freedom, democracy, the dignity of the individual and other historic standards of intellect and conduct." Heider's proposal envisioned a student body of 125; a full-time faculty of ten; an endowment of $10 million; an additional $6 million to build a building on the Drescher Campus; a $2.5 million start-up fund for five years; and an annual budget that ranged from $750,000 in the first year to $2.566 million in year six.[8]

Davenport saw to it that the School of Public Policy was a priority of the $300 million Challenged to Lead campaign, and its inclusion pretty much assured the success of the fund-raising effort. The Olin Foundation agreed to fund the $2.5 million start-up costs; in return, Pepperdine promised to establish John M. Olin Professorships and the John M. Olin Distinguished Lecture Series.[9] The foundation, said executive director James Piereson, liked the "religious background at Pepperdine" and believed that the public policy school there was "pretty unique," unlike some of the university's other graduate programs. Other notable funders included Edward L. Gaylord, newspaper publisher and owner of Opryland in Nashville, and longtime Pepperdine friend Richard M. Scaife.[10] Major contributors also included Robert Dockson of California Federal Savings and Loan, Bill Mortensen of First Fed Financial, Viggo Butler of Lockheed, Thomas P. Kemp of Coca-Cola Bottling Company, Leonard H. Straus of Thrifty Drug Stores, Glenn Campbell of the Hoover Institution, and singer Pat Boone.[11] When the School of Public Policy opened, most of the funds necessary to operate it had been raised.

Constructing Curriculum, Gathering Support

Davenport formed a School of Public Policy advisory committee to identify the school's purpose and construct curriculum and programs to meet that purpose. Among the nationally prominent members were Martin Anderson of the Hoover Institute, Les Lenkowsky of the Hudson Institute, James Q. Wilson of UCLA, Edwin J. Feulner of the Heritage Foundation, and James Piereson of the Olin Foundation. On the political spectrum, all tilted toward the right. Visiting Professor Joel Kotkin, Provost Steven Lemley, Professor of Political Science Stephen Monsma, former Dean and Professor of Business

Administration James Wilburn, and ACE Fellow George Heider represented Pepperdine. Only Monsma was a tenured member of the teaching faculty with a field in public policy.[12]

Ultimately, the blue-ribbon group produced a curriculum notable for a track of core courses both at the beginning (statistics, economics, American political system) and at the end of the program (leadership, administration, application of public policy ideas). Somewhere in between students would take a course on great ideas in public policy utilizing a Great Books approach, and early on they would select one of the three tracks of special emphasis.[13] The committee also finalized plans for the organization of an Institute on Public Policy, which would precede the launching of the school by a year, serving as a platform to allow the emerging school to begin to gain visibility and credibility. The Institute would offer conferences and seminars, encourage publication in the public policy area, draw experts to the university, and communicate Pepperdine's expanded involvement in the field. It would expect to host one or more research fellows.[14]

Meanwhile Provost Lemley was marshaling support for the new school within the university. First, he wrote a conceptual plan for the school, submitting it to the board of regents in June 1995. The regents welcomed the prospect of an additional school and approved the concept with little discussion. The following December, Lemley submitted a strategic plan for the school to the UPC, which approved the plan forthwith. He apparently did not submit it to the University Academic Council, however.

With the support of the regents, the central administration, and the Challenged to Lead campaign, Lemley and Davenport made plans to launch the institute in 1996. To provide some leadership for the institute and to help with the fund-raising, they appointed law school alumnus Brad Cheves as a special assistant to the president for public policy.[15] Lemley soon circulated an announcement that Pepperdine was looking for a dean of its new school of public policy.[16] And in January 1996, *Pepperdine Voice* carried a lengthy article, "University to Open School of Public Policy."[17]

Seaver Faculty Unenthusiastic

With almost everything in place, President Davenport then formally announced the new school to the university faculty. He reminded them that it had been twenty-five years since Pepperdine had launched a new school and that he was committed to building "quality and reputation" of current university facilities and programs rather than starting "something new." Yet, at the same time, it was his sense "that Pepperdine had a distinctive role to play in public policy and that the time [was] right ... to launch a small but important initiative in this area." There were only forty-five schools in the field, just two of which were on the West Coast. Almost all of them focused on federal government policy and training personnel to run the bureaucracy, paying virtually no attention to nonprofit organizations, privately held companies, and local and regional governments.[18]

Above all, "Few, if any, [placed] much emphasis on the ethical, moral or spiritual dimensions of policy, an approach greatly needed in this field." But, Davenport said, Pepperdine's new School of Public Policy (SPP) would operate "within the frame of a Christian university" and place "a unique emphasis on the moral, ethical and spiritual dimension." For that reason, President Davenport was "enthusiastic" about the new school and its related institute.[19]

But the Seaver College faculty was not. By a vote of 67 to 17, the Seaver Faculty Association (SFA) in February 1996 adopted a resolution opposing the creation of another school within the university. The SFA's biggest concern was financial. Since all schools and colleges competed for unrestricted and discretionary funds, since funding for many Seaver academic programs and support services was inadequate, and since lack of funding produced undergraduate programs of "marginal quality," the Seaver faculty "strongly" opposed the formation of the SPP. It also objected strenuously to the school having been formed without any faculty consultation. The resolution requested the university board of regents to reconsider the formation of the school "until comments have been heard from the entire faculty of the University." The major concern of the Seaver faculty, said Dean John Wilson, was "that funds, time, and energy are going to a new program when we have crowded classrooms, inadequate staffing, major programs in trailers, etc., at Seaver."[20]

President Davenport was frustrated by the reaction of the Seaver faculty. He saw their response as falling into two categories, substance and process, but primarily process. He noted that UPC early on had considered the prospect of a new school and that the University Academic Council in due time would consider curriculum. "It sounds as if some may expect," he wrote, "that 'consultation' means that every new idea is to be taken to all faculty of all areas within the University." He noted that "Probably no one would ever undertake a new program or succeed in creating one, if that is the gauntlet that must be run. Perhaps we don't have a clear enough understanding of what consultation means here," he concluded.[21] Davenport's statement echoed ideas often expressed in the Thornton Administrative Center regarding faculty governance.

Provost Lemley sought to calm the troubled waters, arguing in a message to the faculty that the idea of a School of Public Policy was hardly new. It had been studied for two years, published as a priority of the Challenged to Lead campaign, and had already received well-publicized gifts totaling nearly $4 million. The UPC had formally approved the school, the president had mentioned it in various interactions with faculties, and Seaver faculty had been involved in the planning. Elsewhere, Lemley argued that no funds directed toward Seaver College would be redirected toward SPP.[22]

The faculty was hardly satisfied by Davenport's ruminations, if they even heard them, or by Lemley's message. When it came to financing SPP, they were inclined to think the central administration was playing little more than a shell game. In that context, Dean John Wilson reminded Lemley that Brad Cheves's request for office space was at the expense of Seaver College, and that unrestricted gifts had been used to prepare Page Apartments for SPP administration.[23] President of the SFA Cyndia Clegg advised President Davenport that in the judgment of her colleagues the central administration was more concerned about building a new school than in making Seaver College a quality institution. Why was it preferable, the faculty asked, to fund SPP instead of the communication division? Why build a parking lot rather than a communication building?[24]

Forging Ahead

The Seaver opposition did not deter President Davenport from his chosen course. Under the leadership of Cheves, the Institute of Public Policy opened in January 1996 and immediately appointed its first John M. Olin Fellow: Joel Kotkin, a widely acclaimed and UC-Berkeley trained student of urban development. In October of that year, the Institute published Research Fellow Gregory Rodriguez's study, "The Emerging Latino Middle Class" and sponsored a conference on the subject at the Biltmore Hotel in downtown Los Angeles. The conference was well received by 150 attendees, with journalistic coverage in both the *Wall Street Journal* and the *Los Angeles Times* and additional editorial comment in the *Times*.[25] Other conferences followed: the Overseas Security Advisory Council Conference, co-sponsored with RAND; The Pacific Rim in the 21st Century; Southern California as the Epicenter of the Information Age; and The Economic Revival of the Cities. It published two research reports, both by Kotkin: "Southern California Epicenter of the Information Age" and "Can the Cities Be Saved?"

With great anticipation, Davenport also appointed Kenneth Starr, then the U.S. special prosecutor in the Whitewater/Clinton affair, as the inaugural dean of SPP. Starr expected to hold the position in conjunction with the deanship of the School of Law. As noted elsewhere, Starr chose not to resign his special prosecutor's responsibilities and thus could not accept the Pepperdine positions immediately. The unexpected development prompted Davenport to turn to Jim Wilburn, recently retired as dean of SBM, to serve as interim dean of the public policy school until Starr could complete his work in Washington and take up residence in Malibu. Wilburn accepted the interim office as of September 1996; the position soon became permanent and lasted for nearly two decades. His immediate concern was to hire faculty and staff, design the curriculum, and recruit the first class for the fall 1997 semester.[26]

School of Public Policy Opens

Pepperdine's School of Public Policy opened its doors in August 1997. Administrative offices were situated in the Page Apartment Complex, and classrooms were across the street in the law center, where they would continue until they occupied new quarters on the Drescher Campus in 2003. The first class was comprised of thirty-seven students, the average age of whom was twenty-four; the average undergraduate GPA was 3.3, and the average years of professional experience were two. All were pursuing the MPP, the only degree then offered. All but two members of the initial class completed the degree. In addition to Dean Wilburn, there were at least five visiting, part-time faculty members: Distinguished Visiting Professor of Public Policy Kevin Starr, a noted USC professor of American Studies and the California state librarian; Seaver College Professor of Economics Robert Sexton, a respected author and popular classroom teacher; Professor Gordon Lloyd, who was on sabbatical from the University of Redlands; Institute of Public Policy Fellow Joel Kotkin; and Dr. Wayne Walker, who held graduate degrees from the University of Arizona, Harvard Law School, and RAND Graduate School of Public Policy Analysis.[27]

SPP students benefited from learning opportunities beyond classroom interaction. Among the most notable was an October 1997 surprise visit by Mikhail Gorbachev, the last president of the Soviet Union. The closed-door conversation touched upon leadership, economic reform, and family. Before the end of the decade, other dignitaries had made appearances at SPP, including urban reformer Robert Woodson, former Oklahoma Governor David Hall, U.S. Representative David Dreier, television news correspondent Sandy Vanocur, political commentator Bruce Herschensohn, Professor James Q. Wilson of Harvard and UCLA, U.S. Senator Dan Coats from Indiana, philosopher and author Michael Novak, U.S. Representative and vice-presidential candidate Jack Kemp, and University of California Regent Ward Connerly.

Students also had an opportunity to attend two major conferences on Faith and Public Policy hosted by SPP. Featuring Steve Forbes, Jack Scott, and Jean Bethke Elshtain, the first addressed "The Moral Roots of American Society," while the second featured John J. Dilulio, director of the White House office of faith-based initiatives; William Simon, former Secretary of Treasury; and

James Q. Wilson. Dilulio spoke on the efficacy of faith-based programs in the inner city, and Simon delivered a memorable lecture titled "My Faith and I."[28]

Simultaneously, Pepperdine's Institute of Public Policy was busy reaching out to constituencies beyond SPP students. It hosted a series of "Author's Forums" featuring notables such as urban policy analyst Fred Siegel, New York state official Bernadette Castro, and Indianapolis mayor Stephen Goldsmith. It published Kotkin's *Back to the Renaissance* research report and Thomas Tseng's "Common Paths." The former was presented at a formal luncheon at the Biltmore, while the latter was released during a conference on "Rethinking South Los Angeles." Other conferences included "Women in Public Policy" and the "Future of the Center: The Core City in the New Economy."[29]

The Olin Foundation helped with start-up costs but not to the extent that SPP could contribute anything to the university's overhead expenses. The school's expense/revenue (net of financial aid) ratio was 118 percent in FY1998. It averaged 115 percent for the next two fiscal years, on a revenue budget of $1.5 million. Fortunately, friends continued to support the promising work of SPP. In response to a letter from Dean Wilburn, for example, Richard Scaife sent a $225,000 dollar check for the school's unrestricted use.[30]

Growing Pains

Because of the paucity of space, SPP recruited only twenty-five students for its second class and forty-six for its fourth. Anticipating an enrollment of close to 200, Davenport had concerns about the school's long-range viability. He advised successor Andrew Benton to conduct a hard-nosed review of SPP on the school's fifth anniversary. Benton agreed to do so.[31]

Meanwhile, the infant school added three full-time, tenure-track faculty beginning with the second year. These included Gordon Lloyd, who moved permanently to Pepperdine from Redlands; Theodore McAllister, who held a doctorate in history from Vanderbilt; and Charles Van Eaton, who earned his PhD in labor economics from Tulane. Both McAllister and Van Eaton joined the SPP faculty from Hillsdale College, and both were members of Churches of Christ. Kotkin continued as an adjunct, but Kemp, former Secretary of Housing and Urban Development and Republican vice-presidential candidate, replaced Kevin Starr as distinguished visiting professor.[32]

By 2000, Pepperdine University's School of Public Policy was more about promise than reality. It still held classes in the law center; its student body numbered fewer than fifty; it did not contribute to the university's bottom line. But the associated institute had hosted several conferences that contributed to the national conversation on significant public policy issues. Those conferences, along with the Institute's and SPP's choice of fellows and speakers, had defined the institute and the school as politically and socially conservative. It was a brand that President Davenport, Dean Wilburn, and the SPP faculty welcomed. The board of regents appropriately named the Institute of Public Policy after Davenport when he retired as president in 2000.

CHAPTER 48

GLOBAL OPPORTUNITIES
AND LOCAL CHALLENGES

During the Davenport administration, the political landscape of the world changed dramatically, from the thawing of the Cold War, to the collapse of the Berlin Wall, to the emergence of the Pacific Rim. Pepperdine University, eager to seize new opportunities, came to see itself as an advocate of globalism, a perspective that would enable students to pursue lives of purpose, service, and leadership in a worldwide community. At the same time, administrators continued to find themselves mired in local disputes and responding to natural disasters that threatened the very existence of the Malibu campus.

Pepperdine made Soviet connections in the depths of the Cold War, when Norvel Young helped arrange a Soviet–American Writers conference that met in Kiev in 1982 and then in Malibu in 1984. In May 1990, just months after the fall of the Berlin Wall, the conference met again in Moscow, with eighteen well-known writers participating. Two years later, it met for the second time on the Malibu campus, in the immediate wake of the Rodney King riots.

Among the American delegates were Gay Talese, Seymour Hersh, Harrison Salisbury, David Bradley, Sonia Sanchez, Gloria Emerson, and William Gass. Soviets who participated included prize-winning poets Yevgeny Yevtushenko and Andrei Voznesensky, among others.[1] Although the Los Angeles riots hung like a pall, good spirit prevailed throughout the conference, which was strictly limited to a list of stellar invitees. That Pepperdine would host such a conference surprised both its friends and foes in Southern California.

Student Outreach Efforts

Pepperdine students were also influenced by the spirit of glasnost. In fall 1988, Seaver students Scott Talcott, Eric Overman, Jeff Duby, and some of their friends organized IMPAKT as a means to promote world awareness. Their principal objective was to establish an American-Soviet student summit and exchange, and the group wrote Soviet President Mikhail Gorbachev seeking his endorsement. To publicize their petition, they held a candlelight vigil on campus at the foot of the theme tower and in West Los Angeles in front of the federal building on Wilshire for fifty days.[2] They received no response from the Soviet president, who, the students chose to believe, was distracted by an earthquake that had devastated the Soviet Republic of Armenia.

Talcott and his friends switched tactics. With the support of other Seaver students and faculty advisor Dan Caldwell, they spearheaded a campaign for a student journal, *Montage,* that would publish the work of both American and Soviet students in English as well as Russian. The journal would emphasize photography, literary pieces, and political science essays. In his planning, Talcott's partner was Vladimir Tyurenkov, a Soviet citizen and Moscow resident who came to Pepperdine first as a member of the Soviet national debate team. During that visit, the idea of *Montage* was born. Subsequently, Tyurenkov enrolled at Pepperdine as a scholarship student, and his connections in the Soviet Union helped make the journal a reality.[3]

Equally important were grants from Seaver College student government and from the Pepperdine central administration. These resources paid for Talcott's trip to Russia and for desktop publishing equipment for a Moscow office. This cooperation between Soviet and Pepperdine students was surprising to a *Los Angeles Times* reporter, who noted that Pepperdine students went to chapel once a week at a school funded by prominent Republicans where Justice William A. Rehnquist taught law.[4]

Along the way, Talcott sought the advice and cooperation of students attending other universities, including Susan McKean, editor of the Stanford University newspaper and a student of Slavic languages. She thought it was commendable that Pepperdine was "trying to get away from the reputation that most people know about." Then McKean proceeded to muscle herself into a leadership position, assume complete responsibility of the editorial office, and relegate Talcott and his Pepperdine associates to managing the business side of the publication. When the first issue of 10,000 copies (5,000 each for the Soviet Union and the United States) appeared in winter 1991, Pepperdine's name was not to be found in the staff box, presumably because of an "oversight." In barely visible type, Scott Talcott and Vladimir Tyurenkov were identified as founders. Professor Caldwell complained widely that Pepperdine students had not been given sufficient recognition, but Talcott chose to look at the big picture. "We . . . achieved what we wanted. You can afford to go out and make a sacrifice for something you believe in." Although further issues were planned, *Montage* was not published a second time.[5]

Faculty Connections

Pepperdine University faculty members were also involved in the work of glasnost. In addition to supporting the writer's conference and acting as faculty sponsor for *Montage*, Dan Caldwell, professor of political science, held leadership roles in the "Forum for U.S.–Soviet Dialogue," an international group that organized annual exchanges between thirty to fifty American and Soviet delegates, beginning in 1987. The forum, a nonpartisan organization which endorsed no policy beyond a belief in the value of dialogue, met in the Soviet Union and the United States on alternate years. On one of those years it met in Los Angeles, with Caldwell acting as host. His work with the forum put Caldwell and Pepperdine University at the center of perestroika conversations worldwide.[6]

Even more prominent was the work of Jim Wilburn, dean of the School of Business and Management after 1982. As noted elsewhere, one of his major objectives as dean was to globalize the curriculum and programs of SBM.[7] Because of SBM's global strategy, Wilburn saw the fall of the Soviet Union as an opportunity for Pepperdine to exercise leadership in privatizing the formerly collectivist economy. In October 1990, Wilburn proposed that SBM assume a focused and highly visible role in assisting select leaders in the old Soviet Union. If that were done "with a cohesive and rational purpose," Wilburn said, it was "not impractical or overly dramatic to suggest that the Pepperdine business school [could] play a truly historic and significant role in the history of this period." He suggested quarterly visits by a Pepperdine task force to Russia to address issues of privatization, organizational development, commercialization of technology, and launching and managing midsized companies.[8]

SBM Assists Russian Reform

By a fortuitous set of circumstances, as the Soviet Union was disintegrating, Russian Republic officials in the administration of President Boris Yeltsin asked Wilburn to organize a committee of American business leaders to consult with Russian leaders on challenges they expected to face in housing, food distribution, and tourism. They even gave him an official appointment as chairman of the U.S. Committee to Assist Russian Reform, assigning him to work closely with the Russian Committee on Privatization chaired by Valery Chernogorodsky. Coincidentally, Chernogorodsky's assistant was Vladimir Tyurenkov, co-founder of *Montage*. As co-chairs of the committee, Wilburn recruited Tom Kemp, formerly president of Coca Cola Bottling, and Gus Tagliaferri, an SBM graduate and construction contractor.[9]

Pepperdine's mission in Russia was to encourage large military high-tech manufacturers to find peacetime applications for their technology. Since it had international implications, Wilburn secured the financial support of the

U.S. Department of State, which invested $2.5 million in the program between 1992 and 1994. Through the program, Pepperdine taught the Russians how to develop strategic business plans, and over the span of two years brought eighty plant executives from around Moscow to Los Angeles for a two-week crash course. For the most promising business plans, the Pepperdine team acted as mediators between Russian executives and American venture capital bankers. Very good ideas surfaced.[10]

In the process, however, the team asked a lot of questions about particular technologies, leading the KGB at one point to accuse the Pepperdine program of being a front for the CIA. Nevertheless, the university's Russian Conversion Program helped Russia transition to a freer economic system, and Wilburn and Kemp were pleased to introduce Yeltsin's top finance ministers to leading supply-side economists and ideas. When it closed in 1996, Wilburn concluded it had been "one of the most significant programs, though little appreciated, that Pepperdine ever sponsored."[11]

Looking to The Pacific Rim

The globalism so evident in Russian-related activities was apparent in the Far East as well. Since beginning as dean of international programs, William Phillips had wanted to turn Pepperdine's attention from Europe to Asia as he believed the future of the United States lay along the Pacific Rim. He was supported by Professor Glenn Webb, who had joined the Seaver faculty as an Asian art specialist in 1987. Both were delighted when representatives of the Cultural and Educational Promotion Project of Kumagaya City, Saitama Prefecture, Japan, invited Pepperdine to establish a campus to offer two years of general studies for fifty Pepperdine and 200 Japanese students; create a language institute for 750 students; and offer graduate courses in education, business, and law. Phillips and Webb visited the site of the proposed campus in November 1988; other administrators followed. In anticipation of a campus at Kumagaya City, Webb designed a T-shirt with the logo "Pepperdine University, Japan" in Japanese characters.[12]

The Davenport administration as a whole was less sanguine. Similar invitations had been declined by several U.S. universities.[13] What Pepperdine administrators wanted to do in Japan was to provide an educational experience for Pepperdine students in the same manner it was doing in its European programs. The Kumagaya contacts wanted Pepperdine to provide American-style higher education for resident students with full accreditation from Japanese authorities. The administration was willing to consider the proposal if it could be done in cooperation with a Japanese university, but Japanese universities were reluctant to have their undergraduate students study in an American university program. Thus, Pepperdine officials did not feel full accreditation and its costs were justified.

Accordingly, Pepperdine's representatives began looking for a residential campus near Osaka or Kyoto that would accommodate fifty American and fifty Japanese students who would study together with English as the language of instruction.[14] But nothing suitable could be arranged, and in 1990, the Davenport administration terminated their Japanese negotiations, much to the disappointment of Professor Webb.[15]

But Dean Phillips did not give up on his plan to offer some kind of study-abroad program in Japan. Beginning in fall 1991, a Pepperdine program was offered in conjunction with Tokyo International University (FIU). With Professor of Communication Fred Casmir as the inaugural director, eighteen students took classes offered in the facilities of FIU and resided in various homes. By 1994, Phillips had changed the cooperating university to Ibaraki Christian College, the institution associated with Japanese Churches of Christ. The program benefited from the change, but it continued to find tremendous difficulty in accommodating the unique academic calendar in Japan, which began and ended a month later than in the United States. With great regret, Phillips terminated the Japan program in 1996. Thereafter, Pepperdine's Pacific Rim program moved to Hong Kong, in cooperation with Hong Kong Baptist University, and then to Shanghai, in cooperation with Fudan University.[16]

Battles on the Home Front

Ironically, even as Pepperdine University was finding more ways to successfully enlarge its global reach, at home it was facing fierce opposition in its attempts to enlarge its Malibu campus. From the beginning, the university had tried to win approval from proper authorities for a long-range development plan (LRDP) that would authorize a build-out of the physical plant at Malibu. The California Coastal Commission (CCC) was never enthusiastic about such a plan and flatly declined to approve one in 1983.

At that time, however, it did agree to authorize expansion of the campus's sewage treatment facilities, critical to any expansion plan, but only if the university would first cede 150 acres of its campus to the California state parks, promise never to build on an additional 230 acres, and accept a moratorium of at least fifteen years before building on another 120 acres of the campus. As if that were not enough, Pepperdine would also have to develop a plan to hold traffic in the Pepperdine/Malibu Civic Center area to its current level and to develop and pay for plans to bring 5,000 youngsters from the inner-city to Malibu each year.[17] From Pepperdine's perspective, the mitigations were "arbitrary and unreasonable" and obviously designed to prevent the university from doing anything.[18] University officials withdrew the LRPD from further consideration and managed other arrangements for its necessary wastewater treatment.

After many further frustrations with the CCC, the Malibu community, the County of Los Angeles, and the California State Legislature, Pepperdine administrators proposed another version of a LRDP in 1988. In November, the CCC again rejected Pepperdine's proposal for lack of specificity on a number of issues. The rejection essentially sent the message that the university should limit its growth to the build-out of the footprint of its current campus.[19]

Under the leadership of a "cool and calm" Andy Benton, Pepperdine submitted a revised LRDP to the CCC almost immediately. It did not come up for consideration until September 12, 1989. Following a five-hour hearing, the CCC adopted Pepperdine's development plan by a seven-to-five vote. Included in the approved plan was consent to develop seventy-two of the university's 600 undeveloped acres in Marie Canyon—what would become Drescher campus. It authorized removal and recompacting of three million cubic yards of dirt

William B. Phillips joined the Pepperdine community in 1982 as a professor of physics and vice president for academic affairs, serving under Presidents White and Davenport. He subsequently served as dean of international programs for almost two decades, working to integrate an ever-growing number of programs into the Seaver College culture and academic curriculum.

and the building of 385,000 square feet of facilities. Furthermore, the plan approved a doubling of the university's student body to 5,000 full-time equivalent students on the Malibu campus and authorized adding another 850,000 square feet of academic and housing projects. In return, the LRDP called upon Pepperdine to provide a public, open-space easement to more than 500 environmentally sensitive acres and increase the capacity of its planned sewage treatment plant if certain conditions triggered that necessity.[20]

As the vote suggested, the CCC commissioners were sharply divided over Pepperdine's LRDP. Opponents like Madelyn Glickfeld saw Pepperdine as nothing more than a "land developer." Commissioner John Hisserich argued that construction in Marie Canyon would mar the view and glut Pacific Coast Highway with traffic. On the other hand, Commissioner David Malcolm backed expansion because the university offered cultural and educational opportunities for youth and provided an extensive program for minority students. Commissioner Donald McGinnis agreed: "Pepperdine is a world-class leader in higher education, and the expansion is vital to the university."[21]

The Malibu Township Council (MTC), of course, was adamantly opposed to any plan that would permit Pepperdine to expand, accusing the university of being a bad neighbor and a "predatory" consumer of limited resources. Benton responded to all such criticism by saying Pepperdine wanted to develop only seventy-two of 600 currently undeveloped acres. "We don't believe that is unreasonable," he said. "We pledge to care for [the campus] in the way we have in the past."[22] Although the MTC sued to block Pepperdine's LRDP, courts rejected the suit and its appeals, and the Los Angeles County Board of Supervisors finally approved Pepperdine's LRDP in October 1992.[23]

Pepperdine and its Malibu neighbors were involved in other heated disputes during the Davenport administration, with conflicts arising regarding the cityhood of Malibu, the university's sewage treatment plans, and some land development investments. It was not always easy to negotiate with local neighbors who despised the university's existence, but the Davenport administration worked diligently to ease the tensions while asserting Pepperdine's rights to independently control certain aspects of its current campus operations and its future growth. Those efforts required negotiations with the County of Los Angeles, the CCC, the newly incorporated city of Malibu, the state legislature, the Sierra Club, and other local and regional agencies and groups.

Facing so much local hostility and so many regulatory requirements, final approval of the Drescher graduate campus was not won easily or quickly. More than six years after the LRDP was approved, in January 1999, the regional planning commission approved the Drescher site plans. The coastal commission did not approve them until October that year. The Sierra Club tried to stop the project, insisting development would damage rare grassland on the site.

Pepperdine responded by agreeing to harvest the seed of the grass in question and replant it in protected locations. Grading on the site finally began in spring of 2000; by then the university had spent some $15 million to acquire necessary regulatory approvals.[24]

Dealing with Mother Nature

If world affairs and local tensions complicated David Davenport's administration, so too did natural disasters. No more than two weeks before his inauguration as president on October 14, 1985, the Malibu campus was surrounded by the "Piuma Canyon" fire. Ignited when Santa Ana winds knocked high-voltage power lines into dry brush, the Piuma blaze quickly consumed 2,000 acres surrounding the campus. The forty-foot wall of fire that swept down from the canyon crest did an estimated $250,000 worth of damage to university property. Flames damaged the irrigation system, trees, a warehouse, the law school's air conditioning system, and one faculty condominium.[25]

During the fire, there was considerable confusion on campus. With flames visible from residence hall windows, panicked students did not know whether to evacuate or stay on campus; those who attempted to leave by car found parking lot exits blocked by campus security officers, who were directing students to take refuge in Firestone Fieldhouse. The security officers were acting under the orders of Vice President for Student Affairs John Watson. Although the Los Angeles County Fire Department believed the entire campus was safe, Watson had made the decision to evacuate dorms and apartments and shelter students at Firestone. Because of the lack of information and contradictory directives, confusion prevailed within the campus community.[26]

The takeaway from the Piuma fire was that the Malibu campus was not prepared to deal with a major emergency. Almost immediately, Watson led a campaign to update Pepperdine's emergency preparedness plan. Thus, the university was fully prepared eight years later when it suffered its next big fire.[27]

That fire, named the Old Topanga fire, raged between November 2 and 4, 1993. Fanned by Santa Ana winds reaching sixty miles per hour, it torched 18,000 acres and burned 359 homes in the Malibu area. Four hundred fire companies and 6,100 firefighters—with a command post in Alumni Park—were involved in the fight to control it. The firestorm burned to the edges of the Malibu campus but caused no structural damage. Following a predetermined plan executed via a control center supervised by legal counsel Gary Hanson, students and faculty "sheltered in place," evacuating their residences and occupying Firestone Fieldhouse or the campus center cafeteria.[28]

With the fire making national headlines, Davenport, Andy Benton, and Jeff Bliss, Pepperdine's public information officer, were frequently interviewed for television and radio newscasts. They were inevitably asked why students were gathered in a big box within sight of the flames. The Pepperdine spokespersons always responded with assurance that there was no safer place to be: just outside that "box" were some 1,000 firefighters who had gathered to get instructions and rest.[29]

Expressing Gratitude

The rescue of Pepperdine, of course, was due largely to the university's fire-prevention plans and strategies and the tenacious work of the firefighters. All of the Pepperdine community warmly thanked the firefighters in a special convocation on November 8 and then inscribed the names of the fire service agencies involved on bricks embedded on the sidewalk at Ralphs-Straus tennis center.[30] More than 400 Pepperdine students subsequently participated in all manner of clean-up tasks for the city of Malibu and its residents.[31]

In the aftermath of the Old Topanga fire, President Davenport observed to the Pepperdine community that Thanksgiving had come early. He was thankful to God and to the countless people who worked so hard to protect the Malibu campus, but he was especially thankful to the "people and plans that made it possible for us to prevent a real disaster. . . . Every expert I know," he said, "has indicated that the University has done the best job they know of in developing plans that address the needs of our people as well as protect our property." That plan included counseling sessions for students suffering from post-traumatic stress. He added that "One of the things our campus community does best is handle these kinds of emergency situations."[32]

Pepperdine alumni and friends around the globe were thankful that the campus had escaped without significant damage. But alumnus and associate minister of the Torrance Church of Christ, Walter Surdacki, was "disheartened by the lack of any reference to prayer, God or the like in any of the five [television] interviews" that he heard during the fires. He asked if Pepperdine had a policy not to mention such things during such an event.[33]

The Malibu campus endured another firestorm in 1996, but the university's experiences in 1985 and 1993 enabled it to survive once again without significant damage to life or property.[34]

Temblors and Torrential Downpours

The same was true with the Northridge, California, earthquake on January 17, 1994. That 6.7 quake left more than fifty people dead and did more than $500 billion in damages in the Los Angeles area. Although its epicenter was only a few miles north and east, the Malibu campus experienced the quake with no losses other than electrical power for a time and a crack here and there in stucco finishes. Shortly after the quake hit, the emergency operation team met to check the vital signs of the institution, and finding them strong, adjourned to meet another day. In the meantime, the university volunteer center helped students get involved in area earthquake relief efforts, and the Seaver College SGA organized a benefit rock concert at Firestone Fieldhouse. Other students pitched in to feed hungry refugees from the quake at Tent City in Los Angeles' Lanark Park.[35]

They volunteered their services again when Malibu suffered from a once-in-500-year rainstorm during January 1995. Beginning on the tenth, the deluge flooded Malibu Canyon Creek and Las Flores Creek, so weakening Pacific Coast Highway bridges that officials closed them—and all of PCH. The raging waters turned recently burned canyons into mudslides; washed away a Malibu landmark, Cosentino Nursery, at the mouth of Las Flores Creek; and interrupted sources of power. Upon the advice of the emergency preparedness team, university administrators closed the campus for all academic purposes, although it permitted state authorities to use it as a safe harbor for evacuees from nearby canyons. As generally happened in flooding situations, at least 100 students living on campus volunteered to fill sandbags for the community.[36]

Three years later, in February 1998, Malibu suffered from pounding surf that included fifteen-foot waves and another downpour that also resulted in extensive mudslides, road closures, and cancellation of classes. Again, the university's emergency preparedness committee served the community well.[37]

In confronting global realities, local challenges, and natural disasters, Pepperdine University during the Davenport presidency was opportunistic, innovative, and resilient. Institutional adaptability, originality, and buoyancy— at home and abroad—would continue to characterize Pepperdine leadership into the twenty-first century.

CHAPTER 49

REVAMPING SEAVER COLLEGE

J ohn F. Wilson served as dean of Seaver College from 1983–1998, beginning his term shortly before Davenport was named president and stepping aside shortly before Davenport did. During his fifteen-year tenure, Wilson thought deeply about the purpose and character of higher education in general and Christian higher education in particular. He eagerly embraced the notion that Seaver College was offering a "values-centered education," but he wanted to define what that meant, just whose values it embraced. The *Los Angeles Times*, he noted, considered Pepperdine's core values to be mere trivialities that focused on chapel attendance and restrictions on drinking, dancing, and dorm visitation. The student magazine, *Oasis*, agreed with the *Times*, but added one of its own, affluence.[1]

For Wilson, however, the essential values of a Christian college had to be those of Jesus Christ: being right rather than rich, serving rather than being served, loving rather than winning.[2] Those were the values that the faculty manifested when they participated in communities of faith, and which they affirmed by leading a spiritual life and modeling everyday Christ-like interactions.[3]

Wilson also had a clear vision of Seaver as a liberal arts college. It was to embody academic excellence, student centeredness, social involvement, technological literacy, and religious and ethical values. Students and faculty should be representative of the prevailing demographic and committed to cooperative or workplace learning.[4] It would also feature a curriculum with a strong general education component (breadth) and with focused and cohesive majors (depth). Like President Davenport, he envisioned the faculty's priority as "quality teaching" rather than "quality research." Wilson saw the teacher serving as a model of what it meant to be a human being of value. To him, teaching was not simply a job, but a way of being. The task of a quality teacher was "not to fill a bucket, but to light a fire." It irked him that faculty spoke of teaching "loads" but research "opportunities." Teaching and not academic research, Wilson believed, was "Seaver's best hope for academic greatness."[5]

From Wilson's perspective, there were several concepts that must be understood for the college to encourage high student performance and satisfaction. He identified five of them:

- students perform best in a "culture of high expectations";
- the freshman year is crucial in ensuring student success;
- general education and the major must blend into a coherent curriculum;
- students learn more when the classroom extends out into the world through internships, practice, action, and fieldwork; and
- quality instruction involves active learning.

But Wilson also believed that in the equation of quality learning, students have responsibilities to exercise: they must find creative ways to synthesize, apply, and use the information shared in a classroom setting. If not, the faculty's brilliant lectures and written masterpieces would be "delivered to the wind and engraved on the tide."[6]

Distinctive Agendas

Wilson had two major agendas when he assumed leadership of Seaver College. One was for the college "to stand out in the U.S." academically; the other was for it to stand out because of its Christian values.[7] Neither of these agendas was achievable, in his view, given the way the college currently delivered its liberal arts program. Thus he advocated reducing units of credit given per course from four to three units and returning to the semester as opposed to the trimester system. He envisioned a semester calendar that lengthened fall and spring terms by one week each and permitted summer sessions of two six-week or three four-week terms.[8]

Wilson also supported a teaching assignment of four classes, or twelve units each semester and one class, or four units each the summer. He opposed faculty teaching overloads and taking on administrative and other tasks in lieu of teaching. Such practices, he believed took teachers out of the classroom and contributed to an embarrassing faculty/student ratio.[9]

Seaver faculty endorsed Wilson's proposals to return to a semester system, which, despite the reservations of Norvel Young and Howard White, university authorities adopted with the 1989–1990 academic year. With it came an overall course reduction of thirty-two to twenty-eight units or a 12–12–4 course assignment. But the faculty had reservations about changing the number of units granted for a typical class from four to three; that change would mean each faculty person would be responsible for *four* three-unit classes rather than the typical *three* four-unit classes. With little support from the faculty, Wilson had to table that proposal.[10]

The Seaver faculty was even less enthusiastic about Wilson's notion that academic excellence required some personal commitment. As the dean put it, excellence required giving full time and value for money the university paid; creating a community of scholars who loved to learn rather than just publish; and demonstrating "singularity of purpose, intellectual interaction, and the celebration of ritual."[11] Wilson did not understand how faculty members could feel themselves to be a part of the inner life of the college and not attend convocation and graduation ceremonies, for example.[12]

Revising Seaver Curriculum

As part of the university-wide strategic planning process, Dean Wilson charged an academic program task force to review Seaver College's liberal arts curriculum within the context of current national debate. The National Endowment for the Humanities, the Association of American Colleges, and

John F. Wilson was the third and longest-serving dean of Seaver College, arriving at the school in 1983 after a national search and holding the position for fifteen years. Wilson worked throughout his term to enhance academic excellence and foster a Christian environment at Seaver.

the National Institute of Education all had expressed concern with deficient writing skills in the general public; disinterest in foreign languages and cultures; and disregard for self-discovery, critical thinking, and values clarification as educational outcomes.

Wilson charged the task force to discern whether the college's twelve-year-old curriculum had been more concerned with balancing the unit-load distribution among the divisions than achieving "sound theoretical and academic goals." Omitting mathematics, foreign languages, and speech from the general education curriculum seemed pedagogically unconscionable to him. It also seemed that some of the core lectures had lost their interdisciplinary orientation; that freshman seminars were neither attended by freshmen nor organized as seminars; and that language composition instruction was divorced from literature instruction. Altogether, he feared that the Malibu GE curriculum was little more than a shell of what its founders had intended and had lost its power to unify fragmented knowledge around Christian truth.[13]

After a careful review of the general studies program during the 1984–1985 academic year, the task force proposed a complete revamping of the GE curriculum. Among other things, it recommended a three-course lecture/discussion sequence in Western heritage (twelve units); a two-course sequence of English composition/literature (eight units); and a two-course—later three—sequence in religion (eight/nine units). The committee also proposed an enhanced freshman seminar that would emphasize oral and written skills as well as instruction on how to navigate the first-year experience.[14]

Furthermore, it advocated a laboratory course in the natural sciences; a psychology, sociology, or anthropology course; a course in speech and rhetoric; two courses selected from among American history, economics, or political science; a mathematics or computer science course; and an upper-division seminar in any discipline outside the student's major as a capstone (subsequently changed by the Seaver academic council to one course in non-Western cultures). The committee also recommended that students take four units of physical education and establish competency in one foreign language.[15]

Although the total number of units devoted to general education courses did not change substantially from the previous curriculum (50 percent of the 128 units required for graduation), the proposed course of study required a program of predetermined core and distributed courses. The emphasis upon Western heritage, foreign languages, mathematics, and non-Western heritage placed the new Seaver curriculum on a level of its own nationally.

Although the Seaver Academic Council (SAC) approved the curriculum changes in July 1985, three years passed before they were fully operational. Launching the freshman seminars proved especially controversial. The faculty disagreed as to whether the seminars were to emphasize academic *content* or experiential *context*. Introduction of the Western heritage sequence and the speech courses was only slightly less controversial. Everything required more space, faculty, and money than was available.

How to fit the Great Books Colloquium, an innovative four-semester sequence inaugurated in 1985, into the curriculum represented another challenge, as did the new non-Western heritage requirement. The gift of a tea house valued at $200,000 by the Uransenke Foundation of Kyoto, Japan, gave the latter a particular luster. Helpful in these transitions, however, was a new freshman advising program that featured in-office counseling by faculty. Because that feature proved so beneficial, Seaver College was nationally recognized for its "Outstanding Institutional Advising Program" in 1990.[16]

Major—and Majors—Changes

The Wilson deanship also instigated a close study of the structure of majors. Like higher education critics nationwide, Wilson did not see that faculty had put much effort into presenting the major as the "method by which a certain discipline searches for truth," or a structured way of thinking. Moreover, there seemed to be little coherency within each discipline or similar requirements from one major to another, with some requiring twenty-four units, while others required seventy-two. In Wilson's judgment, faculty seemed not to appreciate that students forgot 80 to 90 percent of data within a year of when they first learned it, which called into question the pedagogical methods that merely poured facts into student heads.

While the new general education curriculum pruned some programs in the interest of efficiency (human values, leisure sciences), others were planted and cultivated vigorously. Among these were programs in the religion division, then chaired by biblical scholar and teacher Thomas Olbricht, who had arrived in 1986. In the next decade he managed to transform the division's curriculum and personnel. Initially students could fulfill their two-course, eight-unit GE requirement by taking a course entitled "Jesus the Christ" and another from a menu of religion courses. Working with Dean Wilson, Olbricht got college approval, despite some faculty objection, for a three-course, nine-unit GE requirement with one course covering the Old Testament, another covering the New Testament, and a third concerned with religion and culture.

There were also changes in the graduate program. Since 1944 the religion faculty had offered a MA degree that was mostly restricted to the Pepperdine campus. Olbricht was eager to develop a graduate degree that could work effectively at off-campus locations, and he proposed an MS degree of thirty-six units, with comprehensive exams. Each of the nine courses would be taught over four weekends, making it possible for a student to complete the work in two years. The program was launched in Seattle in the facilities of the Northwest Church of Christ in 1988. Thirty students began; twenty-four graduated two years later.[17]

The off-campus degree program was not without its critics. Vice President Michael Adams considered it a "welfare program" for the church leadership because of reduced rates of tuition and unadulterated "featherbedding," presumably because students could complete a course in four weekends. Provost Bill Adrian, however, was a strong defender, seeing the program as a service to the church and worthy of discounted tuition because the division's best faculty taught without compensation.[18] Adrian's position prevailed, and the program continued through 2007 with stops in cities like Portland, Fresno, Phoenix, Albuquerque, Boise, and Kansas City.

In 1989, Olbricht, Wilson, and Adrian successfully introduced a master of divinity (MDiv) degree, a seventy-six-unit, three-year professional degree. It won approval from SAC and the University Management Committee (UMC) despite serious reservations about its economic viability. The program began with thirteen students and became so popular that over time most students pursuing a graduate degree in religion opted for the MDiv program.[19]

International Studies

Courses offered by the Institute for the Study of Asian Cultures (ISAC) provided another addition to the Seaver curriculum. This program was one of the benefits that arrived with Glenn Webb in 1987. He came to the Seaver faculty to head up the new Fine Arts Division that would include music, art, and theater, and have responsibility for the fall musical. He brought with him an expertise in Asian culture that promised to enrich Seaver's general education curriculum.

After 1988, he organized ISAC and offered an introductory course on the sources of Asian tradition and a series of advanced courses on Japan and China. Additionally, he and his wife, Carole, taught courses on "The Way of Tea," or Chado, utilizing the historic tea house and utensils that the Uransenke Foundation had given to the university. The tea house was first lodged on the upper floor of the Weisman Museum, and then moved to the upper level of Payson Library. Following the retirement of the Webbs in 2004, instruction in tea ended, and the university gifted the house to the Huntington Museum in Pasadena, California.[20]

Complementing ISAC, Seaver College inaugurated a new interdisciplinary international studies program in 1989. It was proposed by Professor of Communication Fred Casmir, who was known internationally for his work in cross-culture communication. In concert with the national push to globalize and "interdisciplinize" the higher education curriculum, the new

major enabled students to specialize in Asian studies, international business, European studies, and intercultural communication studies. Its work
was facilitated by a generous gift of $100,000 from William H. Williams III,
a parent of one of Casmir's students. The program sparked some opposition,
however, as the political scientists saw international studies as part of their
discipline and found the Seaver interdisciplinary approach unsatisfactory.[21]

Internships and Honor Programs

Within the context of collaborative learning, an emphasis of President
Davenport and Dean Wilson, Seaver launched an undergraduate internship
program, or "workplace education," in Washington, D.C., in the summer of
1992. It was designed to serve all students and majors. As director, the administration appointed John Watson, former vice president for student affairs
whose position had just been restructured out of existence. Watson organized
"Pepperdine on the Potomac" with the assistance of the Center for Strategic
and International Studies and the Heritage Foundation.

The long-range plan was for the program to resemble Seaver's year-round
European programs with students and a faculty member living in a univer-
sity-owned residential facility. In the meantime, students filled summer
intern positions, enrolled in academic coursework to parallel the internship,
had guest speakers, experienced a weekly convocation, participated in common co-curricular activities, and lived in the Virginian hotel in Arlington,
Virginia, near a Metro station. Turning the program into a successful year-
round enterprise was difficult, however, primarily because it was virtually
impossible to meet the curricular preferences of each student. The university
in 2007 purchased an elegant and centrally located building on Pennsylvania
Avenue—just three blocks northwest of the White House—to house the students and most program activities. But the building did not solve the core program problem.[22]

With strong encouragement from Dean Wilson, Seaver College also
launched a three-year "Honors" program in 1994. As described in the college
catalog, it was designed to further challenge scholarship-level students and
enhance "an already rigorous curriculum at Seaver College." A faculty mentor
would guide participants in personalized tutorials that explored the humanities and cultivated critical thinking and reasoning skills. The expected attrac-
tion was that participants could complete their undergraduate work of 128 units
in six semesters plus two six-week summer sessions, saving a year's worth of
board and room charges. However, course scheduling problems often required
faculty and staff to make programmatic accommodations for students, who

frequently decided to return for their fourth year anyway. No more than two cohorts actually completed the program before it was abandoned.[23]

A more successful and sustainable curricular initiative allowed undergraduate students to engage in serious research. Dean Wilson may have had misgivings about faculty research, but he had none about student research, which met his criterion for active learning. Student research as a pedagogy was well established in the natural sciences, but it became more entrenched with the Summer Undergraduate Research-Biology (SURB) program that was funded by the National Science Foundation (NSF) from 1989 through 2014. Early principal investigators in the program included biologists Stephen Davis, Gary Tallman, Dwayne Simmons, and Lee Kats. From the beginning of SURB, undergraduates in the natural sciences were authors and co-authors of ninety publications, made 320 presentations at professional meetings, and wrote fifty honors theses. Given the program's success, the Seaver Dean's office generalized the program and offered grants to involve students and faculty from other disciplines during the first decade of the twenty-first century.[24]

Structural Changes, Reorganizations

Initially, Seaver College had been divided into six traditional academic divisions: business administration, communication, humanities and fine arts, natural science, religion, and social science and teacher education. In 1985, a faculty committee chaired by Professor of Math Carol Adjemian recommended creation of a new fine arts division that would contain art, music, and theater and creation of an unnamed division that would include physical education, leisure science, and sports medicine. Other recommendations included a rearrangement of several disciplines.[25]

Dean Wilson had reservations only about the proposal to create two new divisions. He preferred only one, a new fine arts division that would contain art, music, theater and subsequently art history, the leadership of which would be assigned to Glenn Webb beginning in 1987. But Wilson did support moving the composition faculty from the communication to the humanities division. It disappointed him, however, that most of those composition faculty members soon migrated to teaching literature, leaving composition instruction primarily to adjuncts. Subsequently, foreign languages migrated from the communication division in 2005 to merge with international studies and form the Center For International Studies And Languages (CISL), which would later become a full division. Robert Lloyd was the founding chair.

Structurally, the administrative reorganization imposed upon the university by President Davenport in 1992 had major implications for Seaver College. It required Seaver to operate in a manner more consistent with the three professional schools, having managerial responsibility for the student's entire educational experience, both curricular and co-curricular. It brought under the supervision of Dean Wilson the offices of student affairs, admissions and financial aid, and international programs. Upon the advice of faculty, he created within his own office the position of dean of faculty, to whom the division chairs reported, and who supervised the SAC, the RTP committee, and the academic budget.[26]

Added too was the position of dean of academic administration, who had responsibility for academic advising, cultural enrichment, general education, first-year programs, academic computing, and the academic services budget. As the "Dean of Deans," Wilson organized Seaver College's other deans (Dean of Students D'Esta Love, Dean of Admission Paul Long, Dean of International Programs William Phillips, Dean of Faculty Dwayne Van Rheenen, and Dean of Academic Administration Carolyn Vos Strache) into an administrative team that met regularly to coordinate the activities of the college.[27]

Programs to Support Students, Mission

During his tenure as dean, Wilson inaugurated several notable student support programs. To improve a student's composition skills, Seaver College opened a writing center under the direction of Cynthia Novak in 1988. The following year, the college also scheduled a "dead week" at the request of the students and the instigation of the provost.

A volunteer center was designed to support what President Davenport called values-centered education.[28] Opening under the direction of the Office of Student Affairs in the fall of 1988, the center had its origins in the American Humanics program. Students Scott Pitts and Christy Hogan acted as co-chairs, with Sara Jackson serving as staff advisor. The center got its first recognition by sponsoring "Step Forward Day" the following fall, when students departed the Malibu campus to engage in volunteer work that ranged from picking up trash to weeding school yards. Some 150 participated. That number went up each year: 417 in 1991, 600 in 1993, 750 in 1996, and 1,000 in 1999. Through the volunteer center, Seaver students also assisted teenagers at Kid's Club on Skid Row, entertained inner-city youth on the Malibu campus, helped with the cleanup and social displacement following the Rodney King riots, and offered assistance to victims of the Northridge earthquake. As early as 1990, some students used their spring vacations to participate in "Project Serve," a program that allowed students to participate in nonprofit work in a variety of locations—including eight students who went to Uganda. Project Serve participants were so selfless that the *Malibu Times* bestowed its Dolphin

Award upon them in 1992, a heartening moment given Malibu's ongoing negativity toward Pepperdine.[29]

Not until 1996, however, did values-centered education actually become part of the academic curriculum as "service-learning." An aspect of the "learn by doing" pedagogy then popular in higher education, service learning integrated community service activities with academic study. At the request of President Davenport, Sheila Bost pioneered service-learning at Seaver College, and by spring 1999, some fifty classes had service-learning components. Professors Cynthia Novak, Lorie Goodman, Regan Schaffer, and Jeff Banks, among others, embraced the new pedagogy eagerly. Their 1997 outreach to the homeless community in Los Angeles through a forty-hour "Urban Plunge" project demonstrated service-learning at its best.[30]

And Seaver also offered its students many extra-curricular opportunities that supported learning, including two annual lectures offered to the Pepperdine community by the religion division. The first of these was the Thomas F. Staley Lecture, which featured a scholar from the larger Christian community. The William M. Green Lecture highlighted notable Church of Christ scholars. What became the Thomas F. Staley Lecture had its beginning with Elton Trueblood, the well-known Quaker divine, in 1978. There was a succession of distinguished Staley participants during the Davenport years, including Os Guinness, Roberta Hestenes, Philip Yancey, William Willimon, Elizabeth Achtemeier, Fred Craddock, and Dallas Willard. The Green lecture opened with a presentation by J. P. Sanders, former dean of Pepperdine College and president of Columbia Christian College, in October 1980. Lecturers in this series included Howard White, Richard Hughes, David Davenport, Carl Holladay, and Fred Gray.[31]

In addition to the Staley and Green lectures, students also had the benefit of the Dean's Distinguished Lecture series that began in January 1999. When I followed Wilson as dean, I promoted the series as a means of enriching the intellectual discourse of the college with presentations by scholars, public figures, and opinion makers. Michael Dukakis, former governor of Massachusetts and 1988 presidential candidate, delivered the inaugural lecture. He was followed by Jared Diamond, Ron Hansen, and Chris Matthews. Joyce Appleby, Martin E. Marty, John Vickers, and Juan Williams gave the lectures the next year. Other notable participants included Carlos Fuentes, Barbara Boxer, Robert N. Bellah, Laura Skandera Trombley, William Cronon, Jack Hanna, John Kerry, Philip Jenkins, Cornel West, and Condoleezza Rice. After 2008, the lecture was named the W. David Baird Distinguished Lecture Series and generously endowed by Melanie and Richard Flamminio.

A unique measure of academic support came through the Student Portfolio Assessment Project, which was devised in 1994 with the help of the general education committee and led by the associate dean of Seaver College, Don Thompson. The project was designed to improve teaching and learning by exploring how students experienced college life both in and out of the classroom. Forty-six first-year students, or two from each freshman seminar, agreed to collect their academic work including syllabi, notes, tests, and papers and turn them over to a faculty team researching critical reasoning and the moral and ethical development of students. Students got one unit of academic credit, and the faculty got interesting insights to the teaching-learning processes that were later presented to conferences nationwide.[32]

The data spoke to matters of ethnic diversity, writing across the curriculum, undergraduate research, service learning, and connecting general education with the major. Faculty from all seven divisions participated in the analysis, making it an interdisciplinary project that built collegiality and intellectual capital. It also became the basis for general education reform at Seaver College in the late 1990s and a model for e-portfolios at institutions across the country. Significantly, WASC saw the project as a cutting-edge effort to evaluate the effectiveness of the curricular changes under way at Seaver College.[33]

Did the curricular reform and extra-curricular opportunities improve the academic record of Seaver College during the Wilson era? Data suggested that it did. In 1983, only 51 percent of freshmen entering graduated five years later, a ratio well below Stanford (88 percent), Biola (71 percent), LMU (62 percent), and USD (58 percent). By 1998, however, the five-year graduation rate had increased to 71 percent, an improvement of 20 points. Of the 1983 freshman class, only 75 percent came back for the sophomore year. By 1998, the freshman to sophomore retention rate had risen to 86 percent.[34] A more robust financial aid program likely contributed to graduation and retention rate improvements as well.[35]

Faculty Matters

During the Davenport era, the size of the Seaver College professoriate grew from 118 full-time and 132 part-time members to 171 full-time and 138 part-time. Accordingly, faculty/student ratios improved from 1:16 to 1:12. Nineteen percent of the full-time faculty was female in 1986; 24 percent by 1998. No more than 6 percent of the Seaver faculty was other than Caucasian in 1986, a figure that almost doubled by 2000. Fifty-nine percent of Seaver's tenured or tenure-track faculty members were members of Churches of Christ in 1985, a rate that slipped to 55 percent in 2000.[36]

Seaver tenured or tenure-track faculty members enjoyed an array of benefits initiated in the Davenport administration. As has been noted, their salaries rose in those years to the top quartile nationally.[37] Moreover, beginning with the academic year 1996–1997 they were no longer required to teach one four-unit course during the summer term, being contracted to a so-called 3–3 load as opposed to a 3–3–1 load. The faculty managed the change by giving up a 1.5 percent salary increase and accepting an additional revenue obligation for the summer budget of $230,000. Seaver Faculty Association President President Cyndia Clegg and her colleagues promoted the load reduction, which was also warmly embraced by Deans Wilson and Van Rheenen.[38]

The Seaver Faculty Association had become the voice of the Seaver College professoriate by the mid-1990s. It was made up of all members of the Seaver College faculty, met only on special occasions, and vested its authority through an executive committee of officers and one elected representative from each division. This executive committee replaced the faculty organization committee that had represented faculty interests in the 1970s and 1980s. The new governance system reduced the number of standing faculty committees to thirteen.[39]

A task force chaired by Norman Hughes reviewed all academic personnel policies and procedures pertaining to Seaver College in 1989 and found a number of issues that needed attention, most notably the credentials and time in service requirements for professorial rankings and the nature of tenure reviews. The task force recommended that assistant professors hold doctorates or their equivalent, that associate professors have six years of prior service as an assistant, and that professors have six years of teaching and scholarly excellence as associates. It also endorsed a pre-tenure review process during the candidate's third year of service, commended a post-tenure review for professors of all ranks, and urged creation of a title "Distinguished Professor" to honor exceptional faculty who had nine years of service as a professor. Both faculty and administrators embraced these recommendations. They also accepted a mandatory retirement age of 70, but administrative voices nixed task force proposals for an early retirement option.[40]

Examining Faculty Morale

Although Seaver faculty were pleased with their competitive salaries, reduced teaching workloads, attractive benefits package, and clarified professional guidelines, many seemingly remained unhappy with their circumstances. In 1992, Dean Wilson expressed his dismay at how badly Seaver faculty treated each other via a sermon-like address delivered at the opening convocation of the faculty. Using the biblical book of Ephesians as his text, he urged members of the faculty to set aside lying, bitterness, rage, slander, and malice and rededicate themselves to the bonds of peace which unity of the Spirit provided.[41]

The address resonated with many, but it aggravated others. One professor protested that the Seaver faculty was "the closest thing to a Christian community that [he had] ever experienced" and that it appeared that Wilson's "acquaintances on the faculty [were not his]."[42] Wilson did not back down. "Good people, with good motives, are constantly maligned, called liars, ridiculed, etc.," he wrote. He just wanted everyone to analyze their hearts and 'see if there be any sin.'"[43]

Over the years, Wilson expressed great concern about the low level of faculty morale that he felt pervaded the Seaver College campus. Following a faculty survey designed to gather information on the matter, he met with the faculty advisory committee in the fall of 1995. Based on his research, Wilson attributed low morale to the widespread perception that the Seaver faculty was overworked, specifically that the teaching load of seven courses was too high. He also attributed the morale problem to the mysterious way in which the university did its budgeting without any faculty input. He noted the anxiety generated by the promotion and tenure process, especially as it related to scholarship. According to Wilson, the faculty felt that the rules were unclear and that the criteria constantly changed. And, finally, he attributed it to a student advising system—the very system that had brought national acclaim to the university—which the faculty believed reduced them to mere clerks. Interestingly, he did not report any linkage between low morale and the institutional connection with Churches of Christ.[44]

Understanding the causes of low faculty morale and making it go away, of course, were two different things. Encouraged by Wilson's office, the Davenport administration agreed to reduce the teaching obligation to six classes per year and added faculty representatives to the University Planning Committee, which handled budget issues. A task force clarified rank, tenure, and promotion guidelines. And Wilson and members of the faculty adopted strategic plans that restated the mission, goals, objectives, and priorities of Seaver College.

But all of these efforts seemingly raised faculty morale on campus just barely. In 1998, one writer blamed that on workloads and teaching expectations. How could a normal teacher in a single syllabus connect the content of his or her course to Christian mission, incorporate the advice of the center for teaching and learning excellence, and research collaboratively with students, he asked? How could each major program develop both a capstone course and an internship? And what was the meaning of a critical mass requirement of 60 percent Church of Christ faculty as stated in the assumptions document when it came to hiring qualified academic specialists? On the other hand, faculty members like Professor of Great Books Darrell Colson found Seaver College "a really comfortable place to be." In a survey sponsored by the Higher Education

Research Institute (HERI) of UCLA in 1999, Seaver faculty confirmed Colson's attitude and declared themselves generally pleased to be where they were— despite, presumably, low morale.[45]

Unprecedented Strategic Plan

Seaver College created two integrated strategic plans during the Davenport years, one adopted in 1988 and the other in 1997. The first was without precedent in the history of the college. It resulted from the work of thirty-two evaluation committees, whose multiple reports Dean Wilson blended into a single, integrated plan.[46] The overall strategy of the academic plan, Wilson told the faculty, was "to continue to offer a comparatively small number of programs, but to ensure that *every single one of them* is excellent." Wilson did not think that Seaver College wanted "'throwaway' programs . . . purposely kept weak in order to provide resources for other, more favored majors."[47]

The 1988 plan included an eloquent mission statement for Seaver. The college existed, it stipulated, "to provide a link between the knowledge and wisdom of the past and present with the challenges of the future." The plan defined the college as undergraduate and residential, whose task was "to prepare persons of diverse economic, social, and religious backgrounds to become moral and intellectual leaders and to challenge them to value service above material success." As a liberal arts college, moreover, Seaver was "to nourish and transmit the noblest ideas of Western culture, while not eschewing those of the East." Its curriculum was "to sharpen the mind, ennoble the heart, broaden the vision, and cultivate the arts of speaking and writing."[48]

"Devoted to the relentless search for truth in an atmosphere of freedom of inquiry," Seaver's degree programs were to train students "to think, to question, to doubt, to believe, and to affirm." Above all, Seaver was a Christian college, affirming in its programs that there were "sources of truth deeper than those of secular culture." Indeed, "A commitment to Judeo-Christian beliefs regarding the origin, nature, and destiny of humanity permeate the curriculum," while "The College's ties to the Churches of Christ call it to a serious commitment to authentic biblical Christianity."[49]

According to the 1988 strategic plan, Seaver College faculty members were part of a community of scholars who drew strength from certain commonalities and diversities. Commonalities included belief in the primacy of undergraduate teaching, the completion of a rigorous doctoral program, defining oneself as both an academician and a role model, an inquisitive spirit, devotion to Christian moral and ethical values, and a sense of servanthood. Diversities were represented at Seaver in age groups, levels of experience, rank and tenure status, gender, ethnicity, areas of expertise, and different Christian traditions.

The plan defined Seaver College students as "the heart of the enterprise." They were expected to have outstanding records of academic performance and service activities, be of strong moral character, possess inquisitive minds and a willingness to learn, be creative, and be imbued with special talents, especially the capacity for leadership. Incoming classes should be diverse in economic and social status, geographical origins, and racial and cultural heritage. They should also reflect diversity in religious traditions, while at the same time confirming the university's relationship with the Churches of Christ. Graduating students would leave with a passion for lifelong learning; an ability to think clearly, logically, independently, and critically; and a capacity to communicate effectively. They would also depart with a broad cultural perspective, moral integrity, and an enhanced potential for service.

The academic component of the strategic plan was premised upon the assumptions that Seaver College could be truly selective in its undergraduate admission, that the full-time student numbers would be constant, that resources would be finite, that the college was the "flagship" school within the university, and that "better, not bigger" described it. The plan envisioned a student body of 2,600, 95 percent of whom would be full-time, residential, and "traditional" undergraduates. With a stipulated student/faculty ratio of 16:1 rather than 19:1, the plan called for adding 27.6 additional full-time positions over the next five to six years. The plan analyzed every Seaver College major in terms of numbers of students and faculty, setting five- to six-year targets for each.

Because the strategic plan was so explicit in its objectives, it generated a lot of discussion at Seaver College, and tensions ran high in more than one faculty gathering. Nonetheless, the SAC adopted the plan, as did the university strategic planning committee in November 1988. Dean Wilson took some satisfaction in that action, believing the plan's details committed the university's central administration to increasing resources for Seaver College over the next five to seven years.

He was quickly disabused of that expectation, however. In deliberations over annual financial plans, the university budget committee more often than not acted as if there were no approved strategic plan that envisioned at least five new faculty positions per year for Seaver College. Wilson was mystified. During discussions over the 1990–1991 fiscal year budget, he lamented to Provost Adrian that "I think this is the first time in my seven years here when, despite the strategic plan, we will apparently make no progress at all toward building a full-time faculty of adequate size."[50]

Vice President for Finance Mike O'Neal tried to placate him. He regretted that the budgetary process "occasionally" seemed to "drive wedges between various segments of University management," but he wanted Wilson to know "that our ultimate goals for properly financing Seaver College operations are not very different."[51]

Despite Wilson's concern over inadequate funding, the strategic plan remained a viable planning document through the duration of his deanship. Updated and supplemented by sections on enrollment management and student life and reaffirmed by the university strategic planning committee in 1995, the Seaver Integrated Strategic Plan provided an especially useful context for reviewing Seaver College's general education program, inaugurating first-year programs, and adding a Great Books program. It was a constant reminder that the student was at the heart of the educational enterprise, that Seaver was a liberal arts college rather than a pre-professional one, that it was a residential rather than a commuter college, that it had a Christian mission, and that it had historic, worthwhile ties to Churches of Christ. Its characterization of the Seaver student rationalized admission policies for the first time in the history of the college, making plain that the admission's office was tasked not just to fill a class, but also to shape it. The plan also influenced faculty hiring during the 1990s.[52]

Updating the Strategic Plan

The 1988 Seaver College plan was designed to guide the college for a period of six to seven years, so in 1995, Dean Wilson appointed a task force to review and rewrite the academic segment of the integrated plan. Members included June Payne Palacio and Don Thompson, who represented the faculty, and Sherry Woodroof and Mark Davis, who represented the offices of admissions and student affairs. Don Shores and I represented division chairs; and Dean of Faculty Dwayne Van Rheenen represented Dean Wilson and co-chaired, with Palacio, the panel. (When Van Rheenen took a position at Abilene Christian University, Richard Hughes replaced him as a member, and I replaced him as co-chair.) The task force held a series of meetings in late 1995 and early 1996 while a four- to five- person faculty committee performed program reviews of each major. These audits were designed to exemplify a grassroots approach to strategic planning, with an overarching objective of involving faculty early and systematically in the process. The resulting thirty-one reports were forwarded to the chairs of the divisions, who had the responsibility of folding them into a coherent report and action plan by August 1, 1996.[53] Those divisional documents were the subject of sub-meetings at the annual faculty retreat later that month.

The reviewed and edited divisional studies and action plans were then forwarded to the task force, which over the next year condensed them into a college-wide plan that emphasized fifteen different "key elements of quality" (KEQ). The college-wide plan was created in the context of a presidentially commissioned blue ribbon report on Liberal Learning in the Twenty-first Century and Pepperdine's "University Assumptions for Strategic Planning."

Taking Christian mission and academic excellence as givens, the task force grouped the KEQs into three categories: developing the community of scholarship, balancing the learning process, and transforming the student. To each category were attached five KEQs, which ranged from excellence in the classroom, to co-curricular learning, to outcomes assessment. The task force presented the plan to the faculty at its fall retreat August 19, 1997.[54]

Although the faculty had played a large role in shaping the academic plan, its criticisms of the document were sharp, with complaints about too much or too little emphasis on this or that program. To some, the articulation of five to six goals per KEQ was impractical; the approach was shotgun-like rather than rifle-like. Good strategic plans were written on the back of an envelope rather than thirteen single-spaced pages. Moreover, critics said, another plan was unnecessary because it duplicated the work of the Blue Ribbon Commission on Liberal Learning in the Twenty-first Century.

The criticism was so withering that task force members covered their heads with sacks when they presented the final report to faculty in an October 1997 meeting, hoping for a bit of comic relief. The strategy worked. In its laughter, the faculty concluded there was no conspiracy afoot and that the academic strategic plan was worthy of support. The document was then incorporated into an integrated strategic plan and approved by the university strategic planning committee in March 1998. It was one of the final accomplishments of John Wilson's deanship, standing the college in good stead through the WASC review in 2000 and my years as Seaver dean, or for another decade.[55]

CHAPTER 50

TRANSITIONS

By any measure, fifteen years as a college administrator is a long time. John Wilson served that long as dean of Seaver College, and David Davenport served a similar length of time as president of Pepperdine University. By the end of their terms, both had compiled records of impressive accomplishments that reflected thoughtful, effective, and committed leadership. Their legacies provided foundations upon which their successors could build an even better Pepperdine in the twenty-first century.

Dean Wilson in 1998 told the Pepperdine board of regents that he never intended to be a dean nor serve as one for so many years. But in his years of service, he had come to understand that academic administration was "mostly helping other people to do what you'd really like to be doing yourself . . . teaching, writing, creating new ideas, and mentoring students." It also helped if you talked little.[1]

Wilson told the board he could list some achievements that had made him proud. These included

- an international studies program ranked as best in the nation;
- an increase of the number of faculty and administrative positions held by women and ethnic minorities;
- creation of the Great Books program;
- establishment of the Seaver Board of Visitors as a support group;
- organization of the fine arts division and a greatly increased emphasis on the arts;
- establishment of volunteer and academic advising centers;
- major reorganization of the general education program and the entire area of student life;
- massive infusion of computers into the life of the college;
- improvements in the budgeting system of Seaver College; and

- a successful first-year seminar program.[2]

Wilson asked the board to hold firm in its support for the fundamentals upon which he had built his deanship: a broad liberal arts-oriented undergraduate curriculum, a learning environment designed to educate the whole person, a faculty willing to serve as role models, a vital spiritual heritage, and the importance of maintaining strong roots in Churches of Christ in an inclusive, open atmosphere. "Schools which cut their roots," he warned, "like cut flowers, are beautiful only temporarily."[3]

Executive Vice President Andrew Benton heard Wilson's assessment of his tenure as dean and offered a gentle qualification. "Although I know you would be the first to share the credit with the faculty and your other administrative colleagues within Seaver College, the fact is that it has been your leadership and vision that has enabled the remarkable progress of Seaver College over the past fifteen years."[4] David Davenport agreed. Wilson brought to the administrative table, he said, "a breadth of knowledge about higher education, a scholarly bent and an insight to the educational process" that was unmatched. "I do not know anyone in the country who really has a clearer vision of what it means to be a Christian liberal arts college."[5]

Wilson retired as dean as of July 31, 1998, transitioning into a new role as director of the Institute for the Study of Archaeology and Religion, continuing the work in which he had developed an international reputation. He had recently been appointed as Kershaw Lecturer by the American Institute of Archaeology and the American Schools of Oriental Research and after a sabbatical in London would also take on additional teaching assignments as professor of religion at Seaver.

Dean Search Launched

When the Davenport administration launched a search for Wilson's successor, it followed closely the "Procedures for the Selection of Specified Personnel and Faculty of Pepperdine University." Provost Steven Lemley appointed a seven-person review committee made up of chairs and faculty members and published an announcement of the search in national education journals and papers circulated in the Church of Christ community. One of the necessary credentials was that the dean must be an active member in a congregation of Churches of Christ. Faculty and staff who had been critical of previous administrator searches were heartened by the national search and review committee although some were disheartened by the Church of Christ stipulation. Professor Dan Caldwell asked Lemley to explain why, especially "when two of the present five [Pepperdine University] deans or dean-appointees do not fill this requirement."[6]

Lemley replied that it was important to have a "critical mass" of deans associated with Churches of Christ just as it was of faculty. Moreover, it was important for the university to maintain close ties with Churches of Christ and as the "flagship" of the university it was important for Seaver's most visible leader to be an active member of a congregation of the Churches of Christ.[7] Caldwell thought differently, saying the Church of Christ stipulation would mean that distinguished Seaver faculty leaders "would not even be considered to fill this position," and calling the policy "unfair, demoralizing and inconsistent."[8]

Lemley chaired the screening committee, and four candidates were invited to interview in March 1998. With input from faculty colleagues, members of the committee described their opinions of the candidates' strengths and weaknesses to the provost and president, who made the final decision. I was their choice. At the time, I was chair of the Humanities and Teacher Education Division, having come to Pepperdine in 1988 to fill the Howard A. White chair in history.

I had held appointments on the University Planning Committee, as chair of the Blue Ribbon Commission on Liberal Learning in the Twenty-first Century, co-chair of the Seaver College Strategic Planning Committee, and had served as a Fulbright scholar in New Zealand. An Oklahoma native, I had taken undergraduate degrees from George Washington University and the University of Central Oklahoma and graduate degrees in Western American history from the University of Oklahoma. Before coming to Pepperdine, I had served on faculties at the University of Arkansas, Fayetteville, and Oklahoma State University. At OSU, I had also served as chair of the History Department.

I was also a lifelong member of the Churches of Christ. John Wilson had thought deeply about what that membership meant within the context of Christian education; I had not. To me it was primarily a practical matter of the school remaining true to its historic tradition via a critical mass of church members, while earning the respect of students and academic peers via inspired teaching and solid, publishable scholarship. This practical outlook took on different colors over the years as I came to understand more about the integration of faith and learning, but during my ten years as dean, the substance of my work changed little.[9]

Death of "Mr. Pepperdine"

Another 1998 event marked a transition point for Pepperdine when Norvel Young suffered a fatal heart attack on February 17 in his on-campus home. Young, 82, had been one of Pepperdine's most visible figures since arriving as president in 1957, and his role in the survival and evolution of the institution could hardly be overstated.

The *Los Angeles Times* quoted Pepperdine President Davenport as saying that "Norvel Young was the heart of the institution. He had truly become thought of as our 'Mr. Pepperdine.' Davenport noted that it was Young's "vision that transformed Pepperdine from a small liberal arts college to a larger university with multiple schools and campuses around the world."[10]

Friends and admirers filled Firestone Fieldhouse later that week to honor Young's life and his lifelong commitment to Pepperdine.

Davenport's Stunning Announcement

In 1999, after fourteen years as president, David Davenport announced that following one more year of service he would leave Pepperdine University to become CEO of Christianity.com, a Silicon Valley start-up. The campus was stunned; Davenport was, after all, not quite fifty years of age, and still vital, effective, and visionary. But Davenport was ready for a new challenge, especially one that would allow him to work at the intersection of Christianity and culture. He had served ten years longer than the average college president, and he believed that institutions needed "the opportunity to grow around new leaders."[11]

The year 2000 seemed like an appropriate time to make a transition. Clearly, much of what he had set out to do at Pepperdine had been accomplished. The new mission statement and strategic plan assumptions declared that the institution was deeply committed to academic excellence and a Christian world view. The university generally accepted that the student was the heart of the educational enterprise and that teaching was its principal function. It also widely embraced servant leadership as a pedagogy, "lean and clean" as a system of management, and service and volunteerism as a way of relating to the world.[12]

Looking back over his years as president, Davenport could see some significant academic developments. The general education component of the undergraduate curriculum was stronger, more students were involved in international programs, learning was technologically assisted more fully, cultural enrichment was accepted as an institutional goal, and service was recognized as a method of learning.[13] Pepperdine offered nationally recognized programs in dispute resolution, school safety, and organizational development. Its master's and doctoral degrees were the best in the country in combining new technologies and face-to-face learning, and, most importantly, Davenport had presided over the founding of the School of Public Policy. In addition, athletic teams had won seven national championships in four sports, helping to make Pepperdine an "impact" player in higher education circles.[14]

There were many specific accomplishments. Because of two success-ful campaigns, the $130 million "Wave of Excellence" and the $313 million "Challenged to Lead," the endowment had increased sixfold to $386 million, the construction of major new buildings had increased facility space by 51 per-cent, a new graduate campus was under development, and permanent cam-puses in London and Florence had been procured. University enrollment had increased by 15 percent to 7,800; Step Forward Day had been institutionalized; 50 percent of Seaver students participated in an international program.[15] It was an admirable record.

But according to Davenport, the real genius of Pepperdine was not its inter-national programs, volunteer center, bricks and mortar, or Malibu address. It was instead "its foundation of classic knowledge and ancient faith, distilled from the centuries." Its genius was "the best of all worlds, yesterday, today, and tomorrow—the ancient paths of Galilee, the hallow halls of Oxford, the shimmering campuses of Pepperdine on the rim of the Pacific."[16] If his admin-istration had experienced any success, said the president, it was because it had utilized that genius.

The campus community said farewell to President Davenport in a con-vocation on March 29, 2000. The ceremony included a performance by the a cappella group Won by One, a message of thanks from Ken Durham, minis-ter of the University Church, and two videos summarizing Davenport's time at Pepperdine and his competitive spirit, especially at table tennis. With grati-tude, SGA representatives presented a mosaic of Davenport playing a saxo-phone and a book of memories; and Athletic Director John Watson presented a baseball jacket and lifelong athletic passes to Pepperdine events. Declaring a heart full of orange and blue, Davenport assured his audience that "Whatever we've meant to Pepperdine, Pepperdine has meant more for us."[17]

Unprecedented Presidential Search

Unlike Davenport or his predecessors, his successor was chosen through a process that involved regents, administrators, faculty, university friends, and students. Board of regents chair Tom Bost gave the responsibility for screen-ing candidates to a seven-person subcommittee chaired by Edward Biggers.[18] Biggers announced that the committee wanted "Pepperdine [to] continue to enhance its academic excellence" and did "not want there to be any sacrifice or loss in the Christian focus or mission of Pepperdine." He published and circu-lated a formal announcement of the search and expected qualifications of the candidate, including required membership in a Church of Christ.[19]

Biggers also asked Provost Lemley to identify the top institutional issues that should be of concern to the search committee as it interviewed presidential candidates. The provost prepared a list of six:

- new mission and assumption statements
- the focus on educational quality
- the challenge of ethnic diversity
- the role of faculty in governance
- the sustainability of financial resources
- the trials of assessment.

Lemley also identified some strategic issues that should be of concern: allocation of resources in the face of declining revenues, the blessing and burden of technology, the library, the new graduate campus, linking mission to educational programs, and needs specific to the five schools.[20]

The call for nominations generated a candidate pool of forty individuals, which the search committee then narrowed to five by November 1999. The finalists came to campus for a series of interviews with representatives from a wide array of interests both on and off campus. Those interviewed included L. Randolph Lowry, director of Pepperdine's Straus Center for Dispute Resolution; Jerry Hudson, former Malibu campus provost and president of Willamette University; John Wilson, former dean of Seaver College; Carl Holladay, professor of religion at Emory University; and Andrew K. Benton, executive vice president of Pepperdine University. Interviewers submitted their evaluations and rankings to Biggers. After sifting through the feedback, the search committee recommended and the board of regents endorsed the appointment of Benton.

On December 7, 1999, Tom Bost announced to a full house in Smothers Theater that Andrew K. Benton would be Pepperdine University's seventh president. "I believe," said Bost, "that Andy will not only bring a unique depth of understanding of our Christian mission, but also an impressive vision for continuing our ascension in stature and academic excellence."[21]

Andrew K. Benton

Benton had been part of Pepperdine's central administration since 1984. A native of Kansas, he held an undergraduate degree from Oklahoma Christian University and a law degree from Oklahoma City University. He served as a longtime assistant to the president of Oklahoma Christian while simultaneously maintaining a private practice of law. After coming to Pepperdine, he served first as assistant vice president, then vice president for administration (1987), then vice president for university affairs (1989). During those years, his greatest contribution was managing the university's relations with the state of California, the county of Los Angeles, and the city of Malibu, especially as it related to Pepperdine's long-range development plan.

Benton also served as CEO during President Davenport's two sabbaticals. Appointed executive vice president in 1991, he oversaw the university's financial affairs, the athletic department, personnel services, general counsel's office, physical plant and construction operations, as well as its governmental and public affairs efforts. He also taught both graduate and undergraduate classes. In the year before he was president, Benton successfully shepherded an $80 million, fifty-acre graduate campus development project through a controversial and complex approval process. Not only was Benton well prepared for the presidency, he was also deeply invested in the growth plans of the central administration.[22] He would be the one to determine the course of the university in the twenty-first century.

Andrew K. Benton joined Pepperdine University as assistant vice president in 1984 and was called upon to represent the university before various legislative and regulatory agencies in what was called locally the "sewer war." Subsequently he served as vice president for administration, vice president for university affairs, and executive vice president before being named Pepperdine president, where he has served since 2000.

CHAPTER 51

PROMISES TO KEEP

At the onset of the twenty-first century, George Pepperdine's dream of
founding a distinctive college that would prepare young men and
women for lives of usefulness and a life of service to God lived on. The
university's nationally recognized undergraduate and graduate academic programs demonstrated that his dream was realized. So too did opportunities for
international education; a co-curriculum filled with leadership training opportunities; nationally competitive athletic programs; a succession of forty-two
balanced budgets; competitive faculty salaries; a healthy endowment generated
by a legendary development team; its affirmation of the American Way and
free-enterprise system; and one of the most beautiful campuses in the world.

In certain areas, however, the dream had lost power. The original inner-
city campus had been abandoned in, according to some, a white flight to the
suburbs; student costs were among the highest in the nation; ethnic and gender diversity within the student body and faculty was minimal; the university's relationship with the Malibu community was problematic; WASC visiting
teams constantly nagged.

Some critics even saw the university's Christian mission as problematic,
that the influence of the cross was too subtle or too prominent. The first group
thought the university spoke ambiguously about "values-centered" education
rather than clearly about "Christ-centered" education, made few distinctions
between the fathers of the Christian faith and the fathers of the American
Way, and tended to think of religious frills (social regulations on campus,
chapel attendance, censorship of the *Graphic*) as the sum of Christian education. The second group thought the university unfairly favored members of
Churches of Christ in hiring and promotion practices, enforced out-of-date
social and behavioral conventions, and were too often guilty of double standards between their words and deeds.

But others found Christian mission alive and well. A new mission statement had been adopted; the integration of faith and learning was a viable

option; campus ministry was effective; the University Church was growing; women were leading prayers in convo; a substantial number of faculty with an active Christian faith, although not necessarily associated with Churches of Christ, had been appointed; an "assumptions document" actually defined "critical mass" of Church of Christ faculty for various schools.

All of this provided context for Andrew Benton's inaugural address in September 2000. Well aware of the strengths and weaknesses of the university, he saw five challenges looming on the horizon. He identified these as:

- strengthening the institution's resources with a billion-dollar endowment;
- strengthening its diversity by adding more qualified women and minorities to the faculty, staff, and student body;
- strengthening the connection to its religious heritage, specifically Churches of Christ;
- strengthening the sense of community that called the institution to both academic excellence and Christian mission; and
- strengthening Pepperdine's emphasis on scholarship and culture by emphasizing both research and teaching.

These challenges notwithstanding, Benton believed that the university began the twenty-first century stronger and more capable than it had ever been. Although the school had experienced remarkable growth and transformation in its first sixty-three years of life, its new president sensed that the institution did not have time to ponder the successes of its past. For there was a glorious morning ahead, he was certain, although reaching it would require a lot of hard work. As he contemplated Pepperdine University's future, therefore, he quoted with conviction the words of Robert Frost:[1]

> The woods are lovely, dark and deep,
> But I have promises to keep,
> And miles to go before I sleep,
> And miles to go before I sleep.

KEY DATES IN PEPPERDINE'S TWENTIETH CENTURY HISTORY

Spring 1937	George Pepperdine agrees to establish college; Batsell Baxter chosen first president
Sept. 21, 1937	Dedication ceremony for George Pepperdine College
Sept. 27, 1937	Classes begin
April 5, 1939	GPC is fully accredited by Northwest Association of Secondary and Higher Schools
Aug. 1, 1939	Hugh Tiner becomes second president
Jan. 1943	First Bible Lectures First graduate degree, in religion, offered
Dec. 1950	Pepperdine Foundation declared insolvent
April 5, 1951	Accrediting agency (WCA) denies request for accreditation
Summer 1957	M. Norvel Young becomes third president
Nov. 21, 1958	Young inaugurated as Pepperdine president
Fall 1959	Continuing education program established
Fall 1963	Study-abroad program launched in Heidelberg
Fall 1966	Moore Haus opens to Pepperdine students
Dec. 17, 1968	Board of Trustees approves separate School of Business, which became School of Business and Management in 1971
June 1, 1968	William S. Banowsky returns to Pepperdine as executive vice president
Oct. 2, 1968	Trustees officially accept donation of land in Malibu
Oct. 7, 1968	President Young publicly announces Malibu land acquisition
Mar. 12, 1969	Larry Kimmons killed on campus by security guard

May 6, 1969	Pepperdine acquires Orange University, College of Law
Feb. 9, 1970	"Birth of a College" gala in Los Angeles
April 5, 1970	University Church of Christ organized in Malibu
May 23, 1970	Dedication ceremony for Malibu campus
Dec. 10, 1970	Student lockout on Los Angeles campus
Jan. 1, 1971	Pepperdine College becomes Pepperdine University; School of Education opens;
	William Banowsky becomes fourth president; Norvel Young becomes chancellor
Sept. 6, 1972	Malibu campus officially opens
1973–1974	First version of Affirms Statement published in Malibu-campus catalog
Feb. 9, 1977	Pepperdine Associates meet for first time
Oct. 30, 1974	California Attorney General's office issues final report on governance matters
Mar. 12, 1975	*Sacramento Bee* writes story describing attorney general report about Pepperdine
April 20, 1975	Frank R. Seaver College of Liberal Arts dedicated
Sept. 16, 1975	Norvel Young involved in fatal car crash
Sept. 20, 1975	President Gerald Ford visits Malibu campus
Jan. 17, 1976	Pepperdine board opens to non-Church of Christ members
Feb. 12, 1976	Malibu campus faculty conduct a teaching walkout, demanding higher pay
August 1978	Banowsky accepts presidency at University of Oklahoma
Sept. 13, 1978	Howard A. White inaugurated as fifth president of Pepperdine
June 22, 1981	Sale of Los Angeles campus finalized
March 1982	School of Education becomes Graduate School of Education and Psychology
Sept 14, 1983	Pepperdine University adopts its first official mission statement
Spring 1984	Seaver College London study-abroad program begins
Summer 1984	Pepperdine helps host the Olympic Games in Los Angeles

June 12, 1984	David Davenport designated president-in-waiting
Summer 1985	Seaver opens study-abroad program in Florence, Italy
Oct. 21, 1985	David Davenport officially sworn in as sixth president of Pepperdine
Sept. 12, 1989	Long Range Development Plan approved by Coastal Commission
August 1992	Women lead in convo for first time
1994	Seaver opens study-abroad program in Buenos Aires, Argentina
Fall 1997	School of Public Policy opens
January 1999	Coastal Commission approves Drescher site plans
Mar. 26, 1999	Revised version of mission statement adopted
Dec. 7, 1999	Andrew K. Benton announced as seventh president of Pepperdine
Spring 2000	Grading begins on Drescher site
Sept. 2000	Andrew Benton inaugurated as Pepperdine president

Endnotes

Most of the primary sources cited in this book are housed in Pepperdine University's department of Special Collections and University Archives in Payson Library on the Malibu campus. Although served by dedicated personnel, that office had been long overwhelmed when this project began. Archival boxes were stacked six feet high and five feet wide, and only two or three collections had been fully cataloged.

Thanks to new leadership, all of that changed. But those changes—welcome as they are—have created complications for this project. After they were used for this study, many archival files were rearranged and even created from loose papers. Box numbers I have cited for files and papers in some collections (Young, Banowsky, White, Roper, and Nicks) are no longer relevant. But I am reassured by the university archivist that the names of cited files and collections are still valid and the sources can be found.

Knowing that such changes might be taking place, I attempted to document all sources in great detail to make it more likely that they can be relocated in the future. However, in interest of space and readability, I have employed abbreviations for frequently used sources, shortened some document titles, and utilized a slightly modified notes style that should reduce repetition.

ABBREVIATIONS

Unless otherwise specified, all sources are located in Special Collections and University Archives, University Libraries, Pepperdine University, Malibu, CA

BAIRD: Baird (W. David) Book Materials
BB: *Bible Banner*, 1939–1958
BOR: Board of Regents, President's Office, Pepperdine University, Malibu, CA
BOT: Minutes, Board of Trustees, President's Office, Pepperdine University
COON: Coons (R.R.) Papers, Center for Restoration Studies, Abilene Christian University
FF: *Firm Foundation*, 1948–1952, 1976
GG: *Gospel Guardian*, 1950–1953

GRAPHIC: *The Graphic*, 1937–2000
GPFP: George Pepperdine Family Papers
HAWP: White (Howard A.) Papers
IV: *The Inner View*, 1973–1976
JCM: Moore (James C.) Papers
JLP: Lovell (James L.) Papers
JRC: Rushford (Jerry) Collection
JWP: Wilson (John F.) Papers
LAT: *Los Angeles Times*, 1920–2008
LACU: Lovell (James L.) Papers in Center for Restoration Studies, Abilene Christian University
MFA: Adams (Michael F.) Papers
MILL: Miller (Donald V.) Papers
NICKS: Nicks (John D. Jr.) Papers
OHC: Oral History Collection
OIE: Office of Institutional Effectiveness, Pepperdine University, Malibu, CA
PAH: Pepperdine Archives H-Series
PO: Provost's Office, Pepperdine University, Malibu, CA
PUA: Pepperdine University Archives
PULL: Pullias (Earl Vivon) Papers
SCUA: Special Collections and University Archives, University Libraries, Pepperdine University, Malibu, CA
SCP: Seaver College Papers
SRP: Roper (Shirley) Papers
SUB: Subject Files, President's Office, Pepperdine University. Malibu, CA
TINER: Vertical Files, Hugh Tiner, Center for Restoration Studies, Abilene Christian University
WAP: William B. Adrian Papers, Office of the Provost Papers
WAR: Western Auto Supply Co. Records, The State Historical Society of Missouri Research Center, Kansas City, MO
WCA: Western College Association Collection, Special Collections, Hannold Library, The Claremont Colleges, Claremont, CA
WSB: Banowsky (William S.) Papers
YOUNG: Young (M. Norvel and Helen) Papers

Endnotes

CHAPTER 1

1 GPFP: "California is the Land for Me," #1, file 4, Box 1, Series 4.

2 Youngs, *Faith Was His Fortune*, chap. 20. For more on the "motorized civilization" see Starr, *Material Dreams*, 78–84.

3 Bates and Clark, *Faith Is My Fortune*, 10–11.

4 Ibid., 39–40.

5 Youngs, *Faith Was His Fortune*, 83–86.

6 Bates and Clark, 64–65. The 1900 U.S. Census for Missouri shows the Baker family living in Joplin, some fifty miles distant from Parsons, Kansas. In 1910, they were living in Kansas City, MO.

7 GPFP: George Pepperdine and Lena Rose Baker Marriage License, October 17, 1907, Kansas City, Kansas, #1, file 1, Box 4, Series 6.

8 Ibid.: "A Pioneer Woman—In a Modern Version," Secrets of Charm, 1 (Nov. 1924): 5 & 12, #2, file 1, Box 4, Series 6. See also, LAT: "Woman Active in Affairs of Huge Company," May 18, 1924, F7. Current money values are calculated from "Inflation Calculator," retrieved from www.davemanuel.com/inflation-calculator.php (accessed Oct. 14, 2015).

9 Articles of Incorporation, Western Auto Supply Company, Kansas City, Missouri, Nov. 6, 1914; retrieved from http://www.sos.mo.gov/BusinessEntity/soskb/corp.asp?29506 (accessed Nov. 8, 2009). George Pepperdine was director, controlling 19,998 shares of stock; Lena Pepperdine and her brother Ernest Baker were also directors of the corporation, controlling one share of stock each.

10 Youngs, *Faith Was His Fortune*, 110.

11 Ibid., 110–14.

12 The $10,000 figure is the recollection of Don Davis, who came to believe that he had offered too much for the corporation, since George Pepperdine had accepted it so readily. See "Western Auto Supply: Merchant on the Make," *Fortune*, 20 (Oct. 1939): 81.

13 Youngs, *Faith Was His Fortune*, 118–24. See also LAT: "Form Huge Corporation," Oct. 24, 1920, F4.

14 LAT: "Mammoth Store Is Proposed," Feb. 11, 1923, F13.

15 Starr, *Material Dreams*, 78–94; LAT: Chester Hanson, "Crowds Join Chain Store Tax Battle," July 12, 1935, A1.

16 LAT: "Saving Sam Builds Car," Feb. 15, 1920, F14.

17 Ibid.: "Western Auto Gives Bonus," Jan. 3, 1926, G5; and Youngs, *Faith Was His Fortune*, 131–37.

18 YOUNG: Norvel Young to Esther and Kendall Thurston, Oct. 28, 1970, Tabor–Tyson file, Box B28.

19 LAT: Katherine Lipke, "Sketches of Big Man in Industrial Life," Oct. 21, 1923, E14.

20 Ibid.: "Woman Active in Affairs of Huge Company," May 18, 1924, F7; "Auto Camping Now Easy For Women [&] Nature Lovers," July 18, 1926, G19; "Commute Across Ocean Wave," Aug. 27, 1926, A6; "Auto Supply Chain Grows," Sept. 12, 1926, G11; Valerie Watrous, "Meet Your Neighbor," March 7, 1927, A6; and WAR: "A Pioneer Woman," "Western Auto Supply Company, Special Section," *Los Angeles Express*, Nov. 11, 1922, 2, c. 4, Box 19.

21 LAT: Alma Whitaker, "Sugar and Spice," June 20, 1926, D34; "Rose Pageant to Have Theme," June 13, 1926, B1; "Sunland Lures Women of Note," Jan. 15, 1927, A8; "Dinner Tonight Launches Move of Green Cross," Apr. 27, 1927, A23; and Starr, *Material Dreams*, 110.

22 JLP: Jimmy Lovell to G. C. Brewer, July 18, 1935, #7, file 1, Box 1.

23 LAT: "Protestant Laymen To Hold Rally," May 22, 1927, B3; "Brotherhood Will Assemble," Apr. 8, 1940, A17; "Plan Saving of Boys And Girls," May 17, 1923, A17; "Dry Law Held Commerce Aid," Mar. 15, 1925, B1; "Church Brotherhoods Urge Local Option at Pomona Convention," Mar. 15, 1936, A10.

24 Starr, *Material Dreams*, 138–39. Starr writes that Porter was "a church–going used-automobile-parts dealer from Iowa . . ." who "was a nobody: an anonymous, tee totaling, clumsily mannered, poorly educated evangelical Midwesterner typical of the million or so who had poured into greater Los Angeles since the war." I have found no evidence that George Pepperdine had any interaction with Bob Shuler or held parallel views on the KKK. For the connection between Shuler and the KKK see Daniel Cady, "Bringing in the Sheets, Robert Shuler, the Ku Klux Klan and the Southernization of Southern California," in *Race, Religion, Region, Landscapes of Encounter in the American West*, ed. Botham and Paterson, chap. 2. For the grand jury experience, see LAT: "Fitts and Jury Unite on Quiz," Nov. 19, 1930, A1.

25 JLP: Lovell to G. C. Brewer, July 18, 1935, #7, file 1, Box 1.

26 GPFP: "James Smythe, "Church Chat," Southwest Church of Christ (June 17, 1956), 1, Unprocessed Papers, Box 3.

27 See Bates and Clark, chap. 16, for a reprinted copy of the tract. George also wrote articles for religious periodicals like the *Firm Foundation* and *Power for Today*. That figure of 4.5 million copies of the tract circulated is based upon the calculation of Jimmy Lovell, who arranged for the publication of the tracts through the Vermont Avenue Church of Christ in Los Angeles. See JLP: Lovell to George Pepperdine, Jan. 7, 1936, and Sept. 14, 1942, and Reuel Lemmons to George Pepperdine, Nov. 28, 1950, #9, #19, and #29, file 1, Box 1; also see Youngs, Man of Action, 121. According to Lovell, Hugh Tiner helped Pepperdine write the tract; see OHC: Interview with Jimmy Lovell by Dot Moore, Apr. 18, 1980.

28 LAT: "Orphanage To Be Given Start," July 4, 1930, A7.

29 GPFP: [Reuel Lemmons,] "Obituary," *Firm Foundation*, [1962], in Unprocessed Papers, Box 3.

30 Stevens, *Before Any Were Willing*, 181.

31 LAT: Scott Harris, "Days Are Numbered for Historic Mansion," Apr. 11, 1991, A1. Lena never lived in the West Adams house.

32 Ibid.: "Popular Subdebs Home Today," Sept 16, 1927, A6.

33 Ibid.

34 GPFP: His travel letters are items #5–10, file 1, Box 7, Series 12; "World Travel Letters," Unprocessed Papers, Box 1; and Scrapbook of 1928 trip, Unprocessed Paper Box 3.

35 Ibid.: Clipping, *Los Angeles Harold Examiner*, Jan. 1, 1930, file 1, Box 4, Series 6.

36 Geo. Pepperdine v. L. Rose Pepperdine, Jan. 14, 1929, Case No. D71262, First Series, Records of the Superior Court, Hall of Records, Los Angeles County, Los Angeles, CA. The petition for divorce read in part: "[The] defendant for more than one year . . . has willfully and without cause deserted and abandoned this plaintiff and still continues to willfully and without cause desert and abandon this plain-tiff to live separate and apart from against his will and without his consent." Jimmy Lovell, a longtime confidant of George Pepperdine, subsequently wrote that Lena had been "untrue" to George. See JLP: Lovell to Brewer, July 18, 1935, #7, file 1, Box 1.

37 LAT: "Angeleno Dies, Parrot Blamed," Jan. 20, 1930, A1; "Tournament of Roses Mourns Mrs. Pepperdine," Jan. 21, 1930, A1; "Ship With Body Sails Saturday," Jan. 21, 1930, A1.

38 Bates and Clark, 166. According to one witness, Pepperdine seriously dated at least two other women before meeting Helen Louise, but members of his church

family thought those women were only interested in his money. See Maurine Reedy Ruzek, "A Personal Account of the Life of George Pepperdine, Founder of Pepperdine University," Oct. 2003, in Vertical Files, SCUA.

39 Bates and Clark, 291; and GPFP: Christmas card, George to Helen Pepperdine, 1956, Unprocessed Papers, Box 3.

40 PAH: Marilyn, Melon, Lady Bug to Daddy, [no date], "Faith Is My Fortune" Corres. file, Box H01.

41 GPFP: Clipping, Pepperdine Obituary, *Firm Foundation*, [1962], in Box 2, Unprocessed Papers; and LAT: "Death Takes Pepperdine School Founder," Aug. 1, 1962, A1; Kenneth Crist, "Money Has No Value Unless," July 24, 1938, H8.

42 GPFP: A. E. Hedden, "$5 and an Idea," Unidentified newspaper clipping, [1936], #9, file 2, Box 7, Series 12.

43 Bates and Clark, 165. A brochure titled "Interesting Facts about the George Pepperdine Foundation," dates the foundation's origin as 1932. See PAH: Pepperdine Foundation file, Box B68.

44 BB: Ted W. McElroy, "The Pepperdine Foundation," Sept. 1940, 21ff.

45 Bates and Clark, 158.

46 In 1960, *Fortune* magazine reported that Bertin Gamble and Phil Skogmo bought two-thirds of Western Auto Supply (Los Angeles) common stock for "about $2 million" in 1939. Presumably, the company had gotten "into serious trouble" during the Depression and welcomed a buyout. There was no reference to preferred stock or the remainder of the common stock. See Katharine Hamill, "Bert Gamble, Main Street Merchant," *Fortune*, 62 (Oct. 1960): 228.

47 GPFP: Newspaper clipping, "Pepperdine Starts to Recoup," [*Los Angeles Herald Examiner*], Feb. 15, [1951 or 1952], #4, file 1, Box 1, Series 1.

48 LAT: "Dissolution Plea for Pepperdine Foundation Filed," Dec. 20, 1950, B8.

49 By 1953, creditors lodged claims totaling $733,369, with the court allowing $592,486. Claims in the amount of $140,822 were pending. See LAT: "Suit Attacks Transfer of Funds to College," Dec. 1, 1953, A16.

50 Ibid.: "Pepperdine Says He's Penniless Now," Feb. 15, 1951, A1. See also Bates and Clark, 236.

51 See George Pepperdine Foundation v. George Pepperdine, et al., 271 *Pac. Reporter* 2nd 600–606 and/or 126 *Cal. App.* 2d 154 (1954).

52 LAT: "Suit Attacks Transfer of Funds to College," Dec. 1, 1953, A16.

53 Ibid.: "Pepperdine College Suit Settled Out of Court," Sept. 26, 1956, A4; and BOT: Aug. 10, 1956, vol. 3, 198.

54 GPFP: George Pepperdine] to Flossie [Pepperdine], Jan. 3, 1953, and George Pepperdine to Dora Pepperdine, May 1, 1955, #6 and #7, file 2, Box 7, Series 12; and PAH: Ledger/Schedule of Investments, 1956–1981, Investment Record Book file, Box H03.

55 GPFP: George Pepperdine to Dora Pepperdine, May 1, 1955, #7, file 2, Box 7, Series 12; and. newspaper clipping, "Pepperdine Starts to Recoup" [*Los Angeles Herald Examiner*], Feb. 15, [1951 or 1952], #4, file 1, Box 1, Series 1.

56 PAH: See a series of letters between George Pepperdine and Jack Bates between 1957–1958, in "Faith is My Fortune" Corres. file, Box H01.

57 Ibid.: Pepperdine to George Benson, Sept. 1, 1958, Founder's post, 1937 Corres. file, Box H03.

58 LAT: "Supervisors Pay Tribute to Pepperdine, 70," June 20, 1956, A4; "Pepperdine Feted For Distinguished Service," May 16, 1961, A17. See also GPFP: Clipping, Morningside News-Advertiser, Mar. 3, 1960, Box 2, Unprocessed Papers.

59 Youngs, *Faith Was His Fortune*, 215, 223.

60 Ibid., 225.

61 GPFP: "Philanthropist George Pepperdine Dies," *Los Angeles Herald Examiner*, Aug. 1, 1962, A7, clipping in Box 2, Unprocessed Papers.

CHAPTER 2

1 Bill Barol, "The Year of Living Nervously," *Newsweek*, June 8, 1987, 84–85.
2 OHC: Lola Tiner interview by Robert Sanders, Long Beach, CA, May 9, 1984. See also GRAPHIC: "Church Broadcast on KFVD Sundays," Oct. 20, 1937, 1; and [Jimmy Lovell], "Hugh M. Tiner," *West Coast Christian*, April 1943, 1.
3 Tiner became a member of the Churches of Christ when in high school and subsequently accompanied two of his friends, Foy Moody and Hubert Derrick, to Abilene Christian College. See H. G. Derrick, *Why I Have To Believe*, 11. See also Lovell, "Hugh M. Tiner," 1.
4 BB: A. L. Harbin, "Dangers Emanating from Christians," July 1940, 3–4.
5 Stevens, *Before Any Were Willing*, 128.
6 Hall, *Sixty Years in the Pulpit*, 91.
7 Stevens, Before Any Were Willing, 128; LACU: Clinton Davidson to James L. Lovell, Nov. 26, 1956, "GPC Council" file, Box 32.
8 OHC: T. W. Phillips interview by Robert Sanders, Apr. 17, 1984.
9 GRAPHIC: "Pepperdine Is Honored By Warner Bros. in College Broadcast Friday," Nov. 10, 1940, 1. See also OHC: Lola Tiner interview; Youngs, *Faith Was His Fortune*, 199–200.
10 Youngs, *Faith Was His Fortune*, 197.
11 Ibid., 201.
12 Ibid., 200.
13 PAH: George Pepperdine to Hugh Tiner, [March 1937], Founding Corres. file, Box H03.
14 Ibid: MILL: Hugh M. Tiner to Christian Parents and Friends in California, March 15, 1937.
15 LACU: Lovell to Trustees, March 9, 1945, Corres., 1930–1959 file, Box 33.
16 See LAT: "Structures Will Rise for Extensive New College Here," May 23, 1937, F1; and "George Pepperdine Funds L.A. College," *Los Angeles Herald and Express*, May 22, 1937, A7; and "Education: New Colleges," *Time Magazine*, June 14, 1937, 48–49; and Lovell, "Praise the Lord," *Colorado Christian*, April 1, 1937, 1–2.
17 FF: George Pepperdine, "George Pepperdine College," Apr. 8, 1952, 6.
18 BOT: "President's Report, 1938," June 6, 1938, vol. 1, 47; and GRAPHIC: Irene Willingham, "Campbell Traces History of Site For Pepperdine," Dec. 7, 1938, 3; and Youngs, *Faith Was His Fortune*, 204–5.
19 LAT: "Structures Will Rise," F1–1 & 3.
20 In July 1937, Pepperdine clarified what it meant to be a member of the Church of Christ: Such a person accepted the deity, virgin birth, miracles and atoning blood of Christ; the inspiration and authority of the Bible; the doctrine of the church and conversion of sinners (meaning belief, repentance, confession, and baptism); regular observance of the Lord's Supper; and worship without instrumental music. See BOT: George Pepperdine to Batsell Baxter, July 21, 1937, Sept. 15, 1937, vol. 1, p. 22.
21 Ibid.: July 7, 1937, vol. 1, p. 1–3.
22 GRAPHIC: "Campbell Traces History of Site For Pepperdine," Dec. 7, 1938, 3; and BOT: GPC Salaries, 1937–38, Sept 15, 1937, vol. 1, 18.
23 PULL: Baxter to Pullias, July 20, 1937, #40, file 2, Box 2, Series 7.
24 See COON: Baxter to Dr. Coons, July 20, 1937, Box 1; and PULL: Baxter to E.V. Pullias, July 20, 1937, #40, file 2, Box 2, Series 7.
25 BOT: Sept. 15, 1937, vol. 1, p. 18.
26 PULL: Pullias to Baxter, April 20, 1937, #6, file 2, Box 2, Series 7.

27 BOT: George Pepperdine to Batsell Baxter, July 21, 1937, vol. 1, Sept. 15, 1937, vol. 1, p. 22.

28 PULL: Baxter to Pullias, May 19, 1937, #10, file 2, Box 2, Series 7.

29 Ibid., Pullias to Baxter, June 14, 1937, #35.

30 BOT: June 6, 1938, vol. 1, 47; and LAT: "Structures will Rise," May 23, 1937, F-1; and GRAPHIC: Irene Willingham, "Campbell Traces History of Site For Pepperdine," Dec. 7, 1938, 3.

31 *Bulletin*, 1 (June 1937), [14], and 1 (July 1937), 14.

32 *Bulletin*, 8 (July 1944), 35. Former Pepperdine student and professor, William Stivers, remembered fifty years after the fact that nonwhite students began living on the Los Angeles campus a year after the college opened. With the restriction in the catalog until 1944, it seems more likely that it remained a factor until World War II. See Steve Gobbell, "50 Years of Change in Student Life," *Oasis* (1986–1987): 22.

33 *Bulletin, 1937*, [15–16].

34 GRAPHIC: "Radio Program Is a Major Gift," May 4, 1938, 1; "Pepperdine Has Publicity On Two Radio Programs," Mar. 1, 1939, 1; "Foundation Radio Broadcast Led By Ray Simpson," May 2, 1940, 1.

35 *Promenade*, 1 (1939), 50; BOT: "President's Report, Sept. 14, 1938," Sept. 14, 1938, vol. 1, 52.

36 GRAPHIC: "George Pepperdine College Begins First Session With Capacity Student Body," Oct. 20, 1937, 1, 2.

37 GRAPHIC: "Here's a Record of Our First Week," Oct. 20, 1937, 3; and YOUNG: George Pepperdine College Physical Plant Survey, 1952, Box 58.

38 LAT: "College Ready for Dedication," Sept. 20, 1937, B10; and JLP: "Dedicate School Today," Angelas Mesa News, Sept. 21, 1937, news clipping, #18, file 2, Box 6.

39 George Pepperdine, "Founder's Address," Youngs, *Faith Was His Fortune*, 204–5. See also "Welch's Memoirs," in possession of Kanet Welch Thomas, Westlake Village, CA.

40 *George Pepperdine College Catalog, 1949–1950*.

41 PULL: Batsell Baxter to E. V. Pullias, Feb. 20, 1939, #49, file 2 (Pepperdine Years), Box 2, Series 7.

42 BOT: "President's Report to the Trustees, Sept. 14, 1938," Sept. 14, 1938, vol. 1, 53.

43 GRAPHIC: Oct. 20, 1937.

44 Ibid.: "Pepperdine Teams To Be Known as 'Waves,'" 7; and YOUNG: "Some Other Traditions," *Student Handbook, Pepperdine College*, 1963–64 (Los Angeles: Pepperdine College, 1963), 15, in Student Activities file, Box 4.

45 GRAPHIC: "Students to Pick School Colors," Nov. 17, 1937, 1; "Rising Vote in Chapel Tuesday Gives Approval," Nov. 24, 1937, 1.

46 Ibid.: "Seniors Name College Yearbook 'The Promenade,'" Mar. 29, 1939, 3.

47 Ibid.: "Constitution of the All-Student Association," Nov. 9, 1938, 6; John Rettberg interview with author, Jan. 26, 2011, Long Beach, CA.

48 Ibid.: "Six Basketball Lettermen Return," Nov. 30, 1938, 1; "Wade Ruby Remembered As First Wave Basketball Coach," Nov. 25, 1953, 7.

49 Ibid.: "Pepperdine Nine Drops Three Games in Vacation," Apr. 12, 1939, 4.

50 Ibid.: "Four Seniors Form College's First Graduating Class Friday" and "Seniors are Cosmopolitan Class with Majors in Four Separate Departments," June 6, 1938, 1. See also LAT: "George Pepperdine College Awards Degrees to Four," June 11, 1938, A8.

51 *Bulletin, 1938*, 31, 45–47; *Bulletin, 1939*, 31, 70–71. During the first year of the college, eighteen units of religion were required for graduation. See *Bulletin, 1937*, 29.

52 GRAPHIC: "Chapel Programs for this Quarter Are Announced," Jan. 19, 1938, 4; "The Religious and Cultural Life," July 1938, 2.

53 JLP: [Lovell] to Hugh M. Tiner, Aug. 16, 1938, and Mr. and Mrs. James L. Lovell to W. Edgar Miller, et al., Sept. 12, 1938, Corres., 1930–1959 file, Box 33; J. P. Sanders to Jimmy Lovell, July 17, 1939. A document bearing the signatures of charter members of the Vermont Avenue congregation is in Historical Misc. file, Box 1.

54 JLP: Lovell to George Pepperdine, Jan. 7, 1936, #9, file 1, Box 1; and OHC: James Lovell interview with Dot Moore, Apr. 18, 1980. According to Lovell, Hugh Tiner helped Pepperdine write the tract.

55 LACU: Lovell to Albert Lovelady, Alonzo Welch, Howard Horton, Dec. 26, 1938, Corres., 1930–1959 file, Box 33.

56 Ibid.: J. Herman Campbell to Hugh Tiner, Aug. 16, 1939, Corres., 1930–1959 file.

57 BOT: March 13, 1940, vol. 1, 126.

58 PULL: Batsell Baxter to E. V. Pullias, May 11, 1938, #46, file 2, Box 2, Series 7; and GRAPHIC: "Inspectors Well Pleased in Tour Of College Plant," March 2, 1938, 1; "N.A.C. to Act on G.P.C. Bid," March 30, 1938, 1; "Recognition of G.P.C. Unusual," April 27, 1938, 1; and Proceedings of the Twenty-First Annual Meeting of the Northwest Association of Secondary and Higher Schools, April 4 to 6, 1938, 16.

59 BOT: "President's Report, Jan. 10, 1938"; "Board Report, June 6, 1938," Jan. 10, 1938, and June 6, 1938, vol. 1, 29 and 47.

60 Ibid.: "Board Report," June 6, 1938, vol. 1, 47; and GRAPHIC: "Saturday Night Games to Dedicate Gym," Nov. 30, 1938, 1.

61 Ibid.: "Ground Broken for New Library," Dec. 14, 1938, 1.

62 Over the years, George Pepperdine was at pains to increase the holdings of the college library. In June 1941, he purchased for it the 8,000 volumes in the personal library of B. C. Goodpasture, giving the GPC library one of the most complete collections of Restoration history literature among Churches of Christ colleges. He also purchased thirty-seven leaves from famous and rare Bibles and Testaments, including an Armenian Manuscript Bible dated 1121 A.D. and "Eliot's Indian Bible" dated 1685. See GRAPHIC: "College Buys Goodpasture Complete Library," June 4, 1941, 23; "Rare Collection Given Library," Nov. 5, 1941, 1.

63 Ibid.: "Pepperdine Announces Plans to Double Student Living Quarters by Fall," Mar. 1, 1939, 1.

64 BAIRD: Baxter to W. H. Free, Aug. 15, 1938, 1937–1938 file; and Northwest Association of Secondary and Higher Schools, 16.

65 Horton, et al., "From Pepperdine," 29–30, 33.

66 BOT: Mar. 8, 1939, vol. 1, 69–70; and GRAPHIC: "Trustees Grant Baxter Leave of Absence," Mar. 15, 1939, 1; "Baxter's Work Lauded At Service Clubs' Banquet," May 3, 1939, 1.

67 BOT: George Pepperdine to Batsell Baxter, Jan. 8, 1940, Jan. 8, 1940, vol. 1, 117.

68 Ibid.: Mar. 13, 1940, vol. 1, 125–26.

69 BB: Foy E. Wallace Jr., "The George Pepperdine College," Sept. 1940, 4. Wallace attributed Baxter's leaving to "the ambitions of younger men."

70 HAWP: Lovell to Reuel [Lemmons], et al., Jan. 9, 1976, Governing Board Records file, Box 25. See also YOUNG: Maurine Reedy Ruzek, "A Personal Account of the Life of George Pepperdine," Oct. 2003, Pepperdine History file, Box 58; and BAIRD: James Lovell to A. M. Burton, [1939], College founding, 1937–1945 file.

CHAPTER 3

1 OHC: E. V. Pullias interview with Mrs. J. C. Moore, Mar. 25, 1982; Howard Horton, et al., "From Pepperdine," 101–10.

2 The board appointed Tiner president on April 13, 1939, well before he actually took office.

3 LAT: "Unethical Conduct Laid to Kenny and Bowron," June 24, 1943, A3; "Allied Nations Group to Dance," Mar. 7, 1945, A5; "Rotary Chief Cites Problem Before World," Apr. 30, 1946, A2; "U.N. Bill of Rights Forum," July 17, 1949, A2; "Republicans Call Sessions," Apr. 13, 1952, B2; "UNESCO Friends, Foes Clash," Aug. 26, 1952, A2, 5; "Turbulent School Session," Dec. 23, 1952, A2. See also TINER: Campaign Brochure, Tiner for State Legislature; and "Southland Votes On County Posts," June 8, 1960, A23. See also PUA: newspaper clippings file, Box B71.

4 BB: Foy E. Wallace Jr., "The George Pepperdine College," Sept. 1940, 4.

5 [Lovell], "Hugh M. Tiner," *West Coast Christian*, April 1943, 1.

6 GRAPHIC: "E. V. Pullias Selected As Dean," Apr. 11, 1940, 1.

7 OHC: Pullias interview.

8 GRAPHIC: "Pepperdine Climbs Ladder," Jan. 15, 1941, 2.

9 Ibid.: "College Association Elects Pres. Tiner," Apr. 1, 1942, 1.

10 OHC: Pullias interview.

11 LAT: "Pepperdine Progress Told," Aug. 25, 1940, D7.

12 *Bulletin, George Pepperdine College, 1944–1945*, 8 (July, 1944).

13 GRAPHIC: "To The Basketball Fans," Mar. 5, 1941, 2.

14 *Bulletin, George Pepperdine College, Student Handbook, 1945–46*, 9 (July 1945), 8. See also BOT: Faculty List and Salaries, 1940–1941, Mar. 30, 1940, vol. 1, 135–6; and George Pepperdine College Faculty Proposed, 1945–1946, July 23, 1945, vol. 2, 60–63.

15 *Bulletin, The George Pepperdine College Catalogue*, Numbers 1940, 1941, 1942, 1943, 1944, 1945, and 1946.

16 *Student Handbook, 1945–46*, 8.

17 BOT: Faculty List and Salaries, 1940–1941, Mar. 30, 1940, vol. 1, 135–6.

18 Ibid.: Minutes, Board of Regents, Oct. 9, 1944, vol. 2, 33.

19 Ibid.: Retirement Resolution, Jan. 14, 1946, vol. 2, 70.

20 Ibid.: President's Annual Report for 1939–1940, June 19, 1940, vol. 1, 148; Faculty List and Salaries, 1941–42, Mar. 31, 1941, vol. 1, 193, and *1941–1942 Catalogue*, 5 (July 1941).

21 *Student Handbook, 1945–46*, 8.

22 GRAPHIC: "Scholarship Committee Reveals Awards," Dec. 4, 1940, 1; "Committee Announces Scholarships," June 4, 1941, 1; "School to Grant New Scholarships," Jan. 15, 1943, 1; and "Planning for the Future," *Bulletin, George Pepperdine College*, 7 (Nov. 1943), [9].

23 *1943–1944 Catalogue*, 7 (June 1943).

24 "'It Beats Working'—Dean Tegner," *Pepperdine People*, Winter 1979, 22; and Bill Henegar, "Oly, After 50 years," *Pepperdine People*, Fall 1989, 2–5. See also Richard Suenaga, "Family Man," *Pepperdine Colleague*, 20, Spring 2002, 16–17. In some stories, Tegner interacted with President Baxter and J. C. Moore; given the timeline it was more likely Tiner. Neither Baxter nor Moore were on campus when Tegner enrolled as a freshman.

25 GRAPHIC: "Cast Primed for Opening," Dec. 4, 1940, 1; "Hill Opera is Great Success," Oct. 5, 1943, 1; "Graduates May Now Secure Teaching Credentials Here," Oct. 5, 1943, 1.

26 Ibid.: "Baxter Heads Big Debate Tournament," Oct. 8, 1941, 1; "Debate Tourney To Begin Here Tomorrow," Feb. 24, 1942, 1. See also Baxter, *Every Life A Plan of God*, 58.

27 GRAPHIC: "Debate Squad To Be Host," Feb. 18, 1942, 1; "Debate Tourney To Begin Here Tomorrow," Feb. 24, 1942, 1; "Speech Tournament To Begin Tomorrow," Dec. 10, 1942, 1.

28 Ibid.: "Final Preparations Made For Admittance to Pi Kappa Delta," April 22, 1942, 1.

29 *Student Handbook, 1945–46*, 93–94. See also GRAPHIC: "Concert Series Opens," Jan. 8, 1941, 1; "Presentation of The Don Cossack Chorus," Nov. 10, 1944, 1.

30 BOT: Dec. 6, 1943, vol. 2, 5; and Jan. 10, 1944, vol. 2, 12–13; and GRAPHIC: "Religion Graduate School Starts," Apr. 14, 1944, 1; *Catalogue, 1944–1945*, 8 (July 1944).

31 GRAPHIC: "Thirty-Two Seniors," Feb. 18, 1944, 1.

32 Ibid.: "First Summer Session," Feb. 4, 1942, 1; and BOT: July 10, 1944, vol. 2, 23.

33 Ibid.: "Pepperdine Grows Up," June 4, 1941, 3.

34 *Student Handbook, 1945–46*, 8.

35 Ibid., 9–17.

36 *Promenade, 1942*, 5. The initial statute had a water pipe that exited at the bottom of the towel, which once operational looked like a small boy relieving himself. The maintenance crew removed that pipe and ran it up the statue's back and over its head, with water showering down. PUA: C. H. Shipp to Helen Young, May 15, 1975, Young's Corres. (recent) file, Box 32.

37 *Student Handbook, 1945–46*, 90.

38 GRAPHIC: "First Band Is Formed," Nov. 29, 1939, 1.

39 *Student Handbook, 1945–46*, 67.

40 Ibid.

41 GRAPHIC: "To Leave For KC Tourney," Feb. 18, 1944, 1; "Waves To Compete In NCAA Tournament," Mar. 3, 1944, 3.

42 Ibid.: "Bobby Riggs Gives Exhibition," Oct. 18, 1939, 1; "Bobby Riggs Appears," Oct. 22, 1941, 4.

43 Ibid.: "Weems Expresses Pride," May 16, 1940, 1.

44 Ibid.: Tiner, "President Sets Forth Christian Aims," Nov. 4, 1940, 4.

45 PAH: "Faculty Bulletin," 1 (Oct. 20, 1941), in Faculty Bulletins file, Box H03.

46 GRAPHIC: "Chapel Means the Most," June 4, 1941, 3; L. Arnold Watson, "Why Should We Go To Chapel," Oct. 15, 1943, 2; Dan R. Post, "Soldier Looks Back on His Misspent Days," Oct. 5, 1943, 2.

47 *George Pepperdine College, Catalogue, 1943–1944*, 7 (July 1943).

48 GRAPHIC: WRN, "Letters To The Editor," Oct. 15, 1943, 2.

49 BOT: "President's Annual Report for 1939–1940," June 19, 1940, vol. 1, 148.

50 *Bulletin, George Pepperdine College, Catalogue, 1940–1941*, 4 (Mar. 1940), 24.

51 BOT: "President's Annual Report for 1939–1940," June 19, 1940, vol. 1, 148.

52 OHC: Pullias interview; "Planning for the Future," *Bulletin, George Pepperdine College*, 7 (Nov. 1943).

53 BB: "Disturbing Reports from the West," Aug. 1942, 13–14.

54 Ibid.

55 *College Catalogue, 1940–1941*, 4 (March 1940); and *1951–1952-* (Jan. 1951), 3.

56 BOT: Apr. 13, 1942, vol. 1, 252.

57 GRAPHIC: "Dr. C. R. Nichol To Begin Forum," Jan. 22, 1943, 1.

58 BOT: "President's Report," Jan. 10, 1938, vol. 1, 31; Agreement, July 12, 1943, Apr. 12, 1943, vol. 1, 284–87.

59 Ibid.: Apr. 10, 1944, vol. 2, 1.

60 LACU: Lovell to Trustees, Mar. 7, 1945, Corres., 1930–1959 file, Box 33.

61 JRC: L. O. Forsythe, "Facts Uncovered About Conditions at George Pepperdine College," Mar. 13, 1945.

62 BOT: Apr. 9, 1945, vol. 2, 4.

63 YOUNG: Batsell Barrett Baxter to Helen and Norvel, Feb. 17, 1945, Batsell Barrett Baxter file, Box 68.

64 JRC: C. R. Nichol to Members of the Church of Christ, in "Facts Uncovered."

65 PULL: George Pepperdine to . . . Nichol, July 25, 1945, #12, Box 2, Series 7.

66 Underwood, *C. R. Nichol*, 94–95. See also YOUNG: Batsell Barrett Baxter to Helen and Norvel, Dec. 8, 1944, Batsell Barrett Baxter file, Box 68.

67 BOT: Balance Sheet, Dec. 31, 1939, Mar. 6, 1940, vol. 1, 122; Balance Sheet, June 30, 1942, July 27, 1942, vol. 1, 269.

68 Ibid.: Estimated Income, 1941–1942, Sept. 9, 1941, vol. 1, 230; Balance Sheet, June 30, 1942, vol. 1, 269; Summary of Income and Expenses, July 8, 1946, vol. 2, 85.

69 Ibid.: Estimated Income, 1941–1942, Sept. 9, 1941, vol. 1, 230; Summary Statement of Income and Expenses, June 30, 1944, July 10, 1944, vol. 2, 22, "President's Annual Report, 1939–40," June 19, 1940, vol. 1, 150.

70 Ibid.: Balance Sheet, June 30, 1942, June 30, 1942, vol. 1, 269. One half of the securities held by the foundation were Western Auto stock; another fourth was in The Plomb Tool Company and Pacific Rubber & Tire Man. Co. Ibid.: Oct. 11, 1943, vol. 1, 300.

71 Ibid.: Summary of Income and Expenses, July 8, 1946, vol. 2, 85.

72 For example see BB: Ted McElroy, "Interesting Facts About The George Pepperdine Foundation," Sept. 1940, 22.

73 BOT: June 16, 1941, vol. 1, 216.

74 Ibid.: Jan. 15, 1945, vol. 2, 40.

75 GRAPHIC: "Pullias Presents Unique Viewpoint," Nov. 23, 1938, 1.

76 Ibid.; "Charles Stivers," Mar. 30, 1945, 2; "J. Eddie Weems, "I Am An American," May 27, 1942, 2; and *Promenade, 1944,* 3, 148–49.

77 BOT: Oct. 9, 1944, vol. 2, 33; and *Promenade, 1947,* np.; and GRAPHIC: Rudy, "Letters to the Editor," Mar. 30, 1945, 2.

78 *Bulletin, George Pepperdine College, Blueprint for Character Building* (Apr. 1945), 9; and BOT: J. Eddie Weems to President Tiner, et. al., vol. 1, 240.

79 BOT: July 27, 1942, vol. 1, 271.

CHAPTER 4

1 BOT: President's Annual Report, 1948–1949, 15; and LACU: Trustees file, Box 31.

2 *Bulletin, George Pepperdine College, 1951–1952 Catalog,* 15 (Jan. 1951), 170. Enrollment figures between 1950 and 1957 came from references in Trustees, vol. 3. For causes of the drop in enrollment in 1950–1951, see ibid., Aug. 15, 1950, vol. 2, 243.

3 LACU: "Survey of Races represented on campus, Fall 1956," Box 32; and Facts about Pepperdine College, [Fall 1954], Box 7, Misc. Administrative Records, SCUA.

4 GRAPHIC: Sylvester Obi, "Letters to the Editor," Apr. 26, 1957, 3.

5 BOT: July 3, 1946, vol. 2, 81.

6 YOUNG: "Report of Pepperdine College to the California State Board of Education and to the Western College Association" (hereafter, "Report to WAC"), October 1953, 25, in Box 58.

7 LACU: President's Annual Report, 1948–1949, 15, Trustees file, Box 31; and GRAPHIC: "Men Outnumber Women by 637," Nov. 9, 1949, 1.

8 LACU: President's Annual Report, 1948–1949, 38, Trustees file, Box 31.

9 *Pepperdine College Bulletin, 1956–1957, 1957–1958 Catalog,* 20 (March 1956), 16–21.

10 GRAPHIC: "Army Engages GPC Chemistry Research Department," Oct. 15, 1952, 1.

11 BOT: E. V. Pullias to Trustees, March 1955, Apr. 19, 1955, vol. 3, 148ff.

12 Ibid.: Apr. 15, 1952, vol. 3, 11.

13 YOUNG: "Report to WAC," October, 1953, 9, in Box 58; and BOT: Oct. 14, 1947, vol. 2, 137 and Oct. 11, 1948, vol. 2, 177.

14 BOT: Apr. 15, 1952, vol. 3, 11.

15 GRAPHIC: "School Given $142,900 by Ford Foundation," Jan. 6, 1956, 1; and BOT: Jan. 17, 1956, vol. 3, 174.

16 WCA: "Response by Pepperdine College," Sept. 1, 1951, file 57, Box 3.

17 PULL: Entry for Dec. 1952, #20, "Thoughts of Probable Value," Journal N, May 13, 1934-July 26, 1954 file, Box 3, Series II. See also entry for Apr. 15, 1954.

18 "Facts About Pepperdine College, [1954/57], Board of Trustees, Misc. file, Box 7, Misc. Administrative Records, SCUA; and LAT: "Sports Briefs," July 18, 1982, C3; "Loyola, Pepperdine Rest For CBA Campaign," Dec. 22, 1955, C4.

19 WCA: Response by Pepperdine," p. 6; and GRAPHIC: "CCAA Drop . . . Good, Bad, or ?" Jan. 13, 1954, 8.

20 *Student Handbook, 1945–1946*, 9 (July 1945), 16.

21 LACU: President's Annual Report, 1948–49, Oct. 10, 1949, p. 88, Trustees file, Box 31.

22 Ibid.: "Dear Pepperdine Booster," July 1, 1957; Booster News, nd, in Pepperdine file, Box 32; and BOT: Feb. 8, 1949, vol. 2, 184–85, and May 27, 1949, vol. 2, 189.

23 LACU: President's Annual Report, 1948–49, Oct. 10, 1949, p. 88, Trustees file, Box 31; and Promenade 1949, np; and GRAPHIC: "397 Receive Diplomas in Record Breaking Graduation," May 24, 1950, 1.

24 GRAPHIC: "New Office Established for Student Affairs," May 6, 1949, 1.

25 Ibid.: "Plan Revealed to Use Semester System Here, Apr. 22, 1949, 1; and *Bulletin George Pepperdine College, Catalog 1949–1950*, 13 (Jan. 1949), np.

26 GRAPHIC: "School Will Be Held Four Weeks," Mar. 8, 1950, 1; "Camp Charity Show Set," Nov. 14, 1951, 1.

27 WCA: "George Pepperdine College," Oct. 15, 1948, 52–65 in file 79, Box 1; and GRAPHIC: "UN Rip-Snorting Success," Sept. 26, 1974, 1.

28 Ibid.: "James Roosevelt Is To Be Main Speaker," Feb. 13, 1948, 1; "Myrna Loy Will Speak," Apr. 23, 1948, 1.

29 Ibid.: "Famed Durant To Speak," Feb. 11, 1949, 1.

30 *Promenade, 1950*, np.

31 GRAPHIC: "Forum-Arts Procedures," Sept. 30, 1950; and *Bulletin George Pepperdine College, Catalog 1951–1952*, 15 (Jan. 1951), 49.

32 GRAPHIC: Advertisement to hear Norman Rockwell, Mar. 4, 1949, 2; "Special Sale of Laughton Tickets Told," Sept. 30, 1950, 1; "Mead to Speak," May 15, 1951, 1; "Estes Kefauver Talks on Crime," Nov. 21, 1951, 1; "Lord Balfour's Lecture," Feb. 6, 1952, 1; "Brannan Pays Surprise Visit," Oct. 22, 1952, 1; "Senator Douglas Speaks," Nov. 19, 1952, 1; "Chet Huntley To Appear," Jan 27, 1954, 1; "Forum Event Will Feature Philosopher," Mar. 4, 1955, 1.

33 Ibid.: "Boy's Town Choir Opening Program," Oct. 10, 1947, 1; "Official U.S. Navy Band Gives Concert," Nov. 15, 1950, 1; see also *Promenade, 1947*, np.

34 GRAPHIC: "Tiner To Attend UNESCO Meeting," Mar. 12, 1948, 1.

35 Ibid.: "GPC Students Urge Government To Get Behind United Nations," Mar. 26, 1948, 1; WCA: "George Pepperdine College," Oct. 15, 1948, 52–65 in file 79, Box 1.

36 *Promenade, 1950*, np.

37 GRAPHIC: "Banquet Will Initiate United Nations Week," Oct. 14, 1949, 1; "Tiner Speaks Tonight," Oct. 22, 1952, 1; "Intercultural Understanding," Oct. 14, 1949, 1; "International Relations Conference Starts," Dec. 6, 1950.

38 Ibid.: "Whitten Announces Pre-Travel Institute," Mar. 18, 1953, 1.

39 BOT: Dec. 6, 1955, vol. 3, 170; and GRAPHIC: "Pepperdine Will Offer New Summer School Plan," Dec. 10, 1954, 1; *Pepperdine College Bulletin, 1956–1957, 1957–1958*, 22 (March 1956), 43.

CHAPTER 5

1 LAT: "Pepperdine Says He's Penniless Now," Feb. 15, 1951, A5; "Dissolution Plea for Pepperdine Foundation Filed," Dec. 20, 1950, B8; "Pepperdine Offers Records in Probe," Feb. 17, 1951, A3.

2 Ibid.

3 GRAPHIC: "Pepperdine Accredited in Three New Fields," Jan. 21, 1949, 1.

4 Ibid.: "Pepperdine Unable to Offer Secondary Credential, 1949–1950," Mar. 11, 1949, 2; and BOT: Nov. 16, 1948, vol. 2, 182.

5 BOT: Mar. 7, 1950, vol. 2, 226; May 16, 1950, vol. 2, 230.

6 WCA: Gordon S. Watkins, UCLA, to Charles T. Fitts, Pomona College, Dec. 17, 1940, #25 file, Box 1.

7 Ibid.: "Western College Association: Origin and History, 1924–1954," file 1, Box 1.

8 BOT: Feb. 20, 1951, vol. 2, 268.

9 WCA: "A Report by George Pepperdine College," #5 file, Box 16.

10 Ibid.: Charles Fitts to Hugh Tiner, Feb. 9, 1951, #3 file, Box 16. See also PULL: Monroe E. Deutsch to Dean Pullias, July 16, 1951, #12 file, Box 2, Series 7.

11 WCA: Paul A. Dodd, et al., "Western College Association, Report to George Pepperdine College," March 5 and 6, 1951, #4 file, Box 16.

12 Ibid.

13 Ibid.: Minutes of the Executive Committee, April 6, 1951, #56 file, Box 3.

14 Ibid.: Hugh M. Tiner to L. E. Nelson, University of Redlands, June 18, 1951, #3 file, Box 16.

15 Ibid., Aug. 14, 1951.

16 Ibid.: Tiner and E. V. Pullias to the Executive Committee, Sept. 1, 1951, #57 file, Box 3.

17 Ibid.

18 Ibid.

19 Ibid.

20 Ibid.

21 Ibid.: Minutes of Committee on Membership and Standards, San Francisco, Nov. 2, 1951, #17 file, Box 12.

22 Ibid.: #57 file, Box 3.

23 PUA: Minutes, Faculty Meeting, Jan. 7, 1952, Faculty Minutes/Faculty Affairs file, Box 84.

24 WCA: J. Paul Leonard, et al., "Report of the Visiting Committee to George Pepperdine College," Los Angeles, California, March 5–6, 1952, #4 file, Box 16.

25 Ibid.

26 Ibid.: Minutes of Committee on Membership and Standards, Phoenix, Arizona, Apr. 4, 1952, #22 file, Box 12; #62 file, Box 3.

27 BOT: Apr. 15, 1952, vol. 3, 11.

28 GRAPHIC: "Accrediting Group Visits," Nov. 25, 1953, 1; and WCA: Minutes of Committee on Membership and Standards, Los Angeles, Jan. 28, 1954, #27 file, Box 12. With this decision, GPC was technically accredited by two regional associations, the Western and the Northwestern. Pepperdine was still in good standing with the Northwestern Association in 1954, but it does not seem to have continued its membership for long thereafter.

29 GRAPHIC: "GPC Offers Credential," Jan. 13, 1954, 1; and *Pepperdine College Bulletin, 1956–1957, 1957–1958 Catalog*, 20 (Mar. 1956), 71.

30 BOT: May 26, 1947, vol. 2, 116; Nov. 3, 1947, vol. 2, 140; Jan. 20, 1948, vol. 2, 149; Jun. 27, 1947, vol. 2, 124ff; Sept. 7, 1951, vol. 2, 283; Nov. 25, 1952, vol. 3, 44.

31 Ibid., July 19, 1955, vol. 3, 155.

32 Ibid., Nov. 3, 1947, vol. 2, 138; and LACU: George Pepperdine to James E. Lovell, et al., Mar. 4, 1949, Miscellaneous file, Box 3.

33 BOT: Aug. 10, 1956, vol. 3, 198; Feb. 20, 1951, vol. 2, 268–269; Dec. 15, 1953, vol. 3, 90; and Mar. 18, 1952, vol. 3, 4–5.

34 LACU: Meeting, May 22, 1952, Board of Trustees file, Box 31.

35 BOT: Nov. 25, 1952, vol. 3, 44; June 21, 1955, vol. 3, 153.

36 Ibid.: July 10, 1950, vol. 2, 236; June 11, 1951, vol. 2, 277; Sept. 7, 1951, vol. 2, 283; Nov. 25, 1952, vol. 3, 44; Apr. 20, 1954, vol. 3, 106.

37 For an example of this practice, see BOT: Feb. 26, 1957, vol. 3, 221.

38 YOUNG: Report of Pepperdine College to the California State Board of Education and to the Western College Association, October, 1953, 17–18 file, Box 58.

39 BOT: Aug. 30, 1955, vol. 3, 161; Oct. 10, 1949, vol. 2, 205; and LACU: "President's Annual Report, 1948–1949," Board of Trustees file, Box 31.

40 LAT: "Warren to Talk at Pepperdine," June 1, 1948, B16.

41 LACU: Facts About Pepperdine College, GPC Council file, Box 32.

42 BOT: Jan. 18, 1951, vol. 2, 260, and Dec. 15, 1953, vol. 3, 95.

43 Ibid., Jan. 18, 1951, vol. 2, 260, and June 11, 1952, vol. 3, 19.

44 GRAPHIC: "Drive Underway to Raise Funds for Pep Debaters," Mar. 8, 1950, 1.

45 LACU: Hal C. Thomas, "Prospectus for Campaign," Jan. 11, 1951, Board of Trustees file, Box 31.

46 Youngs, Man of Action, chap. 9.

47 Ibid., chap. 16.

48 Hicks, Sometimes in the Wrong, 19, 141.

49 Youngs, Man of Action, 106–8.

50 Copies of the first edition do not seem to have survived.

51 "Recognition Night," America's Builders, 1 (May 1953): [1–3].

52 LAT: "Coliseum Builder Given Degree at Pepperdine," June 2, 1956, A1. See also LACU: American Builder's file, Box 31.

53 GRAPHIC: "America's Builders Night," 5/19/1954, 1; and LAT: "800 Attend Construction Fete," May 28, 1955, A2; June 2, 1956, A1; "Edgar Kaiser Given Honorary Law Degree," June 1, 1957, A7; and BOT: June 19, 1956, vol. 3, 192; "Coliseum Builder Given Degree at Pepperdine."

54 Dam, bridge, and ship builder Daniel V. McEachern of Seattle, Washington, for example, gave the college 1,000 shares of Kaiser stock valued at $44,500 in 1957. See BOT: Jan. 22, 1957, vol. 3, 217. See also "College Gets $50,000 Gift," Alumni Voice, 19 (Jan. 1957).

55 BOT: July 21, 1953, vol. 3, 77.

56 Ibid., Apr. 20, 1954, vol. 3, 109.

57 Ibid., Oct. 1, 1954, vol. 3, 124.

58 Ibid., Feb. 25, 1955, vol. 3, 141; and LAT: "Business Chiefs Unite," Feb. 23, 1955, A23. See also GRAPHIC: "Council Formed to Assist College," Feb. 25, 1955, 1.

59 LACU: Report to President's Council, Oct. 1, 1955, GPC Council file, Box 32.

60 OHC: Interview with Lola Tiner by Robert Sanders, May 9, 1984. Tiner almost apologized when he asked R. E. Smith, a Texas friend he had met in Rotary, to join the President's Council. He wanted permission to put Smith's name on the roster of members and assured him, "We shall not have many meetings as a group. . . . [and] you would [not] have to come to Los Angeles to attend regularly called meetings. YOUNG: Tiner to Smith, Jan 13, 1955, R.E. Smith file, Box B21.

61 BOT: Mar. 20, 1956, vol. 3, 182; June 19, 1956, vol. 3, 192; and ca. May 1955, vol. 3, ca. 150.

62 LACU: Davidson to Tiner, Oct. 12, 1956, GPC Council file, Box 32.

63 Ibid.: James Lovell to Clinton Davidson, Nov. 21, 1956.

64 Ibid.: Davidson to Lovell, Nov. 26, 1956. Davidson reminded Lovell that George Pepperdine had made a definite agreement to join Benson and Harding College in the venture that subsequently paid such big dividends to Harding, but upon consultation with staff members Mr. Pepperdine had walked away from the deal in 1938.

CHAPTER 6

1 Bulletin George Pepperdine College, Pictorial Edition, 13 (Nov. 1949), [1].

2 Bulletin, George Pepperdine College, 1953–1954 Catalog, 17 (April, 1953), 5.

3 LACU: President's Annual Report, 1948–1949, 22, Board of Trustee file, Box 31.
4 GRAPHIC: Gripes Aired," Mar. 11, 1949, 2; and *Bulletin, George Pepperdine College, 1951–1952 Catalog*, 15 (Jan. 1951), 46–47; and *Pepperdine College Bulletin, Student Handbook, 1954–55*, 18 (Nov. 1954), 5.
5 GRAPHIC: "New Schedule for Classes After Chapel," Sept. 13, 1950, 1.
6 LACU: Mrs. Charles Davis to James L. Lovell, July 20, 1955, GPC Council file, Box 32.
7 Ibid.: Lovell to Donald V. Miller, Sept. 15, 1956.
8 Ibid.: Walter E. Adams to James L. Lovell, Aug. 2, 1956.
9 GRAPHIC: "Kappas Show Bathing Suits," Feb. 25, 1953, 3.
10 BB: O. L. Castleberry, "Is George Pepperdine College Sound," Mar. 1948, 1; and LACU: Religious Affiliation of Students, Fall, 1956, Box 32.
11 BOT: May 27, 1949, vol. 2, 189, and Mar. 20, 1956, vol. 3, 182.
12 *Bulletin, George Pepperdine College, 1951–1952 Catalog*, 15 (Jan. 1951), 3. Elimination of references to the Church of Christ probably had more to do with winning accreditation from secular academics, namely the WCA, than the administration's preference for a generic, as opposed to a denominational Christianity.
13 *Pepperdine College Bulletin, 1956–1957, 1957–1958 Catalog*, 20 (Mar. 1956), 6.
14 BB: John F. Wolfe, "What I Found At George Pepperdine," May 1947, 12–15.
15 Ibid.: Hugh M. Tiner, "Reply to Brother Wolfe's Criticism," Feb. 1948, 8–9.
16 Ibid.: Wolfe, "Brother Wolfe's Comments," "Wolfe's Letter to Tiner," and John F. Wolfe to Roy E. Cogdill, Jan. 17, 1948, 7, 10–12.
17 Ibid.: Roy E. Cogdill, "Some Teachers at George Pepperdine Reveal Their Attitude," Mar. 1948, 13–15; Cogdill, "Brother Ruby Misrepresented?" 10 (May 1948), 2–5, 10; Jack G. Dunn, "The Skeptical Religious Student," 11–12.
18 GRAPHIC: "Conclave Here of Biblical Instructors," Sept. 24, 1948, 1.
19 BB: Castleberry, "Is George Pepperdine College Sound?" 1–4.
20 Ibid., 4.
21 Ibid.: Tiner, "Brother O. L. Castleberry's Article," 5–9.
22 Ibid.: Castleberry, "Reply to Hugh M. Tiner," 9–13.
23 Ibid.: Luther Blackmon, "Brother Hugh Tiner's Easter Speech," Apr. 1948, 15–16.
24 GRAPHIC: "Annual Lectureship Slated," Jan. 18, 1946, 1; "Sixth Annual Biblical Forum and Lectureship," Jan. 9, 1948, 1.
25 Ibid.: "Full Program Planned For First Christian Youth Festival," Apr. 2, 1947, 1; LAT: "College Plans Youth Institute on Bible Today," Jan. 29, 1949, A3.
26 Dean Pullias was most prolific in writing for the *Firm Foundation*. He published at least five articles in 1948, including a case against universal military conscription; fourteen articles in 1949 on the Christian college; two articles in 1950 on the dangers to democracy; and five in 1951 on great issues facing the Church of Christ. Ralph Wilburn published four articles in 1948, one on the law and the gospel. Wade Ruby defended himself in 1948 in an article titled "One Is Sometimes Amazed," *Firm Foundation*, June 1, 1948, 4–5.
27 FF: G. H. P Showalter, "George Pepperdine and the Religion of Christ," Feb. 24, 1948, 8; "George Pepperdine College," Mar. 2, 1948, 8–9.
28 George Pepperdine, "What Is A Christian College?" in "The Church and Sound Doctrine," *Bulletin George Pepperdine College*, 13 (May, 1949), 45–47. For a similar but later defense, see YOUNG: "A Word from George Pepperdine, The Founder of the College," [ca. 1955], Pepperdine-Young Corres. file, Box B25.
29 Ibid.
30 GG: T[ant], "A California Tragedy," Mar. 22, 1951, 4, 5b.
31 Ibid.: "The Pepperdine Problem," Feb. 21, 1952, 4–6, 9b.
32 Ibid.: E. V. Pullias, "Second Reply to Brother Tant's Accusations," Mar. 27, 1952, 1, 13.

33 Ibid.: George Pepperdine, "George Pepperdine College, A Report on Fifteen Years of Progress by Its Founder," Apr. 24, 1952, 1, 9b-11. The same article was published in two installments for the *Firm Foundation*, Apr. 8, 1952, 6–7, and Apr. 15, 1952, 6–7.

34 GG: Tant, "That Pepperdine Problem—No. 4," Apr. 24, 1952, 4–5, 13b.

35 Ibid.: "We Saw It Coming," Nov. 15, 1951, 4–5.

36 FF: "W. B. West, Jr. To Head Bible Department at Harding," June 5, 1951, 4.

37 GG: Tant, "That Pepperdine Problem—4."

38 BOT: Tiner, "Christian College Dilemmas," Feb. 14, 1952, vol. 2, 299–300 and vol. 3, 1–3. The published version of this article has not been found.

39 Ibid.

40 Ibid.

41 *Bulletin, George Pepperdine College, 1953–1954 Catalog*, 17 (Apr. 1953), intro.

42 *Bulletin, Pepperdine College, 1956–1957, 1957–1958 Catalog*, 20 (Mar. 1956), 6. This language persisted until the 1963–64 catalog, when any reference to Churches of Christ was eliminated from the "Our Heritage and Our Philosophy" section.

43 MILL: E. W. McMillian to Don Miller, Oct. 1, 1956.

44 LACU: Tiner to Goodpasture, May 13, 1955, Correspondence, 1930–1959 file, Box 33.

45 Ibid.: Lovell to Goodpasture, July 21, 1955, Goodpasture to Lovell, July 25, 1955, and Goodpasture to Tiner, May 31, 1955.

46 Ibid.: Lovell to Don Miller, Sept. 15, 1956, GPC Council file, Box 32.

47 BOT: Apr. 15, 1952, vol. 3, 10; May 22, 1952, vol. 3, 16; and June 11, 1952, vol. 3, 20.

48 Ibid., Apr. 20, 1954, vol. 3, 110; July 19, 1955, vol. 3, 157; Mar. 27, 1956, vol. 3, 184ff.

49 LACU: Lovell to Don Miller, Sept. 15, 1956, GPC Council file, Box 32.

50 BOT: Mar. 27, 1956, vol. 3, 184–85; and FF: George Pepperdine, "Pepperdine College," 736; and LACU: "One of the situations of my life," July 1957, Pepperdine file, Box 32.

51 Ibid.: Lovell to Don Miller, Aug 4, 1956, GPC Council file, Box 32.

52 Ibid.

53 Ibid.: Jimmy to Deak [Don Miller], Aug. 8, 1956; Don to Jim, Aug. 1, 1956.

54 BOT: Aug. 10, 1956, vol. 3, 199.

55 LACU: Jimmy to Deak, [Aug. 1956], and Clinton Davidson to Hugh Tiner, Oct. 12, 1956, GPC Council file, Box 32. See also YOUNG: R. E. Smith to Tiner, Aug 8, 1959, R. E. Smith file, Box B21.

56 LACU: Lovell to Miller, Dec. 11, 1956, GPC Council file, Box 32.

57 BOT: Mar. 5, 1957, vol. 3, 224B, and Mar. 9, 1957, vol. 3, 226B.

58 YOUNG: "President Tiner's Statement to Faculty," March 12, 1957, Faculty Meeting 56–57 file, Box B23; and GRAPHIC: "Tiner Takes Leave of Absence," Mar. 23, 1957, 1.

CHAPTER 7

1 LACU: Lovell to Norvel and Batsell Barrett, Dec. 27, 1956, GPC Council file, Box 32.

2 Ibid.: Young to Lovell, Jan. 18, 1957; Baxter to Lovell, Jan. 14, 1957.

3 Henegar & Rushford, *Forever Young*, 135–39. The projects in Texas included Lubbock Christian College and Lubbock Children's Home.

4 BOT: Mar. 28, 1957, vol. 3, 226D; and MILL: Review by the Board of Trustees of Pepperdine College of the AAUP, Pepperdine Chapter Report 1957/58, [Summer 1958], 3.

5 Ibid.

6 MILL: Correspondence between Miller, Morris, Lemmons, and Benson, Mar. 30 and 31, 1957; and YOUNG: Miller to Young, Mar. 17, 1957, Move to Pepperdine #2 file, Box 58.

7 MILL: Logan J. Fox to Miller, April 6, 1957; Harry Robert Fox Jr. to Miller, Apr. 3, 1957; and Pullias to Logan J. Fox, Apr. 15, 1957. See also BAIRD: Logan Fox, My

Personal Observations on George Pepperdine College, 1957; Harry Robert Fox to Pullias, Apr. 8, 1957; Pullias to Harry Robert Fox, Apr. 26, 1957; Logan Fox to Pullias, June 16, 1957, 1956–1957 file.

8 MILL: Harry Robert Fox Jr. to Miller, Apr. 3, 1957.

9 Ibid.

10 Ibid.

11 BAIRD: Pullias to Logan Fox, Apr. 15, 1957; Pullias to Harry Robert Fox, Apr. 26, 1957, 1956–1957 file.

12 BOT: Mar. 11, 1957, vol. 3, 228B. The inference that the "disturbing reports" involved accreditation concerns is deduced from the fact that the trustees wrote the Northwest Association of Higher and Secondary Schools and the Western Association of Colleges within three days of the resignation of Tiner, informing them of the transition and the nature of the changes contemplated. See BOT: Apr. 22, 1957, vol. 3, 234. This was a point that Dean Pullias made regularly. See BAIRD: Pullias to Harry Robert Fox., Jr., Apr. 26, 1957, 1956–1957 file.

13 BOT: Apr. 16, 1957, vol. 3, 233; YOUNG: Lovell to Norvel and Helen, Apr. 15, [1957], Tiner to Board of Trustees, Apr. 14, 1957, Move to Pepperdine #2 file, Box 58; and LAT: "Dr. Tiner Quits as Pepperdine College Head," Apr. 18, 1957, B1.

14 YOUNG: Don [Miller] to Norvel, Apr. 19, 1957, Move to Pepperdine #2 file, Box 58; and LAT: "Dr. Tiner Quits" and "Hunt Begins for New President," Apr. 22, 1957, B8; and GRAPHIC: "Mystery Solved," Apr. 26, 1957, 2.

15 GRAPHIC: "Committee Serves While Board Seeks Top Man"; "Mystery Solved"; Anita Deeter, "After Deadline," Apr. 26, 1957, 1 & 2; *Alumni Voice*: "To Pepperdine Alumni," (May 1957), 3.

16 TINER: Campaign brochure for Hugh Tiner; LAT: "Southland Votes on County Posts," June 8, 1960, A23.

17 LAT: "Assembly Unit Kills Funeral Bill Proposal," Mar. 31, 1965, A10.

18 YOUNG: Young to Tiner, May 4, 1965, Tiner to Edwin Pauley, Sept. 30, 1969, Hugh Tiner file, Box 66; and Young to R. E. Smith, Dec. 16, 1966, Smith to Young, Dec. 19, 1966, R. E. Smith file, Box B21. See also JLP: Lovell to R. E. Smith, Oct. 10, 1966, file 3, Box 1.

19 Jack W. Bates, "News," *California Christian*, July 1957, 4.

20 YOUNG: [Ruby Young] to Children, Mar. 18, 1957, Move to Pepperdine #2 file, Box 58.

21 Ibid.: The undated list is on a piece of scrap paper giving instructions regarding Sunday School roles.

22 Ibid.

23 Ibid.: Woodrow Whitten to Norvel Young, May 3, 1957, Move to Pepperdine #2 file, Box 58.

24 Ibid.: Some Recommendations for the Development of Pepperdine College, [Apr. 13, 1957].

25 Ibid.

26 BAIRD: Fox to Pullias, Apr. 8, 1957, 1956–1957 file.

27 FF: Reuel Lemmons, "Pepperdine College and Its New Administration," July 9, 1957, 434.

28 LACU: Lovell to Don Miller, Aug. 4, 1956, GPC Council file, Box 32.

29 Ibid.: Lovell to [Miller], Apr. 25, 1957. The president's committee correctly assumed that Lovell was a major force for change at the college. To blunt his influence, members apparently suggested that Lovell's outspoken and controversial support of R. N. Hogan, the noted black evangelist, was hurting the college. See YOUNG: Pepperdine Conf. Correspondence file, Box 58.

30 PULL: Journal entry Apr. 16, 1957, #23 file, Box 3, Series 11.

31 BOT: May 2, 1957, vol. 3, 235; YOUNG: Unsigned notes to [Miller], April 29, [1957], Move to Pepperdine #2 file, Box 58; LACU: Lovell to [Miller], Apr, 25, 1957, GPC Council file, Box 32; Lovell, Pepperdine: Lovell to [Young], Jan. 21, 1984, #61, file 1, Box 3.

32 YOUNG: [Miller] to Norvel, May 11, 1957, Move to Pepperdine #2 file, Box 58.

33 MILL: Pullias to Donald Miller, May 7, 1957. Don Miller sent a copy of this letter to Norvel Young for his comment. Young was not particularly impressed with Pullias's desire to personalize the resignation and to bargain over its terms. Moreover, he was suspicious of a love that threatened "to destroy accreditation, to take away the faculty and ruin the reputation of the institution rather than resign in honor with a year's full pay." Ibid.: A critique of the [Pullias] letter of May 7, 1957.

34 YOUNG: Joseph W. White to J.P. Sanders, Move to Pepperdine #2 file, Box 58.

35 BOT: Wade Ruby, et al. to Board of Trustees, May 2, 1957, May 2, 1957, vol. 3, 236B-239.

36 Ibid.: Board of Trustees to the Faculty, May 7, 1957, May 26, 1957, vol. 3, 240B-242.

37 Ibid.

38 Ibid.

39 YOUNG: [Unsigned] to Gentlemen, [May 1957], Move to Pepperdine #2 file, Box 58. This letter was written doubtlessly by Woodrow Whitten.

40 MILL: E. V. Pullias to Alumni, May 10, 1957.

41 Ibid.: George J. Niedermann to Don Miller, May 23, 1957, but also Evelyn Bills et al to Don Miller, May 15, 1957, and Mrs. Louie H. Moore, to Don Miller, May 25, 1957.

42 YOUNG: [Norvel Young], "Notes made in regard to talks with Logan Fox and Kenneth Hahn," May 17, [1957], Move to Pepperdine #3 file, Box 58.

43 BOT: May 28, 1957, vol. 3, 243. See also MILL: Review by the Board of Trustees of Pepperdine College of the AAUP, Pepperdine Chapter Report 1957/58, 4, [Spring 1958].

44 BOT: June 6, 1957, vol. 3, 244B.

45 Womack, J. P. Sanders, 72–76.

46 YOUNG: Reuel Lemmons to J. P. Sanders, May 22, 1957, Move to Pepperdine #1 file, Box 58.

47 BOT: June 15, 1957, vol. 3, 244F; and YOUNG: Jack Bates to Norvel, June 3, 1957, and Joseph W. White to Norvel Young, Jun. 11, 1957, Move to Pepperdine #2 file, Box 58.

48 MILL: R. C. Cannon et al. to Don Miller, Jun. 10, 1957.

49 YOUNG: [Whitten] to [Young], Jun. 9, 1957, Move to Pepperdine #2 file, Box 58.

50 Ibid.: Wade Ruby to Norvel Young, [June 1957].

51 BOT: June 15, 1957, vol. 3, 244F and June 20, 1957, vol. 3, 248B; and MILL: R.C. Cannon et al. to Don Miller, June 19, 1957, and Review by the Board of Trustees of Pepperdine College of the AAUP, Pepperdine Chapter Report 1957/58, 4.

52 YOUNG: [Whitten], "Quo Vadis, Pepperdine College?" [June 1957], Move to Pepperdine #2 file, Box 58. This is a typewritten document that is actually unsigned, but a pencil notation says "W.W. June 1957." I, therefore, attribute the document to Whitten, but not only because of the notation. Language used in the document also appears in other manuscripts that Whitten actually signs.

53 Ibid.

54 Ibid.

55 Ibid.

56 Ibid.: [Young] to [Miller], Jun. 17, 1957, Move to Pepperdine #2 file, Box 58.

57 Ibid.: [Young], Ideas on Pepperdine Situation as of June 19, 1957, and From the Desk of M. Norvel Young, [June 1957]. See also unsigned and undated note on stationary of La Posada de Santa Fe, [May 1957].

58 Ibid.: E. V. Pullias to Board of Trustees, Jun. 24, 1957.
59 BOT: To the Board of Trustees, June 21, 1957, June 25, 1957, vol. 3, 248D-252.
60 Ibid.
61 Ibid.: Minutes of the Special Meeting, June 25, 1957, vol. 3, 251–252. Jimmy Lovell thought that Slane's management of the meeting was "possibly the greatest contribution" the attorney had ever made to Christianity and that without it the meeting would have failed. See YOUNG: James L. Lovell to Harold Slane, June 27, 1957, Move to Pepperdine #3 file.
62 BOT: June 27, 1957, vol. 3, 252B-53.
63 FF: "Pepperdine College and Its New Administration," July 9, 1957, 434.
64 YOUNG: George Pepperdine to Board of Elders, Aug. 10, 1957, Pepperdine, Helen & George file, Box B25.
65 LACU: [Lovell] to Norvel and Sandy, June 21, 1957, Pepperdine file, Box 32.
66 PULL: Journal entry, Sept. 26, [1956], Vol. 1 (6/54–12/30/56), #22 file, Box 3, Series 11.
67 Ibid.: Entries for Apr. 18, 1957 and May 10, 1957, Journals, #23 and #24 files, Box 3, Series 11.
68 LAT: "Pepperdine Ex-Dean's Son Drowns," Aug. 30, 1957, 1A.
69 MILL: E. V. Pullias to Norvel Young, Sept. 13, 1957; and LAT: "Pullias Named To SC Faculty," Sept. 17, 1957, A17; and "Luncheon Honors George Pepperdine Centennial 1886–1986, *Pacific Church News*, 4 (Summer 1986), 3.
70 OHC: Don Miller interview by James Smythe, Nov. 29, 1996.

CHAPTER 8

1 BOT: Jan. 20, 1959, vol. 4:45.
2 YOUNG: [Helen Young] typewritten notes, Nov. 1961, History file, Box 74.
3 HAWP: Mabel Bean to Young, Oct. 8, 1969, Letters Sent, Box 17.
4 Ibid.: Glover Shipp to Young, et al., Oct. 1, 1961, Finance (Budget) file, Box 2.
5 YOUNG: George Pepperdine College Balance Sheet, Aug. 31, 1957, 1957–1958 file, Annual Report of the President file, Box 43.
6 Ibid.: Norvel Young, "Special Report of Members of the President's Council," [Sept./Oct. 1957], Move to Pepperdine #2, Box 58; James Lovell to Norvel Young, et al., Jan. 17, 1958, Jimmie Lovell file, Box B22; and *President's Annual Report to the Board of Trustees, 1957–1958*, Annual Reports of the President, Box 43.
7 Ibid.: "Fact Sheet for Members of the Advisory Board," [Fall 1957], Board of Counselors file, Box B25.
8 Ibid.: Norvel Young, "Special Report to Members of the President's Council," [Sept./Oct. 1957], Move to Pepperdine #2 file, and "Facts-Religious Affiliation, Fall 1956," Pepperdine Move #1 file, Box 58.
9 Ibid.: "Report for the Accreditation Committees of the Western College Association/California State Board of Education, Dec. 1, 1958," State. Dept. of Edu. file, Box B25.
10 FF: M. Norvel Young, "Accepting A Challenge," July 16, 1957, 456, and *California Christian*, July 1957, 4.
11 "The Nondenomination," *Time Magazine*, Aug. 5, 1957, 58.
12 LAT: "Pepperdine New President Full of Ideas," Aug 4, 1957, A1.
13 "Facts About Pepperdine College," *Pepperdine College Bulletin*, 22 (Jan. 1958), 4.
14 J. P. Sanders, "From the Dean," *Alumni Voice*, 20 (Sept. 1957).
15 LAT: "2000 at Reception for Pepperdine's New Chief," Aug. 18, 1957, A30. According to Mr. Pepperdine, the 2,000 figure was an exaggeration and only 1,000 went through the reception line. See YOUNG: George Pepperdine to Alvin T. Hamilton, Aug. 23, 1957, Helen and George Pepperdine file, Box B25.

16 MILL: Young memorandum to the Board of Trustees, Aug. 29, 1957, 3; and GRAPHIC: "Dr. Young Will Speak in Bay City," Oct. 5, 1957, 1.

17 MILL: Young memorandum to the Board of Trustees, Aug. 29, 1957, 4; and YOUNG: Letter to church leaders, May 21, 1959, Pepperdine Move #1 file; "From the Dean," *Alumni Voice*, 20 (Sept. 1957). For bulletins of "The College of Baton" see PUA: Baton, College of file, Box B49.

18 "Spiritual Emphasis Surges Ahead," *Pepperdine College Bulletin*, 26 (May 1963), 4.

19 See FF: "Special Pepperdine Issue," Feb. 5, 1963, 81–93.

20 YOUNG: Minutes, Administrative Council, Feb. 7, 1961, Administrative Committee Minutes file, Box B26, and Young to George Hill, Nov. 1, 1962, George Hill file, Box B24.

21 BOT: June 24, 1968, vol. 5:152.

22 YOUNG: Minutes of the Administrative Committee, June 18, 1965, Adm. Com. Minutes file, Box B26.

23 Ibid.: Report on the Past Year, Sept. 5, 1964; Roster of Preachers, [1965]; Roster of Faculty, 1969, Faculty file, Box 3.

24 Email from Sara Young Jackson to author, May 1, 2014.

25 YOUNG: Minutes, Board of Trustees, July 15, 1958; Minutes, Board of Counselors, Mar. 18, 1965, Board of Counselors file, Box B25. This program was so welcomed that the Southwest Church of Christ in Los Angeles, Mr. Pepperdine's home congregation, established a scholarship at the college for Church of Christ members interested in missions. So far as I know, this was one of the few times that the school ever accepted money from a working congregation of Churches of Christ. See Ibid.: Suggestions Concerning Southwest Church of Christ Gift for Scholarships, [1968], Fundraising 1968 file, Box 83.

26 Ibid.: *Annual Report, 1962–1963*, 12, in Annual Reports file, Box 43, and A Tabulation of Donors, 1966–1968, Dan Benefiel file, Box B26.

27 Ibid.: Summer Workshop, 1968, Don Gardner file, Box 66.

28 PUA: See Teaching Team's correspondence file, Box B17.

29 YOUNG: Ashby to Administration, Nov. 25, 1968, Home Economic file, Box 2.

30 Ibid.: Lovell to Mr. Derrick et al., Aug. 26, 1957; Lovell to Board of Trustees, Aug. 28, 1957; Development Program, Fall 1957, p. 6; Lovell to Deak [Don Miller], Nov. 15, 1957; Lovell to Deak and Norv, Sept. 19, 1958, Jimmie Lovell file, Box B22. See also Roster of Board of Counselors, Mar. 25, 1964, Board of Counselors file, Box B25.

31 Ibid.: "Faith in Action," *Christian Women*, Spring 1958, 22, clipping in file 6, Box 2, James L. Lovell Papers; Report to Counselors, Aug. 9, 1958, Board of Counselors file, Box B25; *Annual Report to the Board of Trustees, 1963–1964*, 5, Annual Reports file, Box 43; and GRAPHIC: Ron Ellerbe, "Campus Face Lifting Financed by AWP," Sept. 12, 1968, 1.

32 YOUNG: *Annual Report of the President to the Board of Trustees, 1964–65*, Annual Reports file, Box 43; and FF: Glover H. Shipp, "Pepperdine's Supporting Boards," Feb. 5, 1963, 84; and Shipp, "Current Highlights," *Alumni Voice*, 27 (Winter 1964), 24.

33 As examples, see FF: Reuel Lemmons, "Pepperdine College and Its New Administration," July 9, 1957, 434; and YOUNG: Glenn L. Wallace to Norvel Young, July 3, 1957, and Homer Hailey to Norvel Young, July 11, 1957, Congratulations on move to Calif. 1957 file, Box 68.

34 YOUNG: Young to James Baird, Mar. 31, 1958, James O. Baird file, Box 66.

35 Ibid.: Young to Baird, Mar. 31, 1958, James O. Baird file, Box 66.; and GRAPHIC: "1960 Lectures Begin Tomorrow," Mar. 1, 1960, 1; "2500 Expected to Attend Lectureship," Mar. 11, 1966, 1; and FF: Fred Davis, "Sports Arena Lectureship Climax," Feb. 5, 1963, 89.

36 YOUNG: Young to Robert Box, July 3, 1957, Move to Pepperdine #1 file, Box 58.
37 MILL: Young memorandum to Board of Trustees, Aug. 29, 1957, 4; and YOUNG: Young to James Baird, Sept. 3, 1957, James O. Baird file, Box 66.
38 Ibid.: Young, "Talk to Faculty," Sept. 10, 1957, Norvel Young Talks file, Box 57.
39 Ibid.: Resolution passed by a majority of the members of the Faculty Organization, Sept. 10, 1957, Faculty Minutes 57–58 file, Box B23; and PUA: Box 84. The resolution was probably written by Woodrow Whitten, whose selection of a catalog to quote was calculated. Had he chosen earlier catalogs, the Church of Christ would have been mentioned by name in the passage cited. That reference clarifies that subsequent language stating that the college would be unconnected with "any church" actually meant unconnected to any Church of Christ congregation.
40 YOUNG: Robert O. Young to Reuel Lemmons, July 11, 1957, Move to Pepperdine #2 file, Box 58.
41 Ibid.: Jimmie Lovell to Norvel Young and Don Miller, July 8, 1957, Move to Pepperdine #1 file, Box 58.
42 Ibid.: D. M. Morandini to Norvel Young, Sept. 10, 1957, Faculty Minutes 57–58, Box B23, and L. C. Houser to Norvel Young, Feb. 22, 1958, Miscellaneous Letters, 1957–58 #2 file, Box 68; MILL: Eiji C. Amemiya to J. P. Sanders, Jan. 1, 1958, and Lonnie Vanderveer to Norvel Young, Dec. 9, 1957; and GRAPHIC: "Emmett T. Long Joins Polly Staff," Oct. 11, 1957, 3.
43 GRAPHIC: "Resignations submitted by 11 on Faculty," Feb. 14, 1958, 3; and SRP: [Woodrow Whitten,] "Report of Pepperdine College Chapter," [May 29, 1958], AAUP file, Box 28.
44 LAT: "Pepperdine Losing 17 From Teaching Faculty," Apr. 17, 1958, A5; "Pepperdine Group Tells Reasons for Leaving," Apr. 19, 1958, A5. Those who apparently did resign included the following: adjunct professors D. M. Morandini and Eiji C. Amemiya, Professor and Head of Education Lonnie Vanderveer, Director of Admissions Emmett Long, Director of Public Relations Robert O. Young, Dean of Students R. C. Cannon, Head of Home Economics Nona Cannon, Head of Math and Physics Frances Amemiya, Chair of Languages Julian Enguidanos, Professor of Social Science Woodrow Whitten, Head of Chemistry Walter Magnuson, Head Librarian Pearl Ward, Reference Librarian Fina Ott, Social Science Instructor Robert Box, Professor of Education Francis Easley, Assistant Professor of Music Mary Phillips, Assistant Professor of English Milton Rickles, Associate Professor of History Richard L. Clark, Drama Professor James Young, Home Economics Instructor Verda Griner, Visiting Lecturer in French Helene Adcock, Chief Business Officer L. C. Houser, and Associate Dean of Students Margaret Walker.
45 YOUNG: Woodrow Whitten to S. H. Hall, May 29, 1958, Miscellaneous Letters, 1957–58 #2 file, Box 68.
46 SRP: [Whitten,] "Report of Pepperdine College Chapter," [May 29, 1958], AAUP file, Box 28.
47 Ibid.: See "Review by the Board of Trustees of Pepperdine College of the AAUP," Dec. 27, 1958, Board of Trustees, Misc. file, Box 58; and YOUNG: Joseph W. White, et al., Resolution American Association of University Professors, [Fall 1958], AAUP file, Box B26.
48 GRAPHIC: "Five Instructors, Dean Named," Feb. 14, 1958, 3; and FF: "Pepperdine Has Large Faculty," Aug. 26, 1958, 453; and YOUNG: "Report of the Western College Visiting Committee on Pepperdine College, January 12, 13, 1959," 2, History 1957 file, Box 74.

CHAPTER 9

1 "We've Got to Do Something for the College," *Pepperdine People* (Fall 1987), 33.

2 YOUNG: Program, "Inauguration of M. Norvel Young as President of Pepperdine College," Nov. 21, 1958, and Marshon DePoister to J. P. Sanders, Nov. 24, 1958, Inauguration (Dr. Young) file, Box 66; and LAT: "Dr. Young Inaugurated as Head of Pepperdine," Nov. 22, 1958, A8; and GRAPHIC: "President's Inauguration Set for Today," Nov. 21, 1959, 1.

3 YOUNG: M. Norvel Young, "Inaugural Address," Nov. 21, 1958, Inauguration (Dr. Young) file, Box 66.

4 Ibid.

5 Since the 1954 Pepperdine report to WCA has not been found, the concerns expressed in that document have been inferred from the report prepared for the WCA visit in January 1959. See OIE: "Report for the Accreditation Committees," Dec. 1, 1958; and YOUNG: Jimmy Lovell to Young, et al., Jan. 1, 1958, Jimmy Lovell file; and President's Annual Report to the Board of Trustees, 1957–1958, Annual Reports of the President file. See also PUA: Minutes, Faculty Meeting, Nov. 11, 1958, Faculty Minutes/Faculty Affairs file, Box 84. The particular Faculty Handbook in question was compiled by Fred Casmir in Jan. 1957. It may have been the first such document.

6 YOUNG: Young to Briggs, June 28, 1957, Pepperdine Move file, Box 58.

7 GRAPHIC: "Dr. Squire in New Job," Feb. 7, 1958, 1; and OHC: Interview with Dr. Russel Squire by Dorothy Moore, Mar. 20, 1979.

8 WSB: Young, Confidential notes on interview with President Glenn Dumke, June 23, 1958, Misc. D file, Box 19a/b.

9 YOUNG: George S. Benson to Young, Dec. 22, 1958, George Benson file, Box B26.

10 OIE: "Report for Accreditation Committees," Dec. 1, 1958.

11 YOUNG: "Report of the Western College Visiting Committee on Pepperdine College," January 12, 13, 1959, History 1957 file, Box 74.

12 Ibid.

13 Ibid.

14 Ibid.: Faculty Meeting Minutes, Mar. 3, 1959, Faculty Minutes 58–59 file, Box 23.

15 BOT: Mar. 1, 1961, vol. 4:124.

16 YOUNG: "Report to the Committee on Accreditation," January 1959, State. Dept. of Edu. file, Box B25.

17 Ibid.: "Report of the Western College Association Committee," Dec. 4, 5, 6, 1960, Accreditation file, Box 1; OIE: "Report for the Accreditation Committees," Nov. 1965, 1ff, in Records of Accreditations-1965.

18 Ibid.: "Report of the Visitation Committee," December 5–6, 1960, State. Dept. of Edu. file, Box B25.

19 Ibid.: "Report of the Accreditation Committees," Jan. 16, 17, 18, 1961, Box 1.

20 In addition to George and Helen Pepperdine, Don Miller, Jimmy Lovell, Robert P. Jones, and O. V. Melton, the board was expanded in these years to include A. E. Acklin, Nile Yearwood, Lipscomb Crothers, George Evans, Arnold Sallaberry, Ira North, Reuel Lemmons, and Jim Bill McInteer. George Pepperdine served on the board until his death in 1962.

CHAPTER 10

1 "Millions Willed To Right Wingers," *New York Times*, May 4, 1966, 35.

2 GRAPHIC: "$1 Million Declined," May 6, 1966, 3.

3 Smoot, *People along the Way*, 237–45.

4 YOUNG: Bill Teague to D. B. Lewis, May 11, 1964, D. B. Lewis file, Box B24.

5 Ibid.: Arlie Hoover, et al., Faculty Petition, [May 5, 1966], $1 Million Dollars file, Box 4; and GRAPHIC: "$1 Million?" May 6, 1966, 6.

6   Ibid.: Norvel Young, "A Statement From Pepperdine College," [May 5, 1966], D. B. Lewis file, Box B24.

7   Ibid.: Clipping, "Offer Tempting," *Dallas Times Herald*, [May 1966], D. B. Lewis Clippings file, Box B24.

8   Ibid.: Kirk, "All Honor to Pepperdine College," *Helena Independent Record*, May 25, 1966; Morrie Ryskind, "A Few Still Resist Great Society Life," *Los Angeles Herald Examiner*, May 25, 1966; Walter Winchell, "New Yorkers Are Talking," *New York Times*, May 23, 1966, in D. B. Lewis file, Box B24.

9   FF: Reuel Lemmons, "On Turning Down A Million Dollars," June 2, 1966, 354.

10 YOUNG: Clipping, Ronald Buel, "Passing the Buck," *Wall Street Journal*, Aug. 2, 1966, 1, D. B. Lewis file, Box B24.

11 Budget data comes from multiple sources, Board of Trustees minutes, the President's Annual Reports to the Trustees, and loose documents in a variety of files in the M. Norvel and Helen Young Papers. Gifts for capital improvements are not included.

12 YOUNG: John Price Jones Company, "A Special Report," Jan.–Feb. 1960, in J. P. Jones file, Box B22.

13 Ibid., 10–13. See also HAWP: Box 28.

14 YOUNG: John Price Jones, "Special Report," 14–17, in J. P. Jones file, Box B22.

15 Miles, *John Scolinos*, 34.

16 YOUNG: *President's Annual Report to the Board of Trustees, 1959–1960*, 23, in Annual Reports file, Box 43; Minutes, Administrative Council, Jan. 14, 1959, Administrative Council Meeting file, Box B26; and BOT: Oct. 20, 1959, vol. 4:80ff.

17 GRAPHIC: "Pep Names Dacus New Grid Coach," Nov. 20, 1959, 8; and YOUNG: Dacus to Brother, Oct. 13, 1960, Pence Dacus file, Box B23.

18 YOUNG: Opinion poll, [1961], Faculty file, Box 3; and GRAPHIC: "Tuition Increase Possible If College Keeps Football," Oct. 27, 1961, 1; "Football Debate in Chapel Today," Nov. 3, 1961, 1.

19 YOUNG: Bob Pratt to Mr. Miller, Nov 1, [1961], Pepperdine Athletics file, Box 1; and Elmer Noonan, "Voice of the President: The Decision to Drop Football," *Alumni Voice*, 24 (Jan.-Feb. 1962): 3.

20 LAT: "Pepperdine Drops Football Team," Dec. 21, 1961, C1; and GRAPHIC: Brad Shaw, "Football Dropped," Jan. 5, 1962, 1; and BOT: Dec. 18, 1961, vol. 4:155; and YOUNG: Young to Dacus, Feb. 1962, Pence Dacus file, Box B23.

21 YOUNG: Digest of an Address by Benson, Oct. 7, 1958, George Benson file, Box B26.

22 Ibid.: Benson to Young, Aug. 12, 1958.

23 Ibid.: [Young], Comments to Third Annual Freedom Forum, Mar. 1961, Forum file, Box 2.

24 PUA: Transcript of interview with M. Norvel Young by Brett Landis, Oct. 29, 1985, Freedom Forum (MNY) file, Box B53.

25 YOUNG: Benson to Young, Oct. 16, 1959, George Benson file.

26 Programs for virtually all of the forums are found in YOUNG: Forum file, Box 2; "Annual Report of the President to the Board of Trustees, 1960–1961," 18, Annual Report file, Box 43.

27 BOT: Feb. 27, 1962, vol. 4:161.

28 YOUNG: George Todt, "Value of Freedom Forum," *Los Angeles Herald-Express*, Apr. 4, 1961, clipping, Americanism file, Box 79.

29 LACU: Young to Jimmy Lovell, Sept 23, 1970, Box 3; BOT: Mar. 17, 1962, vol. 4:164; and Patricia Yomantas, "How to Succeed in Business," *Pepperdine People*, 4 (Winter 1981), 3–4; and NICKS: M. Norvel Young, "Pepperdine University, A Place, A People, A Promise," a speech delivered to the Newcomen Society, Nov. 1, 1981, Box 13.

30 BOT: Apr. 21, 1959, vol. 4:57 and Jan. 11, 1960, vol. 4:84.

31 GRAPHIC: "Dorm Groundbreaking Ceremony Today," Feb. 12, 1960, 1; and YOUNG: "Pepperdine College's Declaration of Independence," Feb. 12, 1960, Forum file, Box 2.

32 YOUNG: Young, "Education Without Federal Aid," Jan. 20, 1961, Young Addresses, Printed file, Box B14.

33 87th Cong., 1st sess., *Congressional Record*, June 19, 1961, vol. 107, pt. 9, 11844–11845.

34 Norvel M. Young, "Education Without Federal Aid," *Vital Speeches*, June 1, 1961, 492.

35 "Crises for Americans," *Alumni Voice*, 25 (Sept.–Oct., 1961), 15.

36 BOT: Dec. 9, 1965, vol. 5:68.

37 Ibid., Nov. 18, 1958 and July 20, 1961, vol. 4:40 and 145; Oct. 8, 1963, vol. 5:9.

38 Ibid., Mar. 14, 1966, vol. 5:78; and YOUNG: Faculty Meeting Excerpt for Jan. 20, 1966, Government Money for Pepperdine College, Gilbert Richardson file, Box 66.

39 "Federal Aid, Going It Alone," *Time Magazine*, 91 (Feb. 23, 1968), 48 & 53; and GRAPHIC: John Davis, "HUD to probe Chicano charge," June 10, 1971, 1.

40 BOT: Apr. 18, 1961, vol. 4:137–38.

41 Ibid. See also June 27, 1964, vol. 5:26 and Dec. 9, 1965, vol. 5:68.

42 Ibid.: Aug. 4, 1967, vol. 5:126c. The four films are available through the Special Collections and University Archives Division of Pepperdine's University Libraries.

43 GRAPHIC: "College Again Receives Freedom Medals," Feb. 22, 1963, 1.

44 Kirk, *Roots of American Order*, front material.

45 Hoffert, Review of *The Root of American Order*, in *American Political Science Review*, 640–42; and YOUNG: Morris Pendleton to William Banowsky, June 20, 1975, Morris Pendleton file, Box 47.

CHAPTER 11

1 YOUNG: *Annual Report of the President to the Board of Trustees, 1960–1961*, 18, Annual Reports file, Box 43; "Crisis for Americans," *Alumni Voice*, 24 (Sept.–Oct. 1961), 15.

2 GRAPHIC: "Coe Offers Fellowships to Teachers," Mar. 25, 1960, 2; "90 Teachers Coming Here," June 11, 1965, 1; "Coe Grants Again To Be Given Here," Nov. 16, 1962, 3; "Coe Fellowship Program Opens," June 17, 1966, 2; "Coe Foundation Gives Fellowships," Jan. 29, 1971, 4. See also Glover H. Shipp, "Current Highlights," *Alumni Voice*, 27 (Winter 1964), 24, and "Teaching Teachers," 31 (Summer 1968), 28.

3 GRAPHIC: "Robert Taft Institute Fellowships Available," June 10, 1966, 1; "Teaching Teachers," *Alumni Voice*, 31 (Summer 1968), 28; and HAWP: Young to Marilyn Chelstrom, Apr. 18, 1968, Chron. Corres., Apr. 4 1968–Oct. 1968 file, Box 1; and BOT: June 19, 1969, vol. 5:187.

4 BAIRD: Brochure, "'Pepperdine College Points The Way'," [Spring 1962], 1961–1962 file; and GRAPHIC: Paul Wolfe, "College, Dr. Young get 'Freedom' Award," Feb. 23, 1962, 1; and Glover H. Shipp, "The Pepperdine Story," *Alumni Voice*, 26 (May-June, 1963), 4.

5 LAT: Morrie Ryskind, "Through Rose-Colored Glasses," Apr. 5, 1961, B4.

6 LAT: Ryskind, "Pepperdine Points the Way, Sept. 1, 1961, B4.

7 YOUNG: *President's Annual Report to the Board of Trustees, 1959–1960*, 5, Annual Reports file, Box 43; and LAT: "George Elkins to Head Pepperdine Advisory Board," May 10, 1965, A2; and HAWP: Bill Banowsky to George Elkins, June 16, 1970, Chron. Corres., May 29-June 30, 1970, Box 2. At the time, Banowsky wrote to Elkins, "When the history of the College is written, your leadership of the President's Board during the past 10 crucial years will be a major chapter of the success story." Forty years later, Elkins got no more than a line in Banowsky's *Malibu Miracle* (2010).

8 PUA: Young to Miller, July 5, 1961, Miller-Donald (1 of 2) file, Box B97; Young to Scaife, Oct. 2, 1962, Hornbaker Files (File Cabinet F-201B-F286C).

9 BOT: Feb. 27, 1962, 5:160, and Oct. 4, 1965, vol. 5:63; and YOUNG: Young to Robert Jones, Jan. 23, 1962, Robert P. Jones file, Box B24, and Financing for Malibu, Dec. 31, 1970, Management file, Box 66; Richard M. Scaife, "People Who Care," *Alumni Voice*, 29 (Dec. 1965), 9; and HAWP: Young to Scaife, Oct. 11, 1967, Chron. Corres., Oct 2 to Apr. 4, 1968 file; Young to Scaife, Feb. 6, 1969, Chron. Corres., Oct 28 to Feb. 17, 1969, Box 1.

10 HAWP: Young to Charles Ford, May 9, 1968, Chron. Corres., Apr. 4 to Oct. 1968, Box 1; Bill Banowsky to Richard Scaife, July 7, 1970, Chron. Corres., July 1 to 31, 1970 file, Box 2.

11 Among Scaife's many gifts to Pepperdine, one was unique. In 1967, he feared that social unrest in Europe would spread to the U.S., so he and his colleagues envisioned an operative on the ground who would gather information on subversive activity before it reached U.S. shores. They identified Carl von Armfelt, a European-born, multilingual journalist as the agent, then asked Young and Pepperdine College to provide cover for Armfelt while the Allegheny Foundation provided the money. Beginning January 1, 1968, the college hired Armfelt on a one-year contract to be its representative in Heidelberg and "assist us with our Year-in-Europe program and to help us to identify an appropriate site for expansion." A year later, Armfelt's contract was renewed.

   If Armfelt ever appeared in Heidelberg, it was only for a brief moment. Instead he sent Young and the Allegheny Foundation lengthy reports on communist activities, from Sweden to Czechoslovakia, from England to Germany, and points in between. As a whole, Armfelt's reports were less the work of a writer or educator than a covert agent. The whole project was foreign to the objectives of Pepperdine College, although it was germane to an institution that wanted the patronage of Richard Scaife. As President Young told him, "We stand ready to work with you in the fullest." HAWP: Young to William Gill, Oct. 20, 1967; Young to Finance, Dec. 6, 1967, Chron. Corres., Oct. 2 to Apr. 4, 1968 file; Young to Honorable W. W. Heath, Apr. 18, 1968, Chron. Corres., Apr. 4-Oct. 1968 file; Young to Gill, Dec. 24, 1968, Chron. Corres., Oct. 28, 1968 to Feb. 17, 1969 file, Box 1. Armfelt's reports are in YOUNG: Carl von Armfelt files 1, 2, and 3, Box B26.

12 Youngs, *The Legacy of Frank Roger Seaver.*

13 YOUNG: Young to Salvatori, May 1, 1975, Henry Salvatori file, Box 21B.

14 Ibid.: California Teachers Association Research Department, "The Patterns of Attack," Mar. 27, 1961; James H. Corson to CASA Individual Membership, Mar. 27, 1961, Forum file, Box 2.

15 Ibid.: Minutes of Departmental Council Meeting, Apr. 16, 1961, Dept. Council file, Box B23.

16 Ibid.: Garford G. Gordon to Members of State Council of Education, Apr. 13, 1961.

17 LAT: Ryskind, "Pepperdine Points the Way to Self-Reliance," Sept. 1, 1961, B4.

18 YOUNG: [Notes by Helen Young], Nov. 1961, History-1957 file, Box 74; Minutes, Administrative Council Meeting, Apr. 10, 1961, Adm. Council Meeting, Aug. 1957 file, Box B26.

19 Ibid.: President's Message to Pepperdine Student Body, [1969], M. Norvel Young Talks, Box 57.

20 GRAPHIC: Ron Stump, "New 'Debate Challenge' Issued," Sept. 27, 1968, 1; Ron Ellerbe, "PC Political Club Aids Campaign," May 15, 1968, 2.

21 YOUNG: "We have honored both political liberals and conservatives," [Jan. 1970], Student Affairs file, Box 4.

22 Ibid.: Casmir to Young, Sept. 26, 1966, Gov. Reagan file, Box 90.

CHAPTER 12

1 YOUNG: George Benson to Norvel Young, Oct. 16, 1959, and Jan. 7, 1963, George S. Benson file, Box 43.

2 Ibid.: James L. Atteberry to Clifton Ganus, Aug. 8, 1969, and James D. Bales, "Dr. James L. Atteberry and Harding College," Searcy, AR, 1969, in Faculty-Harding Issues file, Box 3; see also HAWP: Young to Bill Banowsky, et al., June 24, 1969, Chron. Corres., Apr. 24 to July 25, 1969, file, Box 1, and Young to Alan Highers, Sept. 3, 1969, Chron. Corres., July 25 to Oct. 31, 1969, file, Box 2.

3 GRAPHIC: "Quiz Show Hobby Pays Off for Dr. Wade Ruby," Sept. 19, 1958, 2; Dr. Wade Ruby, "Inside The Isolation Booth," *Alumni Voice*, 21 (Sept. 1958), 10–11; and LAT: "Angeleno Steps Up Quiz Winnings to $46,000," Aug. 12, 1958, A2; "Dr. Ruby Quits TV Quiz—$67,000 Ahead," Aug. 19, 1958, A5; "Quiz Show Twenty-One Under Investigation," Aug. 29, 1958, A1. Previous to "Twenty-One," Ruby appeared on the "Groucho Marx Show," "Break the Bank," "It's News to Me," "Pillsbury House Party," "Life with Linkletter," and "It Pays to be Married."

4 YOUNG: Hollywood Visitor, Mar. 30, 1966, in church bulletin in Faculty file, Box 3; and GRAPHIC: Noel Beasley, "Dr. Wade Ruby Laid to Rest at Camden, Arkansas"; Phil Pennington to the Editor; Jon Washington to the Editor, Mar. 25, 1966, 1 & 2; and BOT: July 21, 1966.

5 GRAPHIC: Bill Garaway, "Professor Authors Book," Nov. 20, 1964, 2; and YOUNG: Richardson to Mrs. George Pepperdine, Apr. 4, 1966; Richardson to Young, May 4, 1966; Young to Members of the Board of Trustees, July 8, 1966; Richardson to Brother Nichol, Aug. 15, 1966, Gilbert Richardson file, Box 66.

6 YOUNG: Richardson to Brethren, June 24, 1966; Sanders to Friends of Pepperdine College, July 13, 1966; Suggested Proposal for Mr. Gilbert Richardson, [Aug. 1966], Gilbert Richardson file, Box 66; Rex Johnston to Don McGaughey, July 8, 1966, Faculty file, Box 3; and BOT: July 21, 1966, vol. 5:91.

7 YOUNG: Pepperdine College, *Faculty Handbook*, Sept. 1965, 3–5, in Faculty Salaries file, Box 2.

8 Ibid.: Minutes of the Departmental Council, July 14, 1964, Departmental Council file, Box B23.

9 Ibid.: Memo to Dean Sanders from Fred Casmir, Mar. 22, 1960, Fred Casmir #2 file, Box B22.

10 Ibid.: Pepperdine College, *Faculty Handbook,* Sept. 1965, 14–15, 18, & 27 in Faculty Salaries file, Box 2.

11 Ibid.: *President's Annual Report to the Board of Trustees, 1957–1958,* 11–12, in Annual Reports file, Box 43.

12 Ibid.: Professional Problems Committee to Administrative Committee, Apr. 19, 1965, Faculty file, Box 3; J. C. Moore to Young, Feb. 18, 1965; AAUP Survey for average salaries for church related colleges, Feb. 7, 1967, Faculty Salaries file, Box 2; Mabel Bean to Casmir, May 17, 1965, Fred Casmir file, Box B22.

13 BOT: Aug. 11, 1965, vol. 5:58; Aug. 4, 1967, vol. 5:123; July 21, 1970, vol. 5:216. The possibilities of sabbatical leaves grew out of a study by an ad hoc committee of the college's AAUP chapter in 1967. See SRP: "Report of the Committee on Sabbatical Leave," n.d., AAUP file, Box 28.

14 JCM: "Faculty-Student Research Potential . . . 1961–1962."

15 BOT: Mar. 14, 1966, vol. 5:78.

16 Ibid.; and GRAPHIC: "Research Group Receives $77,000," June 29, 1967; "Grant Awarded for Drug Study," July 13, 1967, 1; and HAWP: Sanders to Pournelle, Dec. 15, 1967, Chron. Corres., Oct. 2, 1967–Apr. 4, 1968 file; Young to Robert P. Jones, Aug. 14, 1968, Chron. Corres., Apr 4-Oct. 1968 file; Young announcement, July 7, 1969, Chron. Corres., Apr. 24-July 25, 1969, file, Box 1; and *Pepperdine College Bulletin, 1969–70 Catalog,* 31 (Feb. 1969), 225; and BAIRD: Ruth D. Atteberry, "Pepperdine

University School of Business and Management," [1999], 43, in GSBM file. For quoted material see PUA: Unnamed to John Bolinger and J. Dan Benefiel, Sept. 11, 1968, PRI file, Box CO2–4.

17 BOT: Nov. 18, 1958, vol. 4:40a-b.

18 YOUNG: Pepperdine College, *Faculty Handbook*, Sept. 1965, 7, in Faculty Salaries file, Box 2.

19 Ibid., 9.

20 Ibid.: "Pepperdine College, *Faculty Handbook*," Sept. 1965, 7, in Faculty Salaries file, Box 2.

21 Ibid.: Faculty Committees, 1964–1965, Administrative Council Minutes file, Box B26.

22 See Pepperdine University, AAUP Institutional Files, 1951–1975, Box 41, Special Collection Research Center, Gelman Library, George Washington University, Washington, D.C.

23 YOUNG: Office of the President, Guidelines and Objectives, [Spring, 1959], Norvel Young talks file, Box 57.

24 *Pepperdine College Bulletin, 1958–1959*, 22 (May, 1958), 37; and *1969–1970*, 32 (Feb. 1969), 44.

25 YOUNG: *Annual Report of the President to the Board of Trustees, 1964–1965*, 2, in Annual Reports file, Box 43; "5 New Degree Programs," *Alumni Voice*, 28 (Spring 1965), 8; and BOT: Mar. 14, 1966, vol. 5:79.

26 *Pepperdine College Bulletin, 1958–1959*, 22 (May, 1958), 43; and *1969–1970*, 32 (Feb. 1969), 48.

27 BOT: June 8, 1967, vol. 5:120.

28 YOUNG: *President's Annual Report to the Board of Trustees, 1958–1959*, 6, in Annual Reports, Box 43; and Pepperdine College Bulletin, 1968–1969, 31 (March 1968), 230.

29 *Pepperdine College Bulletin, 1958–1959*, 22 (May, 1958), 43; and *1969–1970*, 32 (Feb. 1969), 48.

30 PAH: John Price Jones, A Special Report to the President of Pepperdine College, Jan.-Feb., 1960 in Box H03; and *Pepperdine College Bulletin, 1958–1959*, 22 (May, 1958),75; 1964–1966, 27 (March 1964), 64; and 1969–1970, 32 (Feb. 1969), 96.

31 Ibid., *1958–1959*, 26–27 (May, 1958), 43; and *1969–1970*, 32 (Feb. 1969), 19.

32 YOUNG: *President's Annual Report to the Board of Trustees, 1958–1959*; Memo from Administrative Officer to Faculty, [Fall 1962]; Memo from Jennings Davis, Mar. 22, 1966; Gardner to Young, May 15, 1967, Jennings Davis #3 file.

33 Ibid.: Young to Davis and Hill, Aug. 13, 1964; Memo from Jennings Davis Jr., March 22, 1966; Davis to Young, Oct. 20, 1966, Jennings Davis #3 file, and General Information, Fall 1968, March 12th Incident file, Box 3.

34 Ibid.: Casmir to Sanders, July 17, 1959, Fred Casmir #2 file, Box B22.

35 Ibid.: Minutes of the Departmental Council, July 14, 1964, Dept. Council file, Box B23.

36 Ibid.: Mar. 10, 1964.

37 HAWP: Young to Sanders, Jan. 23, 1968, Letters Sent, Chron. Corres., Oct 2, 1967 to Apr. 4, 1968 file, Box 1.

38 YOUNG: *President's Annual Report to the Board of Trustees, 1959–1960*, 21, Annual Reports file, Box 43.

39 Ibid.: Casmir to Members of the Administration and the Faculty, [1964–1965], Fred Casmir file.

40 Ibid.: Davis and Todd to Pepperdiner, [Fall 1968], Jennings Davis 66–68 file, Box B23.

41 Ibid.: *Annual Report of the President to the Board of Trustees, 1959–1960*, 21, Annual Reports file, Box 43.

42 "Education: Speed-up at Pittsburgh," *Time*, July 11, 1960, 84.

43 YOUNG: *Annual Report of the President to the Board of Trustees, 1962–1963*, in Annual Reports file, Box 43; FF: Ladis D. Kovach, "Trimester . . . Sign of Progress," Feb. 5, 1963, 87; "Transition to Trimester," *Alumni Voice*, 28 (Spring 1965), 3–6; and LAT: Dick Turpin, "Pepperdine Launches Full-Year Curriculum," Sept. 8, 1963, N4.

44 LAT: "William Trombley, "Regents Press for Year-Round UC Classwork," Sept 16, 1966, A3.

45 GRAPHIC: "Trimester 'Success'," June 2, 1964, 2; and BOT: May 19, 1964.

46 BOT: Dec. 9, 1965, vol. 5:65–66. See OIE: WASC, "Report on visit to Pepperdine College, Nov. 3–5, 1965," 1965 Visit Report file.

CHAPTER 13

1 GRAPHIC: "Annual European Tour to Be Conducted by Tegner," Jan. 8, 1960, 1. This was the 8th annual tour, which included a six-week pre-travel institute and an 8-week travel schedule. Tegner had taught at the University of Lausanne in 1955 and 1956.

2 BOT: Oct. 23, 1962, vol. 4:175; Feb. 12, 1963, vol. 4: 181–82.

3 GRAPHIC: "Heidelberg is Selected As German School Site," Feb. 15, 1963, 1; FF: "Pepperdine Plans 'Year in Europe' Program," Feb. 5, 1963, 80, 83; and LAT: Turpin, "Pepperdine Launches Full-Year Curriculum," Sept. 8, 1963, N4; and YOUNG: *Annual Report of the President to the Board of Trustees, 1962–63*, 4, in Annual Reports file, Box 43.

4 This was the memory of George and Sarah Cooper, members of the first YIE class. See "The Heidelberg program," *Pepperdine People* (Summer 1987), 10.

5 JCM: [J. C. Moore], Mimeographed document without a heading, Jan. 28, 1965, J. C. Moore #3 file; and BOT: May 4, 1965, vol. 5:53–55, and Oct. 4, 1965, vol. 5:61. Henegar and Rushford state inaccurately that the proceeds of the Frankfurt church building sale were "donated" to Pepperdine, with the provision that Pepperdine should organize a Bibelschule for aspiring German ministers. See Henegar and Rushford, *Forever Young*, 184.

6 BOT: A Report to the Board of Trustees Regarding the Heidelberg Property, in Dec. 9, 1965, vol. 5:69a, b, c; and GRAPHIC: Julie Ryan, "German 'Dorm' Purchase Told," Oct. 29, 1965, 1.

7 GRAPHIC: "James C. Moore Memorial Held," July 17, 1969, 1; "Pepperdine Has Renamed Honoring Late J. C. Moore," Jan. 22, 1970, 4.

8 Ibid.: "Germans Will Train To Preach," May 28, 1970, 1; Kenny Waters, "Ministers Train On YIE Campus," Jan. 14, 1971, 1; and HAWP: Herbert Luft to White, Dec. 22, 1970, attached to White to Young, Jan. 13, 1971, Norvel Young '69–'70 file, Box 33; and BAIRD: Herbert Luft, The Heidelberg Bible School, 1970–1985, [Oct. 2010] and email from Glenn Boyd, Searcy, AR, to author, Dec. 7, 2010, in 1970–71 file.

9 HAWP: [Luft] to Dr. White, Aug. 3, 1968, Heidelberg Bible School file (2 of 2), Box 31; and SRP: "Facts of German Preacher Training School (Commonly referred to as the German Bible School)," [Fall 1980], Herbert Luft file, Box 25.

10 BAIRD: Hans Rollman, email communication with the author, July 29, 2010, in 1970–71 file; and YOUNG: Herbert Luft to Howard White, July 5, 1971, Heidelberg file, Box 45.

11 In 1971, seven German nationals enrolled in the Bibelschule were in the field preaching: Werner Fuss, Klaus Gobbels, Karl-Heinz Ignatzi, Dieter Meyer, Hans Rollman, Fred Schickling, and Manfred Schulz. See WSB: "copy for bibelschule heidelberg brochure," [Spring 1974], attached to White to Young, Feb. 26, 1974; White to Young, Nov. 21, 1974; White to Banowsky, June 12, 1975, Howard White file, Box 39/44A. See also HAWP: White to Young, Oct. 30, 1973, Norvel Young '73 file, Box 33, and Feb. 14, 1976, Corres. Feb. 14 to Apr. 5, 1976 file, Box 6. Because of the close relationship between the Bibelschule and the undergraduate program

at Moore Haus, the faculty in charge of that program were always members of Churches of Christ. See HAWP: White to James and Connie Greer, Mar. 20, 1976, Chron. Corres., Feb. 14–Apr. 6, 1976 file, Box 6; and SRP: White to Luft, Sept. 30, 1978, Herbert Luft Corres. '78-'80 file, Box 14 and White to David Davenport, Feb. 14, 1989, Bible School file, Box 18.

12 SRP: White to Luft, Jan. 17, 1977, Herbert Luft Corres. '76–77 file, Box 14.

13 HAWP: Young to William Gill, Feb. 3 and 4, 1969; Young to Trustees, Feb. 18, 1969, and Young to Scaife, Feb. 13 and 18, 1969, Chron. Corres., Oct. 28, 1968–Feb. 17, 1969 file, Box 1. For quotation see BOT: June 19, 1969, vol. 5:188. Charles J. V. Murphy, "The Mellons of Pittsburgh," *Fortune*, 76 (October 1967) 120–29, gives good insight to the source of the Scaife fortune.

14 BOT: Jan. 27, 1969, vol. 5:167.

15 YOUNG: Clipping, "Business Center Downtown," *Los Angeles Herald-Examiner*, Jan. 23, 1970, in Board of Trustees-Misc. file, Box 58. According to David Reagan, subsequently the director of CIB, the Mellon foundation objected to the institute being made "largely into a chamber of commerce type operation for Pepperdine's benefit." See HAWP: Confidential memo to file, Mar. 7, 1975, Ex. VP Corres., Feb. 20–Apr. 30, 1975 file, Box 5.

16 YOUNG: Arthur L. Peterson to Young, Mar. 27, 1970, and May 14, 1970, Arthur Peterson file, Box 66. See also BOT: Jan. 27, 1969; and GRAPHIC: "College Establishes Downtown Center," Jan. 29, 1970, 3.

17 See YOUNG: Four files marked "Center for International Business" in Box 43. See also Clipping, "Business Center Downtown"; and BOT: Sept. 29, 1970; and GRAPHIC: Marsha Teems, "CIB Extension Inaugurates Economic, Political Studies," May 27, 1971, 1. Among some of the publications of the Center was Dennis Ray, et al., *The New Internationalism and the Multinational Firm: Cooperation and Conflict* (Los Angeles: Pepperdine School of Business and Management, c. 1975).

CHAPTER 14

1 GRAPHIC: "44 Regions Represented," Oct. 14, 1960, 3.

2 PUA: "Federal Survey of Negro Undergraduate Enrollment, 1969," Washington, DC: Government Printing Office, 1969, in Box B104.

3 YOUNG: "Traditional Activities" and "General Regulations," *Student Handbook, Pepperdine College, 1963–64*, 14 & 18, in Student Activities file, Box 4; and Pepperdine College Bulletin, 32, Feb. 1969: 28–32; and GRAPHIC: John Davis, "Chapel Heads Conversation 'Gripes'," Oct. 8, 1970, 1.

4 GRAPHIC: "ASB Board Airs Women's Smoking Issue," Oct. 23, 1964, 1; and YOUNG: Lucille Todd to Head Resident, May 2, 1966, Jennings Davis, 65–66 file, Box 79; Todd and Davis to All Faculty, Sept. 28, 1966, Jennings Davis, 66–68 file; White to Banowsky, Nov. 2, 1971, Dean of Student's Office file, Box 79; and GRAPHIC: "'Campus Deterioration,' Stivers Seeks Answer to Smoking Problem," July 29, 1971, 2; and WSB: Banowsky to Young, June 7, 1972, Chronological June–Aug., 1972 file, Box 6BCH (20 A, B & C).

5 GRAPHIC: John Davies, "SA Back Dorm Visitation Rights," Nov. 19, 1970, 1; Davies, "Small College Survey; 80% Conduct Visitation," Feb. 11, 1971, 1; Davis, "Dorm Faces Further Delays," Feb. 18, 1971, 1; "Parents Judge Visiting," May 6, 1971, 1; "Mike Daugherty, "Visitation Defeated by Council," Dec. 9, 1971, 1; Daugherty, "Board Rules No Visitation," Jan. 13, 1971, 1; and WSB: Minutes, Administrative Committee, May 6, 1971, Administrative Com. file, Box 4 A-W (24); and BOT: Dec. 17, 1971, vol. 5:252; and HAWP: White to Parents, Oct. 12, 1971; Ron Woolfolk to Parent, Oct. 27, 1971, Dorm Visitation Policy '71 file, Box 25.

6 BAIRD: "In a Nutshell," [1964–65] ("wool dresses" is not a mistake); "Your New Address, Baxter Hall, Lawhorn Hall, 1964–65," in Dean of Student's file, Box 2 (also in 1964–65 file); and YOUNG: "Dress Guide," *Student Handbook, Pepperdine College, 1963–64*, Los Angeles: Pepperdine College, 1963:19, in Student Activities file, Box 4.

7 Steve Gobbell, "50 Years of Change in Student Life," *Oasis* (1987–1988): 23.

8 SRP: White to Young, Jan. 24, 1972, Howard White '71–'75 file, Box 14. The so-called policy was probably more customary than official in that the Faculty Handbook published in 1970 has no reference to a dress code for faculty.

9 *Pepperdine College Catalog, 1964–1965*, 27 (Mar. 1964): 28.

10 *Pepperdine College Catalog, 1966–1967*, 29 (Mar. 1966): 30; YOUNG: Minutes, July 20, 1965, Administrative Council Meetings file, Box B26.

11 Ibid.: Davis to Faculty, Sept. 15, 1967, Jennings Davis, 66–68 file, Box B23.

12 HAWP: Minutes of the Administrative Committee, Dec. 31, 1969, Chron. Corres. Nov. 1, 1969 to Jan. 30, 1970 file, Box 2; and YOUNG: "Chapel Assembly Attendance Policies," July 1970, Dean of Students Office file, Box 2; and GRAPHIC: John Davis, "Chapel Heads Conversation 'Gripes'," Oct. 8, 1970, 1.

13 YOUNG: Minutes, Administrative Council Meeting, Nov. 16, 1960, Administrative Council Meetings file, Box B26.

14 GRAPHIC: John Huether, "Needed: Initiative," Feb. 12, 1970, 8.

15 BOT: June 19, 1969, vol. 5:186.

16 A faculty committee reported in May 1971 that some students felt "that Church of Christ doctrines [are] strongly imposed, while students of other persuasions are put down and offended." See GRAPHIC: John Huether, "Report Defines Major Campus Issues," May 6, 1971, 1.

17 HAWP: Minutes, Administrative Council Meeting, Dec. 31, 1969, Chron. Corres., Nov. 1, 1969–Jan. 30, 1970 file, Box 2; Young to Sanders, Jan. 23, 1968, Chron. Corres. Oct. 2, 1967 to Apr. 4, 1968 file, Box 1; Young, Statement on Chapel Participation, Oct. 30, 1969, Chron. Corres. July 25–Oct. 31, 1969 file, Box 2.

18 BOT: June 19, 1969, vol. 5:186.

19 GRAPHIC: Kenny Waters, "The Sunshine Corner, Multi-mixup," July 1, 1971, 4; and HAWP: Minutes of Student Board, June 23, 1970, Corres. May 1–28, 1970 file, Box 2.

20 GRAPHIC: Elain Heck, "Survey Outlines Student Needs," June 10, 1971, 1; Kenny Waters, "Poll Reveals Problem: No Freedom of Choice," July 1, 1971, 1; Waters, "Survey Brings 'Mixed' Results," July 15, 1971, 1.

21 Ibid.: Tal Campbell, "Non-Conformity Here?" Apr. 7, 1961, 2.

22 Ibid.: Ron Stump, "New 'Debate Challenge' Issued," Sept. 27, 1968, 1.

23 YOUNG: Manuscript by TCB, "Kalish Refused—Is Money #1?" Nov. 1969, Student Affairs file, Box 4.

CHAPTER 15

1 LAT: Valerie Reitman & Mitchell Landsberg, "Watts Riots, 40 Years Later," Aug. 11, 2005, http://articles.latimes.com/2005/aug/11/local/me-watts11 (Jan. 11, 2011); and Stanford University, Martin Luther King, Jr. Research Institute, "Martin Luther King, Jr. and the Global Freedom Struggle, Watts Rebellion, Los Angeles, 1965," http://mlk-kpp01.stanford.edu/index.php/encyclopedia/encyclopedia/enc_watts_rebellion_los_angeles_1965/ (Jan. 11, 2011); and Banowsky, The Malibu Miracle, 52.

2 Henegar and Rushford, *Forever Young*, 186; and Banowsky, *The Malibu Miracle*, 53–54.

3 Military Support of Law Enforcement During Civil Disturbance: A Report Concerning the California National Guard's Part in Suppressing the Los Angeles Riot, August 1965 (Sacramento: California Office of State Printing, 1966); and LAT:

William Trombley, "Pepperdine U. Torn by Tragedy, Internal Dissent," April 18, 1976, C1.

4   In the district between Florence Avenue on the north, Manchester Avenue on the south, Harbor Freeway on the east, and Western Avenue on the west, population increased from 31,646 to 38,638 between 1960 and 1970. During that period, black population increased from 18 percent to 80 percent, and black housing units increased from 958 to 4,084. White housing units decreased from 5,360 to 1,519 units. Eighty-five percent of the families in the area had income levels of less than $15,000 annually in 1970, which was higher than a decade earlier. Twenty-five percent of the employable were without jobs. See WSB: McArthur Byrd, "A Revitalization Design" (Report for MBA School of Business, Pepperdine University, Jan. 1974), in LA Campus file, Box CO2–4.

5   YOUNG: Dean of Students [Jennings Davis Jr.], "Recommendations on Race Relations for Pepperdine College," Fall 1968, 3, March 12th Incident file, Box 3.

6   Ibid.: Brochure, "National Negro History Week," Feb. 12–17, 1968, in Student Activities file, Box 4.

7   LAT: Dart, "Church of Christ Starts to Change Racial Position," July 30, 1968, A6.

8   YOUNG: Dean of Students, "Recommendations on Race Relations."

9   BOT: Mar. 14, 1969, vol. 5:170; and YOUNG: Davis to Fellow minister and brother, June 3, 1969, Jennings Davis 66–68 file, Box B23. For the significance of "Operation Brotherhood" in one person's life, see Meeks, *I Want Somebody to Know My Name*, 57.

10 YOUNG: Dean of Students, "Recommendations on Race Relations."

11 GRAPHIC: "Handsome Harry," Mar. 2, 1967, 1.

12 Ibid.; and BOT: Dec. 17, 1968, vol. 5:163–164. See also YOUNG: Faculty Minutes, Dec. 2, 1968, Faculty file, Box 3, and "So You've Said It Loud...," [Nov. 1968], Dean of Student Affairs file, Box 8; and HAWP: "Pepperdine Project, Preliminary Report No. 1," Jan. 20, 1973, 7, in Box 31.

13 HAWP: Young to Jay Durbin, Dec. 6, 1968, Chron. Corres. Apr. 24, 1969–July 25, 1969 file, Box 1; and YOUNG: Robert P. Jones to Pepperdine College Board of Trustees, Dec. 31, 1968, an addendum to the minutes of the Board of Trustee's meeting, Dec. 16 [or 17], 1968, Confidential: RE Board of Trustees file, Box 74; and HAWP: "Pepperdine Project, Preliminary Report No. 1," Jan. 20, 1973, 7, in Box 31.

14 BOT: Dec. 17, 1968, vol. 5:163–164; and LAT: "Threats Halt Pepperdine Newspaper," Nov. 23, 1968, A16. Only a few issues of the Graphic survive for the 1968–1969 academic year, none for November 1968. Some are quoted, however, in HAWP: "Pepperdine Project, Preliminary Report No. 1," Jan. 20, 1973, 7, in Box 31.

15 YOUNG: "So You've Said It Loud" [Nov. 1968], Dean of Students file, Box 8; and PUA: Campus (Student Unrest) file, Box CO2–1.

16 HAWP: "One Nigger to Another," *Black Graphic*, Nov. 25, 1968, quoted in "Pepperdine Project, Preliminary Report No. 1," Jan. 20, 1973, 9, in Box 31. An original copy of the April 1, 1969 issue is in Black Students, 1969–1971 file, Box 18.

17 BOT: Dec. 17, 1968, vol. 5:163–164.

18 See YOUNG: Addendum to Minutes of Meeting of Board of Trustees, Pepperdine College, Dec. 16, 1968, attached to Robert P. Jones to Board of Trustees, Dec. 31, 1968, in Trustee—Misc. #1, Box 85.

19 HAWP: Young to Board of Trustees, [Feb. 1969], Chron. Corres.,Oct. 28–1968-Feb. 17, 1969 file, Box 1; and YOUNG: Young, Interim Report to the Board of Trustees, Mar. 6, 1969, Board of Trustees-Misc. file, Box 58.

20 LAT: "High School Youth Killed in Struggle With College Guard," Mar. 13, 1969, A3; "Pepperdine Security Officer Jailed in Slaying of Student," Mar. 14, 1960, A3; Robert Rawitch, "Conflicting Stories Given at Inquest in Pepperdine Slaying," Apr. 11, 1969, B1; Rawitch, "Youth Killed Without Warning, Four Testify," Apr. 11,

1969, C8: William Endicott, "Slaying of Boy at Pepperdine Ruled a 'Criminal Act',"
Apr. 12, 1969, A1; "College Guard Who Killed Boy Charged With Manslaughter,"
Apr. 24, 1969, B1; Stanley O. Williford, "Pepperdine College to Resume Classes
Today," Mar. 19, 1969. See also YOUNG: EKT, "March 12, 1969...," *Black Graphic*, 2,
Apr. 1, 1969, 1; W. O. Fudge to LAPD Patrol Divisions, Mar 13, 1969, March 12th
Incident file, Box 3. For the time of day of the incident, I follow the announce-
ment issued by the Los Angeles Police Department (cited above) and the report
Bill Banowsky gave to the Board of Trustees on March 14. See BOT: Mar. 14, 1969,
vol. 5: 171.

21 Henegar and Rushford, *Forever Young*, 197. Within a year the family sued the
College for $2 million. BOT: June 19, 1969, vol. 5:187.

22 YOUNG: Black Students to Drs. Young and Sanders, [Mar. 13, 1969]; Young to
Members of the faculty, Mar. 13, 1969, and EKT, "March 12, 1969," *Black Graphic*,
March 12th Incident file, Box 3.

23 Ibid.: "Summary of the Meeting Between President Young and Members of
ABS," Mar. 13, 1969; Young to Members of the Faculty, Mar. 13, 1969, March 12th
Incident file, Box 3. James Kimmons's induction into the U.S. Army was deferred
for thirty days. He first enrolled in Pepperdine College in 1970 but did not
become a serious student until 1973. Neither he nor his sister, Betty, completed
their degrees. See SRP: Kimmons family file, Box 25 (J-M).

24 PUA: Minutes, President's Board, Mar. 18, 1969, Presidential Board Minutes 60–71
file, Box CO5.

25 YOUNG: "Demands of the B.S.U. of Pepperdine," [Mar. 14, 1969], March 12th
Incident file, Box 3. Faculty and staff targets were Jerry Pournelle, Warren Jones,
James Kinney, Ted Starnes, Tom Nelson, Harry Walker, and Garnie Hatch.

26 BOT: Mar. 14, 1969, vol. 5: 171, 175–76. The full document Davis prepared in late
1968 was titled "Recommendations on Race Relations for Pepperdine College"
and is preserved in YOUNG: March 12th Incident file, Box 3.

27 YOUNG: H. E. Acklin to Young, June 2, 1969, Acklin file, Box 3. See also WSB: Young
to Acklin, Apr. 3, 1970, Acklin file, Box 1 A-C; Thomas P. Breslin, II to Charles
Lane, Sept. 22, 1970, March 12th Incident file, Box 3. Candace Denise Jones,
"White Flight? George Pepperdine College's Move to Malibu, 1965–1972" (MA
thesis, Pepperdine University, 2003), 59ff, gives full coverage of Lane's trial.

28 YOUNG: "Faculty Ad Hoc Committee on Black Students," [Mar. 1969], March 12th
Incident file, Box 3; and HAWP: Black Students, 1969–71 file, Box 18.

29 YOUNG: Young, handwritten notes on "Thoughts," Mar. 17, 1969; Bulletin by
Norvel Young, Mar. 16, 1969, March 12th Incident file, Box 3.

30 Ibid.: EKT, "March 12, 1969," *Black Graphic*; and HAWP: Black Students, 1969–71
file, Box 18.

31 YOUNG: Harry McDevitt to Dr. Young, Mar. 17, 1969, March 12th Incident file, Box
3.

32 Ibid.: Untitled Resolution, Student Affairs Committee, Mar. 19, 1969.

33 Ibid.: Press Release, Pepperdine College News Bureau, Mar. 18, 1969, and
"Pepperdine Reopens; 'Won't be Coerced'," *Los Angeles Herald Examiner*, Mar. 19,
1969, clipping; and LAT: Stanley O. Williford, "Pepperdine College to Resume
Classes Today," Mar. 19, 1969, A29.

34 YOUNG: EKT, "March 12, 1969," *Black Graphic*.

35 Ibid.

36 Ibid.: Young to Russell Coe, Mar. 25, 1969, March 12th Incident file, Box 3.; and
BOT: June 19, 1969, vol. 5:185; and HAWP: "Pepperdine Project, Preliminary Report
No. 1," Jan. 20, 1973, 9, in Box 31. Editors of the *Black Graphic* were inconsistent in
numbering and dating their issues: Vol. 1, No. 1 carries the date of May 8, 1969,
while Vol. 2, No. 3 is dated April 1, 1969. There is also secondary reference (see

"Preliminary Report No. 1" cited above) to an earlier issue dated Nov. 25, 1968. The numbering suggests that more than just these three issues were published, but if they were, they have been lost.

37 GRAPHIC: "Glass Design Class to Aid Unemployed," Jan. 29, 1970, 6; and YOUNG: Bill Dicke and Kathleen Kelly, "Pepperdine Problems," *SoCal*, May 5, 1969, 4, clipping in March 12th Incident file, Box 3.

38 HAWP: Hubert G. Locke to Jennings Davis, Jr., May 5, 1969, attached to Davis to Young, May 27, [1969], Black Students (1969–71) file, Box 18.

39 Ibid.: Young to Vincent Fowler, Sept. 2, 1969, Chron. Corres., July 25–Oct 31, 1969 file, Box 2; and GRAPHIC: "Ethnic Studies Offers Undergraduate Degree," Nov. 12, 1970, 1.

40 YOUNG: Black Faculty Members, Sept. 1969, in Faculty file, Box 3; and HAWP: Press Release, undated, Black Students, 1969–71 file, Box 18.

41 Ibid.: Young to Lorene Henderson, May 19, 1969, Chron. Corres., Apr. 4-July 25, 1969 file, Box 1.

42 Ibid.: Banowsky to White, May 13, 1969.

CHAPTER 16

1 YOUNG: Dicke and Kelly, "Pepperdine Problems," clipping in March 12th Incident file, Box 3.

2 GRAPHIC: John Huether, "Schiffer Resigns ASB Post," Oct. 9, 1969, 2. HAWP: Jerry Hudson, et al., Report of Athletic Committee, [Dec. 1969], Athletic Committee file, Box 61; Larry Wurth to Walter Glass, Dec. 5, 1969, Bert Brewer file, Box 61; and LAT: "8 Pepperdine Blacks Seek Coach Firing," Nov. 22, 1969, B5; and YOUNG: Statement by Dr. M. Norvel Young, Nov. 24, 1969, M. Norvel Young Articles on Pepperdine, Box 79; and HAWP: Minutes of the Administrative Committee, Dec. 2, 1969, Chron. Corres., Nov. 1, 1969-Jan. 30, 1970 file, Box 2.

3 YOUNG: "Before responding...," [Dec. 8, 1969], M. Norvel Young Articles on Pepp. file, Box 79. Paid receipts of Mrs. Kimmons's funeral expenses are in HAWP: Black Students, 1969–71 file, Box 18.

4 YOUNG: "Monday, I made the best...," Dec. 10, 1969, Talks to Faculty file, Box 79. For a copy of *The Sandwich*, Dec. 5, 1969, see Student Activities file, Box 4.

5 Ibid.: Data sheet, Sept. 1970, Campus Problem 12/70 file, Box 90.

6 GRAPHIC: Julie Ryan, "Additional Campus Considered: Growth Causes New Expansion," Jan. 26, 1967, 1; and YOUNG: "Minutes of the Administrative Committee, June 18, 1965, Adm. Com. Minutes file, Box B26.

7 YOUNG: "Malibu Campus Acquisition," [1969], Pepperdine Univ. Board file, Box 47; and BOT: Apr. 14, 1966, vol. 5:84–85; and HAWP: Don Miller to Board of Trustees, Feb. 6, 1968, Chron. Corres., Oct. 2, 1967 to Apr. 4, 1968 file, Box 1.

8 HAWP: Banowsky to Young, Mar. 1968, Press Release file, Box 27.

9 Ibid.: Young to Scaife, Aug. 29, 1968, and Oct. 10, 1968, Chron. Corres., Apr. 4 to Oct. 1968 file, Box 1.

10 Banowsky, *The Malibu Miracle*, 174–75.

11 Editor, "Cathy Meeks and the Great Band Aid on Racism," *Mission Magazine* (Feb. 1979): 4; Jones, "White Flight?"

12 YOUNG: Willie Davis, et al. to Howard A. White, Dec. 2, 1970; handwritten petition signed by 50 students, ca. Dec. 3, 1970, Campus Problem 12/70 file, Box 90.

13 Ibid.: "A committee composed of Calvin Bowers, Oly Tegner, Bill Satterfield and Hubert Derrick...," [Dec. 11, 1970]; "A Message to all Pepperdine Students," [Dec. 1970]; and LAT: Eric Malnic, "Black Students' Strike Forces Pepperdine College Shutdown," Dec. 11, 1970, 1; and GRAPHIC: John Huether, "Administration Considering Demands by Student Strikers," Dec. 10, 1970.

14 YOUNG: Deposition of Jerry Hudson, Pepperdine University v. Chuck Smith, et al., No. 991957, Superior Court of California, Dec. 10, 1970 and First Amended Complaint for Injunction..., Dec. 11, 1971, in Campus Problem 12/70 file, Box 90; and GRAPHIC: John Huether, "Administration Considering Demands by Student Strikers," Dec. 10, 1970, 1. Henegar and Rushford in *Forever Young* (1999), p. 197, place this strike as a "few days after" the Kimmons tragedy. It was actually twenty months later.

15 LAT: Robert Kistler, "Pepperdine College Closes in Wake of Black Student Strike," Dec. 11, 1970, A3; and YOUNG: "UMOJA (Unity)," [Dec. 9, 1970], Campus Problems 12/70 file, Box 90. Presumably one of the black activist students, Cookie Williams, called Hudson "baby face." See HAWP: Zane Reeves to Jerry Hudson, Feb. 22, 1971, Old Corres. from Jerry Hudson file, Box 31. For Norvel Young's version of the events see PUA: "A Confidential Report to Pepperdine University's President's Board Concerning December 10 [1970] disturbances," Mar. 9, 1971, Student Problems file, Box CO2-5.

16 YOUNG: Deposition of Jerry Hudson.

17 Henegar & Rushford, *Forever Young*, 198–99; and YOUNG: "From the Desk of Helen Young: Lessons from Our Crisis," [Dec. 1970], Campus Problem 12/70 file, Box 90.

18 Banowsky, *The Malibu Miracle*, 200–01.

19 Ibid.: Banowsky remembers that his speech was a little longer and more dramatic, 201–2. See LAT: Eric Malnic, "Black Students' Strike Forces College Shutdown," Dec. 11, 1970, A1, for the newspaper account.

20 LAT: Robert Kistler, "Pepperdine College Closes in Wake of Black Student Strike," Dec. 11, 1970, A3.

21 Ibid.: Lee Dye, "Pepperdine Will Handle Student Discipline Itself," Dec. 12, 1970, B1.

22 WSB: Allan [E. Hoffenblum] to Bill, Dec. 12, 1970, Allen Hoffenblum file, Box BPO F-L (38A & B).

23 Banowsky, *The Malibu Miracle*, 204.

24 YOUNG: "Talk With Faculty," Jan. 15, 1971, Talks to Faculty file, Box 79; and GRAPHIC: "Faculty Ratio Drops in Hiring Stalemate," May 6, 1971, 1.

25 YOUNG: Howard A. White to All Faculty Members, Dec. 14, 1970, Campus Problems 12/70 file, Box 90; Young to The Faculty, Jan. 14, 1971, Faculty (general) file, Box 3.

26 Ibid.: "This report reflects...," Dec. 11, 1970, Campus Problems 12/70 file, Box 90.

27 Ibid.: "The President's Response to Certain Student Concerns," Dec. 11, 1970; and GRAPHIC: John Huether, "Administration Considering Demands by Student Strikers," Dec. 10, 1970, 1.

28 Henegar & Rushford, *Forever Young*, 198.

29 OHC: Oral interview with Don Miller, April 15, 1980; and Banowsky, *The Malibu Miracle*, 190. Ironically, the board of trustees did not confirm the appointment to president until six weeks later. See BOT: Feb. 18, 1971, vol. 5:226.

CHAPTER 17

1 HAWP: Howard A. White, "Summary of the Self-Study Report of Pepperdine College...," attached to White to Young, Nov. 18, 1970, in Norvel Young '69-'71 file, Box 33; and BOT: Oct. 31, 1969, vol. 5, p. 198; and Pepperdine University, Report for the Accreditation Committees of Western Association of Schools and Colleges, Part I, Schedules A-K (Oct. 1970), 3–4, Accreditation Materials, Harold Holland Collection, SCUA. The School of Education had not yet been organized.

2 HAWP: Banowsky to Jack Scott, Oct. 19, 1970, Corres. Aug-Oct 1970 file, Box 3; and WSB: Dorothy Batterson to Banowsky, [Jan. 1972], Dorothy Batterson Letters file, Box 3 A-Con (8).

3 YOUNG: Helen Young, Notes from the closed trustee meeting, Nov. 18, 1972, Confidential, RE Bd. of Trustees file, Box 74.

4 Ibid.

5 Ibid.; Helen Pepperdine to Helen Young, Nov. 29, 1972.

6 WSB: White to Banowsky, Oct. 5, Howard White file, Box 39/44A; YOUNG: Oct. 20, 1972, and White to Scott, Nov. 1, 1972, Los Angeles Campus-Misc. file, Box 46; and IV: "Scott resigns to take post at Orange Coast," Dec. 8, 1972, 3; "Provost Scott resigns amid campus frustrations, richness," Jan. 12, 1973, 5; and BAIRD: [Scott], "Address before the Christian Scholars Luncheon," Nov. 19, 2011, Biographies file.

7 IV: "Future L.A. Provost," Jan 12, 1973, 3; John Davies, "Provost Candidates Revealed," Feb. 2, 1973, 3; "Wilburn named L.A. provost," Feb. 16, 1973, 3.

8 Ibid.: Arline Ubry, "Wilburn—A Modern Tom Sawyer," Mar. 23, 1973, 5; and James Wilburn, "Editorial," *Urbis*, 2 (Fall 1973): 20.

9 HAWP: Minutes of a confidential meeting, Apr. 10, 1970, Mrs. Frank R. Seaver file, Box 27.

10 Ibid.: White to Banowsky, Nov. 11, 1970, Norvel Young '69-'71 file, Box 33; Young to Blanche Seaver, June 26, 1970, May 1970 file, Box 2. See also GRAPHIC: Dee Manges, "Rumbling Bulldozers Clear Land for Learning Center," Jan. 14, 1971, 1.

11 GRAPHIC: Bob Eisberg, "Building's Dedication Marks Urban Concept," Oct. 28, 1971, 1; Elaine Heck, "Protest Disrupts Event," and Mike Daugherty, Senate Decries Action," Nov. 4, 1971, 1. See also "Vermont Campus Gets New Center," *Alumni Voice*, 34 (Spring 1971): 5, and BOT: Dec. 17, 1971, 5:250.

12 YOUNG: Jack Scott, "A New Direction," remarks delivered Oct. 30, 1971, Los Angeles Campus-Misc. file, Box 46.

13 Ibid. See also IV: "Viki Brown, "Cooperative Ed. Program Underway on L.A. Campus," Jan. 18, 1974, 3.

14 GRAPHIC: Chuck Wright, "Task Force to Define Vermont Campus Role," Mar. 25, 1971, 1; and Kent Smoak, "Co-option of Programs," *Urbis*, 2 (Fall 1973), 12.

15 SRP: Pepperdine University, Report for the Accreditation Committee of Western Association of Schools and Colleges, Part 1, (Jan. 1970), 93, in Box 4.

16 GRAPHIC: "1972–73 Requirements Altered," Sept. 30, 1971, 1.

17 WSB: White to Banowsky, Oct. 13, and Nov. 24, 1971, Task Force-LA Campus file, Box 4 A-W (24).

18 In the adopted version, the task force increased the number of general education units required for graduation from forty-two to forty-six, added three units each of Advanced Composition and Quantitative Reasoning, and eliminated two units of PE.

19 *1972–1973 Catalog, Los Angeles Campus, Pepperdine University Bulletin*, 35 (Mar. 1972); and IV: "Three Courses Added for Fall," July 8, 1972, 4; and WSB: Larry Keene to Young, Sept. 27, 1973, K'73 file, Box 1 G-L (14).

20 WSB: Banowsky to Wilburn, Apr. 24, 1973, Corres. Apr.-June 1973 file, Box BCH Corres. (9).

21 Ibid.: Banowsky to Reeves, July 23, 1975, R'75 file, Box B6 PR-SA (28).

22 HAWP: White to Goyne, Feb. 19, 1976, Correspondence Feb. 14-Apr. 5, 1976 file, Box 6; WSB: Lyle Knowles, Survey of MPA Program Graduates, Jan. 1975, in Dr. Lyle Knowles file, Box 4 A-W (24); Wilburn to Banowsky, Jan. 15, 1976, MPA Program file, Box 4 A-W (24).

23 IV: "LEEP Awards Pepperdine an Additional $133,000," May 25, 1973, 3; "Federal Aid Cut $150,000," Oct. 12, 1973, 2; "Pep LEEP Program Receives Award," May 24, 1974, 3; and HAWP: White to Banowsky, Apr. 7, 1975, Correspondence Feb. 20-Apr. 30, 1975 file, Box 5; and WSB: White to Banowsky, Nov. 12, 1975, Howard White '75 file, Box 1 U-W (7).

24 PUA: University Year in Action, Pepperdine University, "University Year For Action," [1972], and *1000 Volunteers, University Year in Action* (U.S. Government Printing Office, [Oct. 1972]), 17, in Action brochures file, Box B53; and GRAPHIC: "Reaction to ACTION 'Amazing'-Ventre," Nov. 4, 1971, 4; and IV: Jack Scott, "Pep Assumes New Image," Aug. 1972, 2.

25 IV: "30 Pep Students Enter ACTION's Orientation," Jan. 12, 1973, 2; "Students Get Real Working Experience," July 27, 1973, 4; "ACTION Phasing Out," Nov. 15, 1974, 3; "UYA Enhances Pep Education," June 20, 1975, 4; "ACTION Funds Discontinued," June 11, 1976, 2; and WSB: White to Banowsky, Dec. 11, 1973, Action file, Box 4 A-W (24); Ralph Beck to Banowsky, Jan. 18, 1976, B file, Box 1B A-E (35).

26 IV: "Urban Center Runs Business Program," Aug. 1972, 8.

27 Ibid.: "Insufficient Funds May End Model Neighborhood Program," Oct. 26, 1973, 3; and WSB: Banowsky to Floyd L. Pierce, Aug. 15, 1972, Corres. June-Aug. 1972 file, Box 6 BCH (20ABC); Banowsky to Pierce, June 1973, Corres. Apr.-June 1973 file, Box BCH Corres. (9); "Charges," Ap. 1972, Bill Satterfield file, Box 4 A-W (24); and GRAPHIC: "Mexican-American Joins Pep Admissions Program," May 25, 1972, 1.

28 "Glass Blowing Pilot Approved," *The Pepperdine News*, 5 (Feb. 1970), 2; and YOUNG: Alexandra Jane Constance, "John Burton Kindles Talent in People Through the Beauty of Glass," *The Christian Science Monitor*, Jan. 22, 1973, 10, clipping in Glass Project file, Box 45. See John Burton, *Glass: Philosophy and Method.* See also PUA: "An Instruction Program in the Art of Glass Design, 27 July 1972," Saxton, Kenneth (Glass Blowing) file, Box CO2–5.

29 LAT: Maggie Savoy, "Whatsies in Demand by Creative Man," Sept. 21, 1969, D-1; and YOUNG: Kenneth Saxton to Young, Aug. 8, 1973, Glass Project file, Box 45; and "An Interview with Suellen Fowler 10/15/96," http://www.mickelsenstudios.com/articles/fowler.htm (July 6, 2011).

30 IV: Lynn McAlister, "Pep Glass Blowing Program Offers a Means of Expression," Nov. 9, 1973, 10; and YOUNG: White to Young, Jan. 2, 1974, Glass Project file, Box 45.

31 IV: "New Program under ACTION," July 8, 1972, 6; and LAT: Betty Liddick, "Betty Ford at Pepperdine," May 21, 1975, F1; and Phillip Brady, "Friend Lost," Nov. 4, 1981, C6; "Centenarian Honored," *Pepperdine People*, Sum. 1977:31. See SRP: Foster Grandparents file, Box 23.

32 IV: "New P.E. Chairman," Sept. 15, 1972, 3; and PUA: James R. Wilburn, "Remarks to the Faculty," Sept. 3, 1974, L.A. Campus file, Box CO 2–4; and HAWP: White to John Tunney, Feb. 26, 1976, Corres. Feb. 14-Apr. 6, 1976 file, Box 6.

33 YOUNG: Wilburn to Banowsky and Young, Nov. 18, 1974, and Wilburn to Banowsky, May 30, 1975, LA Campus-Misc file, Box 46; and WSB: Goyne to Wilburn, Apr. 17, 1975, and "Career Options in the Humanities: A Bibliography and Program Guide" (Dec. 1975), in G 1976 file, Box 4; Zane Reeves to Banowsky, Sept. 29, 1975, attached to Banowsky to Wilburn, Oct. 21, 1975, A-1975 file, Box 1 A-C (46). See also IV: "$3.5 Million Federal Aid Sought for Education," Dec. 6, 1974, 3; "Pepperdine Will Not Receive $1.5 Million AIDP Grant," June 13, 1975, 3. For the reaction of the federal bureaucracy see HAWP: Sheri to Dr. Banowsky, Apr. 9, 1975, James Wilburn file, Box 59.

34 IV: "Veteran Center Opens This Tri," May 25, 1973, 3.

35 Ibid.: "Pepperdine University Hosts Youth Program," July 12, 1974, 6; and WSP: John Watson to Dora Mohit, Feb. 2, 1976; Donald Henson to Banowsky, Sept. 27, 1975, and White to Banowsky, Dec. 15, 1975, U file, Box B6 PR-SA (28).

36 IV: Terrie Roans, "Parolees Live at Halfway House," June 1, 1973, 6.

37 GRAPHIC: "Kairos House Grows," Nov. 4, 1971, 6; and YOUNG: Young to G. R. Holton, July 15, 1972, Criticisms of Pep. file, Box 74.

38 "Lighthouse Assists Youth," *Pepperdine News*, 6 (Nov. 1970), 2; IV: "Lighthouse Day Care May Close," Mar. 9, 1973, 5; Ken Murray, "Lighthouse Youth Program Closes Due to Budget Cuts," Sept. 21, 1973, 3.

39 WSB: Victor Gruen Center for Environmental Planning Library, brochure [PC3/01/F368/nd], in Box 3 A-Con (2). See SRP: Victor Gruen Center file, Box 33.

40 IV: "Ford Donation Assists IUED," Nov. 10, 1972, 2; "New School Opens on Campus," Sept. 21, 1973, 5; "Daycare Center Open," Sept. 20, 1974; and YOUNG: Jesse Jackson to Young, Feb. 9, 1977, LA Campus file, Box 46; and Office of Public Information, School of Education, Pepperdine University, Apr. 6, 1977; and *Pepperdine University Bulletin, Los Angeles Campus 1976–77 Catalog Issue*, 39 (Mar. 1976), 16.

CHAPTER 18

1 WSB: White to Banowsky, Sept. 6, 1972 and Banowsky to Young, Oct. 4, 1972, Howard White file, Box 39/44A; and IV: Carol Clark, "Dr. Clark Resigns as Faculty President," Sept. 28, 1973, 3; and BOT: Dec. 13, 1973, 6:68 exhibit #3; and WSB: "Academic Freedom and Tenure: Rationale for Recommendations of the Administration," attached to White to Banowsky, Jan. 6, 1975, A 1975 file, Box 1 A-OC (46), and White to Banowsky, Mar. 31, 1975, Howard White '75 file, Box 1 U-W (7); and HAWP: White to BB, Nov. 16, 1977, Banowsky '77 file, Box 32.

2 WSB: Banowsky to Todd, Mar. 12, 1973, Corres. Jan.-Mar. '73 file, Box BCH Corres. (9); and IV: Karen Davis, "Administrative Cuts Hit L.A.-Todd Not Returning This Fall," Mar. 23, 1973, 3; Karen Davis, "Movement for Todd is Gaining Momentum," Apr. 6, 1973; and WSB: White to Banowsky, Apr. 4, 1973, Howard White file, Box 39/44A; Banowsky to White, Feb. 8, 1974, Corres. Jan.-Mar. 1974 file, Box BCA Corr. (9); and SRP: Los Angeles Faculty telegram to Banowsky, Apr. 6, 1973, Raymond Jackson to Banowsky, May 7, 1973, White to Banowsky, June 22, 1973, and myriad letters of protest, LA Campus Changes file, Box 4; and "An Evening of Affectionate Farewells," *Pepperdine People*, 3 (Winter 1980): 21.

3 HAWP: Young to White, July 10, 1970, Corr. July 1970 file, Box 2; and YOUNG: Banowsky to Young, Feb. 15, 1972, LA Campus-Misc. file, Box 46; and HAWP: Davis, Jr. to Mrs. Daniel C. Waters, Mar. 9, 1973, attached to memo from Young to White, Mar. 28, 1973, and White to Young, Apr. 2, 1973, Norvel Young '73 file, Box 33; and YOUNG: BB to Young, Feb. 15, 1972, Los Angeles Campus-Misc. file, Box 46; and WSB: Banowsky to Davis, May 26, 1977, D file, Box 2 D-Grad (31).

4 WSB: University Statistics: 1971–1975, Sept. 7, 1976, Enrollment Figures file, Box 4; and YOUNG: Minutes, Univ. Board, Mar. 30, 1976, 2, PU Board Minutes file, Box 47; and BAIRD: Pepperdine University, OIE Research, Enrollment and Faculty Profile for the Oxnard Conference, Oct. 18–19, 1979, Oct. 15, 1979, 1979–1980 file.

5 IV: Richard Alcorn, "Low Academic Rank, Senior Charges at Pep," Oct. 20, 1972, 4; and BAIRD: Academic Profile, July 31, 1974, 1973–1974 file.

6 GRAPHIC: "Commuters Question On-Campus Role," Sept. 30, 1971, 3; and WSB: White to Young, Jan. 2, 1972, Profile of Graduating Seniors, Spring 1973-Los Angeles Campus, S '70-'74 file, Box B6 PR-SA (28).

7 YOUNG: Minutes, Univ. Board, March 30, 1976, 2, PU Board Minutes file, Box 47; and HAWP: White to Wilburn and Goyne, Nov. 13, 1975, Ex. VP Corres., Nov. 11–Dec. 31 '75 file, Box 5; and IV: Viki Brown, "Money Losses Close Cafeteria," Mar. 8, 1974, 3.

8 HAWP: White to Zane Reeves, Mar. 1, 1976, Ex. VP Corres. Feb. 14, 1976–Apr. 5, 1976 file, Box 6; and IV: Steve Adler, "Services Committee Recommends Improvements for L.A. Campus," Jan. 16, 1976, 3; Leon Parker, "Dorms to Close April 16," Feb. 6, 1976, 5; Steve Adler, "'Tent City' Considered As Possible Protest," Feb. 13, 1976, 3;

"Minority Students Protest Pep 'Racism'," Feb. 20, 1976, 2. See also LAT: Tendayi J. Kumbula, "Pepperdine Students Protest Changes," Feb. 14, 1976, A19.

9   HAWP: The Suppressed . . . Students, Mar. 5, 1976, Personal Politics of Presidency, Mar. 1975 file, Box xxx2.

10 Ibid.: White to Wilburn, Mar. 15, 1976, and White to Steve Wilson, Mar. 25, 1976, Ex. VP Corres., Feb. 14–Apr. 5 '76 file, Box 6.

11 IV: Clint C. Wilson, II, "Director Views Newspaper," July 30, 1976, 12.

12 IV: Editorial, June 13, 1975, 6; Editorial, June 20, 1975, 6; and YOUNG: Faculty Association to Banowsky, July 30, 1975, Los Angeles Campus file, Box 46.

13 IV: Leon Parker, "Faculty Committee Draft a Letter," and "Last Rites Held for Sport Draft," June 20, 1975, 3 and 6; and HAWP: White to Willie Davis, Dec. 4, 1975, Ex VP Corres. Nov. 11–Dec. 31, 1975 file, Box 5; White to file, Jan. 16, 1976, and Shirley Roper to Phyllis Dorman, Feb. 10, 1976, Ex VP Corres. Jan. 1–Feb. 13, 1976 file, Box 6; White to Davis, Feb. 9, 1976, Ex VP Corres. Feb. 14-Apr. 6, 1976 file, Box 6; White to Goyne, Apr. 24, 1976, Corres., Apr 6–May 16, 1976 file, Box 6.

14 IV: "Religion: Is It Alive or a Drag," Jan. 12, 1973, 4; "Tradition Affects Recruiting," Feb. 16, 1973, 5; "No More L.A. Chapel Required," July 13, 1973, 3; Lynn McAlister, "Classes During Chapel Cause L.A. Controversy," Sept. 20, 1974, 3; Steve Adler, "Dr. Davis-An Atypical Dean," June 6, 1975, 4; and GRAPHIC: Frank Suyraci and Kris Nelson, "L.A. Campus Drifts from Tradition," July 20, 1973, 1; and WSB: Michio Nagai to Banowsky, Jan. 16, 1976, N 1976 file, Box 1 M-V (2).

15 Phyllis Evans, "Faith, Hope and Chapel," *Urbis*, 2 (Fall 1973): 17–19.

16 HAWP: White to Goyne, May 5, 1976, Corres. Apr. 6–May 16, 1976 file, Box 6.

17 Email message from Ken Waters to author, Mar. 19, 2012. Occupants of the house included Ken Waters, David Rice, Craig Brown, John Smart, and David Ogilbe. See also YOUNG: Cross Roads, 1 (Feb. 11, 1972) in Jesus Movement '71 file, Box 94; Young to G. R. Holton, July 15, 1972, Criticisms of Pepperdine file, Box 74. See also HAWP: Campus Ministries file, Box 22; and GRAPHIC: Laura Patrick, "Festival to 'Explode Campus,'" Feb. 10, 1972, 1,

18 YOUNG: Young to G. R. Holton, July 15, 1972, Criticisms of Pepperdine file, Box 74.

19 HAWP: White to Young, Nov. 25, 1970, M.N. Young, '69–'71 file, Box 33.

20 GRAPHIC: Mark Harvis, "Letter Threatens Pep's LA campus," Feb. 22, 1974, 1; and IV: Carol Clark, "Pep-LA Named in Hearst kidnapping," Feb. 22, 1974, 3.

21 BOT: Dec. 17, 1971, 5:250; and WSB: Bill duVernet to Banowsky, Feb. 18, 1971 and May 2, 1971, Misc. D file, Box 7/3 A-Z (19 A&B); Banowsky to William Palmerston, Jan. 7, 1972, Misc. P file, Box 7/3 A-Z (19 A & B); and IV: Letter from Truman Clark, "Prof Criticizes Carmichael Decision," Feb. 23, 1973, 2; "Security Increased; Force under Review," Mar. 9, 1973, 2; M. Rodriguez, "Fire Causes $10,000 Damage to Home Ec," May 4, 1973, 3; Viki Brown, "Arson suspected in L.A. fires," Oct. 23, 1974, 3; "Second Dorm Arson Causes $1000 damage," Dec. 6, 1974, 3; "Radio Station Burglarized," Mar. 28, 1975, 5; Kathleen Jackson, "Residents Evacuated in False Bomb Threat," Apr. 4, 1975, 3; Leon Parker, "Chief Charges University with Gross Negligence," Oct. 24, 1975, 3; "No Leads in Bomb Threats," Mar. 12, 1976, 3; and GRAPHIC: "Los Angeles Campus Robbed," July 7, 1977, 1.

22 HAWP: White to Young, Jan. 18, 1971, Young '69–'71 file, Box 33; White to Young, Jan. 5, 1972, Young '72 file, Box 33; and YOUNG: Program, Presentation Ceremony, Larry Donell Kimmons Memorial Portrait, Dec. 10, 1971, Library Pepperdine file, Box 46; and WSB: White to Banowsky, Mar. 5, 1974, Howard White file, Box 39/44A, and Banowsky to White, June 23, 1976, Howard White file, Box 2-NZ (40). See also GRAPHIC: Mike Martinez, "Security Booth Eases Harassment Problems," Apr. 6, 1972, 4; and LAT: Tendayi J. Kumbula, "Pepperdine Students Protest Changes," Feb. 14, 1976, A19.

23 WSB: Banowsky to Tom Bradley, Apr. 6, 1977, B 1977 file, Box 2 A-C (26); Jennifer Nims to Roper, Apr. 20, 1978, Misc. file, Box B10 (44B). See also IV: "Senate Allocates Publicity Money," Feb. 9, 1973, 3; "Trustees Rule Unanimously; No Carmichael Appearance," Feb. 16, 1973, 3; "Prof Criticizes Carmichael Decision," Feb. 23, 1973, 4. Unhappily, the new security officers were poorly trained for their jobs and not always morally suitable. One was found with marijuana in a room in Lawhorn Hall. See HAWP: White to Ron Stephens, May 6, 1976, Corres. Apr. 6–May 16, '76 file, Box 6.

24 GRAPHIC: Vicki Brown, "Master Plan Needs Approval," Mar. 22, 1974, 3; "L.A. Master Plan Unveiled," Continuum (Apr. 1974): 1 & 2. See NICKS: "A Summary of the Findings of the Five-Year Master Plan Committee of the Urban Campus of Pepperdine University," Feb. 15, 1974 file, Box 13. Members of the committee were Robert Crosby, Jennings Davis, Grover Goyne, Kenneth Hahn, Robert Holland, Chad McCellan, T. Zane Reeves, Kenneth Ross III, Donald Sime, Olaf Tegner, James R. Wilburn, Lloyd Watson, and Norvel Young. Others who served for limited time were Allen Haile, Arthur Smith, Tom Ventre, and Ronald Woolfolk.

25 WSB: Phyllis to Wilburn, June 25, 1974, Urban Task Force file, Box 4 A-W (24); and YOUNG: Agenda, Pepperdine Urban Board, Dec. 13, 1974, L.A. Campus-Misc. file, Box 46; and IV: Viki Brown, "Mayor Bradley To Serve in Honorary Chairman Post," Sept. 13, 1974, 3; Viki Brown, "Pepperdine Urban Board Works To Update L.A. Campus Master Plan," Jan. 17, 1975, 3; and BAIRD: Jim Wilburn, "My Life and Experiences with Pepperdine University," (unpublished MSS in Graziadio file, Mar. 12, 2012, 31–36).

26 The eight departments and majors were art, music, drama, journalism, physical education, English, speech, and natural science.

27 SRP: "Report on the [WASC team] visit to Pepperdine University," Mar. 4–6, 1974, WASC Visit—1974 file, Box 4-S; and BOT: Dec. 12, 1975, 9:19; and GRAPHIC: James Wilburn, "Cutbacks Save Urban Campus," July 23, 1976, 4; and Pepperdine University Bulletin, 39 (Sept. 1976); Unsigned and undated essay titled "Exciting times," probably written by Grover Goyne in Jan. 1976, 1975–1976 file; and BAIRD: Wilburn, "My Life and Experiences," 31–36; and Pepperdine University Bulletin, Los Angeles Campus 1976–77 Catalog Issue, 39 (Mar. 1976).

28 WSB: Pepperdine University, Reaccreditation Report Submitted to the Western Association of Schools and Colleges, Nov. 1978, p. 41, in Box B10 (44B). See also PUA: Academic Program Brochures, Box B53.

29 BAIRD: Wilburn, "My Life and Experiences," 31–36.

30 HAWP: [Linda Salter to Howard White, 1980], Linda Salter file, Box 51.

31 Email communication from John Watson to the author, Sept. 19, 2011.

32 WSB: Banowsky to White, Feb. 4, 1974, Corres. Jan.–Mar. '74 file, Box BCH Corr. (9); Banowsky to Perry Keith, Mar. 16, 1976, K file, Box 2 GR-K (36).

33 NICKS: John Nicks to Olaf Tegner, June 1, 1977, Chron. Corres., Sept. 29, 1976 to June 20, 1977 file, Box 5.

34 SRP: John Watson to White, Oct. 26, 1979, Dr. White 1979 file, Box 14.

35 WSB: Proposal to Develop a Christian Secondary School at Pepperdine University, Los Angeles, Jan. 27, 1976; White to Banowsky, Jan. 30, 1976, N 1976 file, Box 1 M-V (2).

36 GRAPHIC: "Pep Sells Property to Chit for Park," Mar. 9, 1978, 1; and YOUNG: Mike O'Neal to Board of Regents, Feb. 15, 1978, Trustees-Misc. #2 file, Box 64.

37 YOUNG: White to the City of Los Angeles, Oct. 26, 1979, 1979 file, Los Angeles Campus Sale Collection.

38 Ibid.: F. W. Parker to Don Bibbero, Mar. 24, 1980, 1980 file.

39 HAWP: Fred K. C. Price to White, Mar. 27, 1981, and "Offer to Purchase Los Angeles Campus by Crenshaw Christian Center," attached to Warren Dillard to

Executive Committee, Apr. 21, 1981, 1981 file, Los Angeles Campus Sale Collection; "Report on Audited Financial Statements, for the Year Ended July 31, 1989," A file, Box 15. See also GRAPHIC: Lynette Kelly, "LA Campus Sold," July 2, 1981, 3.

40 SCUA: Mike O'Neal to Honorable Robert Farrell, Apr. 10, 1981, 1981 file, Los Angeles Campus Sale Collection.

41 Ibid.: Tom Bost to White, Dec. 10, 1980, 1980 file, and Carl Baccus et al. to White, May 4, 1981, Los Angeles Campus file.

42 Ibid.: White to All University Personnel, June 22, 1981, 1981 file; and HAWP: White to Price, June 22, 1981, Chron. Corres. June 1981 file, Box 10; and Patti Yomantas, "Original Los Angeles Campus Sold," *Pepperdine People*, 4 (Winter 1981), 11.

43 Sandi Linville, "Where Dolores Goes, Memories Will Follow," *Pepperdine People*, 4 (Winter 1981), 9–11.

CHAPTER 19

1 Glover Shipp, "Trying to Get Ahead?" *Alumni Voice*, 27 (Winter 1964): 16–17; and GRAPHIC: "Evening Degree Program Begun," Sept. 10, 1965, 1. The Continuing Education Department began offering evening degree-completion programs for both the BA and MA with the initiation of the trimester system in 1963.

2 In 1974–1975, two contractors enrolled enough students in continuing education units to generate of $500,000 in tuition revenue. See WSB: Continuing Ed. School file, Box B10 (44B).

3 GRAPHIC: "Fall Enrollment is Almost Over 1800," Sept. 28, 1962, 1; "Evening Degree Program Begun," Sept. 10, 1965, 1; "College Classes Offered," Sept. 24, 1965, 1; "Continuing Education Under the Palms," *Alumni Voice*, 31 (Summer 1968): 7–8; *Pepperdine University Bulletin, School of Continuing Education, Fall 1972*, 35 (Aug. 1972): 22–31.

4 GRAPHIC: Lou Ellen Tomlinson, "Cont. Ed Program Booms," Jan. 29, 1970, 3.

5 Sharon House, "Project Ocean Search," *Alumni Voice*, 36 (Winter 1973): 24–25. See WSB: Cousteau project file, Box 4 A-W (24).

6 Ibid.: *Newsletter of the School of Continuing Education*, 1 (Winter 1976): 1, in Continuing Ed. School file, Box B10 (44B).

7 WSB: White to Banowsky, July 17, 1973, Howard White file, Box 39/44A; Phyllis to Banowsky, Aug. 29, 1973, Continuing Ed. School file, Box B 10 (44B); and PUA: R. G. Gordon to White, Dec. 18, 1973, Continuing Ed. Corres. file, Box B60.

8 GRAPHIC: "Johnston new dean at CCSW," Feb. 18, 1966, 1; and YOUNG: Pence Dacus to Young, Jan. 30, 1967, Pence Dacus file, Box B23; "Pepperdine Liberates Women with Cassette Courses," *Christian Chronicle* (Apr. 5, 1971): 7; and GRAPHIC: Robin Johnson, "Motsinger develops Continuing Ed school," May 25, 1972, 4.

9 "Population Explosion," *Alumni Voice*, 26 (Sept.–Oct. 1962): 18–19; *Pepperdine University Bulletin, School of Continuing Education, 1971*, 34 (Dec. 1971): 1; and GRAPHIC: "Extension Sees Enrollment Up," July 31, 1964, 7; "School Finalized Plans for Hawaii Expansion," Nov. 20, 1964, 2; Lou Ellen Tomlinson, "College Program Expands Service," June 19, 1969, 1; and YOUNG: Continuing Education Department Report, 1967–1968, Pence Dacus #2 file, Box B23; "Pepperdine University-Santa Ana Campus, 1974–1976," [1976], Orange Co. Center #2 file, Box 46; and *Pepperdine College, Continuing Education, 1967 Spring Catalog, Off-Campus Courses* (Los Angeles: Pepperdine College, 1967): 4; *Pepperdine University President's Report, 1971–72*, [1972], FC1/D1/F25/71–72, Special Collections; and WSB: White to Dean Russell, Oct. 3, 1975, C '75 file, Box 1 C-E (15).

10 YOUNG: Dacus and Mark Hagar to Young and Dan Benefiel, Aug. 16, 1967, Pence Dacus file, Box B23.

11 Ibid.: Dacus, Proposal to Edwards AFB, July 1967, Pence Dacus file, Box B23; and GRAPHIC: Mary Johnson, "Clinkenbeard Heads New Master's Program," June 17,

1971, 8; and SCUA: *Pepperdine University President's Report, 1971–72*, [1972], FC1/D1/ F25/71–72.

12 SRP: Max Templeman to Pence Dacus, Feb. 4, 1974, attached to School of Ed. staff to WASC, May 21, 1974, WASC 1974 file, Box 4.

13 Ibid.: "Contract for Professional Services," June 25, 1974, and Bob Lee to Eric Jackson, Oct. 5, 1976, Rockport Management '74–'76 file, and Eric Jackson to Pence Dacus, Sept. 27, 1974, Rockport Management Contract file, Box 30.

14 Ibid.: Eric E. Jackson to Pence Dacus, Sept. 27, 1974.

15 YOUNG: Banowsky to Col. Farrell, Aug. 29, 1972, El Toro file, Box 44; and WSB: L. E. Brown to Vic, Oct. 2, 1974, Pence Dacus file, Box 1 C-E (15). The Marine Corps hosted Pepperdine programs at El Toro, Santa Ana, and San Diego, California; Yuma, Arizona; Beaufort, South Carolina; Cherry Point, North Carolina; Kaneoho, Hawaii; and Subic Bay, Manila, Philippines. Pepperdine had programs for the U.S. Army at Fort Jackson, South Carolina, and Fort Stewart, Georgia; for the U.S. Air Force at Travis AFB, California, and England AFB, Louisiana; and for the U.S. Navy at Brunswick, Maine.

16 SRP: Dacus to White, Jan. 18, 1974, WASC 1974 file, Box 4; and HAWP: White to Stickney, Apr. 14, 1975, Ex. VP Corres. Feb. 20–Apr. 30, '75 file, Box 5, and Center for Innovative Education file, Box 22.

17 HAWP.: L. E. Brown to Frank [Robinson], June 5, 1975, and John W. Stanton to Robert W. Lee, Feb. 16, 1976, Center for Innovative Education file, Box 22.

18 Ibid.: White to Zane Reeves, Jan. 5, 1976, Ex. VP Corres. Jan. 1–Feb. 13, '76 file, Box 6; Banowsky to Nathan Altschuler, July 27, 1977, Ex. VP Corres. July–Aug. '77 file, Box 7; and SRP: White to John Nicks, Aug. 6, 1976, Dr. White 1976 file, Box 14.

19 WSB: John Corey to Banowsky, Mar. 10, 1976, N '76 file, Box 2, and W. B. Fleming to Banowsky, Apr. 28, 1976, Continuing Ed. file, Box 4 A-w (24).

20 HAWP: White to Banowsky, Mar. 25, 1976, Ex. VP Corres. Feb. 14-Apr. 6 '76 file, Box 6; and SRP: White to John Nicks, Mar. 29, 1977, Dr. White 1977 file, Box 14.

21 David Halliburton, "Education's Entrepreneurs," *Change: The Magazine of Higher Learning*, 10 (Nov. 1978): 20; and Beverly T. Watkins, "Educational Brokers: Threat to Academic Standards?" *Chronicle of Higher Education*, June 20, 1977, 6; and SRP: White to William E. Williams, May 14, 1979, Dr. White 1979 file, Box 14.

22 HAWP: White to Robert Lee, Nov. 3, 1975, Center for Innovative Education file, Box 22.

23 BOT: Apr. 11, 1974, 6:84; and SRP: White to Faculty Advisory Committee, June 1974, Faculty Advisory Committee file, Box 21.

24 WSB: Dacus to Banowsky, Jan. 31, 1974, Pence Dacus file, Box 1 C-E (15); White to Banowsky, Aug. 22, 1974, Howard White file, Box 39/44A, and Sept. 4, 1976, Folder N 1976, Box 1 M-V (2); and YOUNG: Wilburn to White, Sept. 11, 1974, Orange Co. Center file, Box 46; and SRP: John Nicks to Henry Jackson, July 29, 1977, John Nicks 1977 file, Box 14. *Bulletin, Pepperdine University-Orange County*, 1 (Sept. 1975).

25 YOUNG: Dacus to White, Dec. 11, 1974, L.A. Campus Misc. file, Box 46.

26 PUA: Unsigned letter to Sir, Aug. 22, 1975, and R. G. Gordon to Area Directors, Jan. 29, 1976, Con't Ed Corres. file, Box B60.

27 Ibid.: Minutes of School of Continuing Education Academic Advisory Committee, Feb. 24, 1976, attached to R. C. Gordon to SCE Academic Advisory Committee, Mar. 1, 1976, Con't Ed Corres. file, Box B60.

28 "Pepperdine Opens Orange Center," *Alumni Voice*, 36 (Fall 1974): 7; and WSB: White to Banowsky, Apr. 1, 1976, Howard White file, Box 2 N-Z (40). See also YOUNG: Wilburn to White, Sept. 11, 1974, Orange Co. Center file, Box 46; Wilburn to Young and Banowsky, Oct. 5, 1974, Orange Co. Center #1 file, Box 46; White to Young, Jan. 16, 1975, Business School file, Box 43; White to Young, Dec. 9, 1974, Orange Co. Center #1 file, Box 46.

29 YOUNG: Dacus to Young, Feb. 5, 1975, and L. Alan Stinson to Banowsky, Mar. 5, 1975, Orange Co. Center #2 file, Box 46. And see HAWP: White to Eric Jackson, Mar. 28, 1975, Ex. VP Corres. Feb. 20–Apr. 30, '75 file, Box 5.

30 YOUNG: George Benskin to Dacus, Apr. 9, 1975, attached to Dacus to White, Apr. 10, 1975, Orange Co. Center #2 file, Box 46; and HAWP: Frank Pack to Pence Dacus, June 12, 1973, J. Hedstrom to Pack, Aug. 8, 1974, and White to Pack, Aug. 16, 1974, Frank Pack file, Box 43.

31 WSB: Banowsky to White, June 3, 1974, attached to Banowsky to White, June 15, 1974, Howard White file, Box 39/44A.

32 YOUNG: Young to Dacus, Feb. 11, 1975, Orange Co. Center #2 file, Box 46; and HAWP: Young to White, Feb. 14, 1975, Norvel Young file, Box 33.

33 WSB: White to Banowsky, Aug. 16, 1974, Howard White file, Box 39/44A.

34 YOUNG: White to Banowsky, Nov. 14, 1974, Orange Co. Center #1 file, Box 46; and SRP: Nicks to Jackson, July 29, 1977, John Nicks 1977 file, Box 14.

35 WSB: White to Jackson, Mar. 31, 1975; White to Banowsky, Mar. 31, 1975; Draft of a contract with Pence Dacus, June 11, 1975, Pence Dacus file, Box 1 C-E (15); and YOUNG: Dacus to White, July 21, 1975, Pence Dacus file, Box 44; and HAWP: White to Harold Slane, July 1, 1975, Ex. VP Corres. May–July '75 file, Box 5.

36 SRP: White to Nicks, Oct. 5, 1976, Dr. White 1976 file, Box 14.

37 PUA: White to Burness Beckham, Aug. 3, 1976, Con't Ed Corres. file, Box B60.

38 WSB: White to Banowsky, Apr. 1, 1976, and White to Goyne, Apr. 4, 1976, Howard White file, Box 2 N-Z (40); Banowsky to Spiro, Oct. 6, 1976, and BB to White and Nicks, Oct. 6, 1976, S '76 file, Box 2. See also Ibid.: loose documents, Box 3.

39 Ibid.: White to Banowsky, Apr. 1, 1976, Howard White file, Box 2 N-Z (40).

40 YOUNG: An angry principal to President, Feb. 7, 1968, Pence Dacus #3 file, Box B23; Dacus to J. P. Sanders, May 3, 1967, Pence Dacus file. See also WSB: White to Gordon, Apr. 1, 1976, G '76 file, Box 6 BCH (20 ABC); and HAWP: Ralph D. Mills to Kay Andersen, Feb. 17, 1976, Frank Pack file, Box 43. One student reported that he did nothing more for two classes than sign in on the first day, but still got Bs. See LAT: David Savage, "Colleges May Bar Course 'Brokers,'" Nov. 12, 1981, B3.

41 WSB: White to Banowsky, Apr. 1, 1976, Howard White file, Box 2 N-Z (40); and HAWP: White to Nicks, July 31, 1976, Ex. VP Corres. July–Aug. '76 file, Box 6; and IV: Scott Gray, "Continuing Ed Closing Aug. 31," July 23, 1976, 3; and GRAPHIC: Doug Drigot, "Pep Consolidates Special Programs," July 23, 1976, 1.

42 WSB: White to Banowsky, July 20, 1976, Howard White file, Box 2 N-Z (40); and NICKS: Nicks to Mike O'Neal, June 6, 1978, Chron. Corres., June 1–July31, 1978 file, Box 5; and IV: "Dillard Claims Orange Move To Save Much," July 30, 1976, 2. In fall 1978, the university recycled the idea of an Orange County Center, this time as a resident center that combined activities then offered at Anaheim, Vista, and Newport Beach. See YOUNG: John Nicks to General Distribution, June 15, 1978, Nabaui-Nunn file, Box B28.

43 HAWP: "Institutional Governance and Administration," June 29, 1978, Ex. VP Corres. June–July '78, Box 8.

44 PUA: White to Nicks, Apr. 29, 1980, John Nicks-Off campus programs file, Box B79.

45 NICKS: Nicks to General Distribution, Mar. 17, 1980, Chron. Corres., Jan. 2–Feb. 28, 1980 file, Box 3.

46 Bryan Reeder, Associate Registrar, Pepperdine Univ., personal communication, Jan. 31, 2013.

CHAPTER 20

1 BOT: Sept. 8, 1964, vol. 5:30.

2 YOUNG: [Young], Annual Report to the Alumni, Oct. 10, 1964, M. Norvel Young Talks file, Box 57; and OIE: Pepperdine College, Report for the Accreditation

Committees of [WASC], Part 1, Oct. 1970, 98, in Accreditation Records; and BAIRD: James R. Wilburn, "My Life and Experiences," 20.

3 YOUNG: Notes on talk with Don Sime, Feb. 3, 1972, handwritten notes in Dr. Young file, Box 95; Susan Gibbons Gillespie, "Building from the ground up, Donald R. Sime...," *Pepperdine People*, 3 (Winter 1980): 6–7.

4 *Pepperdine College Bulletin, Catalog 1968–1969*, 31 (Mar. 1968): 81–83; and "Introducing the new Pepperdine School of Business," *Alumni Voice*, 33 (Fall 1969): 2–3.

5 Among the members of this first class (1968) was Shirley Chilton, who later served on the SBM faculty and as Commissioner of Consumer Affairs for the State of California.

6 Billie Silvey, "Business Is Booming," *Alumni Voice*, 32 (Winter 1968): 6; and HAWP: Young to Scaife, Feb. 6, 1969, Chron. Corres., Oct. 28, 1968–Feb, 17, 1969 file, Box 1.

7 John Davies, "Looking Ahead in the World of Business," *Pepperdine News*, 8 (Mar. 1973), insert.

8 BAIRD: Thomas J. Dudley, "The Graziadio School of Business and Management," [Nov. 2010]; Ruth D. Atteberry, "Pepperdine University School of Business and Management, Nov. 19, 1967–May 1, 1999," 38, Graziadio file; and HAWP: Curtis W. Page to Pence Dacus, [1975], Authorization Memorandum #1, School of Business Management '74–'77 file, Box 51.

9 YOUNG: Sime to Young, Proposal to Establish School of Business Administration at Pepperdine College, Dec. 1968, Bus. Ad. & Econ. file, Box 1; and WSB: Sime, Operation Plan, School of Business, 1971–72, School of Bus. '72–'74 file, Box 6 SC-V (30).

10 BOT: Dec. 17, 1968, vol. 5:161–62; and YOUNG: Article draft, "Pepperdine College and the Business Community," [1966], M. Norvel Young Articles in Pepp. file, Box 79.

11 HAWP: White to William E. Williams, May 14, 1979, Dr. White 1979 file, Box 14, Roper Collection; Alternative Strategies for SBM Programs in Texas, [1979], Report of SBM-Jan. 1978 file, Box 51; White to Luft, Nov. 10, 1981, Chron. Corres., Nov.–Dec. 1981 file, Box 11; White to Andersen, Apr. 6, 1981, WASC file, Box 59; and NICKS: Nicks to Students and Alumni in Texas, June 2, 1980, Chron. Corres., May 6 to Oct. 22, 1980 file, Box 3.

12 IV: "First 'presidents' class graduates with MBAs," Dec. 8, 1972, 4; and BAIRD: Dudley, "The Graziadio School of Business and Management," 4, Graziadio file; and "4 Decades of Discernment," *Pepperdine Magazine*, 2 (Fall 2010): 18–21.

13 *Bulletin, Los Angeles Campus 1976–77 Catalog Issue*, 39 (Mar. 1976): 166–67.

14 BOT: Jan. 4, 1969, vol. 5: 166; and *School of Business, Pepperdine Bulletin, 1969*, 32 (Dec. 1969): n.p.; and WSB: "Pepperdine University School of Business and Management, Strategy for the Future," Oct. 9, 1972, attached to Ruth Rockey to Banowsky, Oct. 9, 1972, School of Bus. file, Box 6 SC-V (30); and NICKS: Ruth Atteberry and Patricia Yomantas, eds., *Perspective* (Pepperdine University School of Business Management, 1980), 5, in Box 13.

15 Wiley Harker, "School of Business and Management," *Alumni Voice*, 35 (Sum. 1973): 7–10.

16 *School of Business, Pepperdine Bulletin, 1969*, 32 (Dec. 1969); and YOUNG: "Business Executive Conference, 1968" March 8–April 20, 1968, Business Executive Conference file, Box 1; Bibbero to J. C. Moore, Apr. 22, 1969, Management Center file, Box 66.; and BOT: Apr. 24, 1969 and June 19, 1969, vol. 5:181 & 184.

17 OIE: Report for the Accreditation Committees of [WASC], pt. 1, Oct. 1970, 97 and 162; and WSB: Research Center, "Credit Hours Summary for Whole University: 1972–73," July 12, 1973, attached to White to Banowsky, July 17, 1973, Howard White file, Box 39/44A; "Pepperdine University School of Business and

Management," Oct. 9, 1972, attached to Rockey to Banowsky, Oct. 9, 1972, School of Bus. file, Box 6 SC-V (30).

18 Ibid.: Enrollment Survey, Fall 1975, Loose files, Box 3.

19 OIE: Report for the Accreditation Committees; Institutional Planning and Research, *Pepperdine University Fact Book, 1982–1987* (Oct. 1988), B1.

20 Robert Blair, "The Atteberry Years, a Grateful University Bids 'Farewell' to One of Its Most Valued Couples," *Pepperdine People* (Fall 1988): 22–23.

21 BAIRD: Ruth D. Atteberry, "Pepperdine University School of Business and Management," Nov. 19, 1997–May 1, 1999, unpublished copy in Graziadio file.

22 HAWP: Banowsky to W. E. McKissock, Apr. 20, 1976, SBM Complaints and Criticisms file, Box 51.

23 IV: "Refurbished Buildings Will Be Repainted Gray," May 4, 1973, 6. There is a lot of confusion over who instigated the refurbishment and chose the initial and final colors of the buildings. Ruth Atteberry identifies herself as the instigator, speaks of "Pepperdine Blue or Green" as the initial color, and identifies the new color as the same one on the buildings at Malibu, or Spanish White. Jim Wilburn remembers himself as being the instigator and the traditional color as "Pepperdine green." He does not mention the final color. The Los Angeles campus student newspaper, publishing contemporaneously with the refurbishment, speaks of the final color as gray. I have adopted this version of the story, although admittedly Spanish White might have looked gray to the student journalist. See BAIRD: Wilburn, "My Life and Experiences," 31–36; and Atteberry, "Pepperdine University School of Business and Management"; and HAWP: Report to the Univ. Board., June 16, 1983, Univ. Board Misc. file, Box 74.

24 YOUNG: Page to White, Oct. 8, 1974, Business School file, Box 43.

25 WSB: Banowsky to White, Jan. 30, 1974, and "Honorary Doctorate Degree," n.d., School of Business file, Box 6 SC-V (30).

26 Ibid.: White to Banowsky, May 13, 1976, Howard White file, Box 2-NZ (40), and White to Banowsky, Jan. 29, 1974, School of Bus. '72–'24 file, Box 6 SC-V (30).

27 Ibid.: White to Ruth Atteberry and Curtis Page, Aug. 12, 1974.

28 Ibid.: White to Banowsky, Nov. 3, 1971, and Sime, "Operation Plan, School of Business, 1971–72," School of Bus. '72-'74 file, Box 6 SC-V (30). OIE: Report for the Accreditation Committees; and WSB: White to Banowsky, Nov. 3, 1971, School of Bus. 1972–74 file, Box 6SC-V (30).

29 WSB: Banowsky to White, June 15, 1974, Corres. Apr.-June '74 file, Box BCH Corr. (9).

30 YOUNG: Banowsky to Young, Oct. 2, 1973, Business School file, Box 43. In Fall 1973, most business faculty made from 10 to 40 percent of their base salary in overtime pay, pushing their salaries to and above $30,000. See also WSB: White to Banowsky, May 28, 1974, attached to Banowsky to Young, Oct. 2, 1973, and June 1, 1974, School of Bus. '72-'74 file, Box 6 SC-V (30).

31 BAIRD: Atteberry, "Pepperdine University School of Business and Management," 23.

32 See WSB: handwritten note of Hudson to Banowsky, Jan. 18, 1974, Howard White file, Box 39/44A; Banowsky to Page, June 15, 1974, Corres. Apr.-June '74 file, Box BCH Corr. (9); and YOUNG: Hudson to Banowsky and White, Oct. 15, 1974, Business School file, Box 43.

33 HAWP: Handwritten note on White to Young, Mar. 7, 1972, Norvel Young '72 file, Box 33; Young to White, June 30, 1972, Norvel Young '72 file, Box 33; and WSB: White to Banowsky, Feb. 15, 1973, Howard White file, Box 39/44 A. See also White to Banowsky, Nov. 29, 1971, School of Bus. 1972–74 file, Box 6 SC-V (30).

34 HAWP: Wilburn to White, Mar. 12, 1984, School of Bus. 1980–85 file, Box 51.

35 Ibid.: See correspondence between White, Sime, and Hudson between June & Oct. 1973 in Business at Malibu file, Box 51.

36 SRP: Sime to John Nicks, May 13, 1977, attached to Jere Yates to Sime, Apr. 21, 1977, John Nicks 1977 file.

37 WSB: White to Young, Dec. 27, 1973, Howard White file, Box 39/44A, and "Business Curriculum at Malibu," attached to Banowsky to White, Nov. 13, 1973, School of Bus., '72-'74 file, Box 6 SC-V (30).

38 HAWP: White to Banowsky, Feb. 14, 1976, School of Bus. & Man. 1976–78 file, Box 51.

39 Ibid.

40 WSB: White to Banowsky, May 16, 1974, attached to Banowsky to White, May 17, 1974, Howard White file, Box 39/44A; Banowsky to Sime and Tegner, July 2, 1974, School of Bus., '72-'74 file, Box 6 SC-V (30); and HAWP: Banowsky to Sime, May 3, 1975, School of Bus. Management '74-'77 file, Box 51.

41 SRP: Stewart Fliege to Nicks, Sept. 9, 1977, John Nicks 1977 file.

42 WSB: White to Sime, Nov. 12, 1971, School of Bus. 1972–74 file, Box 6 SC-V (30).

43 HAWP: Banowsky to Sime, Sept. 9, 1973; White to Nicks, May 31, 1978, Ex. VP Corres. Mar-May '78 file, Box 7. Banowsky once recommended for admission into the MBA II program an Assistant VP at Bank of America who was 30 units away from a baccalaureate degree. WSB: White to Sime, Nov. 12, 1971, and White to Banowsky, Nov. 23, 1971, School of Bus. '72-'74 file, Box 6 SC-V (30).

44 HAWP: White to Page, Dec. 14, 1975, Ex. VP Corres. Nov. 11-Dec. 31, '75 file, Box 5.

45 Ibid.: Minutes of the Graduate Faculty Retreat, School of Business, Oct. 30–31, 1970, School of Business (Specific) file, Box 51.

46 BAIRD: Atteberry, "Pepperdine University School of Business and Management," 11 & 17.

47 *School of Business, Pepperdine Bulletin, 1969*, 32 (Dec. 1969): n.p.

48 Thomas Dudley interview with author, Dec. 1, 2010, Calabasas, CA.

49 HAWP: White to Jennings Davis, Oct. 22, 1975; White to Linda Salter, Nov. 8, 1975, Ex. VP Corres. Aug.-Sept. '75 file, Box 5.

50 Ibid.; and BAIRD: Atteberry," Pepperdine University School of Business and Management," 31–34; Sandi Linville, "'A Star is Born'," *Insight* (Fall 1983), 3, in School of Bus. and Man. 1980–85 file, Box 51. See also NICKS: Remarks of Clay McQuiddy upon receiving the Distinguished Alumnus Award, Apr 10, 1993, attached to Wilburn to Distribution, Spr. 29, 1993, Unfiled Misc. Papers, Box 7.

51 WSB: "Final Reports of the Due Process Committee Concerning Dr. Harold Speer, July 28, 1977," Nicks to Charles J. McClain, Mar. 23, 1977; unsigned Release and Settlement, Nov. 23, 1977, S file, Box B10 (44B).; PO: "Second Report of the Due Process Committee on the Functioning of the School of Business and Management, July 28, 1977," Tenure/Policy/1977 file, Old Subject Files.

52 PO: Lemley to Dr. and Mrs. Don Sime, June 26, 1996, Don Sime folder, Old Subject Files.

53 HAWP: White to Banowsky, Nov. 23, 1971, School of Bus. 1972–74 file, Box 6 SC-V (30), Banowsky Papers; Anderson to Luft, June 7, 1982, An file, Box 15.

54 BAIRD: OIE, Enrollment Profile, Fall 1985, Final, Feb. 14, 1986, 14–15.

55 School of Business and Management, Self-Study, [1981], Dec. 1981 file; and HAWP: Luft to White, Nov. 18, 1981; Draft of letter from Jim Wilburn to Hughes Aircraft, [Sept. 1984], School of Business, 1980–85 (1 of 3) file, Box 51. Remarkably, Pepperdine's use of leveraged credit, a practice WASC disdained, was renamed ("prior-learning assessment" and "competency-based programs"), embraced, and incorporated into the mainstream of MBA instruction by 2013. See Steve Kolowich, "SUNY Signals Major Push Toward MOOCs and Other New Educational Models," *The Chronicle of Higher Education*, Mar. 20, 2013, online.

56 NICKS: Patricia L. Yomantas, "It's Up to Me To Be the Gospel Singer," *Perspective*, ed. by Atteberry and Yomantas (Pepperdine University School of Business and Management, 1980), 7, in Box 13; and BAIRD: Wilburn, "My Life and Experiences."

CHAPTER 21

1 Earl J. Ends, et al. to John D. Nicks Jr., Oct. 28, 1980, School of Business 1974–1977 file; and HAWP: Kirk Kaehler to SBM faculty, Nov. 12, 1980, School of Business 1980–1985 (3 of 3) file, Box 57.

2 Joyce Baxter, "Man with a World View," *Pepperdine People* (Summer 1990): 12–14; and BAIRD: Wilburn, "My Life and Experiences," 6.

3 BAIRD: Wilburn, "My Life and Experiences," 7.

4 HAWP: Sandi Linville, "'A Star is Born'," *Insight* (Fall 1983), 4, in School of Bus. and Man. 1980–85 file, Box 51; and SRP: Luft to White, July 10, 1981, Dr. White 1980–1981 file, Box 14.

5 BAIRD: Wilburn, "My Life and Experiences," 11. Wilburn remembered that he was the first to use the "Judeo-Christian" descriptor "in the history of Pepperdine." It may have been true within the context of SBM, but not university-wide. See SRP: Luft to White, July 10, 1981, Dr. White 1980–1981 file, Box 14. Dean of the School of Law Ron Phillips had used it in the early 1970s. See PUA: Ronald Phillips, "Stated Objectives of the Pepperdine University School of Law," Mar. 4, 1971, Law School, Dean Selection file, Box CO 2–4.

6 HAWP: "Mission Statement, Pepperdine University School of Business and Management," [Nov. 1982], attached to Wilburn to White, Nov. 15, 1982, School of Bus. and Man. 1974–77 file, Box 51. See also Michael Bygrave, "Pepperdine U.," *The Executive* (Dec. 1985), 22.

7 HAWP: Tom Redburn, "Pepperdine Business School Dean on Crusade," LAT, Nov. 7, 1982, clipping attached to Wilburn to White, Sept. 11, 1986, W-Wille file, Box 58.

8 Ibid.: Linville, "'A Star is Born'," 4.

9 Bygrave, "Pepperdine U.," 23.

10 HAWP: "A Strategic Plan for the School of Business and Management, Pepperdine University, May 5, 1984," SBM-Strategic Plan 1984–85 file, Box 52.

11 NICKS: "Abbreviated Mission Statement," [1987], SBM Strategic Plan. Com.-87ff file, Box 19, and "Mission Statement, Pepperdine University School of Business and Management," [1987], Unbound Misc. Materials file, Box 7.

12 "School of Business and Management, Pepperdine University, Strategic Plan, 1988–1993 (Revised)," Jan. 1989, Strategic Planning file, Box 19, and "Chosen to Lead, A Statement of Strategic Intent," [1991], PU Pubs.-Misc. file, Box 12.

13 NICKS: Ad hoc Faculty Committee on Strategic Intent, Oct. 8, 1991, Str. Plan-Fac file, Box 19.

14 Ibid.: "Faculty Ad Hoc Committee on Strategic Intent to Full-time Faculty, Oct. 29, 1991.

15 HAWP: Wilburn to White, Aug. 31, 1983, School of Bus. and Man. 1980–85 file, Box 51.

16 Ibid.: Linville, "'A Star is Born'," 3.

17 Institutional Research, Pepperdine University, *University Fact Book 1983–1989* and Institutional Research, Pepperdine University, *University Fact Book [1995]*.

18 PO: School of Business and Management Program Development Office Recruiting Strategy, Nov. 1981, GSBM Advertising file, Old Subject Files; and PUA: Minutes, Graduate School of Education Faculty Meeting, Mar. 17, 1981, Fac. Minutes 72, 79–82 file, Box B15 (Tegner Papers). See also NICKS: Keith McFarland et al., "Task Force on SBM Marketing, Final Report," Feb. 5, 1987, SBM Strategic Plan. Com. 87ff file, Box 19.

19 HAWP: Wilburn to White, Mar. 12, 1984, School of Bus. 1980–85 (1 of 3) file, Box 51.
20 Ibid.: White to Wilburn, Feb. 13, 1983, Chron. Corres. Feb. 1983 (1 of 2) file, Box 12; White to David Davenport, et al., Feb. 11, 1984, Chron. Corres. Feb. 1984 (1 of 2) file, Box 13.
21 NICKS: Richard Rierdan to Members of the Strategic Planning Committee, Feb. 1, 1988, Unbound Corres. file, Box 7.
22 BAIRD: Wilburn, "My Life and Experiences," 14–19.
23 Ibid., 23.
24 Ibid.
25 PO: Wayne Strom, "The Strategic Significance of the Malibu MBA Program," Nov. 10, 1986, GSBM/Residential MBA Program file; Wilburn to Wm. Phillips, Oct. 24, 1985, Committees/Univ./Dean's Council 1985 file, Old Subject files.
26 Ibid.: Wilburn to Wm. Phillips, Oct. 24, 1985, attached to Wilburn to Phillips, Oct. 31, 1985, and Phillips to Davenport and Adrian, Nov. 18, 1985, GSBM/Residential MBA Program file, Old Corres.
27 NICKS: Wilburn to Faculty and Staff, Apr. 14, 1986, Malibu Program Documents, Box 19.
28 BAIRD: Wilburn, "My Life and Experiences," 29–31.
29 PO: Wilburn to Wm. Phillips, Mar. 31, 1986, GSBM/Residential MBA Program folder, Old Subject Files.
30 NICKS: Strom to Wilburn et al., Aug. 18, 1987, Malibu Program File, Box 19.
31 PO: Scott de Ruyter, et al. to Wayne Strom, Feb. 9, 1987, GSBM/Residential MBA Program file, Old Chron. Corres.
32 Ibid.: Davenport to Wayne L. Strom, Feb. 19, 1987.
33 BAIRD: Wilburn, "My Life and Experiences," 31–36.
34 Ibid.
35 MFA: Providing permanent satellite campuses, tab T-1, Executive Committee, Board of Regents Agenda, May 6, 1986.
36 BAIRD: Wilburn, "My Life and Experiences," 42–48.
37 PO: Wilburn to Lemley and Hornbaker, July 21, 1996, GSBM/Rothschild folder, Old Subject files.
38 Ibid.: [James Wilburn], Executive Summary, Second Annual European Conference-1987," July 23, 1987, attached to Wilburn to Adrian, Oct. 2, 1987, Chron. Corres. 1987 file.
39 Ibid.; and NICKS: [Jim Wilburn], "Pepperdine University School of Business and Management and the Soviet Union, Suggested Strategy," Oct. 31, 1990, Misc. Papers, Box 7; and Lara Shoban, "Years of Struggle and People of Hope," *Pepperdine People* (Spring 1992): 6–9.
40 GRAPHIC: Mark Hull, "Officials Deny Spy Charges," Sept. 8, 1994, 1; and LAT: Sonni Efron, "Russia Livid Over Alleged Spying by U.S.," Sept. 7, 1994, 1.
41 NICKS: Wilburn to Steven Lemley, Nov. 3, 1993, Unbound Misc. Documents, Box 7.
42 "Baskin Named Dean of Business School," *Pepperdine Voice*, 14 (July 1995): 1.
43 BAIRD: Email from Otis Baskin to author, Feb. 17, 2012, SBM folder.
44 Ibid.; and "Dean Leads Business School Into New Era," *Pepperdine Voice*, 15 (Apr. 1996): 3.
45 Ibid.; Jeff Bliss, "Business School Receives Landmark Gift," *Pepperdine Voice*, 15 (Apr. 1996): 1–3; and Bill Henegar with Joyce Hutchinson, "Dividend on the American Dream," *Pepperdine People* (Spring 1997): 1–5.
46 Pepperdine University, *The Graziadio School of Business and Management and Seaver College Business Administration Division, Initial Accreditation Self-Evaluation Report*, vol. 1, (Pepperdine University, 1999), 6–7.

CHAPTER 22

1 "'It Beats Working'—Dean Tegner," *Pepperdine People*, 2 (Winter 1979): 22; and Bill Henegar, "Oly, After 50 years," *Pepperdine People* (Fall 1989): 2–5. See also Richard Suenaga, "Family Man," *Pepperdine Colleague*, 20 (Spring 2002): 16–17.

2 Olivia Yates, "Sixty-Six Years with Pepperdine: A Biographical Study of Dr. Olaf Tegner" (Pepperdine University, Graduate School of Education and Psychology, Doctor of Education in Organizational Leadership Dissertation, 2006), 40–81.

3 Quoted in Henegar, "Oly," 4–5.

4 Ibid.: 6, 39, 42, 59.

5 BAIRD: Graduate School of Education, Pepperdine University, *Faculty Handbook* (Sept. 1978): 1.

6 Yates, "Sixty-Six Years with Pepperdine," 42, 64, 65, and 66; and OIE: "Enrollment and Faculty Profile for the Oxnard Conference, Oct. 18–19, 1979," 18.

7 Heneger & Rushford, *Forever Young*, 336.

8 Pepperdine University, Graduate School of Education, *Faculty Handbook* (Sept. 1978): 2.

9 YOUNG: John Nicks to General Distribution, June 15, 1978, Nabaui-Nunn file, Box B28.

10 PO: Tegner to John Nicks, Feb. 28, 1978, Correspondence 1970–79 file.

11 *Pepperdine College Bulletin, 1956–57 [&] 1957–58*, 2 (Mar. 1956): 44.

12 "School of Education," *Alumni Voice*, 36 (Winter 1973): 15.

13 Lluan Jones, "School of Education," *Alumni Voice*, 36 (Winter 1974): 6; and HAWP: Banowsky to Wm. Johnson, Mar. 11, 1975, J '75 file, Box 1 G-L (14), William S. Banowsky Papers; [White], For University Board, May 21, 1981, Univ. Board Remarks '78-'84 file, Box 74.

14 PUA: Tegner to Novotney, et al., Sept. 23, 1974; Novotney to Wm. Clinkenbeard et al., Nov. 5, 1974 and Nov. 27, 1974; "Proposal: Doctorate of Institutional Management in Education," Jan. 20, 1975, Ed.D. Planning Com. file, Box B15. See also Susan Gibbons Gillespie, "Meeting the Urban Challenge: Pepperdine's School of Education," *Pepperdine People*, 2 (Winter 1979): 16–20.

15 IV: Phyllis Evans, "School of Ed proposes Ph.D.," June 6, 1975, 3; and YOUNG: Minutes, University Board, Mar. 30, 1976, p. 3, PU Board minutes file, Box 47; and "First Education Doctorates Awarded," *Pepperdine People*, 3 (Winter 1980): 30; and PUA: Minutes, Doctoral Program Faculty, Feb. 28, 1978, Mar. 28, 1978, and May 23, 1978, EdD Planning Com. file, Box B15.

16 *Pepperdine University Bulletin, School of Education 1977–1978*, 40 (June 1977): 18; Brochure, Distinguished Visiting Professors, [1976]. See also Gillespie, "Meeting the Urban Challenge," 16–20.

17 SRP: White to Grover Goyne, et al., Dec. 6, 1977, C-G file, Box 29.

18 WSB: Tegner to Banowsky, [Dec. 1977], T file, Box 2 N-Z (40).

19 Ibid.: John T. McCarty to Irving Melbo, et al., Apr. 28, 1977, V file, Box 2 N-Z (40); and GRAPHIC: Julio Moran, "Virtue Chair, Ferraro's Conflict of Interests Questioned," May 26, 1977, 1.

20 YOUNG: Young to Ardeshir Zahendi, Apr. 11, 1978, Iranian Corres. file, Box 94; and MFA: "Petrogrants," *Newsweek*, July 4, 1977, 75, clipping Box 2.

21 LAT: Ronald L. Sobel, "Pepperdine Gets $1 Million Gift," May 24, 1977, D1; and YOUNG: Young to Ardeshir Zahendi, Apr. 11, 1978, Iranian Corres. file, Box 94. Oly Tegner subsequently told Jack McManus that when the Shah learned that women were present in the ceremonial chamber he had refused to enter until the Pepperdine delegation made clear they would cancel the presentation if the women had to leave. Jack McManus, personal communication, Mar. 6, 2012.

22 YOUNG: Young remarks, Oct. 10, 1977, and K. Kormi to Young, Oct. 17, 1977, Iranian Corres. file, Box 94.

23 *Pepperdine University Bulletin, School of Education 1977–1978*, 40 (June 1977): 17; and
    YOUNG: Young to Ambassador Ardeshir Zahedi, Apr. 11, 1978, Iranian Corres. file,
    Box 94.

24 YOUNG: Young to Ardeshir Zahedi, Sept. 1978, Iranian Corres. file, Box 94. A copy
    of the check is in ibid.

25 Ibid.: Young to Her Imperial Majesty Sahbanou Farah Pahlavi, July 29, 1980,
    Iranian Corres. file.

26 *Pepperdine University Bulletin, Graduate School of Education, 1978–79 Catalog*, 41
    (June, 1978): 19.

27 Ibid.: *1979–1980 Catalog*, 42 (June, 1979): 19.

28 PUA: White to John Nicks, Dec. 29, 1980, O. Tegner's Memoranda file, Box B16.
    Pepperdine University Bulletin, Graduate School of Education, 1981–82 Catalog, 44
    (May, 1981): 19.

29 Ibid.: *1984–1985*, 47 (March, 1984): 30. Masoud Mahmoud, subsequently an
    Associate Vice President for Construction and Campus Planning, was a recipient
    of a full-tuition scholarship for doctoral study at GSEP from the fund in 1985.

30 YOUNG: White to Banowsky, July 6, 1973, School of Edu. file, Box 44.

31 HAWP: White to Young, Jan. 29, 1971, Norvel Young '69-'71 file, Box 33; and IV:
    "Hawaii Awards 29 Master's," Oct. 13, 1972, 2; and "School of Education," *Alumni
    Voice*, 36 (Winter 1973): 15.

32 "School of Education," *Alumni Voice*, 35 (Summer 1973): 27; and IV: "School of
    Education Expands to New Site," Nov. 2, 1973, 8; and WSB: Max Templemen to
    Pence Dacus, Feb. 4, 1974, Pence Dacus file, Box 1 C-E (15).

33 HAWP: White to Banowsky, Mar. 25, 1976, Ex. VP Corres. Feb. 14-Apr. 6, 1976 file,
    Box 6; White to Deans, Apr. 10, 1976, Ex. VP Corres. Apr. 6–May 15, 1976 file; Nicks
    to Tegner, Aug. 21, 1978, Ex. VP Corres. Aug. 1978 file, Box 8; and WSB: Ralph Mills
    to Kay Andersen, Feb. 17, 1976, attached to White to Grover Goyne, Apr. 4, 1976,
    Howard White file, Box 2-NZ (40).

34 SRP: Pepperdine University School of Education Staff to WASC, May 21, 1974,
    WASC '74 file, Box 26.

35 Ibid.: White to Banowsky, May 3, 1974, Folder B, and May 28, 1974, WASC '74 file,
    Box 4; "Response of Pepperdine University to the report on the visit of the com-
    mittee from the Western Association of Schools and Colleges, March 4–6, 1974,"
    attached to Banowsky to Andersen, June 4, 1974, attached to "[Final] Report on
    the Visit to Pepperdine University, March 4–6, 1974," WASC '74 file, Box 26.

36 WSB: "Report of the Visiting Committee," Feb. 20, 1976, Howard White file, Box
    2-NZ (40).

37 SRP: Bob Holland to White, July 9, 1976, Dr. White 1976 file, Box 14; Tegner to
    Banowsky, July 1, 1976, T '76 file, Box 1 M-V (20); and PO: Tegner to White, July 28,
    1976, GSEP/Center for Professional Development file, Historic Materials.

38 HAWP: White to Tegner, May 14, 1977, Ex. VP Corres. Apr.-June '77 file, Box 7.

39 NICKS: John Nicks to Howard White, Dec. 20, 1979, Chron. Corres. Nov. 29-Dec.
    31, 1979 file, Box 3. See also OIE: "Enrollment and Faculty Profile for the Oxnard
    Conference," Oct. 15, 1979, 5; *Pepperdine University, Graduate College of Education,
    Center for Professional Development Bulletin* (Spring, Summer, & Fall, 1978).

40 OIE: "Enrollment and Faculty Profile for the Oxnard Conference, Oct. 18–19,
    1979," Oct. 16, 3.

41 BAIRD: Institutional Research, *University Fact Book*, 1983–1989 (Dec. 1989): A5, C1-C3.

CHAPTER 23

1 Jim Hedstrom, "The Graduate School of Psychology at Pepperdine: A Personal
   Perspective," in *Graduate Psychology at Pepperdine: A Forty-Year History*, ed. by
   Louis E. Jenkins (Pepperdine University, 1994).

2 Lawrence M. Brammer, "Everett L. Shostrom (1921–1992)," *American Psychologist*, 51 (Jan. 1996): 52; and Hedstrom, "Everett L. Shostrom-Remembrance of a Great Psychologist," *Pepperdine Colleague*, 11 (Fall 1993): 5; and SRP: Robert E. Holland to Howard White and John Nicks, Nov. 12, 1976, Doctoral Program-Psychology #1 file, Box 23.

3 George Pepperdine College, *Report of Pepperdine College to the California State Board of Education and to the Western College Association* (Oct. 1953): 214–28; and Hedstrom, "The Graduate School," 1.

4 Shostrom returned to the university in the late 1980s to teach at the Orange County Center. He died on Dec. 8, 1992.

5 SRP: Holland to White and Nicks, Nov. 12, 1976, Doctoral Program-Psychology #1 file, Box 23.

6 WSB: Banowsky to Young, July 30, 1973, attached to Banowsky to White, July 31, 1973, Howard White file, Box 39/44A, and Hudson to Banowsky, Aug. 16, 1973, Jerry Hudson file, Box 1 G-I (10).

7 HAWP: [Howard White], Progress Report to the Western Association of Schools and Colleges from Pepperdine University, Apr. 1, 1976, p. 7, Ex. VP Corres. Feb. 14-Apr. 6, '76 file, Box 6.

8 Ibid.: Minutes, University Academic Council, Oct. 8, 1975, and Nov. 8, 1975, Ex. VP Corres. Aug.-Sept. '75 file, Box 5.

9 WSB: Hughes to Holland, Oct. 2, 1975, T '75 file, Box 6 SC-V (30).

10 HAWP: [Howard White], Progress Report to the Western Association of Schools and Colleges from Pepperdine University, Apr. 1, 1976, p. 7, Ex. VP Corres. Feb. 14-Apr. 6, '76 file, Box 6.

11 SRP: White to Kay Andersen, June 6, 1976, WASC 1976 file, Box 4.

12 GRAPHIC: Leland Harris, "New Master's Degrees Offered," May 4, 1978, 3.

13 David Nelson and Nancy Hand-Ronga, "Years, 1971–1976," and Jim Hedstrom, "The Graduate School of Psychology at Pepperdine: A Personal Perspective," 43 & 6–7. See also PUA: Minutes, Graduate School of Education Faculty Meeting, Mar. 17, 1981, Faculty Minutes (1972, '79-'82) file, Box B16.

14 "'It Beats Working'—Dean Tegner," *Pepperdine People*, 2 (Winter 1979): 22.

15 PUA: Faculty meeting minutes, Nov. 10, 1981 and Jan. 26, 1982, Faculty Minutes (1972, '79-'82) file, Box B16; and GRAPHIC: Jake McGowan, "Test Results Don't Reflect Malibu Program," Nov. 29, 1984, A3.

16 PUA: Tegner to Michael Dreskin, May 15, 1980 and Oct. 9, 1980, and John D. Nicks to Dreskin, July 7, 1980, O. Tegner's Memoranda file, Box B16.

17 WSB: Handwritten note from Banowsky to Young on White to Banowsky, Dec. 19, 1975, Howard White file, Box 2 N-Z (40).

18 GRAPHIC: "News Briefly," Feb. 10, 1983, A2.

19 Ibid.: Reid Sams, "New VP Chosen," Nov. 29, 1984, A1; and PO: Phillips to Adrian, Mar. 17, 1983, and Michele Stimac to Phillips, Mar. 2, 1983, Wm. B. Adrian, Jr. file, Old Corres.

20 Hedstrom, "The Graduate School of Psychology," 8; and Marilyn Angeletti, "Golden Moments, Psychology Division Celebrates 50th Anniversary," *Pepperdine Colleague*, 19 (Fall 2001): 12–13; and SCUA: Adrian to Hedstrom, Jan. 7, 1992, Chron. Corres. Jan.-July 1992 (1 of 2) file, Box 2, William Adrian Papers; and PO: Wm. Phillips to Operation's Committee, Oct. 31, 1985, attached to Agenda, Dean's Council, Nov. 1, 1985, Committees/Univ. Dean's Council 1985 file, Historical Materials.

21 BAIRD: "Growth at GSEP," Feb. 19, 1992, GSEP file; and *University Fact Book, 1983–1989* (Dec. 1989); and *University Fact Book 1989–1994* (May 1995); and James I. Woodrow, "Graduate Schools Enters its Second Decade with Optimism," *Pepperdine Colleague*, 11 (Fall 1993): 6. In 1989, nearly 24 percent of all education

doctoral students were African American, the highest percentage of any United States school.

22 Pepperdine University, Institutional Research, *University Fact Book, 1983–1989*, Dec. 1989, tab A & B; and OIE: *Pepperdine University, Self-Study Appendices, Submitted to the Western Association of Schools and Colleges, Book Two of Two* (Malibu, 2000) various tabs, in Records of Accreditations.

23 PO: Nick Stinnett to Bill Adrian, June 30, 1987, Nick Stinnett file, Old Corres. See also SRP: Program, June 11–13, 1987, Faculty Misc. file, Box 21; and GRAPHIC: "Campus briefly," Mar. 27, 1986, A2.

24 BAIRD: "Growth at GSEP," Feb. 19, 1992, 11–13, and "GSEP, Strategic Plans: Vision for the 21st Century," Fall, 1995; Maryam Kubasek, "Fagan Looks at Changes in GSEP Programs," *Pepperdine Voice*, 13 (Apr. 1994): 3; and Mary Ammerman, "Technology Face to Face," *Pepperdine People* (Fall 1997): 18–20; and PO: Michele Stimac, "A Modest Assessment and Projection," Jan. 1983, Chron. Corres. 1983 file, Old Subject Files.

25 BAIRD: "GSEP Strategic Plans," 1–2, 12.

26 Ibid.: See also Kubasek, "Fagan Looks at Changes," 3.

27 BAIRD: "GSEP Strategic Plans," 12–13.

28 Ibid.: and MFA: Minutes, Dec. 10, 1985, in Board of Regents Agenda, Mar. 11, 1986, Box 8.

29 Sara Y. Jackson, "Pepperdine's Center for the Family Provides Supportive Environment," *Pepperdine Colleague*, 16 (Summer 1998): 7–8; and BAIRD: Dennis Lowe email to author, Feb. 6, 2014, GSEP file.

30 BAIRD: Jack McManus to Nancy Magnusson Durham, Dec. 10, 2009, GSEP file.

31 OIE: *Pepperdine University Self-Study Appendices Submitted to the Western Association of Schools and College, Book One of Two* (Aug. 2000), 2.1-C, in Records of Accreditations.

CHAPTER 24

1 BOT: Mar. 14, 1969, vol. 5:171, 175–76; and YOUNG: *Pepperdine College President's Report 1969–70: The Multi-Campus Concept*, [Spring 1970], in Annual Reports file, Box 43.

2 BOT: Apr. 24, 1969, vol. 5:178–79.

3 YOUNG: Agreement between Pepperdine College and Orange University, College of Law, May 6, 1969, attached to Larry Hornbaker to Bill Banowsky, Sept. 8, 1974, Law School file, Box 45.

4 Ibid.: Young to Byron Fullerton, July 10, 1969.

5 Ibid.: Pepperdine College, *President's Report, 1969–70*, n.p., in Annual Reports file, Box 43; and BOT: Apr. 9, 1970, vol. 5:205.

6 HAWP: Mable [Bean] to Mrs. Young, Apr. 7, 1970; Banowsky to Chalk and Banowsky to Phillips, May 5, 1970, Chron. Corres., Feb. 1, 1970–Apr. 30, 1970 and May 1, 1970-May 28, 1970 files, Box 2; and YOUNG: Ron Phillips to Howard White, Mar. 6, 1972, Law School #2 file, Box 45; and BAIRD: email note from Ron Phillips to author, June 6, 2010, in 1969–1970 file. Chalk seems to have turned down the offer for two reasons: he had misgivings about accommodating himself to the radical right, the political world view of Orange and Riverside Counties, and he discovered that his elders at the Highland church thought he was in the midst of a two-year contract that did not expire for another year. See HAWP: Chalk to Banowsky, Apr. 30, 1970 and May 1, 1970, and Chalk to Young, June 2, 1970, John Allen Chalk file, Box 23.

7 GRAPHIC: Jackie Moss, "Pepperdine's Orange Law School Receives Provisional Accreditation," June 19, 1970, 1.

8 BOT: Sept. 29, 1970, vol. 5:219. See also GRAPHIC: "College School of Law Launched," Oct. 29, 1970, 1.

9 GRAPHIC: "Kleindienst Views Crime Prevention," Nov. 12, 1970, 1; Program, Inaugural Ceremonies Banquet for Pepperdine School of Law and Remarks for Richard G. Kleindienst Dinner, Nov. 2, 1970, in the personal papers of Dean Emeritus Ron Phillips, Malibu, CA.

10 BOT: Dec. 17, 1971, vol. 5: 245–46 and "Confidential Report-Pepperdine College," n.d.; and PUA: Larry Hornbaker to Dick McAlpin, Feb. 15, 1972; Phillips to Banowsky, Mar. 5, 1973; and "Pepperdine Law School Okayed by American Bar Association," [Mar. 1973], Law School Accreditation file, Box CO2–4.

11 YOUNG: Millard H. Ruud to Young and Phillips, Aug. 21, 1972, Law School file, Box 45; WSB: Ruud to Council of the Section of Legal Education and Admission to the Bar, Jan. 23, 1973, Law School '71-'73 file, Box 1 G-L (14).

12 SRP: Phillips to White, Jan. 15, 1974; Phillips to Young, Mar. 29, 1974; "Reinspection Report, School of Law, Pepperdine Univ., June 4, 5, and 6, 1975," School of Law '75 file, Box 27.

13 *Pepperdine University School of Law, 1971–1974*, [1974], 10, in box 1, Office of Civic Services Collection; and PUA: Ronald Phillips, "Stated Objectives of the Pepperdine University School of Law," Mar. 4, 1971, Law School, Dean Selection file, Box CO 2–4; and YOUNG: Howard White to William S. Banowsky, July 13, 1971, Law School file, Box 45.

14 Ibid.: "Pepperdine University School of Law, Goals and Objectives, 1972–1977, [Feb. 1972], Law School #2 file, Box 45. See also Susan Gibbons Gillespie, "Law School: A Coming of Age," *Pepperdine People*, 2 (Summer 1979): 15.

15 YOUNG: "Goals and Objectives, 1972–1977," Law School #2 file, Box 45; and SRP: [Phillips], Pepperdine University School of Law, Purposes and Goals, [Apr. 1975], Law School '75 file, Box 27. See *Pepperdine University Bulletin, School of Law, 1976–77 Catalog Issue*, 39 (May 1976), 12.

16 Walter K. Neill, "School of Law," *Alumni Voice*, 36 (Winter 1974), 14; and "Dean Ronald F. Phillips Reflects on School of Law's First 25 years," *Pepperdine Law Quarterly* (Summer 1994): 8–10.

17 YOUNG: "Development Report," Feb. 3, 1972, Law School #2 file, Box 45; and WSB: "SA May Lose Chance For Law Center," *[Orange County] Register*, July 31, 1973, clipping, Law School file, Box 1 G-L (14).

18 BOT: Apr. 19, 1975, 8: exhibit A; and SRP: White to Young, Oct. 28, 1974, Law School '74 file, and Phillips to Banowsky, Mar. 26, 1975, Law School '75 file.

19 Ibid.; see YOUNG: Phillips to Banowsky, June 3, 1975, Law School file, Box 45; SRP: Phillips to Richard Seaver, Apr. 28, 1975, and Phillips, Report on Permanent Location, June 1975, Law School '75 file, Box 27. See also email communication from Ron Phillips to author, Mar. 7, 2012.

20 YOUNG: "Prestige" is Sprinkled Throughout "Goals and Objectives, 1972–1977," Law School #2 file, Box 45.

21 Ibid.: Amended Agreement, Apr. 19, 1975, Law School file, Box 45; and LAT: Larry Welborn, "Pepperdine to Move Law School," May 29, 1975, A3.

22 YOUNG: White to Banowsky, July 13, 1971, Law School file, Box 45.

23 Ibid.: Professor Joseph M. Livermore, et al., Report on Pepperdine University School of Law, Apr. 9–12, 1978, for Association of American Law Schools, attached to Millard H. Ruud to Banowsky and Phillips, Sept. 11, 1978, Law School prior to 1979 file, Box 45.

24 WSB: Program, Law School Graduation, May 22, 1976, and June E. Jones to Justice Blackmun, July 15, 1976, Law School Grad. '76 file, Box 2 D-GRAD (31).

25 "Southland Publisher Benefits Area Culture, Education," *Pepperdine People*, 2 (Summer 1979), 20; and GRAPHIC: "Jerene Appleby Harnish . . . dies at 86," July 17, 1980, 1.

26 BAIRD: Email from Ron Phillips to author, Apr. 17, 2013, 1978–79 file.

27 Ibid.: Jim Wilburn, "Random Pepperdine Reminiscences, 1973–1982" (Oct. 2010): 146, in Graziadio file; and GRAPHIC: Sherri Wilson, "Seminar Features Reagan," Jan. 18, 1979, 1; and LAT: "Reagan to Speak at Pepperdine," Jan. 11, 1979, WS8.

28 GRAPHIC: John Hauser, "Justice to Dedicate Facilities," Nov. 15, 1979, 2; Neal Snyder, "National, State and Local Officials Dedicate Center," Nov. 29, 1979, 2; and PUA: Remarks of Mr. Justice Rehnquist, Nov. 17, 1979, William Rehnquist file, Individual files.

29 WSB: Banowsky to Coffman, Apr. 20, 1972, Dale Coffman file, Box 4 A-W (24); Phillips to Young, Dec. 6, 1973, Law School '71-'73 file, Box 1 G-L (14).

30 YOUNG: Livermore, Report..., Apr. 9–12, 1978, Law School prior to 1979 file, Box 45.

31 WSB: Banowsky to Tom Gilo, July 27, 1973; White to Banowsky, Nov. 20, 1973; White to Young, Dec. 3, 1973, L '75 file; Phillips to White, Apr. 6, 1973, Law School file, Box 1 G-L (14).

32 YOUNG: Reinspection Report, School of Law, Pepperdine University, June 4–6, 1975, attached to Reuschlein to Banowsky, June 11, 1975, Law School #2 file; Joseph P. White to Banowsky and Phillips, July 31, 1975, Law School file, Box 45; and SRP: Frederick R. Franklin to Ron Phillips, Aug. 27, 1975, Law School '75 file, Box 27.

33 YOUNG: Phillips to Nicks, Jan. 10, 1978; Willard H. Pedrick to Phillips, Jan. 20, 1978, both attached to Banowsky to D. Lloyd Nelson, Feb. 1, 1978, Law School prior to 1979 file, Box 45.

34 Ibid.: Phillips to White, Mar. 6, 1972, Law School #3.

35 WSB: Law School, Administrative, and Faculty Salaries for 1976–1977 and 1977–1978, n.d., S file, Box B10 (44B).

36 WSB: Banowsky to Young, May 22, 1974; Banowsky to Dean Fred Hart, et al., June 20, 1974, Chron. Apr.-June '74 file, Box BCH Corr. (9); White to Banowsky, Aug. 22, 1974, Howard White file, Box 39/44A; and YOUNG: Livermore, Report..., Apr. 9–12, 1978, Law School prior to 1979 file, Box 45.

37 HAWP: Millard H. Ruud to Ronald Phillips, Nov. 30, 1978, A-Misc. file, Box 15.

38 Ibid.: Ruud to White and Phillips, Dec. 3, 1979, A's file, Box 15.

CHAPTER 25

1 HAWP: James P. White to Howard White, July 23, 1983, Am file, Box 15.

2 Ibid., School of Law (1 of 3) file, Box 52.

3 YOUNG: Ronald F. Phillips, Dean's Report, Pepperdine University School of Law, 1985–1986, Law School 1979–1986 file, Box 30.

4 HAWP: Phillips to Budget Committee, May 31, 1983, School of Law (2 of 3) file, Box 52; and YOUNG: Ron Phillips, Budget Report, 1982–83, May 11, 1982, Law School 1979–86 file, Box 30; Wm. Adrian to Strategic Planning Committee, Feb. 5, 1988, Chron. Corres. Apr. 1987-Feb. 1988 (3 of 3) file, Box 1, William Adrian Papers; and PO: Davenport to Adrian, Feb. 23, 1989, Chron. Corres. 1989 file.

5 HAWP: Mike O'Neal to White, June 28, 1983, School of Law (1 of 2) file, Box 52.

6 YOUNG: Ronald F. Phillips, Dean's Report, Pepperdine University School of Law, 1985–1986, Law School 1979–1986 file, Box 30.

7 HAWP: White to Phillips and Ralphs, Nov. 3, 1981, Chron. Corres. Nov.-Dec. 1981 file, Box 11; [White], Remarks to University Board, Dec. 15, 1983, Univ. Board Remarks, 1978–1984 file, Box 74.

8 BAIRD: Email from Ronald Phillips to author, Feb. 14, 2014, Law School file.

9 HAWP: White to Lloyd Nelson, Dec. 9, 1977, Lloyd Nelson-Bd. of Trustees file, Box 41.

10 Ibid.: Phillips to James P. White, June 15, 1983, School of Law (1 of 3) file, Box 52.

11 PO: Jim McGoldrick to Dean Phillips, Feb. 22, 1985, attached to Ronald Phillips to William Phillips, Feb. 25, 1985, SOL/Bar Exam Self-study file, Old Chron. Corres. file.

12 SRP: McGoldrick to Dean Phillips, Feb. 9, 198[7], attached to Ron Phillips to David Davenport, Feb. 18, 1987, B's file, Box 17; PO: Phillips to Davenport, Feb. 24, 1987, SOL/Bar Exam Self-Study file, Old Correspondence files. See also LAT: Myrna Oliver, "Legal Profession Frets as Bar Exam Failures Soar," Jan. 20, 1985, 3 & 34; "Passing the Bar Exam," Mar. 14, 1991, 2.

13 BAIRD: Ronald Phillips email message to author, Mar. 11, 2015, Law School file.

14 HAWP: White to Phillips, Mar. 12, 1983, Chron. Corres. Mar. 1983 (1 of 2) file, Box 12.

15 Ibid.: Phillips to White, Mar. 17, 1983, School of Law (2 of 3) file, Box 52.

16 Ibid.: White to Phillips, Nov. 30, 1981, Chron. Corres. Nov.-Dec. 1981 file, Box 10; PO: Luft to James McGoldrick, Mar. 17, 1983, SOL/Housing file, Old Subject Files.

17 HAWP: McGoldrick to White, Feb. 9, 1981, James McGoldrick file, Box 39; and NICKS: "Wave of Excellence Report," Fall 1987, Wave of Excellence file, Box 13; and "Notes," Pepperdine People, 4 (Winter 1981): 26.

18 BAIRD: Email communication from Colleen Graffy to author, Mar. 2, 2015, Law School file.

19 Pepperdine University, School of Law, "Certificate in International and Comparative Law," n.d., http://law.pepperdine.edu/degrees-programs/certificates/international-comparative-law/ (Mar. 11, 2015).

20 "Dean Ronald F. Phillips Reflects on School of Law's First 25 years," Pepperdine Law Quarterly (Summer 1994): 8–10. Others of national stature who spoke on campus were Attorney General Richard Kleindienst, Secretary of Treasury William Simon, Attorney General Edwin Meese, Attorney General Dick Thornburgh (1991), Attorney General William P. Barr (1992), U.S. Solicitor General Kenneth Starr (1993), California Governor George Deukmejian (1993), U.S. Senator Fred Thompson, and Judge Alan Page of the Minnesota Supreme Court.

21 "Celebrating 50 Years of Excellence," Pepperdine University Annual Report (1986).

22 "The Institute for Dispute Resolution to Offer Master's Degree in Dispute Resolution," Pepperdine Law Quarterly (Fall 1995): 8; and Trish West, "Master's program added in Dispute Resolution," Pepperdine Voice, 15 (Jan. 1996): 1.

23 BAIRD: Gregory Ogden email message to author, Feb. 17, 2014, School of Law file.

24 "An era ends as Phillips passes the torch," Pepperdine Voice, 16 (Apr. 1991): 3; and Jennifer Smodish, "The Good Person Wins," Pepperdine People (Winter 1999): 22–24; and BAIRD: Strategic Academic Plan, Pepperdine University School of Law, Mar. 26, 1998, School of Law file.

25 GRAPHIC: Dennis Morris, "School of Law dedicates expansion," Sept. 17, 1992, 2. Louis Nizer had given the commencement address in May 1980, being introduced by Armand Hammer. See YOUNG: "Life University, A commencement address by Louis Nizer," May 17, 1980, Pepperdine School of Law, 1979–1986 file, Box 30.

26 "ABA Sabbatical Site Visit Report," [Oct. 1995], ABA Inspection 1995 folder, Subject Matter Files, Dean's Office School of Law, PU.

27 Ibid.: "Site-Visit Report," 9, attached to Ronald Phillips to Faculty, Mar. 5, 1996.

28 Ibid.: Email from Davenport to Phillips, Apr. 11, 1996, ABA Inspection 1995 folder.

29 BAIRD: "Strategic Academic Plan, Pepperdine University School of Law," Mar. 26, 1998, School of Law file.

30 PO: Andrew Mansour to Davenport, n.d., attached to Davenport to Mansour, June 18, 1992, Chron. Corres. 1989–1994 file, Old Chron. Corres.

31 SRP: Phillips to Charles Nelson, Mar 31, 1987, and Nelson to Phillips, Mar. 31, 1987, Ron Phillips file, Box R.

32 Ibid.: "Pepperdine Gets a Starr," *Santa Monica Evening Outlook*, Feb. 20, 1997.

33 "Starr Properly Will Stay and Conclude Investigation," *Washington Post*, Feb. 19, 1997; and Anne La Jeunesse, "Officials, Law Students Understand Quandary," *Santa Monica Evening Outlook*, Feb. 22, 1997. See also, PO: Press Release, Office of the Independent Counsel, Feb. 21, 1997, SOL/Dean's Search/Starr Selection file, Old Chron. Corres.

34 BAIRD: Anthony Lewis, "Starr a Failure as Independent Counsel," *Standard-Times*, Feb. 22, 1997; Joseph Spear, "Ken Starr Tightens the Thumbscrews," *Sentinel*, Feb. 22, 1997; Joe Conason, "The Right Connections, The Starr in Richard Scaife's Eyes," *Washington Post*, Mar. 16, 1997, clipping in Jeff Bliss to Distribution, RE: Kenneth Starr—Packet No. 5, July 8, 1997, 1996–1997 file. See also Eric Pooley and Michael Weisskopf, "How Starr Sees It," *Time Magazine*, 152 (Dec. 28, 1998): 82. Between 1962 and 1997, the Sarah Scaife Foundation, which Richard Scaife headed, had donated $12.7 million to the university. See BAIRD: "Pepperdine Names Donors in Gifts Flap," LAT, March 1997, clipping in Jeff Bliss to Distribution, RE: Kenneth Star.

35 Paul M. Barrett, "Career Limits, Religious Links May Underlie Starr's Deanship Bid," *Wall Street Journal*, Feb. 21, 1997; "Who's Funding Starr's Pepperdine Position?" *Paradise Post*, Feb. 25, 1997; Garry Wills, "Starr's Self-Promotion Efforts Got Ahead of Him," [Austin, TX] *American Statesman*, Mar. 11, 1997; and Joe Conason, "The Starr in Richard Scaife's Eyes," *The Washington Post*, Mar. 24, 1997.

36 BAIRD: Jeffrey Rosen, "Kenneth Starr, Trapped," *The New York Times Magazine*, June 1, 1997, clipping in Jeff Bliss to Distribution, RE: Kenneth Starr.

37 Ibid.: David Davenport email to Steve Lemley, Apr. 8, 1989, and Independent Counsel Ken Starr's Statement to the press, Apr. 16, 1998, 1997–1998 file.

38 Ibid.: Richardson Lynn email to author, Aug. 22, 2013, Law School file.

39 Ibid.: Bob Cochran to Faculty Interested in the Pepperdine/Union Rescue Mission Legal Aid Project, Sept. 1, 1998, Robert F. Cochrane Personal Papers, Law School Folder; email from Robert Cochran to author, Feb. 21, 2014, Law School Folder; and Bill Henegar, "New Hands at the Helms," *Pepperdine People* (Winter 1999): 4; and Carin Chapin, "School of Law Valedictorian Heads Inner-City Legal Aid Clinic," *Pepperdine Voice*, 19 (Spring 2000): 1.

40 BAIRD: Richardson Lynn email to author, Aug. 22, 2013, Law School file.

CHAPTER 26

1 GRAPHIC: Julie Ryan, "Additional Campus Considered: Growth Causes New Expansion," Jan. 26, 1967, 1.

2 YOUNG: "Minutes of the Administrative Committee," June 18, 1965, Administrative Com. Minutes file, Box B26.

3 BOT: Jan. 25, 1966, vol. 5:74; and PUA: Minutes, President's Board, Feb. 7, 1966, Presidential Board Minutes 60–71 file, Box CO5.

4 PUA: Minutes, Confidential Notes, President's Board, Feb. 7, 1966; Minutes, Mar. 26, 1967.

5 YOUNG: Dan Benefiel to Young, July 31, 1967, Dan Benefiel file, Box B26.

6 PUA: Charles Runnels to Dan Benefiel, Apr. 12, 1968, Site Selection Committee file, Box CO5.

7 Ibid.: Minutes, Site Selection Committee, Dec. 6, 1967, Presidential Board Minutes 60–71 file, Box CO5.

8 YOUNG: "Malibu Campus Acquisition," [1969], Pepperdine Univ. Board file, Box 47; and BOT: Apr. 14, 1966, vol. 5:84–85. See also HAWP: Don Miller to Board of Trustees, Feb. 6, 1968, Chron. Corres.-Oct. 2, 1967 to Apr. 4, 1968 file, Box 1.

9 BOT: Aug. 25, 1966, vol. 5:98–100; Nov. 10, 1966, vol. 5:103–104. The full report, "The Financial Development of Pepperdine College," Sept. 1966 [hereinafter Johnston Report, 1966], is in PUA: Johnston, Robert, Co. file, Box CO2-3.

10 YOUNG: Unattached pencil notes, [1967], Box 4.

11 Ibid.: Benefiel to Young and Teague, May 26, 1967, and Office of Development, Staff Assignments, July 5, 1967, Dan Benefiel file, Box B26.

12 WSB: White to Banowsky, Mar. 29, 1976, Howard White file, Box 2 N-Z (40); and BOT: Mar. 15, 1967, 5:111.

13 Patricia Yomantas, "Like Father, Like Family, The Runnels of Pepperdine U.," *Pepperdine People*, 3 (Sum. 1980): 12–15; and Bill Henegar, "The Texan & the Belle," *Pepperdine People* (Spr. 2005): 2–5; and HAWP: *President's Report, Pepperdine College, 1967–1968*, [1968], 2; Young to Runnels, Nov. 7, 1968, Chron. Corres. Oct. 28, '68—Feb. 17, '69 file, Box 1, and Banowsky to Runnels, June 11, 1970, Chron. Corres. May '70 file, Box 2.

14 OHC: Larry Hornbaker, oral interview with Jimmy Smythe, Nov. 18, 2002, Malibu, CA, Pepperdine Oral History project; and Larry Hornbaker, oral interview with author, Apr. 7 & 8, 2012, Loudon, TN.

15 Bill Henegar, "Not in Kansas Any More," *Pepperdine People* (Sum. 2000): 4–7; and GRAPHIC: Donald Risolo, "Hornbaker Accepts Senior Vice Presidential Job; Rounds Out Pep's Administrative Reorganization," Sept. 16, 1976, 1; and HAWP: White to Banowsky, Feb. 12, 1975, Ex. VP Corres. Jan. 2-Feb. 19, '75 file, Box 5.

16 PUA: Robert Johnston, et. al. to Norvel Young, [Sept. 1966], Johnston, Robert Co. file.

17 Ibid.

18 Ibid.; Johnston Report, 1966, p. 6, 17, 24, 25. See also HAWP: "Announcement regarding Board of Governors," [Oct. 1967], Chron. Corres., Oct. 2, 1967 to Apr. 4, 1968 file, Box 1.

19 Ibid.

20 BOT: Dec. 3, 1966, vol. 5:108–109.

21 Ibid., Nov. 10, 1966, vol. 5:103–104.

22 Ibid., Dec. 3, 1966, vol. 5:108–109; and see PUA: Wm. J. Teague, Summary of Remarks, Jan. 16, 1969, Board of Governors file, Box CO2-1.

23 BOT: June 8, 1967, vol. 5: 120; see HAWP: "A Historical Summary (1966–1975) of the Discussions and Actions of the Pepperdine Board of Trustees Pertaining to the Augmentation and Expansion of the Board of Governors, [1975], Boards file, Box 25; and PUA: Minutes, President's Board, Oct. 17, 1967, Presidential Board Minutes 60–71 file, Box CO5.

24 PUA: Robert Johnston to Ashley Hale, June 18, 1966, Case Statement, Corres., Background Memos file, Box CO2-2, Pepperdine Archives; Dan Benefiel to Young, July 31, 1967, in Johnston, Robert, Co. file, Box CO2-3; and YOUNG: Benefiel to Young, July 26, 1967, Dan Benefiel file, Box B26.

25 PUA: Walter Burch to [Norvel Young], [Jan. 1968], Case Statement-The Epic of Pepperdine College file, Box CO2-1.

26 PUA: "Pepperdine College Affirms" (Original), "Pepperdine College Affirms" (Revised Nov. 14, 1967) and Commentary on Revised Credo, [Nov. 14, 1967], attached to Walter [Burch] to Steve [Lemley], Mar. 27, 1998, Mission Statement of Pepperdine folder; Dan Benefiel to Young, Jan. 22, 1968, Case Statement-The Epic of Pepperdine College file, Box CO2-1.

27 Ibid.: Banowsky to Steve [Lemley], Apr. 30, 1998, Mission Statement of Pepperdine folder.

28 Ibid.: "The Affirming College, a case for the dual campus concept of Pepperdine College," Feb. 7, 1969, Case Statement (The Affirming College) file, Box CO2–1; and Master Planning Committee file, Box B10. See also HAWP: Case Statement, First Working Draft, June 1968, Malibu Campus Case Statement file, Box 39.

29 PUA: "The Affirming College," Feb. 7, 1969.

30 Editor, "Cathy Meeks and the Great Band Aid on Racism," *Mission Magazine* 12 (Feb. 1979): 4.

31 Candace Denise Jones, "White Flight? George Pepperdine College's Move to Malibu, 1965–1972" (M.A. Thesis, Pepperdine University, 2003).

32 HAWP: Young to Evans, Nov. 14, 1967, Chron. Corres.-Oct. 2, 1967 to Apr. 4, 1968 file, Box 1. Pepperdine development was to do for Malibu what UCLA had done for Bel-Air. See Banowsky, *Malibu Miracle*, 73.

33 PUA: Minutes, Site Selection Committee, Dec. 28, 1967, Presidential Board Minutes 60–71 file, Box CO5; and BOT: Nov. 17, 1967, vol. 5:128; and YOUNG: Malibu Campus Acquisition, [1969], Pepperdine Univ. Board file, Box 47.

34 BOT: Mar. 20, 1968, vol. 5:137; and YOUNG: Malibu Campus Acquisition, [1969], Pepperdine Univ. Board file, Box 47. See also HAWP: Young to Don W. Darnell, Apr. 5, 1968, Chron. Corres,-Apr. 4 to Oct. 1968 file, Box 1.

35 YOUNG: Melton to Miller, June 21, 1968, Orbin V. Melton file, Box 10; see also Jack R. Newville, Engineering Service Corp., "Pepperdine College Cost Analysis, Malibu and Thousand Oaks Sites," June 10, 1968, Pepperdine Library Vertical File.

36 BOT: June 24, 1968, vol. 5:141–143.

37 YOUNG: Jones to Donald Miller, et al, May 20, 1968, Confidential RE Board of Trustees file, Box 74. Board of trustees chair Don Miller did not believe that the president's board was usurping any of the powers of the trustees, and certainly did not feel that President Young had misled them. See Ibid.: Miller to Orbin V. Melton, May 29, 1968, Orbin V. Melton file, Box 10. For his part, Young had the greatest respect for Jones's integrity and judgment, appreciated his long service to the college, and hoped that service could continue for "a number of years ahead." See HAWP: Young to Jones, Oct. 11, 1968, Chron. Corres., Apr 4 to Oct. 1968 file, Box 1.

38 YOUNG: Melton to Miller, June 21, 1968, Orbin V. Melton file, Box 10.

39 Ibid. See also HAWP: Young and Don Darnell to Merritt H. Adamson and Young and Darnell to John L. Notter, May 23, 1968, Chron. Corres., Apr. 4 to Oct. 1968 file, Box 1. Bill Banowsky writes that fifteen Pepperdine trustees voted against the Malibu site on March 11, 1968 (see Banowsky, *Malibu Miracle*, 81), citing Henegar and Rushford, *Forever Young*, 192–93. There are two problems with that assertion: there is no record of fifteen trustees ever having met during this time frame and there is no record of them having met on March 11, 1968. The negative "vote" Banowsky references must have been the one on June 24, and it really was not a "rejection" of Malibu.

40 HAWP: Banowsky to Young, March 1968, Press Release file, Box 27. Just how much Norvel and Helen Young preferred Malibu over Westlake is evident in their undated list of advantages and disadvantages in YOUNG: Second Campus file, Box 4.

41 HAWP: Banowsky to Young, March 1968, Press Release file, Box 27.

42 Ibid.

43 Ibid.

44 BOT: July 30, 1968, vol. 5:146–147.

45 The Site Selection Committee had resolved to recommend Malibu to the full president's board on July 31, 1968. See PUA: Minutes, Site Selection Committee, July 31, 1968, Presidential Board Minutes 60–71 file, Box CO5.

46 HAWP: Young to Scaife, Aug. 29, 1968, Chron. Corres., Apr. 4 to Oct. 1968 file, Box 1.
47 Ibid.: Young to Scaife, Oct. 10, 1968.
48 BOT: Aug. 13, 1968, vol. 5:153–155; and YOUNG: Malibu Campus Acquisition, [1969], Pepperdine Univ. Board file, Box 47; and HAWP: Merritt Adamson to Pepperdine College, Sept. 20, 1968, Adamson file, Box 27; Young to George Evans, Oct. 3, 1968; Young to Don Miller, Oct. 4, 1968, Chron. Corres., Apr. 4 to Oct. 1968 file, Box 1.
49 YOUNG: President Young's Statement, Oct. 7, 1968, Second Campus file, Box 4.
50 Ibid.
51 Ibid.: Statement by M. H. Adamson, Oct. 7, 1968; and Ron Ellerbe, "The Birth of a College," *Alumni Voice,* 33 (Summer 1970): 11–19.
52 Brenda Zobrist, "The Adamson Legacy, With the Gift of Malibu Land Came a Rich Heritage," *Pepperdine People,* [8] (Summer 1986): 2–5.

CHAPTER 27

1 Patti Youmantas, "Towering Triumphs, the High-Rise Dreams of Charles Luckman," *Pepperdine People* (Fall 1989): 20–22. Later, Luckman funded cash awards for teaching excellence for university faculty.
2 "The Land: The Man with The Plan," *Time Magazine,* 82 (Sept. 6, 1963): 82.
3 Banowsky, *Malibu Miracle,* 171.
4 These included the academic center (Pendleton Learning Center, Payson Library, and Huntsinger Academic center); the science complex (Stauffer laboratories, Elkins Auditorium, Appleby Center), Tyler Campus Center, and sixteen residence halls. The board of trustees approved Pereira's selection as Master Planner on Nov. 11, 1968. See BOT: Nov. 11, 1968, 5:160.
5 Banowsky, *Malibu Miracle,* 174. The dissent is inferred from notes of a talk in which Norvel Young argues that Pepperdine has given doctorates to both political liberals and conservatives, and that Reagan deserves recognition for what he has done for private education. See YOUNG: "We have honored," dated '70, in Students Affairs file, Box 4.
6 Banowsky, *Malibu Miracle,* 174–75. See also HAWP: Young to G.E. Kinsey, Feb. 10, 1970, Chron. Corres. Feb.-Apr. 1970 file, Box 2.
7 GRAPHIC: Shirley Prideaux, "University Plans Revealed at gala Malibu Unveiling," Feb. 12, 1970, 1; and LAT: Robert Kistler, "Private Colleges Win Reagan's Praise for Spirit of Freedom," Feb. 10, 1970, A1. See also HAWP: Young to Blanche, Feb. 12, 1970, and Young to Robert Dean Fisher, Feb. 16, 1970, Chron. Corres. Feb.-Apr. 1970 file, Box 2.
8 HAWP: Howard A. White, "A Historic Evening," [Feb. 1970], Chron. Corres., Feb-Apr 1970 file, Box 2.
9 Bill Youngs, *Legacy of Frank Roger Seaver,* chapter 6 and page 64; and Joyce Hutchison, "The Passing of a Legend," *Pepperdine People* (Summer 1994): 2–3; and LAT: Myrna Oliver, "Blanche E. Seaver, Major Donor to Colleges, Dies," Apr. 13, 1994, B1.
10 Youngs, *Legacy of Frank Roger Seaver,* chapters 13, 14.
11 Ibid., 104–05.
12 YOUNG: Personal Contact Report, Oct. 11, 1967, Henry Salvatori file, Box B21; and Draft of Proposal for Mrs. Seaver, Oct. 11, 1967, Seaver Oct. 1967 file, Box 7, Brock House Collection.
13 Banowsky, *Malibu Miracle,* chapter 7. On a card to Banowsky, Seaver wrote: "My dearest Soaring Eagle, Will you please help me find my little Preacher Boy that I have lost, somehow-somewhere? I need him very much." SRP: Oct. 7, 1976, S file, Box 25, SRP.
14 Banowsky to Blanche Seaver, Oct. 9 and 27, 1969, Blanche Seaver file, Box 7, Brock House Collection.

15 HAWP: Blanche Seaver to Sir Anthony, Dec. 20, 1973, attached to Banowsky to
    Don Miller, Jan. 14, 1974, Blanche Seaver Materials file, Box 27; Mike Antonovich
    to Mrs. Seaver, Aug. 1, 1974, Unidentified file, Box 27; and WSB: Phyllis Schlafly
    and Banowsky, Nov. 28, 1975, and attached notes, Graduation, LA Gen. Studies-
    Aug. 1976 file, Box 2 D-Grad (31); notes to MNY, Sept. 1973, #22, File 6, Box 2, Series
    2; and BAIRD: email from Ronald Phillips to author, Nov. 11, 2014, Law School
    folder.

16 John Alex McCone to Blanche, Jan. 22, 1975, Richard Seaver File, Box 7; Blanche
    Seaver to Kenneth D. Wells, Feb. 21, 1972, Mrs. Frank R. Seaver #2 file, Box 7,
    Brock House Collection; and author's telephone interview with Bill Banowsky,
    Nov. 3, 2011.

17 Charles Runnels, personal interview with the author, Malibu, CA, Apr. 12, 2012.

18 A copy of Mrs. Seaver's will, dated Dec. 3, 1973, is in YOUNG: MNY-WSB file, Box
    56. This edition of her will left $30,000 to Young and $60,000 to Banowsky.

19 HAWP: Banowsky to Runnels, June 11, 1970, June 1970 file, Box 2; Young to Larry
    Hornbaker, et al., Dec. 1, 1970, Mrs. Frank R. Seaver file, Box 27; Banowsky,
    Malibu Miracle, 308.

20 HAWP: Young to Pat and Shirley Boone, Nov. 12, 1969; Draft of a proposal for
    "Seaver College at Malibu, A New Campus of Pepperdine University," [Nov. 1969],
    Mrs. Frank R. Seaver file, Box 27. There is some evidence that these elaborate
    plans never came to fruition, but that the proposal was submitted to both
    Blanche Seaver and her nephew Richard Seaver at an intimate gathering in the
    California Club but within the same time frame. See YOUNG: Young to Richard
    Seaver, Dec. 21, 1969, Criticisms of Pepperdine file, Box 64; Young to Salvatori,
    Mar. 24, 1975, Henry Salvatori file, Box B21.

21 Banowsky, Malibu Miracle, 129. Banowsky dates this moment to late 1967, before
    he actually returned to California. Inasmuch as Mrs. Seaver just a few weeks
    before had entertained and rejected a $4 million proposal to fund a campus at
    Calabasas and the Pepperdine board of trustees did not accept Malibu as the
    future site of the campus until October 1968, that date seems a bit early. (See
    SRP: "First Proposal to name campus for Seaver, $4,000,000, Rejected," Oct. 11,
    1967, Seaver-Oct. 1967 file, Box 29.) But it is true that at a crucial moment in the
    debate as to the location of Pepperdine's suburban campus she promised a gift of
    $1.35 million for site development, a strategic gift that caused reluctant trust-
    ees to embrace Malibu as the site of the new campus, rather than Calabasas or
    Westlake Village. For the value of the property see WSB: Five Year Debt Analysis,
    July 1975, Ex. Com. Meet., July 14, 1975 file, Box Board of Trustees (16).

22 YOUNG: Young and Banowsky to Richard Seaver, Dec. 5. 1972, Chron. Corres.
    Nov-Dec '72 file, Box BCH Corres. (9), William S. Banowsky.

23 HAWP: Minutes, Confidential meeting with Banowsky, et al., Apr. 10, 1970, Mrs.
    Frank R. Seaver file, Box 27.

24 WSB: Banowsky to Hornbaker, Apr. 20, 1972, Chron. Corres., Mar-May '72 file,
    Box 6 BCH (20ABC); and YOUNG: Analyis of will of Blanche Ebert Seaver dated
    October 15, 1971, attached to Hornbaker to Banowsky, et al., May 5, 1972, Mrs.
    Frank Roger Seaver file, Box 10, and May 16, 1972, Development file, Box 44;
    Current Assets, May 8, 1972, MNY-WSB file, Box 56.

25 Not included in the designation were general university structures like the
    Theme Tower, Firestone Fieldhouse, all athletic facilities, and administra-
    tive housing. YOUNG: Will of Blanche Ebert Seaver, Dec. 3, 1973, attached to
    Banowsky to Don Miller, Jan. 14, 1974, MNY-WSB file, Box 56; and BAIRD: email
    message from Larry Hornbaker to author, Oct. 31, 2011.

26 WSB: Banowsky to Hudson, Feb. 17, 1975, Jerry Hudson file, Box 1 G-L (10).

27 Ibid.: [Norvel Young to Banowsky], [1975–1976], "Pepperdine University is still Mr. Scaife's favorite school," MNY Accident file, Box 39/44A.

28 LAT: "Couple Gives $2.5 million, Oct. 3, 1971, A21; and YOUNG: clipping, *Santa Monica Evening Outlook*, June 9, 1973, 13, Alice Tyler file, Box 91.

29 Banowsky, *Malibu Miracle*, 256.

30 Patricia Yomantas, "How To Succeed in Business By Really Trying," *Pepperdine People* 5 (Summer 1982): 3–4.

31 Banowsky, *Malibu Miracle*, 216–17.

32 WSB: Banowsky to Tegner, Sept. 16, 1975, T 1976 file, Box 6SC-V (30); and "Biography of Fritz Huntsinger Sr.," Feb. 27, 1974, and Scrip for introduction, [1973], Frits Huntsinger Sr. file, Donor Records, Nolij Database, Vice President for Development's Office; and GRAPHIC: Keith Sheldon, "Festivities To Honor Huntsinger," Oct. 13, 1972, 1.

33 LAT: Myrna Oliver, "Beverly Hills Realty Agent George Elkins Dies," Feb. 26, 1993, B1. See also WSB: Banowsky to Young, Mar. 30, 1972, Chron. Corres. Mar-May '72 file, Box 6 BCH (20 ABC); and YOUNG: Jerry Hudson to Elkins, June 25, 1974, Criticism of Pepperdine file, Box 64; and HAWP: Banowsky to Elkins, June 16, 1970, June 1970 file, Box 2.

34 The Law School gift was unrestricted and thus used to balance the budget in a very difficult financial year. Ron Phillips to Larry Hornbaker, Sept. 14, 1999, Jerene H. Appleby Corres. file, NOLIJ Collection, Vice President for Development Office.

35 YOUNG: Young to Governor, Oct. 2, 1969, Reagan file, Box 90; Banowsky to Frank L. Wiegand, Jr., Apr. 16, 1970, Wiegand file, Box B21.

36 PUA: Mildred [Phillips] to Bill [Banowsky], Feb. 23, 1970, Hornbaker files (File Cabinet F-201B-F286); and HAWP: Banowsky to Mrs. B. D. Phillips, Jr., Feb. 17, 1970; Banowsky to Eldon Lewis, July 13, 1970, Chron. Corres., Jan 1970 file, Box 2; and LAT: Noel Greenwood, "Pepperdine Campus at Malibu Ready to Open," Sept. 4, 1972, D1.

37 LAT: "John Stauffer of Chemical Company Dies," Dec. 14, 1972, D24; and "Biographical Sketch—Mrs. Beverly M. Stauffer," Oct. 31, 1969, Beverly Stauffer file, Nolij Database, Vice President for Development's Office; and WSB: Banowsky to Joseph Burris, n.d., B 70–74 file, Box 1 A-C (46); and JLP: Banowsky to Beverly Stauffer, Apr. 20, 1976, File 3, Box 3.

38 BAIRD: Wilburn, "My Life and Experiences," 40–41; and Banowsky, Malibu Miracle, 176–77; and LAT: George Ramos, "Leonard Firestone, Tire Executive, Dies," Dec. 25, 1996, A3; and Neva Ann Hash, "Leonard K. Firestone: Industrialist, Ambassador, Regent," *Pepperdine People*, 1 (Summer 1977): 7–11.

39 Joyce Baxter, "Grand Lady of Encouragement," *Pepperdine People* (Fall 1988), 2–5; and LAT: Myrna Oliver, "Margaret Martin Brock: Major GOP Fundraiser," May 14, 1997, A18; and WSB: James E. H. Mayer to Margaret Brock, Dec. 28, 1970, Margaret Brock 1970–74 file, Box 1B A-E (35). See also Youngs, The House That Brock Built.

40 LAT: Myrna Oliver, "George C. Page; Philanthropist Founded La Brea Museum," Nov. 30, 2000, B9; and Page, Life Story; and Patricia Yomantas, "A Page of Los Angeles History," *Pepperdine People*, 3 (Summer 1980): 10–11.

41 "Charles B. Thornton dead at 68: Was a Litton Industry founder," Nov. 26, 1981, *New York Times*, http://www.nytimes.com/1981/11/26/obituaries/charles-b-thorn-ton-dead-at-68-was-a-litton-industries-founder.html (accessed July 22, 2014).

42 YOUNG: John T. McCarty to Banowsky, Oct. 17, 1974, John T. McCarty file, Box 46; and WSB: Banowsky to John Garson, Aug. 2, 1972, Malibu file, Box BSU '69-'72.

CHAPTER 28

1 LAT: "Many Colleges Plan Resumed Classes Today," May 11, 1970, A17; and HAWP: Banowsky to Pullias, June 4, 1970, June 1970 file, Box 2. A copy of the program for the event is in WSB: Malibu file, Box BSU '69-'72.

2 WSB: Vincent Fowler to Nate Charnley, June 15, 1970, Malibu-Flag file, Box BSU '69-'72. The Santa Monica Rotary Club also presented a two by three foot bronze plaque commemorating the occasion, later placed at the base of the flag pole, that also bore Rotary's famous Four-Way Test.

3 Ronald Ellerbe, "The Birth of a College," *Alumni Voice*, 33, (Summer 1970): 19. See also WSB: Clipping, "Pepperdine College's New Malibu Campus Dedicated," *Van Nuys News*, May 24, 1970, in Malibu folder, Box BSU '69-'72.

4 YOUNG: Malibu Construction Project, Apr. 1, 1974, attached to Hudson to Banowsky, Apr. 16, 1974, Malibu. Const., Misc. file, Box 46; Minutes, University Board, Apr. 12, 1973, Univ. Bd. Min. 73–76 (2) file, Box CO5; and WSB: Bill Youngs to Larry Knudsen, Dec. 12, 1973, ICSC file, Box 1 G-L (14).

5 YOUNG: Pepperdine College, Financing for Malibu Campus, Dec. 31, 1970, Management file, Box 66.

6 Ibid.: Young to Richard Seaver, Apr. 26, 1973, Richard Seaver file, Box 85.

7 WSB: White to Banowsky, Sept. 26, 1973, Howard White file, Box 39/44A; Banowsky to Russ Vorwerk, Jan. 16, 1974, Corres. Jan-Mar '74 file, Box BC11; Five Year Debt Analysis, Jan. 1975, Ex. Com. Meet. July 14, 1975 file, Box Board of Trustees (16).

8 Art Detman, Jr., "Pepperdine Starts Fresh at Malibu," *College Management*, 7 (Sept. 1972): 17–22.

9 PUA: "Archaeological Field Catalog, Summer 1970"; Press Release, Aug. 10, 1971, Archaeological file, Box B77; and LAT: "13th Century Artifacts Given to Pepperdine," Aug. 12, 1971, WS3. Those artifacts remained in the provost's office for a short time, and then were turned over to the natural science division where they remained until 2013. A fragment of the original collection now resides with the special collections division of the university library.

10 PUA. Between 1969 and 1973, Pepperdine paid Typodynamics $200,425 for its consulting work. See HAWP: James M. Cowley to Lawrence R. Tapper, July 9, 1974, Cowley Corres. file, Box 28. Both Young and Banowsky were business partners with Andy Rawn, owner of Typodynamics, in non-university related real estate investments, relationships that the California Attorney General's office subsequently frowned upon.

11 WSB: Banowsky to Young, et al., Mar. 10, 1974, Jerry Hudson file, Box 1 G-L (10).

12 Confusion exists as to when site preparation actually began. In *Malibu Miracle*, 236, Banowsky suggests sometime in Jan. 1969, but the *Santa Monica Evening Outlook* reported contemporaneously that it began August 17, 1970. See WSB: "College Cleans Way to Malibu Opening," *[Santa Monica] Evening Outlook*, Aug. 17, 1970, clipping in Malibu file, Box 17, 0002.

13 Detman, "Pepperdine Starts Fresh at Malibu," 17–22.

14 Mike Pollock, "Von Braun at Malibu Launching," *Alumni Voice*, 34 (Fall 1971), 11–13; and GRAPHIC: Keith Sheldon, "Festivities to honor Huntsinger," Oct. 13, 1972, 1. See also HAWP: Academic Complex file, Box 34.

15 YOUNG: David Parry to Bob Bales, Sept. 28, 1971 and attached Press Release, both attached Herbert Wilson to James E. H. Mayer, Sept. 28, 1971, Alice Tyler '71-'73 file, Box 91; and GRAPHIC: "Cornerstone ceremony slated for Tyler Center," Oct. 14, 1971, 1.

16 GRAPHIC: Bob Eisberg, "Harnish Dedication Set," Apr. 6, 1972, 1; LAT: Marshal Berges, "Home Q&A," Home Magazine, June 4, 1978, 49.

17 GRAPHIC: Frank Suraci, "Goldwater Keynotes Pep Open House," Jan. 26, 1973, 1; Bob Eisberg, "Goldwater Praises Pepperdine Ideals," Feb. 2, 1973, 1. See also SRP: Faculty Advisory Committee to Jerry Hudson, May 4, 1973, Faculty Advisory Com. file, Box 21.

18 HAWP: White to Mike O'Neal, Oct. 7, 1984, Chron. Corres. Oct. 1984 file, Box 13. According to White, Murchison had promised to give a million dollars to the university either during his lifetime or through the provision of his will, but qualified the gift with the proviso that the promise was "in no sense a legal commitment." White compared that promise to the man who showed love for a deceased family member by placing in the casket a check in the amount of $1 million.

19 Banowsky, *Malibu Miracle*, chapter 15. See also WSB: Banowsky to Jeremy B. Lewis, Apr. 27, 1972, Chron. Corres. Mar-May '72 file, Box 6 BCH (20 ABC).

20 Ibid.

21 YOUNG: Alvin S. Kaufer to Banowsky, June 2, 1972, Malibu Construction Misc. file, Box 46.

22 Ibid. See also WSB: Banowsky to Young and Hudson, June 13, 1972, Chron. Corres. June-Aug '72 file, Box 6 BCH (20 ABC); and GRAPHIC: Celia Chapman, "Groundbreaking Slated for Malibu," Apr. 6, 1972, 1. Joseph Bentley of the firm of Latham and Watkins would later argue that had the California Coastal Commission been in existence as the Malibu campus was under construction, its history would have been different. See Banowsky, Malibu Miracle, xx-xxi.

23 GRAPHIC: Bob Eisberg, "Theme Tower Delayed by Attorney's Appeal," Feb. 16, 1973, 1. For a picture of the exposed superstructure see SCUA: "Pepperdine Sets Major Key '73 Religious Event," *Palisadian Post*, Apr. 26, 1973, 11, clipping in LE Lectureship folder, Drawer 1, File Cabinet 207A.

24 GRAPHIC: Chris Parker, "Theme Tower Controversy Cools," Sept. 21, 1973, 1; and WSB: Banowsky to Mildred Phillips, May 21, 1974, Corres. Apr-June '74 file, Box BCH Corres. (9). The quotation comes from the dedicatory plaque.

25 WSB: Banowsky to Mrs. Charles Helfrich, Mar. 30, 1973, Corres. Jan-Mar '73 file.

26 GRAPHIC: "Approval Granted for Tower Lights," Jan. 19, 1978, 1; and HAWP: Simon Zimmelman to Banowsky, Feb. 9, 1978, attached to White to Banowsky, Feb. 15, 1978, Dr. Banowsky '78 file, Box 32; and BAIRD: Bob Thomas to Mike O'Neal, Sept. 6, 1978, and O'Neal of Thomas, Sept. 27, 1978, 1978–1979 file; and SRP: White to Thomas, Mar. 31, 1979, Dr. White 1979 file.

27 HAWP: White to Ron Stephens, Feb. 16, 1981, Chron. Corres. Jan.-Feb. 1981 file, Box 10; and GRAPHIC: James Taylor, "Pep Fights for Tower Light," Feb. 6, 1986, A4.

28 HAWP: White to Gerald Treece, Sept. 9, 1983, Chron. Corres. Sept. 1983 file, Box 12.

29 Ibid.: Banowsky to Hudson, Apr. 7, 1971, Malibu-Chapel file, Box BSU '69-'72, William S. Banowsky; and Joyce Hutchison, "Sentimental Journey," *Pepperdine People* (Spring 1995), 6–7.

30 WSB: Banowsky to Young, Sept. 27, 1973; Banowsky to Hudson, Oct. 16, 1973, attached to Young to Hudson, Oct. 9, 1973, Church in Malibu file, Box 4 A-W (24).

31 Ibid.: Hudson to Banowsky, Oct. 10, 1973.

32 GRAPHIC: Lee Ann Park, "Pep Chapel Dedication Scheduled," Nov. 2, 1973, 1. See WSB: Malibu Church of Christ file, Box GR-K (36).

33 YOUNG: Pereira to Young, Jan. 18, 1972, Pereira Assoc. file, Box 47.

34 GRAPHIC: "Rubber Tree," July 11, 1975, 1; and WSB: Dedication program for Firestone Fieldhouse, Sept. 20, 1975, Firestone Fieldhouse file, BSU Ford 41.

35 LAT: "Passings: Wilma Day Mallmann," Nov. 18, 1987, 24; and Wilma Day Mallmann donor files, Nolij data base, Vice President of Development Office, PU, MC. See also SRP: Mallmann House-Wilma Day file, Box 25.

36 Audene Merrill Connor, Mildred Welshimer Phillips (wife of the donor of the theme tower) Edythe F. Pengilly, Ann Pepper, Aileen T. Pauley (Mrs. Harold Pauley, whose husband was once part owner of Los Angeles Rams), Maxcine Feltman White (wife of Howard A. White), James W. Fifield Jr. (minister of the First Congregational Church in Los Angeles and Frank Seaver's spiritual counselor), Richard H. Banowsky (father of William Banowsky), Roy P. Crocker (president of Lincoln Savings and Loan through 1969), Joseph H. Penguilly, Walter Knott (University Board Member and founder of Knott's Berry Farm), Hubert Eaton (University Board Member and founder of Forest Lawn Cemetery), Donald W. Darnell (University Board Member and chair of the Malibu Site Selection Committee), Donald W. Miller (longtime member of the board of regents), and David Emerson Morgan.

37 SRP: Text of Ronald Reagan speech delivered at Seaver Dedication, Apr. 20, 1975, Blanche Seaver #1 file, Box 29. See also GRAPHIC: Cynthia M. Horner, "Pep Honors Seavers at Dedication," May 2, 1975, 1; and "Birth of Seaver College," *Imprints 1975* (Malibu: Office of Student Publications, Seaver College of Pepperdine University, 1975), 6–7.

38 SRP: Banowsky, "A Spirit of Purpose," Apr. 20, 1975, Seaver Dedication file, Box 4,. See also, Banowsky, *Malibu Miracle*, 310–19.

39 Ibid.

40 Kenny Waters, "Grace Abandoned or Received? Pepperdine's Great Experiment," *Mission Magazine*, 10 (Nov. 1976): 102.

41 WSB: Banowsky to Ford, April 8, 1975, Firestone Fieldhouse Dedication file, Box 6 BCH (20 ABC).

42 Ibid.: Banowsky to Alumni, Sept. 26, 1975, Misc. file, Box BSU Ford (41); Banowsky to John Goplen, Dec. 5, 1975, G '76 file, Box 4. The 1975–1976 issue of the student yearbook, *Imprints*, placed the cost of the presidential visit at $200,000.

43 GRAPHIC: "Fatal Accident," Sept. 19, 1975, 1.

44 WSB: Ralph and Barbara Edwards to Bill and Gay Banowsky, Sept. 22, 1975; Mrs. Brock's Comments, Sept. 20, 1975, Dedication of Firestone Fieldhouse file, Box BSU Ford (41).

45 Ibid.: Program, Leonard K. Firestone Fieldhouse dedication, Sept. 20, 1975, Dedication of Firestone Fieldhouse file, Box BSU Ford (41); and IV: "Architect Designs New Flag," Oct. 17, 1975, 3. The fact that the Malibu campus had its own flag galled *Inner View*, which saw that fact as an example of inequality between the Los Angeles and Malibu campuses. See IV: editorial, "Flag," July 2, 1976, 4. Copies of Ford's speech in what appears to be Banowsky's hand are in WSB: Firestone Fieldhouse Program file, Box BSU Ford (41). A minute-by-minute account of the president's visit is in the Banowsky papers, "The Daily Diary of President Gerald R. Ford," Sept. 20, 1975, Daily Diary of Pres. Ford file. A printed copy of President Ford's address is contained in WSB: Gerald R. Ford Address file, Box 28. See LAT: Kenneth Reich, "President Vows He'll Fight for Private Colleges," Sept. 21, 1975, 1, for another account of the event.

46 WSB: Clarence Honig to Banowsky, Sept. 22, 1975; Marion to Banowsky, Oct. 7, 1975; Banowsky to Alumni, Sept. 26, 1975, Misc. file, Box BSU Ford (41). In a compilation prepared for Richard Scaife, the cost of President Ford's visit was placed at $539,947. That sum included not only one-time costs of the visit, but grading of tennis courts, grading of parking lots, landscaping, stairs from field house to main campus under the bridge, stables, and Seaver College sign on the bridge. See HAWP: Construction Costs for President Ford's visit, n.d., Ford Visit Costs file, Box 62.

47 PUA: Minutes, Pepperdine University Board, May 23, 1978, Univ. Bd. Min.-78–79 (1) file, Box CO5; and GRAPHIC: "Pep Breaks Ground," Oct. 27, 1977, 1; and Frances D. Smothers files, Nolij Data Base, Vice President for Development Office.

48 WSB: Banowsky to Richard Seaver, Apr. 1, 1974, and Sept. 17, 1974, Corres. July-Sept '74 file, Box BCH Corres. (9); and SRP: Richard Seaver to Mrs. Frank R. Seaver, Apr. 18, 1978, Blanche Seaver #1 file, Box 29.

49 GRAPHIC: Rich Taylor, "Field To Dedicate Baseball Stadium," May 19, 1977, 3; and WSB: see F file, Box 2 D-Grad (31); and HAWP: Field Baseball Stadium file, Box 34; Runnels to Bob Thomas, Jan. 29, 1979, Charles Runnels file, Box 47. See "Eddy D. Field Baseball Stadium Dedicated," *Pepperdine People* (Summer 1977), 34; and Patricia Yomantas, "Dream Realized for Pep Friend Eddy D. Field," *Pepperdine People*, 3 (Summer 1980): 6; and LAT: "Eddy Field; Realty Agent, Philantropist," Nov. 12, 1994, A26.

50 WSB: Runnels to Banowsky, Apr. 4, 1972, Malibu Campus file, Box BSU 69–72 (45); and YOUNG: Elaine Farley to Young, May 19, 1972, Fine Arts file; and LAT: Betty Liddick, "Two Projects," June 1, 1972, I1. See also YOUNG: Malibu Township Council Bulletin, Mar. 1972, Forum file, Box 45.

51 LAT: Standalone photo, Nov. 3, 1972, C5; and YOUNG: E. Dale Click to Lowell Thomas, Nov. 8, 1972, Tree Project file, Box 46; clipping, *Santa Monica Evening Outlook*, Nov. 10, 1972, 1; and GRAPHIC: "A Hard Day's Night," Nov. 10, 1972, 3; "Landmark," Oct. 24, 1975, 1.

CHAPTER 29

1 HAWP: White to Mrs. Mayo Dowdle, Apr. 29, 1978, Ex. VP Corres. Mar-May '78 file, Box 7; and BOT: Feb. 18, 1971, vol. 5:226; and GRAPHIC: Greg Krikorian, "Howard White, 'INSIDE PRESIDENT,' Keys Pep's direction," June 22, 1973, 1; and C. Thomas Nelson, "Banowsky Is 4th President; Young Becomes Board Chairman, Chancellor," *Alumni Voice*, 34 (Spring 1971): 5; and Bill Youngs, "Dr. Howard White, Executive Vice President," *Alumni Voice*, 36 (Winter 1973): 6–7.

2 WSB: Resume for Jerry E. Hudson, [1973], Jerry Hudson file, Box 1 G-I (10).

3 Ibid.: Banowsky to Hudson, Dec. 17, 1969, Malibu Personnel file, Box BSU '69-'72 (45); Don Miller to Jerry and Ann, Aug 2, 1975, Jerry Hudson file, Box 1 G-L (10); and HAWP: Zane Reeves to Hudson, [Spr. 1971]; Hudson to Banowsky, Aug. 19, 1971; Hudson to 1973 file, Box 31; and GRAPHIC: Editorial, "The Stubborn Optimist," Oct. 6, 1972, 4.

4 WSB: Banowsky to Hudson, Oct. 9, 1974, Jerry Hudson file, Box 1 G-L (10); and YOUNG: Hudson to Banowsky and White, Oct. 15, 1974, Business School file, Box 43; Hudson to Banowsky, July 9, 1975, Jerry Hudson file, Box 45; and GRAPHIC: Neva Hash, "Provost Resigns Malibu Offices," July 11, 1975, 1.

5 HAWP: White to Kenneth C. Williams, Feb. 14, 1975, Ex. VP Corres, Jan. 2-Feb 19 '75 file, Box 5.

6 YOUNG: Press Release, [July 1976], Jerry Hudson file, Box 45; and HAWP: White to Hudson, May 20, 1984, Box 31. Most Seaver College faculty had high regard for Hudson, but not all. The minority was mortified when he was invited back in 1976 and delighted when he was passed over for president in 1984.

7 Kelli M. Fast, "Pepperdine: 10 Years of Growth and Success," *Oasis* (1981–1982): 13–15.

8 BOT: Nov. 11, 1968, 5:159.

9 YOUNG: Minutes, Malibu Action Committee, Oct. 18, 1968, in unlabeled folder; Malibu Curriculum Planning Committee, "Progress Report and Initial Recommendation," [Apr. 1969], 46, Box 75; Young to Faculty, Nov. 7, 1968, Second Campus file, Box 4.

10 Former Pepperdine Dean E. V. Pullias told the committee that "The over-all environment educates more than any single course or activity." And, thus, a "Christian college must remain genuinely Christian, or it has nothing to offer." See WSB: Minutes of Academic Planning Committee #20, May 6, 1969, Malibu Planning Committee file, BSU '69-'72-'72 (45). The schools visited included the University of Houston; Weber State University, Ogden, Utah; Hampshire College, South Amherst, Massachusetts.; Stephens College, Columbia, Missouri.

11 Ibid.: "Working Paper-January La Costa Meeting," Jan. [1969], Pence Dacus file, Box 1 C-E (15); and YOUNG: Malibu Curriculum Planning Committee, "Progress Report and Initial Recommendation," [Apr. 1969], 94–98, Box 75. Minutes of the Planning Committee between Dec. 1968 and June 1969 are found in WSB: Malibu Planning Committee file, Box BSU '69-'72 (45).

12 The humanities "area" included religion, music, art, literature, philosophy, history, and drama; social science included economics, political science, sociology, psychology, anthropology, and home economics (family living); natural science included chemistry, biology, physics, mathematics, astronomy, physical education, home economics; and communications included foreign languages, speech, journalism, education, and English.

13 JCM: Minutes of Faculty Meeting, June 20, 1969; and HAWP: Wyatt Jones et al. to Young, June 30, 1969, Correspondence Apr. 24 to July 25, 1969 file, Box 1; and YOUNG: Young to Gentlemen, July 2, 1969, Faculty file, Box 3; and WSB: Wyatt Jones, et al, to Young, July 9, 1969, Malibu Curriculum file, Box BSU. See also BOT: June 19, 1969, 5:188.

14 WSB: Banowsky to White, July 25, 1972, attached to Banowsky to Young, July 25, 1972, Law School '71-'72 file, Box 1 G-L (14).

15 Ibid.: Minutes of Academic Council, June 17, 1969, Malibu Planning Committee file, Box BSU '69-'72 (45); Norvel Young Proposal, [1968–1969], Pence Dacus file, Box 1 C-E (15).

16 YOUNG: Pence Dacus, et al., to All Faculty, July 24, 1969, Faculty file, Box 4.

17 Ibid.: Wyatt Jones, et al., "Report of the Committee for the Formulation of an Alternative Proposal for the Malibu Campus, [Aug. 1969], Faculty file, Box 3. See also WSB: untitled interim report beginning with "This is not the final report," [July, 1969], Malibu Curriculum file, Box BSU.

18 Ibid.

19 HAWP: Young to Sister Banowsky, et al., June 24, 1969, Corres. Apr. 24-July 25, 1969 file, Box 1; Banowsky to Vince Fowler, July 31, 1969, Corres. July 25-Oct. 31, 1969 file, Box 2; and Young to Board of Trustees, July 7, 1969, Chron. Corres. Apr. 24-July 25, 1969 file, Box 1.

20 BOT: Aug. 7, 1960, 5:189–191.

21 HAWP: Banowsky to Action Committee, Aug. 5, 1969, Corres. July 25-Oct. 31, 1969 file, Box 2.

22 WSB: From Dr. Jack Scott, Nov. 5, 1970, Malibu Program Statement file, Box BSU.

23 Ibid.: "Report for the Accreditation Committees," Oct. 1970, 129, Accreditation files.

24 Ibid.: Statement attached to Banowsky to Norman Hughes, Dec. 8, 1970, Malibu Program Statements, Box BSU.

25 GRAPHIC: "Clear Understanding Sought by Banowsky," Sept. 23, 1971, 1.

26 HAWP: Frank Pack to Jerry Hudson, Nov. 2, 1971, Frank Pack file, Box 43.

27 WSB: Banowsky to Hudson, Sept. 19, 1972, Chron. Corres. Sept-Oct '72 file, Box BCH Corres. (9).

28 YOUNG: Banowsky to Dacus, Dec. 17, 1969, Chron. Corres. Nov. '69-Jan. '70 file, Box 2, White Papers; Pendleton to Banowsky, Jan. 19, 1973, Morris Pendleton file, Box 47.

29 YOUNG: A confidential document probably written by Jerry Hudson entitled "Blueprint for Transitional Year," [Sum. 1971], Jerry Hudson file, Box 45, lists thirty-four Los Angeles faculty that would be invited to move to Malibu, many of whom chose not to leave the Los Angeles campus. The document seeks a student to faculty ratio of 20:1.

30 Ibid.: Banowsky to Dacus, Dec. 17, 1969, Chron. Corres. Nov. '69-Jan. '70 file, Box 2, White Papers; Pendleton to Banowsky, Jan. 19, 1973; Young to Pendleton, Feb. 13, 1973, Morris Pendleton file, Box 47.

31 HAWP: Banowsky to Dacus, Dec. 17, 1969, Chron. Corres. Nov. '69-Jan. '70 file, Box 2.

32 BAIRD: Silas Shotwell, "Reflections on my year at Pepperdine, 1971–1972," June 15, 2013, 1971–72 file. See also, Bill Henegar, "Big Don," *Pepperdine People* (Winter 1990): 22–23.

33 WSB: Hudson to Banowsky, June 8, 1971, Malibu recruitment file, Box '69–72; and "Why is Ira North Recruiting Students for Pepperdine?" *Christian Chronicle*, Nov. 8, 1971, 12. For other *Chronicle* ads see issues for Nov. 22, 1971, Dec. 6, 1971, Dec. 20, 1971, Jan. 3, 1972, Feb. 14, 1972, and May 8, 1972. See also BOT: Dec. 17, 1971, vol. 5:247; and YOUNG: Report to Pepperdine Faculty, Mar. 2, 1972, Faculty file, Box 44; and WSB: Banowsky to Young, June 7, 1972, Chron. Corres. June-Aug. '72 file, Box 6 BCH (20 ABC).

34 YOUNG: Notes from the closed trustee meeting by Helen Young, Nov. 18, 1972, Confidential, RE Board of Trustees file, Box 74; and WSB: Misc. stats. for speech, [Fall 1974], D file, Box 2 D-Grad (31). The quoted material is scrawled on the latter document in Banowsky's hand. Records in the Seaver College admission office place the number of Church of Christ students in the first Malibu class as 30.3 percent; among freshmen there only were 25.6 percent.

35 BAIRD: Shotwell, "Reflections"; and SRP: Don Williams to White, et al., May 4, 1972, LA Campus Changes file, Box 4.

36 WSB: New student survey, Fall 1973, attached to White to Banowsky, Jan. 28, 1974, Howard White file, Box 39/44.

37 Ibid.: Malibu Program, Fall 1971, Malibu file, Box BSU '69-'72 (45). Of the 147 enrolled in the pilot group, 47, or 28.5 percent, would complete their bachelor's degree at Pepperdine. Registrar Hugh Mingle considered this retention rate problematic. See Ibid.: Mingle to Hudson, Mar. 19, 1975, Grad. Malibu, Apr. 13, 1975 file, Box 2 D-Grad (31).

38 Malibu Fall Enrollment Statistics, Dec. 9, 1972, 1972 Admission Stats, pp. 4–7 (digital), Enrollment Management, Seaver College. Of the 904 students who applied for entry to Malibu in 1972, all but 4 percent were admitted. And only 56 percent of those who were admitted actually enrolled. There was even less selectivity in the fall 1973 and 1974, although it did improve the following year with almost one in ten applications being rejected.

39 1972 Admission Stats, pp. 89, 92, 95 (digital), Enrollment Management Office Records, Seaver College.

40 GRAPHIC: Mark Harvis, "Survey Reveals Attitudes," Nov. 7, 1975, 6. Previously, the *Graphic* had discerned that only 50 percent of the student body at Malibu had supported Nixon's re-election in 1972; 27 percent had favored McGovern; Bob Eisberg, "Nixon Holds Clear Edge, Poll Reveals," Oct. 13, 1972, 1.

41 GRAPHIC: Bob Eisberg, "Dream Campus Opens Its Doors," Oct. 6, 1972, 1; PUA: Minutes, University Board, Oct. 15, 1972, Box CO5.

42 Ralph Beck, "In the Beginning," *Alumni Voice* 3 (No. 2, 1984), 5.

43 WSB: Bob Thomas to Young, et al., Nov. 11, 1973, S '70-'74 file, Box B6 PR-SA (28); and GRAPHIC: Pat McConahay, "McClung Talks Dormitories; Resident's Problems Voiced," Feb. 2, 1973, 6; Neva Hash, "Homecoming Revival Slated," Feb. 23, 1973, 1.

44 GRAPHIC: Bob Eisberg, "Precedents Emerging-Hudson," Apr. 6, 1973, 1; Editorial, "Malibu's First Year," Apr. 6, 1973, 4.

45 Robert Fraley, Seaver Enrollment, Feb. 4, 1976, 1976 Admission Stats, p. 47 (digital), Admissions Office, Seaver College; and OIE: Enrollment and Faculty Profile for the Oxnard Conference, Oct. 18–19, 1979, 1.

46 WSB: Banowsky to White, May 17, 1974, Howard White file, Box 39/44A. The faculty of the professional schools strongly objected to liberal arts faculty controlling general education requirements for their majors, but Howard White insisted to the contrary, citing WASC, costs, and proliferation of GE courses as reasons. WSB: White to Banowsky, Oct. 30, 1973, and White to Young, Dec. 27, 1973, Howard White file, Box 39/44A; White to Banowsky, Jan. 31, 1976, MPA Program file, Box 4 A-W (24); and HAWP: White to Goyne, Apr. 30, 1975, Ex. VP corres. Feb. 20-Apr. 30 '75 file, Box 5; Jerry Hudson to Banowsky, July 18, 1973, School of Business '69-'75 file, Box 51.

47 Enrollment Statistics, Malibu Campus, Spring 1974, 1974 Admission Stats, pp. 6–7 (digital), Enrollment Management Office, Seaver College.

48 WSB: N. Hughes to Banowsky, Dec. 8, 1975, H 71–75 file, Box 1 G-L (10); White to Banowsky, Feb. 21, 1976, Howard White file, Box 2 N-Z (40); and HAWP: Consolidation of Undergraduate Business and Teacher Education Courses Taught at Malibu into Seaver College, Feb. 29, 1976, Ex. VP. Corres. Feb. 14-Apr. 6 '76 file, Box 6; and GRAPHIC: Kathy Graenicher, "Spike Team Grabs Consolation Title," May 12, 1977, 3.

49 WSB: Major Goals, [1971], Malibu Curriculum file, Box BSU '69-'72 (45); and GRAPHIC: Laaura Patrick, "Faculty Views Pass-Fail Theory," June 15, 1973, 4; "Individual Progress Courses 'Strengthened'," July 18, 1975, 1; NICKS: Biographical Sketch of Nicks, [June 28, 1977], Chron. Corres.-Sept. 29, 1976 to June 29, 1977 file, Box 5. For a copy of the syllabus of "American Ideals and Institutions" see PUA: AI&I file, Box 89.

50 GRAPHIC: Keith Sheldon, "Malibu Offers Masters'," May 11, 1973, 1; HAWP: Tabulation attached to Hughes to White, Jan. 10, 1977, Ex. VP Corres. Jan.-Mar. '77, Box 7.

51 GRAPHIC: Neva Hash, "Nine Receive Degrees at Malibu Ceremony," Apr. 6, 1973, 1. Initially, the University reserved the Santa Monica Civic Auditorium for the graduation ceremony, but subsequently switched venues. See HAWP: Santa Monica Civic Auditorium file, Box 51.

52 Kenny Waters, "The Scene Has Changed," *Alumni Voice*, 36 (Fall 1974): 20.

53 WSB: Richard Ware to John T. McCarty, Aug. 28, 1974, attached to Banowsky to Young, Sept. 9, 1974, E '72-'74 file, Box 1 C-E (15).

54 Ibid.: Honor document in May 1978, 1977–1978 file; and *Pepperdine University Bulletin, Seaver College 1979–80 Catalog*, 42 (Feb. 1979), 66.

55 WSB: Banowsky to Distribution List, Dec. 18, 1973, College Rater File, Box 4 A-W (24); Faculty Advisory Committee to Hudson, Aug. 5, 1974, attached to Banowsky to Hudson, Aug. 21, 1974, Jerry Hudson file, Box 1 G-I (10); White to Banowsky, Jan. 30, 1974, College Rater file, Box 4 A-W (24), and College Rater, Inc., Where Do Colleges Rank (Allentown, PA, 1973), pamphlet in College Rater file, Box B10 (44B). Highest ranked in California were Harvey Mudd, Pomona, Claremont Men's College, and Occidental. Below those but above Pepperdine were Loyola, Chapman, Laverne, and California Lutheran.

56 WSB: Banowsky to Abram Samuels, Mar. 1, 1974, College Rater file, Box 4 A-W (24); Samuels to Banowsky, Mar. 4, 1974, C '70-'74 file, Box 4 A-W (24); Roe Darnell to Wilburn, Feb. 12, 1974, and James Kellett to Wilburn, Feb. 11, 1974, College Rater file, Box 4 A-W (24).

57 SRP: "[Preliminary] Report on the visit to Pepperdine College," Dec. 1–4, 1970, Folder B; Pepperdine University, *Report for the Accreditation Committee of the Western Association of Schools and Colleges* (Malibu: Pepperdine University, Jan. 1974), 111, in WASC '74 folder, Box 26. Howard White always believed that WASC's special interest in Pepperdine's programs in Hawaii came from Kay Andersen, the Executive-Secretary of the commission. Andersen had roots in Hawaii and thought that the University of Hawaii should be servicing the program at Schofield Barracks. See Ibid.: White to Banowsky, Nov. 20, 1973, B file.

58 Ibid.: *"Report for the Accreditation Committee."* Dr. Ann Heiss, an educational consultant from Del Mar, California, chaired the team.

59 SRP: "[Final] Report on the Visit to Pepperdine University," Mar. 4–6, 1974, attached to Evelyn Thorne to Banowsky, Apr. 24, 1974, WASC '74 file, Box 26; and WSB: Pepperdine University, *Reaccreditation Report Submitted to the Western Association of Schools and Colleges* (Malibu: Pepperdine University, Nov. 1978), pp. 16–33, in Box B 10(44B).

60 SRP: "Response of Pepperdine University to the Report on the Visit of the Committee from the Western Association of Schools and Colleges, Mar. 4–6, 1974," attached to Banowsky to Andersen, June 4, 1974, attached to "[Final] Report on the Visit to Pepperdine University," Mar. 4–6, 1974, WASC '74 folder, Box 26.

61 YOUNG: Banowsky to Young and White, Apr. 29, 1974, MNY-WSB file, Box 56.

62 SRP: Kay Andersen to Banowsky, June 13, 1974, WASC '74 folder, Box 26; and YOUNG: Banowsky to Board of Trustees, Sept. 30, 1974, Accreditation file, Box 43.

63 HAWP: [Howard White,] "Progress Report to the Western Association of Schools and Colleges from Pepperdine University, Apr. 1, 1976, Ex. VP Corres. Feb. 14-Apr. 6, 1976, Box 6. See also WSB: Appendix A, *Reaccreditation Report Submitted to the Western Association of Schools and Colleges*, Nov. 1978, in Box B 10 (44B).

64 Ibid.; and HAWP: White to Andersen, Oct. 18, 1974, attached to White to Young, Nov. 12, 1974, Norvel Young '74–'78 file, Box 33.

65 WSB: Distinguished Visiting Professors brochure [1975], Box 4 A-W (24).

66 WSB: Young to Banowsky, June 3, 1975, and Bob Bales to Banowsky, June 5, 1975; Pepperdine News Release, Oct. 3, 1975, T '75 file, Box 6 SC-V (30); Banowsky to Spitzer, Sept. 23, 1973, S '75 file, Box B6 OR-SA (28); and LAT: "Naturalized Citizen was Benefactor of the L.A. Arts," Dec. 8, 2003, B9; and "News Briefs," *Pepperdine People*, 4 (Winter 1981): 22–23.

67 GRAPHIC: Cynthia M. Horner, "Pep Establishes a Science Position," Nov. 7, 1975, 1; and WSB: W.F. Libby to Banowsky, Aug. 1, 1975, and White to Libby, Sept. 8, 1975, and Pepperdine News Release, Oct. 29, 1975, L '75 file, Box B6 PR-SA (28).

68 WSB: John T. McCarty to Melbo, et al., Apr. 28, 1977, V file, Box 2 N-Z (40).

69 Ibid.: Young to Banowsky, Mar. 20, 1974, and White to Young, Sept 4, 1974, C '70-'74 file, Box 1 A-C (46); May 15, 1975, Norvel Young '74-'78 file, Box 33; White to Banowsky, June 19, 1974, Howard White file, Box 39/44A; White to Young, May 15, 1975, C '75 file, Box 1 C-E (15); and HAWP: Stephen Sale, Report to the Coe Foundation, [1974], attached to White to Young, Aug. 30, 1974, Norvel Young '74-'78 file, Box 33.

70 WSB: Report from the Director, "Robert A. Taft Institute of Government," June 23, 1975-July 11, 1975, Steve McHargue file, Box 4 A-W (24).

71 Ibid.: Bob Bales to Banowsky, Nov. 8, 1973, attached to Hudson to Banowsky, Nov. 13, 1973, H '71-'74 file, Box 1 G-L (10); Hudson to Banowsky, Jan. 31, 1974, Jerry Hudson file, Box 1 G-L (10); [Robert J. Dyer], Humanics at Malibu 2 (Feb. 1976), in H '76 file, Box 2 GR-K (36). See PUA: Norman Hughes to White, Nov. 20, 1978, American Humanics file, Box B6; and WAP: Adrian to Holden, Dec. 2, 1988, Chron. Corres. Nov. 1988-Mar. 1989 (3 of 3) files, Box 1.

72 YOUNG: Banowsky to Hudson, [Fall 1973], and John Bowls on Equestrian
Program, May 24, 1974, Equestrian Program, Box 44; and Chris Parker,
"Education Equestrian Style," *Oasis*, 9 (1974–75): 34–35; and GRAPHIC: Barbara
Jennings, "Equestrian Education," Oct. 13, 1972, 4.

73 YOUNG: Hudson to John Bowles, et al., July 31, 1974, Equestrian Program-Malibu
file, Box 44; and WSB: Young to Robert Yeary, Oct. 29, 1974, S '70-'74 file, Box B6
PR-SA (28); and SRP: McCarthy to Banowsky, Sept. 23, 1976, Alphabetical files, Box
1.

CHAPTER 30

1 HAWP: Norvel Young to William Banowsky, Mar. 6 and Mar. 22, 1968, Corres.
Oct. 2, 1967-Apr. 4, 1968 file, Box 1.

2 Ibid.: Banowsky to Young, March 1968, Press Release file, Box 27.

3 Ibid.: Bill [Banowsky] to Brother [Young], May 1, 1975, MNY '74-'78 file, Box 33;
and WSB: Young to Banowsky, Sept. 29, 1975, Misc. Corres. file, Box 39/44A.

4 YOUNG: Notes of talk between Young and Banowsky, Apr. 13, 1972, MNY-WSB file,
Box 56; HAWP: Wilburn, Young Opinion, Aug. 17, 1977, Young Misc. file, Box 27.

5 WSB: William S. Banowsky, "The Abuse of Freedom," [June 1968], in Series 5, Box
4, File 1, item 6.

6 GRAPHIC: Diane Piper, "Versatile Banowsky Debates Bishop Pike," Dec. 5, 1968,
2; LAT: John Dart, "Pike Pitted Against Pepperdine Official in Debate on Sex,"
Jan. 13, 1969: C1. HAWP: See also Young to Blanche Seaver, Jan. 15, 1969; Banowsky
to Darrel Rickard, Jan. 15, 1969; Banowsky to Archie Luper, Jan. 15, 1969, Chron.
Corres. Oct. 28, 1968-Feb. 17, 1969 file.

7 YOUNG: Clipping, *Muncie Star*, Apr. 22, 1969, in Univ. Hist. Archives 1969 file, Box 2.

8 HAWP: Young announcement, "Banowsky Named Director of Malibu Campus,"
Dec. 26, 1968, Chron. Corres. Oct. 28, 1968-Feb. 17, 1969 file.

9 HAWP: Announcement, Sept. 17, 1969, Presidential Correspondence, July 25-Oct.
31, 1969 file, Box 2; and BOT: Sept. 16, 1969, vol. 5:194 and Apr. 9, 1970, vol. 5: 209.

10 HAWP: Young to Bill Banowsky, et. al., June 24, 1969, Chron. Corres. Apr. 24-July
25, 1969 file, Box 1; YOUNG: Helen Young notes, "Talk Sept. '69 with Fred Davis,"
Faculty file, Box 3.

11 BOT: Feb. 18, 1971, vol. 5:225–27; and GRAPHIC: "Banowsky Thrives on 'Challenges'
of Post," May 6, 1971, 8.

12 LAT: John Dreyfuss, "Banowsky: He's a Man at the Crossroads," Feb. 18, 1975,
C1&6; and GRAPHIC: Editorial, "The Other Side," Apr. 6, 1972, 4.

13 Student journalists readily saw the value of Banowsky's high profile to the university. See GRAPHIC: Editorial, "The Other Side."

14 "Banowsky TV Host," *Pepperdine News*, 6 (Mar. 1971), 6; and WSB: see Pat Mounts
file, Box BPO L-O (43) and Wally Arno file, Box 3 A-Con (2). Banowsky even
contemplated having a ghost, Doyle Swain, write an article for the *Southwestern
University Law Review*, but determined ultimately not to do so. See Ibid.:
Banowsky to Ron Phillips, Jan. 24, 1973 and Mounts to Swain, Mar. 14, 1974,
Chron. Corres. Jan-Mar 1973 file, Box BCH Corres. (9).

15 SRP: Banowsky to Richard Seaver, Feb. 1, 1972, Blanche Seaver #1 file; and WSB:
Banowsky to Asa V. Call, Feb. 2, 1972, Asa V. Call file, Box 3 A-Con (2); Banowsky
to Young, Mar. 30, 1972, Chron. Mar-May 1972 file, Box 6 BCH (20ABC); Banowsky
to Mr. and Mrs. Robert Nachman, June 5, 1972, Chron. June-Aug. 1972 file, Box 6
BCH (20 A,B. & C); Banowsky to Young, Oct. 11, 1972, place before Banowsky to
Eiden, June 12, 1973, Corres. Apr-June '73 file, Box BCH Corres. (9); and GRAPHIC:
Greg Krikorian, "Banowsky To Get GOP post," June 8, 1973, 1.

16 Among these were Nancy Meyers, Lauritz Miller, Pat Mount, Charlotte Brewer, Dudley Lynch, June Fleming, Walter Arno, and Sheri Keyser. See WSB: Banowsky to Pat Mounts, Oct. 16, 1976, Pat Mounts file, Box BPO L-O (43).

17 Ibid.: Banowsky to Ralph Peterson, Feb. 15, 1972, Ralph Peterson file, Box 4 A-W (24); Banowsky to Carl Terzian, Feb. 14, 1972, Chron. Mar-May 1972 file, Box 6 BCH (20 ABC).

18 YOUNG: Young to Board of Trustees, Mar. 9, 1972, Board of Trustees-Misc. file, Box 58; Morris Pendleton to Banowsky, Dec. 26, 1972; file attached to July 20, 1976, Morris Pendleton file, Box 47; and IV: John Davies, "Banowsky Considers San Francisco Post," Jan. 12, 1973, 3; and GRAPHIC: Bob Eisberg, "No Plans To Accept CSU Post-Banowsky," Jan. 12, 1973, 1; and WSB: Banowsky to Glenn S. Dumke, Jan. 24, 1973, Chron. Corres. Jan-Mar 1973 file, Box BCH Corres. (9); Banowsky to Gov. Reagan, Jan. 30, 1973, Chron. Corres. Jan-Mar 1973 file, Box BCH Corres. (9); Banowsky to Brokaw, Jan. 31, 1973, Media Contacts file, Box BPO L-O (43).

19 YOUNG: Banowsky to Seaver, Oct. 24, 1969, Bill Banowsky file, Box 2.

20 WSB: Banowsky to Herbert Kalmbach, Dec. 2, 1972, and Jan. 22, 1973, and Banowsky to June Fleming, Feb. 10, 1973, Corres. Nov-Dec 1972 file, Box BCH Corres. (9).

21 Ibid.: See VP Spiro Agnew file, Box 39/44A.

22 Ibid.: Banowsky to Richard Nixon, Nov. 6, 1973, Corres. Oct-Dec '73 file, Box BCH Corres. (9).

23 Ibid.: Gordon Luce to Banowsky, Aug. 7, 1974, LA Times articles responses file, Box BPO L-O (43); and LAT: Kenneth Reich, "Party Must Admit Nixon Was a Threat, GOP Official Says," Nov. 14, 1974, C1.

24 WSB: Senate Survey, Los Angeles and Orange Counties, 2nd Quarter, 1973, Operation Sunup file, Box BPO L-O (43).

25 Ibid.: Banowsky to Swain, June 1, 1973, Corres. Apr-June '73 file, Box BCH Corres. (9).

26 Ibid.: Rickard to Banowsky, July 23, 1973, R '73 file, Box B6 PR-SA (28).

27 YOUNG: Young to Young, Feb. 27, 1974, MNY-WSB file, Box 56.

28 WSB: Banowsky to David Reagan, Nov. 19, 1973, Correspondence Oct-Dec 1973 file, Box BCH Corres. (9).

29 LAT: John Dreyfuss, "Banowsky: He's a Man at the Crossroads," Feb. 18, 1975, C1 & 6. Dreyfuss analyzes Banowsky's internal struggle between the sacred and the secular and winning and losing. Although some friends thought the article was negative, readers like Rabbi Magnin found it as an opportunity to speak favorably of Pepperdine's president. See WSB: Letters to the Editor, Feb. 18, 1975, B1; Jack Eiden to Letters to the Editor, Feb. 19, 1975, and Helen Pepperdine to Banowsky, Feb. 24, 1975, L.A. Times Article file, Box BPO F-L (38 A&B). That a possible political career in Texas was a factor is made clear in YOUNG: Young to Banowsky, Aug. 23, 1973, MNY-WSB file, Box 56.

30 HAWP: [White], [Journal entry for] Feb. 13, 1974, Church Relations-Major Issues, Feb. 1974 file, Box xx1.

31 YOUNG: Young to Banowsky, Apr. 13, 1972, MNY-WSB file, Box 56.

32 HAWP: Typewritten note titled "Handwritten note from WSB to MNY, Aug. 19. 1973"; [White], [Journal entry dated] Feb. 16, 1974, Church Relations-Major Issues, Feb. 1974, Box xx1.

33 Ibid.

34 LAT: Dreyfuss, "Banowsky."

35 "200 Faces of the Future," *Time Magazine*, 103 (July 15, 1974).

36 In this conclusion, Devenney stood alongside some educational and women's groups (Pro-America). See WSB: Banowsky to J. D. Bales, Jan. 14, 1972,

Conservative file; and two letters from Dorothy Battersea to Banowsky, [1972], Dorothy Battersea letters file, Box 3 A-Con (8).

37 HAWP: Denny Walsh, "Report Criticizes Pepperdine Aids," *Sacramento Bee*, June 16, 1975, 1, clipping in Newspaper & Magazine articles file, Box 28.

38 LAT: Cliff Tarpy, "Banowsky Rules Out Bid For Senate," May 15, 1975, A1; WSB: "Banowsky Forgets Senate," *Sacramento Bee*, May 17, 1975, clipping, in Banowsky Won't See Senate file, Box 3 A-Con (2); IV: Frank Bies, "University Awards Banowsky Contract," May 23, 1975, 3; BOT: Jan. 17, 1976, vol. 9, p. 1.

39 LAT: Richard Bergholz, "Longtime Reagan Backers Join Ford," July 10, 1975, A1; and Banowsky, *Malibu Miracle*, 105. Banowsky erroneously dates this event as May 10. It is not clear whether the Ford administration offered the undersecretary position to Banowsky as quid pro quo for his endorsement, but the chronology supports that conclusion.

40 Editorial, "Mr. Hathaway Resigns," *New York Times*, July 26, 1975, 22; Ben A. Franklin, "Hathaway Resigns as Secretary for Reasons of Health, and President Accepts," *New York Times*, July 26, 1975, 10. LAT: Gaylord Shaw, "Banowsky: Why Nomination for U.S. Post Didn't Come Off," July 29, 1975, B6. The Pepperdine University board of trustees had granted Banowsky a year's leave of absence from Sept. 1, 1975 to Sept. 1, 1976. See YOUNG: Don Miller to Friends of Pepperdine University, Aug. 1975, MNY-WSB file, Box 56.

41 GRAPHIC: "Banowsky Denies Accepting Post," July 25, 1975, 3; WSB: Banowsky to Carl Gregory, Aug. 27, 1975, Interior Dept. Appointment file, Box BPO F-L (38A&B).

42 HAWP: [White], [Journal entry for] July 26, 1975, Church Relations-Major Issues, July 1975 file, Box xx1.

43 WSB: Horace Busby to Banowsky, July 28, 1975, attached to Banowsky to Buzz, Aug. 1, 1975, Horace N. Busby file, Box 3 A-Con (8).

44 Banowsky, *Malibu Miracle*, 323. See also GRAPHIC: Lee Ann Park, "Ford encourages Support of Independent Education," Sept. 26, 1975, 1.

45 WSB: Dave Reagan to Bill, Aug. 23, 1975, and Banowsky to Dave, Sept. 3, 1975, David Reagan file, Box B6 PR-SA (28); and GRAPHIC: "Banowsky Resigns Party Post," Nov. 7, 1975, 1.

46 WSB: Banowsky to Wally Arno, Jan. 19, 1976, Wally Arno file, Box 3 A-Con (2).

47 Ibid.: Dick Cheney to Banowsky, July 24, 1976, Bohemian Grove 75–76 file, Box 2 A-C (26).

48 Ibid.: John Marin to Jerry Brown, Oct. 10, 1975, Gerald Ford file, Box BPO F-L (38 A&B).

49 HAWP: Banowsky to Lloyd Nelson, Aug. 16, 1978, Banowsky '78 file, Box 32; GRAPHIC: "Banowsky Reviews Past and Present," Sept. 14, 1978, 5.

50 LAT: Marshall Berges, "Home Q & A, Gay and William Banowsky," Home Magazine, June 4, 1978, 48. See also YOUNG: Pros and cons on move to Oklahoma, July 1978, MNY: private memos file, Box 2.

51 HAWP: Banowsky to Scaife, Aug. 17, 1978, Banowsky '78 file, Box 32. Banowsky never claimed to be born in Oklahoma, but he liked to say he was conceived there.

CHAPTER 31

1 HAWP: Trent Devenney to Dr. Young, May 22, 1961, attached memo to President Banowsky from Hugh Mingle, Sept. 7, 1973; Application for Admission, Jun 7, 1961; Devenney to Gentlemen, June 1, 1961, Trent Devenney Misc. file, Box 56.

2 Ibid.

3 Ibid.: [Trent Devenney], Pepperdine Project, Preliminary Report No. 1, R/D No. 2, Jan. 20, 1973, Jerry Hudson file, Box 31; Devenney to Ben McMichael, Apr. 20, 1973, A.G. Invest. (Misc.) file, Box 28. In typing Banowsky as a moderate,

Devenney was probably correct. Certainly that was how Banowsky typed himself. See WSB: Banowsky to Jim Bevis and Rex Vermillion, Mar. 4, 1969, Misc. U-V
file, Box 7/3 A-Z (19A&B).

4   WSB: Banowsky to Ron Phillips, Jan. 24, 1973, and Patricia Mount to Doyle T.
    Swain, Mar. 14, 1973, Letters Sent, Jan.-Mar. '73 file, Box BCH Corres. (9).

5   GRAPHIC: Neva Hash, "Pepperdine Critics Exposed," Mar. 21, 1975, 1; and HAWP:
    Doyle to Mrs. Seaver, Oct. 24, 1973, Trent Devenney Misc. file, Box 56.

6   HAWP: Banowsky to Young, Apr. 4, 1975, A.G. Invest. (Misc.) file, Box 56.

7   Ibid.

8   Ibid.: [Doyle Swain], "The Odyssey of Pepperdine University," R/D No. 2, Mar.
    19, 1973, p. 1–10, in Odyssey of Pepperdine file, Box 56. For substantiation of
    authorship, see Ibid.: Devenney to Dan McMichael, Apr. 20, 1973, attached to
    [Larry Hornbaker], SUMMARY FOR Jerene Appleby Harnish of Trent Devenney
    Activities, June 20, 1973, Mrs. Harnish file, Box 56.

9   Ibid. For the quotation, see p. 44.

10 Ibid.

11 Ibid. For the quotation, see p. 55.

12 See "Pepperdine ($) Christian (?) University (!), Peppergate, Watergate—Which
    $?!," *Contending For The Faith*, 4 (Dec. 1973); "Truth—Not Executive Privilege—Is
    the Issue," *Contending For The Faith*, 5 (Apr. 1974); "And Now For Archie W. Luper's
    52 Questions," *Contending For The Faith*, 5 (Nov. 1974); Dan Flournoy, "Pepperdine
    Versus Christian Education," *Contending For The Faith*, 6 (April 1975); and "Is
    Pepperdine Cutting Umbilical Cord With The Churches of Christ," *Contending
    For The Faith*, 7 (Mar. 1976) in HAWP: Contending For The Faith file, Box 57.

13 GRAPHIC: Hash, "Pepperdine Critics Exposed,"; and HAWP: Luper to Evelle
    Younger, Feb. 8, 1974, attached to Luper to Neva Hash, Apr. 7, 1975; Luper to Reuel
    Lemmons, Oct. 24, 1973, Archie Luper file, Box 56; and YOUNG: Devenney to
    Young, Sept. 14, 1973, and Luper to Young, Oct. 12, 1973, Devenney Affair #1 file,
    Box 64.

14 HAWP: Phyllis to Dr. Banowsky, May 17, 1973, Trent Devenney Misc. file, Box
    56; Devenney to Dan McMichael, Apr. 26, 1973, attached to [Larry Hornbaker],
    Summary for Jerene Appleby Harnish of Trent Devenney Activities, June 20,
    1973, Mrs. Harnish file, Box 56.

15 GRAPHIC: Hash, "Pepperdine Critics Exposed."

16 HAWP: Donations from R&R Four Slide Corp. and R & R Tool and Die Corp [Feb.
    1972], Gordon Del Faro File, Box 57 and Devenney to Dan McMichael, Apr. 20,
    1973, attached to [Larry Hornbaker], SUMMARY FOR Jerene Appleby Harnish of
    Trent Devenney Activities, June 20, 1973, Mrs. Harnish file, Box 56.

17 Ibid.: Helen Pepperdine to Trent, May 4, 1973; Devenney to Dan McMichael,
    Apr. 20, 1973, attached to [Larry Hornbaker], SUMMARY FOR Jerene Appleby
    Harnish of Trent Devenney Activities, June 20, 1973, Mrs. Harnish file, Box 28;
    and YOUNG: Helen Pepperdine to Young, Sept. 19, 1973, Devenney Affair #1, Box
    64.

18 HAWP: Trent to Mrs. Harnish, May 4, 1973; Wm. H.Wilson to Devenney, draft let-
    ter attached to Wilson to Banowsky, July 11, 1973.

19 YOUNG: Doyle to Mrs. Seaver, Oct. 24, 1973, Trent Devenney Misc. file; Devenney
    to Mrs. Seaver, Oct. 30, 1973, Trent Devenney file; Note appended to Banowsky
    to Young, Oct. 30, 1973, Devenney/Tapper Rept. File, Box 56; Devenney to Mrs.
    Seaver, Sept. 12, 1973, Devenney Affair #1 file, Box 64.

20 HAWP: Doyle Swain to Richard Larry, Feb. 22, 1973; Devenney to Larry, Mar. 2,
    1973; Devenney to Dan McMichael, Apr. 25, 1973, Apr. 26, 1973, May 1, 1973, and
    May 11, 1973, all attached to [Larry Hornbaker], SUMMARY FOR Jerene Appleby
    Harnish of Trent Devenney Activities, June 20, 1973, Mrs. Harnish file, Box 28.

21 WSB: Banowsky to Jimmy Lovell, May 25, 1973, Corres. Apr.-June '73 file, Box BCH Corres. (9).

22 YOUNG: Banowsky to Swain, July 13, 1973, Corres. July-Sept. '73 file; Mrs. Doyle Swain to Banowsky, Nov. 1, 1973, and Richard King to Swain, May 25, 1973, Devenney Affair #1 file; and King to Swain, June 27, 1973, Banowsky to Young, Sept. 20, 1973, Young to Banowsky, July 30, 1973, and Banowsky to Young and White, Nov. 15, 1973, Devenney Affair #2 file, Box 64.

23 Ibid.: Devenney to Young, Apr. 30, 1973, Devenney Affair #1 file, Box 64.

24 HAWP: Devenney to Mr. and Mrs. W.B. Camp, Feb. 2, 1976, attached to Devenney to Richard M. Scaife, Feb. 3, 1976; Devenney to Mrs. Helen Young, Apr. 25, 1973; Devenney to Norvel Young, Apr. 30, 1973; Leonard Castro to Devenney, May 7, 1973, Trent Devenney file, Box 56.

25 WSB: Larry Hornbaker to Lawrence R. Tapper, Nov. 7, 1973, #63, file 1, Box 3, Series 3.

26 HAWP: Larry Hornbaker to Lawrence Tapper, Nov. 6, 1972, Attorney General file, Box 57; Hornbaker to John Fiscus, July 31, 1973, A.G. Invest. (Misc.) file, Box 56.

27 Ibid.: "Pepperdine University—Investigation," n.d., attached to Lawrence R. Tapper to Leonard E. Castro, Apr. 4, 1974, Attorney General's Preliminary Report file, Box 56.

28 JLP: Young to Lovell, July 22, 1974, #40, file 1, Box 3.

29 Although the supporting document has been misplaced, the university was at pains to shred all copies of the preliminary report but three—one each for the two law firms and one for the university. That action may have delayed the *Sacramento Bee* report for as long as it did.

30 YOUNG: Musick, Peeler & Garrett, et al., to Lawrence R. Tapper, May 29, 1974, Devenney/Tapper Rept. File, Box 56.

31 Ibid. Subsequently, in *Malibu Miracle,* p. 73, Banowsky would argue that George Evans was the unsung hero in the sequence of events that brought Pepperdine to Malibu.

32 Ibid. See also YOUNG: Young to Banowsky, Oct. 17, 1968, Ex. Comp. file, Box 64.

33 Ibid. See also YOUNG: Young to Banowsky, Dec. 3, 1974, Vista del Malibu file, Box 64. Young paid Banowsky nearly $40,000 for his interest. As early as September 1972, Banowsky had told Rawn that he wanted out of the "Malibu Partnership," having at that point invested $31,800. See WSB: Banowsky to Rawn, Sept. 11, 1972, Corres. Sept.-Oct. '72 file, Box BCH Corr. (9).

34 HAWP: Arthur Tapper to James M. Cowley, Mar. 25, 1975, Latham & Watkins file, Box 57.

35 LAT: "Norris Raps Younger on 3 Investigation," Aug. 21, 1974, A10; and HAWP: Banowsky to Young, Aug. 27, 1974, Norvel Young '74-'78 file, Box 33; and Associated Press Statement, Oct. 22, 1974, Publicity file, Box 28.

36 YOUNG: Copies of both documents are attached to Banowsky to Board of Trustees, Oct. 30, 1974, Devenney/Tapper Rept. file, Box 56; and HAWP: Donald V. Miller to Editor, Mar. 20, 1975, Sacramento Bee file, Box 56.

37 For materials regarding this audit, see Ibid.: Box 56.

38 HAWP: [White,] [Journal entry for] Feb. 21, 1974, Church Relations-Special Issues, Feb. 1974 file, Box xx1. Of Banowsky's presentation, White wrote, "if I am capable of seeing the truth, he did not tell it in this meeting."

39 Ibid., Jan. 18, 1974; Denny Walsh, "Pepperdine Prexy's Fund," *Sacramento Bee,* Mar. 12, 1975, A1 & 10, in HAWP: Sacramento Bee file, Box 56.

40 Ibid.; and GRAPHIC: "What else did the investigation find?" Mar. 21, 1975, 1.

41 "Younger Probing Pepperdine, Chief," *San Francisco Examiner,* Oct. 22, 1974, and "Pepperdine Probed—for Something," *San Francisco Chronicle,* Oct. 23, 1974, clipping in HAWP: Publicity file, Box 28.

42 Ibid.: and LAT: Richard Bergholz, "Younger Knew of Possible Bank Scandal—Norris," Oct. 5, 1974, B1, attached to Banowsky to Young, Oct. 5, 1974, A.G. Invest. (Misc.) file.

43 LAT: John Dreyfuss, "Secret Fund Paid $247,100 to Top Pepperdine Officials," Mar. 13, 1975, A27; and IV: Leon Parker, "Top University officials Receive Secret Bonuses," Mar. 14, 1975, 3; and GRAPHIC: Editorial, "Yesterday's News," Mar. 14, 1975, 6.

44 "A Salary by Any Other Name," *The Chronicle of Higher Education*, Mar. 31, 1975, 6.

45 GRAPHIC: Mark Harvis, "Pep Investigation Brings Changes," June 25, 1976, 4.

46 Ibid.: Larry Marscheck, "Profs Confront Banowsky Today," Mar. 21, 1975, 1.

47 HAWP: Donald J. Miller to The Faculty and Staff of Pepperdine University, Mar. 18, 1975, Sacramento Bee file, Box 56; Faculty Association, Los Angeles AAUP chapter telegram to Donald Miller, Apr. 2, 1975.

48 Ibid.: A Concerned Faculty Member to Reverend Banowsky, Mar. 17, 1975, Sacramento Bee file, Box 56.

49 Ibid.: Mitchell to Banowsky, Mar. 21, 1975, F-M file, Drawer 2, File Cabinet 207A.

50 Ibid.: A Concerned Pepperdine Student to Banowsky, [Mar. 1975], Sacramento Bee file, Box 56.

51 HAWP: Luper to Young, Mar. 13, 1975, attached to Luper to Neva Hash, Apr. 7, 1975; and Ira Y. Rice, Jr., "Truth—Not Executive Privilege—Is the Issue," *Contending for the Faith*, 5 (Apr. 1974): 1 in Archie Luper file, Box 56.

52 GRAPHIC: Hash, "Pepperdine Critics Exposed." For Banowsky's handwritten notes see HAWP: Graphic file, Box 56.

53 HAWP: Donald J. Miller to The Faculty and Staff of Pepperdine University, Mar. 18, 1975, Sacramento Bee file, Box 56.

54 YOUNG: [Don Miller] to Editor, Mar. 20, 1975, Devenney/Tapper Report file, Box 56.

55 HAWP: Carl Mitchell to Banowsky, Mar. 21, 1975, and [White], [Journal entry for] Mar. 22, 1975, Church Relations-Major Issues, March 1975 file, Box xx1.

56 WSB: Donald V. Miller to The Editor, "Pepperdine Replies," *Fresno Bee*, Apr. 7, 1975, clipping in Banowsky Won't Seek Senate file, Box 3 A-Con (8).

57 HAWP: Denny Walsh, "Report Criticizes Pepperdine Aids," *Sacramento Bee*, June 16, 1975, 1, clipping in Newspaper & Magazine articles, file, Box 57.

58 LAT: William Trombley, "Pepperdine U. Torn by Tragedy, Internal Dissent," Apr. 18, 1976, Part II, 4.

59 Conversation with Bill Banowsky, Pepperdine University, no date.

60 LAT: Trombley, "Pepperdine U. Torn" 4; and WSB: Banowsky to All Full-time Faculty and Staff, Mar. 25, 1976, S '76 file, Box 2.

61 LAT: Trombley, "Pepperdine U. Torn," 1–6.

62 HAWP: Banowsky to WilIliam Trombley, Apr. 21, 1976, and Banowsky to Fritz Huntsinger, Jr., May 5, 1976, Bill Trombley file, Box 57.

63 Ibid. See also YOUNG: Young to Banowsky, Oct. 17, 1968, Ex. Comp. file, Box 64.

64 YOUNG: Devenney to Rice, Feb. 25, 1975, Devenney/Taper Report file, Box 56.

CHAPTER 32

1 HAWP: Larry Hornbaker, "To Whom It May Concern," Nov. 18, 1975, Young, M. Norvel-car accident file, Box 60. For a look at the financial crisis as of mid-May 1975 see Ibid.: White to Banowsky, May 14, 1975, Personal Politics of Presidency, May 1975 file, Box xx2.

2 WSB: [Norvel Young], "To Whom It May Concern," [Nov. 1975], MNY Accident file, Box 39/44A.

3 Ibid.

4 M. Norvel Young, "Ordeal at Sunset," *Guideposts* (Aug. 1975): 16–19. High winds pulled the catamaran into the Pacific Ocean with Young clinging to one of the pontoons. Only with great struggle was he able to get on top of the pontoon and await rescue. He nearly drowned.

5 LAT: John Kendall, "Pepperdine's Young Given 1 Year, Stay of Sentence," Jan. 28, 1976, B24, c. 1.

6 WSB: Francis A. Sooy to Frank Morgan, July 2, 1974, #60, File 3, Box 3, Series 2. Banowsky, *Malibu Miracle*, 333–37, addresses Young's developing taste for alcohol, which Banowsky attributes to depression.

7 WSB: [Norvel Young], "To Whom It May Concern," [Nov. 1975], MNY Accident file, Box 39/44A. Young would tell a somewhat different story to student reporter Larry Marscheck. See "Alcohol, Stress and Traffic Accidents," *Oasis*, 11 (1976–1977): 44–47.

8 GRAPHIC: "Young faces charges," Sept. 19, 1975, 1; and WSB: Robert Marshall, Chancellor's Council release, Sept. 19, 1975, attached to Banowsky to Douglas Dalton, Sept. 24, 1975, Misc. Corres. File, Box 39/44A; and HAWP: Orman Day, "Car's Design Partly Blamed in Fatal Crash," *Santa Monica Evening Outlook*, Sept. 20, 1975, Misc-Young file, Box 27.

9 WSB: Helen Young to Banowsky, Nov. 28, 1975, Misc. Corres. File, Box 39/44A; and HAWP: [James Wilburn], Young-Opinion, Aug. 17, 1977, attached to Wilburn to Banowsky, Aug. 23, 1977, Young Misc. file, Box 27; and YOUNG: Young to Banowsky, Mar. 28, 1986, Jan.-Mar '86 binder, MNY Chron. files.

10 LAT: Grahame L. Jones, "Chancellor of Pepperdine Held After Car Crash," Sept. 17, 1975, D1; "College Official Faces Charges: Case Prepared in Car Accident That Killed 1," Sept. 20, 1975, A1; and WSB: Fritz and Nancy [Huntsinger] to Banowsky, Sept. 17, 1975, Misc. Corres. file, Box 39/44A.

11 WSB: John and Marge Menick to Dr. and Mrs. Young, Oct. 8, 1975, Misc. Corres. file, Box 39/44A.

12 YOUNG: Meador to Don Miller, Nov. 14, 1975, Methvin-Morningstar file, Box B28.

13 WSB: Autry to Whom It May Concern, Jan. 21, 1976, attached to Autry to Banowsky, Jan. 21, 1976, MNY Accident file, Box 39/44A. For other letters see WSB: Misc. Corres. file, Box 39/44A.

14 YOUNG: Pendleton to Mrs. Seaver, July 20, 1976, Morris Pendleton file, Box 47; and WSB: Mrs. Seaver to Banowsky, May 26, 1979, File 5, Box 4, Series 2.

15 WSB: Mrs. Fred Holloway to Bro. Banowsky, Sept. 24, 1975, Misc. Corres. file, Box 39/44A.

16 Ibid.: Sam Kline to Banowsky, Oct. 3, 1975, Misc. Corres. file, Box 39/44A.

17 BAIRD: Email from Archie Luper, Jr., Rockvale, TN, to author, Mar. 23, 2015, 1975–1976 file.

18 JLP: Miller to Lovell, Oct. 13, 1975, #46, file 1, Box 3. See also BOT: Oct. 10, 1975, 8:1–2. In *Malibu Miracle*, Banowsky mistakenly identifies the chair as Bob Jones in 1975 (p. 339). Jones would not serve in that capacity until the next year.

19 HAWP: Helen Young to Those Who Are Concerned, Oct. 31, 1975, Young, M. Norvel-car accident file, Box 60. See also LAT: Kathy Burke, "Chancellor of Pepperdine U. Pleads Guilty," Oct. 31, 1975, A3.

20 WSB: John T. McCarty to Richard M. Larry, Feb. 9, 1976, MNY Accident file, Box 39/44A. In Malibu Miracle, Banowsky remembers that there were three such sessions, all of which would have been most extraordinary in the justice process (p. 340–41).

21 LAT: Kendall, "Pepperdine's Young Given 1 Year, Stay of Sentence," Jan. 28, 1976, B26, c. 1.

22 See also WSB: Jerrold K. Footlick and Martin Kasindorf, "A Double Standard?" *Newsweek*, 87 (Feb. 23, 1976):49, in #38, File 3, Box 4, Series 9.

23 HAWP: Norvel to Helen Young, Nov. 10, 1974, M. Norvel Young file, Box 74. Young felt that his own ambition and ambivalence had disappointed his wife.

24 Ibid.: Handwritten notes on legal paper, [ca. 1973], MNY-WSB file, Box 56.

25 WSB: Jerrold K. Footlick and Martin Kasindorf, "A Double Standard?" *Newsweek*, 87 (Feb. 23, 1976):49, in #38, File 3, Box 4, Series 9; and HAWP: Judge Young, For Immediate Release, Jan. 27, 1976, Young Misc. file, Box 27.

26 Ibid. See also Stella Zadeh, "Pepperdine's Young Tells of Depression," *Santa Monica Evening Outlook*, Jan. 28, 1976, 2, clipping in HAWP: MNY 74–78 file, Box 33. See also LAT: Kendall, "Pepperdine's Young Given 1 Year," Jan. 28, 1976, B1.

27 LAT: Kendall, "Pepperdine's Young Given 1 Year," Jan. 28, 1976, B1.

28 LAT: Ben Bycel, "A Case of Real, if Unequal, Justice," Feb. 4, 1976, D5; Pearce Young, "Equal Justice Is Not Equal Sentencing," Feb. 10, 1976, C7.

29 WSB: Pendleton to Banowsky, et al., Feb. 18, 1976, MNY Accident file, Box 39/44A.

30 HAWP: News Release from the Court, July 28, 1976, Young, M. Norvel-car accident file, Box 60; and BOT: Sept. 14, 1976, 10:7–8, and Mar. 8, 1977, 10:12–13.

31 HAWP: Pike to Ernest Noble, Mar. 21, 1977, with transcript of hearing attached, Probation Report file, Box 56, Young Collection; [M. Norvel Young], "Proposed Research and Community Service Project on High-Effective Performers and their Proneness to Become Involved in Traffic Accidents, Submitted to the Honorable Judge Pearce Young," Jan. 10, 1976, Young, M. Norvel-car accident file, Box 60. See also Ibid.: [James Wilburn], Young-Opinion, Aug. 17, 1977, attached to Wilburn to Banowsky, Aug. 23, 1977, Young Misc. file, Box 27.

32 WSB: Thomas P. Pike to Banowsky, July 13, 1976, P file, Box 2; LAT: William Trombley, "Chancellor Youngs Pays His Penalty," May 9, 1976, B1.

33 HAWP: Carbon copy statement of Malibu Elders, [Dec. 14, 1975], M. Norvel Young '74-'78 file, Box 33.

34 WSB: See, for example, "Statement From Norvel Young, Malibu Elders," *Broadway Bulletin*, 32 (Jan. 18, 1976): 1–2, in MNY Accident file, Box 39/44A.

35 YOUNG: Box 93 is filled with letters of concern from Christians around the world. For an account of Young's redemption among Churches of Christ, see also Henegar & Rushford, *Forever Young*, chapter 13.

36 YOUNG: Childress to Young, May 26, 1976, Cheeves-Cushman file, Box B27.

37 WSB: Norvel Young, "To Our 20th Century Christian Family, " *20th Century Christian* (March 1976), page proofs attached to Jim Bill McInteer to *20th Century Christian* Staff, Feb. 13, 1976, MNY Accident file, Box 39/44A; and HAWP: Young to Nile [Yearwood], Feb. 18, 1976, Young, M. Norvel-car accident file, Box 60. Identical letters were also sent to other members of the board of trustees.

38 YOUNG: Pike to Ernest Noble, Mar. 21, 1977, with transcript attached, Probation Report file.

39 HAWP: Mike O'Neal to White, Mar. 5, 1980, MNY Personal Items-Apr. 1980 file, Box xx2.

40 WSB: Paul Harris to Phil Younces, Feb. 3, 1976, Y file, Box 6 BCH (20 ABC.

41 HAWP: Helen Dorris to Larry Hornbaker, May 23, 1983, Norvel Young-1982 to 85 file, Box 60.

42 Ibid.: [White], [Journal entry for] Sept. 18, 1975, Church Relations-Major Issues, Sept. 1975 file, Box x1; and handwritten notes dated June 25, 1976, Personal Politics of the Presidency, May 1976 file, Box xx2.

43 Ibid.: Young to Banowsky, Jan. 13, 1976, Young-Misc. file, Box 60.

44 "The Last Resort," n.d., http://www.learningfromlyrics.org/lastresort.html (Jan. 30, 2012); "The Last Resort by Eagles," n.d., http://www.songfacts.com/detail. php?id=3072 (Jan. 30, 2012).

45 According to one of the mythologizers, "This is a song about a girl from Providence, RI that went to college at Pepperdine University in Malibu, CA. [It is]

a Church of Christ school that is on the land donated by The [sic] Seaver Family and named for George Pepperdine founder of Western Auto Supply. They are the "Jesus People"[; t]he little boxes are the dorms and buildings all surrounding a giant cross on the hill. This girl was walking or riding a bike down PCH and was strruck [sic] and killed by the President of the school who was drunk. There's no drinking in the Church of Christ and the fancy Republican layers [sic] got him off without any charges. // Every year the mother of this girl spills red paint on PCH where her daughter was struck. [I]f you play this song on the campus radio station . . . you get expelled." See schools [sic], July 31, 2006, http://www.songmeanings.net/songs/view/4800/ (Jan. 30, 2012).

46 HAWP: Norman Hughes to Banowsky, Mar. 4, 1976, Ex, VP Corres., Feb. 14- Apr. 6, 1976, Box 6.

47 Ibid.: [James Wilburn], Young-Opinion, Aug. 17, 1977, attached to Wilburn to Banowsky, Aug. 23, 1977, Young Misc. file, Box 60.

CHAPTER 33

1 HAWP: Progress Report to the Western Association of Schools and Colleges, Apr. 1, 1976, Ex. VP Corres. Feb. 14-Apr. 6, '76 file, Box 6.

2 WSB: Bruce Bradberry to White, Nov. 7, 1975, attached to White to Banowsky, Nov. 19, 1975, Howard White '75 file, Box 1 U-W (7).

3 Ibid.: White to Tegner, Nov. 13, 1975, Ex. VP Corres. Nov. 11-Dec. 31, '75 file, Box 5.

4 Ibid.: Bruce Bradberry to White, Nov. 7, 1975, attached to White to Banowsky, Nov. 19, 1975, Howard White '75 file, Box 1 U-W (7).

5 HAWP: White to David Reagan, Dec. 2, 1975, Ex. VP Corres. Nov. 11-Dec. 31, '75 file, Box 5.

6 WSB: Young to Banowsky, Mar. 29, 1976, Howard White file, Box 2 N-Z (40).

7 HAWP: White to Banowsky, Feb. 12, 1975, Ex. VP Corres. Jan. 2-Feb. 19, '75 file, Box 5.

8 Ibid.: White to Banowsky, Sept. 17, 1977, Banowsky '77 file, Box 32, and White to Banowsky, Sept. 7, 1977, Ex. VP Corres., Sept.-No. '77, Box 7; YOUNG: David Reagan to Young, [1975], Center for Int. Bus. File, Box 43.

9 YOUNG: "Strengthening the Foundation for Continued Successful Growth," May 7, 1976, attached to Banowsky to Young and White, May 14, 1976, McKinsey Report file, Box 46. See also Steve Gray, "Pep Management Study Gets Funds," *The Pepperdine News*, 10 (Mar. 1976), 1; and HAWP: Pepperdine Press Release, Apr. 17, 1973, John McCarty file, Box 39.

10 YOUNG: McKinsey & Company, Inc., "Strengthening the Foundation for Continued Successful Growth, Pepperdine University," May 3, 1976, McKinsey Report '76 file, Box 46; and HAWP: McKinsey Study file, Box 39.

11 YOUNG: McKinsey & Company, Inc., "Strengthening the Foundation for Continued Successful Growth, Pepperdine University," May 3, 1976, McKinsey Report '76 file, Box 46.

12 Ibid.: White to Banowsky, Apr. 18 and 23, 1976, McKinsey Report file, Box 46.

13 BOT: Mar. 11, 1976, 9:1.

14 HAWP: Handwritten notes, June 6, 1976, Personal Politics of the presidency, June 1976 file, Box xx2; and BAIRD: White to Bill, Oct. 19, 1989, 89–91 file.

15 WSB: White to Banowsky, Mar. 29, 1976, Howard White file, Box 2 N-Z (40).

16 BOT: June 8, 1976, 11:2–3.

17 HAWP: Richard Larry to Banowsky, May 13, 1976, McKinsey Study file, Box 39.

18 Ibid.: Richard Scaife to Banowsky, Aug. 26, 1976, Personal Politics of Presidency, Aug. 1976, Box xx2.

19 Ibid.: Banowsky to Bob Jones, May 28, 1976, McKinsey Study file, Box 39.

20 Ibid.

21 WSB: Goyne to Banowsky, Apr. 8, 1977, G file, Box 2 D-Grad (31).
22 HAWP: A Report on Organizational Changes Related to the Former Orange Center, Oct. 15, 1976, Ex. VP Corres. Sept. 1-Nov. 11, '76 file, Box 6.
23 Ibid.: White to Banowsky, Mar. 15, 1977, Ex. VP Corres. Jan.-Mar. '77 file, Box 7.
24 YOUNG: Banowsky to Mr./Mrs. Warren Dillard, May 19, 1975, Dacus-Dye file, Box B27.
25 HAWP: [White], Special Report on Student Accounts Receivable, Feb. 1, 1977, Ex. VP Corres. Jan.-Mar. '77 file, Box 7.
26 GRAPHIC: Keith Seldon, "$5 Million Tyler Fund Boosts Ecology Drive," Feb. 23, 1973, 1; and LAT: Sharon Fay Koch, "Checks and Cheer at Ecology Awards," Feb. 12, 1974, IV:2; and BAIRD: Bob Bales, "The Tyler Ecology Award," May 1997, in 1972–1973 file; press packet regarding the Tyler Ecology Award, [Feb. 1974], Tyler Award file, Box 6 SC-V (30); Jan Everett, "Tyler Ecology Award Becomes Southland's Most Prestigious," *Orange County Illustrated*, 13 (Jan. 1975): 59, in Tyler Ecology file.
27 The 1978 award winner was Russell Train, director of the Environmental Protection Agency. He arrived late to the reception being held in his honor at the Beverly Hills Wilshire Hotel because he had first stopped by the bank to see if his award check was valid. See BAIRD: Jody Jacobs, "Pepperdine Firing Line: It's a Gas," *Los Angeles Times*, Apr. 3, 1978, OC C2; and Bales, "The Tyler Ecology Award," May 1997, in 1972–1973 file.
28 WSB: Tim Pownall to Bob Thomas, Oct. 5, 1976, P '76 file, Box 1 M-V (2); and GRAPHIC: "Networks' Battle," Oct. 29, 1976, 1.
29 "Network Stars," *Pepperdine People*, 1 (Summer 1977): 33; and BAIRD: Wilburn, "Random Pepperdine Reminiscences, 1973–1982," Oct. 2010, 141, Graziadio file.
30 GRAPHIC: Karen Cotter, "Network Stars Draw 2100 People," Oct. 13, 1977, 1.
31 WSB: Hughes to Banowsky, Oct. 9, 1977, H file, Box 2 GR-K (36); and HAWP: Donald Finney to Brethren, May 5, 1980, Charles Runnels file, Box 47.
32 PUA: Benefiel to Hornbaker, Apr. 2, 1971, and Banowsky comments on J. Robert Fluor to Mrs. Lee Stanley Meeks, Nov. 28, 1972, Support Groups file, Box C02–5. J. Dan Benefiel had recommended an Associates Group to Larry Hornbaker as early as April 2, 1971.
33 WSB: Banowsky to Packard, Dec. 27, 1976, P file, Box 2.
34 Ibid.: Banowsky to John Stevens, Jan. 28, 1977, S file, Box 2-NZ (40).
35 BAIRD: Jim Wilburn, "Random Pepperdine Reminiscences, 1973–1982," Oct. 2010, 93–97, Graziadio file.
36 "The Founding Four Hundred," *Pepperdine People*, 1 (Sum. 1977): 2–5.
37 HAWP: Program, Box 34.
38 Dochuk, *From Bible Belt to Sun Belt*, 376–96.
39 GRAPHIC: Valerie Roberts, "Kick-Off Dinner Assembles Associates' Founding 400," Feb. 11, 1977, 1.
40 YOUNG: Mike O'Neal to Banowsky, Feb. 21, 1977, MNY-WSB file, Box 56.
41 BAIRD: Jim Wilburn, "Random Pepperdine Reminiscences," Graziadio file; and "Pepperdine Associates reach 600 membership," *Pepperdine People*, 1 (Summer 1977): 6–7; and GRAPHIC: Scott Grant, "Debate Triggers Faculty Proposal," Apr. 6, 1978, 1. The Seaver faculty protested that students and teachers were barred from the debate unless they paid to become Associates.
42 *Pepperdine People*, 1 (Summer 1977): 2–3.
43 HAWP: White to Dillard, Mar. 19, 1977, Jan.-Mar. '77 file, Box 7; and GRAPHIC: Diana Sol Tesz, "University Utilizes Management System," Oct. 8, 1977, 2; and HAWP: The System and the Schools of Pepperdine University, July 1977, Ex. VP Corres. July-Aug. '77 file, Box 7.

44 YOUNG: Banowsky to Pendleton, June 10, 1977, Morris Pendleton file, Box 47; and WSB: Pendleton to Banowsky, July 7, 1977, S file, Box 2 N-Z (40).

45 HAWP: White to Banowsky, Sept. 17, 1977, Ex. VP Corres. Sept.-Nov. '77 file, Box 7.

46 Ibid.: Banowsky to White, Jan. 11, 1978, Banowsky '78 file, Box 32.

47 WSB: Banowsky to Larry Craft, July 19, 1978, Larry Craft file, Box A-W (24). Howard White considered Craft "one of the most able and skilled professional persons in our entire organization" and it would be a "very severe blow" should he leave. See HAWP: White to Banowsky, Aug. 12, 1978, Larry Craft file, Box 24; White to Banowsky, Feb. 23, 1978, WSB-Various Personal Items-Feb. 1978 file, Box xx2. Craft held a bachelor's degree from Lincoln Memorial University and a doctorate in curriculum and instruction from the University of Kentucky.

48 WSB: Craft to Banowsky, July 21, 1978, Larry Craft file, Box 4 A-W (24).

CHAPTER 34

1 GRAPHIC: Donald Risolo, "Faculty Contemplates Unionization," Oct. 15, 1976, 1; Fred Casmir, "Unionization Unavoidable," Nov. 5, 1976, 6.

2 BAIRD: Banowsky to Baird, May 19, 2012, Banowsky-Baird Corres.

3 HAWP: White to Young, Feb. 16, 1971, Norvel Young '69-'71 file; and NICKS: Cora Sue Harris to AAUP, Nov. 1, 1972, AAUP file, Box 11; and "AAUP Election Results," Seaver College Faculty Newsletter, 1 (Apr. 6, 1976, 1, in Faculty Newsletter file, File Cabinet 20 &A, Drawer 2.

4 NICKS: Cora Sue Harris to all AAUP members, Mar. 29, 1973, AAUP file, Box 11.

5 Ibid.: Minutes of AAUP meeting, July 18, 1974 and Ola Barnett to AAUP members, June 25, 1974.

6 Ibid.: Barnett, Government of Colleges & University, AAUP, 1971, and Seaver College AAUP chapter to Full Time Faculty Members, Mar. 17, 1976.

7 YOUNG: McCommas to Norvel Young, May 10, 1973, Fine Arts file, Box 45.

8 SRP: Recommendations of the Salary Scale Committee, [Dec. 1972], attached to White to Banowsky, Jan. 3, 1973, Faculty Salaries file, Box 4.

9 WSB: White to Banowsky, Oct. 27, 1975, and Ola Barnett to Banowsky, Oct. 29, 1975, N.O.W. file, Box 4 A-W (24); Mrs. Arthur Hughes to Banowsky, Nov. 10; and Banowsky to Mrs. Hughes, Banowsky to Beverly Stauffer, and Banowsky to Blanche Seaver, Nov. 17, 1975, Equal Rights Amendment file, Box 7/3 A-B (19 A&B); and telephone conversation with Charles Runnels, Apr. 2, 2015.

10 WSB: Barnett to Banowsky, Oct. 23, 1975, B '75 file, Box 1 A-C Corres. (46), and White to Banowsky, Oct. 27, 1975 and Barnett to Banowsky, Oct. 29, 1975, NOW file, Box 4 A-W (24); and SRP: OIE, "Enrollment and Faculty Profile for the Oxnard Conference," Oct. 15, 1979, Box 4; and GRAPHIC: Chris Parker, "Hughes Named Assistant Dean," June 28, 1974, 1; Valerie Roberts, "Pep Women Speak Up," Oct. 24, 1975, 1. Mrs. Pepperdine did not like Hughes either, but not because he was a man but because he wore a beard.

11 WSB: Banowsky to Hudson, May 26, 1972, Chron. Mar-May '72 file, Box 6 BCH (20 ABC).

12 Ibid.: Yelder to Donald Miller, et al., Oct. 28, 1975, Yelder to Banowsky, Nov. 4, 1975, and White to Banowsky, Nov. 12, 1975, Y '75 file, Box 39/44A.

13 Ibid.: Banowsky to Floyd L. Pierce, June 1973, Corres. Apr.-June 1973 file, Box BCH (9).

14 HAWP: White to Banowsky, Oct. 24, 1975, Ex. VP Corres. Aug.-Sept. '75 file, Box 5; and WSB: Ola Barnett to White, Oct. 23, 1975, B '75 file, Box 1 A-C Corres. (46); White to Banowsky, Oct. 24, 1975, attached to White to Banowsky, Nov. 20, 1975, Howard White '75 file, Box 1 U-W (7); Josephine Yelder to Donald Miller et al., Oct. 28, 1975, and Yelder to Banowsky, Nov. 4, 1975, both attached to White to Banowsky, Nov. 12, 1975, Y '75 file, Box 39/44A.

15 Ibid.: White to Banowsky, Nov. 12, 1975, Y '75 file, Box 39/44A.

16 Ibid.; White to Banowsky, Nov. 20, 1975, Howard White '75 file, Box 1 U-W (7). In 1978, then President White gave instructions to all academic deans not to enter into a contract with the federal government for more than $50,000 "because it would require the adoption and administration of an Affirmative Action plan." They could apply for grants in any amount. See NICKS: White to All Academic Deans, July 7, 1978, Faculty Research Project file, Box 13.

17 SRP: Pepperdine University Policy of Non-discrimination and Program of Affirmative Action, Mar. 1976, attached to Banowsky to All Supervisors, Mar. 23, 1976, Affirmative Action file, Box 30.

18 HAWP: White to Affirmative Action Committee, Mar. 12, 1977, Ex. VP Corres. Jan.-Mar. '77, Box 7; White to Banowsky, Apr. 30, 1976, Ex. VP Corres. Apr. 6-May 16, 1976 file, Box 6.

19 Ibid.: White to Banowsky, May 5, 1976, Ex. VP Corres. Apr, 6-May 16, '76 file, Box 6.

20 Ibid.: Banowsky to Martin H. Gerry, Sept. 27, 1976, Ex. VP Corres. Sept. 1-Nov. 11, '76 file, Box 6.

21 Ibid.: "Pepperdine University Policy of Nondiscrimination and Program of Affirmative Action," attached to White to Banowsky, June 13, 1977, Banowsky '77 file, Box 32.

22 Ibid.: White to Bowers, Feb. 1, 1977, and White to All University Personnel, Feb. 18, 1977, Ex. VP Corres. Jan.-Mar. '77, Box 7.

23 Ibid.: FAC to Banowsky, July 17, 1973, Norvel Young '73 file, Box 33; and WSB: Loyd Frashier to Banowsky, Oct. 11, 1976, 1978 Filing file, Box 2-NZ (40); GRAPHIC: Doug Drigot, "Pep Board Ends Freeze, Grants Tenure to 7 Profs"; "Faculty Ask for Cut in Teaching-Unit Load," Mar. 19, 1976, 1.

24 SRP: Young to Banowsky, Jan. 14, 1974, Faculty Salaries file, Box 4; HAWP: Hughes to Banowsky, Feb. 19, 1975, Church Relations-Major Issues, Feb. 1975 file, Box xx1.

25 YOUNG: Among independently supported colleges, the conventional wisdom was that tuition should furnish no more than 2/3rds of the annual operating budget. See Report to Pepperdine Faculty, Mar. 2, 1972, Faculty file, Box 44.

26 YOUNG: Minutes, University Board, Mar. 30, 1976, PU Board file, Box 47.

27 HAWP: Young to White, Jan. 3, 197[1], M. Norvel Young '69-'71 file, and Young to White, June 30, 1972, M. Norvel Young '73 file, Box 33; WSB: White to Banowsky, Mar. 23, 1971, Howard A. White file, Box 39/44A; YOUNG: Proposal for Salary Increments, 1972–73, Faculty and Staff file, Box 83.

28 YOUNG: AAUP to Jerry Hudson, Jan. 9, 1973, Faculty file, Box 44, and Truman Clark to Wilburn, Mar. 27, 1973, Personnel-Misc. file, Box 47. See also IV: Arline Ubry, "No Faculty Raise Next Year," Mar. 30, 1973, 3; Vikki Brown, "No New Tenure for Two Years," June 8, 1973, 3; Carol Clark, "Dr. Clark Resigns as Faculty President," Sept. 28, 1973, 3; Leon Parker, "Faculty Submits Salary Proposals," Mar. 16, 1973, 3; and GRAPHIC: Greg Kirkorian, "Controversy Sparks Tenure Moratorium," June 15, 1973, 1. Howard White supported the moratorium on tenure as a way of economizing. See HAWP: White to Banowsky, Mar. 9, 1973, and Banowsky to White, Mar. 16, 1973, Memos between Banowsky and White, 1973 file, Box 4.

29 WSB: Banowsky to White, Nov. 21, 1972, Corres. Nov.-Dec. '72 file; SRP: Don Miller to Faulty, May 25, 1973, attached to White to Perrin, June 18, 1973, Tenure Policy & History file, Box 2.

30 HAWP: Ken Perrin to White, June 11, 1973, attached to ibid; White to Young, Oct. 9, 1973, Norvel Young '73 file, Box 33. See also BOT: Mar. 11, 1976, 9:19; and GRAPHIC: Drigot, "Pep Board Ends Freeze," Mar. 19, 1976, 1.

31 BOT: Dec. 13, 1973, 9: exhibit 3; and Pepperdine University, *Faculty Handbook, Malibu Campus*, Sept. 1974, 5ff.

32 Ibid.

33 PO: Ola Barnett to RT & P, et al., June 13, 1978, Tenure/Policies/1978 file, Tenure Summaries; and BOT: Aug. 2, 1975, vol. 8:4.

34 WSB: Board of Trustees, Aug. 3, 1974 file, Box BOTrustees (13A); and BOT: Aug. 2, 1975, 8:4; and GRAPHIC: Doug Drigot, "Pep Trustees Approve Stricter Tenure Policy," Oct. 3, 1975, 1; and HAWP: Academic Freedom and Tenure (Recommendations of the Administration), Aug 2, 1975, Academic Freedom & Tenure file, Box 15. See also PO: Tenure/Academic Freedom and Tenure Statement 1973 file, Tenure File, and "Academic Freedom and Tenure (Recommendation of the Administration)," attached to BOT: Aug. 2, 1975, Tenure/Policies/1975 file, Tenure Summaries.

35 Doug Drigot, "Tightening Up on Tenure," *Oasis* (1975–76): 16–20.

36 PO: Los Angeles campus College of Arts and Sciences Faculty Response to the Proposed University Academic Freedom and Tenure Statement, attached to James Wayland to Howard White, Dec. 8, 1975, and John Nicks to White, Oct. 24, 1975, Tenure/Policy/1975 file; Faculty Advisory Committee to Seaver College faculty, Apr. 5, 1977, attached to Loyd Frashier to Seaver College Faculty Organization, Apr. 5, 1977, and White to Banowsky, Oct. 31, 1977, Tenure/Policy/1977 file; and Ola Barnett to RT& P, June 13, 1978, Tenure/Policy/1978 file, Tenure Summaries.

37 HAWP: White to Nicks, Mar. 19, 1977, Ex. VP Corres. Jan.-Mar. '77, Box 7.

38 NICKS: Malibu AAUP to Jerry Hudson, Jan. 9, 1973, AAUP file, Box 13.

39 SRP: White to Banowsky, Mar. 13, 1973, Faculty Salaries file, Box 4.

40 YOUNG: Faculty Salary Committee to Banowsky, Sept. 26, 1973, Faculty file, Box 44; and GRAPHIC: Bob Eisberg, "Trustees Refuse Salary Increase," Oct. 12, 1973, 1; Bob Eisbert, "Salary Decision Assured," Oct. 26, 1973; John Ince, "Trustees Approve Faculty Pay Hike," Nov. 16, 1973, 1; and BOT: Oct. 8, 1973, 6:56. The AAUP chapter at Los Angeles argued strongly for salary increases as well, noting that tuition had gone up but not salaries. See SRP: AAUP at Los Angeles to Jim Wilburn, [Feb. 1973], attached to Gary Hart to Wilburn, Feb. 20, 1973, Faculty Salaries file, Box 4.

41 WSB: Banowsky to Young, Oct. 1, 1973, Corres. Oct.-Dec. 1973 file, Box BCH Corres. (9); Banowsky to White, Oct. 23, 1973, Howard White file, Box 39/44A.

42 BOT: Dec. 13, 1973, 6:61, 63, and exhibit #3; IV: Margarita Rodriquez, "Board Adopts New Policies," Jan. 11, 1974, 3.

43 GRAPHIC: Ince, "Trustees Approve"; YOUNG: Young to Banowsky, Nov. 19, 1974, Banowsky file, Box 42; Dave Reagan to Banowsky, Nov. 20, 1974, Center for IB file, Box 43.

44 HAWP: White to Banowsky, May 5, 1975, Ex. VP Corres. May-July 1975 file, Box 5.

45 YOUNG: Banowsky, "Statement to Malibu Faculty," [Fall 1974], Faculty file, Box 44.

46 JLP: Miller to Jimmy Lovell, Oct. 13, 1975, file 1, Box 3; and WSB: Loose files, Box BOTrustees (21). What raised Miller's hackles was the "inadvertent" capitalization as construction in process of some $1.7 million of charges relating to Malibu campus loans.

47 IV: "Editorial," Mar. 12, 1976, 10.

48 GRAPHIC: Neva Hash, "Cash-Flow Problems Cause Administrative Cutbacks, Nov. 21, 1975, 1; and YOUNG: Minutes, University Board, Nov. 20, 1975, PU Board file, Box 47; and WSB: Banowsky memorandum, Nov. 12, 1975, Trustee minutes Dec. 12, 1975 file, Box BOTrustees (16), and Banowsky to Hudson, Jan. 23, 1975, Jerry Hudson file, Box 1 G-I (10), and Banowsky to Hughes, Nov. 14, 1975, H 71–74 file; and BOT: Dec. 12, 1975, 9:20, and Mar. 11, 1976, 9:19.

49 WSB: Handwritten note on memo Sime to Warren Dillard, Nov. 17, 1975, W 1975 file, Box 39/44A.

50 Ibid.: Loose files, Box BOTrustees (21); and *Pepperdine University President's Report, 1975–76*, 19.

51 BOR: June 8, 1976, 9:7.

52 NICKS: Seaver College AAUP to Fulltime Faculty, Feb. 6, 1976 and Mar. 17, 1976, AAUP file, Box 11.

53 HAWP: White to Banowsky, Mar. 1, Ex. VP Corres. Feb. 14-Apr. 5, 1976 file, and Apr. 9 and 10, 1976, Ex. VP Corres. Apr. 6-May 16, 1976 file, Box 6.

54 LAT: Trombley, "Pepperdine U. Torn by Tragedy," Apr. 18, 1976, C4. The disparity had a long history. Three years earlier, Occidental paid its full, associate and assistant professors $22,400, $16,900, and $13,300 respectively. Pepperdine paid its full, associate and assistant professors $16,400, $13,900, and $11,200 respectively. See LAT: Trombley, "Faculty Salaries at UC Rank 42nd Nationally," May 7, 1973, part II, 1.

55 GRAPHIC: Jack Mulkey, "No Salary Raises for Pep Professors," Mar. 30, 1973, 1; "Faculty Salaries," 4.

56 HAWP: White to Hudson, Jan. 14, 1976, Ex. VP Corres. Jan.-Feb. 13, '76 file, Box 6.

57 Ibid.: [White], [Journal entry for] Feb. 21, 1974, Church Relations-Major Issues, Feb. 1974 file, Box xx1; and GRAPHIC: "Attorney General Drops Pep Investigation," Nov. 8, 1974, 1.

58 GRAPHIC: Larry Marshek, "Profs Confront Banowsky Today," Mar. 21, 1975, 1; Pat McConahay, "Faculty Communicates Problems to Banowsky," Mar. 28, 1975, 1; and HAWP: Denny Walsh, "Pepperdine Prexy's Fund," *Sacramento Bee*, Mar. 12, 1975, clipping in Church Relations-Major Issues, Mar. 1975 file, Box xx1; and LAT: John Dreyfuss, "Secret Fund Paid $247,100 to Top Pepperdine Officials," Mar. 13, 1975, A27.

59 GRAPHIC: "Symbolic Protest Called Responsible," Feb. 6, 1976, 1; and LAT: William Trombley, "Pepperdine U. Torn by Tragedy, Internal Dissent," Apr. 18, 1976, C1. See also PO: Ginger Terry, "Pepperdine Firm On Pay," *[Santa Monica] Evening Outlook*, Feb. 13, 1976, Tenure/Policies/1976 file, Subject matter materials.

60 GRAPHIC: "Symbolic Protest," Feb. 6, 1976, 1.

61 Ibid.: Doug Drigot, "Faculty Elected to Panel"; "A Necessary Approach," Mar. 12, 1976, 1 and 6; Donald Risola, "Faculty Contemplates Unionization," Oct. 15, 1976, 1.

62 WSB: Banowsky to Faculty and Staff, Mar. 17, 1975, President's Office Budget '75-'76 file, Box 4 A-W (24); and HAWP: White to Nicks and Sale, Feb. 25, 1976, Ex. VP Corres. Feb. 14-Apr. 6, 1976, Box 6; BOT: Mar. 14, 1975, 8:12.

63 HAWP: Faculty Salary Schedule, 1976–1977, Ex. VP Corres. Apr. 6-May 15, 1976 file, Box 6, and clipping enclosed in White to Banowsky, July 18, 1978, Banowsky '78 file, Box 32; Faculty Salary Schedule, 1976–1977, Ex. VP Corres. Apr. 6-May 15, 1976 file, Box 6; and WSB: Agenda book, Board of Regents, Dec. 14, 1976, Box BOTrustees (21).

64 GRAPHIC: Donald A. Risolo, "Administration, Faculty Reach Accord," Nov. 19, 1976, 1. The Seaver negotiating team included Ola Barnett, Royce Clark, Ken Perrin, Stephen Sale, and James Smythe. See also SRP: John Nicks to Faculty Advisory Committee, July 11, 1977, Dr. White 1977 file, Box 14.

65 BOR: Dec. 14, 1976, 10:4.

66 WSB: Runnels to Luther C. Anderson, Nov. 4, 1977, AAIPCU folder, Box 2 A-C (26).

CHAPTER 35

1 WSB: "'A Spirit of Place,' Inaugural Address of Dr. William S. Banowsky as Founding Chancellor of Pepperdine College at Malibu," May 23, 1970, Item #1, File 5, Box 4, Series 5.

2 Ibid.

3 Ibid.

4 SRP: Pepperdine ad in *La Miranda Herald American & Call-Enterprise*, Apr. 18, 1971, clipping in Affirm Statement file, Box 2.

5 A complete version of the statement is at *Pepperdine University Bulletin, Malibu Campus 1973–74 Catalog*, 36 (Feb. 1973), 151. This was one of the earliest published versions.

6 SRP: Banowsky to White et. al., Apr. 23, 1976, Affirm Statement file, Box 2; and WSB: White to Banowsky, Dec. 6, 1976, Howard White file, Box 2 N-Z (40); and *Pepperdine University Bulletin, Seaver College 1978–79 Catalog*, 41 (Feb. 1978), 261. For Burch's role, see Banowsky, *Malibu Miracle*, 214.

7 BAIRD: "'A Spirit of Purpose:' The Address of Dr. William S. Banowsky, President, Pepperdine University at the Dedication of Frank R. Seaver College, April 20, 1975," 1974–1975 file.

8 YOUNG: President's Message to Pepperdine Student Body, 1969, M. Norvel Young Talks file, Box 57, and M. Norvel Young, Thoughts on Directions for Pepperdine University, [July 1971], Goals and Objectives file, Box 45.

9 Ibid.: Jerry Hudson, Random Thoughts on the Future of Pepperdine, Apr. 17, 1972.

10 PULL: Pullias to Della C. Pack, Apr. 22, 1976, file 11, Box 2, Series 7.

11 YOUNG: E. V. Pullias to Banowsky, [Feb. 1977], Christian Emphasis at Pep. file, Box 68. Pullias held a considerably different position with regard to a church relationship when he was acting as dean in the 1940s and 1950s.

12 HAWP: Howard White, For Christian College Presidents' Meeting, Oct. 29, 1975, Ex. VP Corres. Aug.-Sept. '75 file, Box 5.

13 Ibid.: McKinsey & Company, Inc., "Strengthening the Foundation of Continues Successful Growth," May 3, 1976, Management Studies 1976 file, Box 24; and YOUNG: Richard Larry to Banowsky, Feb. 27, 1976, and Banowsky to Richard Larry, Apr. 5, 1976, McKensey Rept. '76 file, Box 46.

14 YOUNG: Banowsky to Dick [Richard Larry], Apr. 5, 1976, McKenzie Report '76 file, Box 46. Banowsky would use these same words in his article, "The Spiritual Mission of Pepperdine University," *Mission Magazine* (Sept. 1976): 51–52.

15 YOUNG: Robert Scott to Religious Standard's Committee and Steering Committee of Chancellor's Council, Feb. 7, 1977, MNY-WSB file, Box 56.

16 HAWP: White to Banowsky, Apr. 17, 1978 and White to Douglas Chong, May 3, 1978, Ex. VP Corres., Mar-May 1978 file, Box 7; White to Banowsky, Feb. 21, 1976, Ex. VP Corres. Feb. 14-Apr. 6 '76 file, Box 6. See also Ibid.: White to Participants in Systems Seminars, Jan. 3, 1978, Ex. VP Corres., Dec. '77-Feb. '78 file, Box 7; White to Mitchell, et. al., Aug 1, 1977, Ex. VP Corres. July-Aug. '77 file, Box 7; White to Mike O'Neal, July 18, 1978, Ex. VP Corres. June-July '78 file, Box 8.

17 FF: Carl Mitchell, "The Uniqueness of Pepperdine," 93, Oct. 12, 1976, 646. See also HAWP: Lovell to [Lemmons], et al., Jan. 9, 1976, Governing Board Records file, Box 25.

18 HAWP: Banowsky to Fred Wyatt, Apr. 6, 1972, Corres. Mar.-May '72 file, Box 6BCH (20 ABC).

19 Ibid.; and WSB: Minutes, Personnel Practices Committee, Aug. 30, 1975, Trustee Meeting Oct. 10, 1975 file, Box BOTrustees (16).

20 HAWP: Howard White, Confidential memo to the file, Mar. 14, 1975, Ex. VP Corres. Feb. 20-Apr. 30 '75 file, Box 5.

21 WSB: Jerry Hudson to Banowsky, Dec. 9, 1974, attached to Banowsky to Hudson, Dec. 17, 1974, Jerry Hudson file, Box 1 G-I (10).

22 YOUNG: Young to David Malone, June 18, 1974, attached to Floyd Lord to Malone, May 11, 1974, McPherson-Malouf file, Box B28.

23 NICKS: Hoover to Clark, Mar. 24, 1976 and Feb. 18, 1977, attached to Clark to Norman Hughes, Feb. 23, 1977, Seaver College Faculty file, Box 12.

24 WSB: Runnels to Banowsky, Apr. 2, 1970, Banowsky to Betty Glass, Apr. 6, 1970, and Banowsky to Sam Miller, June 3, 1970, Church in Malibu file, Box 4 A-W (24).

25 Steven S. Lemley, "Reflecting on Pepperdine's Past," *Currents* (Fall 2002): 7–9.

26 BOR: Minutes, Religious Standards Committee, Sept. 13, 1977, vol. 10:1; and HAWP: White to Banowsky, Sept. 5, 1977, Dr. Banowsky '77 file, and White to Banowsky, Feb. 28, 1978, Banowsky '78 file, Box 32; White to Brethren, Mar. 19, 1977, Ex. VP Corres. Jan-Mar '77 file, Box 7; White to Bob Thomas, Apr. 28, 1978, and White to Banowsky, Apr. 28, 1978, Ex. VP Corres. Mar-May '78 file, Box 7; and GRAPHIC: Buck Fielding, "Bowman Duo Begins Campus Ministry," Sept. 28, 1977, 3; and BAIRD: emails from Rich Dawson to author, July 8, 2012, and Craig Bowman to author, June 17, 2013, 1977–78 file.

27 HAWP: White to Crawford, Sept. 14, 1982, Chron. Corres. Aug. 1982 file, Box 11; and BAIRD: email from Craig Bowman to author, June 17, 2013, 1977–78 file.

28 GRAPHIC: Morrie Goldman, "Campus Minister Aids Student after Inspiration," Nov. 3, 1983, A5; and BAIRD: email from David McMahon to author, May 22, 1013, 1977–1978 file; and HAWP: Education Sunday Announcements, Jan. 1986, Chron. Corres. Jan. 1986 file, Box 14. Bob Thomas, one of the elders of the University church, was the first to envision SHARE.

29 BAIRD: Silas Shotwell, "Reflections on My Year at Pepperdine, 1971–1972," June 15, 2013, 1971–72 file.

30 HAWP: White to Banowsky, Aug. 17, 1977, Dr. Banowsky '77 file, Box 31; Church Relations Budget, [Oct. 1977], Ex. VP Corres. Sept.-Nov. '77 file, Box 7; and GRAPHIC: Bruce Gilbert, "University, Church Communication Evaluated by Chancellor's Council," Sept. 26, 1975, 3.

31 HAWP: [White], [Journal entry for] April 23, 1978, WSB Various Personal Items-Apr. 1978 file, Box xx2.

32 Following one of Ira Rice's diatribes, church criticism was nationwide, from as far away as Connecticut and as near as California. A stack of critical letters are collected in YOUNG: Criticism of Pepperdine file, Box 64. See also Ibid.: Wm. Green to Young, Apr. 2, 1973, Personal, Misc. file, Box 47; as well as Banowsky to Young, June 7, 1972, Chron., June-Aug. '72 file, Box 6BCH (20A,B,C); and WSB: V. Glenn McCoy to Banowsky, May 25, 1973, A-Z file, Box 39/44A; Banowsky to Tracy Crosslin, Dec. 9, 1975, C '75 file, Box 1 C-E (15).

33 JLP: Jimmy Lovell to Helen Pepperdine, Oct. 11, 1972, Item 50; and YOUNG: George Watson to Young, Feb. 11, 1974, Waggoner-Welshimer file, Box B28; and HAWP: White to R. Phillips, Sept. 6, 1976, Ex. VP Corres. Sept. 1-Nov. 11 '76 file, Box 6; Otis Gatewood, "Editorial," *World-Wide Contact*, [1978], FC3/D1/F368/1978.

34 YOUNG: Don Williams to Banowsky, et al., Jan. 14, 1974, Tyler Ecology Fund file, Box 91.

35 HAWP: President Banowsky assured Mrs. Pepperdine that he reviewed all new appointments and that no "liberals" were being hired. See Banowsky to Helen Pepperdine, Feb. 9, 1972, Corres. Jan.-Feb. '72 file, Box 4. Presumed liberal faculty included James Atteberry, Larry Keene, Royce Clark, and Richard Hughes. Reuel Lemmons, editor and regent, came down hard on Clark, wanting him removed from the religion department. Banowsky defended him, however. See WSB: Lemmons to Robert P. Jones, Mar. 1, 1977, and Banowsky to Jones, Mar. 31, 1977, C '77 file, Box 2 A-C (26).

36 Founding board members of *Mission Magazine* were Bill Banowsky, Frank Pack, and Don Sime.

37 Conservative minister Yater Tant asserted that only two of Pepperdine's science teachers accepted the Genesis version of creation. See JLP: Tant to Jimmy Lovell, Feb. 4, 1972, Misc. file, Box 3.

38 Among these were Mrs. Pepperdine. See YOUNG: Areas of Concern from Helen Pepperdine, [Jan. 1972], Dean of Students Office file, Box 79.

39 Ira Rice, "Is there really going to be 'a new face' at Pepperdine?" *Contending for the Faith*, 3 (Apr. 1972), 1–8; Celia Chapman, "A 'Jesus Music Festival'— Pepperdine's First," ibid., 3 (May 1972), 8; Rice, "Is Pepperdine Cutting Umbilical Cord With The Churches of Christ?" ibid., 7 (Mar. 1976): 12–13.

40 YOUNG: Mayeux to Banowsky and Young, Apr. 27, 1975, Criticism of Pepperdine file, Box 83.

41 WSB: Schulze to Banowsky, Apr. 14, 1976, attached to Banowsky to Schulze, Apr. 20, 1976, S '76 file, Box 2.

42 YOUNG: Mary Alice Richards to Young, Aug. 11, 1975, Rafaedier-Ryskind file, Box B28.

43 HAWP: [White], [Journal entry for] October 27, 1976, MNY Personal Items-Oct. 1976 file, Box xx2.

44 YOUNG: Green to Young, Apr. 2, 1973, Personnel-Misc. file, Box 47.

45 Ibid.: Gary Duke memorandum, Feb. 27, 1975, and Petition to Banowsky, Feb. 28, 1975, Confidential '75 file, Box 83. Among those signing were Glenn Boyd, William N. Stivers, Fred Casmir, Morris Womack, Stewart Hudson, Larry McCommas, Wyatt Jones, Della Pack, Louise Thomas, Carl Mitchell, Tony Ash, Dorothy Moore, Stephen Sale, Arlie Hoover, James Smythe, and John McClung.

46 HAWP: Letters dated Mar. 9, 1977 and Mar. 14, 1977, Bost, Thomas (2 of 2) file, Box 64.

47 Ibid.

CHAPTER 36

1 WSB: Banowsky to David Reagan, Nov. 19, 1973, David Reagan file, Box B6 PR-SA (28).

2 William S. Banowsky, "The Spiritual Mission of Pepperdine University," *Mission Magazine*, (Sept. 1976): 51–54.

3 HAWP: [White], Meeting with Norvel, Jan. 12, 1974, and [White], Notes, Jan. 15, 1974, Church Relations-Major Items-Jan. '74 file, Box xx1.

4 Historian Norman Parks described all of this as being "caught in the toils of Caesar's law," in a famous article with the same title in *Integrity*, 8 (Mar. 1977), 115–18. In an ironic voice, he lamented that the "pursuit of mammon," that is, federal aid, had led college executives "to soft-pedal or even alter the basic propositions of their institutions." He had expressed similar concerns in an earlier article, "Heroin for Our Colleges," *Mission Magazine*, 6 (Feb. 1973): 227–34.

5 HAWP: White to Banowsky, July 28, 1977, and Sept. 24, 1977, Dr. Banowsky '77 file, Box 31, and White to Mitchell, et. al., Aug 1, 1977, Ex. VP Corres. July-Aug. '77 file, Box 7.

6 Ibid.

7 BOR: Banowsky to Ken Ross, Sept. 19, 1977, Ken Ross file.

8 YOUNG: Robert E. Scott to Religious Standards Committee and Steering Committee of Chancellor's Council, Feb. 7, 1977, MNY-WSB file, Box 56. See also NICKS: Robert E. Scott, News Release, May 20, 1975, Church Relations file, Box 13. For an early interim report see HAWP: "Prepared for the University/Church Liaison Task Force of the Chancellor's Council of Pepperdine University, by Robert E. Scott, Oct. 1974," Chan-Chap file, Box 20.

9 HAWP: David Malone to M. Norvel Young, Feb. 7, 1977, Chan-Chap file, Box 20.

10 Ibid.: [Robert Scott], "The Christian Emphasis of Pepperdine University," [Fall 1977], The Christian Emphasis of Pepperdine University file, Box 52.

11 Ibid.

12 WSB: White to Banowsky, Mar. 8, 1971, Howard White file, Box 39/44A; and White, confidential memo to the file, Mar. 14, 1975, Ex. VP Corres. Feb. 20-Apr. 30, '75 file, Box 5.

13 Ibid.: Banowsky to Young, Nov. 7, 1973, Corres. Oct.-Dec. 1973 file, Box BCH Corres. (9).

14 HAWP: [White], [Journal entry for] May 18, 1974, Church Relations-Major Issues, May 1974 file, Box xx1.

15 WSB: Joseph Bentley to Robert Jones, Feb. 6, 1973, Bd. of Trustees, Aug. 4, 1974 file, Box BOTrustees (13A).

16 Ibid.: M. Norvel Young, "Educators in a Secular Society," *World-Wide Contact*, [1978], FC3/D1/F368/1978.

17 BOT: Mar. 14, 1975, 8:2–13; and YOUNG: Banowsky, Handwritten comments on the draft of Sec. 6.6, dated Oct. 21, 1974, Employees file, Box 44. Banowsky's reservations about article 6.6 became clearer in 1976 when he reported outside income of $55,020, mostly from speaker fees but also from directors fees. By way of comparison, Charles Runnels reported $6,000, Don Sime reported $2,790, and Norvel Young reported $1,440. Young also reported investments with Trustee Robert Jones and stock in the Westlands Bank, with whom Pepperdine had substantial loans. See WSB: Lectures/Outside Income file, Box BOTrustees (21).

18 GRAPHIC: Scott Grant and Bill Johnson, "Banowsky Resigns; White Installed," Sept. 14, 1978, 1.

19 YOUNG: Minutes, University Board, Mar. 30, 1976, University Board Minutes file, Box 47; Confidential: WSB file, Box 56; and HAWP: By-Laws and Articles file, Box 31. For Larry Hornbaker's contribution see WSB: Banowsky to Hornbaker, Oct. 30, 1975, Amended Bylaws and articles file, Box BOTrustees (16).

20 BOT: Dec. 12, 1975, 9:3–5.

21 BAIRD: Helen Pepperdine to John [Katch], Mar. 19, 1975, 1975–1975 file.

22 Ibid.

23 BOT: Jan. 17, 1976, 9:5; and GRAPHIC: Steve Gray, "New Regents Chosen, Expansion Plan Begins," Mar. 5, 1976, 2; and William S. Banowsky, "The Spiritual Mission of Pepperdine University," *Mission Magazine* (Sept. 1976): 51–54; and SRP: Richard Seaver to Robert P. Jones, Apr. 13, 1976, S file, Box 25.

24 YOUNG: Banowsky to Norvel and Helen Young, Jan. 16, [1977], Confidential: WSB file, Box 56.

25 SRP: Banowsky to Richard Seaver, Oct. 6, 1976, S file, Box 25.

26 YOUNG: Norvel to Banowsky, Jan. [20, 1977], Confidential: WSB file, Box 56.

27 The change probably had to do with Jones's "arbitrary personality." See YOUNG: Mrs. William S. Banowsky to Lloyd Nelson, Apr. 7, 1977, D. Lloyd Nelson-Bd. of Trustees file, Box 41.

28 Ibid.: Banowsky to Nelson, Nov. 17, [1977].

29 Ibid.: D. Lloyd Nelson biography, [Mar. 1980], and Nelson to Banowsky, Mar. 16, 1978.

30 WSB: Banowsky to Jones, Feb. 10, 1978, Special Confidential file, Box BOTrustees (48).

31 Ibid.

32 Ibid.

33 BOT: June 13, 1978, 11: exhibit A. See WSB: also Tom Bost to Members of Board of Regents, May 26, 1978, Special Confidential file, Box BOTrustees (48).

34 HAWP: Bob Douglas to Sub-committee of the Religious Standards Committee, [Mar. 3, 1978], attached to Banowsky to Lloyd Nelson et al., Mar. 23, 1978, Ex. VP Corres. Mar.-May '78 file, Box 7.

35 Ibid.: Banowsky to Nelson et al., Mar. 23, 1978, Ex. VP Corres. Mar.-May 1978 file, Box 7.

36 Ibid.: White to Lemmons, Dec. 29, 1977, Ex. VP Corres. Dec. '77-Feb. '78 file, Box 7.

37 HAWP: [White], [Journal entry for] July 25, 1978, Church Relations-Major Issues, July 1978 file, Box xx1.

38 BAIRD: "Standards and Procedures for Faculty Selection," Dec. 11, 1979, attached to Minutes, Religious Standards Committee, Board of Regents, Dec. 11, 1979, vol. 1, in 1979–1980 file.

39 Ibid.

40 GRAPHIC: Grant and Johnson, "Banowsky Resigns," Nov. 7, 1978, 1. Just what he meant about "going into the courts" is unclear.

41 HAWP: Lovell to [Lemmons], et al., Jan. 9, 1976, Governing Board Records file, Box 25.

CHAPTER 37

1 HAWP: White Journal notes from Tower Hotel, London, Aug. 21, 1978, Journal file, Box xx2.

2 Ibid.; and PUA: Bob Gilliam and Kenneth Perrin to Lloyd Nelson, Aug. 15, 1978, Faculty Org., 1960–1969 (2 of 2) file; Rod Gaudin to Charles Runnels, Nov. 13, 1978, Ron Gaudin file, Box 29.

3 HAWP: White Journal notes from Tower Hotel, London, Aug. 21, 1978; Dick Scaife to James Wilburn, June 21, 1979, and Diary entry, Feb. 4, 1979 and Mar. 22 and 23, 1979, Box xx2.

4 Ibid.: White Journal notes from Tower Hotel, London, Aug. 21, 1978.

5 Ibid.: White note, Jan. 1, 1985, attached to Young to White, Dec. 24, 1984; Diary entry, June 6, 1984, Church Relations-Major Items file, Box xx1; White Journal entries, May 28, 1979 and Feb. 16, 1980; and Donald Collins to White, Aug. 7, 1984, MNY Personal Items-Aug. 1984 file, Box xx2.

6 Ibid.: White Journal entry, Oct. 15, 1981.

7 Bill Henegar, "A Gentleman and A Scholar," *Pepperdine People* (Summer 1991): 2–5; and HAWP: [Howard White], Outline of My Career, Feb. 8, 1985, Chron. Corres.-Feb. 1985 file, and White to Brethren, Feb. 16, 1986, Chron. Corres.-Feb. 1986 file, Box 14. White's dissertation was on the history of freedman's bureau in Louisiana, which, after additional research, he published as a monograph in 1970.

8 Bill Youngs, "Dr. Howard White, Executive Vice President," *Alumni Voice*, 36 (Winter 1973): 6–7; and Susan Gibbons Gillespie, "Dr. Howard A. White as Pepperdine's Fifth President," *Pepperdine People*, 2 (Winter 1979): 2–6.

9 HAWP: Program, Inaugural Convocation, Howard Ashley White . . . at Seaver College, Sept. 13, 1978, Howard A. White Inauguration file, Box 75; White to Herbert Luft, Sept. 16, 1978, Presidential Corres.-Sept.-Oct. 1978 file, Box 8; and White to Bill Henegar, Jan. 4, 1983, Chron. Corres.-Jan. 1982 file, Box 11.

10 Ibid.: Inaugural Speech of Dr. Howard Ashley White, Sept. 13, 1978, Howard A. White Inauguration file, Box 75. White made similar points in an address to the University Board a few days earlier. See PUA: Transition at Pepperdine University, Sept. 5, 1978, attached to Minutes, Pepperdine University Board, Sept. 5, 1978, Univ. Board. Minutes (1978–84) file, Box C05.

11 HAWP: Inaugural Speech, Sept. 13, 1978, Howard A. White Inauguration file, Box 75.

12 Ibid.: [White], Notes, July 1, 1976 entry; Journal entry, Apr. 23, 1978, Box xx2.

13 BOR: White to Ken Ross, Mar. 30, 1982, Ken Ross file.

14 HAWP: White to Tom Bost, Oct. 18, 1980, Tom Bost, 75–80 file, Box 32, and [Howard White], The Mission of Pepperdine University for Faculty Meeting, Nov. 25, 1980, Mission Statement file, Box 39. The reference to raising salaries and hanging the dean is attributed to Jacque Barzun.

15 Ibid.: White to Bost, et al., May 21, 1980, Mission Statement file, Box 40; White to Bost, Aug. 18, 1981, Chron. Corres.-July-Aug. 1981 file, Box 10; and [Howard White],The Mission of Pepperdine University for Faculty Meeting, Nov. 25, 1980, Mission Statement file, Box 39.

16 Ibid.: "The Mission of Pepperdine University," adopted by the Board of Regents, Sept. 14, 1982, Mission Statement file.

17 Ibid.

18 BAIRD: [Howard White], Convocation [Address], Sept. 10, 1980, 1980–1981 file.

19 HAWP: White to Lloyd Nelson, Jan. 13, 1979, D. Lloyd Nelson file, Box 33, and Entry, White Journal, Mar. 22, 1979, and Feb. 4, 1980, and Bost to White, Sept. 3, 1982, Box xx2; Commentary on the Unique Character and Mission of Pepperdine University, attached to White to Distribution, June 1, 1982, Chron. Corres.-June 1982 file, Box 11. Both David Davenport and Jerry Rushford contributed to the position paper, but its language was reminiscent of speeches delivered or articles written in previous years by both Bill Banowsky and Howard White. In it White described the university's spiritual heritage, its emphasis upon a value-centered education, and "its commitment to the highest ideals of American free enterprise."

20 HAWP: "A Commentary on the Unique Character and Mission of Pepperdine University," July 28, 1982, attached to White to Bost, July 28, 1982, Tom Bost '81-'85 file, Box 32.

21 Ibid.

22 "Standards and Procedures for Faculty Selection," attached to Minutes, Religious Standards Committee, Board of Trustees, Dec. 11, 1979, Vol. 1, President's Office.

23 HAWP: White to Nicks, Oct. 17, 1978, Chron. Corres.-Sept.-Oct. 1978 file, Box 10; White to Bost, Oct. 18, 1980, Tom Bost, 75–80 file, Box 32; White to Davenport, Nov. 2, 1981, Chron. Corres.-Nov.-Dec. 1981 file, Box 11; White to Luft, Jan. 12, 1982, Chron. Corres.-Jan. 1982 file, Box 11; and SRP: Minutes, Religious Standards Committee Meeting, Sept. 11, 1979, attached to Ken Ross to Members of Committee, undated, Mike O'Neal Corres.-1978–1987 file, Box 14; and YOUNG: Mike O'Neal to Religious Standards Com., Dec. 4, 1979, Trustees-Misc. #2 file, Box 85; and NICKS: Nicks to White, Apr. 3, 1980, Chron. Corres.-Mar. 1 to Apr. 22, 1980 file, Box 3.

24 Draft of a chart regarding opportunities to hire Church of Christ faculty, 1976–1980, and draft of a chart comparing hiring statistics between 1976–1977 and 1980–1981, SRP: Studies/Profiles (Instit. Res.) file, Box 31.

25 NICKS: Nicks to White, Apr. 3, 1980, Chron. Corres.-Mar. 1 to Apr. 22, 1980 file, Box 3; Nicks to Nelson, Apr. 18, 1978, Chron. Corres.-Apr. 7, 1978 to May 31, 1978 file, Box 5; and SRP: Various statistical tabulations, 76–77 and 81–82, Studies/Profiles (Instit. Res.) file, Box 31; HAWP: Minutes, Religious Standards Committee, Religious Standards Com. file, Box 47; White to Hudson, May 15, 1983, Personal Politics of the Presidency, May 1983 file, Box xx2.

26 HAWP: White to Davenport, Mar. 27, 1986, Chron. Corres.-Mar.-Apr. '86 file, Box 14.

27 Ibid.: White to Luft, Feb. 11, 1981, and For the Executive Committee, Feb. 11, 1981, Chron. Corres.-Jan.-Feb. 1981 file, Box 10; White to Luft, Jan. 7, 1981, Presidential Corres.-Jan.-Feb. 1981 file, Box 8; and "News Briefs," *Pepperdine People*, 4 (Summer

1981): 22. White flew to Germany at the end of 1980 to offer the position to Luft. BAIRD: email message from Luft to author, Oct. 20, 2010, 1978–79 file.

28 HAWP: White to Luft, Jan. 7, 1981, Presidential Corres.-Jan-Feb. 1981 file, Box 8; White to Nicks, Jan. 16, 1982, Presidential Corres.-Jan-Feb. 1981 file, Box 8; and SRP: Notes from memory on discussions between Dr. White and Herbert Luft, Dec. 28-Jan. 1, 1980/81, Dr. White 1980–81 file, Box 14.

29 GRAPHIC: John Secia, "Nicks Steps Down; Luft Takes New Post," Jan. 29, 1981, A1.

30 Dan Caldwell to White, Jan. 30, 1981, Personal Papers, Dan Caldwell Materials, Malibu, CA.

31 GRAPHIC: John Selindh, "White Denies Faculty Power To Question His Decisions," Feb. 5, 1981, A1. See also HAWP: White to Jon Johnston, Feb. 9, 1981, Chron. Corres.-Jan.-Feb. 1981 file, Box 10.

32 GRAPHIC: John Secia, "Nicks Steps Down; Luft Takes New Post," Jan. 29, 1981, A1; and HAWP: White to Luft, Feb. 11 & 14, 1981, and Jon Johnston, Feb. 9, 1981, Chron. Corres.-Jan.-Feb. 1981 file, Box 10.

33 SRP: Various statistical tabulations, 76–77 and 81–82, Studies/Profiles (Instit. Res.) file, Box 31; OIE, Faculty Profile, 1982–83 file, Box 21.

34 HAWP: White to Collins, May 26, 1981, Chron. Corres.-May 1981 file, Box 10; Nov. 30, 1981, Chron. Corres.-Nov.-Dec. 1981 file, Box 11; and Aug. 2, 1982, Chron. Corres.-Aug 1982 file, Box 11.

35 SRP: Mayeux to Luft, Oct. 7, 1981, Herbert Luft file, Box 14.

36 Nancy Magnusson interview with author, June 15, 2012, Nashville.

37 NICKS: Dan Caldwell to Glenn Boyd, Nov. 30, 1979, Jan. 3, 1980, Nov. 19, 1980; Boyd to Caldwell, Jan. 8, 1980, Feb. 3, 1981; Caldwell to M. Norvel Young, Feb. 23, 1981, and Young to Caldwell, Mar. 23, 1981; Caldwell to White, Feb. 23, 1981, and White to Caldwell, Apr. 1, 1981, New YIE file, Box 11. The first non-Church of Christ faculty member to serve in Heidelberg was Professor of Political Science Chris Soper. For administrative reaction, see JWP: Wilson to Phillips, Aug. 30, 1995, 1995–1996 file, Box 2.

38 HAWP: Phillips to David Davenport, et al., Jan. 16, 1989, Bible School file, Box 18.

39 Ibid.: White to Davenport, Feb. 14, 1989.

40 Ibid.: White to Michael Adams, May 29, 1984, Chron. Corres.-May 1984 (2 of 2) file, Box 13.

41 Ibid.: White, "Administrative Responsibility and Academic Freedom," n.d., Speeches-misc. 1971–84 file, Box 74.

42 Ibid.: White to Kenton Anderson, Mar. 31, 1981, Chron. Corres.-Mar. 1982 file, Box 11. See also PO: Luft to Anderson, Feb. 6, 1982, Tenure Summary Materials.

43 JWP: Wilson to Phillips, Apr. 16, 1985, 1984–1985 file, Box 1.

44 Ibid.: Davenport to Wilson, May 7, 1985, attached.

45 Bill Henegar, "Golden Year of the Story of Weavers," *Pepperdine People* (Spring 1993): 6–8.

46 HAWP: "Activities in Pepperdine University related to members of churches of Christ," [1977–1978], Church Relation 1970–78 (2 of 2) file.

47 Ibid.: White to Rushford, May 14, 1986, Chron. Corres.-May '86 file, Box 14; and "Spiritual Feast, Spiritual Beginning," *Pepperdine People* [8](Fall 1985): 23–24.

48 HAWP: White to McGoldrick, Dec. 26, 1984. Chron. Corres.-Dec. 1984 (1 of 2) file, Box 13.

CHAPTER 38

1 PUA: Pepperdine University, Reaccreditation Report (Nov. 1978), 6, in Box B10 (44B).

2 NICKS: "Western Association of Schools and Colleges, Accreditation Review of Pepperdine University," 1979, 1–6 file, Box 17.

3 Ibid.
4 HAWP: Howard A. White to Herbert Luft, Nov. 8, 1982, Chron. Corres. Nov. 1982 file (1 of 2), Box 11.
5 NICKS: Pepperdine University, Western Association of Schools and Colleges, Accreditation Review (1979), 1–6 file, Box 17.
6 HAWP: Andersen to White, June 28, 1979, An file, Box 15.
7 Ibid.: [John D. Nicks, Jr.], "A Report to the Senior Commission of [WASC] from Pepperdine University," Dec. 1, 1980, WASC file, Box 59.
8 For a copy of the analyses see SRP: Phillips to White, Oct. 31, 1984, Strategic Planning #3 file, Box 29 and "A Report of the University-wide Academic Review Committee to the University's Strategic Planning Committee," attached to Davenport to All Faculty Members, May 3, 1985, Univ.-wide Academic Program Review file, Box 33, and Strategic Planning file. As an example of one school's strategic plan see HAWP: "A Strategic Plan for the School of Business and Management," May 5, 1984, SBM-Strategic Plan 1984–85 file, Box 52.
9 HAWP: White to Distribution, Jan. 3, 1978; White to All Pepperdine Staff, Feb. 7, 1878, Dr. White 1978 file, Box 14.
10 Ibid.: "Policy of Nondiscrimination and Program of Affirmative Action,' attached to White to Don Merrifield, July 12, 1980, attached to White to Tom Bost, July 23, 1989, Tom Bost 75–80 file, Box 32; White to Lewis Nobles, Nov. 10, 1981, Chron. Corres. Nov.-Dec. 1981 file, Box 11; White to Phillip Sirotkin, Mar. 4, 1981, Presidential Corres. Mar. 1981 file, Box 8; White to Alan Cranston, Apr. 21, 1984, Chron. Corres. Apr. 1984 (2 of 2) file, Box 13.
11 Ibid.: [John D. Nicks, Jr.], "A Report to the Senior Commission of [WASC] from Pepperdine University," Dec. 1, 1980, WASC file, Box 59.
12 Ibid.: White to Loyd Frashier, Apr. 27, 1981, Chron. Corres. Apr. 1981 file; White to Frashier, Aug. 20, 1981, Chron. Corres. July-Aug. 1981 file, Box 10; White to Luft, Jan. 7, 1981, Pres. Corres. Jan.-Feb. 1981 file, Box 8; White to Faculty Advisory Committee, June 30, 1982, Faculty Advisory Com. file, Box xx2; and SRP: Frashier to White, Apr. 13, 1981, and Paul Randolph to White, May 19, 1982, Faculty Advisory Committee file, Box 21.
13 BAIRD: *Pepperdine University, Self-Study Report* (July 1, 1982), 33.
14 Ibid., 34.
15 HAWP: White to Ronald Phillips, June 2, 1981, Chron. Corres., June 1981 file; White to Robert Dockson, Aug. 10, 1981, Chron. Corres. July-Aug. 1981 file, Box 10.
16 PO: Draft, Tenure Policy, July 1, 1980, Tenure/Policy/1981 (Developmental Process) file, Tenure Summary Material; and NICKS: Key Issues, 10/31/80, Tenure-Pepperdine Univ. 1979–1981 (2 of 2) file.
17 HAWP: White to Bost, May 18, 1982, Tom Bost 1981–85 (3 of 3) file, Box 64; White to O'Neal, May 18, 1981, Chron. Corres. May 1981 file, Box 10; White to Father Donald Merrifield, Oct. 7, 1983, Chron. Corres. Oct. 1983 (2 of 2) file, Box 12; and BOR: Minutes, Sept. 8, 1981, vol. 14:C-17ff; White to Ken Ross, Aug. 221, 1981, Ken Ross file. For a copy of the 1981 tenure policy see PO: Tenure /Policy/1981 file, Tenure Summaries Materials.
18 GRAPHIC: Jim Benson, "New Tenure Policy Wins Faculty Approval," Oct. 8, 1981, A3.
19 BOR: Minutes, Sept. 8, 1981, vol. 14:C-17ff; and PUA: Minutes, Graduate School of Education faculty meeting, Sept. 16, 1980, Faculty Minutes-72,79–82 file (Tegner Papers), Box B16. For a definition of "due process," see *School of Business and Management, Faculty Handbook*, August 1975, 15; and BOR: White to Kenneth Ross, Aug. 21, 1981, Ken Ross file.

20 HAWP: White to Davenport, Oct. 30, 1981, Chron. Corres. Sept.-Oct. 1981 file, Box 10; White, "Administrative Responsibilities and Academic Freedom," [Apr. 30, 1975], Speeches-Misc. 1971–84 file, Box 74.

21 White, Administrative Responsibility and Academic Freedom, [1981], Speeches-Misc. 1971–84 file, Box 74, and Arn-Arz file, Box 15. White used similar language in an article for the Church of Christ faithful: "The Mission of Pepperdine University," *Firm Foundation*, 96 (May 8, 1979): 3 & 11.

22 Ibid.

23 HAWP: Caldwell to White, Feb. 3, 1981, Feb. 23, 1981, Apr. 1, 1981, Oct. 2, 1981, and Oct. 13, 1981; White to Caldwell, Mar. 23, 1981, Apr. 1, 1981, and May 11, 1981; Caldwell to Luft, Sept. 25, 1981, Dan Caldwell 79–84 file, Box 21.

24 Ibid.: White, "Notes for meeting with Dr. Dan Caldwell, 2–8–82," Dan Caldwell file.

25 Caldwell, "Notes to the File, Re Conversation with Dr. White, Feb. 8, 1982," Personal Papers, Dan Caldwell; and HAWP: Caldwell to White, Mar. 2, 1982; Caldwell to Norman Hughes, Apr. 27, 1981, attached to White to Davenport, Mar. 10, 1982; White to Caldwell, Mar. 10, 1982, Dan Caldwell file, Box 21.

26 HAWP: Caldwell to Hughes, May 12, 1982, attached to Hughes to Caldwell, May 17, 1982; Luft to Caldwell, May 21, 1982; Caldwell to Luft, May 27, 1982, Dan Caldwell file, Box 21.

27 Ibid.: White to Tom Bost, June 2, 1982, and White to Caldwell, Sept. 20, 1982, Dan Caldwell file, Box 21. White was not pleased with Caldwell's affirmation of the relationship with Churches of Christ, but once tenure was granted he extended all the benefits of academic freedom to him, defending him against external criticism for his progressive political views. See Ibid.: Robert C. Walker to Jim Wilburn, attached to Wilburn to White, Mar. 17, 1983, Dan Caldwell file, Box 21.

28 GRAPHIC: Ola Barnet, "Letters from Readers," Nov. 12, 1981, A6; and SRP: Recommendations of the Salary Scale Committee, [Dec. 1972], attached to White to Banowsky, Jan. 3, 1973, Faculty Salaries file, Box 4.

29 HAWP: Draft of memo from Gary Hanson to Ola Barnett, Apr. 27, 1983, attached to Hanson to Luft, Apr. 27, 1983, B file, Box 16; and GRAPHIC: Dwayne Moring, "Religion, Location Cited for Low Minority Faculty," Oct. 27, 1983, A1.

30 GRAPHIC: Nanette Bidstrup, "Pep Women Challenge Traditional Church Roles," Jan. 21, 1982, A5.

31 Ibid.

32 Ibid.

33 Ibid.

34 *Pepperdine University, University Fact Book, 1983–1989* ([Malibu]: Institutional Research, Dec. 1989), B7; and GRAPHIC: Moring, "Religion, Location Cited," Moring, "Better Reputation Will Lure Stronger Minority," Nov. 3, 1983, A1.

35 HAWP: White to Davenport, May 30, 1983, Chron. Corres. May 1983 file, Box 12.

36 PAH: John-Eugene Wilhelm, Sept. 29, 1976, Nicks, John-Eugene Wilhelm file, Box B78; HAWP: Minutes, Pepperdine Univ. Board, Feb. 15, 1979, Univ. Board Remarks 1978–84 file, Box 74.

37 HAWP: White to James Wilburn, July 22, 1983, Chron. Corres. July 1983 (2 of 2) file, Box 12.; PO: Office of Academic Affairs, Hawaii Report, Mar. 20, 1981, Corres. 1980–81 file, Historic Subject files.

38 "Some Colleges Are Bobbing Up Everywhere," *New York Times*, Jan. 7, 1979, EDUC20.

39 NICKS: Nicks to Kay Andersen, Jan. 7, 1980, Chron. Corres. Jan. 2-Feb. 28, 1980 file, Box 3, and Mike O'Neal to Luft, Apr. 11, 1981, Hawaii Report file, Box 13; and HAWP: White to Young, Mar. 30, 1981, Pres. Corres.-Mar. 1981 file, Box 8; PO: Office

of Academic Affairs, Hawaii Report, Mar. 20, 1981, Corres. 1980–81 file, Historic Subjects.

40 HAWP: Ed Rockey to Luft, Aug. 2, 1982, School of Business, 1980–85 (1 of 3) file, Box 51.

41 PUA: Michaek Dreskin to Olaf Tegner, May 27, 1980, O. Tegner Memoranda file, Box B16.

42 SRP: Psychology Faculty to John Nicks, Mar. 24, 1980, SOE-Psychology Program file, Box 29 (G-I).

43 NICKS: Nicks to Grover Goyne and Nicks to Oly Tegner, Jan. 3, 1976, Chron. Corres. Sept. 29, 1976-June 29, 1977 file, Box 5.

44 Ibid.: Nicks to White, Dec. 20, 1979, Chron. Corres. Nov. 29-Dec. 31, 1979 file, Box 3; and HAWP: [White], For University Board, May 21, 1981, Univ. Board Remarks '78-'84 file, Box 74.

45 Ibid.: [White], For University Board, May 21, 1981, Chron. Corres. May 1981 file, [White], Report to the Regents, Sept. 8, 1981, Chron. Corres. Sept.-Oct. 1981 file, Box 10.

46 Ibid.: White to Luft, Nov. 8, 1982, Dr. White 1982–84 file, Box 9.

47 BAIRD: *Pepperdine University Self-study Report* (July 1982), Publications.

48 WAP: Pepperdine University, Fifth-Year Report (Oct. 1987), 8–35, attached to Adrian to WASC Task Force Chairpersons, Nov. 15, 1990, Chron. Corres. Nov. 1990—Feb. 1991 (1 of 2) file.

49 Ibid.

50 HAWP: White to Tom Bost, Feb. 4, 1983, Tom Bost 81–85 file, Box 32; Report to Regents, Mar. 8, 1983, Remarks to Regents 1978–1984 file, Box 74.

51 Ibid.: Kay Andersen to White, Feb. 18, 1983, attached to White to Bost, Feb. 26, 1983, Tom Bost 81–85 file, Box 32; White to Luft, Nov. 8, 1982, Chron. Corres. Nov. 1982 (1 of 2) file, Box 11; White to Luft, Feb. 26, 1983, Chron. Corres. Feb. 1982 (2 of 2) file, Box 12; White to Luft, Nov. 8, 1982, Chron. Corres. Nov. 1982 (1 of 2) file, Box 11.

CHAPTER 39

1 HAWP: [Howard A.White], A Commentary on the Unique Character and Mission of Pepperdine University, attached to White to Distribution, June 1, 1982, Chron. Corres. June 1982 file, Box 11.

2 Ibid.: White to Richard Scaife, Dec. 11, 1981, Chron. Corres. Nov.-Dec. 1981 file, Box 11.

3 Ibid.: White to Thomas L. Connelly, Dec. 24, 1983, Chron. Corres. Dec. 1983 (2 of 2) file, Box 12.

4 FF: White, "The Mission of Pepperdine University," 96 (May 8, 1979), 3.

5 GRAPHIC: Rick Cupp, "Pepperdine's Ideology a Major Experiment," Dec. 3, 1981, A7.

6 GRAPHIC: Mychel Walker, "Luft Moves Leaving Important Improvements Behind," June 19, 1983, 2; and HAWP: White to Whom It May Concern, June 18, 1983, Chron. Corres. June 1982 (2 of 2) file, Box 12; and SRP: Jim Hedstrom to Luft, May 13, 1983, Herbert Luft Corres. 1983 file, Box 14.

7 PAH: Minutes, Grad. School of Education, May 19, 1981, Fac. Minutes (1972, 79–82) file, Box B16; and HAWP: White to Jerry Hudson, May 15, 1985, Personal Politics of Presidency May 1983 file, Box xx2; and [White], Note to File, Mar. 31, 1981, Chron. Corres. Mar. 1982 file, Box 11.

8 HAWP: White to Luft, Apr. 28, 1983, Dr. White 1982–84 file, Box 9; White to Univ. Community, May 5, 1983, Herbert Luft Corres. 1983 file, Box 15.

9 GRAPHIC: Michael Dunn, "Regents Unanimously Reinstate Young to Post," Sept. 14, 1978, 1.

10 HAWP: White to Norvel and Helen Young, Sept. 21, 1978, Chron. Corres. Sept.-Oct. 1978 file, Box 10, and White to Helen Young, July 30, 1983, Chron. Corres. July 1983 (2 of 2) file, Box 12.

11 Ibid.: White to Young, Mar. 30, 1981, Presidential Corres. Mar. 1981 file, Box 8.

12 Ibid.: Arthur Spitzer to Young, Feb. 20, 1981, Spitzer-Stahl file, Box 49.

13 Ibid.: White to Tom Bost, Mar. 31, 1982, Chron. Corres. Mar. 1982 file, Box 11; White to Bost, June 4, 1983, Chron. Corres. June 1983 (1 of 2) file, Box 12; White to Young, June 4, 1983, Norvel Young, 1982–85 file, Box 60; [White], The Chancellor of Pepperdine University, [after Sept. 13, 1984,] Misc. file, Box 61. For a partial list of recipients see YOUNG: Distinguished Diploma of Honors, [nd.], D4 file, Box 123.

14 HAWP: Helen Dorris to Larry Hornbaker, May 23, 1983, Norvel Young-1982 to 85 file, Box 60.

15 Ibid.: Robert Dorris, Sr. to White and Bost, Jan. 26, 1984, Dorris to White and Bost, Feb. 1, 1984, and Young to Bost, Apr. 3, 1983, M. Norvel Young-1982 to 85 file, Box 60; White to Dorris, July 3, 1985, Chron. Corres. July 1985 file, Box 14.

16 Stefanie Hein, "Beating the Addiction," *Oasis* (Spring 1988): 22–23.

17 HAWP: White to Jerry Hudson, May 15, 1983, Personal Politics of Presidency-May 1983 file, Box xx2.

18 Ibid.: [White], The Chancellor of Pepperdine University, [after Sept. 13, 1984,] Misc. file, Box 61; and Patricia Yomantas, "Like Father, Like Family: The Runnels of Pepperdine U.," *Pepperdine People*, 3 (Summer 1980): 12–15; and Bill Henegar, "The Texan & the Belle," *Pepperdine People* (Spring 2005): 2–5.

19 HAWP: Job Description of Chancellor Emeritus, Dec. 10, 1984, Chron. Corres. Dec. 1984 (1 of 2) file; and GRAPHIC: Mychel Walker, "Runnels Takes Over Chancellorship," Jan. 24, 1985, A1.

20 Ibid.: Dr. Charles B. Runnels, [no date], attached to White to Bost, Oct. 24, 1984, Thomas Bost 1981–85 (1 of 3) file, Box 64.

21 Howard White, "The Future Is Not What It Used To Be," *Pepperdine People*, 6 (Fall 1983): 8–11; Jennifer Atzen, "Computer Literacy: On-Line with the Times," *Oasis* (Fall 1983): 2–4.

22 White, "Future," *Pepperdine People*; and PO: Mike E. O'Neal to Distribution, Apr. 15, 1985, Computers file, Historic Materials.

23 SRP: William B. Phillips to Operations Committee, May 23, 1986, Fs file, Box 21.

24 Ibid.: Luft to Ron Stephens, Mar. 30, 1981, Herbert Luft 1981 file, Box 14; and GRAPHIC: Lynette Kelley, "Year-in-Europe Program Expands and Changes," Oct. 8, 1981, A5.

25 HAWP: McGoldrick to White, Feb. 9, 1981, James McGoldrick file, Box 39; and NICKS: "Wave of Excellence Report," Fall 1987, Wave of Excellence file, Box 13.

26 HAWP: White to Luft, Mar. 12, 1983, Chron Corres. Mar. 1983 (1 of 2) files, Box 12.

27 WSB: [White,] Comments to Executive Committee, Nov. 14, 1984, Regents, Remarks file, Box BOTrustees (48).

28 [Colleen Graffy,] "London Program Report," [2000], and "History of 56 Prince's Gate and the South Kensingston Area," [2000], attached to email communication from Carolyn Vos Strache to author, April 1 and 2, 2013.

29 GRAPHIC: Kathy Lawrence, "Academic Program in Italy Offered in Spring," Dec. 6, 1984, A3.

30 WAP: "Fifth-year report to the Accrediting Commission for Senior Colleges and Universities of [WASC]," Oct. 30, 1987, 53, attached to Adrian to WASC Task Force Chairpersons, Nov. 15, 1990, Chron. Corres. Nov. 1990—Feb. 1991 (1 of 2) file.

31 "University on the Move," *Pepperdine People* (Summer 1996): 26; and Bill Henegar, "An American Love Affair," and "A Pepperdine Home in Florence Italy," *Pepperdine People* (Winter 1996): 2–5 and 6; SRP: various materials, Florence file, Box 23.

32 NICKS: "Pursuing Academic Excellence, Pepperdine University Distinguished Professors," [1982–1984], Box 13; WSB: [White], The Chancellor of Pepperdine University, [post Sept. 13, 1984], 9, Misc. file, Box 61.

33 SRP: Faculty Salaries Increased, a Ten Year Perspective (1971–1980), Faculty Salary #1 file, Box 14.

34 HAWP: Tabulation for 1979–1980 academic year, Faculty Salaries file, Box B63, Pepperdine University Archives; Minutes, Operation Com., Mar. 2, 1981, Chron. Corres. Mar. 1981 file, Box 10; [White], Regents, Sept. 13, 1983, Remarks to Regents 1978–1984 file, Box 74, and Wm. B. Phillips to White, July 23, 1984, Am file, Box 15; and GRAPHIC: Reid Sams, "Eleven Percent Raise Puts Faculty among Highest Paid," Sept. 23, 1982, A2; and BAIRD: "Fifth-Year Report to the Accrediting Commission for Senior Colleges and Universities of the [WASC]," Oct. 30, 1987.

35 Sandi Linville, "Stalking the Elusive Stomata," *Pepperdine People*, 4 (Winter 1981): 16–19; Brenda Zobrist, "The Greening of Malibu, Student Research Chaparral Regrowth after Wildfire," *Pepperdine People*, [8] (Summer 1986): 7–9; and BAIRD: Stephen Davis to author, email communication dated Apr. 2, 2013, 1988–1989 file.

36 PAH: See "Publications and Scholarly Activities of Faculty Members of Pepperdine University, Vol. II," Nov. 1982.

37 Howard A. White, *The Freedman's Bureau in Louisiana* (1970).

38 HAWP: Caldwell to White, Oct. 2, 1981, Caldwell, Dan 1979–84 file, Box 21.

39 SRP: Phillips to Operations Com., Jan. 9, 1986, Dean's Council 1986ff file, Box 20; and BAIRD: "Fifty-Year Report to the Accrediting Commission for Senior Colleges and Universities of the [WASC]," Oct. 30, 1987, 75. Beginning fall 1988, the university received 45 percent of overhead and the department just 10 percent.

40 HAWP: Hughes to White, Mar. 5, 1982, Richard Hughes file, Box 32.

41 The faculty dining room opened in Tyler Campus Center just after Thornton Administrative Building opened in fall 1984. See SRP: Faculty Dining Room file, Fs file, Box 21. For Pendleton Entertainment fund see HAWP: White to Faculty of Seaver College and School of Law, Mar. 18, 1981, Chron. Corres. Mar. 1981 file, Box 10.

42 "Exclusive National Surveys: Rating the Colleges," *U.S. News & World Report*, 95 (Nov. 28, 1983), 42, and "Best Colleges in America's," *U.S. News & World Report*, 97 (Nov. 25, 1985); WSB: [White], Report to Board of Regents, June 14, 1983, Remarks to Regent's file, Box BOTrustees (48).

43 PUA: Pepperdine University, Reaccreditation Report, (Nov. 1978),102–11, Box B10 (44B); NICKS: Nicks to Ron Phillips, Mar. 27, 1981, Chron. Corres. Mar. 2-Apr.20, 1981 file, Box 3.

44 NICKS: Pepperdine University, Western Association of Schools and Colleges Accreditation Review (1979), 109–13, Box 17.

45 GRAPHIC: Iris Yokoi, "Payson Library Chosen To House Public Documents," Nov. 3, 1983, A2.

46 Ibid.: Parris Ward, "Library Installs Computer System," Mar. 28, 1985, A1.

47 BAIRD: Fifth-Year Report (October 1987), 66–67; and SRP: Payson Library file, Box 27; GRAPHIC: Neal Snyder, "Library Director Back from Leave," Sept. 24, 1981, A2.

CHAPTER 40

1 HAWP: "Che fior fiore de campus," *Capital*, Sept. 1984, 59, translation in Chron. Corres. Nov. 1984 (1 of 2) file, Box 13; and WSB: [White], Report to Board of Regents, June 14, 1983, and Comments to Ex. Com., Nov. 14, 1984, Regent Remarks file, Box BOTrustees (48).

2 NICKS: Wilburn, The Case for a Center for American Private Enterprise, [1978], Center for American Private Enterprise (CAPE) file, Box 13.

3   PAH: See Private Enterprise Award file, Box B77; and BAIRD: Jim Wilburn, "Random Pepperdine Reminiscences, 1973–1982," Oct. 2010, 159, Graziadio file.

4   Wilburn, "Center Fosters Appreciation for Private Initiative," *Pepperdine People*, 2 (Summer 1979): 6–7; "Furthering the cause of Private Enterprise, Corporate Associates Launch CAPE," *Pepperdine People*, 3 (Winter 1980): 8; NICKS: "Center for American Private Enterprise: a Profile," attached to Wilburn to Distribution, July 18, 1981, Center for Am. Private Enterprise file, Box 17. In its fifteen (1966–1980) years of operation, the Taft Institute reached 375 teachers who in turn returned to their classrooms and influenced some 150,000 students. See PUA: Minutes, Pepperdine University Board, Oct. 2, 1980, U.B Executive Com. file, Box C05.

5   Wilburn, "The Importance of Corporate Support," *Pepperdine People*, 4 (Winter 1981): 4. Wilburn addressed many of these same themes in his 1982 book *Freedom, Order, and the University.*

6   The Youth Citizenship Seminar is still an active program on the Malibu campus, faithfully supported by Charles Runnels and his family.

7   "A Pepperdine Alumnus in the White House," *Pepperdine People*, 4 (Winter 1981): 2–3.

8   HAWP: [White], Comments for Executive Committee, Feb. 11, 1981, Chron. Corres. Jan-Feb. 1981 file, Box 10; and WSB: [White], Report for Ex. Com. [of Regents], Oct. 14, 1981, Remarks to Regents file, Box BOTrustees (48).

9   HAWP: See Honorary Degree file, Box 32.

10 HAWP: Nicks to Bob Thomas, Oct. 4, 1977, John Nicks file, Box 14; "Agreement in Principle," attached to Harry L. Usher to Howard White, Sept. 15, 1981, 1984 Olympic Contracts file, Box 42; White to Harry Usher, Mar. 14, 1983, Chron. Corres. Mar. 1983 (1 of 2) file, Box 12; and SRP: Russell Snyder, "Pepperdine Water Polo," *[Santa Monica] Evening Outlook*, [1984], Olympics file, Box 26.

11 HAWP: White to Distribution, Apr. 6, 1982, 1984 Olympics contract file, Box 42.

12 See Carolyn Vos Strache, ed., *Purposes, Principles and Contradictions of the Olympic Movement: Proceedings of the United States Olympic Academy VI* (United States Olympic Committee Educational Council and Pepperdine University, [1982]), in PO: Corres. 1983 file; and HAWP: 1984 Olympic Contracts file, Box 42; and BAIRD: email from Carolyn Vos Strache to author, Apr. 9, 2013, 1981–1982 file.

13 GRAPHIC: Jake McGowan, "Pep Scores Olympic Victory," Sept. 27, 1984, A2; and HAWP: White to John Watson, Dec. 3, 1985, 1984 Olympic Contracts file, Box 42; White to Gentlemen, Mar. 9, 1984, Chron. Corres. Mar. 1984 (1 of 2) file, Box 13; and PUA: Minutes, University Board meeting, Oct. 3, 1984, Univ. Board Minutes (1978–84) file, Box C05.

14 HAWP: White to Ginie Braun, Mar. 224, 1984, Chron. Corres. Mar. 1984 (2 of 2) file, Box 13.

15 Ibid.: Young to White, May 7, 1982, Russian Writers Conference file, Box 47. See YOUNG: Russian Writers Folder and Russian/American Writers Conference file, Box 28.

16 Emma Daly, "Revelations: The roots of Invention," *The Independent* (June 2, 1997) at http://www.independent.co.uk/news/media/revelations-the-roots-of-invention-1253929.html (accessed Apr. 8, 2013).

17 HAWP: Young to White, Aug. 17, 1982, Russian Writers Conference file, Box 47.

18 Ibid.: Young to White, June 29, 1983; Adams to White, Sept. 21, 1983; and White to Adams, Oct. 2, 1983, Chron. Corres. Oct. 1983 (1 of 2) file, Box 12.

19 Ibid.: Guest list, Soviet/American Writer's luncheon, Brock House, Mar. 15, 1984, Russian Writers Conference file, Box 47; and LAT: Kathleen Hendrix, "U.S. and Soviet Writers Break the Ice," Mar. 21, 1984, V-1ff.

20 HAWP: White to James Lee Mcdonough, Mar. 18, 1984, Chron. Corres. Mar. 1984 (1 of 2) file, Box 13.

21 LAT: Hendrix, "U.S. and Soviet Writers Break Ice."

22 See also Maryam E. Kubasek, "The Red and the Red, White, and Blue," *Pepperdine People* (Summer 1990): 9–11; and LAT: Mathis Chazanov, "Perestroika Prospers at Pepperdine: Joint Soviet-U.S. Projects Bely Campus's Conservative Image," Jan. 14, 1990, WSJ, 1.

23 HAWP: White to Meese, Dec. 15, 1983; White to Deaver, Dec. 16, 1983, Chron. Corres. Dec. 1983 (1 of 2) file, Box 12.

24 SRP: National School Safety Center file, Box 26; and LAT: Mark Gladstone, "Counsel Says Meese Had No Grant Role," Oct. 10, 1984, C2; and George Nicholson, "NSSC Report," *School Safety* (Fall 1984): 2.

25 SRP: "Safe schools, Quality schooling," [1986], brochure in Nat. School Safety Center file, Box 26.

26 MFA: Regarding the School Safety Center, tab W-1, Executive Committee, Board of Regents Agenda, Aug. 6, 1985.

27 Joyce Baxter, "Making a Difference, The National School Safety Center," *Pepperdine People* (Summer 1990): 20–22.

28 WAP: Adrian to Stephens, Jan. 5, 1988, Chron. Corres. Apr. 1987-Feb. 1988 (3 of 3) file; and BAIRD: email from Ronald Stephens to author, Apr. 22, 2013, 1997–2000 file.

29 WSB: [White], Report to the Executive Committee, Nov. 11, 1981, Remarks to Regents file, Box BOTrustees (48); and HAWP: "Decade of the Eighties Campaign for Regents," Mar. 10, 1981, Pres. Corres. Mar. 1981 file, Box 8; White to Robert Anderson, July 10, 1981, Chron. Corres. July-Aug. 1981 file, Box 10.

30 MFA: Brakeley, John Price Jones, Inc., "Pepperdine University," Sept. 1981, Pepperdine Capital Campaign file, Box 5.

31 WSB: Brakeley, John Price Jones, Inc., Report to the Executive Committee, Nov. 11, 1981, Remarks to Regents file, Box BOTrustees (48); and Michael F. Adams, "Commitment to the Counter Tide," *Pepperdine People*, 5 (Spring 1983): 9–10.

32 WSB: [White], Report to the Executive Committee, Nov. 11, 1981, Remarks to Regents file, Box BOTrustees (48); and HAWP: White to Richard Ralphs, Nov. 30, 1981, Chron. Corres. Nov.-Dec. 1981 file, Box 11.

33 BOR: Minutes, University Board of Regents, Dec. 8, 1981, 15:260; and HAWP: [White], Report to the University Board, Dec. 10, 1981, Remarks to Univ. Board 1978–84 file, Box 74.

34 NICKS: "Wave of Excellence Report, Special Edition," [1985], Wave of Excellence file, Box 13; and "Campaign Totals Rise," *Pepperdine People*, 7 (Fall 1984): 7.

35 NICKS: "Wave of Excellence Report," Fall 1985, Winter 1985 and Summer 1987; and WSB: [White], Remarks to Board of Regents, June 8, 1982, Remarks to Regents file, Box BOTrustees (48); and "Notes," *Pepperdine People*, [8](Fall 1985): 17.

36 WSB: Remarks to Board of Regents, Sept. 8, 1981, Remarks to Regents file, Box BOTrustees (48).

37 BAIRD: Revenue from Tuition & Fees, Auxiliary Enterprises as Percentage of Total . . . FY ending 1979, attached to John Sasileski to White, Aug. 29, 1980, 1980–81 file. Endowment figures come from financial statements included in Reaccreditation Report (Nov. 1978), and Fifth-Year Report (Oct. 1987). See also HAWP: White to Students, Feb. 15, 1983, Chron. Corres. Feb. 1983 (1 of 2) file, Box 12.

38 WSB: Comments to the Regents, Sept 13, 1983, Financials, Regents Remarks file, Box BOTrustees (48); and HAWP: White to Senator Alan Cranston, Feb. 24, 1981, Chron. Corres. Jan.-Feb. 1981 file, Box 10; and GRAPHIC: Greg Rudder, "Federal Aid Cut 17 Percent Nationwide," Sept. 23, 1982: A8; and Torrie Dorrell, "Reaganomics Leaves Students Grasping for . . . Financial Aid," *Oasis* (1981–1982): 16–17; and

Sandi Linville, "Searching for Alternative Ways to Fund Student Aid," *Pepperdine People*, 5 (Summer 1982): 22–23.

39 SRP: Mike O'Neal to Student, June 29, 1979 and White to Robert Thomas, Jan. 9, 1979, Dr. White 1979 file, Box 14; PUA: Minutes, Pepperdine University Board, Sept. 13, 1979, Univ. Board Minutes (1978–1984) file, Box C05.

40 HAWP: White to Young and Runnels, May 28, 1983, M. Norvel Young 1982–1985 file, Box 60; White to Young, May 18, 1983, Chron Corres. May 1983 file, Box 12; and WSB: Comments for the Regents, Sept. 13, 1973, Regent's Remarks file, Box BOTrustees (48).

41 HAWP: Minutes, Operations Committee, Feb. 13, 1981, Chron. Corres. Jan.-Feb. 1981 file, Box 10, and White to Davenport, Sept. 9, 1983, Chron. Corres. Sept. 1983 file, Box 12; and SRP: Press Release, "Pepperdine University Announces 1986–87 Tuition," Feb. 24, 1986, Flat-Rate Tuition file, Box 3.

42 PUA: "Proposal to System Development Foundation," Nov. 1980, Misc. file, Box B62 (Hughes Collection).

43 SRP: Mike O'Neal to Student, June 29, 1979; White to Robert Thomas, Jan. 9, 1979, Dr. White 1979 file, Box 14; and PUA: Minutes, Pepperdine University Board, Sept. 13, 1979, Univ. Board Minutes (1978–1984) file, Box C05.

44 HAWP: [White], Remarks to Associates Dinner, Apr. 13, 1981, Chron. Corres. April 1981 file, Box 10; and GRAPHIC: Eleaine Vorkink, "New Apartment Housing Uproots Students," June 29, 1983, A3. The University had tried to sell Latigo since 1980. It was complicated because of Coastal Commission policies and because the complex had initially been purchased with CEFA money. See GRAPHIC: Valerie Edison, "Latigo Debate Is Over: It's Sold for $16 Million," Sept. 25, 1980, A1.

45 SRP: White to O'Neal and Thomas, Feb. 27, 1979, Dr. White 1979 file, Box 14.

46 HAWP: White to Caldwell, May 11, 1981, Dan Caldwell 1979–84 file, Box 21.

47 BAIRD: email communication to author from Ron Stephens, April 22, 2013, 1981–1982 file.

48 PUA: Larry Hornbaker to William E. Gross, Sept 15, 1981, Gross Construction Communications file, Project Archives, Office of Planning, Operations, and Construction.

49 HAWP: White to John T. McCarty, Nov. 16, 1981, Chron. Corres. Nov.-Dec. 1981 file, Box 11; and GRAPHIC: Shelli DeWeerd, "Some Faculty Housing Units Ready for Occupancy," Feb. 4, 1982, A2; and WSB: [White], Remarks to the Board of Regents, June 8, 1982, Remarks to Regents file, Box BOTrustees (48).

50 HAWP: [White], Report to the University Board, June 10, 1982, University Board Remarks 1978–84 file, Box 74; White to Davenport, Aug. 26, 1984, Chron. Corres. Aug. 1984 (2 of 2) file, Box 13; and GRAPHIC: Nancy Leong, "On-campus Faculty Use Condos for More Interaction with Students, Survey Says," Oct. 20, 1983, A1.

51 WSB: [White], Report to Board of Regents, June 12, 1984, Remarks to Regents file, Box BOTrustees (48); and GRAPHIC: Reid Sams, "Ground Broken for New Administration Building," Sept. 27, 1984, A1; and "The Making of an Administrative Center," *Pepperdine People*, 7 (Fall 1984): 6–7.

52 SRP: Patti Yomantas to Michael Adams, Jan. 16, 1987, Chronology TAC file, Box 32.

53 Ibid. Ironically, there had been a separate water main break earlier in the year in the Pendleton Computer parking lot, when a backhoe cut into the main, flooding the first floor of the computer building. See SRP: Bill Salyer to Charlie Roberts, July 31, 1985, attached to John Watson to William Adrian, Aug. 2, 1985, Chron. TAC file, Box 32.

54 SRP: Bob Thomas to White, Aug. 9, 1979, Dr. White 1979 file, Box 14; and "Board Accepts Park Proposal," *Pepperdine People*, 2 (Winter 1979), 9.

55 HAWP: White to Keith McFarland and Robert Fraley, Feb. 9, 1981, Presidential Corres. Jan.1981 file, Box 8; and "Pepperdine's Louisiana Purchase," *Pepperdine People*, 4 (Summer 1981): 22.

56 Quoted in GRAPHIC: Jim Benson, "Seaver Academics Rated Equal to UCLA," Jan. 21, 1982, A1.

57 WSB: [White], Comments to the Board of Regents, Dec. 13, 1983, Box BOTrustees (48).

58 "Exclusive National Survey: Rating the Colleges," *U.S. News & World Report*, 95 (Nov. 28, 1983): 42, and "The Best Colleges in America," *U.S. News & World Report*, 97 (Nov. 25, 1985): 48.

59 GRAPHIC: Shelly Ngo, "Pepperdine Ranks in Second Quartile in U.S. News Study," Sept. 26, 1991, 1; and "America's Best Colleges, 2001" *U.S. News & World Report*, 112 (Sept. 1, 2000).

CHAPTER 41

1 GRAPHIC: Iris Yokoi, "Wilson Takes Crack at Seaver's Challenge," Sept. 29, 1983, A2.

2 JWP: [Wilson], Building Academic Excellence at Seaver College, 1984–85, 1984–85 file, Box 1.

3 Robert Thomas (1972–1976) and Steven Lemley (1976–1978) served prior to the White presidency.

4 Institutional Research, *University Fact Book, 1983–1989* (Dec. 1989); and GRAPHIC: Teri Bruce, "Seaver Minority Enrollment Rapidly Declining," Nov. 29, 1984, A1.

5 GRAPHIC: Jaunie Lane, "Studying Abroad," Jan. 20, 1983, A4; Mike Farber, "Seaver Site Transcends International Boundaries," Sept. 22, 1983, A6; Conny Romero, "View of Life for Iranian Students at Pep-Malibu," Feb. 8, 1979, 1; Rick Cupp, "Carter's Asset Freeze Puts Iranian Student in Bind," Nov. 15, 1979, 1.

6 Institutional Research, *University Fact Book, 1983–1989*.

7 Ibid.

8 GRAPHIC: Jake McGowan, "Republicans Maintain Stronghold," Oct. 11, 1984, A1; Dan Guzman, "Where Are They?" Sept. 23, 1982, A6.

9 Ibid.: "SGA Misses Chance To Act," Mar. 1, 1984, 12. Perhaps it was for ethnic insensitivity of this kind in the Office of Student Affairs for which Dean of Students Carl Mitchell apologized a year later. See GRAPHIC: Carl Mitchell, "Failure to Screen Events," Mar. 21, 1985, A7.

10 HAWP: "Facts Concerning Pepperdine," attached to White to Flora Thornton, Jan. 26, 1982, Chron. Corres. Jan. 1982 file, Box 11; and WSB: [White], Report to Regents, Dec. 14, 1982, Remarks to Regents file, Box BOTrustees (48), Banowsky Papers; and PUA: Minutes, University Board, Oct. 3, 1984, Univ. Board Minutes (1978–1984), Box C05.

11 SRP: Norman Fischer to Wm. Adrian, Oct. 5, 1990, G file, Box 23.

12 See different editions of *Handbook Rank, Tenure, and Promotion Committee, Seaver College of Pepperdine University* (Aug. 27, 1982), (Sept. 1984), (Sept. 1986), (Sept. 1987), (Sept. 1993), (1996–1997), and (2005–2006).

13 See various editions of the *Seaver College Faculty Handbook* (Sept. 1978), (Sept. 1980), (Sept. 1985), (Sept. 1988), (Sept. 1989), (Sept. 1991), (Sept. 1998), and (Sept. 2000).

14 GRAPHIC: Jim Benson, "Hayden To Speak on America's Future Monday," Mar. 4, 1982, A1; Benson, "Hayden Pays 'Long-Planned' Visit," Mar. 11, 1982, A1; and HAWP: White to Luft, Mar. 11, 1982 and White to Pendleton, Mar. 31, 1982, Chron. Corres. Mar. 1982 file, Box 11; White to Wm. Phillips, Feb. 10, 1983, Chron. Corres. Feb. 1983 (1 of 2) file; White to Bost, Feb. 26, 1983, Chron. Corres. Feb. 1983 (2 of 2) file, Box 12.

15 HAWP: Warren Robak, "An Inquiry into the Firings of Five Members of the Pepperdine University Student Publication Office," Jan. 13, 1979, in Graphic file, Box 30; Nick De Bonis to the Editor, Jan. 10, 1979, attached to De Bonis to Deane Funk, Jan. 10, 1979, D. Lloyd Nelson file, Box 33; Ames to White, Sept. 30, 1982, Steven Ames file, Box 16; and GRAPHIC: Conny Romero, "Student Publications Editors Fired," Jan. 11, 1979, 1; Wayne Overbeck to the Editor, Jan. 17, 1980, 8.

16 HAWP: Editorial, "Pepperdine Tarnishes College Press Freedom," *Daily Trojan*, Feb. 22, 1979, 4, clipping in D. Lloyd Nelson-Bd. of Trustees file, Box 41; PAH: Overbeck to John Nicks, Jan. 3, 1979, Student Publications file, Box B64; and GRAPHIC: Merdies Hayes, "Reasons?" and Scott Grant, "Letters," Jan. 18, 1979, 8; "Letters," Jan. 25, 1979, 8; "Letters," Feb. 1, 1979, 6.

17 PAH: Hudson to Ames, Apr. 10, 1979, Student Publications file, Box B64; and HAWP: White to Ames, Feb. 1978, Steven Ames file, Box 16.

18 Email communication from Jeff Bliss to the author, Jan. 17, 2013. GRAPHIC: Rusty Reed, "Graphic Gets New Look," Sept. 17, 1981, A3; Jim Benson, "Delegation Accepts Pacemaker," Nov. 5, 1981, A3; "Graphic Called 'Gem' among Papers," July 8, 1982, 2; "Pacemaker Awarded to *Oasis*," July 27, 1983, A2.

19 PUA: Faculty-Regents Committee—Report and Recommendations, [1978], Faculty-Regents Committee file, Box B62; BAIRD: Seaver College Scenario for the 1980's, A study of the Constraints and Opportunities for the decade, July 1981, 1980–1981 file.

20 WAP: Strategic Planning Documents of Seaver College, included as Appendix B in Fifth-year Report (Oct. 1987), 135–44, attached to Adrian to WASC Task Force Chairpersons, Nov. 15, 1990, Chron. Corres. Nov. 1990—Feb. 1991 (1 of 2) file. Wilson and his colleagues added an "academic plan" in 1987, which was revised in 1995.

21 Ibid. In addition to sections on mission and faculty, the Seaver College Integrated Strategic Plan also had segments on administrative staff, the Seaver student, enrollment management, academics, student life, and international programs.

22 PAH: Ralph Beck to Norman Hughes, Aug. 24, 1979, Campus Life file, Box B64.

23 SRP: Ralph Beck to John Nicks, Jan. 3, 1979, John Nicks Corres. 1979 file, Box 14.

24 SRP: Ron Fagan to Herbert Luft, Sept. 8, 1981, Herbert Luft 1981 file.

25 PAH: Nicks to Phil Garr, Feb. 28, 1980, O Student Gov't file, Box B64; and GRAPHIC: Jo Lieberman, "Unique Chapel Policy Results from Diversity," Feb. 16, 1984, A2.

26 HAWP: White to Luft, Nov. 27, 1982, Chron Corres. Nov. 1982 (2 of 2) file; White to Luft, Dec. 31, 1982, Chron. Corres. Dec. 1982 (2 of 2) file, Box 11.

27 Rick Cupp, "How Firm a Foundation," *Oasis* (1981–82), 21, 46.

28 GRAPHIC: Rick Cupp, "Popularity of Christianity Booms," Feb. 24, 1983, A1

29 GRAPHIC: Kathy Barton, "Committee Probes Grade Inflation," Oct. 12, 1978, 1.

30 PAH: See General Education Retreat file, Box B63; and GRAPHIC: Curtiss Olsen & Lisa Vanco, "Academic Change May Hit Seaver," May 15, 1980, 1.

31 HAWP: White to Davenport, Nov. 25, 1983, Chron. Corres. Nov. 1983 file, Box 12.

32 NICKS: Nicks to White, Mar. 10, 1980, Chron. Corres. Mar. 1-Apr. 22 1980 file, Box 3.

33 HAWP: White to John Wilson, Dec. 3, 1985, Chron. Corres. Dec. 1985 file, Box 14.

34 Ibid.: White to Davenport, Dec. 19, 1983, Chron. Corres. Dec. 1983 (2 of 2) file, Box 12.

35 GRAPHIC: Dwayne Mooring, "New Class Schedule To Increase Time," Feb. 2, 1984, A1; and HAWP: Academic Advising Committee to John Wilson, May 15, 1984; White to Davenport, Sept. 22, 1984, Academic Advising file, Box 15; and [Davenport], Notes on Proposed Changes in Seaver College," Oct. 29, 1984, Strategic Planning #3 file, Box 29.

36 *Pepperdine University, Seaver College, 1986–1987 Catalog*, 49 (Feb. 1986), 78–80.

37 "Great Books of the Western World," Apr. 10, 2013, http://www.ask.com/wiki/ Great_Books_of_the_Western_World?o=2800&qsrc=999 (accessed May 2, 2013).

38 HAWP: White to Adler, Oct. 19, 1984, Ad file, Box 15.

39 *Pepperdine University, Seaver College, 1986–1987 Catalog*, 49 (Feb. 1986), 80; and BAIRD: email from Michael Gose to Sarah R. Fisher, Sept. 20, 2011, 1984–1985 file.

40 University of South Carolina, "History of the First University Seminar & the University 101 Program," (nd.), http://www.sc.edu/univ101/aboutus/history.html (May 2, 2013); *Pepperdine University, Seaver College, 1987–88 Catalog*, 50 (Mar. 1987), 85.

41 HAWP: White to Wright, Oct. 4, 1982, Chron. Corres. Oct. 1982 file, Box 11.

42 Ibid.: White, Statement of news coverage, Mar. 15, 1983, Chron. Corres. Mar. 1983 (1 or 2) file, Box 12.

43 GRAPHIC: David Morgan, "Bigger Is Not Always Better," Oct. 11, 1984, B1; "Athletic Program Records Winning Marks," June 27, 1984, 11.

44 WSB: [White], Remarks to Board of Regents, June 8, 1982 and Sept. 11, 1984, Remarks to Regent's file, Box BOTrustees (48).

CHAPTER 42

1   HAWP: White to Luft, Feb. 11, 1981, Chron Corres. Jan.-Feb. 1981 file; White to Hazelip, Mar. 16, 1981, Chron. Corres. Mar. 1981, Box 10.

2   Ibid.: White to Hazelip, Mar. 24, 1982, Chron. Corres. Mar. 1982 file, Box 11; White to Joe Barnett, Feb. 13, 1984, Chron. Corres. Feb. 1984 (1 of 2) file, Box 13.

3   Ibid.: White to Jerry Rushford, Feb. 13, 1984, Chron. Corres. Feb. 1984 (1 of 2) file, Box 13.

4   Ibid.: White to Hazelip, June 18, 1985, Chron. Corres. June 1985 file, Box 14.

5   Serving were Tom Bost (chair), Joe Barnett, William Stevens, Leonard Straus, and John Vaughn.

6   The fifteen included Michael F. Adams of Pepperdine; David Davenport of Pepperdine; Harold Hazelip of Harding Graduate School; Larry Hornbaker of Pepperdine; Jerry Hudson of Willamette University; J. Terry Johnson of Oklahoma Christian; Gary D. McCaleb of Abilene Christian; Ronald R. Phillips of Pepperdine; William B. Phillips of Pepperdine; Joe D. Schubert of Houston; Carl H. Stem of Texas Tech; William J. Teague of Abilene Christian; Robert H. Thomas, University of Montana West at Dillon; R. Gerald Turner of University of Mississippi; and James Wilburn of Pepperdine. See HAWP: [White], Choosing a New President at Pepperdine University, Apr. 7, 1984, Special Adm. file, Box xx2.

7   Ibid.: White to Hudson, May 15, 1983, Personal Politics of Presidency May 1983 file, Box xx2; White to Hazelip, June 12, 1984, Chron. Corres. June 1984 file, Box 13; White to Davenport, Aug. 22, 1984, Chron. Corres. Aug 1984 (2 of 2) file, Box 13; MFA: Minutes, May 9, 1984, 2–3, in Executive Committee, Board of Regents Agenda, Nov. 14, 1964, Box 8.

8   Ibid. "

9   HAWP: [White], Choosing a New President at Pepperdine University, Apr. 7, 1984, Special Adm. file, Box xx2.

10 Ibid.

11 Ibid.: Bost to White, Mar. 23, 1984, attached to White to Runnels, Aug. 20, 1983, Charles Runnels file, Box 47.

12 Ibid.: Bost to University Personnel and White to University Personnel, June 12, 1984, Chron. Corres. June 1984 file, Box 13.

13 Ibid.: White to Frederick Ness, Oct. 30, 1985, Chron. Corres. Oct. 1985 file, Box 14.

14 "About Pepperdine, Howard A. White," Pepperdine University website, (n.d.), http://www.pepperdine.edu/president/past-presidents/white.htm (accessed June

20, 2013); HAWP: Bost to University Personnel, June 12, 1984, Chron. Corres. June 1984 file, Box 13.

15 WSB: [White], Report to the Board of Regents, Mar. 12, 1985, Regents Remarks file, Box BOTrustes (48). See also HAWP: White to Willard Collins, June 18, 1985, Chron. Corres. June 1985 file, Box 14.

16 GRAPHIC: Editorial, "Students Will Remember White's 'Personal Touch,'" Sept. 27, 1984, A6.

17 MFA: Adams to White, Mar. 1, 1983, MFA to Howard White 1984 file; and HAWP: White to Adams, July 14, 1984, Chron. Corres. July 1984 file, Box 13.

18 HAWP: White to Carl Ruggles, Jan. 15, 1985, Chron. Corres. Jan. 1985 (1 of 2) file, Box 14.

19 Ibid.: White, Personal Reflections, Jan. 27, 1977, Church Relation-Major Items 1977 file, Box xx1.

20 Ibid.: White to Davenport, July 7, 1986, Chron. Corres. July/Aug. 1986 file, Box 14.

21 Ibid.

22 Ibid.

CHAPTER 43

1 David Leaser and Tammy Clarke, "Dr. David Davenport," *Oasis* (Spring 1985): 10–13.

2 WAP: Adrian to Michael Adams, Oct. 25, 1985, Chron. Corres. Apr. 1985—Apr. 1986 (2 of 3) file, Box 1; and BAIRD: "Presidential Inauguration, Pepperdine University," Oct. 21, 1985, program, 1985–1986 folder.

3 HAWP: David Davenport, "Lighting the Way," Oct. 21, 1985, Pepperdine Hist.-Misc. 73–79 file, Box 76.

4 LAT: Gary Libman, "Pepperdine's Davenport: Of Law and Gospel," Apr. 15, 1985, F1.

5 GRAPHIC: Liz Sarafian, "Davenport Shows Christian Values, Perspective," Feb. 4, 1988, A2, A6.

6 Ibid.

7 Ibid.: Sandra Lunt, "Pepperdine's First Lady," Nov. 7, 1985, B4-B5.

8 Bill Henegar, "The Courage to be Unique," *Pepperdine People* (Summer 1994): 4–7.

9 PO: Davenport to All University Personnel, Nov. 27, 1984, Corres. 1984 file, Historic Records; and WAP: Adrian to James Billington, Nov. 9, 1988, Chron. Corres, Nov. 1988-Mar. 1988 (1 of 3) folder, and Adrian to Davenport, July 9, 1992, Chron. Corres. Jan.-July 1992 (2 of 2) file, Box 2.

10 GRAPHIC: Shelly Ngo, "Provost Search Comes to an End," Jan. 14, 1993, 1; Jennifer Isom, "Seaver Administration Welcomes New Provost," Sept. 23, 1993, 4.

11 Joyce Hutchison, "Lighting the Flame of Leadership, *Pepperdine People* (Fall 1997): 10–12; Charlotte Allen, "A Place in the Sun," *University Business*, 2 (May 1999), 35.

12 MFA: Davenport to Adams, Jan. 31, 1989, Compensation file, Box 6; and HAWP: White to Davenport, Nov. 26, 1985, Pumpkin Papers file, Box xx2.

13 Jan Turner, "Just Like the Movies," *Pepperdine People* (Spring 1992): 12–14; Bill Henegar, "Not in Kansas Any More, Larry Hornbaker's life has been a wonderful whirlwind," *Pepperdine People* (Summer 2000): 4–7.

14 WAP: Adrian to Watson, Mar. 11, 1992, Chron. Corres. Jan.-July 1992 (1 of 2) file, Box 2; and GRAPHIC: Lisa Wahla, "In Mild Surprise, Watson Named AD," Jan. 15, 1998, A1; and "After Twenty-One Years as Athletic Director, Wayne Wright Retires," *Pepperdine Voice* (Oct. 1997): 1.

15 Abigail Salaway, "Passing the Presidential Baton," *Pepperdine People* (Summer 2000): 2–3.

16 PO: Dwayne Simmons to Davenport, Nov. 24, 1985, Chron. Corres. 1985 file, Historic Materials.

17 JWP: Wilson to Tom Bost, '93-'94 file, Box 2.

18 Allen, "A Place in the Sun," *University Business*, 2 (May 1999): 35.

19 JWP: Wilson to Tom Bost, Feb. 7, 1994, '93-'94 file, Box 2; and PO: Norman Fischer to Davenport, Oct. 27, 1992, Corres. 1992 file.

20 PO: Davenport to Adams and Phillips, Feb. 8, 1985; Davenport to Phillips, Feb. 18, 1985; Davenport to Wilson, Feb. 25, 1985; Davenport to Distribution, Apr. 25, 1985; Phillips to Davenport, May 20, 1986, Corres. 1985 file. See also Ibid.: Davenport to Phillips and Wilson, Jan. 3, 1986, Corres. 1986 file, Historical Materials; Davenport to Distribution, Mar. 10, 1994, and Davenport to Nancy Fagan, Mar. 30, 1993, Corres. '92-'94 file.

21 WAP: Adrian to Distribution, Oct. 27, 1986, Chron. Corres. May 1986-Mar. 1987 (2 of 3) file, Box 1.

22 JWP: Wilson to Davenport, Oct. 29, 1987, 1987–1988 file, Box 1.

23 Ibid.: Davenport to University Community, Oct. 1, 1991, 1991–92 file; Wilson to Davenport, Feb. 27, 1996, 1995–1996 file, Box 2.

24 Ibid.

25 SRP: Benton to Distribution, Oct. 3, 1991, BSI/Civic Center file, Box 20; and LAT: Ron Russell, "Pepperdine Secretly Tied to Developers," Oct. 7, 1991, 1.

26 JWP: Transcription of strategic vision address, Oct. 16, 1990, attached to Davenport to Univ. Com., Oct. 1, 1991, 1991–92 file, Box 2. For a polished statement of the Twin Peaks see BAIRD: Third-Year Interim Report to the Western Association of Schools and Colleges, Nov. 8, 1995, attached to Steve Lemley to Steven S. Weiner, Nov. 8, 1995, xiii-xiv, WASC reports.

27 JWP: Transcription of strategic vision address, Oct. 16, 1990, attached to Davenport to Univ. Com., Oct. 1, 1991, 1991–92 file, Box 2.

28 Ibid. See also NICKS: Davenport to Full-Time Faculty, Feb. 12, 1990, Values in the Classroom file, Box 9.

29 Richard T. Hughes, "Faith and Learning at Pepperdine University," in *Models for Christian Higher Education*, ed. Hughes and Adrian, p. 436. Confirmed also in Davenport interview with author, Jan. 29, 2015, Palo Alto, CA.

30 SRP: Davenport to Distribution, Oct. 20, 1992, David Davenport file, Box 1; and JWP: Wilson to Davenport, Apr. 5, 1993, 1992–93 file; Remarks of John Wilson, Aug. 17, 1993, 1993–94 file, Box 2; and Davenport, "Reflections from a President's Sabbatical," *Pepperdine Voice*, 16 (Oct. 1997), 4.

31 BAIRD: Davenport, "Coming of Age," Sept. 17, 1994, 1992–97 file.

32 Jeff Bliss, "Davenport Talks about Pepperdine, His Role," *Pepperdine Voice*, 13 (Jan. 1994): 1.

33 *Pepperdine University, Self Study* (Aug. 1992), vol. 1, 47–48; and PO: Wm. Phillips to Univ.-Wide Academic Program Review Committee, Sept. 18, 1984, and Nov. 2, 1984, Committees/Univ.-wide Academic Planning Review Com. file, Historic Materials.

34 BAIRD: "A Case For A Pepperdine Vision," attached to Davenport to Policy Committee, May 15, 1990, 1989–1992 file.

35 "University Assumptions for Academic Strategic Planning," Oct. 15, 1997, and amendments of Dec. 13, 1999, contained in *Pepperdine University, Self-Study*, appendix 1.2, Book 1 of 2 (Aug. 2000).

36 Ibid.

37 Ibid.

38 Ibid.

39 Ibid. By the time of the 2000 WASC self-study, the 60 percent figure for Seaver College had been changed to 50–60 percent.

40 LAT: Pepperdine President Speaks Out," Mar. 7, 1993, J1; and Davenport, "How Ross Perot Might Get My Vote," *USA Today*, June 9, 1992, 11A; and SRP: Jeff Bliss to Benton, June 25, 1992, George Bush file, Box R; and GRAPHIC: Liz Krow, "Clinton

Lands at Pepperdine," Mar. 14, 1996, 1; Arie Weedman, "Davenport, Caldwell Represent Dole, Clinton," Oct. 31, 1996, A2.

41 BAIRD: Mark Davis, ed., "Faith Is Our Fortune: Recommendations from the Spiritual Development Task Force" (Seaver, Apr. 1998), 1997–2000 file.

42 "The Mission of Pepperdine University" ([Malibu, CA: Pepperdine University,] Mar. 26, 1999); Allen, "A Place in the Sun," *University Business*, 2 (May 1999): 31–36. One major friend of the university objected to including the "Affirms" statement in the published version of the new missions statement because the language that "God is revealed uniquely in Christ" disenfranchised the beliefs of other religions. See BAIRD: email from Lisa Cappelli to Marnie Mitze, Jan. 29, 1999, 1998–2000 file.

CHAPTER 44

1 GRAPHIC: Steve Gobbell, "Anders Appointed Minister," Sept. 26, 1985, A4.

2 The figures come from various church bulletins gathered for 1985–1986 and 1997 among the Records of the University Church of Christ.

3 WAP: Proposal for a Joint Use Facility, Malibu Church of Christ, May 19, 1990, attached to Adrian to Policy Committee,, Oct. 4, 1990, Chron. Corres., June-Oct. 1990 (3 of 3) file, Box 2; and John Wilson to Univ. Policy Committee, Feb. 11, 1993, 1992–1993 file, Box 2; and GRAPHIC: "News Brief," Feb. 25, 1999, A2.

4 GRAPHIC: Stefanie Hein, "Women's Roles in Church, Convo Discussed," Feb. 2, 1989, 1.

5 Ibid.: Shelly Nego, "Women's Role in Church of Christ Re-evaluated," Oct. 24, 1991, 1.

6 JWP: Wilson to Davenport, Nov. 14, 1991, 1991–1992 file.

7 PO: James Thomas to Members of Faculty Organization, et al., Dec. 5, 1991, attached to Thomas to Davenport, et al., Dec. 8, 1991, Seaver/Committees/Faculty Org. file, Historic Materials.

8 Ibid.: Davenport to Distribution, Nov. 7, 1991, 1991–1992 file.

9 GRAPHIC: Ron Stearns, "D'Esta Love Gives First Female Convo Prayer," Sept. 3, 1992, 1.

10 Ibid.: "Seaver College Enters the 90s," Sept. 21, 1995, A9; Holly Hagler, "'Big Don' Williams resigns," Oct. 1, 1992, 1.

11 Interview with Scott Lambert by author, Aug. 21, 2013; and JWP: Minutes, University Church elders' meeting, May 15, 1998; and GRAPHIC: Nina Lora, "Campus Church Sets New Course," Sept. 24, 1998, A1.

12 GRAPHIC: Kristin McCary, "Care Group Grows in Numbers," Feb. 8, 1990, 2; Louise Brancato, "Care Group Promotes Fellowship," Feb. 20, 1986, A4; Melanie Sanders, "Designing Woman LaJuana Gill Gives New Look," Oct. 24, 1991, 4; Dwayne Jones, "Faith Not a Factor in All Admissions," Oct. 13, 1988, A6.

13 GRAPHIC: Candi Wright, "150 Projected To Attend Fall Retreat," Oct. 3, 1985, A4; Christina Littlefield, "Campus Ministry Retreat Productive," Sept. 24, 1998, A4; Jason Covington, "Christian Students Feed Homeless," Feb. 9, 1989, 5; Erin Lawler, "Students Will Travel South of the Border," Nov. 15, 1990, 5; Kari Johnson, "Campus Ministry Holds 24-Hour 'Hunger Strike,'" Nov. 12, 1992, 2; Schelly Jackson, "Students Sacrifice Food for Rwandan Cause," Oct. 27, 1994, 2; Katja Siegert, "Campus Ministry To Welcome 400 Christians," Oct. 18, 1990, 1; Rebecca A. English, "'The Call' Leaves Lasting Impression," Oct. 25, 1990, 1; Leslie Beville, "On a Mission from God," Oct. 23, 1997, A1; Kellie Heath, "Group Prepares for Brussels Summer Session," Mar. 15, 1990, 6; and Lara Shoban, "Year of Struggle and People of Hope," *Pepperdine People* (Spring 1992): 6–9.

14 GRAPHIC: Lauren Waldvogel, "Students Cross Oceans with Lord's Word," Aug. 29, 1994, 2; Waldvogel, "Students Start Talking," Sept. 14, 1995, 3.

15 Richard T. Hughes, "Faith and Learning at Pepperdine University," in *Models for Christian Higher Education*, ed. Hughes and Adrian, pp. 437–38.

16 GRAPHIC: Michelle Sullivan, "Church of Christ Not Affiliated," Oct. 21, 1993, 1.

17 Ibid.: Rachel Horton, "This Church Never Stops Giving to the Poor," Sept. 26, 1996, A8; Mark Ross, "New Malibu Church: Cult Or Not?" Feb. 25, 1999, A1.

18 Ibid.: Angela Tarantino, "Won by One, One of a Kind," Sept. 26, 1996, B4.

19 PO: Wm. Phillips to Distribution, Apr. 24, 1992, and Phillips to International Programs Advisory Council, Sept. 21, 1992, Ibaraki Christian College file, Old Corres.

20 BOT: Minutes, Religious Standards Committee, Sept. 9, 1980, 2:129–30.

21 GRAPHIC: Agnes Barthelemy, "AWP Funds Awarded to 225 Pep. Students," Oct. 21, 1993, 2; Lauren Waldvogel, "AWP Endowment Nears $1 Million," Nov. 10, 1994, 2; and SRP: Random notes, FAF file, Box 6 (F-L); and JWP: Wilson to Paul Long and Israel Rodriguez, Feb. 24, 1993, 1992–1993 file, Box 2.

22 Pepperdine University, Office of Institutional Research: Enrollment Profile, Fall 1985, Final, (Feb. 14, 1986), 24; *University Fact Book, 1983–1989* (Dec. 1989), A20–21; *University Fact Book [1988–1994]* (May 1995]), A20–21; and *Pepperdine University, Self-Study* (Aug. 2000), 1:67 & Appendix 7.3; and PO: Norman Fischer, "August 17, 2001 Cabinet Retreat," Aug. 2001, attached to Fischer to Andrew K. Benton, Aug. 10, 2001, Steve Hewgley's files.

23 Full-Time Tenured and Tenure Track Instructional Faculty by Religious Preference, Fall 1998, in Pepperdine, *Self-Study* (Aug. 2000), 1:73–74.

24 WAP: Adrian to Nancy Magnusson Fagan, Feb. 17, 1992, Chron. Corres. Jan.-July 1992 file, Box 2.

25 Ibid.: Adrian to Fagan, et al., Jan. 15, 1992; Adrian to Bob Cochrane, Jan. 30, 1992.

26 GRAPHIC: Mark Mallinger, "Can Seaver Survive Diversity?" Feb. 10, 1994, 11.

27 JWP: Wilson to Lemley and Baird, Nov. 12, 1997, 1997–1998 file, Box 2.

28 Allen, "A Place in the Sun," *University Business*, 2 (May 1999): 35.

29 JWP: Speech, "What Do We Mean, 'Christian Values'?" Mar. 4, 1988, 1987–1988 file, Box 1.

30 Ibid.: John Wilson, Notes of comments made to Univ. Policy Com., Oct. 18, 1989, 1989–1990 file, Box 2.

31 Ibid.

32 WAP: Adrian to Arlin G. Myers, Aug. 8, 1991, Chron. Corres. July-Dec. 1991 (1 of 2) file, Box 2.

33 Ibid.

34 GRAPHIC: Bryan Zug, "University Plans Summer Seminar on Christian Worldview," Mar. 5, 1992, 2.

35 Richard T. Hughes, "A National Conversation, Grants from the Lilly Endowment Enhance Christian Higher Education," *Pepperdine People* (Spring 1998): 22–23.

36 SCP: Hughes, "The Idea of a Christian University," Sept. 19, 2000, Center for Faith and Learning file, Drawer 2.

37 Ibid.: Center for Faith and Learning, "Faith and Learning at Pepperdine University" (Mar. 2001).

38 Ibid.

CHAPTER 45

1 YOUNG: Michael Adams to John B. Sample, Oct. 1, 1986, attached to Bob Woodroof to Distribution, Oct. 9, 1986, 50th Anniversary File, Box 13; and "Quest for a Rose Float," *Pepperdine People* (Summer 1987): 15–17.

2 Ibid.

3 GRAPHIC: Cyndee Jackson, "Students Question Float Venture," Jan. 29, 1987, A8.

4 SRP: See 50th Anniversary file, Box 12; and "Alumni Scene," *Pepperdine People* (Fall 1987): 30; and Program, Golden Wave Weekend, Sept. 20, 1987, Pepperdine 50th Anniversary file, Box 15, Public Affairs Records.
5 Chosen from an alumni base of nearly 35,000, the twelve were Gary L. Brinderson (MBA '82), a heavy constructor; J. Richard Chase (BA '53, MA '54), president of Wheaton College; Christopher Chetsanga (BA '64), a Nobel Prize nominee for cancer research; Ressel Fok (BA '54), an international banker; Terry M. Giles (JD '74), an attorney and entrepreneur; Kenneth Hahn (BA '42), Los Angeles County Supervisor; Dorcas R. Hardy (MBA '76), commissioner of Social Security; Darwin Horn (BA '49), member of U.S. Secret Service; Dennis Johnson, professional basketball player; Mike Scott, professional baseball player; Linda M. Thor (BA '71, EdD '86), president of West Los Angeles College; and Helen M. Young (BA '39), founder of AWP and wife of President Norvel Young."
6 SRP: Program, "Pepperdine University 50th Anniversary Convocation, September 21, 1987," 50th Anniversary file, Box 12. See also GRAPHIC: Jennifer Burry, "Pep Celebrates Half a Century," Sept. 24, 1987, A4 & 5.
7 SRP: Jack Searies, "At Age 50, Pepperdine Still Makes the Grade," *[Los Angeles] Herald Examiner*, Sept. 13, 1987, E1, clipping, 50th Anniversary file, Box 12.
8 Rushford, *Crest of a Golden Wave.*
9 SUB: *Fifth-Year Report* (Oct. 30, 1987), WASC 1983–1989 folder.
10 Ibid.: "Report of the Expanded Fifth-Year Visit to Pepperdine University," Dec. 8–11, 1987, WASC 1983–1989 folder; and WAP: Adrian to Distribution, June 7, 1988, Chron. Corres. Mar.-Oct. 1988 (2 of 3) file, Box 1.
11 SUB: Kay Andersen to David Davenport, Mar. 1, 1988, WASC 1983–1989 folder.
12 Ibid.: Davenport to Raymond Bacchetti, Jan. 28, 1988.
13 BAIRD: "Campaign for Pepperdine University," [1984], 1984–1985 folder; and NICKS: "Wave of Excellence Report, Special Edition," [1985], Wave of Excellence file, Box 13; and HAWP: "The Wave of Excellence, Statement from the Vice President for University Affairs," [Mar. 1984], Chron. Corres. Mar. 1984 (2 of 2) file, Box 13; and Michael F. Adams, "The 'Wave of Excellence' Phenomenon," *Pepperdine People* (Fall 1987): 2–5.
14 HAWP: Adams to Davenport, Nov. 6, 1985, White to Davenport, Nov. 26, 1985, Pumpkin Papers file, Box xx2.; and PO: Adams to Davenport, Nov. 23, 1987, Pumpkin Papers file, Historic Correspondence.
15 Principal benefactors were Flora L. Thornton, George C. Page, Mrs. Burtie G. Bettingen, Morris B. Pendleton, and Carl F. Braun Trust Estate.
16 The foundations included Jones, ARCO, W. M. Keck, Kresge, Weingart, and James Irvine.
17 Celebrities participating were singer John Raitt, actor Jimmy Stewart, singer Constance Towers, actress Florence Henderson, actor Rod Steiger, and street painter Kurt Wenner.
18 NICKS: "Wave of Excellence Report" (Fall 1984, Fall 1985, Winter 1985, Summer 1987, Fall 1987, and Winter 1987), Wave of Excellence file, Box 13.
19 SRP: See Payson Library file, Box 27; and Louella Benson, "Payson Plugs In, Computerization Is the First Step in Library Improvement and Expansion," *Pepperdine People* (Summer 1986): 21; WAP: Adrian to University Librarians and Members of the Search Committee, June 9, 1989, Chron. Corres., Apr.-Nov. 1989 (1 of 3) file, Box 1.
20 *Pepperdine University, Self-Study* (2000), 1:84–89; GRAPHIC: Jennifer Cole, "Library Gets New Research Systems," Oct. 2, 1997, A3.
21 *Pepperdine University, Self-Study* (2000), 1:90–96; and Mark Ross, "Y2K: Pepperdine Converts to New Systems," Aug. 30, 1999, A3.
22 These records are maintained by the Office of Admission, Seaver College.

23 In admitting better qualified students, Seaver College had to compete for recruits with some of the best endowed institutions in the country.

24 *Pepperdine University, University Fact Book, 1988–1994*, B1; and PO: Norman Fischer, "August 17, 2001 Cabinet Retreat," Aug. 2001, attached to Fischer to Andrew K. Benton, Aug. 10, 2001, Steve Hewgley's files; and BAIRD: Pepperdine University, Educational Effectiveness Review, Submitted to the Western Association of Schools and Colleges, July 2012, Exhibit D1, 2000ff file.

25 Ibid.

26 Ibid.; and BAIRD: "Third-Year Interim Report to the Western Association of Schools and Colleges," Nov. 8, 1995, table 1–3, attached to Steven Lemley to Steven S. Weiner, Nov. 8, 1995, 1992–1997 file.

27 GRAPHIC: Teri Bruch, "Faculty Salaries Score Within Nation's Highest," Feb. 27, 1986, A1.

28 Linda A. Bell, "More Good News, so Why the Blues?: The Annual Report on the Economic Status of the Profession, 1999–2000," *Academe*, 86 (Mar.–Apr., 2000), pp. 11–95.

29 PO: Davenport to Charles Carpenter, Oct. 19, 1989, Chron. Corres. 1989 file, Historic Materials. See also Ibid.: Davenport to All Full-Time Faculty, Jan. 18, 1989, Tenure/Process/Supp. Info. File, Tenure Summaries.

30 JWP: Wilson, "Remarks to Faculty of Seaver College," Sept. 4, 1984, 1984–1989 file, Box 1.

31 The first recipients were Stephen Davis, Bob Gilliam, and V. Seshan (Seaver); Mary Miller (SOL); Arthur Adams (GSEP); and Wayne Gertmenian (SBM).Other winners were Dan Caldwell, Carol Adjemian, June Payne-Palacio, Lydia Reineck, Harry Caldwell, Janet Kerr, Wayne Strom, Stephen Brown and David Elkins in 1991; Farrel Gean, Michael Gose, Gary Hart, Victoria Myers, Robert Privitt, Jennings Davis, Robert Weathers, Robert Wright, and Wayne Estes in 1992; Mark Mallinger, James Tomas, Louis Jenkins, Owen Hall, James Martinoff, Clifford Darden, Charles Nelson, and Robert Popovich in 1993.

32 WAP: Adrian to Distribution, Jan. 12, 1987, Chron. Corres. May 1986-Mar. 1987 (3 of 3) file, Box 1.

33 JWP: Wilson to Davenport, Apr. 5, 1993, 1992–93 file, Box 2.

34 PO: Davenport to All Full-Time Faculty, Jan. 18, 1989, Tenure/Process/Supp. Info. File, Tenure Summaries; and Mychel Walker, "Double Meaning Intended," *Oasis* (Fall 1985): 18–19; and BAIRD: "Third-Year Interim Report to the Western Association of Schools and Colleges," Nov. 8, 1995, 4–5, attached to Steven Lemley to Steven S. Weiner, Nov. 8, 1995, 1992–1997 file.

35 PO: Wm. Phillips to Connie James, Feb. 19, 1985; Phillips to Davenport, Sept. 15, 1987; Adrian to Edu. Com., Sept 21, 1992, Committees/University/Research Council file; and Davenport to Phillips and Adrian, Feb. 4, 1986, Chron. Corres. 1986 file, Old Subject Files; and GRAPHIC: Angela Louie, "Research Fund Supplies 'Seed Money,' Oct. 10, 1985, A3.

36 Pepperdine University, "University Assumptions for Academic Strategic Planning," Oct. 15, 1997, and amendments of Dec. 13, 1999, contained in *Self-Study*, appendix (2000), 1.2.

37 PO: Dwayne Van Rheenen vita, [1996], D. Van Rheenen file, Old Subject Files; and "Civil War Expert Named First White History Professor," *Pepperdine Voice* (Aug. 1986), in PO: Correspondence 1986 file, Historic Records; and JWP: Wilson to Tom and Dorothy Olbricht, Mar. 24, 1994, 1993–1994 file, Box 2.

38 Mychel Walker, "Journey Back to Academia Leads Wright to Portugal," *Pepperdine Voice* (Aug. 1986), in PO: Correspondence 1986 file, Historic Records.

39 Robert Blair, "Pepperdine's Fulbright Scholars," *Pepperdine People* (Fall 1988): 11–13. Faculty Fulbright scholars included William Adrian, Krakow, Poland;

Byron Lane, University of Latvia in Riga; Frank Novak, University of Maribor in Slovenia; Carolyn Vos Strache, Korea International Educator; Darlene Rivas, Argentina Council for International Relations; and myself, University of Canterbury, Christchurch, New Zealand.

40 PO: Wm. B. Phillips to Distribution, Apr. 18, 1984 and Gary Hanson to Phillips, May 22, 1984, Tenure/Policy/1984 (Review Process) file, Historic Materials.

41 Ibid.: Wm. B. Phillips to Howard White and Davenport, Aug. 6, 1984, Tenure/Policy/1984 (Review Process) file, Historic Correspondence; and *Seaver College Faculty Handbook, 1985*, 8.

42 PO: Tenure/Policy/1986 (Review Process) file, Historic Materials.

43 Ibid.: Hanson to Adrian, Apr. 25, 1991; Adrian to University Tenure Committee, Jan. 22, 1993, Tenure/Policy/1993 (Development process) file.

44 Ibid.: Mike Kinsman to Adrian, July 7, 1992. See also WAP: Adrian to Academic Affairs of the Board of Regents, Dec. 18, 1992, Chron. Corres. Aug.-Dec. 1992 (2 of 2) file, Box 2.

45 BOT: Tenure Policy Statement, June 8, 1993, 25:K-1.

46 BAIRD: "Third-year Interim Report."

47 Ibid.

48 BAIRD: *Pepperdine University, Self-Study* (Aug. 2000), 31, 2000ff file.

49 BAIRD: *Self Study* (Aug. 1992), C6-C13, 1992–1997 file; *Self-Study* (Aug. 2000), 1:114–15, 2000ff file.

50 NICKS: Matthew Lincoln to Charles J. Pippin, Aug. 23, 1990, Fin. & Strat. Plan. file, Box 7.

51 Ibid.

52 Ibid.: Adrian to Policy Committee and Provost's Cabinet, Jan. 9, 1990, Strategic Planning, Box 19.

53 Pepperdine University, *Self Study for Reaffirmation* (1992), appendices, B, C1.

54 "Comprehensive Institutions," *U.S. News & World Report*, Nov. 25, 1985: 48.

55 *The Golden Wave and Beyond, Pepperdine University Annual Report, 1987.*

56 GRAPHIC: Shelly Ngo, "Pepperdine Ranks in Second Quartile in U.S. News Study," Sept. 26, 1991, 1.

57 SUB: Norman Fischer to Andrew K. Benton, et.al., Mar. 12, 2001, WASC 1999–2000 folder. Pepperdine was ranked 51 of 229 schools in 1995, 1996, and 1997, but still in the second quartile.

CHAPTER 46

1 WAP: William Adrian to Alexander Astin, Oct. 1, 1991, Chron. Corres. July-Dec. 1991 (1 of 2) file, Box 2; Adrian to University Community, Sept. 10, 1992, Chron. Corres. Aug.-Dec. 1992 (1 of 2) file, Box 2; and SUB: Pepperdine University, Self Study (1992), 1:ix-xiii, WASC 1992 Folder.

2 SUB: *Self Study* (1992), 1:15–29, WASC 1992 Folder.

3 Ibid.

4 Ibid.

5 Ibid.: "WASC Team Reaffirmation Accreditation Visit, October 20–23, 1992," attached to Stephen Weiner to Davenport, Jan. 5, 1993, 1990/91/93 folder; "Third-Year Interim Report," attached to Lemley to Stephen Weiner, Nov. 8, 1995, WASC 1995–1997 folder.

6 Ibid.: "WASC Team Reaffirmation Accreditation Visit," attached to Stephen Weiner to Davenport, Jan. 5, 1993.

7 Ibid.

8 Ibid.

9 Ibid.

10 Ibid.: Davenport to Weiner, Feb. 2, 1993.

11 Ibid.

12 Ibid.

13 Ibid.: Stephen Weiner to Davenport, Mar. 10, 1993.

14 Ibid.

15 GRAPHIC: Mark Hull, "WASC Adopts Diversity Statement," Mar. 3, 1994, 1; and SUB: Accrediting Commission for Senior Colleges and Universities, "Report on the Future of Self-Regulation in Higher Education," Dec. 1993, and Lemley to Davenport, Dec. 9, 1993, WASC 1990/91/91 folder, and Davenport to Faculty, Feb. 21, 1994, WASC 1994 folder. Davenport was only one of many skeptics of the WASC report on self-regulation. See "Controversy Over an Accreditor's Blueprint for Change," *Chronicle for Higher Education*, July 6, 1994.

16 SUB: Davenport to Donald Gerty, Nov. 11, 1993, WASC 1990/91/93 folder; and GRAPHIC: Mark Hull, "Davenport Disagrees with WASC Proposal," Mar. 10, 1994, 1.

17 Ibid.: Draft of unsigned letter to Donald Gerth, Mar. 18, 1994, attached to Davenport to Geoffrey Cox, Mar. 29, 1994, WASC 1994 folder.

18 Ibid.

19 SRP: Davenport to Steve Lemley, et al., Mar. 28, 1994, A-R Subject files, Box R; and SUB: Donald Gerth and James Appleton to Chief Executive Officers et al., Mar. 28, 1994, and Steve Lemley's comments as a member of a panel discussing "Report on the Future of Self-Regulation in Higher Education" at a meeting of WCA on Maui, Apr. 13, 1994, WASC 1994 folder; and BAIRD: email from Steve Lemley to author, Nov. 18, 2013, 1992–1997 file.

20 SUB: "Third-Year Interim Report," Nov. 8, 1995, i-ii, attached to Lemley to Stephen Weiner, Nov. 8, 1995, WASC 1995–1997 folder.

21 Ibid. See also *Leadership in the New Millennium: Pepperdine University Annual Report, 1994* (1994).

22 Ibid.

23 Ibid.

24 BAIRD: Stephen Weiner to David Davenport, Jan. 4, 1996, attached to Lemley to Reviewers, Jan. 23, 1996, 1992–1997 file.

25 LAT: Judy Pasternak, "Pepperdine: Party School by the Shore," Sept. 19, 1987, 1.

26 Allen, "A Place in the Sun," *University Business*, 2 (May 1999): 34–35.

27 JWP: Wilson to Davenport, June 24, 1993, 1992–1993 file, Box 2.

28 Bill Henegar, "The Next Wave, Jones, Raitt and Runnels lead as Pepperdine's Newest Initiative Roars in," *Pepperdine People* (Spring 1995): 3–5. Larry Hornbaker prepared detailed minutes of the meeting held on Mar. 17, 1994. They are available in SRP: Campaign (Challenged to Lead) file, Box 19. See also Case Statement, "Challenged to Lead, the Campaign for Pepperdine: Campaign Workbook," [Oct. 1994], Case Statement Tab; *Leadership in the New Millennium*.

29 Henegar, "Next Wave," *Pepperdine People*, 3–5; and BAIRD: Davenport, "Coming of Age," Sept. 17, 1994, 1992–1997 file.

30 *Leadership in the New Millennium*.

31 *Promises to Keep, Pepperdine University Annual Report, 2000* (2000): 8–11.

32 Ibid.

33 Allen, "A Place in the Sun," *University Business*, 2 (May 1999): 37.

34 BAIRD: George L. Graziadio to Andrew K. Benton, Mar. 24, 1997, 1992–1997 file.

35 *Advancing the Changeless, Pepperdine University 1999 Annual Report* (1999): 14–15; *Promises to Keep, Pepperdine University Annual Report, 2000* (2000): 8–11.

36 Colleen Cason, "Weisman Museum Opens to Rave Reviews," *Pepperdine Voice*, 11 (Oct. 1992):1, Cason, "The Art of Collecting and Giving," *Pepperdine People* (Spring 1993): 2–5; and GRAPHIC: Sandra Tapia, "Controversial Photograph Removed from Exhibit," Nov. 3, 1994, 1.

37 "Cultural enrichment plan to aid campus diversity," *Pepperdine Voice*, 11 (Jan. 1992): 1; and Pepperdine University's Cultural Enrichment Initiative Notes/ Remarks, [1991], Cultural Enrichment Initiative file, Box 1, David Davenport Papers.

38 Colleen Cason, "Irvine Grant Supports Cultural Enrichment Initiative," *Pepperdine Voice*, 11 (Oct. 1992): 2; PO: Davenport to Faculty and Academic Deans, Sept. 2, 1992, Grants/President's Discretionary Fund file, Old Subject files.

39 *Pepperdine University, Self-Study* (Aug. 2000), 18.

40 Ibid.

41 SUB: Lemley to Tom Corts, Oct. 27, 2000, WASC 1999–2000 folder.

42 Ibid.

43 Ibid. The letter was written at considerable personal and professional risk, for it could have been interpreted as "tampering with the jury." But Lemley was emboldened by the high stakes and because he was already at the end of his term as provost. Within three hours of the WASC team making its final oral report, Lemley had packed up his personal belongings and left the provost's office to assume responsibilities as associate professor of communication in Seaver College. He was succeeded by Darryl Tippens, recently of Abilene Christian University, who had been selected to take over the provost's role. BAIRD: email message from Lemley to author, Nov. 22, 2013, 2000ff folder.

44 SUB: "WASC Team Reaffirmation Accreditation Visit, October 24–27, 2000," WASC 1999–2000 folder.

45 Ibid.

46 Ibid.: Wolff to Benton, Mar. 6, 2001.

CHAPTER 47

1 PO: David Davenport to Adrian, Feb. 17, 1992, Chron. Corres. 1992 file, Old Corres. Files.

2 Ibid.: Davenport to Ron Fagan et al., Feb. 2, 1993, SPP Corres. 1992–1998 folder, Old Subject Files.

3 Ibid.: Steven Lemley to Davenport, May 16, 1994.

4 Interview with Steven Lemley by author, July 7, 2012, Malibu, CA; interview with David Davenport by author, Jan. 29, 2015, Stanford, CA.

5 PO: Davenport to Lodwrick M. Cooke, Aug. 25, 1993; executive summary of the Reagan School of Public Policy, attached to Larry Bumgardner to Davenport and Lemley, Oct. 25, 1993, SPP Corres. 1992–1998 folder, Old Subject Files.

6 Ibid.: George C. Heider, "Review of Existing Graduate Programs in Public Policy," 1994.

7 Ibid.: "The Pepperdine University School of Public Policy," [Aug. 1, 1994]. The MAPP degree was never offered.

8 SRP: Conceptual Outline, School of Public Policy, May 1995; "Pepperdine University," attached to Davenport to James Piereson, Sept. 13, 1994, School of Public Policy, Box 29. See also Jeff Bliss, "University To Open School of Public Policy," *Pepperdine Voice*, 15 (Jan. 1996): 1.

9 PO: Davenport to James Piereson, Sept. 13, 1994, SPP Corres. 1992–1998 folder, Old Subject Files.

10 Unhappily, the $1.1 million Scaife gift to SPP ignited conflict-of-interest charges against Kenneth Starr because of Scaife's funding of pointedly anti-Bill Clinton ventures.

11 Allen, "A Place in the Sun," *University Business*, 2 (May 1999): 37.

12 PO: Davenport to Edwin J. Feulner, Mar. 8, 1995, SPP Corres. 1992–1998 folder, Old Subject Files.

13 Ibid.: Davenport to Piereson, Sept. 13, 1994.

14 Ibid.: Davenport to the Faculty, Jan. 9. 1996.
15 Ibid. See also Patti Yomantas, "Rising to the Challenge of Leadership in America," *Pepperdine People* (Summer 1996): 18–19.
16 PO: "Dean, School of Public Policy," [Feb. 9, 1996], SPP Corres. 1992–1998 folder, Old Subject Files.
17 *Pepperdine Voice*, 15 (Jan. 1996) 1.
18 PO: Davenport to the Faculty, Jan. 9. 1996, SPP Corres. 1992–1998 folder, Old Subject Files.
19 Ibid.
20 Ibid.: email from John Wilson to Steve Lemley, Feb. 8, 1996.
21 Ibid.: email from Davenport to Lemley, Feb. 22, 1996.
22 Ibid.: Lemley to Seaver Faculty, Feb. 12, 1996.
23 Ibid.: email from Wilson to Lemley, Feb. 8, 1996.
24 Ibid.: email from Cyndia Clegg to Davenport, Mar. 27, 1997, Seaver/Committees/ Faculty Org. file.
25 See LAT: Patrick J. McDonnell, "New Latino Middle Class on the Rise, Study Finds," Oct. 10, 1996, 1; Editorial, "New Latino Role in Middle Class," Oct. 11, 1996, 8; and Joel Kotkin, "The Emerging Latino Middle Class," *Wall Street Journal*, Oct. 9, 1996, A22.
26 PO: Davenport to Benefactors, Founders Cabinet, and Friends of the Institute and School of Public Policy, Oct. 28, 1996, Seaver/Committees/Faculty Org. file, Old Subject Files.
27 Ibid.: School of Public Policy, Academic Affairs Report, Fall 1997, SPP Corres. 1992–1998 folder, Old Corres. files. See also SCP: "Five-Year Program Review and Assessment, School of Public Policy, Pepperdine University, April 2002."
28 BAIRD: [Kelo] Time Line, 1996–2011, [Sept. 2011], SPP folder.
29 Ibid.
30 PO: Scaife to Wilburn, June 8, 1999, SPP Corres. 1992–1998 folder, Old Corres. files, Provost Office.
31 Ibid.: Email from Davenport to Lemley, Mar. 12, 1998, and email from Wilburn to Davenport, Apr. 23, 1998. See also SCP: "Five-Year Program Review and Assessment, School of Public Policy, Pepperdine University, April 2002."
32 BAIRD: email from Jim Wilburn to author, Mar. 15, 2014, SPP file.

CHAPTER 48

1 Dan Caldwell, Conference notes, May 5–6, 1992, Cousins' Writers Conference file, Dan Caldwell personal papers. See also Maryam E. Kubasek, "The Red and the Red, White, and Blue," *Pepperdine People* (Summer 1990): 9–11.
2 GRAPHIC: Janna Anderson, "Vigil Held To Better Relations," Oct. 27, 1988, A1; and LAT: Kenneth Garcia, "Making Waves: Christian University Gets First Taste of Protest as Students Fight Apathy," Nov. 3, 1988: 1.
3 Kubasek, "The Red and the Red, White, and Blue," *Pepperdine People* (Summer 1990): 9–11; and GRAPHIC: Mathis Chazanov, Tami Marko, "Moscow Student Bridges East-West Gap, Offers Insight," Feb. 1, 1990, 1.
4 LAT: "Perestroika Prospers at Pepperdine," Jan. 14, 1990, J1 & J10;
5 GRAPHIC: Amy Hannis, "Talcott's Dream for International Student Awareness," Feb. 14, 1991, 8.
6 "Dan Caldwell: Eyeing the Soviets," *Pepperdine People* (Fall, 1986): 12; and LAT: "Malibu Professor to Head Forum," Oct. 12, 1989, 2.
7 PO: Wilburn to Rothschild, Aug. 31, 1994, GSBM/Rothschild file, Old Corres.
8 NICKS: "Pepperdine University School of Business and Management and the Soviet Union, Suggested Strategy," Oct. 31, 1990, Misc. Papers file, Box 7.

9 BAIRD: James R. Wilburn, draft of "My Life and Experiences with Pepperdine University," Mar. 12, 2012, Graziadio file. See also GRAPHIC: Kelly Tate, "Dr. James Wilburn Heads Board," Oct. 3, 1991, 1.

10 BAIRD: Wilburn, draft of "My Life and Experiences."

11 Ibid. See also, GRAPHIC: Mark Hull, "Officials Deny Spy Charges," Sept. 8, 1994, 1; and LAT: Sonni Efron, "Russia Livid Over Alleged Spying by U.S.," Sept. 7, 1994, 1.

12 WAP: Wm. Adrian to Stephen Weiner, Aug. 9, 1989, Chron. Corres. Apr.-Nov. 1989 (2 of 3) file, Box 2; and MFA: "Report of the Academic Affairs Committee on the Program in Japan," Feb. 3, 1988, Executive Committee, Agenda, Feb. 8, 1988, Box 8.

13 LAT: Kenneth J. Garcia, "Pepperdine Pursues Japan Campus," Feb. 2, 1989, 3.

14 WAP: Wm. Adrian to Yoshihisa Okugawa, Nov. 10, 1989, Chron. Corres. Apr.-Nov., 1989 (3 of 3) file, and Jan. 24, 1990, Chron. Corres. Dec. 1989-May 1990 (1 of 3) file, Box 2.

15 Ibid.: Adrian to Steve Weiner, Aug. 28, 1990.

16 GRAPHIC: Shelly Nego, "Japan Added to List of International Programs," Sept. 5, 1991, 2; Elisa Bearly, "Japan Program Continues Despite Cancellation," Jan. 18, 1986, 1; and PO: Wm. Phillips to International Programs Advisory Council, Sept. 21, 1992, Ibaraki Christian College folder, Old Correspondence.

17 HAWP: White to Deane Dana, Nov. 21, 1983, Chron. Corres. Nov. 1983 file, Box 12; and PO: California Coastal Commission, Revised Findings, Feb. 21, 1984 (Hearing Date), Sewage Plant Expansion file, Old Corres.

18 HAWP: [White] Interview [with] *Santa Monica Evening Outlook*, Feb. 24, 1984, Chron. Corres. Feb. 1984 (2 of 2) file, Box 13.

19 PO: "Summary of Past Efforts regarding the Pepperdine University Long Range Development Plan" attached to ADK to Policy Committee, Nov. 7, 1988, Committees/Univ./Policy Com. file, Old Subject files. See also MFA: "Campus Development Plan," tab L, in Board of Regents Agenda, Mar. 10, 1987, Box 8.

20 LAT: Kenneth J. Garcia, "Coastal Panel Oks Expansion for Pepperdine," Sept. 14, 1989, A13; and Anne Morgenthaler, "Pepperdine Wins Expansion Fight," *Santa Monica Outlook*, Sept. 13, 1989, A1 & A12; and Juley Harvey, "Pepperdine Expansion Plan Approved," *Malibu Times*, Sept. 14, 1989, 1 & 18–19, clipping in SRP: Long Range Development file, Box 25.

21 SRP: Harvey, "Pepperdine Expansion Plan Approved," *Malibu Times*, Sept. 14, 1989, 1 & 18–19, clipping in Long Range Development file, Box 25.

22 Anne Soble, "Pepperdine Development Plans Aired at Task Force Forum," *Malibu Surfside News*, Dec. 12, 1991, p. 2, in Malibu Land Development newspaper clippings, 1987–1991 file, Box 1, David Davenport Papers.

23 SRP: Clipping, Joe Bel Bruno, "University Expansion Allowed," *The [Santa Monica] Outlook*, Apr. 1, 1992, Long Range Development file, Box 25.

24 GRAPHIC: Lisa Wahla, "Pep Presents Plan for 'Upper Campus,'" Sept. 17, 1998, A1; Wahla, "New Campus OK'd," Jan. 14, 1999, A1; Wahla, "Project OK'd, Grading Set for Spring," Oct. 28, 1999, A1; Wahla, "Sierra Club Sues Pep over Rare Grasslands," Jan. 20, 2000, A3; Wahla, "Sierra Club Fails To Halt Grad Campus," Apr. 6, 2000, A3.

25 GRAPHIC: Mychel Walker and Kelley Farley, "Containment Expected Today in Malibu Fires"; Wendy Estes, "Students' Panic Needless According to Fire Official"; Keith Sloane, "Faculty Endures Fiery Wall"; and Iris Yokoi, "Brush Fire Causes Confusion among Students," Oct. 17, 1985, A1 & A3.

26 Ibid.

27 Ibid.

28 GRAPHIC: Special Edition, Nov. 8, 1993, 1ff.

29 Ibid.

30 GRAPHIC: Cinnamon Atchley, "Students Say 'Thanks' for Saving University," Nov. 11, 1993, 1.

31 Maryam Kubasek, "Student Volunteers Aid in Recovery Efforts," *Pepperdine Voice*, 13 (Jan. 1994): 1.

32 SRP: Davenport to the Pepperdine Community, Nov. 5, 1993, Pepperdine Fire, Nov. 2–4, 1993 file, Box 22.

33 Ibid.: Walter Surdacki to Jeff Bliss, Nov. 8, 1993, Pepperdine Fire, Nov. 2–4, 1993 file, Box 22.

34 GRAPHIC: Bryan Boettger, "Firestorm Rings Campus Again," Oct. 24, 1996, 1.

35 Ibid.: Lauren Lum, "Campus Organizations Join Forces," Jan. 20, 1994, 1; Joy Bringer, "Dramarama to rock for quake benefit," Mar. 17, 1994, 1; and "University on the Move," *Pepperdine People* (Summer 1994): 23.

36 LAT: "Soaking Wet," Jan. 11, 1995, 1; and GRAPHIC: Arie Weedman, "Volunteers Answer Call," Jan. 12, 1995.

37 Ibid.: Arie Weedman, "El Nino Reigns for a Day," Feb. 5, 1998, 1.

CHAPTER 49

1 JWP: John Wilson, "Remarks to the Seaver Faculty, Aug. 26, 1986, 1986–1987 file, Box 1.

2 Ibid.: Wilson, "Faculty Conference Address," Mar. 4, 1988, 1987–1988 file, Box 1.

3 Ibid.: Wilson, "Remarks at Faculty Conference," Mar. 5, 1992, 1991–1992 file, Box 2.

4 Ibid.: Wilson, "A University for the Third Millennium," Nov. 5, 1992, 1992–1993 file; Wilson, "Goals and Objectives-1994–95," 1994–95 file, Box 2.

5 Ibid.: Wilson, "Remarks to the Faculty of Seaver College," Aug. 21, 1990, 1990–1991 file; Wilson, "Comments from JFW to Faculty at Conference," Apr. 1992, 1991–1992 file; Wilson, "Remarks to the Seaver College Faculty," Aug. 22, 1995, 1995–1996 file, Box 2.

6 Wilson, "Remarks to the Seaver College Faculty," Aug. 19, 1996, attached to "Some Reflections on the Proposed New Seaver Academic Strategic Plan," Aug. 19, 1997, 1997–1998 file.

7 GRAPHIC: Iris Yokoi, "Wilson Takes Crack at Seaver's Challenge," Sept. 29, 1983, A2; and WAP: Adrian to Wilson, Sept. 13, 1990, Chron. Corres. June-Oct. 1990 (2 of 3) file, Box 2.

8 JWP: Wilson, Long Range Goals, Aug. 1984; Wilson statement to Board of Regents, Nov. 11, 1984; FAC to Wilson, May 9, 1985, 1984–85 file, Box 1. See also WAP: Adrian to Davenport, Dec. 19, 1987, Chron. Corres. Apr. 1987-Feb. 1988 (3 of 3) file, Box 1.

9 The faculty/student ratio at Seaver College was 1 to 26, while at Occidental the ratio was 1 to 13 and at Pomona 1 to 9.5.

10 WAP: Adrian to Davenport, Dec. 29, 1987, Chron. Files. Apr. 1987-Feb. 1988 (3 of 3) file; and YOUNG: Young to Davenport, Jan. 28, 1986, Chron. Jan.-Mar. 1986 file, Letters Sent; and JWP: Wilson to Seaver Faculty, July 10, 1989, 1988–1989 file, Box 2.

11 JWP: Wilson, Remarks to faculty of Seaver College, Sept. 4, 1984, 1984–85 file, Box 1.

12 Ibid.: Wilson, Remarks to Seaver College Faculty, Aug. 23, 1989, 1989–1990 file, Box 2.

13 Baird, et. al., *Opportunities for Liberal Learning*, 9–13.

14 SRP: Wm. B. Phillips to Davenport and Benton, Nov. 13, 1985, General Ed. Requirements file, Box 23.

15 Ibid.

16 WAP: Adrian to Budget Committee, Apr. 26, 1989, Chron. Corres. Apr.-Nov. 1989 (1 of 3) files, and Adrian to Dwayne Van Rheenen, Aug. 8, 1990, Chron. Corres.

June-Oct. 1990 (1 of 3) file. See PO: Seaver Committees/Academic Advising file, Old. Corres.

17 Olbricht, *Reflections on My Life*, 285–93; and GRAPHIC: Jennifer Burry, "Division Restructures," Mar. 12, 1987, A1.

18 WAP: Michael Adams to Bill Adrian, June 13, 1988; Adrian to Adams, June 16, 1988, Chron. Corres. Mar.-Oct. 1988 (2 of 3) file, Box 1.

19 Ibid.: Adrian to Wilson, July 5, 1988, Chron. Corres. Mar.-Oct. 1988 (2 of 3) file, Box 1.

20 Ibid.: Terry Law to Carol White, Feb. 27, 1987, Chron. Corres. May 1986-Mar. 1987 (3 of 3) file; Adrian to Budget Committee, Apr. 26, 1989, Chron. Corres. Apr.-Nov. 1989 (1 of 3) file, Box 1.

21 GRAPHIC: Michelle Landon, "International Affairs Program Approved," Oct. 20, 1988, A3; and email from Fred Casmir to author, Dec. 19, 2013.

22 GRAPHIC: Jim Radosta, "Wash. D.C. Program Unveiled," Jan. 23, 1992, 1; and Paul Dyer, "In the Thick of Things," *Pepperdine People* (Fall 1992):11–13.

23 JWP: Wilson, "A Three Year Honors-Tutorial Program at Seaver College," Sept. 29, 1993, 1993–1994 file, Box 2.

24 BAIRD: email from Steve Davis to David Baird, Apr. 3, 2013, 1987–1989 file.

25 PO: "Recommendations of the Division Structure Committee: A Report to the Seaver College Faculty," attached to Wilson to William B. Phillips, Apr. 23, 1985, Seaver/Committees/Faculty file, Historic Corres.

26 JWP: Wilson to Pepperdine Community, Mar. 26, 1992, 1991–1992 file, Box 2.

27 Ibid.

28 GRAPHIC: Denise Wasilevich, "Students React to 'Value-Centered Education,'" Mar. 15, 1990, 1.

29 Ibid.: Margo Taylor, "Volunteer Center Now Open at Pepperdine," Nov. 3, 1988, A1; Kristen Scheu, "Student Volunteer Center focuses on Community," June 14, 1989, 2; Beth Gurdock, "Community Gains Helping Hand," Sept. 12, 1996, 6; Tami Marko, "Malibu Meets Skid Row in Christian Outreach," Feb. 8, 1990, 1; Lauren Lum, "Students Volunteer for Kids Klub," Nov. 21, 1991, 1; Shelly Ngo, "Pepperdine Responds to Los Angeles Riots," Sept. 3, 1992, 1; Lauren Lum, "Campus Organizations Join Forces To Assist Earthquake Victims," Jan. 20, 1994, 1.

30 Ibid.: Hannah Duvon, "Service Learning New Buzzword for University," Nov. 9, 1995, A4; Julie Broad, "Service Learning," Mar. 18, 1999, A7; and SRP: Sheila Bost to Shirley Roper, Feb. 6, 1996, Volunteer Center file, Box 33; and Ted Parks, "Putting the Mission to Work," *Pepperdine People* (Spring 1998): 18–19,

31 BAIRD: email from Jerry Rushford to David Baird, June 4, 2013.

32 BAIRD: email from Don Thompson to David Baird, Aug. 15, 2013.

33 Ibid.

34 JWP: Wilson to the Seaver Chairpersons, et al., Sept. 6, 1989, 1989–90 file, Box 2; and *Pepperdine University, Self Study* (1992), 2:A38; *Self-Study* (2000), 2:Ap. 4.4.

35 GRAPHIC: Robert Vogt, "Administrators Startled by Drop in Retention," Oct. 5, 1995, A1; Mari Gutierrez, "Student Retention Rates Increase," Oct. 24, 1996, 2.

36 Pepperdine University, *University Fact Book, 1982–1987* (1988), sec. B; *Self Study* (1992), 2: B1-B7; *Self-Study* (2000), 1:71–82; and JWP: Wilson to Davenport and Adrian, Dec. 20, 1989, 1989–1990 file, and Church of Christ Affiliation, 1984–1994 file, Box 2.

37 GRAPHIC: Teri Bruce, "Faculty Salaries Score Within the Nation's Highest," Feb. 27, 1986, A1.

38 PO: Cyndia Clegg to Wilson, Feb. 22, 1996, Seaver/Committees/Faculty Org. file, Historic Materials.

39 Ibid.: Proposed constitution of the Seaver Faculty Association, attached to Dwayne Van Rheenen to David Davenport and Nancy Magnusson Fagan, June 22, 1993.

40 Ibid.: RTP Task force to Seaver Faculty, Mar. 24, 1989; Norman Hughes to Seaver Faculty, May 4, 1989; Adrian to Nancy M. Fagan, et al., Feb. 13, 1990; Adrian to Seaver College RTP Task Force, Nov. 8, 1990, Seaver/RTP Task Force file, Tenure Records.

41 JWP: Wilson, Remarks to the Seaver College Faculty, Aug. 18, 1992, 1992–1993 file, Box 2.

42 Ibid.: Frank Novak to John Wilson, Aug. 19, 1992.

43 Ibid.: Wilson to Novak, Aug. 20, 1992.

44 PO: Wilson to Davenport and Lemley, Nov. 10, 1995, Seaver/Committees/Faculty Org. file, Historic Materials.

45 Stephanie Carlisi, "Faculty Morale," Currents (Winter 1998), 4–7; and GRAPHIC: Gayle Wheatley and Olivia Neri, "Survey Says: Faculty Is Generally Pleased," Nov. 18, 1999, A3.

46 BAIRD: These can be found in "Major Review Reports, 1988" binder among Seaver College Records.

47 JWP: Wilson, "Remarks to the Seaver College Faculty," Aug. 31, 1988, 1988–1989 file, Box 2.

48 BAIRD: "Strategic Plan, Seaver College, Pepperdine University," Nov. 1. 1988 (Final Draft, 11/09/88), 1988–1989 file.

49 Ibid.

50 Ibid.: Wilson to Wm. Adrian, Jan. 25, 1990, 1989–1990 file, Box 2.

51 Ibid.: Mike O'Neal to Wilson, Oct. 19, 1988, 1988–1989 file.

52 BAIRD: "Integrated Strategic Plan: Seaver College, Apr. 1995," in Seaver College Academic Strategic Plan Task Force, 1996–97, binder, Apr. 6, 1996, tab D; and Tamera Marko, et al., "Religious Diversity: Melting Pot or Boiling Point," Oasis (Spring 1991): 16–19.

53 For an example see BAIRD: "Program Review, Humanities and Teacher Education Division, Fall 1996," attached to W. David Baird to Humanities and Teacher Education Faculty, Aug. 3, 1996, 1992–1997 folder; others are in an undesignated blue binder.

54 Ibid.: "Seaver College Academic Strategic Plan," Oct. 9, 1997, 1992–1997 folder; and JWP: Wilson, "Some Reflections on the Proposed New Seaver Academic Strategic Plan, Aug. 19, 1997, 1997–1998 file, Box 2; Seaver College Academic Strategic Plan Task Force to Seaver College Faculty, Apr. 7, 1997, 1996–1997 file, Box 2.

55 "Integrated Strategic Plan: Seaver College," Mar. 1998, in Self-Study (August 2000), Appendices, Book One of Two, tab 2.1A.

CHAPTER 50
1 JWP: John Wilson, "Remarks to Pepperdine Board of Regents," June 11, 1998, 1997–1998 file, Box 2.

2 Ibid.

3 Ibid.

4 Ibid.: Benton to Wilson, June 16, 1998.

5 Quoted in GRAPHIC: Phil Osterhold, "Wilson Resigns As Dean," Sept. 18, 1997, A1.

6 Dan Caldwell Personal Papers: Lemley to Seaver College Faculty and Staff, Sept. 17, 1997; email from Dan Caldwell to Steve Lemley, Sept. 19, 1997; email from Steve Lemley to Dan Caldwell, Sept. 24, 1997; email from Dan Caldwell to Steve Lemley, Oct. 2, 1997, and clipping of ad "Pepperdine University, Dean of Seaver College," Chronicle of Higher Education, Nov. 7, 1997, B87.

7 Ibid.

8 Ibid.
9 GRAPHIC: Jennifer Smodish, "Dean's List Dwindling, Down to 4," Mar. 19, 1998, 1; Linda Wahla, "3 New Leaders Fill Dean Slots," Aug. 24, 1998, A1; Dawn Safian, "New Dean Encourages Growth," Nov. 5, 1998, A7.
10 LAT: Myrna Oliver, "M. Norvel Young; Led Move of Pepperdine to Malibu," Feb. 19, 1998.
11 PO: Public Information Office announcement from David Davenport, Mar. 29, 1999, and Davenport to Pepperdine Community, Mar. 17, 2000, David Davenport file, Old Corres. Materials.
12 Bill Henegar, "Meeting the Challenge to Lead," *Pepperdine People* (Winter 1996): 7–9.
13 Ibid.
14 Davenport, "The University Emerges As An 'Impact Player,'" *Pepperdine Voice*, 17 (April/May 1998): 4.
15 *The Davenport Years* (2000).
16 David Davenport, "The Changeless Light," *Annual Report, 1999*, 3.
17 GRAPHIC: Christina Littlefield, "Convo Honors Davenport," Mar. 30, 2000, 1.
18 Other members of the committee initially included Robert Dockson, Jerry Hudson, John Katch, Travis Reed, Carol Richards, and Joe Rokus.
19 SRP: Lemley to the Presidential Search Committee, May 13, 1999, P file, Box R.
20 Ibid.
21 BAIRD: Fax Announcement from Thomas G. Bost, Dec. 7, 1999, 1998–2000 file; and Abigail Salaway, "Passing the Presidential Baton," *Pepperdine People* (Summer 2000): 2–3.
22 Ibid.; and GRAPHIC: Julie Broad, "Benton 7th President," Jan. 20, 2000, A1.

CHAPTER 51

1 SRP: Andrew K. Benton, "Promises to Keep: Reaching Deep, Reaching Far" (Sept. 23, 2000), Benton file.

BIBLIOGRAPHY

Manuscript Sources

American Bar Association, Section of Legal Education and Admission to the
    Bar, Chicago, IL
        Pepperdine University School of Law File
California Secretary of State, Sacramento, CA
        Records of Incorporation
Center for Restoration Studies, Brown Library, Abilene Christian University,
    Abilene, TX
        Coons (R. R.) Papers
        Lovell (James L.) Papers
        Lemmons (Reuel) Papers
        Vertical Files
           George Pepperdine
           Hugh Tiner
           Misc. Christian Colleges, Pepperdine University
Enrollment Management, Seaver College, Pepperdine University, Malibu, CA
        Admission Statistics
Hall of Records, Los Angeles County, Los Angeles, CA
        Records of the Superior Court
Missouri Secretary of State, Jefferson City, MO
        Records of Incorporation
Office of Institutional Effectiveness, Pepperdine University, Malibu, CA
        Records of Accreditations
Personal Collections
        Caldwell, Dan, Malibu, CA
        Cupp, Richard "Rick," Malibu, CA
        O'Neal, Mike, Edmond, OK
        Reicheneder, Dale, Calabasas, CA
        Wilburn, James, Malibu, CA
Planning, Operations, and Construction Office, Pepperdine University,
    Malibu, CA
        Project Archives

President's Office, Pepperdine University, Malibu, CA
> Board of Regent's Records
> Brock House Collection
> Minutes, Board of Trustees, 1937–2000
> Minutes, Religious Standards Committee, Board of Trustees, 1977–1987
> Subject Files

Provost's Office, Pepperdine University, Malibu, CA
> Old Chronological Correspondence
> Old Subject Files

School of Law, Dean's Office, Pepperdine University, Malibu, CA
> Subject Matter files

Special Collections and University Archives, University Libraries,
    Pepperdine University, Malibu, CA
> Adams (Michael F.) Papers
> Baird (W. David) Book Materials
> Banowsky (William S.) Papers
> Davenport (David) Papers
> Holland (Harold) Collection (Accreditation materials)
> Los Angeles Campus Sale Papers
> Lovell (James L.) Papers
> Miller (Donald V.) Papers
> Miscellaneous Administrative Records
> Moore (James C.) Papers
> Nicks (John D. Jr.) Papers
> Office of Civic Services Collection
> Office of the Provost Papers
>>   William B. Adrian
>>   Steven S. Lemley
> Office of Public Information
> Office of the Seaver College Dean
>>   Baird (W. David) Papers
>>   Wilson (John F.) Papers
> Oral History Collection
>>   James Lovell, Apr. 18, 1980
>>   Donald Miller, Apr. 15, 1980
>>   Donald and Louise Miller, Nov. 29, 1996
>>   T. W. Phillips, Apr. 17, 1984
>>   Charles Runnels, Apr. 28, 1997 and Oct. 20, 1997
>>   Russell Squire, Mar. 20, 1979
>>   Lola Tiner, May 9, 1984
> Pepperdine (George) Family Papers

Pepperdine University Archives
Pepperdine Archives H-Series
Pullias (E. V.) Papers
Roper (Shirley) Papers
Rushford (Jerry) Collection
Seaver College Papers
University Management Committee
University Planning Committee
University Policy Committee
Vertical Files
White (Howard A.) Papers
Young (M. Norvel and Helen) Papers
Special Collections Research Center, Gelman Library, George Washington
University, Washington, D.C.
AAUP Collection, Box 41
Special Collections, Hannold Library, The Claremont Colleges, Claremont, CA
Western College Association Collection
The State Historical Society of Missouri Research Center, Kansas City, MO
Western Auto Supply Co. Records (K1233)
Vice President for Development, Pepperdine University, Malibu, CA
Nolij Data Base, Donor Records
Raiser's Edge Data Base
Newspapers
Los Angeles Daily Journal, 1986–1987
Los Angeles Times, 1920–2008
The Graphic, 1937–2000
The Inner View, 1973–1976
The Pepperdine News, 1965–1976
Church Periodicals
Bible Banner, 1939–1958
California Christian, 1951–1962
Colorado Christian, 1936–1937
Firm Foundation, 1948–1952, 1976
Gospel Guardian, 1950–1953
Mission Magazine, 1973–1979
West Coast Christian, 1942–1948
Pepperdine Publications
Yearbooks
Impressions, 1977–2000
Imprints, 1973–1976
Promenade, 1939–1970

Catalogs/Bulletins
George Pepperdine College, 1937–1953
Graduate School of Education, 1978–1982
Graduate School of Education and Psychology, 1982–2000
Graziadio School of Business and Management, 1996–2000
Pepperdine College, 1953–1970
Pepperdine University
Graduate School, 1974–1979
Los Angeles Campus, 1973–1982
Malibu Campus, 1973–1975
Orange County, 1975–1976
School of Business and Management, 1968–1996
School of Continuing Education, 1972–1976
School of Education, 1977–1978
Center for Professional Studies, 1976–1978
School of Law, 1973–2000
School of Professional Studies, 1977–1981
School of Public Policy, 1997–2000
Seaver College, 1975–2000
Miscellaneous
Annual [President's] *Reports*, 1948–2000
Alumni Voice, 1982–2000
Currents, 1992–2000
Management Insight, 1983–1988
Oasis, 1966–1991
Pepperdine People, 1977–2000
Pepperdine Colleague, 1983–2000
Pepperdine Law Quarterly, 1990–2000
Pepperdine News, 1965–1975
Pepperdine Voice, 1991–2000
Seaver College, 1976
School Safety, 1984–1993
Urbis, 1972–1976

Interviews

Adams, Michael, Greensboro, GA, December 9, 2013
Adrian, William, Malibu, CA, May 2, 2012
Banowsky, William S., Dallas, TX, Nov. 3, 2011 (telephone)
Davenport, David, Stanford, CA, Jan. 29, 2015
Dudley, Thomas, Calabasas, CA, Dec. 1, 2010

Hopkins, Gail, Malibu, CA, Dec. 16, 2010
Hornbaker, Larry, Louden, TN, April 7 and 8, 2012
Lemley, Steven, Malibu, CA, July 5, 2012
Magnusson-Durham, Nancy, Nashville, TN, June 15, 2012
McManus, Jack, Los Angeles, CA, March 6, 2012
Nelson, Harry, Los Angeles, CA, Dec. 10, 2010
O'Neal, Mike, Edmond, OK, June 22, 2012
Rettberg, John, Los Angeles, CA, Jan. 26, 2011
Rockey, Edward, Woodland Hills, CA, June 18, 2014
Runnels, Charles, Malibu, CA, April 12, 2012

Books

Alexander, Nan Ray. *You're Not Going To Tell That Are You Mom?* Pulaski, TN: Sain Publications, 2000.

Baird, W. David, et al. *Opportunities for Liberal Learning in the Twenty-first Century.* Malibu: Pepperdine University, 1997.

Banowsky, William S. *The Malibu Miracle: A Memoir.* Malibu: Pepperdine University Press, 2010.

Bates, Jack Ward, and Richard L. Clark. *Faith Is My Fortune, A Life Story of George Pepperdine; Actual Experiences, Business Success and Reverses, Stewardship and Philanthropy, which have proved that Strong Religious Faith is a Greater Fortune, More to be Desired than Riches, or any other Assets.* Los Angeles: Pepperdine College Book Store, [1959].

Baxter, Batsell B. *Every Life A Plan of God: An Autobiography of Batsell Barrett Baxter.* Abilene, TX: Zachry Associates, c. 1983.

Benne, Robert. *Quality with Soul: How Six Premier Colleges and Universities Keep Faith with Their Religious Traditions.* Grand Rapids: Eerdmans Publishing, 2001.

Botham, Fay, and Sara M. Paterson, eds. *Race, Religion, Region: Landscapes of Encounter in the American West.* Tucson: University of Arizona Press, 2006.

Burton, John. *Glass: Hand-Blown, Sculptured, Colored: Philosophy & Method.* Philadelphia: Chilton Book Co., 1967.

The Davenport Years. Malibu: Pepperdine University, 2000.

Derrick, Hubert G. *Why I Have To Believe.* Huntington Beach, CA: Geocopy Educational Materials, 1994.

Dochuk, Darren. *From Bible Belt to Sun Belt, Plain-Folk Religion, Grassroots Politics, and the Rise of Evangelical Conservatism.* New York: W.W. Norton & Co., 2011.

Foster, Douglas A., Paul M. Blowers, Anthony L. Dunnavant, and D. Newell Williams, eds. *The Encyclopedia of the Stone-Campbell Movement.* Grand Rapids: Eerdmans Publishing, 2004.

George Pepperdine College. *Report of Pepperdine College to the California State Board of Education and to the Western College Association.* Los Angeles: George Pepperdine College, Oct. 1953.

George Pepperdine Foundation v. George Pepperdine, et al., 126 *Cal. App.* 2d 154 (1954).

Hall, S. H. *Sixty Years in the Pulpit.* Ann Arbor, MI: Cushing-Malloy, Inc., c. 1955.

Handbook Rank, Tenure, and Promotion Committee, Seaver College of Pepperdine University. (Aug. 27, 1982), (Sept. 1984), (Sept. 1986), (Sept. 1987), (Sept. 1993), (1996–1997), and (2005–2006).

Henegar, Bill, and Jerry Rushford. *Forever Young: The Life and Times of M. Norvel Young & Helen M. Young.* Nashville: 21st Century Christian, 1999.

Hicks, L. Edward. *"Sometimes in the Wrong, but Never in Doubt": George S. Benson and the Education of the New Religious Right.* Knoxville: University of Tennessee Press, 1995.

Hughes, Richard T., and Thomas H. Olbricht, eds. *Scholarship, Pepperdine University and the Legacy of Churches of Christ.* Malibu: Center for Faith and Learning, Pepperdine University, 2004.

Hughes, Richard T., and William B. Adrian, eds. *Models for Christian Higher Education: Strategies for Success in the Twenty-First Century.* Grand Rapids: Eerdmans Publishing, 1997.

Iram, Yaacov, et al. *The Role of a Religious University.* Ramat Gan, Israel: Bar Ilan University Press, 2013.

Jenkins, Louis E., ed. *Graduate Psychology at Pepperdine: A Forty-Year History.* n.p., 1994.

Kirk, Russell. *The Roots of American Order.* LaSalle, IL: Open Court Publishers, 1974.

Meeks, Catherine. *I Want Somebody To Know My Name.* Macon, GA: Smyth & Helwys Publishing, 1994.

Miles, Jerry. *John Scolinos: The Man, the Legend.* Upland, CA: Dragonflyer Press, 2007.

Military Support of Law Enforcement During Civil Disturbance: A Report Concerning the California National Guard's Part in Suppressing the Los Angeles Riot, August 1965. Sacramento: California Office of State Printing, 1966.

Nanch, E. C. *The Daniel V. McEachern Story: Saga of a Seattle Scot.* College Place, WA: The College Press, 1958.

Olbricht, Thomas H. *Reflections on My Life, in the Kingdom and the Academy.* Eugene, Oregon: Wipf & Stock, 2012.

George Pepperdine Foundation et al. v. George Pepperdine et al. 271 *Pacific Reporter* 2d, 600–606.

Page, George C. *The Life Story of George Charles Page, In My Own Words.* Glendale, CA: Griffin Publishing, 1993.

Patterson, Franklin, and Charles R. Longworth. *The Making of a College: Plans for a New Departure in Higher Education.* Cambridge, MA: MIT Press, 1966.

Pepperdine College. *Faculty Handbook.* Los Angeles: Pepperdine College, Sept. 1965.

———. *Report for the Accreditation Committees of the Western Association of Schools and Colleges [and] California State Board of Education.* Los Angeles: Pepperdine College, Nov. 1965.

———. *Report for the Accreditation Committees of the Western Association of Schools and Colleges [and] California State Board of Education.* 3 parts. Los Angeles: Pepperdine College, Oct. 1970.

———. *Student Handbook, 1963–64.* Los Angeles: Pepperdine College, 1963.

Pepperdine University. *Educational Effectiveness Review, Submitted to the Western Association of Schools and College, July 2012.* Malibu: Pepperdine University, 2012,

———. *Enrollment and Faculty Profile for the Oxnard Conference, Oct. 18–19, 1979.* Malibu: Pepperdine University, Office of Institutional Research, Oct. 16, 1979.

———. *Faculty Handbook, Malibu Campus.* Malibu: Pepperdine University, Sept. 1974.

———. *Fifth-Year Report to the Accrediting Commission for Senior Colleges and Universities of the Western Association of Schools and Colleges.* Malibu: Pepperdine University, Oct. 1987.

———. *The Graziadio School of Business and Management and Seaver College Business Administration Division, Initial Accreditation Self-Evaluation Report.* 3 vols. Malibu: Pepperdine University, 1999.

———. *Malibu Student Handbook.* Malibu: Pepperdine University, 1972.

———. *Reaccreditation Report Submitted To The Western Association of Schools and Colleges.* Malibu: Pepperdine University, Nov. 1978.

———. *Report for the Accreditation Committees of Western Association of Schools and Colleges.* 2 parts. Malibu: Pepperdine University, 1970.

———. *Report for the Accreditation Committee of the Western Association of Schools and Colleges.* Malibu: Pepperdine University, Jan. 1974.

———. *Seaver College Faculty Handbook.* Malibu: Seaver College, Sept. 1978.

———. *Self-Study Report for Reaffirmation of Regional Accreditation by the Western Association of Schools and Colleges.* Malibu: Pepperdine University, July 1982.

———. *Self-Study, for Reaffirmation of Accreditation by the Western Association of Schools and Colleges.* 2 vols. Malibu: Pepperdine University, 1992.

———. *Self-Study, Submitted to the Western Association of Schools and Colleges.* 3 vols. Malibu: Pepperdine University, 2000.

———. *University Fact Book, 1982–1987.* Malibu: Institutional Research, Pepperdine University, 1988.

———. *University Fact Book, 1983–1989.* Malibu: Institutional Research, Pepperdine University, 1989.

———. *University Fact Book, 1988–1994.* Malibu: Institutional Research, Pepperdine University, 1995.

———. *Western Association of Schools and Colleges Accreditation Review of Pepperdine University.* Malibu: Pepperdine University, 1979.

Pepperdine University Bulletin, Seaver College Student Handbook. Vol. 43. Malibu: Pepperdine University, Mar. 1980.

Pepperdine University, Graduate School of Education. *Faculty Handbook.* Los Angeles: Pepperdine University, Sept. 1978.

Proceedings of the Twenty-First Annual Meeting of the Northwest Association of Secondary and Higher Schools, April 4 to 6, 1938. Spokane, WA: Northwest Association of Secondary and Higher Schools, 1938.

Proceedings of the Twenty-Second Annual Meeting of the Northwest Association of Secondary and Higher Schools, April 3 to 5, 1939. Spokane, WA: Northwest Association of Secondary and Higher Schools, 1939.

Proceedings of the Northwest Association of Secondary and Higher Schools, Annual Convention, 38th Year (Nov. 28–Dec. 1). Salt Lake City: Northwest Association of Secondary and Higher Schools, 1954.

Ray, Dennis, et al. *The New Internationalism and the Multinational Firm: Cooperation and Conflict.* Los Angeles: Pepperdine School of Business and Management, c. 1975.

Richman, Barry M., and Richard N. Farmer. *Leadership, Goals, and Power in Higher Education.* San Francisco: Jossey-Bass Publishers, 1974.

Rushford, Jerry, ed. *Crest of a Golden Wave, Pepperdine University, 1937–1987.* Malibu, CA: Pepperdine University Press, c. 1987.

Seaver College Faculty Handbook (Sept. 1978), (Sept. 1980), (Sept. 1985), (Sept. 1988), (Sept. 1989), (Sept. 1991), (Sept. 1998), and (Sept. 2000).

School of Business and Management. *Faculty Handbook, August 1975.* Los Angeles: Pepperdine University, 1975.

St. John, Adela Rogers. *First Step Up Toward Heaven: Hubert Eaton and the Forest Lawn Story.* Englewood Cliffs, NJ: Prentice-Hall, 1959.

Smoot, Dan. *People Along the Way: The Autobiography of Dan Smoot.* Tyler, TX: Tyler Press, 1993.

Starr, Kevin. *Material Dreams: Southern California Through the 1920s.* New York: Oxford University Press, 1990.

———. *Endangered Dreams: The Great Depression in California.* New York: Oxford University Press, 1996.

———. *The Dream Endures: California Enters the 1940s.* New York: Oxford University Press, 1997.

Stevens, John C. *Before Any Were Willing: The Story of George S. Benson.* Searcy, AR: Harding University, 1991.

Teague, Helen Louise. *A Fortune of Service: The Life of Helen Louise Pepperdine.* Privately printed, April 13, 1981.

Underwood, Maude Jones. *C. R. Nichol: A Preacher of Righteousness.* Clifton, TX: The Nichol Publishing Co., 1952.

Whitten, Woodrow C. *Out of the South: An Autobiography.* Privately published, 1979.

Wilburn, James R. *Freedom, Order, and the University.* Malibu: Pepperdine University Press, 1982.

———. *Productivity, a National Priority.* Malibu: Pepperdine University Press, 1982.

William L. Pereira and Associates. *A Master Plan Report for Rancho Malibu.* Los Angeles: William L. Pereira and Associates, 1965.

Womack, Morris M. *J. P. Sanders: A Champion of Christian Education.* Agoura, CA: Professional Communication Services, Inc., c. 1988.

The Yearbook of Construction. Los Angeles: Pepperdine College Press, 1968.

Young, M. Norvel. *Poison Stress Is a Killer: A Monograph on Physical and Behavioral Stress and Some of Its Effects on Modern Man.* Malibu, CA: Pepperdine University Press, 1978.

Youngs, Bill, ed. *America's Builders: The Gallery of the Greats, 1969.* Los Angeles: Pepperdine College Press, 1969.

———. *Faith Was His Fortune: The Life Story of George Pepperdine.* Malibu, CA: Pepperdine University Press, 1976.

———. *The House that Brock Built.* Malibu, CA: Pepperdine University, 1975.

———. *The Legacy of Frank Rogers Seaver.* Malibu, CA: Pepperdine University Press, 1976.

———. *The Man of Action: The Story of Jimmie Lovell.* Austin, TX: Sweet Publishing Co., c. 1969.

Articles

"A Salary by Any Other Name." *The Chronicle of Higher Education*, Mar. 31, 1975, 6.

Allen, Charlotte. "A Place in the Sun." *University Business* 2 (May 1999): 29–37.

Banowsky, William S. "The Spiritual Mission of Pepperdine University." *Mission Magazine* 6 (Sept. 1976): 51–54.

Barol, Bill. "The Year of Living Nervously." *Newsweek* 109 (June 8, 1987): 84–85.

Bell, Linda A. "More Good News, So Why the Blues? The Annual Report on the Economic Status of the Profession, 1999–2000." *Academe* 86 (Mar.–Apr., 2000): 11–95.

Bygrave, Michael. "Pepperdine U." *The Executive* (Dec. 1985): 22–23.

Bradberry, Bruce. "Pepperdine University: Not Guilty." *Mission Magazine* 12 (May 1979): 9–10.

Brammer, Lawrence M. "Everett L. Shostrom (1921–1992)." *American Psychologist* 51 (Jan. 1996): 52.

Chapman, Celia. "A 'Jesus Music Festival'—Pepperdine's First." *Contending for the Faith* 3 (May 1972): 8.

"Comprehensive Institutions." *U.S. News & World Report* (Nov. 25, 1985): 48.

"Controversy Over an Accreditor's Blueprint for Change." *The Chronicle of Higher Education*, July 6, 1994.

Detman, Art, Jr. "Pepperdine Starts Fresh at Malibu." *College Management* 7 (Sept. 1972): 17–22.

Editor. "Cathy Meeks and the Great Band Aid on Racism." *Mission Magazine*, 12 (Feb. 1979): 3–6.

"Education: New Colleges." *Time* 29 (June 14, 1937): 48–49.

"Education: Speed-up at Pittsburgh." *Time* 76 (July 11, 1960): 84.

"Federal Aid, Going It Alone." *Time* 91 (Feb. 23, 1968): 48, 53.

Halliburton, David. "Education's Entrepreneurs." *Change: The Magazine of Higher Learning* 10 (Nov. 1978): 18–20.

Hamil, Katharine. "Bert Gamble, Main Street Merchant." *Fortune* 62 (Oct. 1960): 228.

"The Harilelas, Leaders of the Indian Community Abroad." *Asia Magazine* 23 (May 19, 1985): 15–18.

Hedstrom, Jim. "Everett L. Shostrom: Remembrance of a Great Psychologist." *Pepperdine Colleague* 11 (Fall 1993): 5.

Hoffert, Robert W. "Review of *The Root of American Order*." *American Political Science Review* 71 (June 1977): 640–42.

"J. L. Allhands." *America's Builders* 3 (1954): 1–15.

Kolowich, Steve. "SUNY Signals Major Push Toward MOOCs and Other New Educational Models." *The Chronicle of Higher Education*, Mar. 20, 2013, online.

Lala, Jack. "Murchison, Clinton Williams, Jr." *Handbook of Texas Online* (June 15, 2010), http://www.tshaonline.org/handbook/ online/articles/fmu32 (accessed Nov. 07, 2011).

Linville, Sandi. "A Star is Born." *Insight* (Fall 1983): 2–4.

———. "The Land: The Man with the Plan." *Time* 82 (Sept. 6, 1963): 68–72.

"Millions Willed to Right Wingers." *New York Times,* May 4, 1966, 35.

Murphy, Charles J. V. "The Mellons of Pittsburgh." *Fortune* 76 (Oct. 1967): 120–29.

"My Son, the MBA." *Forbes Magazine* (March 1, 1977): 41–44.

Pooley, Eric, and Michael Weisskopf. "How Starr Sees It." *Time* 152 (Dec. 28, 1998): 82.

Parks, Norman. "Caught in the Toils of Caesar's Law." *Integrity* 8 (Mar. 1977): 115–18.

———. "Heroin for Our Colleges." *Mission Magazine* 6 (Feb. 1973): 3–6.

"Recognition Night." *America's Builders* 1 (May 1953): 1–3.

Rice, Ira. "Is Pepperdine Cutting the Umbilical Cord With the Churches of Christ?" *Contending for the Faith* 7 (Mar. 1976): 12–13.

———. "Is There Really Going to be 'A New Face' at Pepperdine?" *Contending for the Faith* 3 (April 1972): 1–8.

Telander, Rick. "School of Soft Knocks." *Sports Illustrated* (May 23, 1977): 110.

Tiner, Hugh M. "Let's Start at the Grass Roots." *The Rotarian* 71 (Nov. 1947): 7.

———. "Meals for Millions." *The Rotarian* 96 (May 1960): 51.

"200 Rising Leaders." *Time* 104 (July 15, 1974): 37.

Watkins, Beverly T. "Education's Entrepreneurs." *The Chronicle of Higher Education*, June 20, 1977, 6.

Waters, Kenny. "Grace Abandoned or Received? Pepperdine's Great Experiment." *Mission Magazine* 10 (Nov. 1976): 99–102.

"Western Auto Supply: Merchant on the Make." *Fortune* 20 (Oct. 1939): 81.

Wilburn, James R. "Significant Meanings: The Crisis of the MBA." *Executive* (May/June 1984).

U.S. Congress. *Congressional Record.* 91st Cong., 2d sess., July 1, 1970.

Young, Norvel M. "Education Without Federal Aid." *Vital Speeches* 27 (June 1, 1961): 492.

———. "Ordeal at Sunset." *Guideposts* (Aug. 1975): 16–19.

Theses and Other Unpublished Materials

Atteberry, Ruth D. "Pepperdine University School of Business and Management." Unpublished essay, 1997–1999.

Byrd, McArthur. "A Revitalization Program Design." MBA Report, Pepperdine University, 1974.

Gardner, Audrey. "A Brief History of Pepperdine College." MA thesis, Pepperdine University, 1968.

Horton, Howard, et al. "From Pepperdine into All the World: Conversations on Christian Education, Preaching, Missions & Congregational life." Recorded, transcribed & edited by Marcus Shira, et al. Unpublished MSS, c. 2008.

Jones, Candace Denise. "White Flight? George Pepperdine College's Move to Malibu, 1965–1972." MA thesis, Pepperdine University, 2003.

Rough, Jenny G., and Jim Gash. "It's All About the Students: Pepperdine University School of Law, 1969–2009." Unpublished MSS, Jenny Rough, 2011.

Ruzek, Maurine Reedy. "A Personal Account of the Life of George Pepperdine, Founder of Pepperdine University." Unpublished MSS, Oct. 2003.

Welch, Alonzo D. "Alonzo D. Welch Memoirs." Unpublished MSS, 2011, in possession of Kanet Welch Thomas, Westlake Village, CA.

Wilburn, James R. "My Life and Experiences with Pepperdine University." Unpublished memoir, 2010–2012.

Yates, Olivia. "Sixty-six Years with Pepperdine: A Biographical Study of Dr. Olaf Tegner." EdD diss. in Organizational Leadership, Pepperdine University, 2006.

INDEX

Note: Page numbers in italics indicate photos.